730
EASY SCIENCE EXPERIMENTS
with everyday materials

By E. Richard Churchill, Louis V. Loeschnig,
and Muriel Mandell

Illustrated by Frances Zweifel

Tess
Press

Compilation copyright © 1997 by Sterling Publishing Company

This edition contains the texts of the original editions. They have been reorganized and reset for this volume:
This edition was originally published in separate volumes under the titles:
Simple Science Experiments with Everyday Materials © 1989 by Muriel Mandell;
Simple Weather Experiments with Everyday Materials © 1990 by Muriel Mandell;
Amazing Science Experiments with Everyday Materials © 1991 by E. Richard Churchill;
Simple Chemistry Experiments with Everyday Materials © 1994 by Louis V. Loeschnig; and
Simple Earth Science Experiments with Everyday Materials © 1996 by Louis V. Loeschnig.

Library of Congress Cataloging-in-Publication Data
on file at the offices of Black Dog & Leventhal.

Published by Tess Press, an imprint of
Black Dog & Leventhal Publishers, Inc.
151 West 19th Street
New York, NY 10011

Designed by Liz Trovato

Cover design by Filip Zawodnik

Printed in China

Comb bound ISBN 1-57912-387-2

g f e d c

Hardcover ISBN 1-57912-613-8

f e d c b a

Disclaimer:
Although the advice and suggestions contained in this book have been carefully evaluated by the publishers,
neither the authors nor the publishers accept any responsibility for damage to either persons or possessions
which might result from the experiments.

PART 1

CONTENTS

Introduction *Page 14*

Clutching at Straws *Page 18*

Paper Capers *Page 24*

More than Lemonade *Page 36*

Soap Suds *Page 70*

Slow Start—Fast Finish *Page 81*

Keeping Your Balance *Page 89*

Here's Superman, But Where's Clark?   *Page 283*

Salty Solutions and Sweet Success   *Page 302*

Index   *Page 307*

INTRODUCTION

Science experiments aren't just for scientists and college students. They are fun for everybody—and that includes you. What's even better, all the experiments in this book have a surprise in them. Some of them will surprise you because they work. Others are surprising because of what happens.

You may decide that some of these experiments are really stunts or tricks. That's true. Some of them are, but it is also true that lots of the best stunts and tricks work because they are based on scientific principles. This book just helps you to put science to work in ways that may seem impossible, but which are always fun and entertaining.

The first five chapters show you how the most ordinary materials—drinking straws, paper, lemons, eggs, cooking oil, string, and soap—can be used in extraordinary ways. From these remarkable projects you will learn how to taste electricity with a lemon, make a water trombone with a drinking straw, and use a spot of butter to tell which light bulb is brighter.

The seven chapters that follow include more than seventy easy-to-do experiments that will surprise, astound, startle, and delight you—and your friends. You'll learn how to catch a coin on your elbow, mysteriously balance a dinner fork, amplify sound with a balloon, tune a glass, break up rays of sunlight, and empty a glass by blowing on it. And, best of all, you will learn why each experiment works while you're having a great time!

The next section shows you how, using everyday supplies like bottles, jars, newspaper, magnets, potting soil, clay, and sand, you can explore the mysterious forces that affect the earth. Discover how earthquakes, light, energy, erosion, and other factors change the face of the planet. You'll learn how magnetism and electricity are related earth forces. Make a pin on a thread sway like a dancing cobra and discover how business security people catch fake coins, or slugs, in vending machines—both by using magnetic force. You'll see how earthquakes are produced and tidal waves, too.

The experiments in the next four chapters are related to weather. From these exciting projects you'll find out about many of the mysteries of climate and weather. You'll learn why the North Pole is colder than the equator, why the sun sets, and what causes thunder and lightning. You'll be able to make your own weather station, putting together the instruments you need to keep track of temperature, air pressure, wind direction and speed, humidity and rainfall.

The final three chapters include dozens of sensational experiments and activities that give you a chance to do some real chemistry. A few involve serious chemical changes, like removing salt from water and making your own litmus paper from berries to test for acids and bases. Other experiments may look more like magic tricks, but they all deal with molecules or chemical changes. Try blowing up a rubber glove using a famous gas that chemists study. Pour water into a bottle without actually filling it and make paper worms that really crawl.

You can start with any experiment in any chapter, but you will get the most out of this book if you take one chapter at a time and do most of the experiments in order.

In a few of the projects, you'll need to use a stove, boiling water, or a safety match and these are labelled HOT! You can see them at a glance and get an adult to help you. We'll also let you know when any experiments will involve construction, and alert you to safety concerns.

All the materials needed for the projects are inexpensive and easy to find. You can find most of them around your house. The rest can be found in supermarkets, variety stores, and drugstores. Some materials are used for

many experiments so it might be a good idea for you to begin saving such things as various-size bottles and jars, coffee cans, shoe boxes, small plastic or clay flower pots, plastic spoons, drinking straws, coffee filters, medicine droppers, newspaper, paper clips, quart milk cartons, large plastic soda bottles, a magnifying glass, toy compass, bar and horseshoe magnets, scissors, pencils, paper, protractor, potting soil, gravel, clay, and sand. It is best to check with an adult before using or taking any materials needed for your experiments. You might also want to keep all your science equipment in a special cupboard or box. Besides being safely stored, it will be easy to find and ready for you whenever you want to do some experiments.

All the experiments have been simplified and thoroughly tested—they do work. If one doesn't seem to work for you, just re-read the instructions and try it again. When you get everything just right, the experiment will work. That's a promise! Some of the experiments, however, like those that involve living plants and seeds are long term—take time and patience.

So now the fun will begin and many of the mysteries of science will be revealed to you. We wish you many happy hours and successful experiments! Have fun!

CLUTCHING AT STRAWS

An ordinary drinking straw can become an atomizer, a medicine dropper, an oboe or a trombone, a scale—and more!

About Straws

What is a straw? The dictionary defines it as a stalk or stem of dried, threshed grain, like wheat, rye, oats, and barley. The first drinking straws were cut from stalks of grain. That's how they got their name.

The first paper straw was patented in 1888 by Marvin Chester Stone of Washington D.C. It was rolled by hand from manila paper and coated with paraffin. Drinking straws were handmade until 1905 when Stone's company invented the first successful straw-making machine. Today drinking straws are made of paper or plastic.

1 ◆ Make a Paper Straw

Cut out a strip of paper 2 inches x 10 inches (5 cm x 25 cm). Holding the paper at one corner, start rolling it diagonally in a narrow cylinder shape until it is all rolled up. Then fasten the sides with tape.

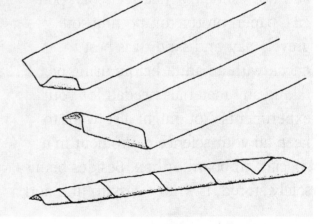

How Does a Straw Work?

Do you think you use a straw to pull liquid up into your mouth? Not so!

What to do: Suck a little water into the straw. Then hold your finger across the top of the straw and take the straw out of the water. Place the straw over the empty glass. Then remove your finger from the top of the straw.

What happens: While your finger covers the top of the straw, the water remains in the straw. When you remove your finger, the water flows out.

Why: Your finger on top of the straw lessens the pressure of the air from above the straw. The greater pressure of air under the straw holds the water inside it.

When you suck through the straw, you are not actually pulling the liquid up. What you are really doing is removing some of the air inside the straw. This makes the pressure inside the straw lower than the pressure outside. The greater pressure of the outside air then pushes the water in the glass up through the straw and into your mouth.

A pipette, a tube scientists use to measure and transfer a liquid from one container to another, works the same way.

Make a Medicine Dropper

You can make a regular drinking straw into a medicine dropper. Suck up some liquid into the straw. Hold it in the straw by covering the top of the straw with your finger. Then bend your finger slightly and raise and lower your fingertip so that the liquid flows out one drop at a time.

Experiment with the straw until you get the knack of it. It's easy to do.

Make a Straw Atomizer

This is the way window-cleaning sprays and perfume atomizers work.

What to do: About one–third of the distance from one end of the straw, cut a horizontal slit. Bend the straw at the slit and slip the short section into a glass of water, keeping the slit about ¼ inch (6 mm) above the surface of the water.

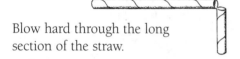

Blow hard through the long section of the straw.

What happens: Water enters the straw from the glass and comes out through the slit as a spray.

Why: As you blow through the long section of the straw, a stream of air flows over the top of the short section, reducing the pressure at that point. As normal pressure underneath forces water up into the straw, the moving air blows it off in drops. In atomizers and spray cans, you use a pump to blow in air.

Make a Straw Oboe

The first wind instruments were probably hollow reeds picked and played by shepherds in the field. You can make music with a straw.

What to do: Pinch flat ½ inch to ¾ inch (12 mm to 19 mm) at one end of the straw. Cut off little triangles from the corners to form wedges, or reeds. Put the straw far enough into your mouth so your lips don't touch the corners. Don't pucker your lips, but blow hard. Cut three small slits along the length of the straw about 1 inch (2.5 cm) apart. Separate the slits so they form small round holes. Cover one of them and blow. Then cover two, then three, blowing each time.

What happens: Each time you blow, you hear a different sound. You can play simple tunes by covering and uncovering the holes.

Why: As in a real oboe, the two wedges, the reeds, opening and closing at high speed, first allow air to flow into the straw and then stop the flow. Vibrating air creates the sound. As you cover and uncover the holes, you regulate the length of the air column and that determines the pitch. The shorter the air column, the faster it vibrates and the higher the note.

Make a Water Trombone

With a soda bottle, some water, and a straw you can make a slide trombone.

What to do: Pour water into the bottle until it is about three-quarters full. Put the straw into the bottle. Blow across the top of the straw. Then either lower the bottle or lift the straw and continue to blow.

What happens: As you lower the bottle, the sound gets lower in pitch.

Why: You are lengthening the column of air in the straw. This is how a slide trombone works.

Bend a Straw Without Touching It

You can "bend" a straw without touching it!

What to do: Half fill the glass with water. Put the straw into the glass. Look at it from the top, the bottom, and the sides.

What happens: When you look at the straw from the side of the glass, it appears to be bent or broken at the point where it enters the water.

Why: We see an object because rays of light come to our eyes from it. Light rays travel more slowly through glass and water than through air. Therefore, light from the part of the straw in the water reaches our eyes later than the part that is above the water, and the straw appears bent.

Straw Balance Scale

8

This balance can actually be a real scale. All you have to do is "calibrate" it—figure out what its movements mean by checking out items you already know.

YOU WILL NEED:

scissors
small paper cup
drinking straw
pencil eraser cap
large needle
index card
pencil
large spool of thread

What to do: Make two oblong notches on opposite sides of the paper cup. (See A.)

Cut away part of one end of the straw to form a little scoop. (See B.) Fit the eraser cap on the other end of the straw. Pad it with a little paper if it is too large. (See C.)

Push the needle through one side of the cup. Pull out the eraser head a little so the straw slants slightly upward. (See E.)

Tape the index card to the pencil and stand it in the spool. Place the spool so the straw's scoop falls across the index card. (See F.) You can mark the weight of things you weigh on the card.

Your scale is finished: Try it out by placing a few grains of sugar in the scoop, or by hanging a paper clip from it.

What happens: The straw moves down.

Why: Your scale is a lever. It acts like a seesaw. The place at which the lever rests (the needle) is called the fulcrum. When the straw lies flat, the distance and the weight on one side of the needle balance out the distance and the weight on the other side. As you add weight, you change the relationship between the two sides of the needle.

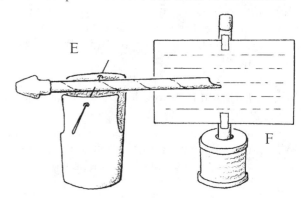

Finding the Center of Gravity

9

Figure out the point at which the straw balances. Do this by hanging the straw on the spine of a book or on the edge of an upright metal ruler. Move the straw about until it doesn't fall off. It will probably be fairly close to the eraser. Mark that point of balance with a pencil.

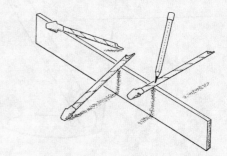

Spear a Potato

Would you think an ordinary drinking straw could pierce a potato without destroying itself?

What to do: Soak the potato in water for about thirty minutes before trying this experiment. Then, with one fast strong push, thrust the straw straight down into the potato.

What happens: The straw pierces the potato without buckling or bending.

Why: Inertia is the tendency of objects to continue whatever they are doing. An object at rest (the potato) tends to remain at rest while an object that is moving (the straw) tends to keep moving in the same direction.

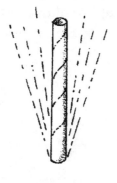

Straws that grow in fields have been driven into—and through—planks of wooden barns and houses when propelled by tornado-force winds.

Straw Wheels

Do wheels make work easier? See for yourself.

What to do: Place the book on a table and try to push it. Then place the straws on the table and put the book on top of the straws. Push the book.

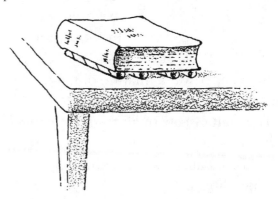

What happens: Without the straws, you have to push hard to move the book. With the straws, the book moves more easily.

Why: When one item rubs against another, it resists moving because both surfaces are not completely smooth. The bumps of one surface (the book) catch against the bumps in the other (the table). The amount of this resistance, known as friction, depends on the kinds of surfaces and the forces pressing them together. The rougher the surfaces, the greater the friction. The greater the weight of the objects, the greater the friction. Rolling results in less friction than sliding.

PAPER CAPERS

Charm a paper snake, electrify an ordinary newspaper, step through an index card, and defy gravity.

About Paper

Paper is believed to have been invented by Ts'ai Lung almost two thousand years ago in China. Chinese paper was a mixture of rags and plant fiber.

The craft of papermaking didn't spread to Europe until twelve hundred years later. Until 1700, paper was made from cotton and linen fibers.

Paper was made by hand, one sheet at a time. In 1798, Nicholas Robert of France invented the first machine to make paper, which he sold to Henry and Sealy Fourdrinier of England. Papermaking machines are still known as Fourdriniers.

Today paper is thin flat sheets of tissue made usually from wood pulp.

The many types of paper include stationery, wax paper, cardboard, contact paper, oaktag, newspaper, wallpaper, index cards, boxes, and wrapping paper.

Shaping Up

Which of these shapes
do you think is the
strongest? No matter
what materials you are working
with you can make a structure stronger by
simply changing its shape.

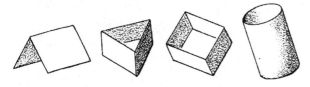

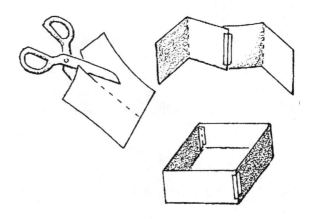

What to do: Fold the sheets of paper into various shapes, such as those shown in the illustrations.

1. Fold a sheet of paper in half and stand it on its edges.

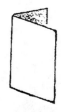

2. Fold a sheet of paper in thirds and tape the ends together.

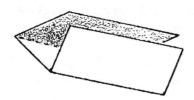

3. Fold a sheet of paper in half lengthwise, cut on the fold, and tape the two halves together at the top and bottom. Then fold the attached halves in half again from top to bottom. Spread the sheets to form the cube.

4. Roll a sheet of paper around the can, secure the paper with tape, then remove the can.

Put a light book on top of each shape. Some will collapse immediately. Keep piling books on the others until they collapse.

What happens: The round paper pillar holds a surprising number of books.

Why: A hollow tube is the strongest because the weight is distributed evenly over it.

Corrugated Paper

What makes a corrugated box strong?

13

What to do: Make a crease about ¼ inch (6 mm) from the edge of one sheet of paper. Fold it down and press down on the folds. Using the first fold as a guide, fold a second crease back. Alternate folding back and forth until the entire sheet is pleated, as in the illustration.

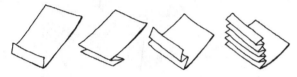

Roll the second sheet of paper around a can and tape the ends together. Remove the can. Do the same thing with the third sheet of paper. Line up the two circles of paper 4 inches (10 cm) from one another on a table. Then place the pleated sheet on them. Rest the jar on top of the pleated sheet.

What happens: The pleated paper holds the jar.

Why: You have added strength by using corrugated paper, which you created by folding the sheet back and forth. An engineer devised this way of making paper stiffer—and stronger.

Powerful Paper

14

Just how strong can paper get?

What to do: Cut a strip about 4 inches x 12 inches (10 cm x 30 cm) from the corrugated carton. Wrap the strip around the can and secure it with rubber bands or masking tape. Then remove the can.

Place a small board on top of the cardboard circle. Stand on it.

What happens: The cardboard circle will hold your weight.

Why: The strength comes from the combination of the circular shape and the corrugated paper.

Tough Newspaper

15

YOU WILL NEED:
wooden ruler
table
newspaper

Your strongest blow cannot budge this fearless newspaper!

What to do: Place the ruler on the table so that 2 inches (5 cm) projects over the edge. Spread a double sheet of newspaper over the ruler so the paper lies flat along the table edge.

Strike the projecting edge of the ruler as hard as you can.

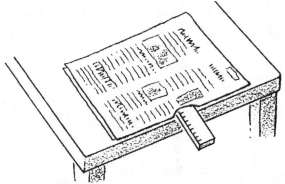

What happens: The newspaper doesn't budge.

Why: Air pressure on the paper prevents it from moving. Air pushes down with almost 15 pounds of pressure on almost every inch of surface (1 kg per square centimeter). For an average sheet of newspaper, the total resistance is about two tons.

Invisible Shield

16

If you've ever been caught in the rain and tried to keep dry by putting a newspaper over your head, you know that water doesn't treat paper very well. But in the following experiment the paper seems to be protected by an invisible shield.

YOU WILL NEED:
sheet of newspaper
empty glass
pot of water

What to do: Crumple the sheet of newspaper and stuff it into the empty glass tightly enough so that it doesn't fall out when you turn the glass upside down. Holding the glass bottom up, sink it deep into the pot filled with water. Hold it there. After a minute or so, pull the glass out of the water and remove the paper.

What happens: The paper is dry.

Why: Water cannot get into the glass because the " empty" glass is already filled with air and the air cannot get out because it is lighter than water.

Why No Flood?

YOU WILL NEED:
piece of cardboard or
large index card
glass of water

Until you learn how to do
this experiment perfectly
(and maybe even then), it's best to do it
over a sink or basin.

What to do: Place the cardboard over the
drinking glass which you have filled to the brim
with water.

Make sure no
air bubbles enter
the glass as you
hold the cardboard
against it. Then
turn the glass
upside down over
a sink or basin.
Take away the
hand holding the cardboard.

What happens: The cardboard stays in
place—and the water stays in the glass.

Why: The pressure of the air outside
the glass is greater than the pressure of the water inside. It is
the air pressure that keeps
the water in the glass.

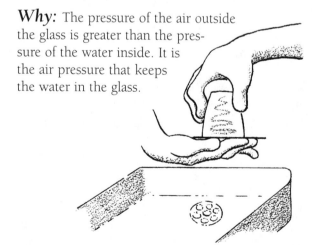

The Paper Napkin Trick

YOU WILL NEED:
paper napkin
plastic cup of water

It's a good idea to
practice this trick, too,
where spilled water
won't do any harm.

What to do: Drape the napkin over the edge of
a kitchen counter or table. Place the plastic cup of
water on one corner of the napkin about 1 inch
(2.5 cm) from the edge.

Pull the napkin quickly away from under the
plastic cup.

What happens: The napkin comes out—without any water spilling.

Why: The cup doesn't overturn because of the
tendency of things at rest to stay at rest. It's that
old law of motion—inertia—at work. If it does
spill it's because you're not pulling the napkin fast
enough or with enough force.

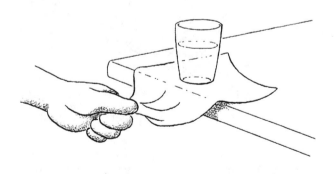

Cantilever Bridge

A cantilever bridge is built with two beams that project toward each other to join and form a span.

What to do: Stack the notebooks on the edge of the table. Slide the top book halfway out from the stack and over the table's edge. When it balances, slide it back a little. Move out the next notebook along with the top one until they balance, and then slide them back a little. Add another notebook and move the top three out and slide them back a little after they balance. Continue in the same way until all six notebooks are staggered.

What happens: The top notebook seems to be suspended in air, but the notebooks do not fall.

Why: You have found the center of gravity, the point at which all the weight of an object seems to be concentrated. Although the top book appears to be suspended in air, more than half the weight of the stack of notebooks is resting on the table.

20 Flash!

You will need a friend to help you with this experiment.

What to do: Rub the sheet of newspaper vigorously with the plastic wrap for about 30 seconds. Then place the top of the can in the center of the newspaper. Holding the newspaper by its edges, lift it while your friend puts a finger near the metal.

What happens: A spark!

Why: When an electrical charge passes between two objects, the result is a spark. As you rubbed the newspaper, you charged it with static electricity. Your friend's touch made the electrical charge jump from the paper to the uncharged can lid.

You may have seen a similar spark when you've walked on a carpet and then touched a doorknob. Or you may have heard a crackling sound while you combed your hair. These are all examples of static electricity.

Lightning is a huge electric spark that results when charges jump from one cloud to another or from a cloud to the ground.

Charming a Paper Snake

It's easier than you think to charm a snake.

YOU WILL NEED:

thin cardboard or heavy paper
scissors
string
lamp or heated radiator
straight pin
pencil with an eraser
spool of thread

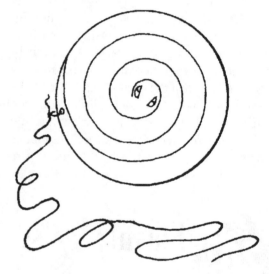

What to do: Draw a spiral snake (as in the illustration) on thin cardboard or any slightly heavy paper, such as oaktag or a large index card.

Cut out the spiral snake and tie a string to its "tail."

Suspend the snake over a lighted bulb or a heated radiator.

What happens: The snake dances.

Why: Hot air is less dense than cold air and therefore it rises. The moving air spins the spiral snake.

To make a stand for your snake: With a pin, attach the head to the eraser end of a pencil, letting the snake curl around the pencil. Stand the pencil in the center hole of the spool of thread.

Dancing Dolls

Did you ever think you'd see paper dolls dance?

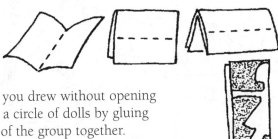

What to do: Fold the stiff paper from top to bottom twice. Draw the right half of a doll along the exposed top fold, extending the doll's arm and leg to the bottom of the exposed fold, as in the illustration.

Cut along the lines you drew without opening the folded paper. Form a circle of dolls by gluing or taping the two ends of the group together. Attach the paper clips so that the dolls stand on them.

Balance the large sheet of cardboard so a portion of it hangs over the edge of a table. Stand the circle of paper dolls on top of the cardboard so that one of the clips is on the overhanging portion.

Move your magnet underneath the cardboard—first to the right and then to the left.

What happens: The paper dolls dance.

Why: The paper clips are made of steel. Therefore the magnet attracts them—even through the cardboard.

YOU WILL NEED:

piece of stiff paper, like oaktag

pencil

scissors

glue or tape

large sheet of cardboard

2 paper clips

magnet

31

Paper Magic: The Moebius Strip

YOU WILL NEED:

sheet of paper
scissors
glue or tape
pencil

You can cause paper to have only one side! This surprising phenomenon was first discovered by a nineteenth-century German mathematician, August Ferdinand Moebius.

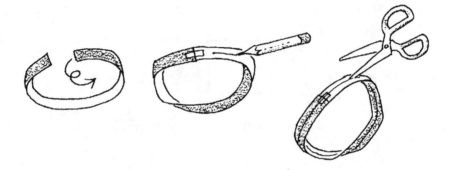

What to do: Cut a strip of paper 1 inch x 10 inches (2.5 cm x 25 cm). Give one end a half twist and tape or glue the ends together to form a loop.

Draw a lengthwise line down the center of the strip until you reach your starting point.

Cut along the line you have drawn.

What happens: There is no side without a line! And you have only one loop, which is twice as long as your original loop.

Why: No one has been able to explain this strange "trick." But it has actually been put to practical use. Ordinarily, the fan belts in cars and factory conveyor belts wear out faster on the inside than the outside. But belts made with a half twist like this wear out more evenly and more slowly.

Through the Index Card

Alice stepped through a magic looking glass—which seemed impossible. You can do the "impossible" too—stretch a very ordinary index card and step through it!

What to do: Fold the card or paper down the middle from top to bottom. Then make seven or nine deep cuts (any odd number will do) alternating with one cut starting at the fold and the other starting at the edge of the card. Unfold the index card and stretch it out.

What happens: You can step through the paper without tearing it.

Why: Because of the way you cut the card, you stretch it first from one side and then from the other. In each case, the opposite side holds firm.

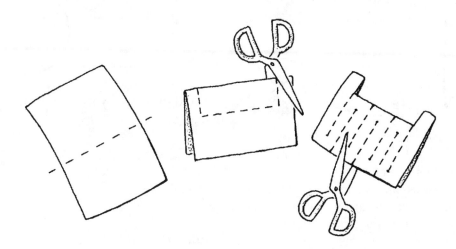

Color Fun

Is green really green?

YOU WILL NEED:

strip of paper towel
green felt-tipped pen
or 1 drop of green
food coloring
jar or glass with
1 inch (2.5 cm) of water

What to do: Make a spot of color about 2 inches (5 cm) from one end of the strip of paper towel. Hang the strip in the jar so that the spot is above the water and the end of the strip is in the water. Let it stand for 15 to 20 minutes.

What happen: The green spot is gone, but above the original spot the paper has turned blue, and above that the paper is yellow.

Why: Most dyes and inks are combinations of coloring substances which can be taken apart by adding water or alcohol. Water moves up the paper in the same way as sap rises in trees. As the water moves up, it dissolves the green spot and gradually moves the color up the strip of paper. But since the colors that make up green—blue and yellow—do not move at the same rate, they separate.

Magic Color

Mix colors the easy way!

YOU WILL NEED:

small plate
cardboard
pencil
scissors
watercolors or
poster paints
hole punch
string

What to do: Using the plate as a pattern, draw a circle on the cardboard. Cut out the circle. Paint one side red and the other side blue. Punch small holes on the opposite sides of the disk, as in the illustration, and thread short lengths of string through each hole.

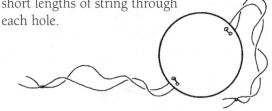

Hold the circle by its strings and twirl it around.

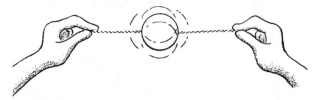

What happens: The color you see is purple.

Why: The eye continues to see each color for a while after it has disappeared, and so your eye and your brain mix the colors of the rapidly whirling disk.

What happens if you make one side red and the other yellow?

Benham Disk

YOU WILL NEED:
white paper
scissors
black-ink marker
cardboard
straight pin
pencil with an eraser

The hand is quicker than the eye. Well, is it really? Is it magic, illusion, or trickery?

What to do: Cut a circle 4 inches (10 cm) in diameter out of white paper. Color one half black. Divide the white half into four equal parts. In each segment draw three black arcs about ¾ inch (19 mm) thick, as in the illustration.

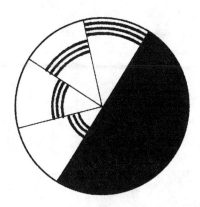

Cut a circle 4 inches (10 cm) in diameter out of the cardboard. Place the paper circle on the cardboard circle.

Mount them together on a pin attached to a pencil eraser.

Spin the disk at various speeds, clockwise and counterclockwise.

What happens:
The arcs seem to close up to form six rings.

At a slow speed, spinning clockwise, the outer rings look blue and the inner rings look red. When you spin them counterclockwise, the colors reverse.

Why: The arcs seem to close to form rings, because the eye continues to see each arc for a short time after it has disappeared.

Why do we see red and blue when the only colors on the disk are black and white? The entire color spectrum is present in white light, but our eyes register the different colors at different lengths of time.

When we spin the disk, light from the colors that make up white reach the eye, but are visible for only an instant before being followed by the black portions of the disk. Our eye is only able to register a part of that color spectrum—the blue, which has the shortest rays, and the red, which has the longest.

Try varying the patterns on the white half of your Benham Disk and see what interesting results you get.

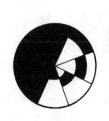

MORE THAN LEMONADE

With a little ingenuity, you can turn an ordinary lemon into invisible ink, cleaning fluid, a rock tester, a rocket launcher, and a wet cell.

About Lemons

The lemon probably came to us from India.

The small thorn-branched lemon tree was first planted in the United States during the California Gold Rush of 1849 to fight scurvy among the prospectors.

Lemon juice will remove rust, ink, and mildew stains. Oil from the lemon skin is used to flavor extracts, perfumes, cosmetics, and furniture polish.

Lemon juice is the main source of citric acid, which is used in textile printing to keep the fabric clear of rust stains from the machinery.

Invisible Ink

28

You can use a lemon to write a secret message.

What to do: Squeeze the lemon juice into the saucer. Add a few drops of water and mix well with the spoon. Dip the swab into the lemon juice. Then use the swab to write a message on ordinary white paper. When it dries, the writing will be invisible. When you want to read the message, heat the paper by holding it near a light bulb.

What happens: The words appear on the page.

Why: The juice of lemons and other fruits contain compounds of carbon. These compounds are nearly colorless when you dissolve them in water. But, when you heat them, the carbon compounds break down and produce carbon, which is black.

Lemon Cleaning Fluid

29

Don't taste! Iodine is poisonous

Write an invisible message with flour and water and make it appear with iodine. Then use lemon to make it disappear again.

What to do: In the saucer, use the teaspoon to mix the flour and water together. When the mixture is smooth, dip a cotton swab into it. Then use the swab to write a message on the paper towel. When the message dries, it will be invisible.

When you are ready to read the message, use a clean swab to apply a few drops of iodine. Your message will appear in blue-black.

Then dab on a few drops of lemon juice.

What happens: Your message disappears.

Why: The iodine reacts with the flour, a starch, to form a new compound that appears as blue-black.

When you apply the lemon juice, the ascorbic acid (Vitamin C) of the lemon combines with the iodine to make a new colorless compound. So, if you spill iodine on anything, you can use lemon juice to remove it. Lemon juice will also remove ink, mildew, and rust stains from paper and cloth.

Bright as a Penny

30

Soap and water won't clean metals very easily. That takes a special cleaner—or you can try lemon juice!

What to do: Squeeze the lemon juice into the glass. Soak the coin in lemon juice for 5 minutes.

What happens: You fish out a shiny coin!

Why: Oxygen in the air combined with the copper to form the dull copper oxide coating. The acid of the lemon acts chemically to remove the oxide—and the result? A bright copper penny. Vinegar will work the same way.

31 Nifty Nail

Dig out that pile of pennies you've been saving and make yourself a copper-plated nail.

What to do: Squeeze the lemon juice into the glass. Put the pennies into the glass a few at a time. The lemon juice should cover them. Add a pinch of salt. Let the pennies stand for 3 minutes.

Meanwhile, clean the nail with scouring powder and water. Put the nail into the glass.

Wait at least 15 minutes, then fish out the nail.

What happens: The nail is coated with copper.

Why: Copper from the pennies interacts with the acid of the lemon juice to form a new compound (copper citrate). When you put the nail into the solution, the compound plates the nail with a thin layer of copper that cannot be rubbed off.

After you've got your copper nail, you might want to wear it on a string.

Lemon— Save that Apple!

32

Lemon can also keep apples fresh.

What to do: Cut the apple into four parts. Put the apple pieces on the plate then squeeze lemon juice on two of them. Let all the apple pieces stand for 3 hours.

What happens: The pieces of apple that were not treated with lemon turn brown. The apple pieces that were doctored with lemon juice do not.

Why: When exposed to air, certain chemicals in the apple react by destroying cells, which turn brown. But the Vitamin C (ascorbic acid) in the lemon slows down the reaction between the chemicals in the fruit and the oxygen in the air. This preserves the color and the taste of the apple.

Make Red Cabbage "Litmus" Paper

YOU WILL NEED:
jar of red cabbage or small head of fresh red cabbage
wide-mouthed jar
paper towels

What to do: Strain the liquid from the jar of red cabbage into another wide–mouthed jar. (Or you can make you own with the help of an adult: Grate half a small red cabbage. Put the grated cabbage into a pot with 1 cup of water. Boil for 15 minutes. Let the red cabbage juice cool and then strain it into a wide-mouthed jar.)

Cut 2 inch (5 cm) strips of paper toweling. Soak the paper strips in the cabbage juice for 1 minute, then let them dry. Your "litmus" paper is now ready for testing. It will turn red-pink in acid and green in alkali. You can also experiment and make indicators from fruits, flowers, other vegetables, and even tea. But the color changes will be different.

The litmus paper used in schools and in chemistry labs is colored by lichen plants, a kind of fungus.

Acid or Base

YOU WILL NEED:
10 tablespoons of red cabbage juice
10 small glasses or paper cups
various fruit juices, vinegar, milk, and household products

Use your red cabbage indicator to determine which foods are acid and which are alkali.

What to do: Pour 1 tablespoon of red cabbage juice into each glass. Add lemon juice to one; grapefruit juice to the second; tomato or pineapple juice to a third; vinegar to the fourth. Then test baking soda, milk, rubbing alcohol, oil, soap, and other household products.

Those that turn pink are acids. Those that turn green are alkali (bases).

Lemon—Life Saver

Poison control centers used to recommend lemon juice or vinegar as an antidote for some poisons. This experiment shows why. You will need "litmus" paper. But that's no problem. You can use the liquid of red cabbage to make your own. (See page 39 for instructions.)

What to do: Apply a few drops of lemon juice to one strip of "litmus" paper. Add a few drops of ammonia to a second strip. Then apply a few drops of lemon juice to the spot made by the ammonia.

What happens: The strip with the lemon juice on it turns pink. The strip with the ammonia added turns green. When you add lemon to the green ammonia spot, it returns to its original reddish purple color.

Why: The pink color indicates the presence of acid because lemon is a mild acid, a nonmetal combined with hydrogen.

The green color indicates the presence of alkali because ammonia is an alkali (otherwise known as a base), a metal combined with hydroxide. The "litmus" paper returns it to its original color when the ammonia is acted against—neutralized—by the lemon, its chemical opposite.

What does all this have to do with poison? Ammonia is poisonous if someone drinks it. Since lemon neutralizes ammonia, it was once recommended as a temporary antidote, just enough to last until the person could get to a doctor. The current emergency treatment for accidentally drinking a poison, like ammonia, is to dilute it in the stomach by drinking large amounts of water or milk.

Blowing up a Balloon

Put chemistry to work for you! This experiment will also work if you substitute 2 ounces (60 ml) of vinegar for the lemon juice.

What to do: Stretch the balloon to make it easier to inflate. Pour the water into the clean, empty soda bottle. Add the baking soda and stir with the straw until it has dissolved. Pour in the lemon juice, then quickly fit the stretched balloon over the mouth of the bottle.

What happens: The balloon inflates.

Why: When you mix the base (the baking soda) and the acid (the lemon), you create carbon dioxide, a gas that rises into the balloon and blows it up.

Rock Tester

How do geologists identify their specimens? This is one way. It is best to do this experiment in a sink or basin. Vinegar may be substituted for the lemon juice.

What to do: Pour the lemon juice over the rocks.

What happens: The liquid bubbles on some, but not on others.

Why: When the lemon juice bubbles, the rock sample is either limestone or marble. Limestone, a sedimentary rock formed under water from mud and silt, contains a carbonate form of calcium, an alkaline earth metal. When you add the lemon (an acid) to the alkaline of the limestone, it forms carbon dioxide. That makes the liquid bubble up, just as pancakes and cakes puff up when you add baking soda to the batter. Actually, baking soda can be made from limestone. Marble is a rock formed under great heat and pressure from limestone. It reacts to acid just as limestone does.

You get similar results if you add lemon juice to chalk, because it, too, is made of limestone.

Turn That Lemon On

You can make electricity with your lemon!

YOU WILL NEED:
2 stiff copper wires
large paper clip
lemon
scissors
galvanometer (see page 43 for instructions to make your own)

What to do: If there is any insulation on the ends of the wire, strip it off. Untwist the paper clip and attach it to an end of one of the wires. Squeeze and roll the lemon to loosen the pulp inside. Make two small cuts in the skin of the lemon about 1 inch (2.5 cm) apart. Insert the bare wire and the paper clip through the skin of the lemon and into the juicy part. The two wires should be close to each other but not touching.

Connect the free ends of the two wires to the terminals of the meter (or to the free ends of the wires of the homemade galvanometer).

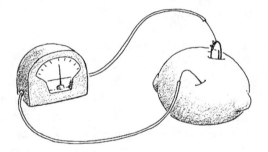

What happens: The meter moves.

Why: Chemical reactions of the two different metals (the copper of the wire and the iron of the clip) in the acid (lemon juice) draw electrons away from one wire toward the other. They flow out of the lemon through one wire, go through the meter, and then enter the lemon by the other wire.

Light Up a Bulb

If your hardware or electrical supply store can provide a bulb of less than 1.5 volts, try connecting several lemons and see how many lemon wet cells it will take to light the bulb. Line up the lemons so you can link them to one another with a bare copper wire and a clip in each, as in the illustration. You should end up with two free wire ends, one attached to a clip. Connect these wire ends to the bulb.

40 | A Taste of Electricity

If you touch the two wires that you've inserted in the lemon to your tongue at the same time, you will taste something metallic and feel a slight tingling sensation. You are tasting and feeling electricity!

YOU WILL NEED:

compass (from a stationery store)

15 feet (4.5 m) of bell wire (from the hardware store)

small rectangular cardboard box

Make a Galvanometer

A galvanometer is an instrument designed to detect electric currents. You can make one with a few simple materials.

41

What to do: Place the compass in the center of the box. Scrape off about ½ inch (6 mm) of insulation from each end of the bell wire. Starting about 6 inches (15 cm) from one end, wind the wire tightly around the box, circling it about twenty-four times. Leave another 6 inches (15 cm) of wire free on the other side of the box.

Rest your galvanometer on the table so it is horizontal and turn it until the compass needle is parallel to the coil of wire.

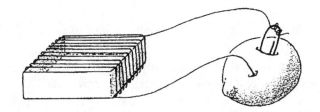

Attach the bell wire ends to the wires of the lemon cell.

Shock Them All!

42

Want to shock your friends? You can do it by repeating an experiment first done two hundred years ago by the Italian physicist Alessandro Volta.

What to do: Squeeze the lemon juice into the small dish. Soak the paper towel strips in the lemon juice. Make a pile of coins, alternating the dimes and the pennies and separating each one with a lemon-soaked strip of paper towel.

Moisten one fingertip on each hand and hold the pile between your fingers.

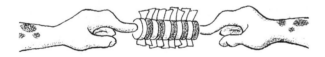

What happens: You get a small shock or tingle.

Why: You have made a wet cell, the forerunner of the battery we buy at the hardware store. The lemon juice, an acid solution, conducts the electricity created by the separated metals of the two coins.

What we call a battery is actually two or more dry cells. In each dry cell, thirty–two metals (a zinc metal container and a carbon rod) are separated by blotting paper soaked in a strong acid.

Make Your Own Lemon Soda

43

You can make a bubbly lemon soda that is tasty enough to drink. You can try this with an orange, too.

What to do: Squeeze the juice from the lemon into the measuring cup. Add an equal amount of water then pour the mixture into the glass. Stir in the teaspoon of baking soda. Taste and add sugar if you like.

What happens: The liquid will be bubbly and taste like lemon soda.

Why: The bubbles are carbon dioxide gas formed when you combine the base (the baking soda) with the acid (the lemon juice).

The bubbles in real soda are also created by carbon dioxide, added under pressure to water and a flavored sweetener.

Lemon Rocket

44

YOU WILL NEED:

empty soda bottle
cork
paper toweling
2 paper towel strips,
1 inch x 10 inches
(2.5 cm x 25 cm)
tape
2 ounces (60 ml)
of lemon juice
water
1 teaspoon of baking soda

Launch a rocket by following instructions exactly. You don't want the rocket to go off before you're out of the way!

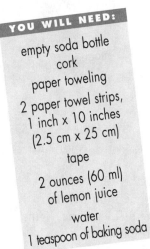

What to do: Fit the cork into the soda bottle, trimming it or padding it with paper toweling, if necessary. Tape the two paper towel streamers to the cork. Put the cork aside; it will be your rocket.

Pour the lemon juice into the soda bottle. Add enough water to fill the bottle halfway. Wrap the baking soda in a little square of paper toweling.

Go outside where your rocket has plenty of space to travel. Drop the wrapped-up baking soda into the bottle and insert the cork loosely. Put the bottle on the ground and stand back.

What happens: The cork will eventually shoot up.

Why: As the water and lemon juice soak through the paper towel, the baking soda reacts to produce carbon dioxide. As more gas forms, pressure builds up inside the bottle and sends the cork flying.

Baby Lemons

45

Don't throw away those lemon seeds. Plant them—and eventually you may even have a lemon tree! At the very least, you can get them to sprout.

YOU WILL NEED:

seeds from
several lemons
water
blotter or paper towel
wide-mouthed jar
bits of paper towel or
absorbent cotton

What to do: Soak the seeds overnight in water to soften the outside layer.

Wet a piece of blotter or paper towel and line the jar with it. Fill the center of the glass with the bits of paper towel or absorbent cotton. Near the top of the jar, push the seeds between the outside of the jar and the blotter or paper towel,. Pour about 1 inch (2.5 cm) of water into the bottom of the jar. Place the jar in a warm dark place like a closet or cabinet. Check it every day and add more water as it dries up.

What happens: In a week or ten days, the seeds will begin to sprout.

Why: Seeds contain "baby plants" or embryos. The embryos in the seeds may grow into new plants if you give them moisture and warm air. The blotter supplies the moisture without waterlogging them.

Lemon Penicillin

Grow your own microbes with a lemon, water, darkness—and patience.

What to do: Place the lemon in the container. Add a few drops of water and cover the container tightly with plastic wrap or aluminum foil. Store it for a week or more in a dark place, like a kitchen cabinet.

Then take out the lemon. Look at it carefully with the magnifying glass.

What happens: You will see soft, green mold growing on the lemon. (Don't touch the mold or breathe on it because you may be allergic to it.)

Why: The green fuzzy mold on the lemons is actually a colony of millions of one-celled plants growing together. They grow on food that is kept too long and make it change color and smell bad.

This particular mold, the same kind that grows on blue cheese, is the one from which scientists make penicillin, the medicine that fights harmful microbes when we're sick.

When you finish examining the moldy lemon (or use it to do the next experiment) place it in the container and replace the wrapping. Dump it in the nearest trash can—and wash your hands.

Ripe Fruit in a Hurry

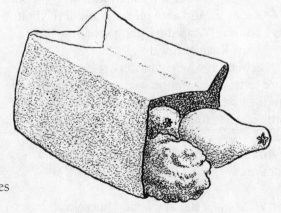

Try putting that moldy lemon in a paper bag with some unripe pears or peaches.

After one day note the results. The green mold on the lemon gives off a gas called ethylene. The mold gives off so much gas that a single moldy lemon can speed up the ripening of hundreds of pieces of unripe fruit.

Be sure to wash the ripe fruit well before eating it and throw the moldy lemon away.

Dairy Dozen

The refrigerator can supply the raw materials for a baker's dozen of fascinating—and useful—experiments. You can construct a plastic toy, etch graffiti on an eggshell, and make a "fat" light meter.

About Milk

Mammals, including people, feed their young with milk from the mother's body. Most of our milk comes from cows, but humans also use the milk of the mare, goat, ewe, buffalo, camel, ass, zebra, reindeer, llama, and yak.

About Butter

Butter—probably from buffalo—was known by 2000 B.C. First used as an ointment to beautify hair, it was also used as a medicine to treat burns, and, melted, as oil for lamps.

Butter is made by churning or agitating milk or cream and separating the solid fatty portion.

About Oil

The word "oil" comes from the Greek word for olive, but we use many different kinds of oils from animals and from such plants as cottonseed, palm, corn, peanut, and soybean.

Margarine is made from cottonseed and other vegetable oils.

About Eggs

Various wild birds were first tamed for use as food—flesh and eggs—in India.

Making Muffet Food

Little Miss Muffet was eating her curds and whey when that spider came along.

Just what are curds and whey?

What to do: Mix the milk and the vinegar together in the jar.

What happens: The milk changes. At the bottom there is a thick substance, the curds. On top there is a watery liquid, the whey.

Why: Vinegar turns the milk sour and separates some of its parts. Curds are made up of the fat and minerals and a protein called casein. Cheeses are made from curds. white glue is made from the casein of the curds. To use the curds as glue, just wash away the liquid.

Make a Plastic Toy

HOT!

Create your own plastic—and mold it into a tiny toy. But don't expect it to look store-bought. Have an adult help you with this experiment.

What to do: Heat the milk in the pan, stirring frequently, until lumps (curdles) form. Ask an adult to slowly pour off the liquid. Put the lumps into the jar and add the vinegar. Let the lumps stand for about one hour.

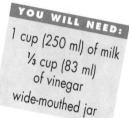

What happens: A rubbery blob forms. Again slowly pour off the liquid. The shape the blob into a ball or a face. Leave it to harden for a few hours in the open jar or on a paper towel. If you wish, you can then color it with acrylic paints.

Why: When the vinegar and milk interact, the milk separates into a liquid and a solid made of fat, minerals, and protein casein (made up of very long molecules that bend like rubber until they harden).

At first, plastics were made from milk and plants. Now they are made from petroleum, and this poses a problem because they don't decompose.

50

YOU WILL NEED:
2 raw eggs
1 hard-boiled egg

Detecting the Hard–Boiled Egg

What a dilemma! You've put a cooked egg in the refrigerator and someone stuck it back among the raw eggs. You need the cooked one for a salad. But which one is it?

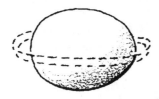 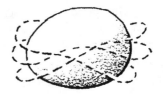

What to do: Spin each egg. Note what happens, Then touch each egg lightly while it is spinning.

What happens: Two of the eggs wobble, but one spins. The spinner is the hard-boiled egg. When you touch the spinning hard-boiled egg lightly, it stops spinning completely. The raw eggs move again after you have tried to stop them.

Why: The loose yolks and whites in the raw eggs revolve slowly because of inertia, the tendency of an object to continue at rest or in motion. This causes the raw eggs to wobble and to continue to move even after you tried to stop them. The solid white and yolk cause the hard-boiled egg to respond more quickly.

How do You Make an Egg Float?

51

YOU WILL NEED:

egg
2 drinking glasses
water
salt

No—this is not a riddle! Find out why it is easier to swim in the ocean than in a freshwater lake or pool.

What to do: Pour water into one glass until it is half full. Put the egg into the water. Notice what happens. Now add 3 tablespoons of salt, stir gently, and observe what happens.

Pour water into the second glass until it is half full. Stir in 10 tablespoons of salt. Slowly add fresh water until the glass is full. Donot stir. Gently lower in the egg.

What happens: In the fresh water the egg sinks. As you add salt, it floats higher and higher.

When you add fresh water to the very salty water, the egg is suspended in the middle.

Why: The denser the liquid the greater its upward life, or buoyancy. Salt makes the water denser.

When you add fresh water to the salty water, it remains on top. The egg sinks through it and floats on the lower, denser salty water.

52 The Egg in the Bottle Trick

Can you really put an egg into a bottle—if the bottle has a neck that is slightly smaller than the egg—without mashing the egg?

YOU WILL NEED:

boiling water
small-necked bottle
like a ketchup bottle or
a baby's bottle
pot holder
hard-boiled egg, peeled

HOT!

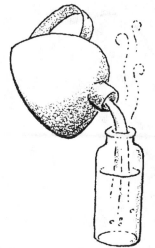

What to do: Pour the boiling water into the bottle. Hold the bottle with a pot holder and shake the water around in it and then pour it out. Quickly place the egg over the mouth of the bottle.

What happens: Although the egg is larger than the opening, the egg drops into the bottle.

Why: The hot water leaves steam in the bottle, which forces out some of the air. As the steam in the bottle cools, it changes into droplets of water and requires less space. This reduces the amount of air pressure in the bottle, and so the pressure of the outside air pushes the egg inside the bottle.

To remove the egg, hold the bottle upside down, place your mouth on the opening of the bottle, and blow into it for 30 seconds. The pressure inside will be greater than the pressure outside—and the egg will be forced out.

Egg Power

Eggshells are fragile, aren't they? Or are they? For this experiment collect the empty eggshells when the family has scrambled eggs or omelets for breakfast.

What to do: Wrap a piece of masking tape around the midsection of each eggshell half. Then, with your scissors, trim off the excess shell so each one has a straight-edged bottom.

Lay out the four eggshells, dome up, so they form a square. Holding a can upright, stand it on the eggshells. Keep on stacking cans on top of that one until the shells crack.

What happens: The "fragile" eggshells can support a surprising amount of weight.

Why: The secret of their strength is their shape. No single point in the dome supports the entire weight of the object on top of it. The weight is carried down along the curved walls to the wide base.

Egg Graffiti

54

Can you etch your initials or a drawing on an ordinary egg—without breaking the shell?

What to do: Carefully draw or write on the eggshell with the crayon. Put the egg into the jar and add enough vinegar to cover it. Let it stand for 2 hours. Then pour out the vinegar. Replace it with fresh vinegar, and allow the egg to stand in it for another 2 hours. Wash the egg and remove the crayon marks.

What happens: The eggshell may be very fragile, but your drawing or writing remains!

Why: The acid in the vinegar combines with the calcium carbonate of the shell and dissolves much of it—but not the part that you wrote on the crayon. The wax in the crayon protects that part of the shell from the vinegar so the section with your writing or drawing is not dissolved.

Oil and Water

55

YOU WILL NEED:

tablespoon cooking oil
water colored with a few drops of food coloring
narrow jar or soda bottle with a lid or a cork

"They are like oil and water!" That's how we describe two people who don't get along. Well, how do oil and water get along?

What to do: Pour 2 tablespoons of oil and 2 tablespoons of colored water into the jar or soda bottle. Cover and shake it hard. Now put it down.

What happens: Although the oil and water seem to mix when you shake the container, they separate when you put it down. The oil floats on top.

Why: Many liquids dissolve in water to form a solution, but water and oil do not mix. The oil molecules have a greater attraction for each other than for the molecules of the water. Oil floats on top of the water because it weighs less. That's why it is so easy to remove the fat from chicken soup and from beef gravy. When these liquids stand for a while, and especially after they have cooled, the fats form a solid layer on top of the other liquids.

Liquid Sandwich **56**

Can you make a sandwich with three liquids?

What to do: Into a narrow jar, pour the oil, the water, and the honey or molasses. Cover the jar.

What happens: A liquid sandwich! The honey or molasses sinks to the bottom; the oil floats on top; and the water remains in the middle.

Why: The honey or molasses sinks because it is denser (it weighs more for the same amount) than water. The oil floats because it is less dense than the water.

How Fat is It? **57**

It is surprisingly simple to find out whether a food has fat in it.

What to do: Draw six small circles on the paper. Label each circle with the name of one of the food you will be testing.
Rub a tiny bit of each food on its own circle. After 10 minutes, examine both sides of the paper.

What happens: Some of the circles will be dry. Others will be greasy and the spots will be spreading.

Why: Both water and fat produce a spot by filling in the spaces between the fibers of the paper. Spots made by water in the food evaporate in the air and dry. But the fat globules remain. They can only be broken down by soap or a solvent like ether.

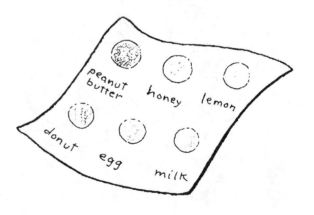

A "Fat" Light Meter

Which light bulb is brighter? What flashlight?
You can figure it out scientifically!

YOU WILL NEED:
cooking oil
sheet of white paper
paper towel
2 unshaded lamps
with light bulbs of
different wattage
ruler or tape measure

What to do: Place a few drops of ordinary cooking oil on the sheet of white paper. Let the oil soak in and then, using a paper towel, blot away the excess so that all that remains is an oil spot on the paper.

In a dark room, set up your light bulbs in the unshaded lamps across a table from each other. Hold the paper close to the bulb on the left and gradually move it closer to the bulb on the right. Keep your eyes on the oil spot.

What happens: The spot disappears when the same amount of light falls on both sides of the paper.

Why: How does that help you to find out which bulb is brighter?

If you measure the distance from the spot to each bulb, and the distances are not equal, one of the lights must be brighter than the other.

For example, if Bulb A is 2 feet (60 cm) away from the paper and Bulb B is 3 feet (90 cm) away, Bulb B is brighter. If you want to know how much brighter, multiply A's distance—2 feet—by itself (2 x 2). Then multiply B's distance—3 feet—by itself (3 x 3). Divide the larger number by the smaller (9 divided by 4). Bulb B gives off more than twice as much light as Bulb A.

Magnifying Glass

A magnifying glass made of water?
Impossible?

What to do: Straighten the paper clip. Form a small loop at one end of the wire and rub a little butter or cooking oil on it. Dip the loop into the glass of water and lift it out. You now have a lens—a kind of frame that holds a layer of water.

Use the lens to read the small print in the telephone directory, the classified ads in the newspaper, and to see the fine details of the postage stamp.

Why: The water lens, just like a glass or plastic lens, has a definite shape. It bends light rays as they pass through it. First, it bends light as the light enters. Then it bends it again as the light leaves. The angle at which the water bends the light depends upon the shape of the lens.

Reflected light spreads out from the object you are look at, hits the lens, and is bent back to your eye. Your eye see the light as though it came on a straight line from the object—and the object seems to be much larger than it actually is.

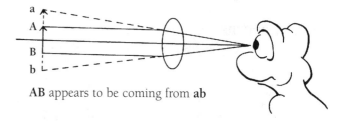

AB appears to be coming from **ab**

How Much Bigger?

You can find out just how much larger a lens makes an object by using a piece of graph paper. You can also use an ordinary sheet of paper, but you have to draw graph lines on it.

Look through your magnifying glass at the lined paper. Count the number of lines you see through the "lens" compared to the number you see outside of it.

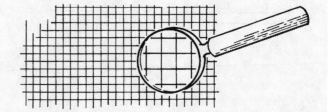

If there are 4 lines outside, compared to 1 line inside, the lens magnifies 4 times.

Adventures with a String

With a piece of string, you can perform all kinds of scientific marvels! You can force water to walk a tightrope, cut a string inside a bottle, lift a heavy weight with a button, make a grandfather clock—and even prove your superior strength!

About String

Through the centuries, string and cord, rope and twine have been made from the fiber of such plants as hemp and flax, jute and sisal. Strands of fiber are twisted or braided together. Today we also use synthetic, or man-made materials, like nylon and polyester to make string and rope.

61 ◆ Cut a String Without Touching It

Can you cut a string without laying a hand on it—when it is inside a covered glass jar? See how easy it is when you "concentrate," but you must do this on a sunny day!

YOU WILL NEED:
small piece of string
jar with a lid
tape
magnifying glass

What to do: Tape one end of the string to the inside of the jar lid. Screw on the jar lid so the string is suspended in the jar.

With the magnifying glass, focus the rays of the sun on the string for a few minutes.

What happens: The string breaks in two.

Why: The magnifying glass concentrates the heat of the sun on the string. The heat becomes intense enough to burn right through the string.

62 Water Walks a Tightrope

Will water travel on a string without falling off? Try this experiment and find out.

What to do: Using the nail, punch a small hole near the top lip of the plastic cup. Dampen the string and thread it through the hole, tying a knot on the inside. Fill the cup almost to the top with water.

Place the pail on the floor near your left foot. Tie the free end of the string to your left index finger and hold it over the pail.

Then hold the cup up in your right hand. Stretch the string taut and slant it down toward the pail. Tip the cup of water and slowly pour the water onto the string.

What happens: The water travels down the string until it reaches your left index finger and the pail.

Why: The molecules near the surface of the water cling together to form an elastic, tubelike skin through which the water flows along the wet string. This elastic skin is known as surface tension.

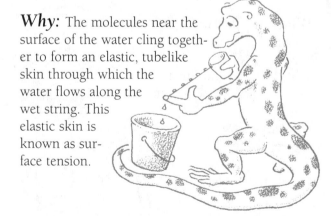

63 Making a Figure 8 Stopper Knot

You can secure the string to the inside of the cup in any way that holds. But if you want to do it with a figure 8 stopper, follow the diagram below.

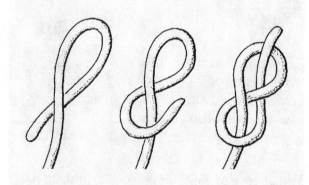

Mining Salt

YOU WILL NEED:

small jar
hot water
tablespoon
salt
nail
small piece of string
pencil

In some tropical areas, salt is not mined from the earth, but is taken from sea water in shallow ponds. You can create your own salt water—and then separate the salt in the form of crystals.

What to do: Fill the jar with hot water and stir in 1 tablespoon of salt at a time until the salt no longer dissolves. It will take about 1 tablespoon of salt for every 1 ounce (30 ml) of water.

Attach the nail to one end of the string. Wrap the other end of the string around the pencil. Rest the pencil on the edge of the jar and suspend the nail in the salted water so it hangs down, but does not touch the bottom of the jar.

Put the jar in a warm place.

What happens: After a few days, the water dries up and crystals form on the string. They taste salty.

Why: Water molecules slowly go into the air as water vapor. As the water evaporates from the salt water, the salt atoms draw close together, forming cube-shaped crystals. When the water is gone, the salt crystals remain.

Make Rock Candy

You can make rock candy, which is really just sugar crystals, the same way you make salt crystals. You will need a jar that is a little larger and a longer piece of string. Add 2 cups of sugar to ¼ cup (125 ml) of hot water and let it stand for a few days.

Rescue an Ice Cube

This is a great "icebreaker" for a party! Challenge your guests to use a string to rescue an ice cube from a glass of water without getting their hands wet. Tell them they may use anything on the party table except the dishes or utensils. After they fail, show them how to do it.

What to do: Float the ice cube in the glass of water. Hang one end of the string over the edge of the glass. Place the other end of it on the ice cube.

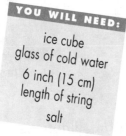

Then sprinkle a little salt on the ice cube and let it stand for 10 minutes.

What happens: The string freezes onto the ice cube. Then you pull on the string and lift the ice cube out of the water.

Why: When the salt strikes the ice, it lowers the freezing point of the water to a little below 32 degrees F (0 degrees C) and causes the surface of the ice cube to melt a little. As the ice refreezes, it traps the string.

Something Fishy

Here is an easy way to spin a sea monster!

What to do: On the cardboard draw and cut out a sea monster, like the one in the illustration. Add three dots, as shown.

Tack up the monster at the top dot and drop the nail from the tack. Draw along the string line. Repeat for the other two dots.

Tack up the monster at the point where the three lines cross. Spin it.

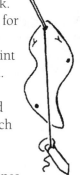

What happens: The cardboard monster spins evenly and stops each time at a different place.

Why: The point where the three lines intersect is the center of gravity. If you hang the shape by any other point, it will be out of balance, spin unevenly, and stop at the same place, where the center of gravity is lowest, every time you spin it.

68 Lazy Bones

In this experiment you might expect the thin threads that support the stick to break, but instead . . .

What to do: Tie a piece of thread to each end of the stick. Then tie the other end of each thread to the hanger so the stick is suspended underneath. Use clove hitch knots (see instructions below) if you like. Strike the stick with the metal edge of the ruler.

What happens: The threads do not break! If you strike hard enough, the piece of wood will break.

Why: You are applying force not to the threads but to the stick. The stick resists moving—so much that it would rather break than move. It is the law of inertia again: bodies at rest tend to stay at rest.

69 Making a Clove Hitch Knot

The clove hitch allows you to join a rope to something else, like a stick or a clothes hanger.

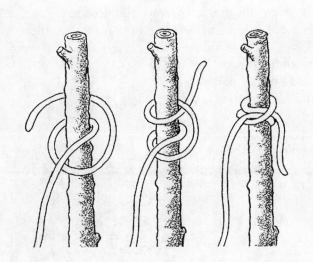

Getting It Straight

70

Bet you can't straighten this string!

What to do: Lay the string out straight on a table or on the floor. Place the book in the middle of the string. Tie the string around the book without making a knot. Lift the book by holding the ends of the string. Then take one end of the string in each hand and pull on it so the two ends of the string form one straight line.

What happens: You cannot pull the string straight—no matter how hard you pull.

Why: You will notice that as you separate the string ends, the book feels heavier and heavier. The greater the angle between the two halves of the string, the greater the force you need to hold the book up. A straight line forms an angle of 180 degrees. You would need an enormous amount of force to hold up the book with the ends of the string at that angle—so much force that the string would break before you got the two ends to form a straight line.

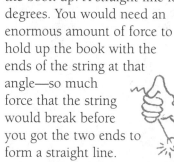

Loop-the-Loop

71

When you are on a loop-the-loop, and it turns upside down, why don't you fall out?

What to do: Tie the rope securely to the handle of the pail. Put the ball into the pail.

Choose a spot where there is no risk of hitting anything—outdoors if possible. Hold the pail by the rope and whirl the pail in circles in the air as fast as you can.

What happens: The ball remains in the pail even when it turns upside down.

Why: Centrifugal force—the force created by that whirling motion—equals the force of gravity and keeps the ball from falling out of the pail. It pulls the object against the sides of the pail rather than down and out of it.

When you get really good at this, you may want to try it with a pail of water—outdoors!

The Talking String

Believe it or not, you can make your string talk!

YOU WILL NEED:
strong, thin string, or thread, 18 inches to 24 inches (45 to 60 cm) long
large two-hole button

What to do:

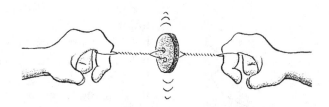

Thread the string through the holes of the button and knot the ends together. Use a bowline knot (see instructions below), if you like. Center the button.

Loop the string on each side of the button on your index fingers. Swing the button around a number of times, either toward you or away from you, but always in the same direction.

When the string is "wound up," separate your hands, pulling the string taut. Then bring your hands together, releasing it. Alternate pulling and releasing until the string unwinds.

What happens: The button spins very fast until it twists in the opposite direction. If you spin it fast enough, you hear a whirring sound.

Why: The law of inertia is at work again: A body in motion tends to continue in motion. The sound comes from the vibration of the air around the string.

Making a Bowline Knot

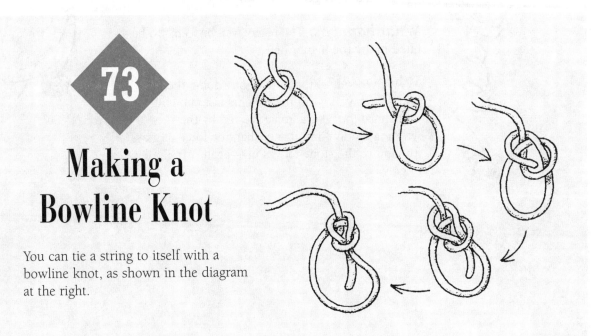

You can tie a string to itself with a bowline knot, as shown in the diagram at the right.

David and Goliath

Can a button lift a stone?

74

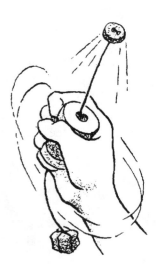

What to do: Thread the string through the spool so about two-thirds of the string is above it. Then tie the button to one end of the string and the stone to the other end. With the button toward the top and the stone toward the bottom, hold the contraption above your head. To do this, hold the spool with one hand and with the other hand hold the string just above the stone. Begin whirling the spool around so both weights move as fast as possible.

Gradually let go of the string below the spool.

What happens: The heavy weight seems to be lifted up by the lighter one.

Why: Of course, the button isn't doing the lifting! When you whirl the weights fast enough, centrifugal force—the force created by the whirling motion—is greater than the force of gravity. and so the stone moves up—against the pull of gravity.

Broomstick Block-and-Tackle

YOU WILL NEED:
jump rope or clothesline
2 brooms or long sticks
2 friends

You are amazingly strong! To prove it do this experiment.

What to do: Give a broomstick to each of your friends and ask them to stand a few feet apart. Then tie one end of the rope to one of the sticks and weave the rope in and around the sticks, as in the illustration. You hold on to the other end of the rope. Now ask your friends to pull the broomsticks apart as hard as they can, while you pull on the rope.

What happens: No matter how hard your friends try to keep the broomsticks apart, you can pull them together.

Why: Each time you wrap the rope around the broomsticks, you increase the distance the rope has to be pulled. When you pull on the end of the rope, you exert a small force—but over a long distance. The resulting force is far greater than the force your friends can exert over a shorter distance.

The broomstick block-and-tackle is a form of double pulley. It is used for loading ships, lifting the shovels of cranes, and lowering and lifting lifeboats, pianos, safes, and machinery.

Blow the
Book Away

YOU WILL NEED:

2 long pieces of
string or rope
book
wooden clothes hanger

Move a book back and forth by blowing on it? Try it!

What to do: Loop the two pieces of string around the book and knot them. Then tie the loose ends of the strings to the rod of the wooden hanger so the book swings freely, as in the illustration.

Blow on the book. Continue blowing on it every time it swings back toward you.

What happens: Even gentle blowing seems to make the book swing vigorously.

Why: It is not only a question of force, but also one of timing, Although you may not be blowing very hard, regular blowing at the right moment sends the book flying.

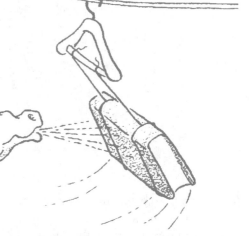

Making a Sheet Bend Knot

If a string or rope isn't long enough, use the sheet bend, a knot for joining two ropes.

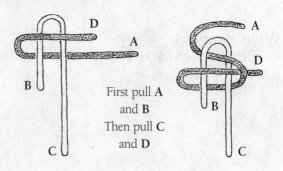

First pull **A**
and **B**
Then pull **C**
and **D**

78

Swing Time

Galileo first performed this amazing experiment
with strings in 1583!

YOU WILL NEED:

4 strings of
different lengths
2 strings of the
same length
teaspoon
5 paper clips
clothesline or
clothes hanger

What to do: Tie the teaspoon to one of the strings
that has another string the same length. Tie the paper
clips to the five other strings. Tie each string to the
clothesline or hanger. Swing the teaspoon.

What happens: All the strings with the paper clips
on them start to swing. But the paper clip on that
string that is the same length as the teaspoon's swings
with more energy than the others—and the string
with the teaspoon winds down. Then the teaspoon
strings picks up vigor and the same-length paper
clip slows down.

Why: The swing of the teaspoon moves along the
hanger and gives all the strings and paper clips a push,
starting them all moving. But each string, depending
on its length, swings back and forth at a different time.
Only one paper clip—the one that swings at the same
time as the teaspoon—gets pushed at the right moment
to build up its swing. It swings with more vigor than
the others—until it loses energy to the teaspoon string,
which builds up its swing again. The teaspoon and
the same-length paper clip continue taking turns
speeding up and slowing down.

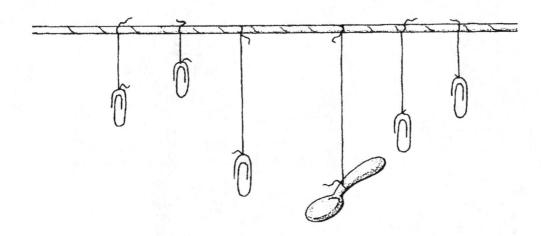

79 A String Grandfather Clock

This experiment will show you how to measure time with a string.

What to do: Tie the weight to the string that is 48 inches (120 cm) long and suspend it from the clothes hanger or ceiling hook. (If you don't have a long enough string, you can use sheet bed knots, see the instructions on page 66, to join strings.)

Pull the string slightly to one side and let it swing. Count the number of swings it makes in 60 seconds. Then pull the string farther over to one side and count the number of swings it makes in 60 seconds. Write down the results.

Now do the same thing with the strings of different lengths: 10 inches; 20 inches; and, finally 39 inches. In each case, count the number of times the weight moves back and forth in 60 seconds and write it down.

What happens: When the string is 39 inches long, the weight moves back and forth 60 times in 60 seconds, or 1 minute.

Why: A pendulum takes the same amount of time to make every swing no matter how far it travels or how heavy the weight at the end of it. But the longer the pendulum, the longer the time it takes to complete its swing, and the shorter the pendulum, the quicker it travels back and forth.

Since a length of string measuring 39 inches swings back and forth 60 times in 1 minute, you know that every complete swing it makes measures one second. You can use that length of string to measure time with great accuracy.

In 1673, Christopher Huygens used this principle in his design for a "grandfather" clock.

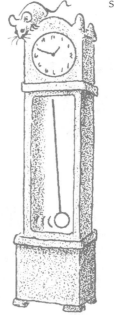

String Balance

You can make your own scale with a few strings and then put it to work weighing small objects.

YOU WILL NEED:
tape
3 strings of different lengths:
4 inches (10 cm);
6 inches (15 cm);
and 8 inches (20 cm)
12 inch (30 cm) ruler
wire clothes hanger
12 small paper clips

What to do: Tape the 6 inch string to the center of the ruler, making sure that it won't come off. Tie the free end of the string to the rod of the hanger, as shown in the illustration.

Attach the other two strings (the 4 inch and the 8 inch strings) so they are the same distance from the ends of the ruler. Knot the free ends of the strings.

Unwind one of the paper clips and bend it so it fits tightly when you hang it over the ruler. Slide it along the ruler until the ruler hangs straight.

Link 2 paper clips and tie them to the 8 inch length of string. Then attach paper clips to the 4 inch length of string until the ruler is balanced again.

What happens: You have to attach 4 paper clips to the 4 inch string to balance 2 paper clips attached to the 8 inch string.

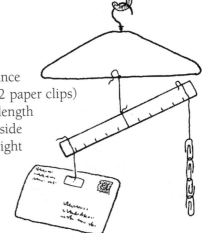

Why: In the balance scale, the weight (2 paper clips) multiplied by the length (8 inches) on one side must equal the weight (4 paper clips) multiplied by the length (4 inches) on the other side.

Using Your Scale

You can use your string scale to weigh various objects. It will make a great postage scale.

How many paper clips will you have to add to the 8 inch string if you attach a 1 ounce letter to the 4 inch string?

When you find out, you can tell in a quick glance whether you have put enough postage on a letter.

SOAP SUDS

Make "blood," sink a ship, power a paper boat, move tooth picks at will, put bubbles to work—all with soap.

About Soap

Ancient peoples washed with water and wood ashes and then soothed their clean but irritated bodies with grease or oil from animals or plants.

About two thousand years ago, the Gauls invented a soap that combined wood ashes and animal fat. They used it to make their hair brighter.

A soap factory and bars of scented soap were found in the ruins of Pompeii, the city that was destroyed in the first century A.D.

Today, commercial soap makers combine fat or grease with lye (an alkali made from wood ash) and salt. They add perfumes, coloring, water softeners, and preservatives before they shape or flake the soap.

Although the word "detergent" actually means anything that will clean things, it is usually used today to refer to a cleaner made from a man-made, or synthetic, substance usually derived from petroleum. Detergent was first developed for commercial use in the 1950s.

Dracula's Favorite Soap

Soapy Shipwreck

1 tablespoon of rubbing alcohol

2 laxative pills, like Ex-Lax or Feen-a-Mint

bar of soap

Terrify your friends with this amazing soap!

What to do: Pour the rubbing alcohol into a small dish and mash the pills into it. Rub the mixture on your hands and let it dry. Then wash it off with soap.

What happens: The soapy water turns bright red.

Why: The laxative contains a compound known as phenolphthalein. This substance turns a brilliant red when it is mixed with an alkali. Soap is made from fat boiled together with a strong alkali. When you add water, you free some of the alkali. This alkali mixes with the phenolphthalein on your hands—and turns them blood red.

What does soap do to water that makes washing easier? Watch!

straight pin

1 cup of water

tweezers

1 teaspoon of liquid soap (either dishwashing or laundry detergent)

medicine dropper

What to do: Float the pin on the water in the cup. It's easiest if you lower the pin with a pair of tweezers. Then carefully add the liquid soap one drop at a time.

What happens: As you add the soap, the pin sinks.

Why: To start with, the pin is not actually floating. It is resting on the water's invisible elastic skin.

Water molecules are strongly attracted to one another and stick close together, especially on the surface of the water. This creates tension—enough tension to support an object you would think would sink. Surface tension also prevents water from surrounding the particles of dirt, soot, and dust on your skin or clothes.

When dissolved in water, soap separates the water molecules, reducing the surface tension. That's the reason the pin sinks—and the reason soapy water washes dirt away.

Soap Power

Can you use soap to power a boat? Well, maybe, a very small one—in a basin or in the bathtub.

What to do: From the index card, cut out a boat approximately 2 inches x 1 inch (5 cm x 2.5 cm), with a small slot for the "engine" in the rear, as in the illustration.

Float the boat in the pot of water. Pour a few drops of detergent into the engine slot.

What happens: The boat travels through the water.

Why: The soap breaks the water's elastic "skin," the surface tension behind the boat. The boat sails forward—and will stop only when the soap reduces the surface tension of all the water in your "lake."

Picky Toothpicks

You can make a circle of toothpicks come and go at will.

What to do: Arrange the toothpicks in a circle in the bowl of water. Place the cube of sugar in the center of the circle.

Change the water and arrange the toothpicks in a circle again. This time place the piece of soap in the center.

What happens: When you place the sugar in the center, the toothpicks are drawn to it. When you place the soap in the center, the toothpicks are repelled.

Why: The sugar sucks up water, creating a current that carries the toothpicks with it toward the center. The soap, on the other hand, give off an oily film that spreads outward. It weakens the surface tension and the film carries the toothpicks away with it.

YOU WILL NEED:

small plastic bag and fastener

wax paper, cut into small pieces

felt-tipped pen

large pan or bowl of water

liquid detergent

Polluting the Duck Pond

86

Is anything wrong with washing your clothes with detergent in a lake or a pond? Take a look!

What to do: Stuff the plastic bag with the small pieces of wax paper. Close the bag with its fastener. Draw a duck on the bag with the felt-tipped pen. Float your "duck" in the pan or bowl. Then add a little detergent.

What happens: The duck sinks.

Why: The wax paper and plastic are water-repellent—just the way a live duck is. A duck's feathers are oily. This oil repels water and helps a duck to float. But a detergent enables water to stick to greasy materials. Detergent may be fine for washing dishes and clothes, but it is deadly for the duck.

Handmade Bubbles

87

Bubbles are globs of air or gas inside a hollow liquid ball. Soap bubbles are globs of air enclosed in a film of soapy water. You can make bubbles by blowing through a pipe or a ring dipped in soapsuds. You can do it with just your hand, too.

What to do: Pour the water into the bowl. Gently stir in the dishwashing liquid. Curl your fingers and dip your hand into the soapy mixture. Blow into your curled hand.

What happens: Bubbles form.

Why: When you blow into the mixture of water and detergent on your wet hand, you add the air that forms the center of the bubble.

Bubble Mix Recipes

Recipes for bubble mix differ, partly because soap powders and detergents vary in strength. Experiment and figure out which ones work best for you. Here are some suggestions that may help:

○ Dishwashing detergent usually works well.

○ Use at least 1 part detergent to 8 to 10 parts of warm water for a normal mix. For example, 1 tablespoon (15 ml) of detergent for every ½ cup (125 ml) of water, or ½ cup of soap to 5 cups of water.

○ A larger proportion of soap to water makes larger bubbles.

○ More detergent than water creates giant bubbles.

○ Add sugar or gelatin powder or glycerin to get longer-lasting bubbles. Bubbles burst when they dry out. These substances slow down the evaporation of water that causes the drying out. Try 1 part sugar or gelatin or glycerin to 1 part soap and 6 parts water.

Bubble Tips

○ Save clean jars of different sizes to hold various bubble mixes.

○ Stir gently so as not to whip up soapsuds. (Suds are actually tiny bubbles.)

○ If possible, let the bubble mix stand for a day or two before using it.

○ Put the bubble mix in the refrigerator for a few minutes before using it. Your bubbles will last longer.

○ For best results, blow bubbles on a rainy day. Because there is more moisture in the air, they will last longer.

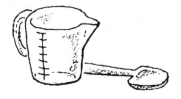

89

Making a Bubble Blower

YOU WILL NEED:

uncoated wire
clothes hanger
circular object, like a
frozen juice can or
a thick crayon
bubble mix

You can make a great bubble blower from a wire clothes hanger. Ask an adult to help you.

With the help of an adult, untwist the wire hanger and then wrap a piece of it around the can or thick crayon. Slip the can out. Leave about 4 inches (10 cm) of straight wire for a handle. Then bend the rest of the wire back and forth until it snaps. And now you have your bubble wand.

Dip the wand into the bubble mix and wave it in the air.

What happens: You get a spray of bubbles.

Why: By waving the soapy wand in the air, you add the air that forms the center of each bubble.

90

Other Bubble Blowers

You can make a bubble blower from almost anything: a drinking straw, a clay pipe, a tin horn, a funnel, a paper cup with the end removed, a juice can with both ends removed, even a cutaway plastic bottle.

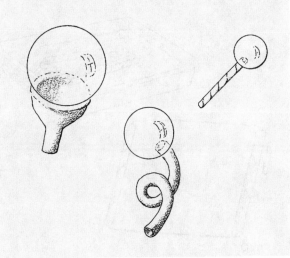

91 ◆ Super Bubble

YOU WILL NEED:
3 foot (90 cm) length of string
2 plastic drinking straws
jar of bubble mix with more
detergent than water
(see page 74)
large baking pan

To create a large bubble, you need a large bubble blower and a strong bubble mix.

What to do: Thread the string through the two drinking straws and tie the ends of the string to one another. Pour the bubble mix into the large baking pan. Wetting your fingers first, hold one straw in each hand and dip the strings and straws into the mixture for a couple of seconds.

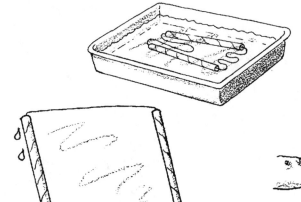

Remove the strings from the mix and pull the straws apart so the strings are taut. Holding the straws as though they were a frame, wave them around several times. Then pull the straws upward and bring them close together.

What happens: You release an enormous round bubble.

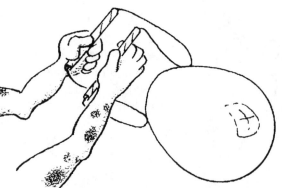

Why: You get a large bubble because you are adding a large amount of air when you wave the straw frame and pull the straws up. As this air pushes out in all directions, you pull apart the molecules of the soapy film. But the molecules are attracted to one another, and the "elastic" skin of the bubble contracts as much as it can to form the smallest surface for the air it contains. The form that has the smallest surface is the sphere. That's why the bubble is round.

Bubble Duet

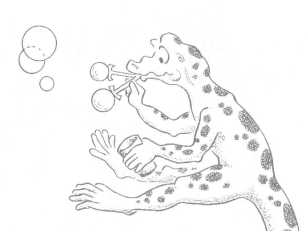

plastic drinking straw
scissors
bowl of bubble mix

Blow two bubbles with one bubble blower—and see how they affect one another.

What to do: Cut four slits about ⅔ inch (17 mm) long at both ends of the drinking straw. Bend the cut strips outward, as in the illustration. Make a small slit in the middle of the straw, and bend it at the slit. You have now made a two-ended bubble pipe.

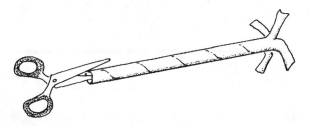

Dip one end of the pipe into the bubble mix. Blow into the middle slit. You'll get a bubble. Blow a second bubble by dipping the other end of your pipe into the mix and blowing the middle slit again. Then seal the slit in the middle of the bubble pipe by covering it with your fingers.

What happens: When you blow the second bubble, the first one gets larger. When the opening is sealed, the smaller second bubble gets ever smaller while the first one gets even larger.

Why: Because a small bubble is more curved than a large bubble, the air pressure exerted by its "elastic" skin is greater than that on a large bubble. Therefore, the small bubble gets smaller. The air from it is forced into the bigger bubble, which then gets even larger.

Make a Bubble Stand

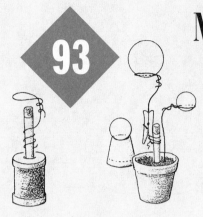

93

To make a stand for your bubbles, all you have to do is place a plastic cup or container upside down.

Or you can put a pencil in the hole of a wooden spool of thread and wind a wire loop around it, as in the illustration at the left. Transfer a bubble from a bubble blower to the stand by simply shaking it off gently. You can then observe the bubble—and make others.

Rainbow in a Bubble

94

A rainbow in a bubble? Yes!

YOU WILL NEED:

bubble mix
1 tablespoon of sugar
refrigerator
bubble blower, like a
wire ring
bubble stand

What to do: Add the sugar to the bubble mix. Put the bubble mix in the refrigerator for 5 minutes. This will make the bubbles last longer.

Dip the bubble blower into the mix. When you have a film of soap on the ring, blow gently. Attach your bubble to the bubble stand by shaking the bubble blower over the stand.

What happens: After a few minutes, you see different colors.

Why: When light hits a bubble, most of it passes through it because the bubble is transparent. But as the air in the bubble evaporates and the bubble gets even thinner, some of the rays that make up white light do not pass through. Instead, they are reflected back from either the outside or the inside. That's why you see various colors of the spectrum. The colors change and disappear, because the bubble's thickness is not the same all over and is constantly changing.

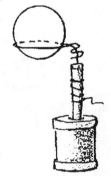

Bubble in a Bubble in a Bubble

YOU WILL NEED:
plastic cup bubble stand
bubble mix
bubble ring
plastic straw

Use a bubble stand to put a bubble in your bubble's bubble.

What to do: Turn the plastic cup upside down and wet the bottom of it, which is now on top. Using the wire ring make a large bubble and attach it to the bubble stand.

   Wet the plastic straw in the bubble mix and gently push it through the large bubble. Blow a smaller bubble inside the large one. Then carefully push the straw through the smaller bubble, and blow an even smaller one.

What happens: You get a bubble in a bubble in a bubble.

Why: Anything wet can penetrate the bubble without breaking it. The wet surface coming into contact with the soapy film becomes part of it. Do not touch the wet wall with your smaller bubble. If you do you will not get a separate bubble.

Putting a Bubble to Work

We can make an ordinary soap bubble do work for us!

YOU WILL NEED:
long needle
½ inch (12 mm) cork
3 inch (7.5 cm) square of paper
empty thread spool
bubble mix

Carefully stick the needle into the cork with the point out. Put the cork on a table or counter.

   Fold the paper diagonally twice. Unfold it. Balance the center of the paper square (where the creases meet) on the point of the needle, as in the illustration.

   Dip the spool in the bubble mix and blow a bubble on one end. Hold the other end toward the paper.

What happens: The paper moves.

Why: Air escaping from the bubble moves the paper.

Take a Bubble Dancing

If you think your bubbles have worked hard enough
and need a little recreation, you can take them dancing.

YOU WILL NEED:

comb
piece of flannel or wool
bubble ring
bubble mix

What to do: Rub the comb several times
against the piece of flannel or wool. Make a
spray of bubbles with the bubble ring and float
the bubbles above the fabric so they land on it.
Then move the comb close to each of the bubbles
in turn.

What happens: Each bubble seems to
dance—moving up and then falling down.

Why: You are using static electricity—electricity
created by friction—to make your bubbles
"dance."

By rubbing the comb on the fabric, you charge
it with static electricity. Because charges of electricity that are not alike attract one another, the
charged comb attracts the uncharged bubbles. The
bubbles then become charged by the comb—and
are pushed away because they have the same
charge of static electricity as the comb. Charges of
electricity that are alike repel one another. Each
time the bubbles come up and touch the comb
they get charged and each time they go down,
they lose their charge and are pulled up again.

SLOW START—FAST FINISH

You know how you feel when you're lying in bed in the morning and you don't want to move? That's inertia.

You're on your bike at the foot of a steep hill and it takes every ounce of strength you have just to get the bike started. That, too, is inertia.

Inertia is a scientific work that says that things that are standing still tend to continue to stand still.

When you are riding your bike along a level road, you don't have to pedal hard every second. You can even stop spinning the pedals and coast a bit. That's inertia.

You see, inertia also means that objects that are moving tend to keep on moving.

These ideas aren't difficult to understand. Of course things stand still until someone or something moves them. What would life be like if you put a pizza on a table and, all by itself, it started to slide to the edge and fall onto the floor?

Engineers found out long ago that an automobile uses only a small part of its power to cruise along the highway. It makes much greater horsepower to get that car moving and up to speed than to keep it going when it is on the open road.

The experiments we are going to do in this chapter show how you can make inertia work for you. Some of the results will amaze you and your friends. If you wish, let them think you are performing a bit of magic.

98 Watching Inertia at Work

YOU WILL NEED:
3 foot (1 m) length of string
book
rubber band

Here is a simple experiment that lets you see inertia at work.

What to do: Tie the string around the book. Then tie the free end of the string to the rubber band.

Put the book on the floor. Rough carpet is best. Just don't use a polished floor that might get scratched. Things look like this now:

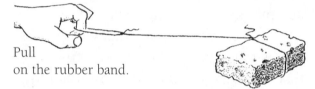

Pull
on the rubber band.

What happens: The rubber band will stretch until you get the load moving. Then, as you continue to pull the weight across the floor, the rubber band won't stretch quite so much as when you started pulling.

Why: Inertia tends to keep motionless things where they are. To get things moving, you have to overcome inertia. The greater stretch in the rubber band show you had to pull harder to get the load started than you have to pull to keep it moving after that.

99 The Amazing Bottom Checker

YOU WILL NEED:
9 to 11 checkers, or a small stack of coins

Can you remove the bottom checker in a stack without touching the other checkers in the stack and without having the stack tip over?

What to do: Build a stack of eight or ten checkers. If you use coins, be sure they are all the same size. Medium-sized coins are best.

Place another checker next to the stack. Leave about 1 inch (2.5 cm) between this checker and the stack.

Flip the single checker hard with your forefinger or your middle finger. Give it a really hard snap.

What happens: The bottom checker will fly out from the stack. If all goes well, the rest will stay neatly in place.

Why: Inertia keeps the stack of checkers from moving even when the bottom one is suddenly snapped away. Because the stack was not moving to begin with, it tends to stay that way. Scientists say, "A body at rest tends to remain at rest."

100 The Amazing Middle Checker

To vary this experiment, you need a pencil in addition to the checkers. Use the pencil to hit one of the checkers in the middle of the stack. Hit it sharply and be sure to hit only one. With a little practice you can knock any checker out of the stack without tipping the stack

Catching a Coin on Your Elbow

Here is a great trick that is also a neat science experiment.

YOU WILL NEED:
coin

What to do: Place one coin on your elbow.

Hold your arm parallel to the floor or the coin will fall off.

You are now going to catch the coin that is on your elbow. That wouldn't be much of a trick except for one thing. You are going to catch the coin in the hand of the same arm.

Here's how it works. In one sudden, very quick move you will drop your arm. This will cause your open hand to snap forward. The arrow in the drawing shows the direction your hand will move.

At the same time, your elbow will fall away from under the coin.

What happens: As your elbow moves from under the coin your hand will come down from it. When you get your timing right, you'll catch the coin every time.

Why: Since the coin is still it tends to remain in that position. Good old inertia again! When your elbow moves rapidly it just drops out from under the coin. This leaves the coin hanging in air. Gravity pulls the coin toward the ground, but inertia gives it a slow start. Your hand is faster than the coin because your hand is already moving.

Catching More Coins

It's not difficult to flip a lot of coins from you elbow into your hand. After you have the hang of catching one coin, add a second on top of the first, and then three or four or more and catch them all at once.

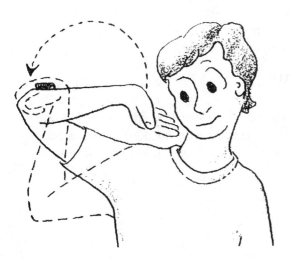

What a Crazy Way to Break Thread

You can cut thread or even break it between your hands. Her's a way to break a piece of thread you never thought of! It's best to do this experiment outside.

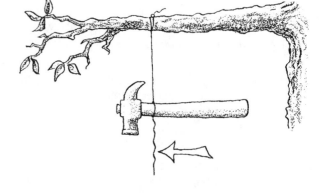

What to do: Choose a hammer or other object that won't break if it is dropped. A heavy wrench or a chunk of wood will work just fine.

Tie a loop of string around the hammer like this:

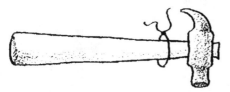

Next, cut the sewing thread in half. Be sure to use cotton thread because the experiment won't work with nylon thread.

Tie the end of one piece of thread to the top of the string loop. Then tie the second piece of thread to the bottom of the loop like this:

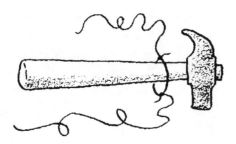

Tie the loose end of the top thread to something solid so the hammer hang below it. A tree branch is great, but any strong support will work fine.

Be sure there is nothing you can break or hurt beneath the hammer.

After you have set up the experiment, get a firm grip on the bottom string. The arrow shows where to grab. Then give a sudden, hard jerk downward.

What happens: You're expecting the hammer to fall on your hand, aren't you? What happens is the thread breaks somewhere between your hand and the hammer. The hammer will continue to hang from the top thread.

Why: Although the hammer doesn't weigh much, it takes a lot of energy to get it moving when it is at rest. The sudden downward pull causes the thread to break because it is not strong enough to overcome the inertia of the hammer.

104

That's a Lot of Work to Put Soap in a Glass

This experiment in inertia is impressive even if there is no good reason to put a bar of soap in a glass.

What to do: Put the glass on the table with the rim up. Put a plastic plate, like the ones from frozen foods, on top of the glass. (If you don't have a plastic plate use the square piece of cardboard.)

Next, put the outside of a small matchbox on top of the plate. If you don't have a matchbox you can make one. Take a look at the instructions on the right.

Now put the bar of soap on the matchbox. The illustration shows how.

Get a firm grip on the glass with one hand.

Strike the edge of the plate or cardboard with your other hand. Make the blow hard and fast.

What happens: The plate flies into the air (so be sure there's nothing breakable near it). The soap holder tumbles off and the soap plops into the glass.

Why: Inertia strikes again!

Making a Matchbox

105

Cut a piece of cardboard 2½ inches by 5 inches (6 cm x 12 cm).

Fold it along each dotted line as shown below. Fasten the overlapping end with tape.

When you finish, your matchbox looks like this:

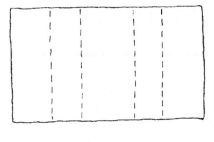

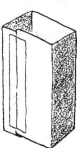

The Strange Case of the Marble in the Bottle

YOU WILL NEED:

empty bottle
piece of cereal box
material
scissors
ruler
marble or coin

Anyone can drop a marble or a coin into a bottle. But can it be done without touching the marble?

What to do: Be sure the open mouth of the bottle is larger than the marble or coin you are going to drop into it.

Cut a piece of cereal box material into a 4 inch (10 cm) square. Place the cardboard square on top of the bottle. Place the marble or coin on the cardboard so it is right over the mouth of the bottle. (It's a good idea to hold off on using a marble until you see how this works. A coin is easier to handle.)

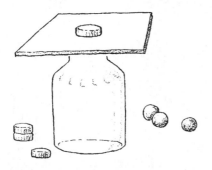

Flip the edge of the card hard and fast with your finger. If you're thinking like a scientist, you'll remember how you flipped one checker into another to move the bottom checker out of the stack.

What happens: The card snaps out from between the marble and the bottle. The marble drops into the bottle without you touching it. Pretty neat!

Why: The marble is standing still. Inertia wants to keep it that way. The card snaps away so quickly that the marble has no chance to follow the card. Gravity pulls it down into the bottle.

If the card moves too slowly, the marble will follow the card instead of falling into the bottle.

What now: If you want to be adventurous, try this with two marbles.

Slow But Steady

Here's an experiment you'll be able to perform only if you're willing to go about it slowly and with a steady hand.

What to do: Cut a strip of paper 3 inches (7 cm) wide and 10 inches (25 cm) long.

Place the bottle upside down on the paper near the edge of a table like this:

Your goal is to remove the paper without tipping over the bottle.

Place the pencil on the loose end of the paper and carefully roll it around the pencil. Keep rolling very slowly until the rolled paper touches the mouth of the bottle. Then, with a steady hand, continue rolling the paper.

What happens: As you slowly and steadily keep rolling, the paper gradually creeps out from under the bottle, which won't tip over.

Why: The unmoving bottle tends to say motionless and upright because of inertia. The bottle's mouth can't move because it touches the rolled paper. It doesn't tip over because inertia tends to keep it exactly where it was to begin with—so long as you don't make any sudden moves.

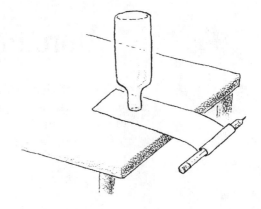

Nail Driving the Hard Way

YOU WILL NEED:

large dictionary and large books
thick newspaper
wooden board
hammer
several nails

It's one thing to drive a nail into a board. It's another to do it while you hold the board in your lap.

What to do: Stack the dictionary and another large book on your lap. If you don't have a large dictionary use three large books. Place a thick newspaper on top of the books to protect them.

Finish off the stack by placing the board on top of the newspaper. Any scrap of lumber will do, but a piece of 2 x 4 is best. Now you are going to pound a nail into the board. That's right. You'll pound the nail while holding the board in your lap.

What happens: As you pound the nail, you feel the force of the hammer blows on your legs, but it won't hurt. Just be sure you don't pound the nail all the way through the board.

Why: Inertia saves the day.

More Impressive Nail Driving

You can experiment with nail driving using fewer books. But if you want to impress you friends, let someone else hammer the nail. Just be sure you always have a thick newspaper pad between the board and the books. Also be sure anyone swinging the hammer holds it so that the hammer head does not come down toward you. The person who is hammering must stand or kneel at your side and aim the hammer away from your face and body.

KEEPING YOUR BALANCE

How many times have you walked along a curb or on top of a stone wall with your arms out at your sides to help keep your balance? Even as a tot you understood that to keep your balance you had to have as much weight on one side of you as on the other. You knew this instinctively.

You also discovered how easy it was to lose your balance when you walked on any wall or narrow line. Instead of stepping off the wall or falling, you bent and twisted and waved your arms a bit. When you did these things your body was regaining its balance by getting its center of gravity right over the curb—or whatever it was you were walking along.

Everyone knows how gravity works. Gravity is that invisible force that keeps us from flying off into space. It's the force that makes your slice of bread fall jelly-side down when you accidentally drop it. Gravity is the pull that turns your home run into a double when the ball falls inside the park. But what is the center of gravity? And what does it have to do with keeping your balance?

The center of gravity is that point in an object where there is as much weight on one side as on the other. When you're walking along a curb or a crack in the concrete, your center of gravity is right on the line where you place your feet. If you stand up straight with your feet spread, your center of gravity is between your feet and straight down in a line from your nose.

When we locate the center of gravity in an object we can get that object to balance. You've balanced a pencil on your finger when things got a little boring in class, haven't you? Its center of gravity is halfway from the eraser to the point— unless you have one of those big erasers. In that case, the center of gravity is closer to the eraser than to the point.

If you want to impress people, you can refer to the center of gravity as the "point of balance." Whichever term you use, there are some really great bits of science that depend on finding where things are in balance.

The Incredible Balancing Hammer

YOU WILL NEED:

hammer
ruler
1½ feet (.5 m) of
strong string

Anyone can stand a hammer on its head and it will balance. But can you tie a hammer to a ruler and balance them both on the edge of a table with only one end of the ruler touching the table?

What to do: Tie one end of the string around the ruler. Tie the other end of the string around the hammer handle. Tie it tightly so it won't slip up and down the handle.

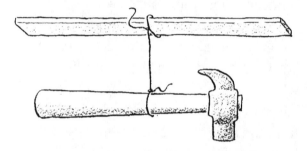

What happens: Now to make things balance. Be sure the end of the hammer handle touches the end of the ruler. Position the ruler so that about 4 inches (10 cm) of it are on top of the table. Carefully test the ruler and hammer to see if they are in balance.

You may have to adjust the string to get the hammer to hang correctly. If you have problems getting things to balance, shorten the string between the hammer and the ruler. Don't give up if things don't balance at first. They will when you adjust the string to the perfect length.

Why: You positioned the hammer and ruler so that the center of gravity is right at the edge of the table. If you look at things from one side, you'll see that the head of the hammer is on one side of the center of gravity and the handle and most of the ruler are on the other.

A hammer with a wooden handle will have a different center of gravity than one with a steel handle because of the heavier weight of the metal handle.

The Amazing Balancing Yardstick

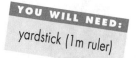
YOU WILL NEED:
yardstick (1m ruler)

It's not difficult to balance a yardstick on top of your hands when you hold your hands apart. The surprising thing is how difficult it is to make that yardstick lose its balance.

What to do: Hold the yardstick between two outstretched fingers as shown below.

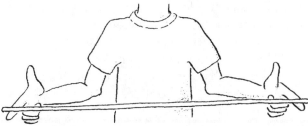

The object of this experiment is to move one finger toward the center of the yardstick until it loses its balance and tips over. Make this move slowly and steadily. It isn't fair to suddenly jerk your finger to the center of the yardstick.

What happens: A strange
thing happens as you move your finger toward the center of the yardstick. You only move one finger along the yardstick, but the other finger moves along, too.

Eventually you find yourself with both fingers side by side and the yardstick still balanced.

Try it and see.

Why: The yardstick's center of gravity is right in the middle. When you slowly move one finger toward the center of gravity the yardstick begins to tip toward that finger because that finger is nearer the center of gravity. When it tips, even slightly, it reduces the weight on the finger that isn't moving.

When less weight presses on the unmoving finger, that finger begins to slide along the yardstick. This is because there is less friction on that finger. The finger you moved first has more friction because more weight is on it. Friction slows down movement, so that less friction results in faster movement.

The yardstick keeps rebalancing itself as your fingers slowly move toward one another.

The Rapid Ruler
and the Slowpoke Yardstick

YOU WILL NEED:
yardstick (1m ruler)
12 inch (30 cm) ruler

Everyone knows that babies are likely to take a lot of tumbles when they are learning to walk. This is because they are learning how to control their bodies. Did you know that people's height has something to do with how fast they fall?

What to do: Begin by standing a ruler and a yardstick side by side with a few inches between them. Steady each of them with just the tip of your finger as shown in the illustration.

If you don't have a ruler and a yardstick, two dowel rods or other straight pieces of wood will work perfectly.

Lean the ruler and yardstick forward just a tiny bit to make sure both of them will fall in the same direction. Be sure they both have the same amount of forward lean. Now let go.

What happens: The ruler will win the race to the ground every time. Try it and see!

What you've just seen helps to explain why if a child and a taller adult start to fall forward at the same instant, the child will finish falling first. This also helps explain why babies sometimes seem to fall so fast.

Why: The center of the balance for the yardstick is higher than it is for the ruler. The farther that center of balance is from the ground the longer it will take the object to complete its fall.

This does not mean that a high center of gravity makes an object steadier than one with a low center of gravity. Just the opposite! Automobile manufacturers try to keep the center of gravity as low as possible so that cars are less likely to tip over. And that's the reason big trucks and trailers are sometimes required to pull off the highway during high winds. Not only do they have lots of surface to catch the wind, but their center of gravity is high. They are, therefore, more likely to turn over than are cars with a lower center of gravity.

The Mysterious Balancing Dinner Fork

YOU WILL NEED:

long wooden pencil
1 very small
potato or apple
newspaper
table fork

Can you balance a table fork, a potato, and a pencil so only the pencil's tip touches the table?

What to do: Press the pencil through the center of the potato or apple. (If anyone objects to your sticking things into the family's vegetables, a lump of soft modeling clay will do just as well.) Be careful doing this: Place the potato on a thick pad of newspapers. Don't hold the potato in the palm of your hand! If you do, you may run the pencil point into your hand.

Slowly and firmly push the pencil point into the potato. When the point pokes through, pick up the potato and hold it by its sides. Carefully push the pencil on through until about 1½ inches (4 cm) stick out.

When you've gotten the pencil through the potato, press the tines of the dinner fork into one side of the potato so the fork is at about the angle shown here.

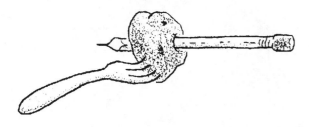

Rest the pointed end of the pencil on the edge of a table as shown below.

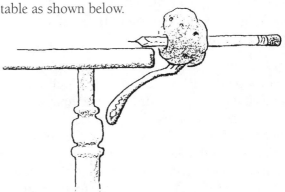

What happens: If you're having a lucky day, the whole thing will balance right away. If it doesn't, try moving the pencil tip farther onto the table or nearer the edge.

You can also slide the potato backward or forward a bit along the pencil. By now this strange combination has probably balanced. If it hasn't, you can begin to feel which direction it is going to move as you steady it with your hands. Don't give up if it doesn't balance the first few times. Keep adjusting it. If necessary, pull the fork out and replace it at a different angle.

When the combination does balance, it looks as if you have found a way to defy the laws of gravity. With a little practice, you can adjust this so the pencil actually slopes downhill and only the point touches the table

Why: This is the same principle as on page 90. You must have as much weight on one side of the center of gravity as on the other.

Twice the Balancing Magic

YOU WILL NEED:

very small potato or apple or a lump of clay
pencil
2 table forks
tall drinking glass

Since you've already messed up a potato or apple, grab another fork and try another impossible feat of balance.

What to do: If you haven't already pulled the pencil out of the potato or the apple from the last experiment, leave it just the way it was. Otherwise, push the pencil through the potato or apple just as carefully as you did before.

You can leave the fork in at the same angle as before if it's still sticking in the potato. Now add a second fork by pushing its tines into the side of the potato opposite the first fork. Try to stick in both forks at the same angle.

Things look pretty much like this:

Turn a tall glass over so you can set the project on top of the glass as seen on the right. (Instead of a glass you can use a soda pop or salad oil bottle or any bottle with a small neck and a wide bottom.)

What happens: By adjusting the angle and location of the forks you can make the pencil stand straight up or lean to one side. Of course, only the point of the pencil touches the glass or the top of the bottle.

It is amazing how far you can get the pencil to lean to one side if you arrange the forks in the right position.

Why: Study the balancing figure and you'll see that there is exactly as much weight on any side of the pencil point as on any other side. The point of the pencil is the center of gravity.

HOW TO HAVE ALL THE MOVES

We already know a lot about motion. We know that many things move. We know that things that are not moving tend to remain still and stay in one place because of inertia. To get something to move that is standing or sitting some kind of force has to be applied to it.

Force can be as simple as giving a toy a push to start it moving. Force can be the wind that fills a sail, carrying a boat across the lake.

Applying force to an object can be complicated, too. It may involve running an engine or motor so that a pulley can turn. That pulley may cause a belt to go around and around, which, in turn, transfers the force to another pulley. This process can go on and become more and more complicated until, finally, a cutting device is put into motion that carefully produces a delicate part for an expensive machine.

We know that when the power of force is applied to an object, that object tends to keep on moving. When the power or force runs out, a moving object begins to slow down and eventually stops. Gravity pulls on objects and helps to slow them down and use up their force. So does air and wind resistance. If it were not for air and wind resistance, you could hit a home run without having to stop and think about it.

We know that movement and motion can change with the center of gravity. By changing the center of gravity, you can turn an object or tip it over. In the last chapter you learned to create objects that stopped moving after you located their center of gravity. Now let's deal with some other things that affect motion and the way things move.

The Turtle and the Hare

Remember the story of the turtle and the hare? When the turtle finally passed the finish line, he said, "Slow and steady wins the race."

YOU WILL NEED:
2 large plastic bottles exactly alike (large soft drink bottles are ideal)
water
2 boards (or a sloping surface)

What to do: Fill one of the plastic bottles half full of water. Screw the lid on good and tight. Leave the second bottle empty.

Place the two bottles side by side at the top of a ramp or slope. A concrete sidewalk or driveway that runs downhill for a few feet and then levels out will be just fine. You can also make a ramp from two boards of the same length. Place one end of each board on a chair and let the lower ends of the boards rest on the floor as shown in the illustration.

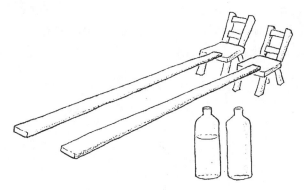

Hold the bottles at the top of the slope and then release them at the same time. Watch carefully as they roll down the slope.

What happens: The two bottles start together. But wait! One bottle starts off faster. That's the hare in this race. When the bottles reach the level floor, however, the slower bottle (that's the turtle) rolls farther than the "hare" that took off faster.

Why: Rub two things together and you create friction. To prove this, just rub your hands together rapidly. Feel the heat that you generate by the rubbing. Heat is created by friction.

The water in the half-filled bottle gives it extra weight. This added weight made it take off faster down the slope. But the water rubbing against the sides of the half-filled bottle created friction. The friction slowed that bottle down.

Friction not only creates heat: it slows movement. Automobile manufacturers use oil in an automobile engine to cut down on friction and heat. They use grease to lubricate other moving parts for the same reason.

Racing Hoops

YOU WILL NEED:
2 sheets of paper
ruler
scissors
tape
4 paper clips
slope or ramp

You've watched horses and cars race. Perhaps you've even watched roller-skaters race. Well, here's a race the likes of which you've never seen.

What to do: For this experiment you need two paper hoops exactly the same size. (It wouldn't be fair to race hoops of different sizes against each other.)

Cut two strips of notebook paper as long as the sheet of paper and 2½ inches (6 cm) wide. Make each strip into a hoop by taping the narrow ends together. Now tape a paper clip inside one of the two hoops.

Be sure the paper clip is in the exact center of the hoop.

Place the two hoops side by side a few inches apart at the top of a slope or ramp. (The ramp you used for the turtle and hare race is perfect, although if there is much of a breeze blowing you'll need to use an indoor ramp.)

Let go of the hoops at the same time.

What happens: If you look closely, you'll see that the hoop with the paper clip doesn't roll at an even speed. It seems to speed up as the paper clip circles down toward the ramp. Then it slows down when the clip climbs back up away from the ramp. Eventually the hoop with the paper clip loses.

Why: It isn't friction that slows down the hoop with the paper clip. It slows down because it is out of balance. This is the reason the wheels on cars and trucks must be balanced.

Balancing the Hoops

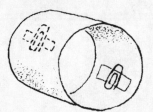

Let's see if we can make the hoop with the paper clip roll at an even speed. Tape a paper clip exactly opposite the first one and repeat the race.

Now add two more paper clips, each one halfway between the clips already in place. The hoop should roll better now.

Why: Objects that turn, like tires and engines, have to be as perfectly balanced as possible. Otherwise, they need more energy to turn and they don't turn easily. This causes extra wear and can even destroy them.

The Astounding Balancing Coin

When was the last time you saw someone balance a coin on a spinning clothes hanger? For that matter, did you ever hear of anyone who tried such a stunt?

YOU WILL NEED:
plastic clothes hanger
coin or washer

What to do: If you can't find one of those thick plastic clothes hangers you can try this with a regular wire hanger, but you'll need a great sense of balance.

Now that you have your coat hanger go outside. Don't be tempted to demonstrate this experiment in a room full of breakable things. If you happen to let the hanger slip off your finger, you better be outdoors! Since you're going to be experimenting outdoors, you're better off using a washer instead of a coin. A dropped coin that is easy to find on the living-room floor may be lost outside.

Loop the hanger over you finger. With your other hand balance the washer or coin on the bottom of the hanger so it looks like this:

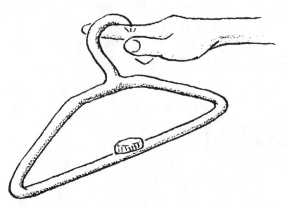

Now you know why it is a good idea to use the thick plastic hanger. It's not hard to balance a washer on a thick hanger, but it's difficult to get it to balance on a thin wire one.

Be absolutely sure to place the coin directly below your finger, which is sticking through the hanger's hook.

When the coin is balanced, begin rocking the hanger gently back and forth on your finger. Speed it up gradually.

When the hanger is swinging well, give it an extra spurt of energy and start it spinning in a circle around your finger.

What happens: The coin will stay in place as long as you keep the hanger spinning and don't jerk it.

Why: Centrifugal force is created when things spin rapidly. It causes spinning things to try to move away from the center around which they are spinning. The coin is pressed against the bottom of the hanger by centrifugal force. It won't slip off unless you slow down or break the smooth spinning motion.

The Spinning Bowl

Scientists demonstrate centrifugal force in huge laboratories. You can do it in your kitchen sink.

YOU WILL NEED:
large mixing bowl or pot
water
dessert bowl
wooden spoon

What to do: Fill the large mixing bowl with about 4 inches (10 cm) of water. If you have a bowl that's about 12 inches (30 cm) across, it will be perfect for this experiment.

Float the dessert bowl inside the large bowl or pot.

Pour enough water into the floating dessert bowl to fill it ¼ inch (1 cm) deep.

Now spin the floating bowl as rapidly as possible using the wooden spoon. Just stick the spoon into the bowl as shown here and begin turning it. If you don't have a wooden spoon, stick your index finger into the bowl to start it spinning. Since the bowl is floating, there is very little friction to slow it down and it will spin easily. Use a little wrist motion and the dessert bowl will pick up speed.

Try to keep it centered in the larger bowl. If the bowls touch, the spinning one will slow down.

What happens: Watch the water inside the floating bowl as you spin it faster and faster. The water will rise along its sides until the bottom of the spinning bowl is completely dry.

Let it slow down and the water will flow down from the sides of the bowl and cover the bottom again.

Why: Centrifugal force works on liquids just as it does on solid things. The faster you spin an object, the more it wants to escape by flying to the outer edge of the circle.

120 Power-Lifting Fingers

YOU WILL NEED:
straight chair
6 people

Your fingers are a lot stronger than you think. This experiment demonstrates that power and it is also a great party stunt.

What to do: One person sits erect in the straight-backed chair with hands clasped, head bent slightly forward, and neck stiff. The sitting person's entire body should be as unbending as possible.

Have each of the other five people extend one index finger. It helps to steady the hand with the other hand like this:

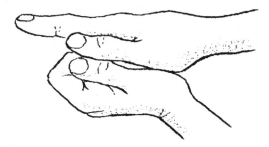

Ask one person to stand beside each of the sitting person's knees. Have them slip their entire index fingers under the sitter's knees.

Two other people will stand behind the chair and place their entire index fingers under the sitter's armpits.

The fifth person may stand beside the sitter or in front, placing an index finger under the sitter's chin.

Tell everyone to take a deep breath and hold it. Count, "One, two, three." All five people lift straight up on "Three." Caution everyone to lift straight up and not to jerk.

What happens: To everyone's surprise the sitting person comes right up out of the chair. Be sure to caution the lifters not to let the person drop when he or she is in the air.

Why: Since the sitter remains stiff, his or her weight is evenly distributed among all five lifters. By having everyone move at the same instant, the weight remains divided evenly, so everyone lifts the same amount So, if the sitter weighs 80 pounds (36 kg) this means each lifter only has to raise about 16 (7 kg) of those pounds.

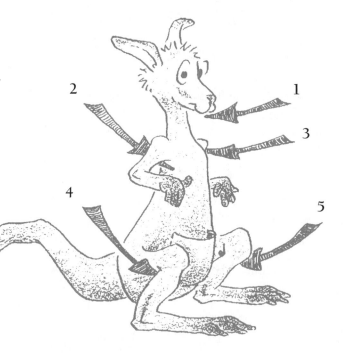

Pulley Power

YOU WILL NEED:
2 wire clothes hangers
2 empty thread spools
2 chairs
broomstick
scissors
10 foot (3 m) length of strong string
book

If you want to pull a string instead of lifting a weight, a pulley is exactly what you need. You will need an adult's help with this experiment.

What to do: To perform this experiment in motion and movement, you have to build some pulleys. An easy way to do this is to unwind the neck of a wire hanger. Ask an adult to help you do this. Push the end through the center of one thread spool. (If you have to straighten the wire a bit to get it through the spool, that's fine.) Then bend the hanger back into shape.

When you've fastened the hanger back together, your pulley looks like this:

Make another pulley with the other hanger and spool. You will need it for the next experiment.

Now place the two chairs back to back and place the broomstick between them. Then tie a loop of string around the stick to hold the pulley. Cut a piece of string long enough to tie around the book, which is the load you are going to lift.

Cut another piece of string 4 feet (1.2 m) long. Tie it to the string on the book and run it over the pulley.

Now pull down on the string.

What happens: The book rises.

Why: Of course it did! What's so great about that? The great thing is that you changed the direction of motion. You pulled down and the book came up. This ability to change the direction of motion lets us set up factories and do the work needed to construct buildings and bridges.

In this experiment you pulled down just as hard as you would have to pull up to lift the book. You didn't gain any mechanical advantage using just one pulley. The next experiment shows you how to get science to improve your lifting power.

Double Power

Here's your chance to be twice as strong as you were before.

What to do: Leave the last experiment set up exactly as it was. Hook the second pulley into the string that is tied around the book you plan to lift. Things should be set up like this:

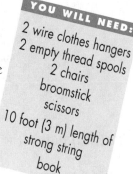

Now pull up on the string that runs around the second pulley. Measure the amount of string you pull up to lift the book 3 inches (7.5 cm).

What happens: You will be using less force to lift the book than you did using only one pulley. You'll also pull 6 inches (15 cm) of string through the pulleys to lift the book 3 inches (7.5 cm)

Why: Using two pulleys gives you what is called a mechanical advantage. This simply means that it is easier to lift the book than it was before. However, you have to pull twice as much string through the pulleys to gain this advantage.

The Mysterious Moving Glass

Can you make a glass of water move without touching the glass?

What to do: Fill both glasses nearly full of water. On a flat surface, like a kitchen counter, place the pencil under the ruler, as shown in the drawing. Put one glass of water at each end of the ruler. Hold onto each glass until it is balanced.

Now move the pencil along under the ruler until the raised end is almost ready to tip downward.

Put two fingers into the water, but don't touch the glass. Push your fingers down into the water.

What happens: As your fingers move down in the water, that glass will move down as shown by the arrow in the drawing. The level of the water will rise in the glass as your fingers push into the water.

Why: As your fingers push into the water they move, or displace, water, which causes the water level to rise. The glass's weight is increased by exactly the amount of water that is displaced.

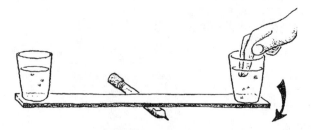

THE SOUND OF SCIENCE

Sounds are all around us. We are used to hearing the sounds of other voices, of a dog's bark, the honking of an automobile horn, or the slamming of a door. Sounds are so much a part of our lives that a sudden, total silence can be frightening. Total silence is so different from what we are used to that some people claim the silence itself creates sound.

Everyone knows how to create sound. Strike one hand against the other and you'll cause sound to be made.

What actually causes the sound of two hands clapping? When two objects come together hard and fast to create a sound, they cause the air to move or vibrate—the result of the force of their coming together. This vibration of the air causes little waves of sound to travel out in all directions.

Some of those sound waves, or vibrations, reach your ear. They cause your eardrum to vibrate, or move back and forth, slightly. This movement causes the tiny bones inside your ear to pick up that vibration and relay it through a tiny tube of liquid to the hearing or auditory nerves. These nerves communicate the sound to your brain and you hear.

When you speak, your vocal cords vibrate in your throats. The force of the air coming out of your lungs and passing the vocal cords creates these vibrations. The moving vocal cords set air in motion and the sound is carried from your mouth.

If you would like to test how this works, try to speak out loud while you are pulling air into your lungs. You can make a sound, but you can't speak when you breathe in. Try it now just to make sure.

In this chapter there are experiments in sound that are fun and offer some surprises. They will also help you understand how you hear.

Noisy Paper

YOU WILL NEED:
2 sheets of notebook or computer paper

Two sheets of notebook or computer paper make a great noisemaker.

What to do: Hold the two sheets of paper up in front of you. The bottom sheet should stick out toward you about ½ inch (12.5 mm) past the top paper.

They should look like this:

Now blow directly toward the two sheets at the point shown by the arrow.

What happens: The two papers will make a strange, noisy sound.

If you don't get some kind of sound from the papers, move your mouth closer and blow again. When you blow between the two sheets of paper they vibrate rapidly back and forth.

If you still haven't created some sound, adjust the way you hold the papers. Move your fingers closer to your mouth or farther back. Blow harder or less hard. Eventually you'll find the right combination.

Don't blow until you get dizzy. Blow, then rest a few seconds.

Why: When the papers flutter back and forth their vibration creates the sound you hear. Their vibration creates sound waves that your ear picks up.

The Screamer

YOU WILL NEED:
piece of cellophane, 2 inches (5 cm) square

Here's your chance to make all the noise you want and do it in the name of science.

What to do: Hold the piece of cellophane stretched tightly between the thumbs and index fingers of both hands.

Place your hands directly in front of your face so the cellophane is right in front of your lips. The set-up looks like this:

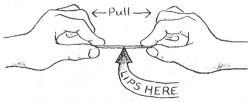

Blow hard and fast right at the edge of the tightly stretched piece of cellophane. Keep your lips close together so you send a thin stream of air right at the cellophane's edge.

What happens: When the jet of air hits the edge of the cellophane you will create the greatest, most terrible sound you've ever heard!

If you don't get a terrible sound, adjust the distance between the cellophane and your lips until the air hits it just right.

Why: The rapidly moving air from your lips causes the edge of the cellophane to vibrate quickly. Because the cellophane is extremely thin, the jet of air makes these vibrations extremely fast. The faster something vibrates the higher the tone it creates.

Balloon Amplifier

YOU WILL NEED:
1 ordinary round balloon

You're used to seeing big sound amplifiers that make sounds louder. These amplifiers are often called "speakers." But did you know a balloon can increase the volume of sound?

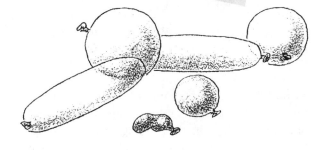

What to do: Blow up the balloon. Hold the blown-up balloon right against your ear.

Tap lightly on the side of the balloon away from your face.

Do not do anything that will make the balloon pop while it's next to your ear. The loud noise of an exploding balloon won't do your ear any good at all.

What happens: The sound you hear is lots louder than the light tapping of your finger.

Why: The air inside the balloon is tightly compressed. When you blew up the balloon you actually let your lungs work as an air compressor, forcing the air to expand the rubber balloon. The air molecules are much closer to each other inside the balloon than they are in the air in the rest of the room. When you crowded the molecules closer together inside the balloon, that air became a better conductor of sound waves than ordinary air.

The Spoon That Thinks It's a Bell

YOU WILL NEED:

scissors
4 foot (1 2 m) length of string
teaspoon
4 feet (12 m) of string

How can a spoon act like a bell? Read on and find out.

What to do: Tie a simple sliding loop in the middle of the string. Do this by simply wrapping one end of the string over the other and pulling the open loop down so that it is halfway between the ends of the string.

Don't tighten the loop into a knot. Leave it open about ½ inch (13 mm) like this:

Slip the handle of the teaspoon through the loop and tighten the loop so the spoon won't slip out. Adjust the spoon so it hangs with the scoop end just a little lower than the handle.

Now press one end of the string against the outside of your right ear and the other string end against the outside of your left ear. Don't put the string into your ear.

Swing the string gently so the scoop of the spoon hits the edge of a table. Listen to the sound you hear.

What happens: By swinging the spoon gently you will hear a sound that is nothing like a spoon striking a table. It's more like a bell, a church bell.

Why: The string conducts the vibration of the spoon. Not only does string carry sound waves better than air, it directs them right into your ear. This accounts for the deep bell-like tone you hear.

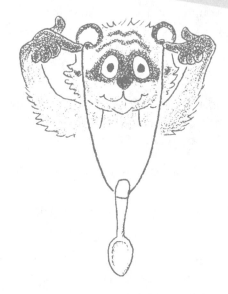

128

Big Bells

Repeat the last experiment using a soup spoon and listen to the deeper tone it creates.

Then, give your ears a treat, and do the experiment with a serving spoon. Because of its greater size its sound is much, much deeper.

The Tapping Finger

Do you know how to make even the lightest taps of your finger sound loud?

What to do: Sit at the table or desk. Place your ear flat on top like this:

Tap with your finger on the surface of the table about 1 foot (30 cm) away from your ear. Tap hard. Then tap softly.

What happens: The sound of your tapping finger is much louder than when you listen to the same tapping with your head not touching the table. Check right now to be sure this is true.

Why: Sound waves don't only travel through air. They also travel through solids, such as a table or desk. Many solids—like wood—carry sound waves much better than air because the molecules in wood are closer together than the molecules in air. This is the reason your tapping finger sounds louder when you hear it through wood than through air.

The Listening Yardstick

Did you ever try to hear through a yardstick? Now's the time!

What to do: A wind-up alarm clock is perfect for this experiment. If you don't have one, then check your electric alarm clock. Does it make a whirring sound? Most of them do if you listen carefully. If it doesn't, find some other appliance in the house that hums or makes a mechanical sound that isn't very loud. If you don't have a yardstick, a ruler will work. So will a wooden dowel rod.

Hold the yardstick so that one end touches the clock and the other end presses against the outside of your ear, like this:

What happens: The sound of the clock is much louder now than when you listen to it without the yardstick. You can check this by using the yardstick to listen to other appliances around the house.

Why: The wooden yardstick carries sound waves better than air. Therefore, you hear the clock's sounds more loudly through the yardstick than when you listen normally.

107

The Strange Vibrating Bowl

Can you hear the sounds from a vibrating bowl? Let's find out. It is helpful to do this experiment with a friend.

What to do: Set the bottle on the table. An empty, large soft drink bottle is great.

Balance the bowl upside down on top of the bottle like this:

Put your ear close to the bowl and tap the edge of the bowl with the eraser end of the pencil. Better still, have a friend do the tapping.

Then repeat the experiment, but this time have your friend touch the edge of the bowl with his or her finger.

What happens: The first time you'll hear a pleasant sound. The second time, when your friend touches the edge of the bowl, you won't hear it.

Why: The sound is created because the bowl is vibrating. When your friend touches the bowl with a fingertip it causes the vibration to stop and the sound to end.

Can You Tune a Fork?

It's sad but true that a piano can be tuned, but no one can tune a fork. However, even an untuned fork is good for a tone, if not a

What to do: Tie one end of the string around the fork, as shown in the illustration. Lift the fork by the string so the tines hang straight down.

Tap the bowl with the pencil and lower the fork so the tines are lightly touching the opposite side of the bowl.

What happens: When the fork touches the bowl its tines begin to vibrate. If you hold your ear close to the tines you can probably hear the tone.

If you're working with a friend, have him or her tap the bowl again. This time press the string holding the fork against the outside of your ear, just as you did with the spoon experiment. Now you can hear the tone more clearly.

Why: The fork tines pick up the vibrations from the bowl. This is called "sympathetic" vibration. The string helps to conduct the sound, just as it did with the spoon that thought it was a bell.

Tuning a Glass

YOU WILL NEED:

8 drinking glasses
water
pencil

We said you can't tune a fork, but who said you can't tune a glass?

What to do: Line up the eight drinking glasses in a row on the kitchen counter. (Plastic bottles won't work this time.) It does not matter if the glasses are all the same size or not. If they are, however, it's quicker to tune them.

Fill the glasses part full of water, so that they look pretty much like those in the illustration:

As you can see, each glass has a little less water in it than the one to its left.

Now use the pencil to gently but firmly strike the side of each glass.

What happens: You will hear a different tone from each of the glasses. The more water there is in a glass, the lower the tone that it makes.

Call the first glass on your left "do," which is the first note of the musical scale. Strike the next glass. If its tone is the next step up the scale move on. If not, either add a bit of water or pour some out until the glass's tone is one step up.

Continue in this manner until you have tuned the eight glasses to play a musical scale.

Why: We know that vibrations cause sound. Striking the side of a glass causes it to vibrate. The speed of the vibration depends upon how much glass and water there are to set in motion. The more water, the slower the vibrations and the deeper the tone.

Tune More Glasses

Now set up eight glasses that are different in size. The more different, the better.

Keep in mind that it is the total amount of water that determines the tone of the glass.

Tune these eight glasses to play a musical scale by adding or pouring out water until each tone is one step above the one to its left.

Seeing Sound Waves

Now is your chance to see sound waves, but you must do this experiment on a sunny day.

What to do: Remove both ends from a tin food can. Wash the can carefully with warm water and soap. Watch out for sharp edges left from the can opener.

Next you need a piece of balloon to fit over one end of the can. It's a good idea to blow up the balloon and play with it a while before stretching it over the can. This makes the rubber easier to pull. Then let the air out and cut the neck off the balloon with the scissors. Stretch a piece of the main part of the balloon over one end of the can. Hold it in place with the rubber band. You'll probably have to wrap the rubber band around the balloon and can several times.

You need a small piece of mirror. (If you don't have an old mirror, use a piece of aluminum foil.) Wrap the mirror in several sheets of newspaper. Then tap it with a hammer. Unwrap the newspaper and carefully pick out a piece of mirror about ½ inch (12.5 mm) square. Wrap up the other scraps in the paper and throw them away.

Use a drop of glue to fasten the mirror to the balloon as shown here.

Stand so the sunlight from a window hits the reflector. Move the can around until the reflection shows up on a wall, like this:

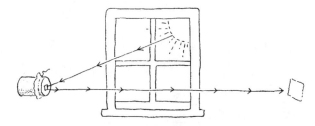

Talk directly into the open end of the can. Shout. Make different sounds. Watch the reflection.

What happens: The sounds you make cause movement of the reflection.

Why: The rubber on the can picks up the vibrations of the sound waves from your voice. As it vibrates, so does the reflector. That's what makes the reflection on the wall move.

Feeling Stressed?
Try Some Surface Tension

Water is an extremely important part of our lives. Without it, human life cannot survive.

Not only do we drink water, but the major part of our bodies is also composed of water.

We bathe in water, we sail across it, we use it as the basis for drinks ranging from sodas and juices to tea and coffee.

Without water we'd have no trees, no grass, no flowers—no life as we know it. Water is essential to living.

In this chapter you will find out some interesting facts about water. You'll see that it can do some amazing things, and that it's great to experiment with. You'll find out something else about water, too. You've probably heard a lot about tension and stress. Water has tension, too, but of a different type than the one that comes with stress.

Water has surface tension. Surface tension is a scientific term that means that the surface of a bowl of water has the ability to hold itself together. This happens because the molecules that make up a container of water tend to cling to one another.

Normally, we don't think of a lake or ocean as having water molecules clinging together to form a covering for the water. But that is exactly what surface tension does. You don't feel it when you poke your finger into a cup of water or when you dive into a swimming pool. But it exists, even if you are not aware of it.

Let's begin this chapter with some experiments that show some of the surprising things water does because of surface tension.

Then we'll move on to some really interesting things below the surface.

Full to Overflowing

YOU WILL NEED:
drinking glass
water
lots of straight pins

Everyone has filled a glass or a cup until the liquid flows over the top. Here's your chance to fill a glass to overflowing without spilling a drop.

What to do: Put the glass on a kitchen counter or in the sink. Add water until the glass is full to the brim.

Now to answer this question: How many pins can you drop into the glass before it runs over? Ten? Twenty? Fifty?

Carefully hold a pin over the glass so its point just touches the surface of the water.

Let go of the pin so it slides into the water. Add another pin and then another until the water finally runs over.

What happens: You'll add more pins than you believed possible. Look sideways at the glass and you'll see the level of the water is above the edge of the glass.

Why: Surface tension keeps the water from overflowing long after it seems possible for the glass to hold any more pins.

137 The Strange Expanding Loop of Thread

YOU WILL NEED:
large bowl
water
1 foot (30 cm)
length of thread
bar of soap

Once something is done to change water's surface tension, strange things happen as you will see.

What to do: Fill the bowl with water nearly to the top.

Form the thread into a loop by lapping one end over the other, but don't make a knot in it. Carefully place the loop on the surface of the water. Keep the loop sort of skinny so it looks like this:

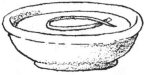

Now touch the corner of the bar of soap to the water inside the loop in the thread.

What happens: The loop will form a circle around the soap.

Why: The soap destroys the surface tension of the water inside the loop. The thread keeps the soap from spreading beyond the loop. Since the water outside the loop still has its surface tension, it pulls away taking the thread with it. This leaves a circular loop around the soap.

138 The Stubborn Cork

YOU WILL NEED:
cork
drinking glass
water
teaspoon

Can a cork be stubborn? Here's how to deal with one that refuses to obey your commands.

What to do: Fill the glass with water almost to the top. Now float the cork in the glass. Within a short time the cork will drift to the side of the glass.

Your challenge is to convince the cork to come to the center of the glass without touching it or taking it out of the water. If you want to blow on it, that's okay, but when it reaches the center of the glass it must stay there after you stop blowing.

Here's how to make the stubborn cork obey. Slowly, one spoonful at a time, begin to add water to the glass. Eventually the water will rise above the top of the glass as surface tension holds it in place.

What happens: The cork drifts to the center of the glass and stays there when the water level rises high enough.

Why: Surface tension lets the water rise above the glass. It causes the water to form a little curved dome whose high point is at its center. The cork seeks the highest point of the water.

A Strainer Full of Water

YOU WILL NEED:
small strainer
cooking oil
empty bowl
glass of water

139

A strainer won't hold water. Or will it?

What to do: Use a small strainer because a large one requires too much cooking oil.

Coat the strainer with cooking oil. A good way to do this is to pour the oil into the bowl and then gently slosh the strainer around in the bowl until it is coated with oil.

Shake the strainer carefully into the bowl so that all the holes are open. (Don't throw away the cooking oil you just used. If you set it aside, you can use it in the experiment on page 120.)

Hold the strainer over the sink. Start pouring water very, very slowly from the glass into the strainer.

What happens:
As you carefully pour the water, you'll see the strainer begin to fill with water. Look  closely and you'll see tiny beads of water pushing through the wires, but very few of them will leak out.

Why: It is the surface tension of the beads of water that makes this experiment work. The oil helps by giving the wires a smooth coating. It also makes the spaces between the wires a fraction smaller, because, even after you shake the oil off, some of it clings to the wires.

The Incredible Upside-Down Bottle

YOU WILL NEED:

bottle with a small mouth and neck

water

small piece of screening or a strainer

6 inches (15 cm) of soft wire or rubber band

Anyone can turn a bottle upside down. But how many people can do it without having the water spill out? This experiment really needs at least three hands some of the time. Unless you happen to have an extra hand yourself, make sure you have a friend around who can help when needed.

What to do: Fill the bottle with water all the way to the top.

Cover the mouth of the bottle with screen wire, if you have a little chunk of screening available. If not, check to see if you have any plastic screen of the type that comes in some frozen dinner cooking pouches. Attach the screen to the top of the bottle with the piece of wire or a rubber band.

If you don't have a piece of screen available, you can hold a strainer tightly against the mouth of the bottle. That's where you need that extra hand your friend will supply.

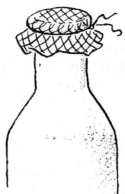

With the screen in place or the strainer held tightly against the bottle's mouth, quickly turn the bottle upside down.

What happens: The water doesn't run out.

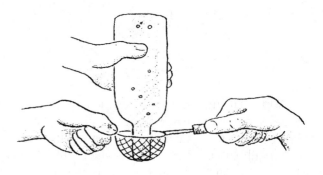

Why: Surface tension is helping. It also helps that the bottle is full so that no air is trapped inside the bottle to push down on the water. The only direction air pressure is pushing is up against the water that might want to run through the screen.

The Hawk and the Sparrows

Hawks often fly into a flock of sparrows and scatter them. You'll see why this experiment was named for them when you complete it.

What to do: Place the dinner plate on a table and pour water into it until the plate is nearly full. When the water is calm, sprinkle a bit of the powder onto the surface of the water—just a pinch of it between your thumb and finger.

The powder will float on the water like this:

The bits of powder are the "sparrows."

Rub the tip of your finger the soap. Touch the surface of the water with your fingertip. Your finger is the "hawk."

What happens: The instant your soapy finger touches the water the powder the "sparrows" scatter.

Why: The soap breaks the surface tension of the water. The water around the edges of the dish pulls away and carries the powder with it.

A Scale You Never Thought Of

Can you use a bowl of water as a scale? Do this experiment and find out.

What to do: Put the bowl in the baking pan. Fill the bowl to the rim with water. Place the apple or the orange in the bowl of water.

What happens: Water will overflow into the baking pan. Carefully lift the bowl of water out of the pan. Pour the water from the pan into the measuring cup. Read the scale on the side of the cup to see how many ounces of water are in it. This reading gives you the weight of the fruit.

Why: The water that overflowed was displaced by the fruit. The amount of water a floating object displaces is the same as the object's weight.

Water's Great Escape

You've heard that water doesn't run uphill. Here's an experiment that shows how you can coax water to do it. Just in case there's a leak it's a good idea to do it in the kitchen sink.

What to do: Fill the glass nearly full of water. Put it next to the bowl.

The plan is to have the water move up and over the rim of the glass and down into the bowl. To do this you need a wick through which the water can travel. A wick is a tight roll of paper or cloth that will absorb water. Just as a candle wick carries melted wax up to the flame, your water wick will carry water along its length.

Twist the paper towels together fairly tightly to form the wick. Bend the wick in the middle. Then place one end in the glass. Be sure the other end reaches into the bowl, like this:

What happens: Within just a minute or so you'll see the wick getting wet as water begins to travel along it. After a few minutes some water will appear in the bottom of the bowl.

Water won't flow from the glass into the bowl. Instead of flowing, it sort of oozes. This experiment takes time. Check back once in a while to see how it is coming.

When the water level in the bowl is as high as the level of the water left in the glass, the water stops moving. If you set the glass on something higher than the bowl you get most of the water out of it.

Why: There are thousands and maybe millions of tiny spaces between the fibers of the paper towel. Water moves into these openings and advances along the twisted material. Its movement is known as capillary action. Moisture moves from plant roots into the rest of the plant in this same way.

Slow But Mighty

Is it possible for a can full of cardboard squares to lift a heavy board?

YOU WILL NEED:
empty can
2 or 3 empty cereal boxes, or pieces of cardboard
scissors
water
dishwashing detergent
piece of wood about 2 feet (.6 m) long or a stack of old magazines

What to do: Wash out the empty can with soap and water. Watch out for sharp metal around the edge.

Cut enough square pieces of cereal box cardboard to fill the can when you stack the pieces on top of each other. Don't worry about making the pieces of cardboard the exact size of the can. It's better and faster to cut them a bit smaller, like this:

 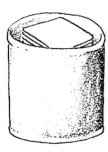

When the stack of cardboard pieces fills the can fill the can with water. Add a squirt of dishwashing detergent or a bit of dishwasher powder. Within a minute or so you'll see that the water level has dropped as much as 1 inch (2.5 cm). This is because the water is seeping into the pieces of cardboard. Add enough water to bring the water level back to the top of the can.

Push down on the cardboard. You can probably add a few more pieces.

Now place the piece of wood on top of the can like this:

What happens: Within a short time the piece of wood will begin to rise. When it stops rising, remove it and try to push the cardboard back into the can. This will be difficult, if not impossible!

Why: Capillary action causes the water to soak into the pieces of cardboard. When each piece of cardboard fills with water it is a fraction thicker than it was without the water. This is what causes the lifting action which raised the piece of wood.

The Case of the Shrinking Tissues

145

YOU WILL NEED:

drinking glass
water
6 facial tissues
pencil

Facial tissues don't get smaller and smaller—or do they? Here's an experiment that asks the question: What happened to the tissues?

What to do: Fill the glass with water to about ¼ inch (9 mm) below the rim.

Tear each of the facial tissues into strips about 1½ inches (3.75 cm) wide. The dotted lines in the illustration show where to tear the tissues. Don't worry if you don't tear them straight.

Now, stuff one strip of tissue at a time into the glass of water. Use the pencil to keep pressing the tissues down toward the bottom of the glass.

What happens: You'll see small bubbles rise through the water from time to time. This is because some air was trapped by the tissue when you pushed it into the water.

As you push the tissues down with the pencil you free the trapped air. This makes room for more tissues in the water.

Why: Highly absorbent products like facial tissues have only a bit of solid material in them. They are made up largely of air space. When the air is gone from the tissues there isn't a lot left. This is the reason you can stuff so many into the glass of water. Cotton balls, incidentally, work the same way.

The Moving Mystery Match

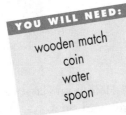

Why does a wooden match suddenly decide to move?

What to do: Bend the wooden match in half. Don't break it in two pieces. Leave several wood fibers holding it together. Place the coin so that just its edges rest on the match.

Run a few drops of water into the spoon. Let a single drop of water fall onto the broken match at the point shown by the arrow.

Drop here

What happens: Almost instantly the two halves of the match will move apart slightly and the coin will fall off at least one of the halves.

Why: Water causes wood fibers to expand or swell, which makes the match move slightly.

If you want to use this experiment to impress your friends, set it up so the match rests on the rim of a bottle. Just be sure the neck of the bottle is large enough so the coin falls into the bottle when the match moves.

You Can't Keep a Good Button Down

If you've ever wanted to see a button rise and fall in a glass of liquid, now's your chance.

What to do: Fill a glass with carbonated soda to about ½ inch (12.5 mm) of the top. (One of the clear sodas is probably best because you can see through it easily.)

Drop the button into the glass. If it floats on top of the soda, give it a tap with your finger and send it to the bottom of the glass.

What happens: Small bubbles begin to form around the button.

Suddenly the button rises to the top of the glass. Give it a tap to knock the little gas bubbles off and it will sink to the bottom

again. This will go on as long as the soda is fizzy. If you wish you can have several buttons rising and falling in the same glass.

Why: The gas bubbles are carbon dioxide, which is what gives soda its "fizz." When the bubbles attach to the button they give it enough lift, or buoyancy, to make it rise.

119

The Great Cooking Oil Trade Off

YOU WILL NEED:
2 small glasses the same size
cereal box cardboard
scissors
water
cooking oil
baking sheet

Can you trade a glass of cooking oil for one of water without pouring one into the other? Have a friend help you try.

What to do: Begin with two glasses exactly the same size. Juice glasses are perfect.

Cut a piece of cereal box cardboard about 4 inches (10 cm) square, large enough so that when you place it over the mouth of a glass, it sticks out ¾ inch (18 mm) on each side.

Fill one of the glasses to the top with water. Fill the other to the top with cooking oil. For safety's sake, set both on a baking sheet.

Place the cardboard on top of the glass of water. Hold the cardboard firmly in place and turn the glass over so it looks like the illustration above.

Put the upside-down glass of water, with the cardboard still in place, on top of the glass of cooking oil. Don't let the cardboard slip!

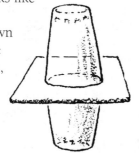

Hold both glasses steady and slowly move the cardboard sideways. Here's where your friend comes in. You need an extra hand to hold things in place. Move the cardboard until its edge is exactly where the rims of the glasses meet, like this:

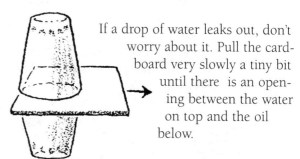

If a drop of water leaks out, don't worry about it. Pull the cardboard very slowly a tiny bit until there is an opening between the water on top and the oil below.

What happens: A few oil bubbles rise into the water glass. They will form a little oil dome on the bottom of the water glass (which is at the top, of course).

Pull the cardboard a bit farther and suddenly you'll see the oil begin to roll upward into the water glass. At the same time, water flows down to replace the oil.

In a minute or less the top glass is full of oil and the water is in the bottom glass.

Why: Because water is heavier than cooking oil, the water flows downward, forcing the lighter weight oil upward. This is why oil and water don't mix and oil floats on water.

SCIENCE CAN GIVE YOU A WARM FEELING

Light is something we take for granted. The sun shines. We turn on an electric light. Light shines through glass. It is light that enables us to see reflections in mirrors.

Light travels in rays that move in a straight line at great speed. When we speak of the speed of light we are talking about a light ray that travels through space at 186,000 miles (297,600 km) per second! To get a good idea of what this speed means, consider that the sun is 93,000,000 miles (148,800,000 km) away from us. Light travels from the sun to the earth in just about eight minutes.

Although light rays travel in straight lines, these rays can be bent, or refracted. When light enters water or passes through glass, the light ray bends at an angle. When it leaves the glass or water the ray again moves in a straight line. However, it is traveling at a different angle than before it encountered the glass or the water.

Our chief source of light is from the sun, but we create light by artificial means, such as electricity, as well.

It is important to remember that light is related to heat. It is the sun's tremendous heat that causes it to give off light. A burning fire also creates light. And if you hold your hand near, but not touching, an electric light bulb you'll feel the heat it gives off.

Heat can also cause light. It is the heating of the filament inside an electric light that creates the artificial light we see in the bulb.

When things are heated enough, they change. Vegetables, for example, become tender when they are cooked. A room gets warm when the furnace comes on. Ice melts and water boils if heated enough. Air and many other materials expand when heated. It is the expansion of air that makes some of the experiments in this chapter work.

Breaking Up Rays of Sunlight

It is possible to break up or separate the sun's rays. When this is done, a ray of light suddenly shows a rainbow of colors. And you can do it in about two minutes on a sunny day.

What to do: Pour about 1 inch (2.5 cm) of water into the baking pan. Now you need a small mirror.

Put the pan of water where the sunlight shines directly on it, either indoors or outside.

Lean the mirror against one edge of the pan, like this:

Direct the mirror's reflection onto a white ceiling or wall or the sheet of white paper. If you are outside, you'll probably have to use the paper as your viewing screen.

What happens: You'll see a rainbow of colors on the ceiling or wall or sheet of paper. These colors start with red and end with violet.

Why: Water causes the rays of sunlight that are reflected from the mirror to bend. When light rays bend, each color in the ray bends at a different angle. This causes the rainbow effect.

All the colors we normally see—red, orange, yellow, green, blue, and violet—are contained in sunlight. We see objects as having color depending upon which light rays they reflect.

Upside Down in a Spoon

YOU WILL NEED:
shiny soup spoon or serving spoon

How can a spoon turn you upside down? This experiment is great fun for younger children you have to entertain.

What to do: The scoop of a spoon makes an interesting mirror. Just be sure the spoon you use is shiny and the larger the better. Hold the spoon up so you see yourself in the scoop.

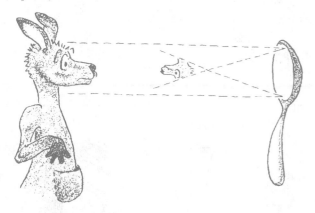

What happens: When you look at the spoon you'll see your reflection upside down. Tip the spoon so it reflects other things that also appear upside down.

Why: Light rays travel in straight lines. They are reflected in straight lines, too. But when light is reflected from a curved surface, the rays leave the surface at different angles. The illustration shows how this works with the spoon. The reflected image appears upside down because of the angle of the reflected rays of light.

151 The Case of the Vanishing Reflection

In this experiment you'll see your reflection one minute and have it vanish the next.

YOU WILL NEED:
10 inch (25 cm) length of kitchen foil
scissors

What to do: Use the scissors to cut a piece of kitchen foil off the roll. Don't tear it. Cut it to avoid wrinkles.

Look at your reflection on the shiny side of the foil. It won't be perfect, but you'll see yourself clearly.

Now crinkle the foil into a loose wad. Don't press it together tightly because you'll have to straighten it out again.

Flatten out the wadded foil, like this:

Now look for your reflection.

What happens: No matter how you turn the foil you won't see your reflection. It has vanished.

Why: Remember that light rays are reflected from a surface in straight lines. The once-smooth foil surface is now a mass of ridges and valleys. The reflected light bounces off it in all directions.

Because these reflected rays are going off at different angles, your image does not form in the way it did when its smooth surface reflected the rays right back to you.

A Water Droplet Magnifier

Yes, it's possible to make a tiny drop of water into a magnifier. You can't use it to read with, but it will magnify one letter at a time.

YOU WILL NEED:
paper clip
pliers
glass of water
newspaper page

What to do: Straighten the paper clip and make a small loop, as round as possible, at one end. You'll need a pair of pliers to form the loop. Paper clips are hard to bend when you work with just the end. The loop should be about 1/8 inch (3 mm) across or just a tiny bit larger.

Dip the loop into the glass of water. You'll see that a film of water fills the inside of the loop. Tap the wire against the side of the glass. This helps form the tiny lens of water.

Hold the loop above a letter on the newspaper page.

What happens: If all went well, the letter you're looking at will appear several times larger than it is.

If the letter seems smaller than usual , the water formed the wrong kind of lens. Tap it against the side of the glass and look again.

If you lose the water inside the loop, just dip the wire again and collect a new water lens.

Why: The drawing above shows how light enters and leaves the lens you just made. Always remember that light rays may be bent by a lens, but they always enter or leave the lens in a straight line.

The Hot Water Tap
Always Leaks

153

It wastes water to have any tap leak. But it's even worse to realize that it is always the hot-water tap that seems to be leaking.

What to do: Right in the middle of the bottom of each paper cup make a tiny pin hole. Then set the paper cups on top of the glasses like this:

Fill one cup half full of cold water. Drop in a couple of ice cubes to make sure it is really cold.

Fill the other cup half full of hot water out of the hot-water tap.

Now sit back and observe the tiny drips from the pin holes in the bottoms of the cups.

What happens: If the holes are the same size, you'll see the hot water leaking faster than the cold water. In fact, if the cold water is cold enough it may not leak at all.

Why: The molecules in hot water move much faster than they do in cold water. The faster they move, the easier it is for them to slip past each other. That's why hot water is more likely to leak than cold.

154 Undersea Water Fountain

YOU WILL NEED:

pot
cold water
small glass bottle
hot water
marbles or washers
ink, food color, or
watercolors

What happens when warm water suddenly appears beneath a mass of cold water?

What to do: Fill the pot nearly full of cold water, the colder the better. If you want, instead of using a pot, just put the stopper in the kitchen sink and run about 5 inches (12.5 cm) of cold water into it.

Next, fill the small bottle about three-quarters full of hot water. A glass bottle works best, but if you only have a plastic bottle it will do. Drop a couple of clean marbles or washers into the bottle. These will give it enough weight so it won't float when you put it into the cold water.

Add a few drops of ink or food color to the hot water. If you don't have any, then use a bit of paint from a set of watercolors.

Immediately put the bottle in the bottom of the pot or in the sink.

What happens: The colored water will rise upward from the bottle toward the surface of the cold water. It looks just like a little underwater volcano erupting. When the colored water begins to cool, it will thin out and settle toward the bottom of the pot.

Why: Hot water rises because the molecules in it are moving rapidly. As they bounce and dart about they expand the water. When water or air expands, it gets less dense, because the same amount of matter takes up a larger space.

This expansion causes warm water or air to rise above colder, denser water or air. This kind of movement is called convection.

What a Way to Cut an Ice Cube

155

YOU WILL NEED:

18 inches (45 m cm) of thin wire or thin nylon cord

2 round pieces of wood (dowel rods) or 2 bolts, 6 to 8 inches long (15 to 20 cm)

ice cube

pieces of wood or a tin can

If you ever need to cut an ice cube in half, here's a way of doing it that has a result so surprising it seems impossible.

What to do: Tie the ends of the wire or nylon cord to the round pieces of wood. Dowel rods are perfect but so are pieces of broomstick. Fairly long bolts will work well, also.

Make sure the wire or cord is tied tightly to the wood rods or bolts. You'll use them as hand-holds so you don't cut your fingers instead of the ice cube. The cutter looks like this:

Put the cube of ice on something solid that is high enough so you can stand over the cube and push down on the cutting tool. Several short pieces of wood work well when stacked on top of each other or you can use a tin can as a cutting stand.

After placing the cube on the wood or can, position the cutting tool like this:

Take hold of the two handles and press down good and hard. Move the wire back and forth over the surface of the ice cube in a sawing motion while you keep pressing down.

What happens: Within a few seconds the wire or cord will begin to work its way slowly into the ice cube. As you continue to push down and the wire cuts deeper, you may wish to stop the back and forth motion and just keep pressing down.

The wire sinks into the ice cube even if you don't keep up the sawing motion! And the amazing thing is that the ice cube seems to freeze over above the wire.

When the wire is nearly through the ice cube, let up just a bit on the downward pressure. This keeps the wire from coming through the bottom of the cube with a sudden jolt.

When the wire is finally all the way through the ice cube wouldn't you think you'd have two cubes? You don't. You still have only one because the two halves froze together.

Why: Pressure on the wire causes the ice under the wire to melt. This is because pressure creates heat. However, the ice cube is cold enough to refreeze when the water oozes its way to the top of the wire where there is no pressure.

Another Way to Cut an Ice Cube

156

Hang two heavy weights on either end of the wire. Then stand back and watch the wire work its way through the ice cube all by itself.

The Hot Air Twirler

Here's a twirling toy that uses the heat from your hands for power.

YOU WILL NEED:
sheet of thin paper
scissors
straight pin
pencil with an eraser

What to do: Begin with a sheet of the thinnest paper you can find. Cut a square that is exactly 3 inches by 3 inches (7.5 cm x 7.5 cm.)

Fold the square diagonally and then unfold it. The solid line in the illustration shows this fold. The dotted line shows the next fold to make.

When the two diagonal folds are in place, push in a little on opposite sides of the paper. This causes the center to rise about ½ inch (1.25 cm) higher than the sides. The arrows in the illustration below show where to push.

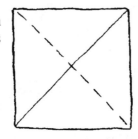

Next, push the straight pin into the eraser of the pencil. Leave 1 inch (2.5 cm) of the pin sticking straight up from the eraser. Sit down and hold the pencil between your knees as seen in the illustration.

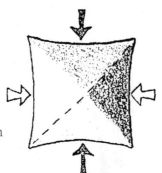

Set the square of paper on top of the pencil so the head of the pin is right at the center peak, where the two folds come together.

Place your cupped hands on either side of the paper so they are about an inch or so away from it.

Now just sit and think warm thoughts without moving your hands or knees.

What happens: Within just a minute the little paper twirler will begin to turn. If you see that the corner of the paper is going to hit your hands when it turns, move your hands back enough to give it room. But keep your hands as close to the paper as possible.

When it gets going, the twirler will spin slowly around and around. The lighter the paper and the warmer your hands, the faster it turns.

Why: The warmth from your hands heats the air near them. Heated air rises. The rising air causes the delicately balanced twirler to spin.

BLOWN AWAY

Air is all around us. We breathe it. We see such things in the air as dust, smoke, and other kinds of pollution we all dread.

Air is moving constantly. We are aware of it when the wind blows. We also see clouds moving rapidly across the sky or watch a plume of smoke or steam as the wind blows it one way or the other.

Automotive engineers design cars so their movement through the air will be smooth. Airplanes fly only because air provides the "lift" necessary for them to remain in flight. It is the shape of their wings that changes the wind speed and results in the lifting effect.

Air also exerts pressure. Anyone who has ever tried to carry a large sheet of cardboard when the wind is blowing knows

how great that pressure can be. And it is the force or pressure of moving air that drives a sailboat across the water.

Air doesn't have to move to exert pressure. Every minute it pushes down on us and from every side as well. We have about 14 pounds (6.3 kg) of air pressure pushing down on every square inch of our bodies at every moment.

What we call a vacuum is really just lower-than-normal air pressure. When you suck on a drinking straw, you are lowering the air pressure inside the straw. Then the normal pressure outside pushes the liquid up into the straw.

Air presses from all sides. So, when something like a kite or an airplane is up in the air, air pressure is pushing up and from all sides as well as pushing down from above.

The things that happen because of air speed and pressure are what make the following experiments work.

158

The Impossible Fluttering Paper

YOU WILL NEED:

strip of paper 4 inches
by ½ inches
(10 cm x 1.25 cm)
large bottle
2 inches (5 cm) of tape
scissors

Do you have enough lung power to make a paper flutter that is hidden behind a bottle?

What to do: Fold the paper strip ½ inch (1.25 cm) from the end so it looks like this:

Place the strip of tape over the folded end and tape the paper onto a tabletop so it looks like the illustration below.

Put the large bottle on the table between you and the paper. Place the bottle about 3 inches (7.5 cm) in front of the paper strip. Blow directly at the bottle in front of you. Keep your eye on the paper strip as you blow hard, then soft, then fast, and then slow.

What happens: When you blow just hard enough, the paper will begin to bend and flutter although you are blowing on the bottle instead of the paper.

Why: Moving air will follow a curved surface. It does not always travel in a straight line the way light rays do. Although your breath of air is deflected when it strikes the bottle, some of the air continues around the bottle, striking the paper strip.

159

The Even More Impossible Fluttering Paper

See how far away from the bottle you can blow and still make the paper flutter. Move the paper closer to the bottle or farther away and check your results. Just remember to rest a minute between blowing efforts so you don't get dizzy.

The Stubborn Ping-Pong Ball

Anyone can blow a ping-pong ball a few inches. Or can they?

YOU WILL NEED:
large funnel
ping-pong ball
sheet of paper and
tape (if you don't have
a funnel)

What to do: Wash the funnel carefully to make certain it is absolutely clean. A funnel used around the kitchen is the only kind to use for this experiment. Don't use a funnel that has been used around oil and gasoline in the garage.

If you don't have a funnel, it takes about ten seconds to make a paper cone. Roll a sheet of paper into a cone that is large at one end and 1/4 inch (6 mm) across at the other. Tape the loose end so your cone looks like this:

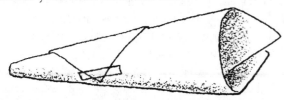

Drop the ping-pong ball into the paper cone or funnel. Hold the funnel directly over your head and blow into the small end. The drawing shows how.

The object is to blow the ball out of the funnel. Blow hard, but steady.

What happens: Unless you are using a very small funnel, you'll find it is impossible to blow the ball out of it.

Why: The passage of air around the ball makes it jump and bounce, but it will not fly out of the funnel. This is because the fast-moving air flows all around the ball instead of pushing it upward. The ball tends to jump up (even higher at times than the rim of the funnel) but it won't jump to one side.

YOU WILL NEED:

sheet of notebook or
computer paper

scissors
tape or glue
drinking straw

Puzzling Paper Loop

161

Here's a paper loop that does just the opposite of what you'd expect it to do.

What to do: Cut a strip from paper about 8 inches (20 cm) long and 1½ inches (3.75 cm) wide. Glue or tape the loose ends together to form a circular loop like this:
The next step requires a drinking straw. If you don't have one, just roll a hollow tube from half a sheet of notebook paper.

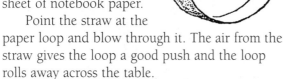

Point the straw at the paper loop and blow through it. The air from the straw gives the loop a good push and the loop rolls away across the table.

Now place the loop on the table in front of you. Aim the straw so it is above the loop, pointing to the side that's away from you at an angle, as shown in the illustration.

Now blow sharply through the straw.

What happens: The loop will either stay where it is or roll away from you. If it doesn't roll away from you, toward the burst of air coming out of the straw, then change the angle of the straw. Blow again.

When you have the correct angle for the straw and get the feel of exactly how hard you need to blow, you can astound friends by making the paper loop follow the air rather than run from it.

Why: Moving air creates a low pressure area as it flows along. The paper loop is moved into that low pressure area by the normal air pressure behind it and on its sides.

The fact that moving air—or something moving through the air—creates a low pressure area is one of the things that enables airplanes to fly. Air flowing past a curved surface tends to speed up.

The faster it flows the lower the pressure it creates. This tells you something about creating low pressure on top of a curved airplane to supply the "lift" the plane needs to fly.

The Great Coin and Paper Race

162

The outcome of this race between a coin and a piece of paper is amazing.

What to do: Cut a round piece of paper that is a little smaller than the coin. It doesn't have to be perfectly round, but keep it as nearly round as possible. Just be sure the doesn't stick out at any point past the edge of the coin when you place the coin on top of it.

You're going to use the coin and the paper in a scientific race. Hold the coin in one hand and the paper in the other about 3 feet (90 cm) above the floor. Drop them both at the same instant.

What happens: The coin takes off for the floor in a straight line while the paper flutters this way and that and reaches the floor long afterward. Their paths look like this:

Why: The coin is heavy enough so its fall is not disturbed as gravity draws it down. The paper is extremely light in weight, but it has about the same amount of surface as the coin. This combination of lots of surface plus light weight causes the paper to flutter because the air pushes at it as it falls.

The Great Coin and Paper Race— Second Stage

163

It's only fair to let the loser in any race have a second chance at winning.

What to do: Hold the paper and the coin in the same hand with the paper sitting on top of the coin. Hold them like this:

Hold the coin by its edges so you don't touch the paper at all. Drop them now.

What happens: The coin and the paper should travel together all the way to the floor. If any air gets between them they will separate and the paper will finish its journey fluttering instead of falling with the coin. If that happens, repeat the experiment.

Why: The paper and the coin travel together because of moving air. When something moves rapidly through the air (such as the falling coin), it pulls some air immediately behind it.

The paper "rides" the coin down because it is caught in the pocket of air traveling with the speeding coin.

The Great Coin Blowing Demonstration

Do you know anyone who can blow hard enough to blow a small coin all the way across the mouth of a glass? Of course you do. You can!

What to do: Put the drinking glass on a table. Balance the coin on the rim of the glass like this:

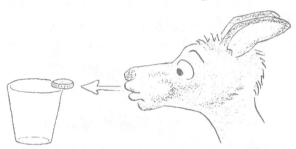

Blow sharply on the edge of the coin. The arrow in the drawing shows where to direct the stream of air.

Now, balance the coin on the rim of the glass again. This time you are going to blow the coin all the way across the open mouth of the glass so it lands on the table on the opposite side of the glass.

Impossible? No, You can do it!

Blow hard. The coin will probably fall into the glass the first few times you try.

You must blow right at the edge of the coin. Check the arrow in the illustration again. Don't blow over the coin and don't blow under it. Don't place your lips too close to the coin. Stay back several inches and blow straight at the coin's edge. Blow hard and fast.

What happens: The first time you tried it, the coin fell off the rim of the glass. It may have fallen into the glass or onto the table. But that's what you expected, wasn't it?

When you lined up everything correctly, the coin sailed across the glass and hit the opposite rim, but the force of the rapidly moving air kept it going.

Why: The coin is light enough for the moving air from your lungs to set it in motion. It had very little friction to overcome, because it was balanced delicately on the rim of the glass.

It's all a matter of directing the coin in the path it needs to take. Air speed does the rest.

165 What's the Matter With This Bottle?

YOU WILL NEED:

large, empty plastic
soft drink bottle
funnel
sticky cloth or plastic tape
large pitcher
water

Here's a bottle of water with an open top, but you can't empty it.

What to do: Place the funnel in the mouth of the bottle. Carefully and tightly seal the funnel onto the bottle as seen here:

Use very sticky black cloth or plastic tape or electrician's tape. Take your time and work with strips of tape 8 or 10 inches (10 or 12.5 cm) long. Make certain you tape the funnel onto the bottle so the seal is airtight. Pull the tape tight and press it down firmly.

Put the bottle and funnel in the kitchen sink. Fill the pitcher with water and start filling the bottle. Be sure you pour water into the funnel fast enough so the water level rises in the funnel. This is extremely important! Keep pouring so the water level is near the top of the funnel.

Now, place your hand tightly over the top of the funnel (which is full of water) and quickly turn the bottle over so it looks like this:

Keep your hand over the mouth of the funnel until the air inside the bottle rises to what is actually the bottom of the bottle. Don't let even a tiny bubble of air get past your hand into the mouth of the funnel.

What happens:
The water stays in the bottle.

Why: With the space between the funnel and bottle taped airtight and the funnel full of water, air is trapped inside the bottle with no way to escape. As water fills the bottle the air molecules are so compressed that the air pressure inside the bottle is equal to the pressure of the water pushing against it.

As long as not even a bubble of extra air works its way into the bottle, the air pressure on the outside will hold the water in the bottle.

166

A Person Could Die of Thirst

YOU WILL NEED:

soda bottle
water
drinking straw
sticky cloth or plastic tape

What could be more annoying than to stick a drinking straw into a bottle and then find it impossible to suck any of the liquid up into your mouth.

What to do: Fill the soda bottle nearly full of water. Place the drinking straw in the bottle.

Pull off a strip of sticky cloth or plastic tape about 8 inches (10 cm) long. Wrap it carefully and tightly around the mouth of the bottle so it forms an airtight seal around the straw. Use a second and maybe even a third strip of tape to make sure no air can get through the seal.

Place your mouth on the end of the straw and begin to suck on it as you normally would. Don't take your mouth away from the straw after you begin trying to drink through it.

What happens: You won't get more than just a tiny bit of water out of the straw, if you get anything at all.

Why: Early in this chapter we mentioned that it is the outside air pressure that enables us to drink through a straw. Unless air can push down on the liquid in a glass or bottle, it is impossible to drink through a straw.

As you suck on the straw you lower the air pressure inside the straw. Outside pressure normally pushes the liquid up into the straw. But, since you sealed the top of the bottle shut, the outside air can't push on the water in the bottle, and you're out of luck when it comes to drinking through that straw.

The Paper Wad That Won't Go Into the Bottle

167

No great effort is required to put a small wad of paper into a bottle. So why won't this paper wad do what you ask it to do?

What to do: Place the bottle on its side on a table.

Wad a small piece of paper into a ball about the size of a green pea. Then place the paper wad in the bottle's mouth as seen here.

Blow hard and fast as shown by the arrow in the drawing.

What happens: Instead of flying into the bottle the paper wad is more likely to fly out of the bottle's mouth and come back toward you.

Why: The fast-moving air goes past the paper wad and strikes the bottom of the bottle. This increases the air pressure inside the bottle. As that compressed air rushes out, it carries the paper wad out with it.

168 How to Empty a Glass by Blowing on It

YOU WILL NEED:

water
2 drinking glasses the same size
pan
drinking straw

It's easy to empty a glass by pouring the water from it. But it's more fun to blow on it to accomplish the same thing.

What to do: Run enough water into the kitchen sink so the water level is a little higher than the width of the glasses when they are turned on their sides. Here's how:

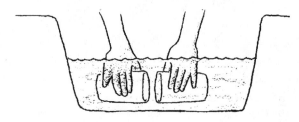

Be sure the glasses are full of water. Press the two rims together. Get a firm hold on both glasses and lift them out of the sink with their rims still pressed together.

Now turn them a quarter turn so that one glass is on top of the other. Set the two glasses in the empty pan.

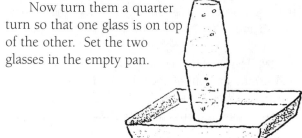

Very carefully slide the top glass a bit to one side so the rims of the glass no longer meet exactly. Do this slowly and no water will run out of the top glass. Here's how the glasses look in relation to each other:

Aim the drinking straw right at the point shown by the arrow where there is a tiny space between the rims of the glasses. Now blow gently through the straw. Then blow a bit harder.

What happens: Air bubbles will rise inside the top glass and a stream of water will flow down the side of the bottom glass into the container. Within a short time the top glass will be totally empty.

Why: Air pressure outside the glasses combines with surface tension to keep the water on the top glass from running out and into the container when you move their rims apart slightly.

When you blow, the air pressure from the end of the straw overcomes the water's surface tension and forces air between the two glasses. Once inside the glasses, the air rises since it is lighter than water.

169   A Great Experiment or a Wet Trick?

YOU WILL NEED:
plastic bottle
pliers
small nail
water

Try this as a great science experiment. Then decide whether to use it as a wet trick.

What to do: Begin by making twelve very small holes in the bottom of the bottle. A small nail is all you need for this. Hold the nail in the pliers and use the pliers to push the nail's point into the bottle's bottom.

After you've made the little holes, set the bottle in the kitchen sink. Run about 2 inches (5 cm) of water into the sink so the water rises well above the holes you just made. Hold onto the bottle to keep it from floating and tipping onto its side.

Now fill the bottle to the top with water. The water in the sink keeps the water you pour in from coming out the holes in the bottom. Lift the bottle above the water in the sink for a second to make sure water comes out the holes. When the bottle is completely full, screw on the cap and slowly lift the bottle up above the water in the sink.

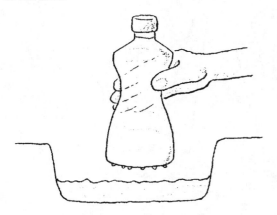

What happens: A few droplets may form around the holes, but the bottle will not leak. While you're still holding the bottle over the sink, remove the cap and the water will flow out through the holes you punched. Your experiment looks like this:

Why: As long as no water can push down through the open mouth of the bottle, the outside air pressure holds the water inside the tiny holes. When you open the cap, air pressure pushes down through the bottle's mouth and out the water comes.

You can use this as a practical joke, but you must do it outdoors. Pretend you can't open the cap, which you have screwed on fairly tight. Ask someone to help. Of course, that person will be able to open the lid and may even laugh at you for being so weak. But when the lid loosens, whoever is holding the bottle is going to get wet.

BEING EARTH CONSCIOUS

The chapters that follow give you a world of information, dozens of earthly exciting activities and experiments, and teach you the hows and whys of becoming a real conservationist—a person who is "earth conscious" and does everything possible to save and protect our lands, forests, and waters.

You'll learn through experimentation how plants give off oxygen and moisture and how, without them, life could not exist. You'll learn how magnetism and electricity are related earth forces. You'll see how earthquakes are produced and even make your own seismograph, the instrument for measuring them, and you'll build a glacier model that melts, moves, and leaves behind the sand and rock it carries.

Learn about soil, sand, the sun, and fossils, and then make a down-to-earth water filter, solar water heater, and a different type of "chemistry volcano" that foams, steams, and hisses.

In addition, you'll learn through facts and experimentation about ozone, fossil fuels, acid rains, rain forests, and global warming. You can even recycle old newspapers to make your own paper and note-cards.

Worldly Matters

The planet Earth—a huge ball with an outer crust, inner mantle, and core—travels through space, as do the sun, stars, and other planets. Beside this movement through space, the surfaces of the earth are also changing constantly. High mountains and deep valleys, both on land and under the oceans, are all part of the earth's movement. Nothing stays the same. Think of the earth as an apple sitting in the sun. As the sun warms and dries the apple, its water is lost and the apple shrinks and wrinkles.

The earth, like the inside of the apple, shrinks or contracts. As the hot interior parts of the earth cool and shrink, the outside covering is forced to move. The apple's surface makes wrinkly peaks and valleys and, similarly, the earth's crust forms mountains, valleys, and breaks or cracks called faults.

In this chapter we'll take a look at some of the forces that affect our earth, as well as other worldly matters.

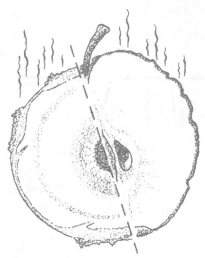

Earthquakes: They're Definitely Not Your Fault!

YOU WILL NEED:

3 similar-size hardcover books

The pressures within the earth cause great forces, which, in turn, break and crack the earth's crust. These cracks are called faults, and movement along a fault produces earthquakes. How does this happen?

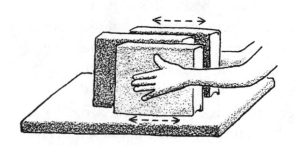

What to do: With the three books held firmly together, bring them close to your chest, book spines (with titles) upward. Reaching under, push upward on the middle book so that it slides upward between the two outer books. Do this several times to make a smooth, straight lift.

Next, firmly hold the books out away from your body, keeping them tightly and evenly together. Hold them sideways again, with the titles up and the pages going down. You'll have to apply a lot of force to keep them from slipping. Now, release some of the pressure so the middle book slips.

Finally, hold the books evenly together, spines upward, and rest them on a table. With your hands holding only the two outer books, slide them back and forth.

What happens: The different movements of the books resemble earthquake faults, with much uplifting and slipping.

Why: In the first two experiments, in which you held the books first close to your chest, and then away from your body, you demonstrated dip slip fault movement, a repositioning up and down. The middle book that was forced up (thrust fault) and the one that slipped down (normal fault) are good examples of this type of fault. The books that rested on the table and were moved to slide past one another show the action of a strike slip fault. In this type of fault, movement is sideways (side by side) or parallel.

Get the Lead Out!—Build a Seismograph Shaker-Maker

YOU WILL NEED:
scissors
shoebox with lid
heavy weight
masking tape
pencil with eraser
weights for the pencil,
like nails or washers
clay
2 paper clips
string
2 sheets of paper

That's right! With a sharp lead pencil with an eraser, you can build a simple seismograph, an instrument used by seismologists (earthquake scientists) to record the strength or intensity of earthquakes. (Adult help may be needed.)

What to do: Carefully cut a tiny slit in the middle near one end of the shoebox lid. Place the open box upright, on one end, and put something small and heavy inside to keep it in position. Tape the lid onto the top of the box forming an upside-down L. (It doesn't matter if the open part of the box or the bottom of it is toward the slit in the lid.)

Now, place the weights near the tip of the pencil point, but do not cover it, and tape them on securely. A small piece of clay around the pencil near the taped weights will keep weights from slipping off. The weights must be fairly heavy so the seismograph recorder pencil will make good contact with the paper and draw fairly dark drag lines on it.

Next, open one end of a paper clip and push it securely into the eraser. Tie the string to the unopened end of the clip. Attach the second paper clip to the other end of the string. Wind the string around the paper clip, as you would wrap a kite string around a stick.

Slip the top clip through the slit and adjust the pencil marker so the tip rests on the table, not perfectly straight but dragging as it moves. Slip the remaining string under one side of the clasp to fasten the upright pencil in place.

Now, cut each paper sheet lengthwise into three strips. These strips will act as roll paper and will record your "earthquake movements."

Place a paper strip against the box (below the slit you made in the lid) and slowly pull the strip forward. Notice how straight the drawn line is as you move the strip of paper.

Have someone bump and shake the table as you pull the paper strips under the dragging pencil marker. Your seismograph makes sideways and up and down movements. Compare the separate strips of paper, how do the lines differ? How do they show the effects of a dip slip fault versus a strike slip fault? (See the experiment opposite.)

172 You Can Move Mountains

YOU WILL NEED:

clay
newspaper

Have you ever wondered how mountains are formed? One way is the great pressures from deep within the earth that cause folds or waves to appear on its surface. These forces cause fold mountains. You can reproduce a version of this force and effect in a simple and easy way. All you'll need is a lump of clay—and a lot of imagination.

What to do: Lay some newspaper on a work table. Place a lump of clay on it and make a clay rope by rolling the lump back and forth over the table with your fingers. When the rope is about 8 inches (20 cm) long, lay it out flat on the newspaper and push inward on the ends, trying to make hills and valleys. After you've done that, roll and smooth out the rope again and place different forces on it. Try to make it bend in new and different ways.

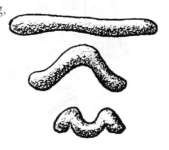

What happens: The clay rope, with its outside forces, demonstrates the hills and valleys of mountain making.

Why: Great broken pieces of the earth's crust, called plates, float on the layer beneath the surface called the mantle. This is similar to cracked sheets of ice floating on water.

When these plates meet, pass, or bump into each other (the science of plate tectonics), great and forceful pressures are created. These tremendously strong forces can fold, bend, uplift, and break the earth's surfaces to form whole mountain ranges.

When the clay rope was pushed and forced inward from the ends, it made hills and valleys similar to mountain building. The hill shape, higher in the middle, is called an anticline formation. If the clay makes a wavy S-like pattern that dips in the center, it is a syncline formation. The North American Appalachian mountain chain is an example of mountains formed by folding.

173

Tsunami: It'll Tide You Over

YOU WILL NEED:
deep baking pan
water
2 blocks of wood

If you receive some money when you're very broke, we say it will "tide you over" or help you out until you get paid. But tsunami, a Japanese term for great ocean waves, will really tide you over . . . tidal wave, that is!

In this activity, you can create conditions that will produce your own tsunami wave, then you'll understand much better how they are formed and the changes these giant tidal waves produce. This is a great experiment for a hot summer day because it's likely you will get very wet! So either wear your old clothes, or be very careful.

What to do: Fill the pan with water, then place the blocks of wood in the bottom of the pan so they are completely below the surface of the water. The object of this experiment is to rapidly compress, or squeeze, the water between the blocks.

So, take hold of the blocks and quickly bring them together. Do it again, and again. Continue the squeezing action until the blocks can no longer compress the water.

What happens: The movement of the two blocks coming together rapidly under the water forces swells of water to the surface, where they form waves that splash over the sides of the pan.

Why: The action of the blocks and the water in this experiment is similar to the conditions in the ocean depths that produce tsunami tidal waves. Great earthquakes and volcanic forces on the ocean floor cause large amounts of ocean water to be compressed, or squeezed together, and pushed to the surface. There, great walls of water are formed and threaten nearby coastal cities. These great waves sometimes reach heights of 50 to 100 feet (15 to 30 m). Because they form so suddenly and without warning they are extremely dangerous and often kill many people.

Photoplay: Say Cheese!

Light energy from the sun is so important that without it there would be no life on earth! Still, we can put this great energy to use right now by making a simple but exciting pinhole camera. It uses light rays from the nearest star—our own sun.

What to do: Prepare your camera by painting the insides and the lid of the shoebox with the black paint.

Cut a 2 inch x 4 inch (5 cm x 10 cm) opening in the middle of one end of the shoebox and tape the larger piece of tracing paper or wax paper over it. You should now have a screen on one side of your pinhole camera.

At the other end of the box, again in the middle of the panel, carefully punch a small ⅜ inch (½ cm) hole in the side with the scissors.

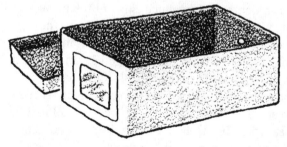

Now you are ready for action. Take your camera outside, find a sunny location, and place something—a friend, a toy, or another object—in front of it. Point the pinhole side of the camera toward the object, and keep the screen in position in front of you for viewing.

The next experiment will tell you about getting picture-perfect images.

What happens: When you aim the small opening of the pinhole camera at something, a fuzzy but noticeable, upside-down image of that object appears on the screen.

Why: The image or picture on the pinhole camera is reversed because light normally travels only in straight lines. Light rays from the top part of the image are reflected to the bottom part of the screen while rays from the bottom part of the image fall on the top.

175 ◆ Picture Perfect: Watch the Birdie!

To view a perfect picture, or image, through your pinhole camera, place a covering over your head. Wrap it around your head and the screen so that it is completely dark. No light is able to get in. (This may remind you of photographers long ago, with their big cameras on tripods, who had to cover their heads with large dark cloths attached to the cameras to take pictures.)

Find something or someone (your subject) in the light through the screen held before your face. A part of a house or a person at sunset is a perfect image. Move the camera away from your face, up or down, closer or farther until the object is in view. Take your time—it may take several trials to adjust your eyes to the dark, get enough light into the box, and find the object, but you will eventually succeed.

176

I Steam Cone

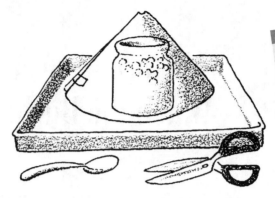

YOU WILL NEED:

strip of lightweight cardboard,
3 inches x 8 inches (8 cm x 20 cm)
small, empty, clean container,
like a spice jar or vitamin bottle
scissors
paper clip or tape
flat tray or pan
½ tablespoon of
quick-rising yeast
½ cup of hydrogen peroxide
metal spoon

In this great party-trick experiment, you'll build a different type of volcano based on earth science and chemistry. It's definitely something to get all steamed up about! It's simple, easy, and you won't need a lot of materials. So, what are you waiting for? Get going and dig in! (Caution! Throw away all chemical solutions and thoroughly wash out all containers when you're finished.)

What to do: With the cardboard strip, form a cone shape that will fit over the small container and fasten it with the paper clip or tape. Cut the end corners off so the cone will stand upright in the tray or pan. Place the small bottle or jar in the tray and get ready for action.

The jar should be large enough to contain the hydrogen peroxide but fit under the cardboard cone or extend slightly above the cone's mouth. With the cone over the small container, pour in the hydrogen peroxide followed by the quick-rising yeast. Stir the mixture thoroughly. (If it is easier, you may place the cone over the bottle after stirring, but you must be quick!) Continue to stir the mixture, for best results, until the experiment is finished.

What happens: The mixture of hydrogen peroxide and yeast causes foam, steam, and a hissing noise to come from the cardboard "volcano."

Why: The ingredients placed in the container under the cone produced a chemical reaction, or change. It is called exothermic because, in addition to foaming, steaming, and hissing, heat is given off. If you touch the rim and sides of the container or the stirring spoon you can feel this warmth.

In a real volcano, hot melted rock called magma, deep within the earth, erupts or shoots through fissures or cracks. This moving rock, known as lava, sometimes flows from openings in the volcano's sides, or explosively shoots or blows out steam, smoke, ash, and rocks. Although your model volcano is small and simple, it does give you a good idea how a real volcano erupts.

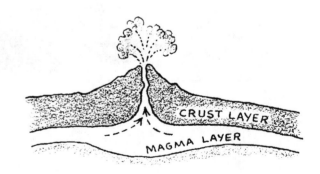

CRUST LAYER

MAGMA LAYER

Hotwire High Jinks

Rocks inside the earth can be changed due to the pressure and folding within the earth. The pressure causes heat. Do this experiment and see what we mean.

YOU WILL NEED:
wire coat hanger
candle

You will need the help of an adult.

What to do: To prepare for this experiment, ask an adult to unhook the wire hanger or cut it apart. Take the hanger and bend one section rapidly back and forth, in the same place, 30 to 50 times. Quickly, place the bent section against the candle. Don't touch the wire.

What happens: The wire has heated up. This warmth placed against the candle causes some melted grooves or ridges to appear in the wax.

Why: Deep within the earth, certain rocks,

called metamorphic rocks, are caused by the constant folding of the earth. This causes heat and changes the composition, or make–up, of the rocks. Marble and quartz are examples of metamorphic rock.

In this experiment, the rapid and constant bending of the wire caused heat that changed or partly melted the wax, the same way that pressure and heat within the earth melts and changes rocks.

An Earth-Shattering Experience

YOU WILL NEED:
piece of chalk
½ cup of white vinegar
small jar

Limestone caves are hollowed out by slightly acid rainwater that, over thousands of years, has gradually dissolved the soft rock.

What to do: Place the piece of chalk in the jar with the vinegar for 5 minutes.

What happens: The chalk dissolves in the vinegar.

Why: School chalk is a form of limestone, or calcium carbonate. It is made up of small bits of sea shells and the mineral calcite and is similar to the soft rock caves of limestone. These caves have been formed when the rock has been dissolved by the acids in rainwater, similar to the chalk that is dissolved by the vinegar, which is acetic acid. England's famed White Cliffs of Dover are made of great sheets of chalk, a form of calcium carbonate.

Shell Shock

179

Replace the chalk with a few sea shells, another form of calcium carbonate and limestone, and see how fast or completely they dissolve.

What to do: Place some sea shells in one jar with the vinegar, and a few in the other jar with the water (as the control, for comparison). Leave the shells sit in the jars for 4 days.

Remove the shells from the jars, place them on newspaper on a counter or worktable, and carefully try to break them with the spoon.

What happens: The shells from the jar of water remain as hard as ever, while the shells placed in the vinegar should break and crumble quite easily. They will also be covered with a white chalky substance (calcium carbonate).

Why: The shells in the water are the experiment's control, to be compared with those in the other jar that were affected by the vinegar. Again, there is acid in rainwater as there is acid in vinegar. Acid will dissolve calcium carbonate whether it is in the form of cave rock, chalk, or shells. In some areas of the world, the rain is as acid as vinegar.

Snow . . . Er! Iceballs!

180

This simple activity can help you to understand how huge glaciers are formed.

Glaciers are created when snow becomes compacted, or packed tightly. During the winter, when snow is on the ground, go outside and get some. At other times, ask an adult to make you some shaved ice in a blender or food processor, so you can learn about glaciers.

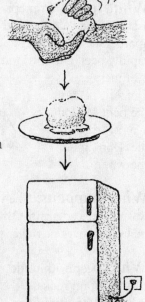

Compact or squeeze the snow or shaved ice into a tight ball (notice how solid it becomes). Let it melt a little and then put it into the freezer for about 30 minutes. When you remove the chunk of snow it will be changed into a solid ball of ice.

Think of all the snow that falls in the mountains, day after day, compressing the snow underneath, and what happens to that snow, and you can imagine how the great glaciers are formed.

Glacier Melt

181

You can learn a lot about glaciers by making a model of one. It's best to do this outside. Adult help may be needed.

YOU WILL NEED:

small cup or clean, empty yogurt container

sand

small pebbles

water

piece of board, to make incline

hammer

thick rubber band

nail

watch

What to do: Place a 1 inch (2.5 cm) layer of sand and pebbles in the cup. Add 2 inches (5 cm) of water. Place the cup in the freezer. When the water has frozen solid, repeat the process, adding sand, pebbles, and water, then freezing. The cup should be filled to the top.

Next, carefully hammer a nail partway into the middle of one end of the board. Place that end against something immovable to create an incline or slant. Now you are ready.

Remove your model glacier from the freezer. Warm the sides of the container under warm tap water, only just enough to get the model glacier to slide out of the cup when tapped. With the sand-side down, place the glacier at the top of the incline and fasten the rubber band around its middle and around the nail. How long will it take your glacier to melt, move, and leave rock and sand deposits? Time it.

What happens: Depending on the weather, melting should begin immediately, even on cooler days. Pebble and sand deposits will fall off in clumps, some will slide down the board, while other separate bits and pieces will form along the

board surface in strange patterns, much like moraine, or glacial matter.

Why: Glaciers are large masses of ice that move down mountainsides and valleys cutting gouges out of the rock and soil. Deposits from glacier movements can be found in such places as the Arctic, Antarctica, Finland, and Greenland.

These giant masses of ice would not move at all if it weren't for the great pressures they also exert. The force of these pressures causes periods of heating and melting. The ice refreezes, but just enough thawing occurs to cause the slipping movement.

As glaciers move, they break off and pick up tons of rock and soil and deposit it someplace else. The unusual rock formations or deposits left behind are called moraine. Like the real thing, our miniature-glacier experiment shows how and why those rock and sand deposits are so unusual and often unevenly placed.

WORLD TRAVELLERS

While the earth's surface, or crust, is always changing, and our planet continues to move through space, time and the seasons go through constant cycles—day after day, year after year.

While reading about the earth and its place in the solar system of planets is good, it is even better to do simple experiments that help you to understand time and space and why things happen as they do.

So, gather up your materials and get ready to do some simple, interesting, and timely experiments. Definitely, a fun time will be had by all!

 **Stick Around**

YOU WILL NEED:

stick
pencil
paper
stones or other markers

Make a simple sundial or sun clock and watch the shadow from its stick or rod, called a gnomon, move around on the ground to tell time. The angle of the shadow produced by the sun will change as the earth rotates, or spins, and changes from day to night. So stick around to watch the shadows, and the time, change—it's time well spent!

This experiment can only be done on a sunny day.

What to Do: Find a sunny location in your yard and push the stick into the ground. On the hour, mark the time of day on the piece of paper and place a stone or marker on the spot where the shadow strikes the ground. Again, one hour later, record the time and mark the shadow with a stone or marker. Continue these steps until you have a completed and marked (calibrated) sun clock.

What happens: The shadow cast by the sun on the gnomon, or stick, will change angle and length as the sun moves from east to west in the sky.

Why: Although the sun appears to be moving from east to west, it is really the Earth that is moving, or revolving, around the sun. Besides orbiting, or circling, the sun, the earth also spins on its axis, or turns like a top. It is this spinning, or rotating, in relation to the sun that makes it possible to record the time, and night and day. Where the sun casts the gnomon's shadow at a certain time of the day, it casts the same shadow the next day, and the day after that.

In the morning, the shadow will be long and narrow and will point to the west. At noon, when the sun appears at its highest point, the shadow will be short and will point north in the northern hemisphere (but south in the southern hemisphere). In the afternoon, the shadow will be directed toward the east.

Time on My Hands

It is important to check and double-check all experiments to make certain that the results come from your hypothesis, or scientific guess, as to what will happen. If you are not careful, other causes or variables could affect the results you get.

To be certain that shadows always perform the same, do the previous experiment again, but this time use the shadow of a hand-held pencil gnomon to compare with your shadow stick. This is a "controlled" experiment, comparing the shadow of the short pencil rod to the longer stick rod.

adjust the shadows of the two gnomon rods so that they are parallel, or next to, one another.)

Is one shadow in alignment or in the same position as the other? Mark the base of your hand gnomon with the side of the other pencil. Put pressure on the clay, marking where the shadow strikes it. Continue to compare the shadow of the pencil gnomon with the rod in the ground. Mark each, with stones and markings, every hour. What are the similarities or differences? Do the shadows change position equally? Do the shadows of the rods grow longer or shorter? If so, when?

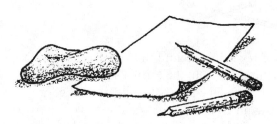

What to do: To make a base, flatten the piece of clay into a disk about 2 inches (5 cm) across. Push the pointed end of the pencil into the clay. You now have a simple hand gnomon. Position the gnomon, aligning and adjusting it according to the shadow cast by the stick version. Write down the exact position in which you place the hand rod next to the shadow stick and keep it in that position every time you do a reading or test the experiment. (Example: Place the clay base of the hand rod next to the ground stick and align or

Spotlight Time Machine

184

YOU WILL NEED:

cardboard square,
about 4 inches x 4 inches
(10 cm x 10 cm)
watch or clock
scissors
tape
2 pieces of paper
pencil

The sun is a kind of time machine, as this simple experiment will show. It will only work, however, on a sunny day.

What to do: Cut a 1 inch (2 cm) hole in the center of the cardboard square. Tape the square on a south-facing window in a position so the spot of sunlight will shine on a clear area of floor. Place the paper where the spot of sunlight hits the floor so that it lands on the paper.

Draw a circle around the spot of light and write the time next to it. Continue to watch the sunlight spots every 30 minutes. Use more paper and record the times and movement as you watch.

What happens: The spots of light move from left to right and change their positions as the time changes.

Why: The earth rotates, or turns, from west to east every 24 hours while it travels around the sun. This movement of the earth causes the spot of sunlight to move across one paper and to the next as your part of the earth moves from sunrise to sunset.

Season Tickets

185

Would the spots of sun fall in the same location at 8:00 A.M. in the summer as they would at 8:00 A.M. in the winter?

If you enjoy long-term experiments, those that take a while, and you can find an unbusy room with a south-facing window, try it! An undisturbed bedroom with plenty of floor space would be an excellent place to do this experiment.

Repeat the last experiment, but this time use pieces of paper about 4 inches (10 cm) square.

Tape them to the floor, over the spots, at the same time at different times of the year. Example: 8:00 A.M., October 1st, and 8:00 A.M., December 22nd.

Is there a difference in the positions of the spots from one season to the next? Record your results.

Skylight Direction-Finder

Early explorers and sailors used a simple direction-finder called an astrolabe to find their location on the open sea. You can make your own astrolabe and find your location on the earth with a few easy-to-find and inexpensive materials.

What to do: Tie a piece of string from the middle of the flat side of the protractor. The string should extend a little beyond it. Now tie the weight to the end of the string and place the flat side of the protractor next to the pencil and tie it to it with two additional short pieces of string.

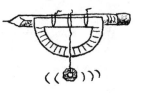

You are now ready to use your astrolabe. On a clear, starry night, point your instrument and center it on the North Star, sometimes called the Pole Star. The weighted string will drop next to the side of the protractor and will show the degree or the number of your latitude. Be patient and do this several times to get an accurate reading.

What happens: Your instrument, when pointed to the North Star, will help you find your latitude on earth. Latitude is a series of imaginary side-to-side earth lines that tell you in numbers where a certain place on earth is located.

Why: The protractor in your astrolabe is a half-circled instrument used to measure angles. It is marked in units of ten called degrees. When you pointed your instrument to the North Star, the weighted string aligned itself to the unit angle on the protractor. This, in turn, gave you your exact location on earth or your latitude.

How to Find the North Star

The North Star, also called the Pole Star, is seen only in the northern part of the sky. This star seems almost fixed in place because of its position above the North Pole. Like a clock, it also appears to change position from hour to hour and season to season. It appears very faint because it is more than four hundred light years away.

The North Star can be found opposite the constellation Ursa Major, commonly known as the Big Dipper. It is seen as a cup with a long handle on it, if you were to draw imaginary lines from each of the seven stars that make up the pattern (as you would in a dot-to-dot puzzle). The stars furthest from the handle, which make up the cup, point directly to the North Star.

Can You Find the Southern Cross?

188

Do people in the southern hemisphere, or the southern half of the world, also see the stars visible from the northern half of the earth?

If you live in the northern hemisphere, you cannot see all the stars in the sky over the southern half of the world. If you live in the southern hemisphere you cannot see all the stars over the northern half of the world.

If you live on or near the imaginary line that circles the middle of the earth, known as the equator, however, you can see all the stars of both halves of the earth.

While people in the northern hemisphere can find Polaris, the Pole or North Star, which appears to be fixed directly above the North Pole, star gazers in the southern hemisphere have no such marker.

The Southern Cross, in the southern hemisphere, is a constellation, or group of stars, made up of four crossed stars and other stars, two of which, like the north's Big Dipper, point to the South Pole. The Southern Cross, however, is not a good locator of its pole. It does not always appear as a cross and it is often hard to find and to see. In addition, the southern hemisphere has no visible "pole" star to mark it in the sky.

Meteor Burnout: Truth or Friction?

189

Meteors are small rocklike chunks, most probably broken fragments of comets or asteroids, tumbling rapidly around the sun in outer space. As they enter and pass through the earth's atmosphere, they burn up. Now you can try this simple experiment and discover how this happens.

What to do: Drop the tablet into the bottle of water and watch what happens as it falls or floats down to the bottom.

What happens: The tablet dissolves or breaks up into many small pieces, or fragments, that disappear as it journeys to the bottom of the bottle.

Why: The water represents the earth's atmosphere and the seltzer tablet, the meteor.

Like a meteor, the tablet breaks up into many

YOU WILL NEED:

large soda bottle filled with water

½ seltzer tablet

small fragments as it drops to the bottom of the bottle (the earth's surface). Unlike the tablet, the meteor rushes through outer space at such great speeds that friction, or the rubbing force of its surface against the earth's atmosphere, causes the space rock to heat up and the white-hot fragment to break up and explode into cosmic space dust.

Most meteors are no bigger than small stones, but every so often a few larger chunks make their way to the surface of the earth as meteorites.

Starry-Eyed

190

Make a star-lit light box and learn about the constellations, groups of fixed clusters of stars. It's fun and it's easy, and you and your friends will be headed for stardom.

YOU WILL NEED:
oatmeal box with lid (several lids are best)
nail
flashlight
pencil

What to do: Using the nail, punch "star" holes in the box lid. Follow your favorite star–chart patterns from astronomy books, or from looking overhead at the night sky where you live.

Depending on the size of the box and the lid, you should be able to punch in a large pattern or two or more smaller constellations on one lid.

Now, press the narrow end or handle of the flashlight against the center of the other end of the box and draw a circle around it. Then cut a hole in it and fit the flashlight into the box. (This can be done by removing the lid and pushing the handle through the hole.)

What happens: Your light box projects groups of small, starlike, light spots on the ceiling or wall.

Why: Different constellations seem to sweep across the sky, and are seen only at certain times of the year. From week to week, and at the same time every night, their positions change, as they move a little farther to the west.

The orbit or path the earth takes around the sun, and its position at certain times of the year, determines whether you can see certain constellations or not. In winter, the summer constellations are blocked out by the sun's light while the winter constellations are blocked out in the summer.

You are now ready to dazzle your friends with your new star-lit light box. By rotating a lid or turning the box, you can even make the constellations move. Take it into a dark room and point it, with the flashlight on, at the ceiling or wall and enjoy the starry-eyed show.

191 Parallax Puzzle

YOU WILL NEED:
pencil

Scientists can calculate, or figure out mathematically, the distances of different stars from the earth.

As we look at the stars, we understand from what we have learned that the stars stay in an exact position and are very far away. But what our eyes and our brains tell us may not be totally correct.

If we walk past a house, the house does not move but the position of it does because the angle we view it from after passing it is different. This is parallax, and this simple experiment will show you how parallax works.

What to do: Hold the pencil out vertically, or straight up and down, right before your eyes. Now, close your left eye, then quickly open it and close your right eye. Do it again. Continue to rapidly close first one eye and then the other and observe what happens to the pencil before you.

What happens:
The pencil jumps, moving from side to side! Where is it really? How can you know?

192 Moving Picture

Do the parallax experiment again the same way, but this time, as you view the close–up pencil, also look at a distant object, like a lamp or a table, in the background. What do you see? Does the position of one object change more than the other?

What happens: Although the pencil appears to shift position, or move, from one side to the other as it did before, the distant object did not.

Why: The pencil did not really move, but the angle of viewing did. The angle between the pencil and your eye changed and so the pencil's position did, but only according to your eyes and your brain. This shift difference is called parallax, and it is the key to finding distance. The closer an object is, the more it will seem to shift, while objects that are farther away do not. In the same way, parallax makes closer stars seem to move and those very far away seem fixed.

To see the shifting of stars, astronomers (scientists who study and observe the universe from our solar system to the farthest galaxies) measure the different positions of stars at two different times of the year as the earth moves in orbit around the sun. In that way they can calculate the stars' exact distances from the earth.

Track Star

YOU WILL NEED:

sheet of paper
drinking glass
half-filled with water

Our sun, a star, is a giant ball of hydrogen gas many million of miles away. Yet it is possible to learn something about the sun from tracking, or following, the wavelengths of light coming from it. This can be done in a simple way in a sunny outdoor location.

What to do: Find a place outside in full sunlight for your experiment. Place the sheet of paper on a table or lay it on the ground where the experiment is to be done.

Now, hold the glass with the water firmly and carefully between your thumb and a finger over the sheet of paper. The glass should be held about 3 to 4 inches (7 to10 cm) above the paper. Do not hold the glass in the usual way, around the glass. It's important that you hold the glass so that your hand does not block the sides.

Move the glass up and down and slant it slightly, focusing the light on the paper until a clear colorful pattern appears.

What happens: The glass of water acts as a prism and casts a rainbow on the paper.

Why: A glass of water is able to act as a prism, or something that can change the direction of light so the bands of color in it can be seen and studied. White light is really a combination of many colors.

When a wavelength of light is split and changed by the glass of water, color occurs. Light from the sun shows many colors. Astronomers can tell what elements or gases make up a star by studying the bands, or spectrums, of the light it gives off.

194

Glassify

Do different types of glass make better prisms for casting rainbow patterns on paper?

Do the same experiment again, but instead, use a different size glass, then use a glass with a different shape. What about colored glass? Will glasses made of colored glass refract, or split, light into colors, too? Will a full glass of water work better than a glass half full of water?

Do a variety of experiments and write down your observations and results. When you're finished, you'll know what glass works best.

195 Highly Focused

YOU WILL NEED:
thermometer
paper
pencil
flashlight
watch or clock
can or other support
for thermometer

The seasons of the year depend on the tilt of the earth and the concentration of sunlight at different times of the year in the northern and southern hemispheres. This simple experiment explains it all.

What to do: Record the temperature on the thermometer. Run the thermometer under warm or cool water to get the temperature where you want it, so that it is easy for you to record and calculate.

Prop the thermometer, glass side outward, against the lighted end of the flashlight. Leave it in that position, timing it with a clock or watch, for 3 minutes. Record the final temperature.

After the first reading against the flashlight, hold the thermometer under cool water until the temperature returns to what it was at the beginning of the first trial.

Now, lean the thermometer against a support to hold it upright and shine the flashlight on it from a set distance away, about 1 foot (30 cm). Again, record the reading after 3 minutes.

What happens: The thermometer leaning against the flashlight and in direct contact with the light, so it was more concentrated or had greater strength, registered a few degrees warmer. No noticeable change was seen when the light was shined on the thermometer from a short distance away.

Why: The concentration of light on various parts of the earth, at any one time of year, is similar to the concentration of light in our experiment.

The greater an area covered by light, the lower the temperature. In our experiment, the thermometer that was farther away from the light was not affected by it as much, if at all.

The northern hemisphere, or upper half of the earth, which is tilted away from the sun in December, receives a greater spread of light, while the southern hemisphere, or lower half of the earth, is tilted toward the sun at that time and receives stronger, more concentrated light. This explains why, in December, it is winter in New York City and summer in Sydney, Australia.

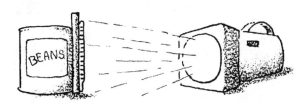

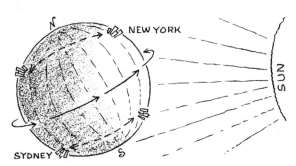

LEAFY LESSONS

We could not live without plants. Consider these facts:

Plants, humans, and animals keep the Earth's atmosphere balanced.

Plants, through photosynthesis, make their own food, while taking in carbon dioxide and giving off oxygen.

Animals and humans need oxygen and breathe out carbon dioxide.

Animals and humans get much-needed sugars and starches from eating plants.

Millions of tons of water are released into the air every day by plants in a process called transpiration.

Some scientists believe that the loss of trees and an increase in human and animal breathing, or respiration, can increase the amount of carbon dioxide in the atmosphere and cause the earth to warm up.

The experiments in this chapter will answer your questions about plant growth, but more important, they'll show you why these living things are so very important to our lives.

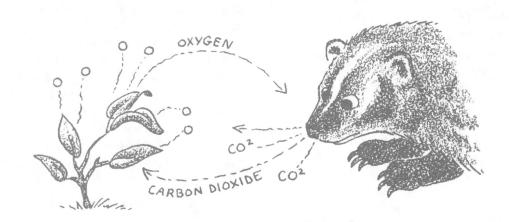

Oxygen Leaves

196

YOU WILL NEED:
1 clear, wide-mouth jar
water
1 leaf
magnifying glass

Oxygen leaves? That's right, oxygen leaves! Leaves what? Confused? Try this experiment and you won't be. You'll also learn about two important plant words—stomata and photosynthesis.

What to do: Fill the jar with water and drop the leaf into it. Place the jar in a sunny location outdoors or on a windowsill. Leave it there in the sun for at least one hour, or until the outside of the jar feels warm. With the magnifying glass look at what happens in the jar.

What happens: Thousands of tiny bubbles appear on the surface of the leaf and inside the jar.

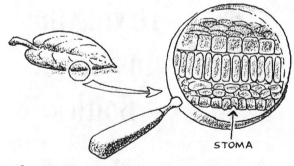

STOMA

Why: The bubbles are formed by the oxygen gas given off by the leaf.

A plant needs certain elements and sunlight to make its food. This process is called photosynthesis. "Photo" and "synthesis" mean "light" and "putting together." When water, air, chlorophyll (which causes the leaf's green coloring), and sunlight are put together in a certain way by the plant, it makes its own food. If any one of these elements is missing, a plant cannot live.

Carbon dioxide, a gas, enters the tiny, pinlike holes, called stomata, in the underside of the leaf. The plant uses sunlight and chlorophyll and, combined with water and carbon dioxide, turns these elements into the food it needs. The food is actually a form of sugar that is eventually turned into starch. Oxygen is given off as a waste product. Now you know why you saw the bubbles in the container and on the leaf.

Don't Leaf Me Alone

197

Now see what happens when you do the same experiment again, but place the jar in the shade.

Does it matter if a leaf is in the sunlight before you test it? Try placing a leaf from outdoors in the sunlight into one container of water. Into a second container of water put a leaf from an indoor plant that is kept in the shade. Put both containers outdoors in the sunlight. Is there any difference?

Try this experiment indoors now. Do bubbles appear on the leaf or container?

Remember always to keep good notes and records and to log, or write down, all your observations and the results of your experiments.

Phototropism: Waiting for the Weekends

198

Plants will always grow toward the sun. They will turn upward, even if they are turned on their sides.

What to do: Take the two flat squares of plastic. Fold the napkin to fit onto one of the plastic squares and arrange the roots of the weed on top of it.

Place the second square of plastic on top, like a sandwich, making sure that the stems and leaves of the plant are outside the plastic sandwich. Wrap the rubber bands tightly around the squares to keep everything in place.

Fill the shallow container with water. Place the "weed sandwich," propped on its side in the container, near a sunny south-facing window. You will have to wait at least four days for results. Make sure there is always ½ inch to 1 inch (1 to 2.5 cm) of water in the bottom of the container. Make drawings showing the position of your plant each day. Be patient.

YOU WILL NEED:

2 small pieces of plastic, about 3 inches (8 cm) square, cut from a plastic container

paper napkin

medium-size weed with well-developed leaves and stems and a good root system

2 rubber bands

small shallow container or a meat tray from a frozen food package

water
pencil
paper
scissors

Why: A plant's leaves and stems always grow toward the sun, no matter if they are placed sideways, or even upside down. This could involve moving, bending, and turning to go toward the light. This process is known as phototropism.

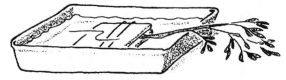

What happens: The leaves and stems of the weed grow upward, toward the sun, even though the weed was placed on its side.

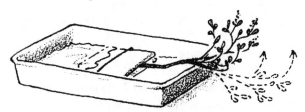

199

Drying the Insides of Bottles

Some experiments call for completely dry soda bottles. But how do you get the inside of a wet soda bottle dry? Just stuff a sheet or two of paper toweling inside the bottle and use a long-handled screwdriver, stick, or something else that is long and thin to press and stir the absorbent paper against the sides and bottom—and slide it up and out of the bottle when you are finished.

Perspiration or Transpiration: Don't Sweat It!

People sweat, or perspire, while plants transpire. A plant gives off water through its stomata, the tiny holes located under the surface of each leaf. Now see what it's all about.

YOU WILL NEED:

lump of clay (golf ball size)

2 short clear soda or water bottles

nail or pencil

broad leaf, or leaflet with stem, which has been exposed to the sun

magnifying glass

What to do: Roll the clay between your hands to form a 2 inch (4 cm) plug. The plug will have to reach about 1 inch (2 cm) into each bottle neck to hold one bottle vertically, upside down, above the other.

Using the nail or pencil, poke a hole in the plug and insert the stem of the leaf through it, being careful not to break the stem or crush the leaf. Now, gently, press the clay plug inward around the stem to seal it in. Fill one bottle with water and push the plug with the leaf in it into the top of the bottle. (The plug should rise above the bottle neck and the stem of the leaf must touch the water.)

Wipe any moisture from the plug and leaf and make certain that the plug itself is not touching the water—this could cause moisture to get into the bottle above and negate the experiment.

Carefully, turn the other bottle upside down on top, working the leaf into it, and the plug into place. Press the clay gently around any opening to seal it. After one hour, take the magnifying glass and observe your experiment closely.

What happens: A small, but noticeable amount of moisture (areas with small water droplets and steamy haze) appears on the glass inside the "dry" upside-down bottle.

Why: Transpiration in plants is much like a person sweating. A plant loses water vapor through holes or pores called stomata. Plants often obtain too much ground water through their roots and get rid of what is not needed through these holes.

All the world's water is always the same—none is ever lost. The earth's waters are naturally recycled through rain, clouds, lakes, rivers, oceans, and especially by plant transpiration.

Although you may not see it, plants give off gallons of water each day. Leaves release millions of tons of water vapor into the air every day. This is an earth process we never consider, but without it we could never live on this planet.

Three Leaves and a Maybe

In the last experiment, you used a broad leaf in a bottle and saw water droplets and steam form. But would the rate of transpiration be the same if different types of leaves were used?

Find more bottles and try the experiment using different leaves—broad leaves, narrow leaves, leaflets, and fern-like leaves. Place one set in the sun, another in the house. Is the amount of water seen in the "dry" bottle more, less, the same? What's your hypothesis?

Doing the same experiment without the leaf can serve as a control, to show that other things are not producing the water droplets.

For the Birds

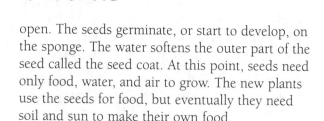

Birdseed, radish seeds, onion seeds, or any other kind of seed will grow if placed on a water-soaked sponge.

What to do: Place the sponge in the container with enough water to soak it. The sponge should rise above the water level. Water should be added to the container from time to time as the water evaporates, to keep the sponge moist.

Sprinkle a small amount of seeds on the surface of the sponge and lightly pat them into it. Place the container of sponge-soaked seeds in a sunny location, perhaps on a windowsill. Check them in two or three days for some cracking and sprouting. You'll need your magnifying glass to see them. The seedlings should be fully developed in five to seven days.

Why: When the dry seeds are placed on the water-soaked sponge, they swell until they break

open. The seeds germinate, or start to develop, on the sponge. The water softens the outer part of the seed called the seed coat. At this point, seeds need only food, water, and air to grow. The new plants use the seeds for food, but eventually they need soil and sun to make their own food.

203 What Now?

Now you have a quick and easy and fun way to sprout seeds, because you can actually see them. After the seeds have sprouted, gently scrape them off the sponge and let them fall into a container of potting soil or another gardening material like vermiculite. (See the next experiment for instructions.)

Waterbed

204

Can plants be grown if you don't have any soil? Hydroponics is the science of growing plants without this needed element! How is it done? Does it really work? You'll find out, dirt free, in this important scientific investigation.

YOU WILL NEED:

flower pots (with holes in the bottoms)

stones or broken pottery, for pot drainage

tray or shallow dishes

spray bottle

flower or vegetable seeds

water-absorbent plant material, like vermiculite, perlite, or peat moss

liquid or granular plant food

What to do: Place the stones or broken pottery in the bottoms of the flower pots, to cover the holes and provide drainage. Fill the remaining areas with the planting material. Put the pots on the tray or on shallow dishes.

With the spray bottle, water the material well—it should be moist but not soaking wet. Now, lightly and evenly scatter the seed over the planting material and press it down. If you have a lot of several kinds of seeds, it is best to use several pots for good spacing and better growth. Place the pots in sunny, south-facing windows and continue to keep the planting materials moist.

What happens: The seeds grow into healthy seedlings or young plants without using any type of soil.

Why: Plants need air, water, and light to grow, but they don't necessarily need soil. Plants can be grown without soil by replacing the minerals they would normally get from the soil with liquid or dry plant food. Hydroponics, or growing plants without soil, may be the new way of growing plants for the future.

After the plants germinate, or sprout, water them with a combination of water and plant food. (See package directions on how to dilute the food with water.) Continue to water the plants whenever more moisture is needed, but be careful not to water them too much.

Phil O. Dandrun's Root Bare

205

A new brand of soda? No. Phil O. Dandrun is our nickname (an alias) for the philodendron. If you have this common house plant at home, try this experiment—if you don't, use a different plant. One way or another, leave it to us and you'll be raising a plant from a stem in no time.

What to do: Cut the stem off the plant below the leaf scar or the bulge, which is called the node, as in the illustration. Remove the side leaves.

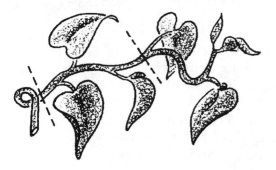

Place the piece of philodendron in the jar of water. Make sure the water covers the spot where the leaves were pulled off. Now you must wait patiently for roots to develop. It may take several weeks for good root growth.

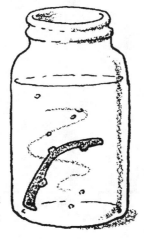

What happens: Long brown, threadlike roots form from the scarred areas where the leaves were removed.

Why: Some plants can grow from roots, leaves, and stems. Philodendron sections or stems, called cuttings, that are placed in water will grow roots from the leaf areas around the bulge or node. Geraniums and other plants also do this, so if yours didn't work, don't give up. Try again.

206 Little Sprouts or Hothouse Tomatoes

YOU WILL NEED:

flower pots
potting soil
spoon
fresh tomatoes, or
packaged tomato seeds
plastic wrap
rubber bands
sunny windowsill

Note: The amount of materials needed depends on how many containers of seedlings you wish to grow.

A greenhouse is a hot, closed space for growing plants. The earth can have a kind of greenhouse effect, too, when gases from burning fossil fuels act as a lid and prevent heat from escaping into space.

Now let's put this greenhouse idea to work for the fun of raising some sweet little sprouts that may even turn into tomatoes. There's nothing like tasting the juicy, sweet, delicious results of this successful experiment.

What to do: Prepare the pots with packed-down potting soil. Scoop the seeds from fresh tomatoes, or use packaged tomato seeds, and scatter them evenly over the soil, avoiding clumps of seeds. Then cover them with a light and thin layer of soil.

Water well, then cover each pot with a piece of clear plastic wrap and fasten it with a rubber band. Place the pots on a sunny windowsill and watch for little sprouts.

207 Planting Seeds and Seedlings

Plant cuttings that have rooted, seeds, and seedlings, can be planted or moved into soil. Easy enough, but some rules must be followed.

For seeds to start growing and plants to grow well they need water—but not too much (they'll "drown" from lack of air) or too little (they'll dry out and die). Good light and soil with the proper minerals are also needed to boost growth.

First, plant seeds, seedlings, and new plants in clay or plastic pots with drainage holes in the bottom. (Egg and milk cartons with holes punched in them also make great planters.) Adding bits of broken clay pots, gravel, or stones also helps the water drain. Use a good potting soil with equal parts of peat moss, sand, bark, wood, and a good nitrogen and iron content.

Containers should be nearly filled and plantings should be given "elbow room" away from other seeds, seedlings, or plants. In other words, don't crowd! A light covering of soil, about ¼ inch (1 cm), should cover seeds or seedling roots and be lightly compressed, or pressed down. New plantings should be placed in a sunny, south-facing window, and the soil should be kept moist. A small sprayer or medicine dropper might deliver just the right amount of water and help prevent over-watering.

If necessary, get an adult to help with your new plantings until you know what to do and how to get the results you expect. Good luck and happy planting!

Dirty Words: Soil, Sand, Humus, and Mud

The next time you fill a pot or planter with soil, think about its properties—how it looks, feels, and smells, what it's made of, and what lives in it. As you investigate, you'll discover bugs, leaves, pebbles, and small rocks, but that is just scratching the surface. You won't see the billions of microscopic plants and tiny animals that live there in the soil, too, but they are responsible for making up good, rich soils.

In this chapter you'll learn about soil, sand, humus, and mud, and how dirt acts under certain conditions. And asking questions about these dirty words won't get you grounded!

Dirty Questions
Call For Dirty Answers

What is soil made of? Is all soil the same? What's the difference? What kind of soil is best for plants ? How can I find out about it?

Read this whole introduction, and then do the "Earthshaking" experiment and you'll definitely dig up more dirt on the subject than you ever imagined was there.

What is known as soil or dirt is made up of broken rocks, minerals, the remains of dead plant and animal life, and germlike plants called bacteria. These tiny, one-celled plants are too small to be seen, unless you look through a good micro-

scope, but they are everywhere in the soil and they do a big job.

Small animals, worms, oxygen, and water are also needed in the soil. With the help of the larger animal life, the bacteria use the air and water to break down and chemically change the soil. When their job is done, poor soil that was not good enough to grow anything becomes a nitrogen-rich fertile soil that can grow just about anything.

Soil by Any Other Name is Still Dirt

Scientists have identified four different kinds of soil according to the way it feels (texture) and what it contains. The types of soil are sand, silt, loam, and clay.

Sand is made up of broken shells and worn-down bits of rock and minerals like quartz and basalt, a volcanic-like rock.

Although all good soils need sand, too much of it can cause too much water to drain away from plant roots, leaving them to dry and shrivel up. Sand is found in deserts, on beaches, and along river bottoms. Larger grains of sand are called gravel.

Silt, on the other hand, is a very fine-grained, sandy soil. Its parts are smaller than sand but larger than particles of clay.

Clay is a fine soil and it is much needed in all soils. Without clay, soils fall apart and fertilizers are washed away. Too much clay in any soil, however, will cause problems with water drainage and eventually produce rotted roots in plants.

The best type of soil for most plants is loam. Loam is a mixture of clay, sand, and silt with enough humus (broken-down plant life and animal matter) to make it rich and fertile.

Sand
Silt
Clay

Loam

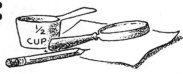

Earthshaking Discovery: It's Sedimentary

208

YOU WILL NEED:

Jars with lids
(depending on how
many soil samples you
wish to test)

½ cup each of soil
sample from different
locations and depths
(topsoil, or upper soil,
and subsoil, or
deeper soil)

water
magnifying glass
paper
pencil

The sediment, or different types of soil particles, and how they float and settle, are unusual and interesting. Just shake up these soil-shakers and watch out.

What to do: Fill each jar with ½ cup of soil. Add water. The jar should be about three-quarters filled. Screw the lid on the jar tightly and shake well. Repeat the procedure with other soil samples to be tested.

Be patient and wait about 2 hours for the soil to settle. (You could sit and watch, but you don't have to.) Then, with the magnifying glass, observe what happened to the soil samples. Draw a picture of the settled sediment in each jar.

What happens: The soil settles into bands, or layers, depending on the content of the soil.

Why: In sandy mixtures, heavier, rocklike particles settle first, followed by light-colored silty, sand-like grains.

In most loamy, gardening top soils, the heavier gravel mix settles to the bottom, while the dark-colored, lighter-in-weight humus floats to the top of the jar. As you see, this is a good test for determining good, loamy, rich soils.

209

More Dirt

Collect soil samples in different areas when you go on long car trips and vacations. When you come home test the soil you have collected and discover how much humus and different kinds of soil are in each sample.

Air Condition

210

What if you can't see what condition the soil is in?

What to do: Place the soil sample in the jar. Pour the cooled, boiled water slowly onto the soil and watch closely.

What happens: Air bubbles appear and circle the top surface of the soil.

Why: All dry soil has air trapped in and around the particles. The bubbles that rise from the soil's surface are formed by air forced from the soil by the water.

Water also normally contains its own air, which is why, for this experiment, it is necessary to use boiled and cooled water. During the boiling, the heated air in the water is boiled away. This experiment, then, reveals that it is the air from the soil that causes the bubbles and not the water.

Bubble Blowers

211

Find some porous rock (rocks that are lightweight, with some holes or spaces in them) and place them in a pan filled with water for a rocky bubble-blower show.

What to do: Place the rocks in the baking pan and pour in enough water to cover them. Using the magnifying glass, observe what happens.

What happens:
Streams of bubbles flow from the rocks. The more porous the rocks, the more bubbles you will see. Depending on the  weight of the rocks and the force of the air escaping from them, the rocks might move slightly, rock back and forth, or bounce and rattle against the pan.

Why: Oxygen is present, even in the rocks. Air bubbles flow from the spaces in the minerals that make up the rocks and rise to the water's surface.

212 ◆ Sand Trap

Quicksand is a thick body of sand grains mixed with water that appears to be a dry hard surface. It may look solid, as if it can be walked on, so it can be unexpectedly dangerous because it really cannot support much weight. People have been known to be swallowed up in quicksand.

In this experiment, you'll make a type of quicksand goop that will magically and surprisingly support your hand one minute but not the next.

What to do: On the newspaper, because this experiment can be messy, combine the cornstarch and water in the bowl and stir with the spoon until the mixture looks like paste. The cornstarch mixture will be hard to stir and will stick to the bottom of the bowl. This is to be expected. Next, lightly and evenly sprinkle the ground coffee on top of the mixture to give it a dry and even look.

Now the fun begins. Make a fist and lightly pound on the surface. Notice what happens and how it feels. Next, lightly push your fingers down into the mixture.

What happens: When you used your fist to hit the surface of the mixture, it appeared to hit the surface only and seemed to be mysteriously and magically stopped from going any further. But when you placed your fingers or hand in the mixture, they easily and readily slid into the bottom of the bowl.

Why: The molecules of quicksand goop behave much like real quicksand. Unlike water molecules, the goop's molecules are larger. They swell and hook together, and seem to act more like a solid than a liquid. In addition, the coffee grains give the mixture a deceptively smooth and dry look, much like real quicksand.

Holding Pattern

YOU WILL NEED:

nail

equal amounts of four different soil samples, like clay, sand, potting soil, and rich loam gardening soil

4 paper cups or the bottoms of waxed cartons

small containers

water

paper

pencil

measuring cup

A soil is called "permeable" when it allows water to pass through it. Which soils are the most permeable? Which soils hold the most water, the least, or just the right amount? For this dirty experiment, it will be best to set up work space outside where you can just dig in!

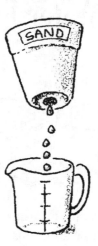

What to do: With the nail, punch about six holes in the bottoms of the paper cups or the carton bottoms. Fill each container about half-full with a soil sample to be tested. Pour ½ cup of water into sample of soil to be tested. Place a small container under each to catch the water. Pour the water that drains into each container into the measuring cup. Record the type of soil tested and how much water the soil held. Repeat this step with other soils and again measure the amount of water.

What happens: There will be noticeably more soil and water in the bottom of some containers than in other. Water will drain faster from some soil samples than from others.

Why: Clay soils retain, or keep, too much water, while sandy soils drain too quickly. Too much water around the tender roots of plants can cause rotting, while with too little water the roots will dry out and shrivel up. Soils with a lot of humus, or decomposed, broken-down plant and animal matter, are best for most plants. It retains just enough water for healthy plant growth while stimulating the roots. Some plants, however, still do well or better in other kinds of soil.

214 ◆ A Down-to-Earth Water Filter

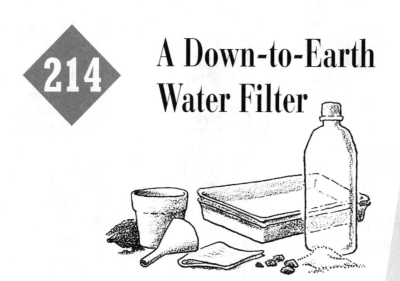

YOU WILL NEED:

medium-size flower pot, or a
cut-down waxed carton with
holes punched in the bottom
coffee filter or paper towel
large soda bottle with cap
2 shallow trays or containers
gravel or pebbles
sand
funnel
dirt
water

Have you ever wondered how water is cleaned before it reaches your home? How about making a simple water filtration system that will answer many questions? You can get lots of down-to-earth information as you test it.

Remember, though, that however good a job you think you have done, the water from this experiment should never be drunk. The experiment will give you a good idea how water filters work, but it is still not a real water treatment plant, and just a few drops of "bad" water can make you sick.

It will be best to do this experiment outside since it can be messy and the dirt you need to use should be easy to find nearby. Clean sand and gravel are available in small bags in garden or variety store.

What to do: Place the filter or a piece of paper towel in the bottom of the pot or carton. Fill the bottom of the pot with gravel or small stones, to a depth of about 2 inches (5 cm). Pour sand into the container until it is about three-quarters full. This is your filter system.

Using the funnel, pour about 1 cup of dirt into the soda bottle and fill it with water. Screw the cap on and shake it thoroughly.

Pour some of the muddy water from the bottle into one of the shallow containers. This will be the control or test container, to compare the filtered water against the original sample. Place your filter system in the other container and pour some muddy water into the top of it. Watch the water as it filters through and compare it to the control sample. Be patient, the first samples will not be as clear as later ones. Repeat this procedure several times until the water comes through fairly clear. Continue to compare these samples with the water in the control pan.

What happens: The first water the trickles out of your filter system will still be fairly dirty. However, as you continue to pour the water back into and through your system, it begins to get clearer. Although the water gets cleaner, there will likely still be a certain amount of sediment that remains.

Why: Although there are similarities, your simple water filter system is not like a city's large water treatment plant. In the city system, water is sprayed into the air to release unwanted gases, and substances are added to clump together dirt particles suspended in the water so that they can be filtered out.

As with your system, the water is also passed through layers of sand and gravel, but also through a layer of charcoal. The water is then chlorinated. The chlorine gas kills bacteria that may be present in the water. Cleaning water is a big job.

Now you know something of how water filter systems work, and why you wouldn't want to drink any water you "clean" yourself.

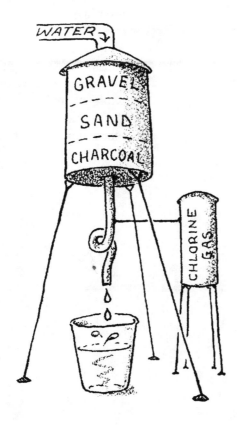

 # Sand-Casting

YOU WILL NEED:
sand or very fine soil
metal baking pan
water

The sea wears away coastal shorelines and rebuilds new sand formations. In this simple experiment, you will see how the earth is constantly being worn away, eroded, and how the process of erosion steadily changes the different shapes and formations on the earth's surface.

What to do: Pile the sand at one end of the baking pan and firmly pat it down. For the purposes of the experiment, this will represent the sandy beach or shore. Pour some water into the middle of the pan until part of the shore is slightly covered. At first gently, then increasingly faster, slide the pan back and forth until small waves are formed that roll up and onto the shore so the sand shifts, or moves.

What happens: The action of the waves in the container gradually changes the shape of the shore, moving the sand down the beach and into the water.

Why: All the seas and oceans of the earth are constantly changing the land they meet. Some wear away or carve out great rocky areas of land while others take away great sections of sand, depositing it elsewhere. This gradual but persistent action of water against land is called erosion.

216

Playing Dirty, or Groovy Soil Boxes

YOU WILL NEED:
scissors
3 1-quart (946 ml) milk cartons
garden soil
water
shallow pan or tray
short stick
measuring cup
paper
pencil

If you liked playing in mud when you were small, you're going to love this experiment. Do it outside wearing old clothes because you can get pretty dirty if you're not careful.

What to do: Cut away one side of each carton, the side away from the opening or spout. (The spout should rest on the ground as in the illustration.) Pack each opened carton with the same amount of soil.

Wet the soil in each carton thoroughly and mix it up. If the soil is too wet, put in some dry soil and mix it thoroughly by hand.

Next, pack down the muddy soil in each container to form a hill, or a slant with the high side toward the unopened end of the container. With your hand or the stick, form sideways, or horizontal, gullies or ridges in one carton, steps in the second carton, and leave the third "hill" alone.

Let the soil containers dry out for about 30 minutes. After they have dried, prop the first carton against something immovable so that it is at a slight slant. Place the shallow container under the spout opening so the opening rests on the bottom of the container.

Measure 1 cup of water and pour it steadily but gently on the top of the soil hill. Wait a few minutes for the water to settle and drain into the pan.

Pour the water from the container back into the measuring cup and see how much you have gotten back, or recovered. Write this down. Repeat this with the other two soil boxes, and again record your results. Make a note of just how clear or muddy the water is, or how much sediment or soil particles are present, as well as how long it took for the water you recovered to flow from each soil box into the drainage container.

What happens: In our experiment, we recovered 1 cup of water from the step and plain boxes but only ½ cup from the box with gullies. Is that what you found?

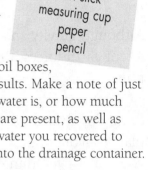

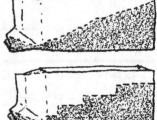

Why: Boxes that keep more of their soil in the boxes and not in the water are definitely experimental winners. Soil erosion, or the wearing away of topsoil, can be lessened by good farming or conservation techniques designed to protect and save the soil. The two such methods used in your experiment were contour farming, in which gullies or horizontal ridges are dug, and terracing, in which steps or elevated planes or levels are formed.

GRAVITY AND MAGNETISM: ATTRACTIVE FORCES

Although gravity and magnetism are different earth forces, they both exert a lot of pull.

Gravity is the force that pulls everything downward, toward the middle of our planet—you, your house, a ball, your bed, your car—everything! Your weight on earth is simply the amount of pull this force has on you.

The planets, the sun, and the moon also have gravities, but with a force lesser or greater than the earth's. The sun's gravity holds the earth and other planets in orbit around it, while the moon's gravity pull lowers and raises the tides of the oceans. Sir Isaac Newton, an English scientist, discovered these and other laws of gravity.

On the other hand, magnets have polar or field forces where an attraction, or pull is stronger. The earth itself, due to its iron center, or core, is also a giant magnet.

The wonderful gravity and magnetic experiments in this chapter will certainly attract your attention and pull you away from anything else you're doing.

Weight Lifter

217

Weight is simply the pull of the force of gravity on you and on other objects. This experiment will demonstrate how this works. To avoid the mess of spills (gravity again), it's a good idea to do this experiment outdoors. You will need a friend's help, too.

YOU WILL NEED:

nail
bottom of a waxed carton
heavy string
paper clip
thick rubber band
ruler
substances to weigh, like stones, gravel, beans, rice, dirt, sand, and marshmallows

What to do: With the nail, poke a hole through one side of the carton about 1 inch (2.5 cm) down from the top and another hole directly across from the first, on the other side of the carton. Thread the ends of the string through the holes and tie them securely to form a handle. Attach the paper clip to the top of the string handle and the rubber band to the other end of the paper clip.

Have your helper hold your homemade spring scale so the top of the carton basket is even with the top of the ruler. From the substances available, select one and pour some of the gravel, stones, rice, dried beans, or whatever you wish to weigh into the carton. Do this gradually as you fill the carton.

Hold the top of the ruler to the top of the

cup and calibrate, or measure, how many inches, or centimeters, the gradually filled cup passes as it drops past the ruler.

What happens: Your homemade spring scale, filled with different amounts of weight, measures the force of gravitational pull on the material in the basket. The carton basket is pulled down past the ruler's measurements according to the amount of force gravity exerts on it.

Why: The earth pulls everything toward its center. The more pull gravity is able to exert on an object, based on its denseness or mass, the heavier the object is. As the basket is filled, and the rubber band stretches, the amount of force measured by the spring scale grows.

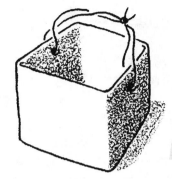

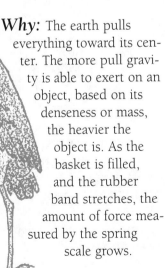

Canned Laughter

THE FORCE

YOU WILL NEED:

2 large, hardcovered, thick books
empty coffee can with lid
clay ball (golf ball size)
pencil

Roll a can uphill and play a trick on a friend while learning about an important force that affects everybody and everything on earth.

What to do: Place one end of a book on top of the other end of the other book to form a ramp. Place the clay ball inside the coffee can and press it firmly against the side so it sticks to the can's surface. The ball should be centered on the can's wall somewhere between the two ends.

On the outside of the can, mark the spot with a pencil so you'll know where the weight of the clay is concentrated.

Now, put the plastic lid back on the can and get ready to amaze yourself with an uphill roll.

Position the can on the lower end of the book ramp and experiment with it until you get it to roll up the book ramp. Now find some friends who are interested in seeing your amazing "scientific magic."

What happens: The can, surprisingly, rolls up the slightly uphill book ramp.

Why: All objects are pulled toward the earth's center by a constant strong force called gravity. The "center of gravity" of any object seems to be the particular place on it where all the weight of the object is "centered." At this one point, the object will balance rather than fall.

The clay ball place inside the coffee can was enough to reposition the can's natural center of gravity. The added off-center weight allowed gravity to pull the can forward and up the ramp.

219 Roll Playing

Test the last experiment using different surfaces. What happens if you place the can in the same "weighted position" but on the "downhill" side of the ramp? What happens if you place it on a flat surface?

Take the lid off the can and watch what happens to the clay weight inside it as you try different things. When the can does not roll, the weight in the can is concentrated in one place. When the center of gravity is shifted, the can is forced by the weight to move.

Where is the center of gravity? Press one end of a short string or piece into the clay ball and watch.

220 Rapid Transit

YOU WILL NEED:
plastic drinking glass
small sphere, like a ball of clay, a small toy ball, or a marble

City subways or monorail trains are often called rapid transit. Now watch how rapidly a ball will transit, or move out of, a drinking glass, and learn about an important earth force.

What to do: Place the sphere in the drinking glass and rapidly slide it, open end forward, across a tabletop or a hard-surfaced floor. Stop the movement suddenly and observe what happens to the ball inside.

What happens: The ball shoots out of the end of the stopped glass and keeps on rolling straight until something in its way stops it or changes its direction.

Why: Sir Isaac Newton, an English physicist, discovered several natural laws of gravity and motion. One of these laws is called inertia. This means that something that is at rest will stay at rest, not moving, until another force works on it or moves it—and it will continue to stay in motion until, again, something works on it to stop it!

The ball in the moving drinking glass stayed in it as long as it was moving. The inertia of this force was not overcome until the movement was suddenly stopped. The sudden stop was the force that overcame the inertia of the ball in the moving container and sent the ball rolling—until a counter-force stopped it.

221 The Dancing Cobra

YOU WILL NEED:
cotton thread, about 8 inches (20 cm) long
straight pin
horseshoe magnet

This experimental trick done with a pin and a magnet will remind you of an Indian snake charmer and his swaying cobra.

What to do: Make a loop in the thread and tie it around the head of the pin.

Hold the end of the thread with the pin attached and, with the other hand, lift it with the magnet. When you get the pin to an upright position, carefully lift the magnet from the pin so it is slightly suspended in midair. Move the magnet slowly in circles and watch the pin and thread, or cobra, follow the movements. Unless you have a very strong magnet, there may be only a very small distance, or break, between the pin and the magnet or the pin and thread will fall.

What happens: The pin and thread floats suspended in the air slightly below the magnet and follows its path as you move it around.

Why: The pin seems to be slightly overcoming gravity, floating below the magnet while not touching it. This is proof that the magnet's attraction can pass through air and, at the right distance, can "balance" the force of gravity.

Needlework on the Santa Maria

Christopher Columbus and other early mariners, or sailors, probably used a wondrous device to help them travel the seas out of sight of land—a magnetized needle floating in a bowl of water.

Modern seafarers now have access to several devices to help them navigate the oceans, even a system of space satellites surrounding the earth. But let's take a close look at that earlier version of the modern compass and see what a simple sewing needle can do.

What to do: Magnetize the needle by rubbing one end of it fifty times with the north end of the magnet. Do the same thing to the other end by rubbing it with the south side of the magnet. Be certain to stroke the needle with the magnet in only one direction, from the center to the end, and lift the magnet away from the needle each time you go to repeat the stroke.

Cut a small circle about 1 inch (2.5 cm) in diameter out of the wax paper. Place the bowl of water on a table or kitchen counter. Carefully stick the needle into the wax-paper circle, as you would a needle into cloth. Float the wax paper with the needle on top of the surface in the middle of the water. Try to move it around on the surface. Observe what happens.

What happens: The needle, when the movement stops, points north and south, no matter how many times you move it around.

Why: Your floating needle is reacting to the earth's invisible magnetic pull, caused by its giant bar-magnet core.

Don't Get Stuck: Control Your Needle!

How do you know if all needles, when movement stops, position themselves in a north-south position? To find out, set up a control compass or one that lets you know if other things are causing results.

Do the same experiment in the same way as in the previous experiment, but now substitute a non-magnetized needle for the magnetized one.

Move the compass to the middle of the water and again move the needle around. Wait patiently for the needle to stop moving. Do several trials or experiments and compare the control compass with the magnetized needle.

Don't Needle Me!

Make a magnetic compass that doesn't look like the usual one. It has no case and you won't have to needle it

YOU WILL NEED:
large piece of modeling clay (to make a stand)
very sharp pencil with an eraser
horseshoe magnet

What to do: Roll the piece of clay into a ball and flatten it to make a sturdy stand; then push the eraser end of the pencil into the clay stand. Carefully balance the magnet on the pencil lead.

What happens: The magnet gradually positions itself into a north-south direction.

Why: The earth is a magnetic ball with north and south magnetic poles. The magnet positioned itself in a north-south direction because magnetic metals and liquids buried within the earth's core have turned

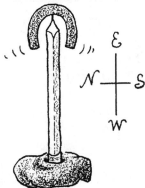

it into a giant magnet that naturally attracts all compasses and magnets. These great magnetic forces are concentrated at its north and south magnetic poles, which, incidentally, are not exactly the same as the North and South Poles we usually speak of, although they are in the same area.

225 What's Your Point?

Magnetized straight pins with like poles repel each other, while unlike poles attract. True?

What to do: Magnetize one straight pin by laying it on a hard surface and rubbing one end of it with the north side of the magnet. Rub from the center to the end, one way only, and lift the magnet between the rubs. Do this about fifty times. Repeat the rubbing action on the other end of the pin using the south end of the magnet. Magnetize the second pin the same way.

Write down which end (point or head) is north or south. Tie 10 inch (25 cm) lengths of thread to the center of each pin and attach paper clips to the other ends. Dangle the two balancing pins about 2 inches (5 cm) apart, one on each thread, from the end of the table. Place the paper-clipped ends of the threads on the table and weight them down with the book. Now, try pushing the pins together.

What happens: Some ends move away from each other, while the other ends jump up at each other and bump.

Why: Like magnetic poles repel away from each other while unlike poles attract or pull together.

226 Bartender

If you tend, or pay attention, to this spinning bar magnet, you will notice some surprising things.

What to do: Tie one end of the long piece of string around the center of the bar magnet. Tie, or tape, the other end up to a light fixture, closet pole, or a rod between chair backs, where it can swing freely. Adjust the magnet so it is properly balanced and does not hang down on one side.

Now spin the magnet and wait about 3 minutes until it has stopped moving. Draw a picture showing its north and south poles as they look to you. Do this five or six times. Does the magnet come to rest, or stop moving, in the exact same position each time, with the poles aligned or the same?

What happens: The bar magnet should continue to align itself up similarly, with the same poles showing, no matter how many times you spin it.

Why: Hanging freely from a string, your bar magnet becomes a compass that aligns itself according to the earth's magnetic pull.

Coin Artist

Many coin-operated food and soda machines, called vending machines, catch fake coins, like slugs or washers, by using a magnetic part. How does this theft preventer work?

YOU WILL NEED:
3 large hardcover books
bar magnet
4 coins, like a dime, penny, quarter, and nickel
3 metal washers

What to do: Stack two books on top of one another and lean the third against the stacked books to form a slide. Hold the bar magnet in the middle of the book forming the slide, while you drop each coin and washer down the side of the book, past the magnets.

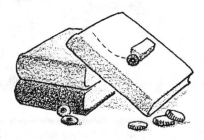

What happens: The coins slide past the magnet, but the washers are caught and held by it.

Why: The bar magnet "picked up" the washers because they are made of steel or iron, but did not pick up the official, government-minted coins because they are minted, or made into coins, from alloys or mixed metals that are non-magnetic.

United States coinage is a combination of copper and other metals. Since magnets will not pick up copper, they are useful in catching all the slugs, or fake coins, made of steel or iron that thieves may drop into vending machines.

228 Drawing Paper

YOU WILL NEED:
2 sheets of paper
old scissors
steel wool pad
bar magnet
magnifying glass

Riddle: What kind of paper can you draw on, but yet never use a pencil nor be an artist? Do this experiment and find out.

What to do: Over one sheet of paper, using an old scissors, cut the steel wool pad into fine small threads. (Be careful of splinters.) Lay the magnet down and place the second sheet of paper over it so that the magnet is underneath in the middle. Now, carefully and evenly, pour the threads onto the sheet over the magnet. Lightly pound the table near the thread-covered sheet with your fist and watch the movement of the threads. Examine the thread patterns through the magnifying glass.

What happens: The fine steel wool threads are drawn to and align themselves around the magnet in a circular pattern.

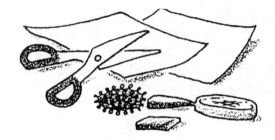

Why: Definite circular lines of steel threads form around the magnet. This pattern is called the magnetic field of force. The steel threads gather more at the magnet's poles, where the force is greater, and thin out in the middle, where the force is less. This is the same magnetic force that encircles the earth. Since the earth is a giant magnet, all steel and iron objects on its surface will behave this way.

DON'T FIDDLE WITH OLD FOSSILS

At one time or another we have all left the lights on when leaving a room or turned on the air conditioner when it wasn't that hot or the heater when it wasn't that cold. It's also very easy to forget to turn off the water promptly when finished, and even easier to just toss away aluminum cans, paper, and glass and plastic bottles when they are empty—without thinking about it. But the earth's resources, the natural substances we use to make energy and put it to work to make life better, are fast being used up. Some scientists predict that the earth's resources will be gone within fifty years—within your lifetime!

The earth resources of coal, oil, and petroleum are used to heat and cool our homes, make electricity, and fuel our cars. They are known as fossil fuels because they are made from the remains of ancient dead plants and animals. When these fuels are gone, they cannot be replaced.

There are other

natural ways to create power. These include tapping into the heated water within the earth (geothermal), nuclear energy, solar panels, windmills, or water-driven devices that move turbines (hydroelectricity) or geared machines that circle back to again produce more energy. Until energy can be fully and inexpensively produced from such sources, however, fossil fuels will not be replaced.

So what can you do to help the earth? You can turn off lights when leaving a room, keep the thermostat or heater controls low so heat energy won't be wasted, dress warmly or use a blanket when it is cold, and drink cool water and wear light clothing when hot. Also, recycle paper, glass, aluminum, plastics, and metals (whatever is being collected where you live). Don't waste water. Use less when washing, take shorter showers, don't flush the toilet unnecessarily, turn water off while you brush your teeth. Just for the record, one leaky faucet can waste thousands of gallons of water each year!

In this chapter you'll learn about conservation, fossil fuels, and recycling. You will even learn to make your own recycled-paper note cards. But remember, it is your efforts to be a conservationist, an earth-conscious, responsible person, that will help to save our planet, so don't fiddle with old fossils—save them!

Housewarming

A greenhouse is a closed glass house used to grow plants, where heat from the sun is trapped inside and moisture cannot escape.

Scientists see the earth today as becoming a type of greenhouse. By burning coal, oil, and other such products known as fossil fuels, by over-using and abusing the use of our cars, and by heating and cooling our homes with electricity or gas, carbon dioxide and other harmful gases are being pushed into the atmosphere. These gases act as a dome, or lid, over the earth's atmosphere, trapping the solar heat and preventing it from escaping into outer space.

When trees are cleared from large land areas, like the tropical rain forests, tons more carbon dioxide gas remains in the atmosphere, instead of being converted into breathable oxygen. It's like putting the earth into a big glass cooker, where heat from the sun is trapped and the air inside gets hotter and stuffier.

229 What Green House?

You may or may not find a greenhouse, or even a green house, on your block, but learning about the greenhouse effect and what it means to you and everything on earth is very important today.

YOU WILL NEED:
glass jar with a cap or lid
1 teaspoon of water
sunny outdoor location

What to do: Pour the teaspoon of water into the glass jar. Replace the lid and tighten it well so that no air can escape. Leave the container outside in a sunny location for about 1 hour.

What happens: Droplets of water form and cling to the sides of the jar.

Why: The sun's heat warms up the jar's atmosphere and the movement of the water molecules in it speeds up. The water then evaporates into the air, but the moisture has nowhere to go, so it gathers into droplets, or condenses, on the cool glass sides. The lid on the jar acts as a greenhouse and produces the greenhouse effect. This is similar to the carbon dioxide gas that is produced by our own personal energy use and by the use of fossil fuels by industry which acts like a lid over the earth and prevents heat that is building up from escaping into space.

230 Greenhouse: An Open-and-Shut Case

Do the last experiment again, but this time don't put the lid on the jar. Try the experiment with different-size containers (with lids and without) and with different amounts of water. Does the heat buildup that causes steam through evaporation occur earlier or later?

What differences do you notice? How do the experiments show what's happening to the earth? Do the results suggest ways to prevent the greenhouse effect?

Warm Up

Measuring the heat energy trapped in a glass container shows us again how the greenhouse effect works and can affect us. You will have to do this experiment on a sunny day

YOU WILL NEED:

2 thermometers
wide-mouth jar with lid
2 small rocks
2 strips of black construction paper or cloth, 2 inches by 6 inches (5 cm x 15 cm) long
paper
pencil

What to do: Make sure that the temperature readings of both thermometers are the same—normal, outdoor temperature. Then find a sunny location outside and place the jar on its side. Put a small rock against one or both sides of the jar to keep it from rolling over.

Take one piece of black construction paper and place a thermometer on top of it, then slide both the thermometer and the material together into the bottle. Screw the lid on tightly but carefully so the thermometer stays in place.

Put the other thermometer on a dark strip next to the bottle. Record both temperatures, wait 10 minutes, then record the temperatures again.

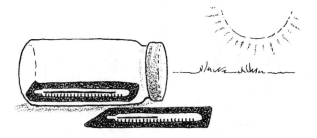

What happens: The thermometer in the closed bottle registers a higher temperature than the one outside.

Why: This closed-environment experiment demonstrates the effect of large amounts of carbon dioxide (CO_2) in the earth's atmosphere. CO_2 gas acts like the glass of the bottle, trapping heat. Although the sunlight falls equally on both sections of cloth, which absorb the light and produce the same amount of heat energy, the heat cannot easily radiate out through the glass barrier.

Carbon dioxide is produced on earth (given off as we breathe), but much more comes from the industrial burning of fossil fuels (smokestacks) and automobile engines, causing pollution and raising heat levels in the atmosphere. This "trapping" of heat by an increasing amount of CO_2 in the atmosphere is known as the greenhouse effect.

Cool Down

Try the same experiment again, but leave out the black strips. Is there a difference? Bring your bottle with the thermometer inside (don't open it) and leave the other thermometer indoors.

Write down the temperature as the thermometers cool down. Is there a difference in the cooling-off time of the thermometer inside the bottle compared to the one outside? Which cools faster, and at what rate?

Oh, Ozone!

233

YOU WILL NEED:
stick of chewing gum
short soda bottle
very hot tap water
magnifying glass

Make a model of the ozone layer, the thin layer of gas in the earth's upper atmosphere that protects us from the sun's damaging ultra-violet rays. Learn about CFCs, those chemicals that make life so much easier and better, but yet do so much damage (they destroy ozone molecules). Then, watch as your ozone–layer model produces holes, gradually tears apart, and finally disappears!

What to do: Chew the stick of gum thoroughly. When it is soft, take it out of your mouth. Flatten it into a small disk between your fingers because you need a thin flat cap to seal the top of the bottle. Now, fill the bottle right to the top with very hot tap water. Take the flat piece of gum and place it over the top of the bottle to seal it. Try to avoid making any holes, and make sure that the water slightly touches the gum cap. Observe what happens closely with the magnifying glass.

What happens: The gum cap, as it touches the hot water, loses its elasticity, or stretchability, and holes begin to form. Eventually the gum cap breaks apart.

Why: In your ozone model the bottle represents the earth while the gum cap represents the ozone layer. The hot water touching the gum cap stands for the CFCs (chlorofluorocarbons), the chemicals that can damage ozone molecules.

CFCs are found in coolants for air conditioners and refrigerators and in the foam–plastic packaging used by some fast–food restaurants. These chemicals are released into the atmosphere as chlorine gas, which eventually destroys ozone.

Stick to It

234

How can you reduce the amount of CFCs in the earth's atmosphere? Of course, you can't do it all alone, but you can do your part. Buy fewer products with CFCs in them, use less air conditioning, and remind others of our responsibilities to Mother Nature. Working together is the way to help save our Earth.

Now, do the same ozone experiment, but instead of filling the bottle to the top with hot water, stop when it is only half full. Does the gum cap still show signs of wearing away? Is there a difference? Now you can see how releasing fewer or no CFCs into the air can make a big difference to the earth's ozone layer.

It's a Solar System

YOU WILL NEED:

8 feet (265 cm) of aquarium air-line tubing (found in aquarium shops or pet stores at low cost)

rubber band

large, short wide-mouth jar

aluminum foil

baking pan

large soda bottle

water

We're not talking about the sun, moon, and planets here, but rather about a solar water heater. In warmer parts of the world, a system of panels can be seen on the roofs of buildings and houses. These panels collect the sun's rays and use the energy to heat water.

Now it's time to make your own solar collector to heat water. It's fun, easy, and it won't take a lot of expensive equipment either. This experiment should be done outside in a warm place where the rays of the sun will fall directly on your solar collector. The best time for the experiment is between 1 and 2 P.M., when the sun is at its strongest. It is important to "preheat" the collector bottle by letting it sit in the sun 30 to 60 minutes before the experiment begins.

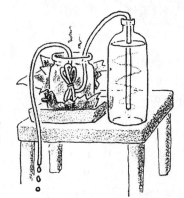

What to do: Coil the plastic tubing back and forth accordion style leaving about 1½ feet (48 cm) of tubing loose at each end. Place the rubber band around the middle of the tubing, then shove the bunched tubing into the jar. Cover it with the foil, sealing the open jar around the tubing. Place the wrapped bottle in the pan on a table outdoors to preheat for about 1 hour.

To complete the experiment, fill the large soda bottle with cool tap water, put it on the table next to your solar collector and place one end of the tubing into it. The other free tube should hang below the table.

Now, to get the water flowing through the collector bottle and out the free end, suck slightly on the end of the tubing as you would on a straw. This should start the water moving from the bottle through the collector and down the tube hanging below the table. The water will leave this tube in a slow, steady drip.

What happens: The water that drips slowly from the tube toward the ground will be slightly but noticeably warmer than the water in the bottle.

Why: Your solar heater is a miniature version of the large solar panels mounted on rooftops. Like the large collectors, your small model captures the sun's energy and heats the water traveling through the tubing. How much warmer the water will get, passing through your collector bottle, depends on a lot of things: the time of year, the time of day, the outside temperature, the location of the collector, how fast or slow the water passes through the system, and how long the collector is allowed to "preheat" before the water starts flowing.

Hot Under the Collar

What's hot under this bottle's collar, or opening? Now's the time to find out. In "It's a Solar System" you really did two experiments. You built a solar collector, but you also made a siphon, a device used to draw off liquids from a higher to a lower place. A siphon works because of an important earth force—gravity!

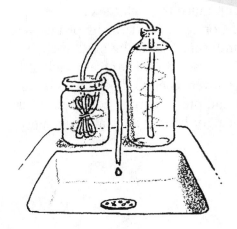

What to do: Remove the foil from the collector bottle. Leave the tubing as it is, and fill the jar with very hot tap water. Fill the soda bottle with very cool tap water.

Place the large soda bottle next to the collector bottle on the sink or on a small table outside. Insert one end of the free tubing into the bottle filled with cool water. The other end should hang down into the sink or toward the ground. Again, suck on the end of the lower tube to get your water moving.

What do you observe? Is the dripping water warmer than the water that came from your solar collector? What things, or variables, could have affected the temperature of the water coming through your collector?

Can you think of something you may have in your home that is similar to this device? How about a water heater?

Fossil Fuelish

Hundreds of millions of years ago great plants like mosses and ferns growing in swamps died and fell one on top of the other. These layers became peat, or decayed plant matter. This process continued through the centuries until great beds, or layers, of decaying plants were formed and were covered by mud, rock, and sediment. Pressed down by great weights, these layers were chemically changed by natural heat and pressure into beds of pure carbon, or coal, or became natural gas, mainly made up of a marsh or swamp gas called methane.

Crude oil was also formed in a similar way—chemically changed from the remains of small sea animals and plants by heat and great pressure. This compression, being tightly pressed together, turned the dead marine plant and animal matter into oil. Much of this chemical change took place under ancient seas—some of which no longer exist.

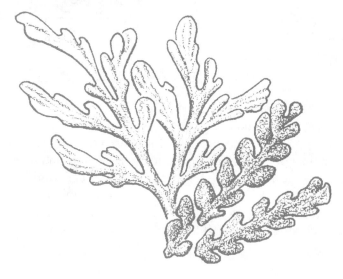

# Spicy Test

You can do an acid-base test to measure pH. In this test liquids are applied to strips of test paper and the color change that results is compared to a pH strip to determine just how acid or alkaline (base) a substance really is.

The pH scale is a range of numbers and colors. Number 1 is extremely acid while 14 is extremely alkaline, or base, which neutralizes acids. Number 7 is considered a neutral number.

Now, make your own test paper by using a spice called turmeric. Since the turmeric solution stains, cover your work area with newspaper; then, in a small cup, make a turmeric-paste solution Add 1 tablespoon of turmeric to 5 tablespoons of hot tap water and stir until smooth.

Cut white construction paper (or thick paper towels) into small strips and dip them into the turmeric paste. Coat them well. The paste will stain your fingers, but it won't hurt you. Lay the golden, yellow-brown strips on newspaper to dry.

When the paper strips are thoroughly dried, test one in vinegar, one in soapy water, another in a baking soda solution, lemon juice, or water with detergent. If the solution is very acidic, the strip will turn yellow; if it is alkaline, it will turn a brownish-red. You can also use the turmeric test papers to test local tap water, the water in lakes and rivers, and soils.

After testing, let your test papers dry and label them, telling what substances they were dipped into.

Rainwear

Is acid rain responsible for a gradual destruction of the world's forests? Perhaps not directly, but most scientists agree that any conditions that affect trees and plants are important to their health and our survival.

Acid rain is made up of nitric and sulfuric acids and produces poisonous metals, like mercury, that can affect plants and animals. It contaminates the minerals in soil that plants need for food and destroys the plants we need for food.

The sulfur and nitrogen elements of acid rain and acid dust, called acid deposition, also affect buildings, cars, statues, and other nonliving objects, causing a lot of damage over the years.

These polluting acids can be found in rain, snow, fog, and the moisture available in the air in different strengths in all parts of the world. Did you know that some European cities have had rains that were as acid as lemon juice (2.3 on the pH scale)? How does the rain in your city compare? See the next experiment.

Papermaking: A Chip Off the Old Block

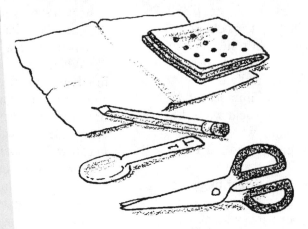

Paper is usually made of tiny slivers of wood and water and processed to produce a pulpy mush. This is spread over a screen, called a deckle, and left to dry. Now you can make your own paper simply and easily, and you won't even have to use a blender for chopping and mixing the glop or a deckle.

This "recipe" makes four 6 inch (15 cm) square note cards. It is a messy activity, however, so do the mixing on a kitchen counter and do the last part outside on a table that can be washed down. Also, be prepared! Paper making is a slow process. This experiment may take all day to complete.

What to do: Cut four pieces of aluminum foil and fold them over to make four 6 inch (15 cm) foil squares. They will be used to make a sieve, or simple deckle, to hold and drain the paper mixture. Punch holes with the pencil in each of the foil squares, about ½ inch (1 cm) apart and in vertical rows.

Next, cut sheets of newspaper into long, thin strips and then cut or tear them into smaller pieces. You'll need about 1½ packed cups of shredded paper.

Place the paper in the jar and fill it three-quarters full of hot tap water. Screw on the lid and let the mixture stand for about 3 hours, shak-

ing the jar from time to time and continuing to beat and stir the pieces with the wooden spoon to break them up. The more you stir and beat the pieces, the more the mixture will become pulpy, gloopy, creamier, and smoother. Add more hot water as the paper absorbs it.

When the mixture is pasty and creamy, pour it into the baking pan. Add a bit more water, if needed. Stir the mixture with the spoon again to be sure all the paper is broken up. Now, dissolve the 3 tablespoons of cornstarch in ½ cup of hot water. Pour the solution into the paper mixture and mix thoroughly.

It's best to do the last part of this activity out-

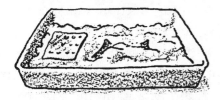

doors where the work area can be washed down. Place the tray with the mixture flat and put a foil square on top of it.

With the palms of your hands, press the foil downward until the mixture covers it. Bring the foil up and place it on the table. Press it flat with your hands to squeeze away the water. Repeat the process, using the other foil squares.

Lay a few sheets of newspaper in a sunny location and let your foil-backed paper dry. As the paper dries, continue to press it down to squeeze out water. While you are doing this, pinch together any holes you notice.

After 3 hours, carefully peel the paper from its

foil backing and trim it neatly into a square note card. With your crayons or paints, colored markers, pencils, or chalk, design a special, homemade recycled card for someone you know. A specially made card from a young, thoughtful conservationist like yourself is sure to be appreciated.

What now: Your recycled newspaper looks and feels much like a gray egg carton. But what would it look and feel like if you used different types of paper?

Collect scrap samples of used white writing paper and recycle it as you did the newspaper. What is the difference in the texture, or feel, and color of the paper?

WEATHER

Why is the North Pole colder than the equator? Why does the sun set? What causes thunder and lightning? From the experiments in the four chapters that follow, you will find out about these and many other mysteries of climate and weather. Climate is the average weather of a region over a long period. Weather has to do with daily changes in the lower part of the atmosphere—the ocean of air that surrounds the earth.

Both climate and weather are created by the interaction of the earth and the sun. Both climate and weather have to do with warmth, wind, and water. The experiments in these chapters all explore how and why.

You will discover why some places and some parts of the year are warmer than others. You may be surprised to know that closeness to the sun is not the reason! You will find out what creates wind and why it is sometimes so destructive. You will learn why cold air usually brings "high pressure" and good weather, while warm air often causes "low pressure," bad weather, and strong winds.

You will come to understand snow, sleet, and hail, lightning and thunder. You will be able to make your own weather station, putting together the instruments you need to keep track of temperature, air pressure, wind direction and speed, humidity and rainfall.

You can begin with any experiment in any chapter, but it is best if you take one chapter at a time and do most of the experiments in order.

In a few of the experiments, you will need to use a safety match or a stove, and these are labeled HOT! You can see them at a glance and get help, if that's the rule at your house.

Some of these experiments are great tricks that you can use to amaze yourself and your friends. But the best part is that they give you hands–on experiences that show the scientific principles behind weather, so that you can understand them—from the ground up.

WEST WIND

Warming Up

What heats our earth? Why are some places warm and some cold? Why do we have tropical deserts near the equator and the frozen tundra at the poles? What causes the seasons? What is the "greenhouse effect"?

Perform the simple experiments in this chapter and discover the answers to these questions—and others!

Earth's Temperature Records

Highest temperature: 136° F (57.7° C)
  Place: Azizia, Tripolitania, Libya
  Date: September 13, 1922

Longest hot spell: 100° F (38° C)
  for 162 consecutive days
  Place: Martin Bar, Western Australia
  Date: October 31, 1923—April 7, 1924

Highest annual mean temperature:
  94° F (34.4° C)
  Place: Dallol, Ethiopia
  Date: 1960–1966

Hottest hot spell: 120° F (48.8° C) or more
  for 43 consecutive days
  Place: Death Valley, California
  Date: July 6–August 17, 1917

Lowest temperature: –129° F (–89° C)
  Place: Vostok, Antarctica
  Date: July 21, 1983

Lowest temperature in an inhabited place: –90.4° F (–68° C)
  Place: Oymyakon, Siberia, Russia
  Date: Feb. 3, 1933

Lowest recorded annual mean temperature: –70 degrees F (–56.6degrees C)
  Place: Pleasteau Station, Antarctica

What Warms Us?

Indoors, we use coal, oil, gas, or electricity to heat and light our homes and workplaces. But what provides the heat and light outdoors? What warms the earth and the objects on it?

What to do: On a sunny day, hold one hand up behind a shaded window. Lift the shade or blind. Now hold your hand up to the window again.

What happens: Instantly, your hand feels warmer.

Why: You didn't touch anything but you felt the heat. It came from the sun—a star 93 million miles away from the earth.

Like all stars, the sun is a great ball of hot gases that pours out huge amounts of heat and light and other energy. Only a tiny part of that energy reaches us. But it is enough to light and warm the earth.

About the Sun

The sun is a medium-sized star—a huge, hot ball of gas. It is one star among billions in the galaxy. Although the sun varies from 90 million miles (144 million km) away in winter to 96 million miles (153.6 million km) away in summer, it is still the closest star to earth.

The sun measures 864,000 miles (1,400,000 km) across—108 times more than the earth.

The sun makes its own light and heat—and provides the light and heat for the earth—by a process that is similar to what happens in the hydrogen bomb.

The sun's extreme heat (millions of degrees at the center) causes its hydrogen atoms to move at such super speeds that they smash together. The nuclei, or centers, of the atoms fuse together, in groups of four, forming a heavier atom called helium. The shock of the collision is so great that part of the atom is converted into energy. It is this energy that provides the light and heat for the earth. It is this energy that causes our weather.

240 Heat Wave

How does heat from the sun reach us?

What to do: Hold one end of the ribbon and shake it.

What happens: The movement you make travels the length of the ribbon, like a wave.

Why: Energy often moves from one place to another in waves. Short waves carry light and heat from the sun to the earth. Longer waves carry other forms of energy. When energy moves by waves it is called radiant energy.

241 Why is Spring Sometimes Late?

Why does spring come later in some places? This experiment will explain.

What to do: Place the pie plate next to the lamp. Fill half the plate with dark soil and the other half with sand. Stick a thermometer into each half.

Write down the temperature of each side. Turn on the lamp and let the plate stand for 30 minutes. Then compare the new temperatures with the starting ones.

What happens: The dark soil gets hotter.

Why: The light sand bounces back the light energy before it can change to heat energy. The dark soil soaks up the light and converts it to heat.

This is what happens when the sun's rays reach the earth. The dark-colored areas absorb the sunlight and heat up quickly. Light-colored areas reflect the sunlight and remain cool.

The earth does not heat up evenly. The air around dark soil becomes warmer than it does around sand or snowcapped mountains. And so spring comes later in snow-covered countries.

Black, White, and Shiny

242

Here is another way to find out how different colors and surfaces are affected by heat.

What to do: Paint one can white, inside and out. Paint the second can black. Leave the third can shiny.

Fill the three cans with warm water of the same temperature. Record the temperature

Cover each can with an index card, and set all three on a tray in a cool place. Record the temperature of the water in each can at 5 minute intervals, for 20 minutes.

Now empty the cans, dry them well, then fill each one with very cold water. Record the temperatures of the water in each can. Cover each can with an index card and place them in a warm place or in the sun. Record the temperature of the water in each can at 5 minute intervals, for 20 minutes.

What happens: In both cases, the water in the black can heats up the most, the water in the shiny can heats up the least.

Why: The dark can absorbs best and turns the light into heat. The others reflect or give back the light before it can turn to heat.

Let it Snow

243

Save this experiment for a snowy day.

What to do: After a snowstorm, when the sun is shining, put the square of aluminum foil and the square of black cloth on the snow. Leave them in the sun for 1 hour. Then see which has sunk the deepest.

What happens: The black cloth will be deeper in the snow than the foil because it has absorbed the most heat.

Why: The dark cloth absorbed the light, which turned into heat—and melted the snow. The foil reflected the light before it turned into heat.

Land versus Water

244

YOU WILL NEED:
2 plastic cups
½ cup of water
½ cup of soil
room thermometer

Which gets hotter—land or water?

What to do: Pour the water into one plastic cup and the soil into the other. Put both cups into the refrigerator for 10 minutes. Then place both cups in sunlight for 15 minutes. Measure and record the temperature of the water and of the soil.

What happens: The soil gets warm, while the water remains cool.

Why: In sunlight, soil heats up faster than water. It's not only because land is darker than water that it retains the heat. In water, the heat can go farther down and spread out. Soil keeps the heat on the surface. If you dig down on a hot beach, you find that the sand underneath is cool. Sunlight can't pass through it. The surface, therefore, becomes very hot.

In addition, the specific heat of water is higher. This means it takes more heat to raise the temperature of water than it takes to raise the temperature of the same amount of soil.

These are the reasons why, on a sunny day, land feels warmer than water.

Water versus Air

245

YOU WILL NEED:
empty drinking glass
drinking glass filled with water

Why is it warmer in summer and milder in winter near the ocean than it is inland?

What to do: Put the two glasses in the refrigerator for 15 minutes.

What happens: The water-filled glass feels warmer than the empty glass.

Why: The "empty" glass is, of course, filled with air. Both air and glass lose their heat much more rapidly than water. The glass filled with water does not let the cold air in and the water keeps the glass warmer longer.

That's the reason the world's oceans help to store up warmth from the sun. In winter, the oceans cool off more slowly than the land, so a city near an ocean stays warmer in winter than an inland city. Oceans also warm up more slowly in summer, so a seaside city has a milder summer, too.

246 Time in the Sun

Why is summer hotter than winter? This experiment will demonstrate one reason.

What to do: Place the black paper in the sun for 1 minute. Feel it. Then place it in the sun for 5 minutes. Feel it again.

What happens: The longer the paper is in the sun the hotter it feels.

Why: The amount of heat increases, because it is absorbed and retained.

One reason summer is hotter than winter is that the sun shines 15 hours a day in July, but only 9 hours a day in December—since every day the sun rises a little later and sets a little earlier. In the Southern Hemisphere, it is the reverse—the sun shines longest in December and least in July.

247 Why is Summer Hotter than Winter?

Here's proof that the direct rays of the sun are hotter than slanted rays.

What to do: Paint both sides of the tin can lids with black paint and let them dry.

Prop one lid up so the sun hits it directly. Place the other lid flat so the sunlight hits it at a slant.

Let both lids stand for 10 minutes and then touch them.

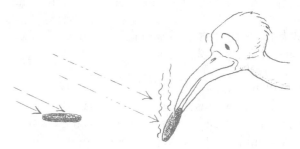

What happens: The lid facing the sun directly gets much hotter than the one the sun hits at a slant.

Why: In summer the sun's rays hit the earth more directly than in winter. That's why summer weather is hotter.

Why the Equator is Hotter than the North Pole

YOU WILL NEED:
flashlight
sheet of paper

Here's why the direct rays of the sun are hotter than slanted rays.

What to do: Shine the flashlight straight down on the sheet of paper. Then tilt the flashlight so its rays strike the paper at a slant, as in the illustration below.

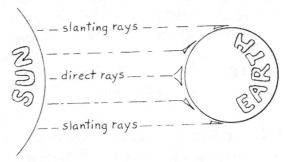

What happens:
When you point the flashlight straight down, it makes a small circle of light on the paper.

When you tilt the flashlight so its rays strike the paper at a slant, it makes a larger, dimmer, oval shape.

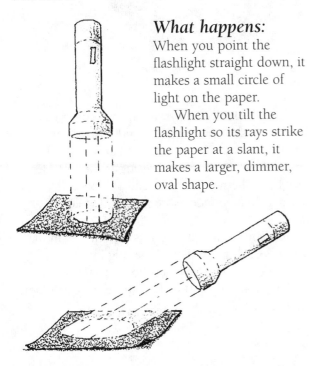

In the same way, a slanted ray of sunlight spreads out more thinly over the earth's surface than a ray that shines straight down. While both rays carry the same amount of heat from the sun, the heat carried by the slanted ray is spread out and less intense.

So, places at and near the equator—where the sun shines directly—get two-and-one-half times as much heat as the North and South Poles where the sun always shines indirectly.

Why: Both the oval and the circle were made by the same source of light (the flashlight). Therefore, the oval has the same amount of light as the circle. But since the oval is bigger, the light in it must be spread more thinly.

249

Make a Shadow Thermometer

The higher the sun is in the sky, the more direct—and the hotter—are the sun's rays on the earth. A simple way to measure the position of the sun in the sky is to measure the length of the shadows it casts.

What to do: Choose a lamppost, a fence post, or a young tree to cast your shadow. Starting in the fall, observe and measure the length of the shadow at noon every week.

Make a chart in a notebook that records the length of the shadow, as in the illustration. Be sure to include the date.

What happens: The shadow gets longer each time you measure it.

Why: The higher the sun is in the sky at noon, the shorter the shadow it casts. The lower the sun is in the sky, the longer the shadow.

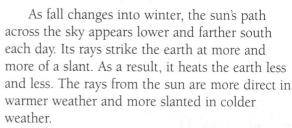

As fall changes into winter, the sun's path across the sky appears lower and farther south each day. Its rays strike the earth at more and more of a slant. As a result, it heats the earth less and less. The rays from the sun are more direct in warmer weather and more slanted in colder weather.

Of course, if you start this experiment in the winter or spring, instead of getting longer, the shadows will gradually get shorter as the sun rises higher in the sky and its rays strike the earth more directly.

250 Length versus Height

Here is a simple way to see how the length of a shadow changes when the source of light changes position.

What to do: Stand one of the pencils in the center of the thread spool on the sheet of paper. Darken the room and hold the flashlight at different angles above the pencil. Record the length of each shadow.

What happens: When the flashlight is high and right above the pencil, the shadow is short. When the light is low and at a slant, the shadow is long.

251 The House is Moving!

Step outside on a clear evening and watch the earth spin!

What to do: On a clear evening set out a chair or lie on the ground facing south with a corner of your house to your right. Pick a star close to the edge of the wall of the house and watch it steadily.

What happens: In a minute or two the star disappears behind the house.

Why: Though the sky seems to move, it is really the house that is moving—as part of the earth that is rotating on its axis.

252 Does the Sun Rise in the Morning?

YOU WILL NEED:

unshaded lamp
orange
knitting needle

What causes night and day? We know that despite what our eyes seem to tell us the sun does not rise in the morning and set in the evening. Here's one way to visualize what really happens.

What to do: Place the unshaded lamp near the center of a darkened room. The lamp represents the sun. Turn on the lamp. Push the knitting needle through the center of the orange. The orange represents the earth.

Holding the orange by the needle, turn it counter-clockwise as though it were a top, and walk around the lamp.

What happens: Different parts of the turning orange are lit and warmed by the lamp.

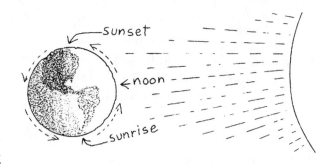

Why: Obviously, the lamp was not moving—the orange was turning. And the sun does not move up in the sky when it rises and down when it sets—it is the earth that is turning. Part of the earth's surface moves toward and then away from the sun as the earth spins toward the east on its axis.

When we are on the side of earth that is in shadow, it is night. When we come back into sunlight, it is day.

The earth spins around completely every 24 hours. Because the earth turns, the sun seems to "set" as we turn away from it and "rise" as we face it again.

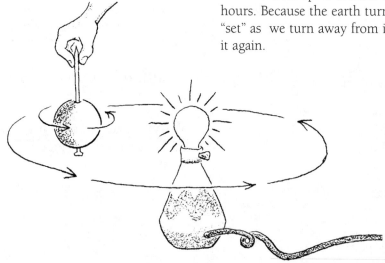

Foucault's Pendulum

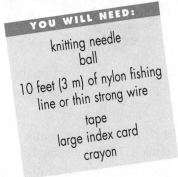

YOU WILL NEED:

knitting needle
ball
10 feet (3 m) of nylon fishing line or thin strong wire
tape
large index card
crayon

To show that the earth rotates, you can repeat an experiment performed in 1851 by the French physicist Jean Bernard Leon Foucault. He suspended a 200 foot (61 km) pendulum from the Pantheon, a huge public building in Paris. The weight traced the path of the earth on sand on the floor.

You can use your living room and trace the same path with a more modest pendulum. You don't need any sand.

What to do: Push the knitting needle into the ball and attach the end of the knitting needle to the length of string or wire. Tape this "pendulum" to the ceiling so it can swing freely.

With the crayon draw a line on the index card and tape it to the floor directly under the knitting needle.

Start the pendulum swinging back and forth following the line on the index card. Note what happens after 2 hours.

What happens: Although the pendulum is still swinging in its original path, it is no longer swinging over the crayon line you made.

Why: Its inertia keeps the pendulum swinging in the same plane. But it no longer swings over the chalk mark because the room has moved! It moved because of the earth's rotation.

A large pendulum demonstrating earth's rotation is kept swinging in the United Nations building in New York City.

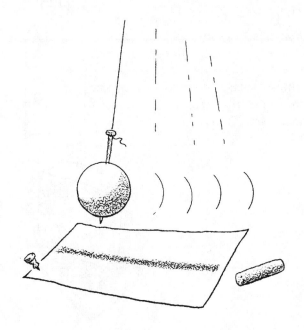

254 Why We See the Sun After it "Sets"

YOU WILL NEED:
tightly covered jar
filled with water
books
unshaded lamp

We see the sun a couple of minutes before it comes up over the horizon at sunrise and after it has set! Here's how!

What to do: Place the jar on its side on a table next to a stack of books. Put the lamp on the opposite side of the table. Stack the books so high that you can't see the light from where you are standing. Then place the tightly covered jar filled with water in front of the stacked books, as in the illustration below.

What happens: You can see the light even though it is below the level of the top of the books.

Why: The rounded top of the jar is like the earth's atmosphere. It bends the rays of light and brings the image of the light into view. It creates a mirage, such as those sometimes seen in the desert, at sea, on hot pavement—and in the sky.

The light from the rising or setting sun passes through a greater thickness of the earth's atmosphere than noontime sunlight does. This bends the rays of the sun. So, at sunrise, when the sun seems to be moving up over the horizon, an image of the sun can be seen on the horizon before the sun actually reaches it. And at sunset, because of those bending rays, we continue to see an image of the sun briefly after the sun has actually set.

As the World Turns

For many centuries, people believed that the sun circled around the earth. Now we know that not only does the earth rotate on its axis, but it also revolves around the sun. All you need for this experiment is a light chair.

What to do: Place a chair in the middle of the room. Move around the chair.

What happens: As you move around the chair, the chair lines up with different things in the room.

Why: The things in the room behind the chair seem to move, although you are actually doing the moving.

In the same way, the sun looks to us as if it is moving, but it is the earth going around the sun that makes it look that way.

The earth completes its journey of 598.3 million miles (965 million km) around the sun in a little more than 365 days, moving about 18½ miles (29.76km) per second. It revolves around the sun in an oval path—an ellipse. Therefore, it sometimes goes a bit faster and at other times a bit slower. The closer the earth is to the sun, the greater the speed.

Sun in Your Room

YOU WILL NEED:
piece of chalk
pen or pencil

Here's more proof that the earth changes position in a simple experiment that will keep you busy for months!

What to do: Mark a chalk line on the floor or wall where the sun shines in your room. Keep a record of the place and the exact hour, day, and month.

A week later, at the same time of day, make another line. Again, jot down the spot and the date.

Repeat this weekly throughout the year.

What happens: The sun shines at a different spot in the room each week.

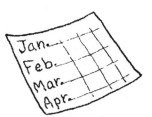

Why: The movement of the earth around the sun causes the change in position of the line from week to week and from month to month.

Why Do We Have Seasons?

YOU WILL NEED:
orange
knitting needle
tall, unshaded lamp
piece of cardboard
marker

Near the equator it remains hot all year round. At the North and South Poles it is always cold. But in most parts of the world there are four seasons every year. Why?

What to do: Push the knitting needle through the orange to represent the earth and its imaginary axis, as in the illustration.

With your marker draw an ellipse (see the next experiment) about 10 inches (25 cm) in diameter on a piece of cardboard to represent the earth's oval orbit. Mark the four quarter points north, south, east and west.

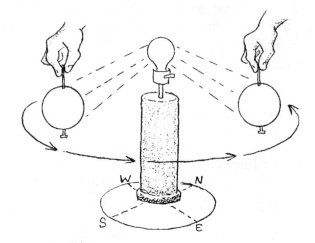

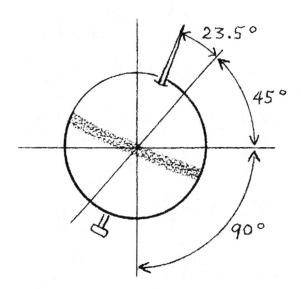

Place the lighted lamp in the center of the cardboard to stand in for the sun.

1. Holding the needle straight up and down, move the orange in turn to each of the four positions. Observe which part of the orange is lit up.

2. Now tilt the orange so that the axis is slanted about 23.5° away from the vertical. (See illustration). Place the orange in turn at each one of the four positions, keeping the needle tilted in the same direction. Look at the lighted section of the orange. In each position observe which part receives the direct rays and which the slanting rays of light.

What happens:

1. When the needle is straight up and down, the same section is lit no matter where the orange is in relation to the light.

2. When the needle is at the 23.5° angle, the amount of light depends on whether the orange is tilted toward or away from the light.

Why: If the earth's axis were vertical, like the orange in the first experiment, there would be no seasons. But the axis of the earth points to the North Star at a 23.5° slant. (See illustration.) It is this slant that makes the seasons change as the earth revolves around the sun.

When the side of the earth we live on is tilted

toward the sun, we have summer because we receive the direct rays of the sun. Six months later our part of the earth is tilted away from the sun—it is winter because we receive the sun's rays at a slant and so get less of the sun's heat.

At the equator, the sun's rays are always direct. There are no seasons. At the poles, the rays always strike at a slant.

You can see, therefore, that seasons are not caused by the distance of the earth from the sun. Actually, in January in the Northern Hemisphere, the earth is closer to the sun than it is in June.

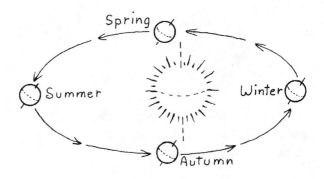

258 ◆ Making an Ellipse

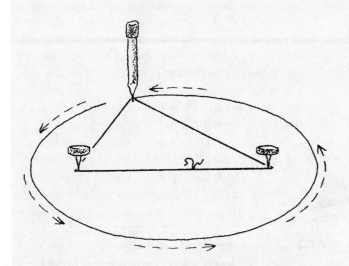

The earth's path around the sun is elliptical. Here's an easy way to make an ellipse.

Place a sheet of unlined paper on a piece of cardboard. Push two tacks (or pins) into the paper about 2 inches (5 cm) apart. Tie the two ends of a 6 inch (15 cm) length of string together and loop the string around the tacks. Insert a pencil in the loop and pull the string tight. Keeping the string tight, move the pencil around and you will draw an ellipse.

The Greenhouse Effect

259

The whole earth is warmed by the greenhouse effect. What is it? This experiment must be done on a sunny day.

YOU WILL NEED:
clear plastic bag
2 room thermometers

What to do: Put a thermometer into the plastic bag. Close the bag and place it on a sunny windowsill. Place the second thermometer on the same windowsill.

After 10 minutes, read both thermometers.

What happens: The thermometer inside the bag reads several degrees higher than the other one.

Why: The sun's rays pass through the bag easily. Once inside, however, they convert into heat, which cannot get out as easily. Therefore, the temperature inside the plastic rises. The bag warms up like a greenhouse, in which gardeners grow plants.

The sun's rays pass through earth's atmosphere in the same way. And when they convert into heat rays, they cannot get out easily. They are absorbed by the surface of the earth, warming it as if it were a large greenhouse.

Some scientists fear that carbon dioxide in the air, from our industrial use of such fuels as oil and coal, have increased the greenhouse effect. Carbon dioxide absorbs heat rays, and so they are radiated back to the earth instead of escaping into space. They believe that this will make the earth warmer, causing the ice at the North and South Poles to melt. They fear sea levels will rise and flood land areas, changing our climate altogether and creating many problems.

Other scientists predict a cooling trend, and suggest that air pollution will block out more of the sun's radiation and prevent the greenhouse effect from increasing.

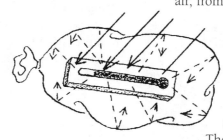

WHIRLING WINDS AND GENTLE BREEZES

We live at the bottom of an ocean of air called "the atmosphere." Most of our weather changes take place in the lower 3 miles (5 km) of this atmosphere. And most of it is caused by the wind—as it spreads the heat of the sun from warm areas to colder ones.

Wind is simply air that moves. But what is air? What gets it moving? Why is it sometimes so destructive?

Earth's Wind Records

Fastest surface wind speed recorded:
231 miles (370 km) an hour
Place: Mt. Washington, New Hampshire
Date: April 12, 1934

Windiest place: gale winds reach 200 miles (320 km) an hour
Place: Commonwealth Bay, Antarctica

Fastest tornado winds: 286 miles (457 km) an hour
Place: Wichita Falls, Texas
Date: April, 2, 1958

World's worst tornado: killed 792 people
Place: South–central United States
Date: March 18, 1925

Fastest hurricane winds near a storm center: more than 74 miles per hour (118 km per hour)

Hurricane with highest wind gusts:
175 to 180 miles per hour (280 to 288 km per hour)
Place: Central Keys and lower southwest Florida coast
Date: August 29 to September 13, 1960

World's worst hurricane (unleashed floods that killed one million):
Place: Bangladesh
Date: 1970

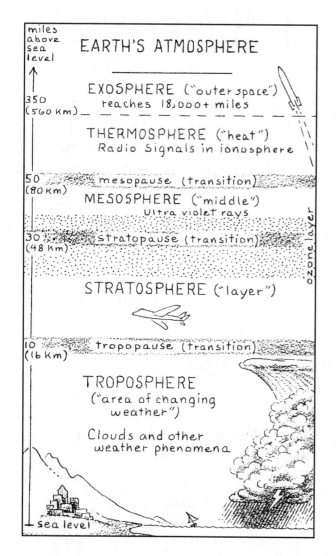

EARTH'S ATMOSPHERE

miles above sea level

EXOSPHERE ("outer space")
reaches 18,000+ miles

350 (560 Km)

THERMOSPHERE ("heat")
Radio Signals in ionosphere

50 (80 Km) — mesopause (transition)
MESOSPHERE ("middle")
Ultra violet rays

30 (48 Km) — stratopause (transition)

STRATOSPHERE ("layer")

ozone layer

10 (16 Km) — tropopause (transition)

TROPOSPHERE
("area of changing weather")

Clouds and other weather phenomena

sea level

260 Air Takes Up Space

YOU WILL NEED:

funnel
empty soda bottle
wide masking tape
or clay
water

How do we know air is really there?

What to do: Put the funnel into the mouth of the soda bottle. Stretch the tape around the funnel and the bottle's mouth, or pack the clay around the neck of the bottle so there is no space between the bottle and the funnel.

Pour water into the funnel.

What happens: The water remains in the funnel. It does not flow into the bottle.

Why: The "empty" bottle is already full of air. It takes up space and prevents the water from entering.

If you remove the masking tape or the clay, the results will be very different because the air will be able to escape!

Air Has Weight

261

YOU WILL NEED:
ruler
clothes hanger
2 balloons
tape
string

Air is a real substance. It not only takes up space, but it has weight. Here's proof.

What to do: Suspend the ruler from the hanger by attaching a string to the middle of it. Then tape each balloon the same distance from the ends of the ruler. Make sure that the ruler is in balance.

Now remove one of the balloons and blow it up. Tie a knot to keep it closed. Replace it at the same place on the ruler.

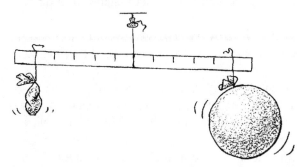

What happens: The balloon filled with air pulls the ruler down.

Why: The balloon filled with air is heavier than the other one. Air has weight. It is actually quite heavy. At sea level air weighs 14.7 pounds (6.6 kg) per square inch (2.5 cm). On a mountaintop, air is a little thinner and weighs less.

A Lot of Hot Air

YOU WILL NEED:
balloon
soda bottle
pan of hot water

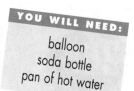

262

Why does warm air take up more space than cold

What to do: Stretch the balloon slightly and pull it over the neck of the soda bottle.

Place the bottle in the pan of hot water and let it stand for 5 minutes.

What happens: The balloon begins to inflate.

Why: The air in the balloon expands when it is heated. The molecules move faster and farther apart. That's what makes the balloon stretch.

And that's exactly how hot air works outside the balloon. Warm air is less dense than cold. It takes up more space than the same amount of cold air— and weighs less than the amount of cold air occupying the same space

263 ◆ Air Currents and Wind

You can create an air current—and see what it does.

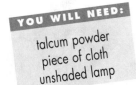

What to do: Sprinkle the powder on the cloth and shake a little of it near the unlit lamp. Notice what happens.

Then light the lamp. After a few minutes, when it is hot, shake some more powder off the cloth.

What happens: Before you turn the bulb on, the powder sinks slowly down through the air. After the bulb is hot, the powder rises.

Why: The air, warmed by the lighted bulb, rises—carrying the powder with it. The denser, cooler air sinks.

This is what happens in nature, too. Warmer air pushes upward because it is less dense, and cooler air flows in to take its place.

Air that moves up and down (vertically) is called an air current. Wind is air that moves on the same level (horizontally).

The speed of the air currents and the wind depends upon how much the temperature of one region differs from another. The direction of the wind depends on the location of these areas.

264 ◆ How Much Oxygen is in the Air?

Air is a mixture of invisible, tasteless gases, including oxygen. How much oxygen is there in air?

What to do: Poke one end of the pencil into the piece of steel wool. Moisten the steel wool. Then prop up the pencil—with the steel wool on top—in the dish of water. Cover it with the measuring cup. Let it stand for 3 days.

What happens: The steel wool rusts—and the water rises until it fills about one-fifth of the cup.

Why: The rusting process uses up the oxygen from the air in the jar, creating an area of low pressure. Water rushes into the cup to take the place of the used-up oxygen. Since oxygen makes up approximately one-fifth of the composition of air, the air rises to the height of one-fifth of the cup.

The rest of the air is mostly nitrogen, with a few traces of several other gases, including carbon dioxide.

What Causes an Air Inversion?

HOT!

What happens during an air inversion? An adult must help you with this experiment.

What to do: Rinse one jar with very cold water, and the other with hot water. Dry them thoroughly.

With the index card between them, place the jars mouth to mouth with the warm jar on the bottom.

Ask the adult to light the end of the twine so it smokes. Direct the smoke into the bottom jar, as you lift the index card. When the smoke fills the bottom jar, pull out the card.

Try the experiment with the cold jar on the bottom and the warm one on top. What happens this time?

What happens: When the warm jar is on the bottom, the smoke rises from the lower to the upper jar. When the cold air is on bottom, the smoke is trapped and cannot rise.

Why: The smoke rises as the warm air rises and the cold, denser air sinks. But when the warm air is trapped below the cold air, the smoke is also trapped.

This is what happens in the earth's atmosphere when a layer of warm air holds down the dust particles. This is an "air inversion." If the air is polluted, your eyes may smart, and you may cough or find it difficult to breathe.

The Air Pollution Control Laboratory records the air pollution index, which is computed based on the amount of sulphur dioxide, carbon monoxide, and smoke in the air. The average daily index is 12. An emergency level is placed at 50.

266 Is Your Air Polluted?

You don't need complicated instruments to find out whether the air around you is dirty!

What to do: Line the can with the white paper. Then place it outside the window for 1 week.

Take the can in and carefully remove the paper. Examine it the paper with the magnifying glass.

What happens: Dust and debris have discolored the paper.

Why: Impurities pass into the air from car exhausts and smokestacks and other sources. They pollute the air and remain there if no wind blows them away—or if a layer of warm air above them acts as a blanket as you learned in the previous experiment. Sometimes this dust in the air causes a haze, in which it is hard to see.

267 Whirling Winds

Why do winds whirl counterclockwise above the equator and clockwise below?

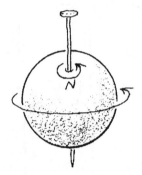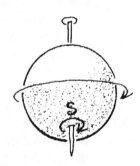

What to do: Push the knitting needle through the ball. Mark the top of the ball "N" for the North Pole and the bottom "S" for the South Pole.

Hold the ball so that the "N" is on top and whirl the ball from west to east. Look at the "N."

Now hold the ball high over your head and continue whirling it in the same direction.

What happens: At the North Pole the globe is whirling counterclockwise—but the area south of the equator is whirling clockwise!

Prevailing Winds

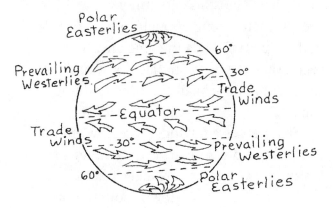

YOU WILL NEED:

1 marble
turntable (a lazy Susan
or stereo turntable)

The earth rotates—spins—from west to east. This affects the direction in which our winds blow. Here's a simple experiment that helps to explain why some winds blow from the same direction most of the time.

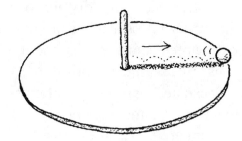

What to do: Roll the marble from the center of the turntable to the edge. Note what happens.

Then start the turntable spinning. Aim the marble at the center to the same point on the edge.

Finally, try rolling the marble from the edge to the center.

What happens: When the turntable isn't spinning the marble rolls in a straight line from the center to the edge. But when the turntable is moving, the marble seems to twist as it rolls from or toward the center.

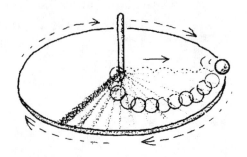

Why: When the turntable is still it is obvious that the marble moves in a straight line. But, even though it doesn't look that way, when the turntable moves, the marble continues to move in a straight line! The marble stops at different places on the moving turntable, and that's why it seems to twist and curve. But it reaches different places because the turntable is curving away from it. This phenomenon is known as the Coriolis effect.

In the same way, it is the spinning of the earth on its axis that makes the winds twist and turn in certain ways. This spin creates world-wide patterns of winds called "prevailing winds"—winds blowing from the same direction most of time. Much of world's weather depends on this great system of winds that blow in set directions.

Local Winds

Some winds are occasional, brief, and gentle. Other winds may last only a few minutes, but are strong enough to hurt people and property. Winds in some areas come regularly every year and last for months so that people must plan their lives around them.

Sea breezes are winds that blow from cooler high pressure areas over water to warmer low pressure areas over land.

Slope winds rush down mountain into valleys or rise up from the valleys. Winds that blow down the slopes of smaller hills are called helm winds.

Foehns are warm, dry winds that occasionally blow from a mountain ridge down the side of a mountain range away from the wind, the leeward side. In the Rockies, a foehn sometimes melts as much as two feet of snow overnight and is known as a *chinook*, the Indian word for snow eater. In South America, a westerly foehn blowing off the Andes is called a *zonda*, and an easterly foehn is called a *puelche*.

A squall blows strong gusts of cold air and lasts only a minute or two. It is usually accompanied by a wall of big black clouds and a short fierce shower. But a squall has been known to capsize hundreds of small boats in its brief life. In Alaska a squall is called a williwaw and in Australia it is called a Cockeyed Bob.

The mistrals blow cold dry air down from the western Alps across southern France in winter, sometimes for months. The monsoons, seasonal winds in the Indian Ocean and Asia, bring torrential rains in summer. Simoons, hot, dry winds in the Sahara and Arabian Deserts, blow up suffocating clouds of sand, sometimes for a few minutes and sometimes for days.

Jet streams are fast winds that start about four miles up in the atmosphere. Caused by the sharp difference in temperature between the air in the troposphere and the stratosphere, they can be thousands of miles long and several miles wide. Sometimes they rise higher into the atmosphere and sometimes they descend toward earth, forming storms.

Airplane pilots like to hitch a ride on these winds when they are going their way.

269 Air Masses and Fronts

An air mass is a body of air thousands of miles across that has about the same temperature and amount of moisture. How does it form? To find out all you need is a radiator or a heater and a refrigerator or air conditioner.

Short, hard rains

Cold air

Cold Front

What to do: First stand in front of the radiator or heater for 2 minutes. Then stand in front of the opened refrigerator or an air conditioner for 2 minutes.

What happens: When you stand in front of the radiator or heater, you feel warm air. When you stand in front of the refrigerator or air conditioner, you feel cool air.

Why: The warm radiator heats the air around it. The refrigerator cools the air around it. Air masses work the same way. Air that lingers above a region without moving forms an air mass with the temperature and moisture of the area.

When an air mass moves on, it influences the weather of the area it passes over.

When cold and warm air masses meet, they don't mix. Instead, they form a zone that is generally hundreds of miles long. That zone is called a "front." It's called a "cold front" when a cold air mass replaces a warm air mass by forcing it to rise. It's called a "warm front" when a warm air mass pushes a cold air mass ahead of it. When neither mass moves, it is called a "stationary front."

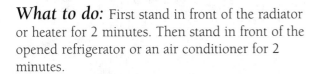

Stationary Front

The arrival of a front indicates a change in the weather.

A cold front moves quickly. If the air is dry, it will become cloudy and the temperature will drop. If the air is moist, a cold front will bring thunderstorms and hail, but they won't last long.

A warm front moves in more slowly. If the air is dry, wispy clouds will form. But if the air is moist, the sky will become gray and the rain or snow that follows may last for many days.

After the front moves on, there will usually be fair weather—warm if the warm air mass remains, cold if the cold air mass remains.

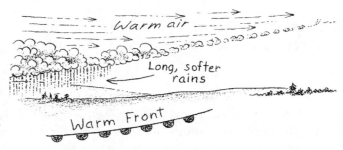

Warm air

Long, softer rains

Warm Front

Air Pressure and Weather Predictions

Air pressure and the way it is changing helps you predict how the weather will change in the next few hours and days.

What to do: Cover the wide mouth of the funnel with the piece of balloon and tape it on tightly.

Suck some air from the narrow end of the funnel and notice what happens to the rubber.

Turn the funnel upside down and suck the air in again. Then turn the funnel sideways and suck in the air.

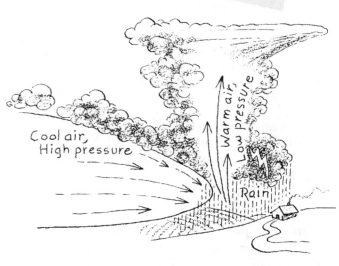

Cool air, High pressure — Warm air — Low pressure — Rain

What happens: When you suck in the air, the rubber is pulled in, whatever the direction of the funnel.

Why: When you suck in the air, you are removing it from the inside of the funnel. When you do that, the push of air outside the funnel is greater than the push of the air from inside, even when you hold the funnel upside down or sideways. Air pushes—presses—equally in all directions.

You already know that the air over each square inch of the earth's surface, pulled by the earth's gravity, weighs 14.7 pounds (6.6 kg). This weight is known as air pressure.

When cool, dense air presses down on the earth, the air pressure is usually high. Warm, less dense air rises away from the earth, and so, when it's warm, we generally have low air pressure.

High pressure usually brings clear weather while low pressure brings bad weather and strong winds. Changing pressure also brings winds.

When there are big differences in air pressure, air rushes out of the high pressure area to fill the low pressure area. Then there are strong, sometimes savage winds. If the difference in pressure is small, air gently drifts toward the low pressure area and we have gentle breezes.

A Trick Can

271

This experiment is best done over a sink or basin.

What to do: Using the hammer and nail, punch a small hole on one side of the can near the bottom. Fill the can with water and quickly screw on the cap. Then remove the cap.

What happens: The water does not flow out from the hole—until you remove the cap.

Why: Air is pressing up harder than the water is pressing down—until you remove the top of the can. Then the air pressing down on the opening in the can, added to the pressure of the water, makes the downward pressure greater than the upward pressure.

Ballot's Law

272

Using Ballot's Law we can find the location of high and low pressure areas.

Buys Ballot, a Dutch scientist, discovered in 1857 that there was a relationship between the direction of the wind and the locations of the high pressure and low pressure areas that were causing it.

In the Northern Hemisphere, if you stand with your back to the wind, the high pressure area will be on your right and the low pressure on your left. In the Southern Hemisphere, it is exactly the opposite.

A change in wind often brings a change in weather. In the Northern Hemisphere a south or west wind brings warm or mild, wet weather. A north or east wind brings colder, drier weather, especially in the winter. All winds are named after the direction from which they are blowing.

273 ◆ Tornado!

YOU WILL NEED:

clean, empty plastic
bottle or jar

Although most of the destruction done by tornadoes is caused by the terrible speed of the whirling winds, lowered air pressure may also cause a great deal of damage.

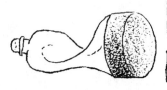

What to do: Remove the air from inside the bottle by sucking on it.

What happens: The bottle collapses.

Why: The air around the outside of the bottle pushes inward because you've removed some of the inside air. Normally, the air inside the bottle would balance the outer force.

The pressure inside the bottle drops, just as it does in the center of a tornado.

A tornado starts when cold dry air coming from the west catches up with unusually warm, moist air from the south. The result is a whirling wind with thick, black clouds and thunderstorms. Water vapor is swept upward as gusts of warm air rise in a spiraling motion. When the air cools, it forms the tornado's twisting, funnel-shaped cloud.

The funnel-shaped wind cloud whirls at enormous speeds and picks up dust, trees, animals, water, automobiles, houses—anything in its path—and whirls them upward. The rapidly rising column of air within the funnel lowers the pressure in the funnel's center as the tornado advances.

A house can be crushed in the midst of a tornado just as the bottle was crushed—because the air pressure in the center of the tornado is lower than the normal pressure inside the house.

The tornado spins, smashing and destroying, until all the heated air that was near land has been squeezed up by the cooler, heavier, inflowing air. Then the air stops flowing and the tornado dies.

More about Tornadoes

A tornado seldom lasts more than an hour and usually covers about two city blocks—less than one-tenth of a mile (158 m). Only 2 per cent of tornadoes are classified as "violent."

Tornadoes may last longer, however, with winds of up to 300 miles (480 km) an hour, and may cover a path of up to 26 miles (42 km) long and a mile wide (1.6 km). They can be the most destructive storms on earth. Most tornado injuries and deaths result from flying objects whirled about by the wind.

Tornadoes are sometimes called cyclones and twisters.

274 Bernoulli's Law

YOU WILL NEED:
2 apples
2 strings about 12 inches (30 cm) long
2 tacks

The air pressure of a tornado is so low that houses in its path may be destroyed. What causes this low air pressure?

What to do: Hang the apples 3 inches (7.5 cm) apart. Blow hard between them.

What happens: Instead of being pushed apart, the apples move toward each other.

Why: By blowing between the apples, you cause the air between the apples to move. This lessens the air pressure between them. Then the air on the

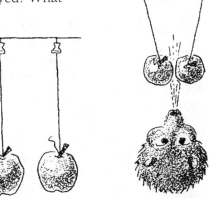

sides of the apples pushes them toward the area of lower pressure.

As the speed of air increases, the pressure of the air decreases. The faster air moves, the less pressure it has. This was discovered in 1738 by the Swiss physicist, Daniel Bernoulli.

This lessening of pressure caused by high-speed air movement is one of the reasons a tornado is so destructive. Objects are propelled into whirling air by the stronger pressure of air around them.

Eye of a Hurricane

YOU WILL NEED:
yo-yo

A hurricane is a violent storm that starts in tropical waters. In the middle of the swirling winds of a hurricane there is the calm "eye."

What to do: Whirl the yo-yo around your head.

What happens: The yo-yo seems to try to pull away from your hand holding its string. The faster you whirl it, the stronger the pull.

Why: The explanation is centrifugal force, the force that pulls an object outward when it is moving in a circle.

In the same way, the winds of a hurricane tend to pull away from the center as their speed increases. When the winds move fast enough, a hole develops in the center—the mark of a full-fledged hurricane.

The eye of a hurricane is a cloudless hole, usually about 10 miles (16 km) wide, within which all is calm and peaceful. But surrounding the eye, howling winds swirl at speeds up to 150 miles (240 km) an hour, with gusts up to 180 miles (288 km) an hour.

Hurricane winds may cover an area up to 60 miles (96 km) wide. They may rage for a week or more, and travel tens of thousands of miles over sea and land.

Hurricanes arise when warm moist air over tropical waters rises above 6,000 feet (1800 m). The water vapor condenses, turns to raindrops, releasing heat energy. This in turn forces columns of air to rise up quickly (updraft) to heights of 50,000 to 60,000 feet (80,000 m) and fluffy, cauliflower-like cumulus clouds become towering thunderheads. (See illustration.)

Then air from outside the storm area moves in to replace the rising air. It begins to swirl around the updraft because of the earth's spin. As it swirls over the surface of the sea, it soaks up more and more water vapor, which then gets pulled into the updraft, releasing still more energy as more of the water vapor condenses. The updraft then rises faster, pulling in larger amounts of air and water vapor from the edge of the storm, and the air swirls even faster around the "eye."

Hurricane winds circulate counterclockwise in the Northern Hemisphere and clockwise in the Southern Hemisphere.

They are called cyclones in the Indian Ocean, typhoons in the Pacific, and willy-willies in Australia.

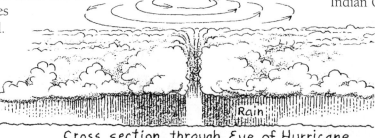

Cross section through Eye of Hurricane

WATER, WATER, EVERYWHERE

How does water get into the air? Why does it come out of the air? Why does it snow? When does it rain? sleet? hail? In this chapter you'll find answers to these questions and more.

Earth's Precipitation Records

Greatest rainfall in one day:
73.62 inches (184 cm)
  Place: Le Reunion, island in the Indian Ocean
  Date: March 15, 1952

Greatest rainfall in one month:
366 inches (915 cm)
  Place: Assam, India
  Date: July, 1961

Greatest rainfall in one year:
1,041 inches (2,602 cm)
  Place: Assam, India
  Date: August, 1880 to August, 1881

Highest average annual rainfall:
460 inches (1,150 cm)
  Place: Mount Waialeale, Kauai, Hawaii

Greatest number of thunderstorms:
322 days a year
  Place: The island of Java, Indonesia

Lowest annual rainfall: 0.03 inches (0.08 cm)
  Place: Arica, Chile

Longest period without rain: 400 years
  Place: Desert of Atacama, Chile

Greatest snowfall in one day:
75.8 inches (189.5 cm)
  Place: Silver Lake, Colorado
  Date: April 14 to 15, 1921

Greatest snowfall in a single storm:
189 inches (472.5 cm)
  Place: Mt. Shasta, California
  Date: Feb. 13 to 19, 1959

276

Water Going into the Air

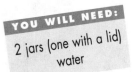

Moisture in the air—humidity—is one part of a great water cycle. The main supply comes from the earth's five oceans and from many smaller bodies of water. How does the water get into the air?

What to do: Pour an equal amount of water into the jars. Put the lid on one of them. Place both jars on a table overnight. Check them in the morning.

What happens: There is less water in the open jar than in the covered jar.

Why: Even at room temperature, the tiny particles, or molecules, of water in the uncovered jar move fast enough to fly out and escape into the air. The water turns into water vapor, an invisible gas. This process is known as evaporation.

If you've ever wondered what happens to puddles when the rain stops, that is the explanation. And that is how water gets back into the air.

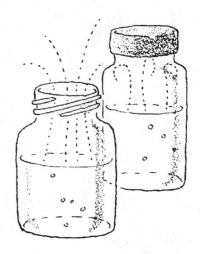

Evaporation Race #1

Which container of water will evaporate faster—the flat disk or the deep jar?

What to do: Pour an equal amount of water into the dish and the jar. Place both, uncovered, on a table to stand overnight. Check them in the morning.

What happens: Less water remains in the flat dish than in the narrow jar.

Why: The molecules of water can escape only from the surface. So water will evaporate faster when the surface is large.

A wide shallow puddle, therefore, will dry up more quickly than a deep narrow one.

Wind and Water

What effect does wind have on the water in the air? Why does fanning a washed blackboard make it dry more quickly?

YOU WILL NEED:
clothesline
piece of cardboard
2 wet handkerchiefs

What to do: Hang the two handkerchiefs to dry. Fan one with the cardboard.

What happens: The handkerchief that is fanned dries first.

Why: Fanning speeds up evaporation by replacing the moist air near the handkerchief with drier air. Blowing winds do the same thing with clouds in the sky.

279 Evaporation Race #2

YOU WILL NEED:
2 dishes
water

What role does the sun play in the evaporation of water in the air?

What to do: Half fill the dishes with water. Place one in the sun or on a radiator, and the other in the shade.

What happens: The dish in the sun dries first.

Why: The warmer the water, the faster the molecules move into the air and the faster they evaporate.

Most water vapor comes from lakes, rivers, oceans, leaves of plants, and wet ground. The heat from the sun causes the water to change from liquid to gas, which goes into the air. As its temperature increases, air can hold more and more water. As it gets colder, it holds less and less.

Evaporation Cools Air

280

Liquids require heat to evaporate—and so
any place where evaporation takes place
becomes cooler.

What to do: Place the thermometer where wind will strike it. Note the temperature after 30 minutes.

Using an eye dropper or a straw, dampen a small piece of cotton and wrap it around the bulb of the thermometer. Secure it with the rubber band. Leave the thermometer in the wind for 30 minutes and again note the temperature.

What happens: The temperature of the thermometer with the wet cotton on it is several degrees lower than it was before.

Why: In the process of evaporation, energy in the form of heat is removed from the thermometer. The hygrometer, one of the most important weather instruments, is based on this fact (see page 254).

Be a Rain Maker!

Make rain in your kitchen!

YOU WILL NEED:
double boiler
water
4 ice cubes

What to do: Boil water in the bottom section of the double boiler. Then pour cold water into the upper pot, add the ice cubes and place the pot over the boiling water. (If you don't have a double-boiler, you can make your own by stacking a small pot on top of a small can in a slightly larger pot.)

What happens: You see—rain!

Why: The cold surfaces of the upper pot cool the steam from the boiling water. The steam changes back into water, collecting in drops. As the drops get bigger and heavier, it "rains."

The boiling water is like the water heated by the sun. The steam is like the water that evaporates into the air as water vapor. As the vapor

HOT!

rises, it cools. You see clouds when droplets form. As these droplets collect more moisture, they become heavy enough to fall to earth as rain.

Measuring the Size of a Raindrop

Hold a piece of cardboard outside your window when it first starts to rain, and you will be able to see the size of a raindrop.

Raindrops may measure from 1/100 of an inch across to ¼ inch (0.25 to 1 cm) across. Each is made up of millions of droplets of water.

Small raindrops—less than 2/100 of an inch (0.5 mm) across—often take an hour or more to reach the ground. Light rain like this is known as drizzle. It usually falls from a layered cloud less than 1.2 miles (2 km) thick.

A heavy, sudden shower of large raindrops or of hail falls from a heaped cumulo-nimbus cloud that might be 9 miles (15 km) or more deep.

283 Water Coming Out of the Air

YOU WILL NEED:

empty tin can
ice cubes
water
food coloring

You found out how water gets into the air. Let's look at how it gets out again.

What to do: Remove the label from the can, then fill the can with ice. Add water and a few drops of food coloring. Let the can stand on a table for 5 minutes.

What happens: The can seems to be "sweating." Drops of water form on the outside.

Why: The drops are not colored, so they couldn't be coming from the ice water leaking out of the can. The water must come from the air.

Water vapor—water in the form of gas—in the air around the can has been cooled by the ice.

Air molecules slow down when they become cold. They move closer together and change into liquid form. This is known as "condensation."

Great amounts of water are always evaporating into the air as the sun warms the earth's oceans, rivers, and lakes. On a day when humidity is high, as much as 5 percent of the air can be water vapor. The water vapor becomes part of the warmer air near the earth's surface. Because it is less dense than cold air, this warmer air tends to rise. It rises to colder and colder levels. When it reaches a cold enough level, the water vapor changes into droplets of water. Cold air can't hold as much water vapor as warm air.

Large numbers of these little drops of water collect on dust particles as the air cools. This forms clouds. The drops fall to earth as rain or snow when they become too heavy to be held up by the pressure of air.

The movement of water through evaporation and condensation is called the water cycle.

Indoor Cloud

YOU WILL NEED:
tea kettle filled with water
metal pie plate

You form a cloud in your kitchen every time you boil water in a tea kettle!

HOT!

What to do: Heat the water in the tea kettle. When it starts to boil, hold the pie plate in the steam.

What happens: When the water boils, a whitish "cloud" forms above the spout. When you hold the pie plate in the "cloud," drops of water form on it.

Why: The clouds in the sky form in the same way. Heated air containing invisible water vapor rises. As it rises, it cools. The water vapor condenses into millions of tiny water droplets, forming a cloud.

On a sunny summer day, the sun heats up the ground quickly. The ground heats the air next to it. Because warm air is less dense than cold air, it rises. As it moves away from the hot ground, it cools. When it rises high enough and becomes cool enough, the water vapor in the air condenses—turns into water droplets. Millions of these droplets together make up one of the fluffy clouds we see in the sky. These fluffy clouds are known as cumulus clouds.

Why Clouds Look White

The white light of the sun is really a mixture of all the colors. When sunlight enters a droplet of water, it is broken up into the different wavelengths that we see as red, orange, yellow, green, blue, indigo, and violet. Some of the colored light is reflected from the far side of the droplet back and out of the droplet.

The blue color of the sky results from the way tiny particles of dust and vapor in the air scatter light rays. The rays of shorter wavelengths (the blues and violets) are spread out more widely than the rays of longer wavelengths (the reds and yellows).

Too much dust, especially in large particles, causes the scattering of many rays—not only the blue ones. Then the sky becomes whitish or hazy. When a cloud forms, there isn't much difference in the scattering of the different wavelengths of sunlight. We see the mixture of all the colors of the spectrum and the clouds look white to us.

The sky appears red at sunset and sunrise when the longer wavelengths (the reds and yellows) are scattered more effectively. This happens because the sun is closer to the horizon, and so its light shines at an angle closer to the surface and through more atmosphere, dust, and water droplets.

285 ◆ What Causes Smog?

HOT!

YOU WILL NEED:

large narrow-mouthed jar
match

Smog is a combination of fog—tiny droplets of water in the air—and smoke from pollutants in the air. Let's see how it happens. (You will need an adult's help with this experiment.)

What to do: Blow hard into a large narrow-mouthed jar and then remove your lips quickly. Ask an adult to light a match and you blow it out. While the match is still smoking, dip it into the jar so that smoke enters. Blow into the jar again and again remove your lips quickly.

What happens: Smog builds up in the jar.

Why: When you stopped blowing the first time, the sudden lessening of pressure produced a cooling effect. This caused a small amount of water vapor to condense—turn back into droplets of water in the jar. When you added the smoke of the match, the droplets combined with tiny particles of dust from the smoke to form smog.

On dry windy days, smoke and soot from factory chimneys and automobile exhaust systems are carried high into the air and blown away. But on cool damp days with no wind, the particles hang low in the moist air to form smog.

286 ◆ Refrigerator Weather

Raid your refrigerator and learn the difference between snow and sleet. If your refrigerator defrosts automatically, wait for a snowy day and collect your specimens outdoors.

YOU WILL NEED:

white frost (from the freezer) or snow (from the ground)
black construction paper or black cloth
magnifying glass
ice cube
large spoon

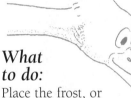

What to do:
Place the frost, or the snow, on the black paper or cloth and examine it with the magnifying glass.

Chip off a small piece of the ice cube with a large spoon and place the sliver of ice on the black cloth. Examine it under the magnifying glass.

What happens: In the frost, or the snow, you see a six-pointed star-shaped crystal. In the ice, you don't.

Why: The frost in the refrigerator and the snowflakes in the sky form in the same way. Water vapor in the clouds—and water vapor in the refrigerator—cools down so much that instead of turning into water, it freezes into snowflakes and frost.

The ice cube forms in the same way as sleet. Both start out as water—and later freeze. Sleet starts as raindrops. When it falls through very cold air, it freezes into little bits of ice.

Dissecting a Hailstone

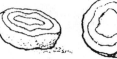

If you've ever been in a hailstorm, you may know how violent they can be. In 1981, in Ohio, a hailstone was found that weighed thirty pounds! What causes hail? Like sleet, hail is made from raindrops that later freeze, but its formation is more complicated.

What to do: Split open the hailstone on a newspaper. Count the number of rings you see.

What happens: You learn how many trips up in the cold air the hailstone made before it fell to earth.

Why: Strong winds pick up raindrops and fling them high up where the air is cold enough to freeze them into ice drops. If they fell to the earth at this point, they would be sleet. But instead of letting them fall all the way down, the winds blow them up again. In the very cold upper air, a new layer of ice freezes around the old. The ice drops fall and are blown up again and again. Finally, when they are too heavy for the up-blowing wind, they clatter to the ground as hail.

Hailstones sometimes get bigger than golf balls and they have been known to do damage to crops or buildings. The largest hailstone on record measured 17.5 inches (44 cm) and fell on Coffeyville, Kansas, on September 3, 1979.

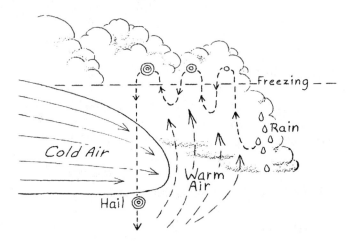

Ozone

Ozone, the main ingredient of smog, is an oxygen with three atoms. It forms when such chemicals as hydrocarbons and nitrogen compounds—released by factories and machines—react to heat and sunlight.

Ozone in the lower atmosphere can make people sick. When the air quality index for ozone climbs to over 200, people are advised to stay indoors, if possible.

In the stratosphere, from 10 to 30 miles (16 to 50 km) above the earth, a layer of ozone forms naturally, shielding the earth from the sun's harmful ultraviolet rays. But there is now evidence of an ozone hole above Antarctica. It has been traced to the use of carbofluorides and similar compounds. These are used in refrigerators and air conditioners, in cleaning electronic equipment, in the manufacture of plastic foam, and in pressurized spray cans. If the ozone layer continues to get holes in it—or the hole that exists gets larger—scientists warn that we can expect an increase in diseases that result from the sun's ultraviolet rays, like skin cancer.

What is Lightning?

288

YOU WILL NEED:

comb
piece of wool
metal doorknob

Make your own lightning! Don't worry—homemade lightning isn't dangerous. You've probably made it many times without realizing it.

What to do: Rub the comb with a piece of wool. Hold the comb near a metal doorknob.

What happens: You produce a small spark.

Why: By rubbing the comb with the wool, you charge it with electricity. The spark is made when the charge jumps to the uncharged, or neutral, doorknob. The spark is the passage of an electrical charge between two objects.

You may have seen a similar spark when you walked over a rug and then touched a doorknob. You may have heard a crackling sound while combing your hair or petting a cat. These are all examples of static electricity.

Lightning is a huge electric spark that results when charges jump from one cloud to another or to the ground. Though lightning may discharge an enormous amount of electricity, it lasts much too brief a time to be trapped into useful energy.

On a hot humid summer day, when hot air climbs quickly, moisture in the air condenses to form billions of water drops and ice crystals. These pick up tiny electric charges as they move through the air. The violent air currents in thunder clouds move different-sized drops and dust particles at different speeds. Those of the same size and with similar amounts of electricity get concentrated in the same part of the cloud. A very high positive electrical charge is often formed in the cold higher parts, while near the ground the thunder cloud is usually negatively charged. The big difference between the charges at the top and the bottom of the cloud creates a powerful voltage or electric pressure. This "push" sends a flash of lightning streaking through the cloud between those parts with opposite electric charges.

Does Lightning Ever Strike Twice in the Same Spot?

Despite sayings to the contrary, lightning may hit the same place or the same person several times. The United States Weather Bureau reports the case of a National Park Ranger who was hit seven times!

Storm Warnings

A summer thunderstorm clears the air and leaves us refreshed. The rumble and roar of thunder is all noise and no bite, and by the time you hear it all danger is usually past. But flashes of lightning may be dangerous. They can start fires, knock over trees, and injure or even kill people.

Lightning takes the shortest path. It hits the highest objects—a tall tree or house, a tower, a person standing alone in a flat field. Modern skyscrapers, however, are built so that lightning may strike them without doing any harm.

Here's what the weather service says to do, if a storm is close.

If You're Outdoors: Go indoors, if possible—inside a house or a large building. If you can't do that, get into an automobile. (Not a convertible!) Don't take refuge in a shed—metal or wood.

Don't stand next to a telephone pole. Keep away from a lone tree. Don't stand on a hilltop. Avoid being the tallest object. Seek shelter in low areas under small trees. If you're in a field, crouch on your knees and bend over.

Keep away from metal pipes, rails, metal fences, and wire clotheslines. Don't carry anything made of metal. Don't ride a bicycle or a scooter. If you're in a group, everyone should spread out. Keep several yards apart.

Keep away from water. If you are swimming, get out of the water. Don't stay out in a boat or stand under a beach umbrella.

If You're Inside: Keep away from windows and doors. Stay away from water taps, sinks, tubs, the stove—anything that could conduct electricity. Don't use electric appliances—the television, an irons, toaster, or mixer.

Don't use the telephone unless there is an emergency.

289 What Causes Thunder?

YOU WILL NEED:
balloon or paper bag

You hear a crackle when you raise a spark. What causes that sound and what causes the roar of thunder?

What to do: Blow up the balloon or the paper bag. Tie it closed with a rubber band or a piece of string. Then place one hand on the top and one hand on the bottom of the balloon or the bag and pop it.

What happens: You get a small clap of thunder.

Why: You created thunder by causing a small quantity of air to move fast. An object produces sound when it vibrates—moves back and forth or up and down. Humans only hear sound when an object vibrates at least 16 times a second—and not more than 20,000 times a second.

When a flash of lightning passes through the atmosphere, it heats the nearby air, and causes it to expand rapidly. It is this movement that causes the sound. A short crash of thunder results from a short flash of lightning. Rolling thunder occurs when lightning covers a large area, or when clouds, mountains, or other obstructions cause echoes.

290 How Far Away is the Storm?

When you see a flash of lightning, start counting seconds like this: "and one and, and two and, and three and"—and continue until you hear a roar of thunder. Divide the number you get by 5 (for miles) or by 3 (for kilometers). That will give you a rough estimate of how far away the center of the storm is.

Why: Lightning and thunder take place at the same time, but light and sound travel to us at different speeds, and so reach us at different times. Light travels at 186,000 miles (300,000 km) per second and takes only a fraction of a second to reach us. We see lightning the moment it flashes.

It takes about 5 seconds for sound to travel a mile (3 seconds for a kilometer).

When a thunderstorm is near, the thunderclap sound is loud and sharp. When it is far away, it is a low rumble. Ordinarily, you can't hear thunder more than 10 or 15 miles (16 or 24 km) away. If you see lightning and hear thunder at just about the same moment, the storm is right above you.

243

291 Make Your Own Rainbow

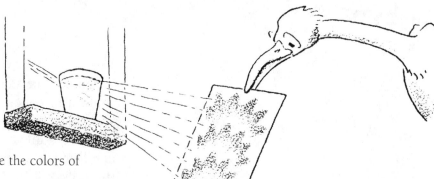

YOU WILL NEED:
glass of water
sheet of white paper

After the storm comes the rainbow. Here's one you can have on any sunny day.

What to do: Stand the glass of water on a windowsill that is in bright sunlight. Place the sheet of paper on the floor.

What happens: You see the colors of the rainbow on the paper.

Why: You are separating the various colors, the spectrum, that make up white light. When light passes at a slant from the air through the glass of water, the rays change direction—they are "refracted." Each color bends differently: violet bends the most and red the least. So, when the light comes out of the glass of water, the different colors travel in slightly different directions and strike the sheet of paper at different places.

It is the same with a rainbow in the sky. It is simply a curved spectrum, made when sunlight shines through water drops in the air at an angle of between 40 degrees and 42 degrees with the horizon. The water drops bend the sun's rays.

The sun has to be behind you if you're going to see a rainbow in the sky. So you'll only see a rainbow early in the morning, when the sun is shining in the east and showers are falling in the west—or in the late afternoon, when the sun is shining in the west and showers are falling in the east.

The arc you see from the ground is just a part of the rainbow. Only if you happen to be flying in a plane will you see a rainbow's full circle.

BUILDING A WEATHER STATION

With everyday materials, you can make the instruments you need to keep track of temperature, air pressure, wind direction and wind speed, humidity and rainfall.

Don't feel too bad if your predictions are not always accurate. Meteorologists, the people who predict the weather, are not always right, either—even with the help of weather satellites circling the earth, radar, balloon-borne instruments, and super-speed computers to help them make their surface observations!

Keeping Records

Weather maps are based on information collected by hundreds of local weather stations. You may want to check the daily findings of your "station" with your local radio and television meteorologists—and with the information published in your local newspaper.

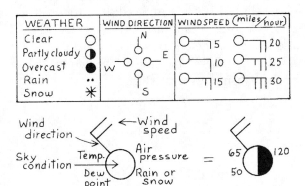

You can keep records and report your findings in several ways.

When you measure the various weather factors, using instruments and observations, make a chart of your findings, like the one on this page.

You may also want to make a station model. It's a handy way to show the same information. It uses a system of symbols that can easily fit on a map. You can adapt the symbols on the left so you can record and compare your daily findings. This sample model is reporting a partly cloudy day, northwest winds at 20 miles (32 km) an hour, temperature of 65 degrees F (18.3 degrees C), and a dew point of 50 degrees F (10 degrees C). Air pressure is reported in millibars (see page 247). You can substitute H (for high) and L (for low), and + for rising and – for falling pressure.

Straw Thermometer

How does a thermometer work? Make your own and find out.

YOU WILL NEED:

medicine bottle or small jar

cork to fit the bottle or jar

nail

glass straw or medicine dropper tube

water

food coloring

felt-tipped pen

What to do: Dig out a hole in the cork with the nail and fit the straw or tube through it.

Fill the bottle to the brim with water colored with a drop or two of food coloring and put the cork in securely. With the felt-tipped pen mark the line the water rises to in the straw or tube.

Note the height of the water in the straw at room temperature and also at different times and places—on a sunny windowsill, in the refrigerator, in a pot of hot water.

What happens: The water goes up the tube when the temperature is warm and goes down when it is cold.

Why: Temperature is measured by the changes made. Temperature is really a measure of whether one object absorbs heat from or loses heat to another object.

Liquids expand when heated and contract when cooled. The liquid of the thermometer absorbs heat. It expands when it contacts anything warmer than itself, and contracts when contacting something cooler. Mercury and colored alcohol are usually used as the liquid in thermometers because they react so quickly.

Makers of commercial weather thermometers use a sealed glass tube that has a little bulb blown out at one end. They mark the thermometer's scale by placing its bulb in contact with melting ice. The point at which the liquid contracts is 32 ° for

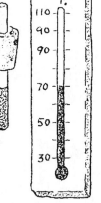

a Fahrenheit scale and 0° for a Centigrade scale. Then the bulb is placed in the steam from boiling water. The point at which it expands is marked 212° F or 100° C.

You can make a scale for your thermometer by comparing its levels with a commercial weather thermometer.

Gabriel Fahrenheit, a German physicist, devised the first commonly used scale in 1714. About thirty years later, a Swedish astronomer, Anders Celsius, established the centigrade scale, also known as the celsius scale.

The first thermometer was invented in 1593 by the Italian physicist Galileo.

°F.
110
90
90
70
50
30

292

◆293 Temperature Conversion

°Fahrenheit		°Centigrade
212	water boils	100
194		90
176		80
158		70
140		60
136	highest Earth temperature ever recorded	57.7
122		50
104		40
98.6	body temperature	37
86		30
68		20
50		10
32	water freezes	0
14		–10
–4		–20
–22		–30
–40		–40
–58		–50
–76		–60
–94		–70
–112		–80
–129	coldest Earth temperature ever recorded	–89
–130		–90

To convert from F° to C°:
Subtract 32° and then multiply by 5. Divide the result by 9.
For a quick estimate of Centigrade:
Deduct 30 and divide by 2.
To convert from C° to F°:
Multiply by 9. Divide the result by 5. Then add 32.
For a quick estimate of Fahrenheit:
Multiply by 2 and add 30.

◆294 Reading a Barometer

At sea level, in normal weather, the mercury in a barometer measures 29.92 inches (1013.2 millibars). In cool, dry weather the mercury level rises. In warm, wet weather, it drops, just the way the water does in the bottle barometer which you will find instructions to make in the next experiment.

The Weather Bureau prefers the mercury barometer to the aneroid (a barometer made without liquid) because it is more accurate. The Bureau finds it more convenient to measure air pressure in millibars. Millibar readings are shortened on weather maps by dropping the first two numbers and the decimal, so that normal pressure—1013.2—for example, is reported as 132.

The lowest barometric pressure ever recorded was 25.59 inches (870 mb) on October 12, 1979, about 300 miles west of Guam in the Pacific Ocean, during a typhoon. The highest barometric pressure recorded was 32 inches (1083.8 mb) in Agata, Siberia, in Russia, on December 31, 1968.

Air pressure is usually lower on stormy days than it is on clear, dry days. So, when air pressure falls, it often indicates that a storm is approaching. A change in pressure of one-tenth of an inch (2.5mm) or more in six hours means there is going to be a fast change in the weather.

To change inches to millibars, multiply the number of inches by 33.87.

Bottle Barometer

295

YOU WILL NEED:
saucer
water
plastic soda bottle
index card
tape

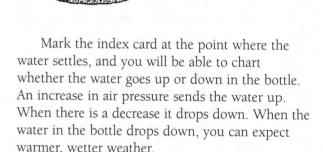

You already know that the layer of air surrounding the earth exerts a pressure of more than fourteen pounds on every square inch.

More than three hundred years ago Evangelista Torricelli, an Italian physicist, first figured out a way to measure this atmospheric pressure. He balanced a column of mercury with a column of air. You can make a barometer with ordinary tap water that will work like his.

What to do: Fill the saucer halfway with water. Pour water into the bottle until it is about three-quarters full. Keeping your thumb on the mouth of the bottle, turn the bottle upside down. Then remove your thumb and quickly put the mouth of the bottle into the saucer of water. Tape a strip of the index card on the outside of the bottle, as it is in the illustration.

What happens: The water doesn't pour out of the bottle. Instead, the water level drops slightly and comes to rest. Then, it moves up or down as the air pressure changes.

Why: Air pressing against the water prevents it from running out. The water stops moving downward when the water pressure is balanced by the pressure of the atmosphere.

Mark the index card at the point where the water settles, and you will be able to chart whether the water goes up or down in the bottle. An increase in air pressure sends the water up. When there is a decrease it drops down. When the water in the bottle drops down, you can expect warmer, wetter weather.

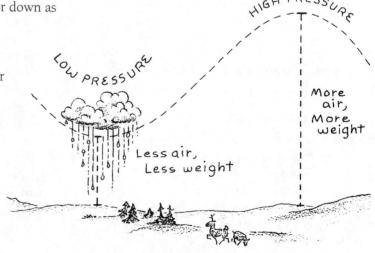

HIGH PRESSURE

LOW PRESSURE

Less air, Less weight

More air, More weight

Balloon Barometer

This crude barometer will also show when there is a change in air pressure.

YOU WILL NEED:

balloon
narrow-mouthed jar
rubber band or
piece of string
glue
drinking straw
straight pin
index card

What to do: Stretch the balloon over the top of the jar. Fasten it with the rubber band or string. Then glue the straw horizontally, starting from the center of the rubber, so it extends beyond the edge of the top of the jar, as in the illustration. Attach the pin to the free end of the straw.

Prop up a marked index card so that you can follow the movement of the straw.

What happens: The unattached end of the straw (the pointer) sometimes moves up and sometimes moves down.

Why: When air pressure increases, the pressure inside the bottle is less than that of the outside air. Therefore the balloon rubber pushes down, and the pointer end of the straw moves up. When the air pressure goes down, the air inside the bottle presses harder than the outside air. The rubber pushes up and tightens, and the pointer moves down.

When your pointer moves down, bad weather is probably on the way. Air pressure usually falls when a storm is approaching. When air pressure rises, it is usually a sign that the weather is going to improve.

Your balloon barometer functions a lot like the aneroid barometer. A flexible top pushes in and out as air pressure changes, and moves the pointer around a scale on the face of the instrument.

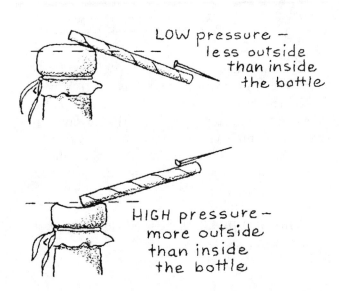

LOW pressure – less outside than inside the bottle

HIGH pressure – more outside than inside the bottle

Weather Vane

YOU WILL NEED:

drinking straw
scissors
index card or piece of light cardboard
straight pin
pencil with an eraser
red marker or crayon
compass
thin wire
straight pin
shallow flower pot full of earth or a lump of clay

If we know the direction the wind is blowing, we can sometimes locate a low pressure system and forecast the bad weather that usually comes with it. A weather vane shows wind direction.

What to do: Make a 1 inch (2.5 cm) vertical slit in one end of the drinking straw. Using the index card or other piece of cardboard, cut out an arrow tail and glue it into the cut end of the straw, as in the illustration. Mark the other end of the straw with the red marker or crayon. Insert the straight pin through the straw about 2 inches (5 cm) from the arrow. Push the pin into the eraser end of the pencil. Be sure the straw can move freely.

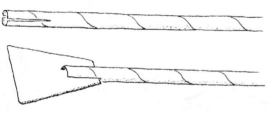

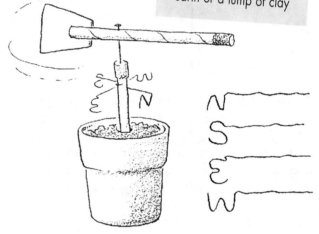

Form the letters N, S, E, and W from pieces of wire. Wind them around the pencil, 1 inch (2.5 cm) below the arrow. Prop the pencil up by its point in a lump of earth in a shallow flower pot or in a lump of clay.

Put the weather vane in a place where the wind is not blocked by buildings. Use a compass to make sure your letters are set up correctly.

What happens: As the wind blows, the weather vane moves.

Why: When the wind blows, it pushes away the larger surface (the arrow). As a result, the other end points into the wind, in the direction from which the wind is blowing.

In the northern hemisphere, a wind that shifts in a counterclockwise direction usually brings a low pressure system and stormy weather along with it. East winds generally bring rain, west winds clearing. North winds mean cold weather, and south winds heat. In the southern hemisphere, it is exactly the opposite for every direction.

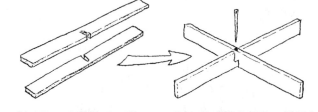

Cup Anemometer

How can you measure the speed of wind? One way is with a cup anemometer. This instrument has three or four small hollow metal hemispheres that revolve around a metal rod and catch the wind. How fast they move reveals the speed of the wind. Our anemometer looks almost like the real thing. But while real anemometers record the revolutions of the cups electrically, you will have to count them yourself.

YOU WILL NEED:

2 pieces of heavy cardboard

scissors

staples or tacks

4 individual metal-foil muffin pans

paint

sharp, thin nail

large needle

pencil with eraser

spool of threed

clay or paper towels

glue or cord

block of wood or flat stone

What to do: Cut out two strips of heavy cardboard, approximately 2 inches x 18 inches (5 cm x 45 cm). Make a slit in the middle of each one so that they fit together to make a cross.

Staple or tack a small metal-foil pan to each end of the cross. If you don't have any old muffin pans around, you can make them by cutting out disks from heavy duty aluminum foil, or cutting down paper cups. Paint one of the pans a bright color. Make a hole through the center of the cross with the sharp thin nail or a large needle.

To make a base, stick the eye of the needle into the pencil eraser. Fit the pointed end of the pencil into the hole of a spool. (You may need the clay or paper towels to make it snug.) Glue or tie the spool to a block of wood or a flat stone.

Attach the cross to the base by placing it on the point of the needle. Blow on the cups. If the cross does not turn easily, make the hole in the crossed strips larger.

Place the base outdoors on a box about 3 feet (1 m) above the ground. Keep a record of the number of revolutions it makes per minute. You can do this easily by counting how many times the colored pan passes you.

What happens: The anemometer sometimes whirls around quickly. At other times it barely moves.

Why: The inward curve of the cups receives most of the force of the wind. That's what makes the cups move. The more revolutions per minute, the greater the wind velocity. A rapid increase in speed can mean approaching rain or snow or thunderstorms.

The Beaufort Scale

The Beaufort scale was originally designed by Francis Beaufort, a British admiral, in the early 1800s to help guide ships. It calculated wind speed at sea, but it has since been adapted for use on land. The Weather Bureau, though it uses an anemometer to measure wind speed, still reports winds to us using the Beaufort Scale.

It gives you a great way to judge the speed of wind—anywhere, any time—by watching the things that the wind moves. Memorize it and you'll be able to amaze people with your accurate readings.

0: Calm
Smoke goes straight up
Wind Speed: Less than 1mph

1: Light air
Smoke drifts in direction of wind
Wind Speed: 1–3mph

2: Light breeze
Wind felt on face; leaves rustle; flags stir; weather vanes turn
Wind Speed: 4–7mph

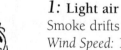

3: Gentle breeze
Leaves and twigs move constantly; light flags blow out
Wind Speed: 8–12mph

4: Moderate breeze
Dust, loose papers, and small branches move; flags flap
Wind Speed: 13–18mph

5: Fresh breeze
Small trees in leaf begin to sway; Flags ripple
Wind Speed: 19–24mph

6: Strong breeze
Large branches in motion; flags beat; umbrellas turn inside out
Wind Speed: 25–31mph

7: Moderate gale
Whole trees in motion; flags are extended
Wind Speed: 32–38mph

8: Fresh gale
Twigs break off trees; walking is hard
Wind Speed: 32–38mph

9: Strong gale
Slight damage to houses—TV antennas may blow off, awnings rip
Wind Speed: 47–54mph

10: Whole gale
Trees uprooted; much damage to houses
Wind Speed: 55–63mph

11: Storm
Widespread damage
Wind Speed: 64–75mph

12: Hurricane
Excessive damage
Wind Speed: more than 75mph

How Cold Do You Feel?

The speed of wind affects how cold you feel. The wind-chill factor is the relationship between the speed of wind and the temperature of the air. A wind chill table tells us the still-air temperature that would feel the same as the temperature and wind speed combined. For example, a temperature of 20° F (–6° C) and a wind of 20 miles (32 km) an hour makes us feel as though it were –10° F (–23° C).

Air Temperature (F°)

Wind Speed (miles per hour)	35	30	25	20	15	10	5	0	–5	–10	–15	–20	–25	–30	–35	–40	–45
0–4	35	30	25	20	15	10	5	0	–5	–10	–15	–20	–25	–30	–35	–40	–45
5	32	27	22	16	11	6	0	–5	–10	–15	–21	–26	–31	–36	–42	–47	–52
10	22	16	10	3	–3	–9	–15	–22	–27	–34	–40	–46	–52	–58	–64	–71	–77
15	16	9	2	–5	–11	–18	–25	–31	–38	–45	–51	–58	–65	–72	–78	–85	–92
20	12	4	–3	–10	–17	–24	–31	–39	–46	–53	–60	–67	–74	–81	–88	–95	–103
25	8	1	–7	–15	–22	–29	–36	–44	–51	–59	–66	–74	–81	–88	–96	–103	–110
30	6	–2	–10	–18	–25	–33	–41	–49	–56	–64	–71	–79	–86	–93	–101	–109	–116
35	4	–4	–12	–20	–27	–35	–43	–52	–58	–67	–74	–82	–89	–97	–105	–113	–120
40	3	–5	–13	–21	–29	–37	–45	–53	–60	–69	–76	–84	–92	–100	–107	–115	–123
45	2	–6	–14	–22	–30	–38	–46	–54	–62	–70	–78	–85	–93	–102	–109	–117	–125

How Hot Do You Feel?

If it is 85°F (29.4° C) how hot do you feel?

Well, if the humidity is 95 per cent—it feels like 105°F (40.5°C). The Heat Index prepared by the weather service shows what the temperature feels like as the humidity changes.

At 110° F (43° C), you only need relative humidity of 50 per cent to feel as if the temperature is 150° F (65° C)!

With a hygrometer, the relative humidity chart, and this index, you can figure out how hot it feels any day.

Relative Humidity (%)

Air Temperature (°F)	25	30	35	40	45	50	55	60	65	70	75	80	85	90	95	100
140																
135																
130																
125																
120	139	148														
115	127	135	143	151												
110	117	123	130	137	143	150										
105	109	113	118	123	129	135	142	149								
100	101	104	107	110	115	120	126	132	138	144						
95	94	96	98	101	104	107	110	114	119	124	130	136				
90	88	90	91	93	95	96	98	100	102	106	109	113	117	122		
85	83	84	85	86	87	88	89	90	91	93	95	97	99	102	105	108
80	77	78	79	79	80	81	81	82	83	85	86	86	87	88	89	91
75	72	73	73	74	74	75	75	76	76	77	77	78	78	79	79	80
70	66	67	67	68	68	69	69	70	70	70	70	71	71	71	71	72

300

301

Milk Carton Hygrometer

302

Humidity is the amount of water vapor, or moisture, in the air. Meteorologists usually report what is called "relative humidity," rather than actual humidity. Relative humidity is a figure they come to by comparing the moisture in the air to the amount of moisture the air can hold. And that amount will change according to the temperature of the air. High humidity combined with high temperatures makes most people uncomfortable.

You can figure out relative humidity with a homemade hygrometer.

YOU WILL NEED:

2 room thermometers
small piece of cotton material
thread
quart milk carton
rubber bands
scissors
water

What to do: Check the two thermometers to make sure they register the same temperature.

Cover the bulb of one of the thermometers with a 2 inch (5 cm) scrap of cotton material (an old handkerchief will do fine). Tie it on with thread and leave a "tail" on one end, as in the illustration.

Using rubber bands, attach the thermometers to two sides of the milk carton. Cut a small hole in the carton just below the thermometer with the covered bulb. Push the tail of cotton through the hole. Fill the carton with water up to the level of the hole so the cotton can be kept wet.

Read the dry bulb and wet bulb thermometers.

What happens: The temperature of the wet-bulb thermometer is always lower.

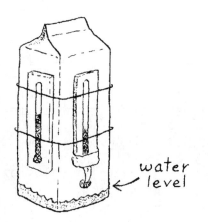

water
level

Why: Water evaporating from the thermometer with the moist cloth uses up heat. Therefore, the temperature drops.

The water in the cloth around the wet-bulb thermometer will keep on evaporating as long as the air can hold more water vapor. Dry air can take on more water vapor than air that is already filled with moisture.

The drier the air (the lower the humidity), the further apart the two temperature readings will be. When the temperatures are exactly the same, the humidity is 100 percent.

The higher the temperature, the more water vapor the air can hold at a particular temperature, the relative humidity is 100 percent. And it is foggy or raining or snowing.

Check the readings of the two thermometers and see the humidity table (below) to find the relative percentage of humidity.

Relative Humidity Table

Difference between dry-bulb and wet-bulb temperatures

Dry-bulb temperature (F°)	1	2	3	4	5	6	7	8	9	10	11	12	14	16	18	20	22	24
10	78	56	34	13														
15	82	64	46	29	11													
20	85	70	55	40	26	12												
25	87	74	62	49	37	25	13	1										
30	89	78	67	56	46	36	26	16	6									
35	91	81	72	63	54	45	36	27	19	10	2							
40	92	83	75	68	60	52	45	37	29	22	15	7						
45	93	86	78	71	64	57	51	44	38	31	25	18	6					
50	93	87	80	74	67	61	55	49	43	38	32	27	16	5				
55	94	88	82	76	70	65	59	54	49	43	38	33	23	14	5			
60	94	89	83	78	73	68	63	58	53	48	43	39	30	21	13	5		
65	95	90	85	80	75	70	66	61	56	52	48	44	35	27	20	12	5	
70	95	90	86	81	77	72	68	64	59	55	51	48	40	33	25	19	12	6
75	96	91	86	82	78	74	70	66	62	58	54	51	44	37	30	24	18	12
80	96	91	87	83	79	75	72	68	64	61	57	54	47	41	35	29	23	18
90	96	92	89	85	81	78	74	71	68	65	61	58	52	47	41	36	31	26
100	96	93	89	86	83	80	77	73	70	68	65	62	56	51	46	41	37	33

303 How Uncomfortable Do You Feel?

The Temperature Humidity Index (THI) shows how heat and humidity combined make us feel.

If you know the temperature and the relative humidity, you can use the chart below and tell just how uncomfortable you are. For example, if the temperature is 81 degrees F (27.2 degrees C) with the humidity at 55 per cent, the THI is 75, and about half the people are uncomfortable. At that same temperature and a humidity of 100 per cent, the THI is 80 and most people are uncomfortable.

If you love math, you can figure out the THI for yourself by using the following steps:
1. Add the wet bulb and dry bulb temperatures.
2. Multiply the sum by 0.4.
3. Add 15.

If you don't have the wet bulb temperature, but you know the temperature and the humidity, you can find the wet bulb temperature by using the relative humidity table on page 255. All you have to do is subtract the "difference" from the dry bulb temperature.

Temperature Humidity Index

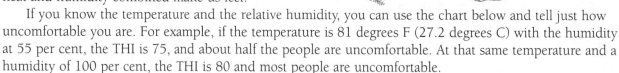

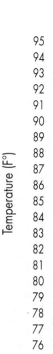

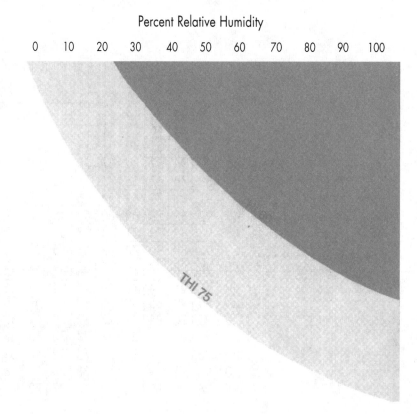

Dew Point

The dew point is the temperature at which the air cannot hold any more water vapor. That's when the moisture in the air begins to condense—to turn back from water vapor to droplets. This temperature will change from day to day depending on the temperature of the air and the amount of moisture in it. The closer the dew point temperature is to the air temperature, the more likely we are to have fog or rain or snow.

You can use simple equipment to determine the day's dew point, but you must set it up outdoors.

What to do: Write down the temperature of the air.

Remove the label from the can. Fill the can with water, and then make sure the outside is dry. Place the thermometer in the can.

Add ice to the water, a cube at a time. Carefully stir the water with the thermometer. Watch both the outside of the can and the thermometer closely.

What happens: Liquid begins to form on the outside of the can—and the temperature goes down.

Why: The temperature—at the point when liquid begins to form—is at or near the dew point—the temperature at which the relative humidity is 100 percent.

When water cools off and condenses on an object, the droplets are called dew. Dew forms when damp air touches anything that cools it to below its dew point—the point at which it cannot hold any more water.

When air currents are rising rapidly, cooling takes place high in the air and clouds form. When gentler air currents mix cool air into warmer air, fog forms.

Dew usually forms on grass or on plants that have cooled off. The temperature at which this happens depends on the amount of water vapor in the air. If it's small, dew may not form until the temperature drops to 32 degrees F (0 degrees C) or even below freezing. When it's that cold frost forms. If the air contains a great deal of water vapor, dew will form at 68 degrees F (20° C).

Rain Gauge

Measure the amount of rain that falls during a period of a week or month, and compare your results with the official statistics.

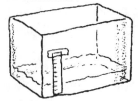

YOU WILL NEED:

ruler
masking or adhesive tape
various empty containers, like a coffee can, a jar, and a cut-down milk carton
pencil
paper

What to do: Using the ruler, measure off inches or centimeters on strips of masking or adhesive tape. Attach the tapes to the various containers.

Put the containers on a flat, level suface outside. It may be wise to place the containers in a box to make sure they remain upright.

Each time it rains, measure the amount of rain in the containers. The levels should be the same whatever the size of the container, provided that its sides are parallel. Record the amount and date.

Compare measurements from one rainfall to the next. And compare your measurements with those announced on television or radio. They may not always agree. Sometimes, the amount of rain varies from one side of the street to the other!

Reading the Clouds

When the air is heavy with moisture and it gets cool, the water vapor in it turns back into droplets and combines with tiny dust particles in the air to form fog. When fog is high in the sky, we see clouds. The type of cloud depends on how the air is cooled and the way the air is moving.

Cirrus clouds are high, feathery clouds.

Stratus clouds hang low in layers or sheets in the sky, causing overcast and fog.

Cumulus clouds look like cauliflowers with flat bases. They usually mean fair weather.

Nimbus clouds are dark gray rain clouds.

Most clouds change shape continually. Parts of them evaporate when touched by warmer air and when winds blow.

Weather is called cloudless when there are no clouds at all, and "clear" when clouds cover less than three-tenths of the sky. It is "partly sunny" when the sky is three-tenths to seven-tenths clouded, and "cloudy," or overcast, when the sky is more clouded than that.

Weather forecasters study clouds carefully. With the help of the Cloud Chart, you, too, can read the clouds!

CLOUD CHART

40,000 ft. (12,000 m)

CIRRUS

CIRRO-STRATUS

CIRRO-CUMULUS

20,000 ft. (6,000 m)

ALTO-STRATUS

ALTO-CUMULUS

CUMULO-NIMBUS

STRATO-CUMULUS

5,000 ft. (1,500 m)

CUMULUS

NIMBO-STRATUS

3,000 ft. (900 m)

STRATUS

1,500 ft. (450 m)

pH Scale

The pH scale, developed by S.P.L. Sorensen, a Danish biochemist, is used to indicate how alkaline or acid a solution is.

All acids contain hydrogen. The stronger the acid, the more hydrogen the solution contains—and the less hydrogen the solution can accept when it combines with another substance. When it can't accept any more hydrogen its ph is 0. The stronger the acid, the lower its pH.

A solution with a pH above 7 is alkaline. A solution with a pH below 7 is acid.

alkaline

- 14.0 drain cleaner
- 13.0 lye/ammonia
- 12.4 lime
- 11.0
- 10.5 milk of magnesia
- 8.5 baking soda
- 8.3 seawater
- 8.0
- 7.4 blood
- 7.0 distilled water
- 6.6 milk
- 6.0
- 5.6 unpolluted rain
- 5.0 tomato juice
- 4.2 coffee
- 3.0 apple juice
- 2.2 vinegar
- 2.0 lemon juice
- 1.5
- 1.0 battery acid
- 0.0

acidic

259

Acid Rain

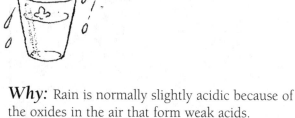

You can test whether the rain that falls in your area is polluted by using pH paper or litmus paper, both of which you can buy from chemistry laboratories or hobby shops. Or you can make your own indicator with juice from a jar of red cabbage.

What to do: Collect rain water in a clean jar.

Line up and number or label the paper cups. Put a tablespoon of red cabbage juice in each. Add rain water to the first, an equal amount of cooled boiled water to the second, milk to the third, apple juice to the next, then lemon juice to the last.

Compare the color of the cup with the rain water with the colors of others. When you find the one that comes closest in color to the rain water, refer to the pH chart on page 259 and estimate the pH of the rain water you are testing.

What happens: If the solution changes color only slightly, your rain water is normal. If it becomes as pink as the lemon solution, it has a very high acid content.

Why: Rain is normally slightly acidic because of the oxides in the air that form weak acids. Unpolluted rain water measures about 5.6 on the pH scale.

If your rain water has a lower pH level, the rain falling in your area is polluted with acids. When the pH of water in lakes and streams drops below 5 on the scale, most fish die.

When the waste from the fuel burned to run our factories—and our cars, trains, and planes—combines with the water in the air, it forms acids that fall to the ground—either in the form of rain or as dry particles.

This new man-made pollution has been called a slow poison from the sky. It harms trees and food crops, and poses a threat to life in lakes and streams, as well on land. It can even cause buildings to crumble.

AIR, H$_2$O, AND OTHER THINGS

Everything in this world takes up space and has weight: you, and even air, as this chapter will show!

The three states of matter are solid, liquid, and gas. This refers to how a thing feels, how hard it is, or how it moves or looks, even if it's invisible, like air. A table is a solid object, water is a liquid, and air is a gas, and these three things are made up of small parts called molecules and even smaller parts called atoms. It is these parts of things that chemists study, and rearrange to create new products that make our lives that much better.

Be Smart/Be Safe

You can be smart and do these experiments safely by following these general rules:

• Always wash thoroughly any kitchen containers, bowls, or tools you use before you put them back.

• Don't leave old chemical solutions lying around the house. Dispose of them carefully.

• Be especially careful using the stove or microwave, or handling boiling water or hot foods. Find a parent or an adult to help you use any appliances needed, or to do experiments you are unsure of.

• Be sure to label the contents of any bottles, jars, and containers you want to keep, and store them in a safe place, away from young children.

• Read through the What to do instructions completely before you start, to make sure you have everything you need and the time to complete the experiment.

• If an experiment may be messy, do it outside or in the sink, or cover your work area with a protective covering or old newspapers.

Atomic Brew: The Molecule and I

A molecule is the smallest part of anything that exists as that thing. You cannot see molecules, but everything in the world is made up of them. The best way to understand this is to imagine yourself shrinking way, way down until you become one. If you were a molecule of something on a tabletop, a salt crystal (one grain of salt) on the table would look like a mountain to you. If you were a molecule of water, you would be the last, littlest part of a drop. The last part of that water drop to evaporate would be you. Now you have a good idea of how small molecules really are. But, while molecules are small, the parts that make them up are even smaller. These very small parts that form molecules are called atoms.

If you were a molecule of oxygen, you would be made up of two of these very small parts, or atoms. You would need two atoms of oxygen, because one atom of oxygen does not behave like oxygen.

A substance with only one kind of atom is called an element. Oxygen, hydrogen, nitrogen, and carbon are all elements. (See The Periodic Table of the Elements on pages 264 and 265.) If you were an element of nitrogen, you would be made up of only nitrogen atoms. If you were an element of carbon, you would be made up of only carbon atoms. You could not be anything else.

Atoms of different elements come together to make different molecules. A molecule of water is made up of three atoms. If you were one atom of oxygen, you would have to be joined by two friends representing hydrogen atoms to make a molecule of water, because water has two atoms of hydrogen and one atom of oxygen. You would now be a substance, made up of two (or more) different elements, called a compound. Water, carbon dioxide, and sugar are all examples of compounds. As a molecule, or small bit of matter, you could exist in three possible forms. Chemists would identify you as one of the three states of matter: solid, liquid, or gas.

If necessary, a scientist, or chemist, could again split you apart, using electricity, into your original parts or atoms. Now you would no longer be water but three separate atoms, two hydrogen atoms and one oxygen atom. The very smallest part of you that could ever exist as water would be a molecule.

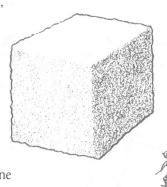

Atom Up!

Everything on the earth is made up of atoms. They are the smallest part of any element, and the atoms of each element are different. If you were to take all the electrons in each element and add'em up, you would get different (atomic) numbers. Now, you know why we titled this section. "Atom Up!"

Each atom has a central point, or nucleus, made up of neutrons and protons. Some atomic parts contain electrical charges: the protons in the nucleus contain positive electrical charges, but the neutrons contain no charge (they are electrically neutral). Spinning around the nucleus, however, are even tinier parts called electrons. These have a negative electrical charge. These positive and negative electrical charges between electrons and protons are what keep the atom whole and together.

It helps to think of the nucleus of an atom as a ball, and the electrons as smaller balls circling it. Chemists sometimes call the paths the electrons take around the nucleus "shells." Better yet, think of the nucleus of the atom as the sun and the electrons as circling, or orbiting, it as its planets. The orbiting planets are attracted to, or pulled towards, the sun just as the electrons are to the nucleus of the atom.

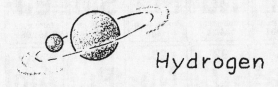

Hydrogen

308 ◆ Charting The Elements

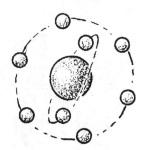

A special table known as the Periodic Table of the Elements can help you better understand atomic chemistry. Dmitri Ivanovich Mendeleyev, a Russian chemist, put together the first table of the elements in 1869. He left some spaces in it so that, when new elements were discovered, they could be placed on the chart. In a modern version (see The Periodic Table of the Elements chart) the seven rows numbered at the left and running across the table, called periods, tell the number of orbits the electrons take in each of the elements.

Period-one elements have only one orbit, period-two have two orbits, period-three have three orbits, etc.

Each element on the chart has a number (atomic number) and a letter symbol as well as an atomic weight. Find oxygen on the chart (period 2, column 16/6A). The atomic number of oxygen is eight. This shows that there are eight protons in the nucleus of the atom. Notice the numbers two and six on the right side of the box. They add up to eight. The two numbers, one on top of the other, represent the number of electrons in the first orbit (2) and in the second orbit (6) of the element oxygen. The number of electrons orbiting the nucleus of an atom is the same as the number of protons in the nucleus.

PERIODIC TABLE

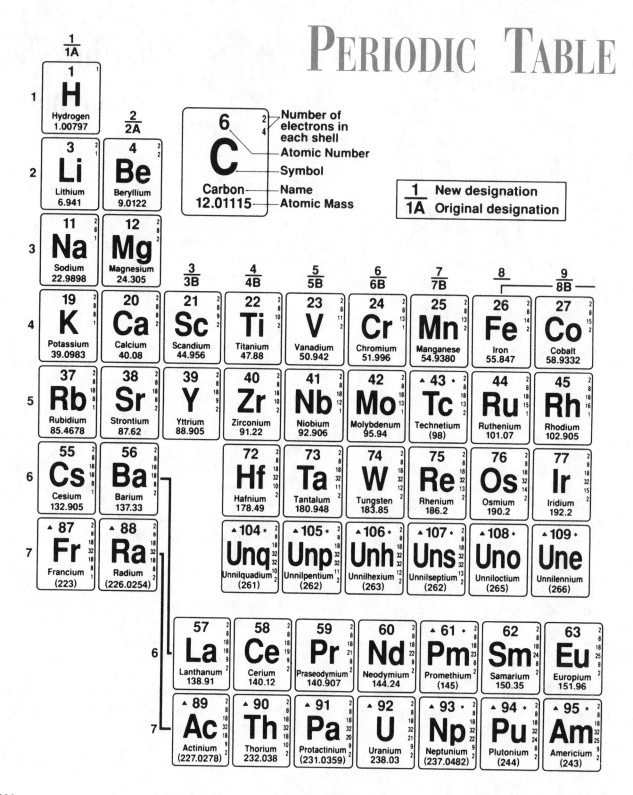

1 / 1A		
1 / **H** / Hydrogen / 1.00797		

6 / **C** / Carbon / 12.01115

- Number of electrons in each shell
- Atomic Number
- Symbol
- Name
- Atomic Mass

1	New designation
1A	Original designation

2 / 2A

| 3 / **Li** / Lithium / 6.941 | 4 / **Be** / Beryllium / 9.0122 |

| 11 / **Na** / Sodium / 22.9898 | 12 / **Mg** / Magnesium / 24.305 |

| 3 / 3B | 4 / 4B | 5 / 5B | 6 / 6B | 7 / 7B | 8 / 8B | | |

Row 4:
- 19 / **K** / Potassium / 39.0983
- 20 / **Ca** / Calcium / 40.08
- 21 / **Sc** / Scandium / 44.956
- 22 / **Ti** / Titanium / 47.88
- 23 / **V** / Vanadium / 50.942
- 24 / **Cr** / Chromium / 51.996
- 25 / **Mn** / Manganese / 54.9380
- 26 / **Fe** / Iron / 55.847
- 27 / **Co** / Cobalt / 58.9332

Row 5:
- 37 / **Rb** / Rubidium / 85.4678
- 38 / **Sr** / Strontium / 87.62
- 39 / **Y** / Yttrium / 88.905
- 40 / **Zr** / Zirconium / 91.22
- 41 / **Nb** / Niobium / 92.906
- 42 / **Mo** / Molybdenum / 95.94
- 43 / **Tc** / Technetium / (98)
- 44 / **Ru** / Ruthenium / 101.07
- 45 / **Rh** / Rhodium / 102.905

Row 6:
- 55 / **Cs** / Cesium / 132.905
- 56 / **Ba** / Barium / 137.33
- 72 / **Hf** / Hafnium / 178.49
- 73 / **Ta** / Tantalum / 180.948
- 74 / **W** / Tungsten / 183.85
- 75 / **Re** / Rhenium / 186.2
- 76 / **Os** / Osmium / 190.2
- 77 / **Ir** / Iridium / 192.2

Row 7:
- 87 / **Fr** / Francium / (223)
- 88 / **Ra** / Radium / (226.0254)
- 104 / **Unq** / Unnilquadium / (261)
- 105 / **Unp** / Unnilpentium / (262)
- 106 / **Unh** / Unnilhexium / (263)
- 107 / **Uns** / Unnilseptium / (262)
- 108 / **Uno** / Unniloctium / (265)
- 109 / **Une** / Unnilennium / (266)

Lanthanides (6):
- 57 / **La** / Lanthanum / 138.91
- 58 / **Ce** / Cerium / 140.12
- 59 / **Pr** / Praseodymium / 140.907
- 60 / **Nd** / Neodymium / 144.24
- 61 / **Pm** / Promethium / (145)
- 62 / **Sm** / Samarium / 150.35
- 63 / **Eu** / Europium / 151.96

Actinides (7):
- 89 / **Ac** / Actinium / (227.0278)
- 90 / **Th** / Thorium / 232.038
- 91 / **Pa** / Protactinium / (231.0359)
- 92 / **U** / Uranium / 238.03
- 93 / **Np** / Neptunium / (237.0482)
- 94 / **Pu** / Plutonium / (244)
- 95 / **Am** / Americium / (243)

OF THE ELEMENTS

★ Synthetic

▲ Radioactive

( ) Indicates atomic weight of most stable isotope

18 / 8A
2 ² / **He** / Helium / 4.0026

13 / 3A	14 / 4A	15 / 5A	16 / 6A	17 / 7A
5 ²₃ / **B** / Boron / 10.811	6 ²₄ / **C** / Carbon / 12.01115	7 ²₅ / **N** / Nitrogen / 14.0067	8 ²₆ / **O** / Oxygen / 15.9994	9 ²₇ / **F** / Fluorine / 18.9984	10 ²₈ / **Ne** / Neon / 20.179

| 13 ²₈₃ / **Al** / Aluminum / 26.9815 | 14 ²₈₄ / **Si** / Silicon / 28.086 | 15 ²₈₅ / **P** / Phosphorus / 30.9738 | 16 ²₈₆ / **S** / Sulfur / 32.064 | 17 ²₈₇ / **Cl** / Chlorine / 35.453 | 18 ²₈₈ / **Ar** / Argon / 39.948 |

10	11 / 1B	12 / 2B

| 28 ²₈₁₆₂ / **Ni** / Nickel / 58.69 | 29 ²₈₁₈₁ / **Cu** / Copper / 63.54 | 30 ²₈₁₈₂ / **Zn** / Zinc / 65.37 | 31 ²₈₁₈₃ / **Ga** / Gallium / 69.72 | 32 ²₈₁₈₄ / **Ge** / Germanium / 72.59 | 33 ²₈₁₈₅ / **As** / Arsenic / 74.9216 | 34 ²₈₁₈₆ / **Se** / Selenium / 78.96 | 35 ²₈₁₈₇ / **Br** / Bromine / 79.904 | 36 ²₈₁₈₈ / **Kr** / Krypton / 83.80 |

| 46 ²₈₁₈₀ / **Pd** / Palladium / 106.4 | 47 ²₈₁₈₁ / **Ag** / Silver / 107.868 | 48 ²₈₁₈₂ / **Cd** / Cadmium / 112.40 | 49 ²₈₁₈₃ / **In** / Indium / 114.82 | 50 ²₈₁₈₄ / **Sn** / Tin / 118.69 | 51 ²₈₁₈₅ / **Sb** / Antimony / 121.75 | 52 ²₈₁₈₆ / **Te** / Tellurium / 127.60 | 53 ²₈₁₈₇ / **I** / Iodine / 126.9044 | 54 ²₈₁₈₈ / **Xe** / Xenon / 131.29 |

| 78 ²₈₁₈₃₂₁ / **Pt** / Platinum / 195.09 | 79 ²₈₁₈₃₂₁ / **Au** / Gold / 196.967 | 80 ²₈₁₈₃₂₂ / **Hg** / Mercury / 200.59 | 81 ²₈₁₈₃₂₃ / **Tl** / Thallium / 204.383 | 82 ²₈₁₈₃₂₄ / **Pb** / Lead / 207.19 | 83 ²₈₁₈₃₂₅ / **Bi** / Bismuth / 208.980 | ▲ 84 ²₈₁₈₃₂₆ / **Po** / Polonium / (209) | ▲ 85 ²₈₁₈₃₂₇ / **At** / Astatine / (210) | ▲ 86 ²₈₁₈₃₂₈ / **Rn** / Radon / (222) |

| 64 ²₈₁₈₂₅₉₂ / **Gd** / Gadolinium / 157.25 | 65 ²₈₁₈₂₇₈₂ / **Tb** / Terbium / 158.9254 | 66 ²₈₁₈₂₈₈₂ / **Dy** / Dysprosium / 162.50 | 67 ²₈₁₈₂₉₈₂ / **Ho** / Holmium / 164.930 | 68 ²₈₁₈₃₀₈₂ / **Er** / Erbium / 167.26 | 69 ²₈₁₈₃₁₈₂ / **Tm** / Thulium / 168.934 | 70 ²₈₁₈₃₂₈₂ / **Yb** / Ytterbium / 173.04 | 71 ²₈₁₈₃₂₈₂ / **Lu** / Lutetium / 174.97 |

| ▲ 96 ²₈₁₈₃₂₂₅₉₂ / **Cm** / Curium / (247) | ▲ 97 ²₈₁₈₃₂₂₇₈₂ / **Bk** / Berkelium / (247) | ▲ 98 ²₈₁₈₃₂₂₈₈₂ / **Cf** / Californium / (251) | ▲ 99 ²₈₁₈₃₂₂₉₈₂ / **Es** / Einsteinium / (252) | ▲ 100 ²₈₁₈₃₂₃₀₈₂ / **Fm** / Fermium / (257) | ▲ 101 ²₈₁₈₃₂₃₁₈₂ / **Md** / Mendelevium / (258) | ▲ 102 ²₈₁₈₃₂₃₂₈₂ / **No** / Nobelium / (259) | ▲ 103 ²₈₁₈₃₂₃₂₈₂ / **Lr** / Lawrencium / (260) |

Atomic Orbits

An easy way to start learning about atoms is to make a model of one. Although electrons and protons are not clay balls (in fact, electrons are fast-moving, electrically charged particles that move faster than you can say "atom"), making a clay model will help you understand what can be a very difficult idea.

What to do: Spread some newspaper over your work area. Select any two colors of clay. We'll use red and blue. Now, make two red clay ropes and a blue rope, rolling them out with your hands. These will show the orbits, or shells, or paths the electrons will take around the nucleus. Make certain that you make the ropes long enough to make complete circles inside the jar lid. Press the first red rope against the inner rim of the lid. Follow it with the blue rope, pressed in next to the red. (When you finish your model, it will have a target pattern.) Now press another circle of red in next to the blue rope; then place a blue "bull's-eye" piece of clay in the middle. When you finish, flatten the clay with your fingers.

Next, make a "yellow" clay ball and stick it on the "bull's-eye." Make two smaller (green) balls and stick these to the outside of the blue bull's-eye, one on each side and in a straight line with the larger ball. Then place eight more green balls in four groups of two on the outer edge of the red ring.

What happens: You now have made a usable atomic model!

Why: Atoms can have no more than seven orbits, or paths, and only so many electrons can fit into each orbit. The larger ball in the "bull's-eye" represents the nucleus of the atom. The two smaller balls on the outer edge of the blue circle show that there are only two electrons in the first orbit. The second orbit, the edge of the red ring, has eight green balls around it, showing that only eight electrons can be in its orbit.

The third orbit of the model (outer edge of the blue clay circle, not filled) can have up to eight more green balls, or electrons, if it is the last orbit, but up to eighteen, if it is not the last. An important thing to remember is that, after the first orbit, each orbit in turn must have eight electrons before another orbit is started.

310 Identify the Model

Look at the Periodic Table of the Elements and identify the model you just made; then add balls, or electrons, to your atomic model to make other elements.

ISO What?

Isomers are essentially compounds, or atoms of two or more elements that chemically unite. Although they have the same number and kinds of atoms as other compounds, they are arranged differently. Scientists have taken compounds and chemically rearranged their molecules to form isomers and make new products. Detergent, paint, gasoline, and aspirin, products we use every day, are but a few examples of products made by this process.

311 Isomer Patterns

Now challenge your brain power. See how many isomer models you can make. Try this with friends. It makes a great brainteaser!

YOU WILL NEED:

6 paper clips
paper
pencil

What to do: Take one paper clip. Place it in front of you. You have made your first pattern. Can you make any more with just the one clip? Select two paper clips and place them end to end to form a chain. Use the same two clips and place one on top of the other to form a cross. How many patterns can you make with these two clips?

Add another clip to the two to make three. How many patterns can you make now, using the added clip? Now add another clip to make four, then five, then six. How does increasing the clips by one increase your chances for making new patterns? Hypothesize, or guess, how many patterns you can make before each activity. Write down your estimate, or guessed number, and draw each pattern you are able to make.

What happens: Every time you add one more paper clip, you are able to make more new patterns.

Why: This experiment is based on a study of probability; in this case, how many patterns you can make in each activity. The more paper clips,

or elements, you have to work with, the greater the number of patterns you are able to make. The number of possible patterns increases faster than the number of clips you add.

312 Pencil Pusher

Most pencils have six flat sides. Number the sides by writing 1 through 6 on them. Place a book on a table and roll the pencil towards it until it stops. What are the possible chances that a certain number will come up?

By chance, each number will come up equally; in mathematics, we say the outcome is "equally likely." Are there any variables, or things that could affect how many times a certain number side on the pencil could come up?

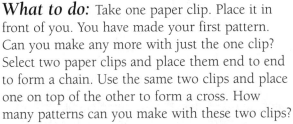

267

Molecules in Motion

You can demonstrate the movement of molecules in solids, liquids, and gases in a simple way.

YOU WILL NEED:

small box lid (or flat box with short sides)

marbles (or any other small spheres or balls)

scissors

What to do: Place a layer of marbles, or balls, in the lid so that they are jammed close together. Move the lid back and forth slowly. Now, take some of the marbles out of the lid and move the lid back and forth again, faster than you did when more marbles were in it.

Take more marbles out of the lid and move it at an even greater speed than before.

Finally, cut a hole in each side of the lid and shake the lid again, and again.

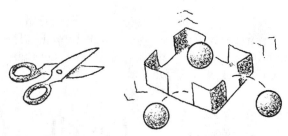

What happens: As the marbles get fewer and fewer, they spread out more easily. Some leave through the holes in the lid.

Why: The "packed marbles" at the start show molecules in a solid substance. This explains why these substances are hard. They move, but they don't move much.

A number of marbles taken out shows molecules in a liquid. They are farther apart and they move more easily.

Finally, the few marbles in the lid demonstrate molecules even farther apart and moving quite rapidly. This represents a gas.

The holes in the sides of the box show what happens when substances break away from substances: water boiling on the stove will turn to water vapor, or steam, and leave the pot. A drop of water left in a dish will evaporate. If one of its molecules is moving fast enough, it will move from the surface of the drop and into the air.

When an ice cube is heated, it changes from a solid form into a liquid state, and then into a gas. The molecules of water never change, but the forms the substance takes do change; for example, from ice to water to vapor.

The Spreading Molecules

YOU WILL NEED:

2 clear glasses
cool and hot tap water
food coloring
medicine dropper

Do water molecules really move? If so, how fast and how slowly?

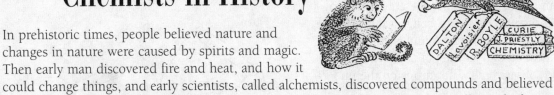

What to do: Fill one glass with cool tap water. Fill the other glass with hot tap water. Now, quickly, place one drop of food coloring in each glass. (Make certain that all the variables are the same. This means that the glasses should have the same amount of water in them and that the same number of food coloring drops are added. Controlling variables is important to make the experiment scientifically correct.)

What happens: The food coloring spreads throughout the water in both glasses, but at different rates.

Why: The cold water eventually becomes completely colored because the water molecules are moving throughout the glass. But when the water is warmer (the hot tap water), the heat energy in it causes the water molecules to move much faster. This makes the food coloring spread out more rapidly.

You might want to chart, or keep a record of, how much time it takes for the food coloring to spread evenly throughout each glass of water.

Chemists in History

In prehistoric times, people believed nature and changes in nature were caused by spirits and magic. Then early man discovered fire and heat, and how it could change things, and early scientists, called alchemists, discovered compounds and believed that metal could be turned into gold. But none of them knew how chemistry really worked.

The chemistry we know (organic chemistry is the study of carbon compounds, while inorganic chemistry deals with all the other elements and compounds) began in the 1600s, when Robert Boyle started charting the list of elements still in use today. Chemists Joseph Priestley and Karl Scheele separately discovered oxygen in the late 1700s. It was then, too, that French chemist Antoine Lavoisier discovered combustion, or what chemical changes happened when things were burned. John Dalton thought elements were made of atoms (1803), while Jons J. Berzelius, a Swedish scientist, believed all atoms were negatively and positively charged (1812). He also gave atomic weights to elements, while Henry Moseley gave them atomic numbers. Finally, the French chemists Marie Curie and her husband, Pierre, discovered radium (1898), an element that is radioactive.

A Matter of Change

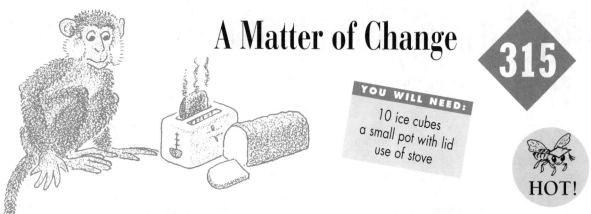

YOU WILL NEED:
10 ice cubes
a small pot with lid
use of stove

HOT!

Sometimes things change. When toast burns it is no longer the same substance. Its molecules have been rearranged by heat. What is left is carbon, an entirely new substance. This is called a chemical change. However, when ice turns to water and then to a gas, the molecules of water do not change. The forms which the substance takes change but the substance, water, does not. This is called a natural change. Let's see how this works.

What to do: Put the ice cubes in the pot and melt them on the stove. Once the cubes turn to water and the water starts to boil, place the lid on the pot. Let it boil for a few minutes, and then turn the heat off and let the pot cool. Then, as you lift the lid, observe the water drops on the underside.

What happens: The ice turns to water, the water to steam, a gas which we sometimes call water vapor, and the steam back into water.

Why: Ice is a solid. Its molecules move slowly but they do move. When you heat the ice cubes, the molecules move faster. The ice gets warmer and melts. When you continue to heat the water further, the molecules move even faster, bump into each other, and escape, leaving the liquid. The water drops that collect on the inside of the lid are a result of water vapor (gas). As the pot cools, the vapor turns back into water (liquid). This process is known as condensation. Chemists identify what happens in this experiment as demonstrating the three states of matter: solid, liquid, and gas.

The Water Factory

316

HOT!

In this experiment, you'll become a wizard of chemistry. You'll distill water, or take salt out of it, and you won't need a lot of expensive chemistry equipment to do it. Impossible, you say! Try it and find out. Adult help is recommended

What to do: Drop a few grains of salt into the jar of water. Stir it with a spoon and take a taste. The water should taste salty; if not, add a few more grains of salt. Put the jar of salt solution in the microwwave (without lid) for about 90 seconds, or until the water comes to a boil.

Do not touch or remove the jar from the microwave! The water is scalding hot!

Carefully reach in with a mitt or folded dish towel and hold the jar while you screw on the lid. (Better yet, get an adult to do it for you.) After the jar has thoroughly cooled, unscrew the lid and taste the water drops under it or on the sides of the jar.

What happens: The water drops on the sides of the jar or under the lid do not taste salty.

Why: The boiling water in the closed jar makes steam (water vapor) that collects as condensation (water drops) that forms on the sides of the jar or under the lid. Salt is a compound that will not leave the water (in steam) when boiled, so the salt is removed from the steam. This is a good way to purify water.

What's the Solution?

Chemists study suspensions and solutions—what are they all about? Try this simple experiment and find out.

What to do: Add the soil to one jar of water, the salt to the other. Stir both. Look through your hand lens at both jars.

What happens: The particles of soil appear to be hanging in the water. Because of their weight, the larger soil particles settle to the bottom of the jar first, followed by the medium particles, and then the smaller ones. The particles of salt in the other jar have disappeared, or dissolved.

Why: The soil did not dissolve, or mix and disappear, into the water, because soil and water are composed of molecules of different types. These different molecules cannot chemically combine. The soil and water are what chemists call a "suspension" because the soil particles spread, or become suspended, throughout the water and then later settle to the bottom of the jar, or come out of suspension. But water and salt do combine. The salt dissolves, or seems to disappear, in the water. Its particles (crystals) do not fall to the bottom of the jar. This is an example of a solution. Chemists call the solid molecules that become part of a solution, such as salt, a "solute," and the liquid molecules, such as water, a "solvent."

Act I: All Mixed Up!

318

YOU WILL NEED:
¼ cup of flour
¼ cup of salt
glass
spoon
hot tap water

Chemists often talk about solutions and suspensions, and also emulsions and mixtures. In a solution, one substance is thoroughly dissolved in another (salt and water). In a suspension, one substance is mixed throughout the other, but is not dissolved (soil and water).

In an emulsion, one liquid "floats" in another, but is not dissolved. The spread mayonnaise is a perfect example of an emulsion. But a mixture, unlike the above, is made up of different substances that do not dissolve into one another or stay together. Salt and flour may be really mixed up, but don't you be! Try this experiment and find out what's going on.

What to do: Stir flour and salt together in the glass (do not add the water yet). Is it thoroughly mixed? Add the hot water to fill the glass. Stir well and wait about 30 minutes; then reach in with your finger and taste the water.

What happens: The water at the top tastes salty, and white covers the bottom of the glass.

Why: Salt and flour is a perfect mixture. These substances are so different that they cannot dissolve or chemically mix in any way. They also react differently to water. While the flour floats and then sinks to the bottom of the glass, the salt dissolves into the water to form a salt solution above the flour.

Save the mixture for the next experiment, "Act II: Bring Back the Substance."

Act II:
Bring Back the Substance

YOU WILL NEED:

wide-mouth jar
coffee filter
salt and flour mixture
(from last experiment)
rubber band
hot tap water
shallow container

Since salt and flour were so good in "Act I: All Mixed Up!" let's bring them back. So, here they are again, folks—salt and flour!

What to do: Place the filter over the top of the jar and put the rubber band around it to keep it in place. Let the filter droop or sag a little in the middle so that it will hold the water more easily. Pour the salty water and flour mixture from the last experiment slowly onto the filter. Very slowly, add a little bit of hot water to help the salt solution break through the flour. Be patient! It will take some time to recover, or get back, a good amount of salt solution. Save as much as you want, and then take the filter off the jar. Pour the salt solution out of the jar into the shallow container. Let it stand in a warm place for 24 hours.

What happens: The flour stays on the top of the filter while the salt in the water passes through it. When the water eventually evaporates from the shallow container, it leaves salt crystals behind.

Why: The molecules of solid salt crystals (called a solute by chemists) that had dissolved in the water (solvent) could pass freely through the filter, while the flour grains, which are much too large and do not dissolve, remained on top.

Because water evaporates but salt cannot, the salt molecules left behind as the water disappeared reformed into crystals.

Drop Out!

320

Water and oil act differently as this experiment will show.

YOU WILL NEED:

2 small shallow containers
2 tablespoons of oil
2 tablespoons of water
white construction paper
scissors
paper towels or napkins
food coloring
medicine dropper

What to do: Place the oil into one shallow container and the water into the other. Cut two small strips from the construction paper. Dip one paper strip into the oil and the other into the water; then place them on the paper towels or napkins. Drop a drop of food coloring on each.

What happens: The drop of food coloring on the oiled paper sits on the surface while the drop on the water-dipped paper spreads out.

Why: The food coloring, which is water–based, sits as a drop on the oiled paper because its water molecules will not combine with the oil. A substance is called "immiscible" with another when it does not combine to become one substance. The food coloring on the water-dipped paper is said to be "miscible" with it. It dissolves on the paper strip and spreads out, even beyond the paper. Its molecules combine as do the molecules in a solution.

321

Chromatography: Watercolor

YOU WILL NEED:

red and blue food coloring
medicine dropper
a small container
2 white napkins or paper towels
newspaper
a cup of water

Chemists needed a way to separate substances such as dyes and chemical mixtures into their separate parts. In this experiment, we'll mix two different food colors and see if we can bring them back. This is a simple version of what chemists call "chromatography."

What to do: Mix 2 to 3 drops each of red and blue food coloring in the same small container. Put the two napkins together and place them on top of the newspaper. Pour the colored mixture in the center of the napkins. With the medicine dropper, squirt water on the food coloring and try to separate the colors.

What happens: The colored mixture separates into purple (red-blue) and light blue areas.

Why: The water acts as a solvent, dissolving the food coloring solution. Because the colors dissolve at different rates, they separate into circular colored areas as the solvent travels through the absorbent, spongelike napkins.

Fluttering Flatworm Marathon

Enter these fantastic paper flatworms in a marathon, or race, and see which one wins. It's all based on molecules, too!

What to do: Fold the strips back and forth, accordion-style. Line them up evenly on the kitchen counter. Load the medicine dropper(s) with water. Let a few drops of water fall on the ends and middle of the paper strips and try to extend, or stretch, the worms across an imaginary finish line.

What happens: The paper worms seem to flutter and turn.

Why: The thousands of open holes in the paper fill with water. This "capillary action" expands, or makes larger, those parts of the paper. As the paper expands, it moves, and so do your flatworms!

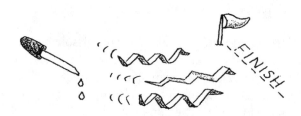

How to Make a Hydrometer

A hydrometer is an instrument that measures the density, or heaviness, of water compared to other solutions. You can make your own with just a few simple materials, but be patient, as it may take a few trials before you get your instrument to float properly.

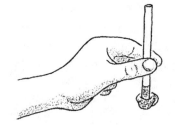

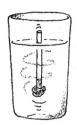

What to do: Cut the straw in half. Close one end of the halved straw with the clay and form it into a small ball. Pour a small amount of salt into the top of the straw to weight it. The salt should rise about a ½ inch (1 cm) in the straw. Hold the straw up to the light to see the level.

Now, gently and carefully, lower the hydrometer into the water. It should float freely and straight up, and should not touch the bottom of the glass. If the straw does not float correctly, straight in the water, adjust the salt in the straw or the water in the glass until it does.

Hydrometer Holdup

This hydrometer experiment is designed to make a real chemist out of you. In the experiments in this book, but particularly this one, you will need to control all the variables. This means that all the materials and measurements will need to be the same. You will need to be patient here, too. It may take a little time to get your hydrometer and measurements adjusted, but you will succeed!

What to do: Put one rubber band around the bottom of the glass of water and the other around the top. Carefully place the hydrometer in the water. Again, it should float freely straight up and should not touch the bottom of the glass. Push the hydrometer close to the side of the glass, being careful not to push the open end of it under the water, and let it float freely. Adjust the bottom rubber band around the glass so that it marks the bottom of the clay ball on the hydrometer. This will measure how far your instrument drops in the water. Move the top rubber band to mark the level of the water in the glass. Now, keep your same position and watch the rubber band

markers as you slowly and carefully add the first tablespoon of salt to the water, followed by the second. Make certain that the hydrometer is above the level of the water at all times and that the top of the straw does not fill with water or salt.

What happens: In the salty water, the hydrometer floats higher and rises above the bottom rubber band. The water level of the salty water also rises above the top rubber band.

Why: Salt water is denser, or heavier, than tap water, so fewer water molecules are displaced, or forced out of position, by the weight of the hydrometer. So the straw sinks less in the salty water and rises above the rubber band.

Sí, C!

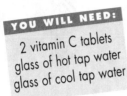

No, you won't learn Spanish from this experiment, but you will learn how long it takes for vitamin C tablets to dissolve in hot or cool tap water (solubility).

YOU WILL NEED:

2 vitamin C tablets
glass of hot tap water
glass of cool tap water

What to do: Drop one vitamin C tablet in the cool tap water and one in the hot water.

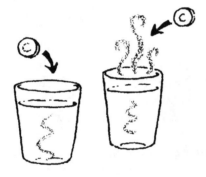

What happens: The vitamin C tablet in the hot water dissolves faster than the vitamin C tablet in cool water.

Why: The solid molecules of vitamin C tablet (solute) in the hot water (solvent) dissolve faster, or are more soluble, because heat energy from the water causes the molecules in the vitamin C tablet to vibrate and move farther apart. Without heat energy, no such sudden change can occur.

326 Tip of the Iceberg

YOU WILL NEED:

glass
warm water
6 to 8 ice cubes

If all the icebergs in the seas were to melt, would the sea level rise? This very simple experiment will give us the answer, and it's based on a very important compound chemists study—water!

What to do: Place as many ice cubes as you can into a glass; then fill the glass to the brim with warm water. Wait.

What happens: When the ice cubes melt, the water does not overflow.

Why: The ice cubes simply displaced the water in the glass, or the amount of ice that melted was exactly equal to the mass of the ice cubes below the water. Like the ice cubes in the glass, the main part of an iceberg is under water. If all the icebergs were to melt, as did the ice cubes in our experiment, the sea level would remain the same.

Air is Real

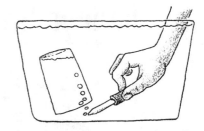

How do you know air is real? Since it is invisible, you certainly can't see it. Can you prove it really exists? The following experiment will give you the answer. Roll up your sleeves for this one!

What to do: Fill the glass with water. Put the water proof pad over the mouth of the glass. Hold it in place with your hand. Now, carefully turn the glass upside down and place it under the water in the pot or basin until it is completely under the surface. Do not remove the pad until the glass is completely under the water and touching the bottom of the pot.

Observe the water level in the glass. Tilt the glass to one side and carefully place the empty medicine dropper under it. Squeeze the dropper. Remove the dropper from the pot and squeeze the water out of it. Repeat what you did before (squeezing the empty dropper under the glass). Do this several times. You'll know you're doing this experiment correctly when, after squeezing the dropper, you see bubbles entering the glass of water.

What happens: Air bubbles move up the inside of the glass, and the water level in the glass gets lower.

Why: Air was in the medicine dropper when you squeezed it. The bubbles on the side of the glass were the air forced out of the dropper. As you "pumped" air into the glass with the dropper over and over, you saw the water level in the glass go down. Since the air had to go somewhere, it displaced some of the water, forcing it out of the glass. Now you know that air is real. It takes up space.

328 Pop Top

When its air is warmed, will a pop bottle pop its top?

What to do: Wet the cap of the soda bottle and place it upside down on the top of the container. Gently place your hands around the bottle. Hold it, but do not squeeze it.

What happens: The cap jumps or pops off the bottle.

Why: When you place your hands around the bottle, you warm the air inside it and the molecules of warm air expand and try to escape. The wet cap at first acts as a seal and keeps the air in place, but eventually some of it manages to escape and pushes the lid to the side or off the top of the bottle. If the cap doesn't fall and you keep your hands placed around the bottle, you can continue to make it jump.

Banana Split

329

Can you place a banana in a bottle without using your hands? Amaze your friends with this party–trick science experiment. Watch carefully, because the banana is quicker than the eye in this split–second surprise. Moreover, it all has to do with molecules and air.

Careful—boiling water involved! Also, it's best to do this in the sink.

YOU WILL NEED:

½ banana, peeled
teakettle with boiling water
clean, long, narrow bottle
(with banana-size mouth)
funnel
dish towel

What to do: Put the funnel into the bottle neck and carefully fill the bottle almost to the top with boiling water (adult help recommended). Remove the funnel. Wrap a dish towel around the bottle and gently swirl the water around; then pour it out. Quickly, fit the pointed end of the half-banana downwards into the bottle neck so that it makes an airtight plug. (Watch the variables—the size of the banana and bottle neck, the amount of hot water, the time it takes—and be patient! You may have to do this experiment several times to get it right, but you will succeed!)

What happens: The banana is sucked down into the bottom of the bottle.

Why: The heat from the boiling water causes the air inside the bottle to expand, forcing some of it out. When the banana is placed into the mouth of the bottle and the cooling air inside the bottle shrinks again, the air pressure inside is reduced, and the greater air pressure outside shoves the banana ahead of it into the bottle. This gives you an idea of what happens when air is removed from a space and nothing takes its place (partial vacuum). Just small differences in air pressure can cause things to move.

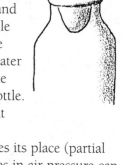

What now: You want to recycle the bottle, but the banana is inside it! What can you do?

Just wait a few days. Let the bacteria in the banana do their chemistry work. Bacteria give off enzymes that break down proteins and starches. The banana will eventually change chemically (ferment) and soften enough to be removed easily.

330 Air Force

YOU WILL NEED:
funnel
small, narrow-neck bottle
small piece of clay
glass of water

Molecules of air not only take up space, they can even stop water from entering a bottle.

What to do: Place the funnel in the bottle. Roll a small clay rope and fit it around the funnel in the bottle neck. Press the clay rope in firmly around the funnel to seal it completely, making the bottle airtight. Now, slowly pour a small amount of water into the bottle, a little at a time. Continue to do this until you've completely emptied the glass.

What happens: At first, water will enter the bottle, but as you continue to pour the water, less will enter. Finally, the funnel will fill up with water and none will enter the bottle.

Why: The molecules of air in the closed bottle will eventually press together and take up all the space there is, and so will stop any more water from entering.

331 Dry Goods

YOU WILL NEED:
small glass
napkin or
paper towel
glass bowl
water

Molecules of air can even stop paper from getting wet in a glass of water.

What to do:
Crumple the paper and place it in the bottom of the glass. Make certain it is tight so that the paper will not fall out. Fill the bowl with water. Now, turn the glass upside down over the bowl and lower it until it touches the bottom of the bowl. Lift the glass straight up out of the bowl. Continue to keep it upside down as you dry around and inside the rim of it. Now, take the paper out of the glass.

What happens: The paper inside the glass remains dry.

Why: When the glass is pushed into the water, the molecules of air do not escape but instead are pressed together and act as a shield between the water and the paper. Some water enters the glass but not enough to wet the paper. The molecules of air take up enough space to block it.

332

Soft-Touch Soapsuds

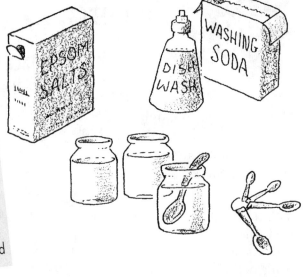

Did you know that water can be hard or soft? What effect does that have on soap-suds? (You'll use two chemical compounds again, Epsom salts and washing soda, or sodium carbonate.)

What to do: Fill all three containers with warm water. Pour the Epsom salts in one container. Stir the solution thoroughly. Do the same with the washing soda in the second container. Add a teaspoon of dishwashing liquid to each container, including the one with plain tap water. Stir each of the solutions and try to make suds.

What happens: Suds form in the water with the washing soda, but few form in the water with the Epsom salts.

Why: Washing soda "softens" water, while Epsom salts is a mineral that makes water "hard."

Tap water often contains calcium salts, which stops soap from making suds. If water has a lot of salts, it is called "hard." Washing soda "softens" or neutralizes the calcium salts in the water and forms a solid substance, called a precipitate, that falls to the bottom of a solution when a chemical reaction takes place. (This is where that ring or scum comes from in the bathtub.)

Epsom salts is a mineral that makes water hard. That is why you couldn't get soapsuds to form. Did your plain tap water make suds? Is your tap water hard or soft, or in between? Now empty the solutions in each glass. What do you see on the sides of the Epsom salts and washing soda containers?

HERE'S SUPERMAN, BUT WHERE'S CLARK?

When Clark Kent changes into Superman, he is no longer the same person. Clark is nowhere to be seen when Superman flies through the air.

In some ways, chemical reactions or changes are like Clark and Superman. After a chemical change or reaction, the molecules of a substance are no longer the same. The substance has changed completely.

Chemical changes occur every day everywhere—even our bodies are chemical factories. The food we eat combines with oxygen and causes a chemical change which releases heat and energy. Other chemical changes include the burning of coal, oil, gasoline, and wood. Chemists also produce chemical changes that make new products such as clothing, plastics, cleaners, paints, and foods.

In this chapter, we'll take oxygen from a compound, produce carbon dioxide from other substances, and even take two substances and make a new chemical compound called a precipitate.

These are just a few of the many exciting experiments which involve atoms being rearranged to make new substances.

333 ◆ Very Berry Litmus Paper

Here is your chance to make your own litmus paper to test for acids and alkalis, called bases. It's done with berries and it's very berry easy!

YOU WILL NEED:

½ cup of berries (blackberries, blueberries, or strawberries)

small strips cut from white construction paper

small bowl

fork

water

teaspoon

paper towels

What to do: Remove any stems and place the berries in a bowl. Crush the berries with the fork until they look like jam. Add a little water to thin the juice. Dip the paper strips in the juice and spoon the juice over them until they are well coated. Slide the strips between your thumb and finger to remove the pulp. Place the strips on paper towels to dry. When they are dry, pick off any big pieces of pulp or berry skins you missed and your Very Berry litmus paper is ready for use.

What Do the Color Changes Mean?

Purple blackberry litmus turns pinkish-red in acids and deep purple in alkali compounds, or bases. These strips work best for litmus testing, for they show the most change.

Purple blueberry litmus turns reddish-purple in acids and light bluish-purple in bases.

Pink strawberry (although not as noticeable as the other two) turns bright pink in acids and light pinkish-blue in bases.

Thoroughly confused? Not to worry! We can tell you how to remember this easily: the paper that has more red in it is reacting to acids, while the paper that has more blue in it is reacting to bases.

Litmus Lotto

334

Why: Vinegar is acetic acid but soapy water is an alkali compound, or base. The berry-colored litmus papers are positive tests to determine which substances are acids or bases.

Note: Keep containers, litmus paper, pencil, and paper for the next experiment.

Are you ready to test your homemade Very Berry litmus paper? By dipping the paper into different solutions, you can find out if the substance is acid or alkali (a substance that can dissolve in water and weaken acids). When we test how much acid or alkali a substance has, we say we are testing for the pH of that substance.

YOU WILL NEED:

2 homemade Very Berry litmus strips

2 small containers, one with a lid

3 tablespoons of dishwashing liquid

½ cup of water

¼ cup of vinegar

paper and pencil

newspaper

What to do: First read "What do the color changes mean?" before continuing. Put the water and dishwashing liquid into the container with a lid, close it up and shake to mix well. Put the vinegar into the other container. Dip strips of litmus paper into the solutions. Hypothesize, or guess, if the color change will show whether that solution is acid or alkali. Write down the name of the solution (dishwashing liquid and vinegar), and record your answers. Now dry the strips of litmus on the paper towels (about five minutes) and label them as to what solutions they were dipped into and what color changes were noticed. Was your hypothesis, or guess, correct?

What happens: The litmus dipped into the vinegar has more red in it. The litmus dipped into the soapy water has more blue in it.

More Litmus Lotto

335

Are you ready to do some more testing with litmus paper? Basically, you'll be doing the same thing as you did in "Litmus Lotto" but with different substances.

YOU WILL NEED:

2 homemade Very Berry litmus strips

½ cup of water, with 2 or 3 squirts of window cleaner with ammonia (Be careful! This solution can be harmful! Dispose of it carefully when finished!)

¼ cup of lemon juice

What to do: Dip the litmus strips and record your guesses and the results of the test as you did under "Litmus Lotto."

What happens: The litmus that was dipped into the lemon juice will have more red in it, but the one that was dipped into the window-cleaner ammonia will show more blue.

Why: Lemon juice is another acid, called citric acid, but the ammonia solution is an alkali compound. Can you guess what other fruits may have citric acid, and test your hypothesis?

pH Power

Use your Very Berry litmus paper again to test your tap water, soil, swimming pool or pond water, even your saliva (spit)!

What to do: Dip the strips of litmus paper into the samples. (See "What to do" under "Litmus Lotto.")

What happens: The strips will change color depending on whether the samples are more acid or alkali.

Why: The litmus papers are positive tests for the acids or bases in substances. (See "What do the color changes mean?")

Starch Search

How do you know if certain substances contain starch? Starch, a substance found in plants, gives us energy (sugars and fats do, too!). Chemists are especially interested in starch because it is a compound made up of carbon, hydrogen, and oxygen. This experiment will help us find out if a solution has starch.

What to do: Spoon the cornstarch into the bottle of water. Add the drops of iodine to the water. Swirl the contents around and then let the solution "rest" for a few minutes.

What happens: The water turns dark blue or purple.

Why: Iodine is a good test for starch. It combines chemically with starch, in this case cornstarch, to produce the dark blue color. Chemists regularly use iodine for this purpose.

Look up iodine on the Periodic Table of Elements chart. What does it tell you about the iodine atom?

Note: Iodine is a poisonous chemical. Get adult help, if needed, and dispose of this chemical experiment carefully when finished! Wash thoroughly any utensils you wish to keep!

Plant Power

Plants don't eat. They make their own food from the energy of the sun (a process called photosynthesis). They change water and carbon dioxide into glucose, a kind of sugar, and oxygen. The sugar is then turned into starch. Both the sugar and the starch help plants live.

338 The Great Oxygen Escape

If you can add an atom, can you subtract one—or release an element from a compound? Watch carefully! Oxygen will actually escape before your very own eyes in this electric and thrilling experiment.

What to do: Stick a small piece of modelling clay on the bottom of the bottle. (This will anchor the bottle down and keep it steady under the water.) Put the hydrogen peroxide into the bottle and then drop in the iron rust. Lower the container into the bowl of hot water and press it against the bottom. Watch the bottle closely through the magnifying hand lens.

What happens: Many small bubbles come from the bottle of hydrogen peroxide.

YOU WILL NEED:

small amount of rust
(scraped from old iron object)
1 tablespoon of hydrogen peroxide
small bottle or jar
(to hold hydrogen peroxide)
small, deep container or bowl filled
with hot tap water
(to submerge small bottle)
modelling clay
magnifying glass

Why: A molecule of hydrogen peroxide (H_2O_2) contains one more atom of oxygen than a molecule of water (H_2O). When you drop the iron rust into the peroxide and place the container into the hot water, a chemical change takes place. The bubbles you see in the peroxide solution are really groupings of those "extra" oxygen atoms being released from the hydrogen peroxide compound.

Flour Power

YOU WILL NEED:
slice of rye bread
paper
pencil

Chemists know proteins as chemical compounds. Protein called gluten is found in grains, especially wheat. Now let's see how we can put the gluten in bread to work as a chemical.

What to do: With the pencil, scribble two or three dark areas on the paper. Tear off a piece of rye bread and rub it hard across the dark scribbled areas.

What happens: The bread works like an eraser and cleans the paper.

Why: The gluten protein in the rye bread is sticky. When you rub the bread across the dark pencilled areas, you lift the marks from the paper using the sticky protein.

Rye Clean

You know now why scientists use gluten in substances to clean things. But what things? The sticky protein in bread will erase pencil marks, but will it remove other spots? Soil your fingers with dirt, oil, or jam. Rub your fingers on the paper to make soiled areas on it. Now test how well the rye bread cleans these.

341

Color Me Gone

What happens to tea when you put lemon into it?

What to do: Squeeze a little of the first piece of lemon into the tea. Continue to increase the amount of lemon in the tea until all of the quarters are fully squeezed and used up.

What happens: The lemon causes the color of the tea to completely fade.

Why: The citric acid in lemon is a bleaching agent that reacts chemically with the dye in the tea to lighten it.

342

Detergent Derby

How do laundry detergents work?

What to do: Add the detergent to one of the jars. Screw the lid on, shake the jar, and remove the lid. The other jar will contain only plain water. Now drop three or four pieces of string into each jar and watch what happens to the strings.

What happens: The strings in the jar of plain water float on the surface, while the strings in the detergent water soon sink to the bottom.

Why: The strings that dropped to the bottom of the glass of detergent water had become water-soaked. The water and detergent mixture is an emulsion, or liquids floating in one another. This emulsion caused the strings to get wetter faster. The simple idea of using detergent as a "wetting agent" helps to remove dirt from clothes.

Keep materials for the next experiment, "Clean as a Whistle."

Clean as a Whistle

343

Now let's really challenge agent detergent, using newly soiled strings.

What to do: Soil pairs of strings in juice, grease, dirt, oil, ketchup, mustard, or whatever you have, and drop one of each pair into each jar or glass. Stir the contents of each container. After ten minutes, remove the strings from the jars.

What happens: The strings in the detergent-water solution appear cleaner, while the strings in the glass of plain water do not.

Why: Again, the emulsifying effect of the detergent in the water thoroughly soaks the strings and easily lifts the dirt from them. This is seen by the now discolored water in the detergent-water solution.

Take it to the Cleaners

344

Chemists are always working with new chemicals and trying to find out which ones clean best. Some everyday foods found around the kitchen make good cleaners, too, but which ones?

What to do: With the margarine, oil, or butter, make several grease marks, or stains, on the cloth. Make certain they are not too close together. Take the cloth and spread it out on a hard kitchen surface. Squeeze some lemon juice onto a paper towel and, while holding the cloth against the hard surface, rub the juice on the towel against one of the marks. Rub hard and try to remove the stain. Crush the onion in another paper towel to make some juice and try to remove a second stain with it in the same way. Do the same with the other two substances. Make certain you record on the cloth which substances you used to clean the different grease stains.

What happens: The lemon, onion, and vinegar remove stains a little, but not as well as the milk does.

Why: The milk does a better job of neutralizing, or canceling out, the stains. This is a case of "Like will dissolve like." The butterfat in whole milk will dissolve grease stains such as that caused by fat in butter or margarine. Substances that have similar fat content will dissolve one another.

345 Put Out the Fire

Make your own fire extinguisher with a few materials you can find around your house.

What to do: First, on a rock outside or on an old workbench or board, turn the lid of the large jar over, and with the hammer and nail pound a large hole through it. (Get adult help, if needed!)

Pour the water into the large jar. Add and mix in the baking soda. Fill the small jar with vinegar and gently place it, without a lid, into the large jar, making certain that the vinegar jar does not spill its contents. Screw the punctured lid onto the large jar. Turn the lid away from your face and tip the jar towards the sink.

What happens: A foamy liquid spurts out of the hole in the lid.

Why: Baking soda (sodium bicarbonate) puts out fires when used in soda-acid fire extinguishers. In your homemade version, the vinegar (acetic acid) mixes with the baking soda to produce the carbon-dioxide gas (CO_2) that smothers fires.

346 Eggs-tra Bounce: What Did You Eggs-pect?

Can an egg be changed chemically by placing it in different compounds?

What to do: Put one egg in a glass of water and let it stand for a full 24 hours. Place the other egg in the vinegar and let it stand for the same length of time.

What happens: The egg in the water remains the same, while the egg in the vinegar compound now feels and looks like a rubber ball, and no longer has a shell! If you drop it a short distance into the sink, it will actually bounce. Now you know how this experiment got its name.

Why: In the vinegar, a chemical change took place in the egg. The acetic acid (vinegar) reacted with the calcium carbonate of the eggshell. The change caused the shell to soften and disappear, while the egg in the glass of water did not chemically change. Chemists would say that the shell of the egg in the vinegar becomes "decalcified."

No Bones about It!

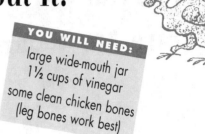

Can you make chicken bones soft and even bend them? Try this experiment and see.

What to do: Place the vinegar in the jar and put the clean bones in it. Make certain the bones are completely covered by the vinegar. Leave the bones to set for two days.

What happens: The chicken bones are no longer hard, but soft.

Why: Bones are chiefly made up of the minerals calcium and phosphorus. When you soak the chicken bones in vinegar (acetic acid), a chemical change takes place and the mineral (stiffening) matter in them dissolves.

Water Softener

How would you like to make your own bath solution? This solution will make your water softer, and soft water makes more suds to clean you better. It's fun and easy, and it's real chemistry.

What to do: Pour some of the washing soda into the saucer. With the back of the spoon, crush the crystals of washing soda into a fine powder. Spoon the washing soda powder into the jar of water a little at a time until no more will dissolve. (If needed, crush more washing soda powder and add it to the jar of water.) You now have a "saturated solution." Store the solution in the jar and add a small amount to the water when you take your bath.

What happens: The washing soda dissolves in the water and creates a natural bathwater softener.

Why: Sodium carbonate, or washing soda, neutralizes, or softens, water by removing hard bath salts, such as calcium. When this happens, chemists call it precipitation, but unlike weather forecasters, they don't mean rain, the soft water that falls from the sky. Here, precipitation is the chemical splitting of the two compounds calcium salts and washing soda into simpler molecules which form a solid substance called a precipitate. (See also "Presto-Perfect Precipitate")

349 Designer Bath Solution

Add special cologne, scents, or other ingredients, such as coloring, to make your solution look and smell good. Put your special bath softener in fancy-shaped bottles or jars, and tie on some colorful ribbons. It makes a great and inexpensive homemade gift, and a little simple chemistry makes it all possible!

350 Shiny Silver Coins

HOT!

Why not make your own silver cleaner? It's cheaper and may be better than cleaner from the store.

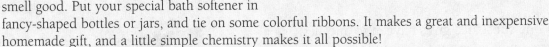

YOU WILL NEED:
small container with water
1 teaspoon of baking soda
1 teaspoon of salt
aluminum foil
small enamel or glass pot
silver coins
water
use of stove
soft cloth

What to do: In the small container, dissolve the salt and soda in a small amount of water. Place the coins in the water so that it covers them. Fill the small glass or enamel pot with water. Tear the aluminum foil into pieces and add them to the pot. Bring the water in the pot to a boil on the stove (you may want to ask a parent to assist you), then turn off the heat and let the water stand and cool. Remove the coins from the salt and soda solution. Rinse the coins in the cooled aluminum water, and dry them with a soft cloth.

What happpens: You are now the proud owner of many shiny, sparkling-clean coins.

Why: Chemical reactions take place among the salt and soda (loosens tarnish) and the aluminum-foil solution. The heat turns the water and aluminum foil into an electrolyte solution, which carries a mild electric current that takes the tarnish off the coins.

Oxidation: Rust Race

When one substance gives oxygen to another, chemists say it is "reduced," and the substance that receives the oxygen is said to be "oxidized." Confused? Think of it this way: You have ten balls that stand for oxygen and a friend takes seven of them. Your friend would be oxidized, because he received extra oxygen from you, but you would be reduced because you lost some of your oxygen. Now you can produce this chemical change, oxidation, and see how it works.

What to do: Place a selection of metal objects into the various jars. Add two tablespoons of one of the liquids to each jar. Screw lids tightly on some jars; leave the other jars without lids. Place some of your experiments in shady, cool places, others in warm, sunny places. Set the experiments aside for one to three weeks. Keep good records: dates and times you started the experiments, substances used, and what happens.

What happens: A reddish-brown or brownish-yellow substance forms on some of the metal objets, but maybe not on all.

Why: Moisture, an oxidizing agent, causes oxygen from the air to attach to certain metals, like iron and steel, to form rust. This chemical change, called oxidation, corrodes, or rots, metals. That is why bridges and fire escapes, which often get wet, must be painted to protect them from being rotted and weakened by oxidation.

Why Rust?

In the last experiment did some objects rust while others didn't? Try to figure out why. Perhaps the oxidation takes a longer time, or the object is protected by a coating of non-rusting material. Redo the experiments exactly, or change one of the variables, and see what happens then. Compare the results.

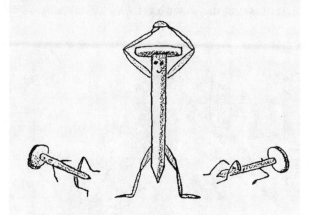

Copperhead

353

YOU WILL NEED:
dark, dull copper coins
small, flat container
2 disposable cups
1 teaspoon of salt
1 tablespoon of water
2 tablespoons of vinegar
medicine dropper
paper towel

Can you see whose head is on the penny or other dark, copper coins? If they are very dark and dull, it may be hard to tell. But it only takes a few minutes and a little simple chemistry to turn that dirty, dull copper into bright, shiny coins.

What to do: Place the coins in the container. In one cup, make a solution with the salt and water. Pour the vinegar into the other cup. With the medicine dropper, drop the salt solution on the pennies, followed by the vinegar. Repeat these steps and keep the pennies in the solution for five minutes. Clean the pennies by wiping them off with a damp paper towel.

What happens: The pennies turn shiny-bright and the dark and dull film is removed.

Why: The vinegar (acetic acid) when combined with the salt (sodium chloride) chemically changes into a weak solution of hydrochloric acid. Hydrochloric acid cleans metals like copper. After a while, the pennies will oxidize, or become dull and dark, again because of the water and oxygen molecules that they come in contact with in the air.

The Gas Guzzler

A car is called a gas guzzler when it wastes gas. In this experiment, gas wastes water. Try it and see!

What to do: Place the baking soda in the middle of the square of the filter. Gather the filter together to make a pouch and fasten the top with a rubber band. Place the baking soda pouch in the tall jar of water and place your hand over the opening. With your hands in place on the bottom and the top of the jar, turn the jar upside down and place its opening in the bowl of water. Remove your hands. Mark the water line on the jar. Watch the glass jar with the hand lens. Be patient; you must wait at least an hour for results.

What happens: Bubbles rise from the pouch in the bottom of the jar to the top of it. Some bubbles cling to the sides of the jar. Within an hour, the water drops slightly, but noticeably, below the marked water line.

Why: As the baking soda in the pouch is dissolved by the water, it produces carbon dioxide gas (CO_2). This gas needs room in the jar, so it displaces the water, or forces some of it out of the jar, lowering the water level.

355 King Kong's Hand

YOU WILL NEED:

disposable latex glove
(available in packages of ten)
¼ cup of baking soda
½ cup of vinegar
brown or black
permanent marker pen
(optional)

King Kong's hand must have been very big to hold a lady in it. Now, you can make your own big hand with just a few simple materials. Without the marker lines, the hand becomes a cow's udder, the bag under the cow that holds its milk—an udderly fantastic trick! Anyway you look at it, it's pure chemistry and it will teach you about an important gas that all chemists know.

What to do: A friend or assistant would be helpful for this experiment, and it's best done over a sink or basin (or outside) as it can be messy!

For a King Kong hand, make short vertical lines with the marker pen on each side of the glove to represent King Kong's hairy hand. If you're making a cow's udder, leave the glove plain.

Have your helper hold the glove over the sink or basin while you pour the baking soda, followed by the vinegar, into the glove. Now, very quickly, close the opening of the glove with your hand to make an airtight seal. Hold it tightly for several minutes.

What happens: The glove blows up like a balloon, then after several minutes goes back to its normal size.

Why: When you mixed the baking soda and vinegar together, you made a very popular gas called carbon dioxide (CO_2). This is why the solution started to fizz and foam up and spill out over the top of the glove before you closed it up. Once the gas is trapped in the glove, it has no place to go, so it blows the glove up. Eventually, the reaction grows less, the gas succeeds in escaping, and the glove returns to its normal size.

What a Gas

Baking soda (sodium bicarbonate) is a compound made up of the elements hydrogen, sodium, oxygen, and carbon. When vinegar is added (water and acetic acid), a chemical reaction takes place; the elements carbon and oxygen link together to make a new gaseous compound called carbon dioxide.

Exothermic Exercise

What kind of chemical change takes place when yeast mixes with hydrogen peroxide? This extremely exciting experiment is bound to warm you up.

YOU WILL NEED:
thermometer
small bowl
1 tablespoon of
quick-rising dry yeast
¼ cup of hydrogen peroxide
spoon
pencil and paper

What to do: Record the temperature showing on the thermometer, and then place it in the bowl. Pour in the hydrogen peroxide, add the yeast, and stir the solution. As you watch what happens, feel the lower sides and bottom of the bowl. Wait a minute or two; then spoon out the thermometer and record the temperature again.

What happens: The solution foams up and bubbles, and the bottom and sides of the bowl feel very warm. Steam can be seen coming from the solution. The higher thermometer reading shows that heat has been produced.

Why: When yeast and hydrogen peroxide mix chemically, the hydrogen peroxide changes into oxygen and water molecules. The bubbles are produced by the oxygen gas escaping during the chemical change. This change also produces heat. When heat is produced in a chemical change, we call the process exothermic.

Endothermic Cold Wave

YOU WILL NEED:

thermometer
1 tablespoon of Epsom salts
tap water, neither hot nor cold
spoon
medium-size jar
pencil and paper

If a chemical change can cause heat (exothermic), can another chemical change make something cold?

Caution: Epsom salts can be a harmful solution. Dispose of it carefully after use.

What to do: Fill the jar with tap water. Place the thermometer in the water. With your hand, feel the coolness of the jar while you wait until the thermometer registers the water's temperature. Write the temperature down. Now stir in the Epsom salts. Feel the jar again. Is there a change? After a couple of minutes, take out the thermometer and record the temperature again.

What happens: The jar feels slightly colder, and the temperature of the water after the chemical change is actually lower.

Why: In the previous experiment "Exothermic Exercise," a chemical change produced heat energy. But sometimes heat is instead used up in the chemical change. When Epsom salts, or magnesium sulfate, is added to water, it uses the water's natural heat energy to split apart ions of sulfate and magnesium. (Ions are positive or negative electrically charged atoms that occur when electrons are lost or gained.)

The chemical change in this experiment is called endothermic because more heat energy is being used up than is being produced. This is why the water gets colder, and why Epsom salts are used to soak a sprained ankle and draw the heat out of an injury.

It's Simply Marbelous!

YOU WILL NEED:

*colored chalk
*half sheets of white paper
*2 to 6 disposable cups

hammer or heavy stone
(for crushing chalk)

2 tablespoons of vinegar
paper towels or napkins

disposable plastic
spoon or fork

large bowl or basin
(plastic or rubber is best)

newspaper

water

cooking oil

*Quantities depend on how
many colors and how much
colored paper you want.

Wrap small presents up in your homemade marbly-colored gift wrap. When dried, this paper is like parchment, a crisp, crinkly, see-through kind of paper. It's crispy, it's streaky, it's simply marbelous!

What to do: Place some newspaper over the kitchen counter. Fill the bowl to the top with water and add two tablespoons of vinegar. Place the bowl in the middle of the newspaper. Lay extra newspaper down to hold drying papers. Place doubled paper towels down and add a small piece of different-colored chalk. Crush the chalk to a fine powder.

Carefully lifting the towels, pour the colored powdered chalk into as many disposable cups as you need colors. Place a tablespoon of oil into each cup, stirring thoroughly with the plastic fork or spoon. Pour the contents of each cup into the bowl of water. The chalky colored oil should form large colored circular pools on the surface of the water. Now, carefully lay each piece of paper on the surface of the water and lift away.

Dry the colored papers on newspaper over the next 24 hours. When they are fully dried, carefully wipe off any surface chalk grains with a paper towel.

What happens: The colored oil sticks to the paper and makes circles and streaky patterns.

Why: Negative- and positive-charged molecules are attracted to one another. The molecules of chalk (a type of calcium carbonate) and vinegar (acetic acid) and water and the surface of the paper all chemically combine to cause a chemical bond which causes the swirling colors to stick to the paper.

Presto-Perfect Precipitate

I bet you can't say that fast ten times! You can, though, make a preipitate in just seconds. If you remember, a precipitate is a substance that forms when a chemical reaction or change occurs. This substance, also, is insoluble. That means it does not dissolve or evenly mix as does a substance in a solution.

What to do: Dissolve the Epsom salts in the jar and add a few squirts of window cleaner.

What happens: The solution becomes milky white.

Why: When magnesium sulfate (Epsom salts) is mixed with ammonium hydroxide (ammonia solution), it forms a new chemical compound. The milky white liquid formed is a precipitate of magnesium hydroxide.

A New Precipitate

Repeat the Presto-Perfect Precipitate experiment, but this time use alum (found in the spice section of the supermarket) instead of the Epsom salts. You'll make a new precipitate called aluminum hydroxide. Compare the color change of the magnesium hydroxide with that of the aluminum hydroxide.

SALTY SOLUTIONS AND SWEET SUCCESS

Without salt and sugar, life would be very dull. Most important, we could not live without a proper balance of sugar and salt in our bodies. Now, we'll find out just what these chemical compounds are all about and what they can do.

Salt and Sugar

Salt (NaCl) is a mineral compound, which in this case means it is a combination of two elements and is a crystal substance. Each salt crystal is made up of millions of atoms that fasten on to one another. Salt is made up of the elements sodium and chlorine (a compound). Sodium is a metal solid and chlorine is a greenish gas. By themselves, these two chemicals are extremely dangerous but when they are combined into a compound, they become common table salt.

Sugar is a carbohydrate, or a chemical compound made up of carbon, hydrogen, and oxygen. Common table sugar is called sucrose. Other sugars are glucose, fructose, lactose, and maltose.

The Sugar Cube Race

361

Will more sugar cubes dissolve, or disappear, in cold water than in hot or warm tap water? Let's have a race and find out.

YOU WILL NEED:

sugar cubes
clear glass of cold tap water
clear glass of very hot tap water
spoon
paper and pencil

What to do: Put a cube of sugar in the cold water and stir until its crystals disappear, or dissolve, completely. Continue to put cubes of sugar into the water one at a time—count them—until no more sugar will dissolve. You'll know when this happens, because the crystal grains of sugar will begin to show in the solution and will start to gather on the bottom of the glass.

Now, repeat this activity using hot water. Make certain you count the number of cubes that dissolve in each glass of water. Record, or write, the number for each. Which can hold the most dissolved sugar cubes?

What happens: Fewer cubes should dissolve thoroughly in the cold tap water than in the hot.

Why: The first sugar cubes dissolve in each glass of water until no more sugar crystals can be seen. Then, as more cubes are added, the solutions reach a point where the crystals can no longer disappear and they can easily be seen. Scientists and chemists call this a saturated solution. More sugar dissolves in the hot water than in the cold because, when water is heated, its molecules move faster and farther apart. As a result, the spaces between the water molecules become larger, allowing room for more sugar molecules.

303

Sweet and Slow

362

Which dissolves faster, a whole sugar cube or a crushed one?

YOU WILL NEED:
2 sugar cubes
small disposable container
hammer or rock (to crush one cube)
2 glasses half-filled with water

What to do: Crush one of the cubes in the container. Leave the other sugar cube whole, as is. Place each in its separate glass of water at the same time.

What happens: The crushed sugar cube dissolves faster.

Why: The water molecules must dissolve all of the outside parts of the solid sugar cube before they can reach and dissolve the inside. This takes longer. Because the water molecules come in contact with more outside surfaces when the sugar cube is crushed, the rate of solubility (or how fast a substance dissolves) is quicker.

Sweet Talk

YOU WILL NEED:
unsalted soda cracker

363

Our bodies are complicated chemical factories, as this simple experiment shows.

What to do: Chew the soda cracker slowly for a few minutes.

What happens: The cracker tastes sweet.

Why: Your saliva has a substance in it called an enzyme. The enzyme stylin breaks down starch or other carbohydrate molecules to a simple sugar called maltose. When you chew the cracker, the starch in it is changed to sugar, so it tastes sweet.

Carbohydrates

The organic compounds called carbohydrates are found in such foods as sugar, bread, potatoes, and crackers. They are made up of carbon, hydrogen, and oxygen atoms.

Sweet Tooth

YOU WILL NEED:

tooth
glass of cola drink (regular)

Want to see how fast a tooth dissolves in a cola drink?

Don't pull out a tooth for this experiment, and don't use Grandma's dentures! But if you happen to have an extra tooth lying around the house, try it!

What to do: Place the tooth in the cola beverage. Leave it in the drink for at least a week.

What happens: The tooth starts to dissolve.

Why: Now you know why your parents and dentists warn you about drinking too many sugary drinks with a high acid content. Even though your teeth wouldn't be constantly sitting in a cola drink, the high sugar and acid content of these drinks can chemically affect your teeth over time. In this experiment, the sugar and acid eventually cause the tooth to dissolve, even right through its hard enamel surface coating.

Watercooler

YOU WILL NEED:

10 ice cubes
2 disposable cups
1 tablespoon of salt
2 thermometers
marker pen
paper and pencil

Which is colder, regular ice water or salted ice water?

What to do: Mark each cup with the pen "Salt," "No salt." Place a thermometer in each cup. Pack the ice cubes around the thermometers, five cubes to each cup. Pour the salt over and between the ice cubes in one cup. Wait about 30 minutes for results. Read the temperature on each thermometer and write it down.

What happens: The temperature in the cup with the salted ice water is colder.

Why: Water freezes at 32 degrees Fahrenheit, or 0 degrees centigrade. In the unsalted water, the temperature is usually above freezing, while the salted water is much below. The salt draws heat from the ice and makes it much colder while lowering the freezing point on the thermometer.

What now: Do this same experiment again but this time substitute crushed ice for ice cubes. Does crushed ice make the water colder? Write down the temperature reading in each experiment and compare the differences if any.

INDEX

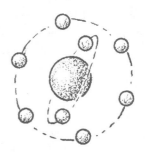

B

C

D

E

F

Fahrenheit, Gabriel, 246
Fat, 54
Faults, 142
Fibers, 57, 119
Finger lifting, 100
Finger tapping, 107
Fire extinguisher, 291
Fissures, 148
Foehn, 224
Force(s)
    of air, 66, 79, 103-104
    centrifugal, 64
    doing work, 62, 65, 66, 95,
        100-102
    gravity, 64, 83, 89, 180-
        183
    magnetism, 180, 183-188
    See also Air, pressure;
        Earthquakes; Erosion
Fossil fuels, 189-190, 191,
    196
Foucault, Jean Bernard Leon,
    211
Foucault's pendulum, 211
Fourdriniers, 24
Freezing point, 60, 305
Friction, 23, 80, 91, 96,
    157

Front, 225
Fruit, 38, 46
    See also Lemons
Fulcrum, 22
Funnel, 135

G

Galileo, 67, 246
Galvanometer, 42-43
Gases, 41, 73, 160, 202, 279-
    280
Geology, 141-151

dissolving chalk and shells,
    149-150
    facts about, 141
    glacier, 150-151
    and pressure, 142-145,
        149, 151
    seismograph, 143
    types of faults, 142
    volcano, 148
    wave, 145
Germination, 166
Gift wrap, 300
Glacier, 150-151
Glasses, 102, 109, 138
Gluten, 288
Gnomon, 153, 154
Gravel, 171
Gravity
    definition of, 89
    facts, 180
    and inertia, 83, 86, 183
    scale, 181
    tricks using, 83, 86, 182-
        183, 195
    See also Center of gravity
Greenhouse effect, 169, 190-
    192, 216
Growth experiments, 45-46,
    164-169

H

Hail, 240
Hammer, 90
Heat
    and expansion of gases,
        128, 279-280
    and expansion of liquid, 126
    facts about, 121
    and friction, 96, 157
    from hands for power, 128
    and greenhouse effect, 191-
        192
    and light, 203-209
    and molecules, 125, 269,
        270, 278, 303
    and pressure, 127, 148,
        149, 280
    from sun, 194-195, 202-
        209
Heat Index, 253
Helium, 202
Hoops, 97
Humidity, 200, 232, 253-256
Hurricanes, 230
Huygens, Christopher, 68
Hydrometer, 276-277
Hydroponics, 167
Hygrometer, 253, 254
Hypothesis, 154

I

Ice, 60, 127, 270, 278
    See also Glacier
Immiscible substance, 275
Inertia, 23, 28, 49, 61, 63, 81-
    88, 95, 211
    definition of, 183
    facts about, 81
    tricks using, 82-83, 85-88
Inorganic chemistry, 269
Invisible ink, 36
Ions, 299
Isomers, 267

J

Jet stream, 224

K

Knots, 58, 61, 63, 66

L

Latitude, 156
Lava, 148
Lavoisier, Antoine, 269
Leaks, 125
Leaves, 163-165
Lemons, 36-46
    as antidote, 40
    as cleaner, 37
    electricity using, 42-44
    facts about, 36
    and fruit, 38, 46
    to identify rocks, 41
    invisible ink with, 36
    make a rocket, 45
    soda with, 44
Lenses, 56, 124
Lever, 22
Lift, 100, 117, 129, 132
Light
    bending of rays, 56, 121-
        122, 124, 212, 244
    facts about, 121
    and heat, 203-209
    intensity of, 55
    reflection of rays, 56, 78,
        121, 123, 146, 203-204
    and seasons, 161, 214-215
    speed of rays, 21, 121, 243

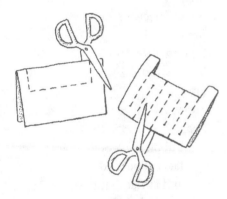

Q

Quicksand, 174

R

Radiant energy, 203
Rain, 236
  gauge, 258
  See also Acid rain;
    Precipitation
Rainbows, 78, 122, 144, 160,
  244
Recycling, 189-190, 198
Red cabbage indicator, 39
Reduction, 294
Reflection, 56, 78, 121, 123,
    146, 203-204
Refraction. *See* Light, bending
    of rays
Relative humidity, 253-255
Resistance, 23
Respiration, 162
Robert, Nicholas, 24
Rock candy, 59
Rocket, 45

Rock(s)
  composition of, 149
  limestone, 41, 149
  metamorphic, 149
  and pressure, 141-142,
    144-145, 148-149
Rotation, of earth, 153, 155,
    209-211
Rust, 220, 294-295

S

Safety rules, 261
Salt, 59-60, 271, 273-275, 303,
    305
Saturated solution, 303
Scales, 22, 69, 115, 181
Scheele, Karl, 269
Sea breeze, 224

Seasons, 161, 206, 214-215
Sedimentary rocks, 41
Sedimentation, 172
Seeds, 45, 166
Seismograph, 143
Shadows, 153-154, 208-209
Shapes, 25
Shells, electron, 263
Simoons, 224
Siphon, 194-195
Slope wind, 224
Smog, 239
Snow, 204
Soap, 71-73, 85, 282
  bubbles, 73-80
  facts about, 70
  and surface tension, 71-73,
    112, 115
  See also Detergent
Soda, 44
Sodium carbonate, 282
Soil
  box, 179
  composition of, 173
  erosion, 178-179
  facts about, 170-171
  permeability, 175
  quicksand, 174
  sedimentation, 172
  types of, 170-172, 174
Solar collector, 194
Solubility, 304
Solutes, 272, 274, 278

T

Y

PART 2

Published by Tess Press, an imprint of
Black Dog & Leventhal Publishers, Inc.
151 West 19th Street
New York, NY 10011

Designed by Liz Trovato

Printed in China

Comb bound ISBN 1-57912-387-2

g f e d c

Hardcover ISBN 1-57912-613-8

f e d c b a

Disclaimer:
Although the advice and suggestions contained in this book have been carefully evaluated by the publishers,
neither the authors nor the publishers accept any responsibility for damage to either persons or possessions
which might result from the experiments.

CONTENTS

Plenty of Plants *Page 198*

Wonderful Wildlife *Page 212*

INTRODUCTION

365 Simple Science Experiments was the first book in this series and it taught many people about science. Science, however, includes so many topics that we needed to create *365 More Simple Science Experiments*. Now you can fill more of your days with fun and entertaining activities. All of these experiments have a surprise in them. Some of them will surprise you because of how they work. Others are surprising because of what happens.

These experiments come in the form of projects, stunts, tricks and even games. The one thing that they all have in common is that they are based on scientific principles. This book helps you to put scientific ideas to work in ways that may seem impossible, but which are always interesting and enjoyable.

The first seven chapters talk about physics. It's a marvelous world that we live in. A world filled with rainbows and rockets, with echoes and electric sparks, with atomic particles and planets, and with invisible forces and vibrations that affect you without your even knowing they exist.

Physics comes from the Greek word *physica*, meaning "natural things." Learning about the natural things of this world, what is happening every second all around us, is what physics is all about. What better way to learn about physics than in our everyday laboratory—the world itself—where it can be experienced and not just studied.

These hands-on experiments put the natural world at your fingertips. And you don't have to spend time and money at the store buying expensive equipment and supplies. You can do all of these experiments using just odds and ends that you probably have around your home. (If you don't have an eyedropper, use a straw. See instructions on page 44.) Use whatever you have available and, if necessary, adjust or substitute using the experiment's instuctions as a guide. Most likely the experiment will work just as

14

well. And if it doesn't, with some thought you'll discover why it doesn't and be well on your way to becoming a problemsolver (someone who gets things done no matter what).

Several of these experiments require the use of heat. Where possible, the heat needed comes from a 100-watt light bulb with a foil shade (the shade makes its easier on your eyes and the light bulb is safer to use). A symbol reminding you to be careful marks those experiments using heat.

The next eight chapters focus on learning about science using everyday foods. What makes you hungry or thirsty? Does water always boil at the same temperature? Why is a tomato called a fruit? Is a raw carrot healthier than a cooked one? Why do we cry when we peel an onion?

These are a few of the questions the experiments in this section will answer. We'll be working with carbon, hydrogen, oxygen, nitrogen, phosphorus and sulphur—the elements that play a leading role in the chemistry of the kitchen. They combine to make up the food we eat: carbohydrates such as sugars and starches; fats and oils; proteins such as meat and eggs; and water.

When we cook, we're actually preparing chemical compounds in a form our body can use safely—with enough good taste so that we're willing to eat them. This book will help you discover both the how and the why of doing this. The eating is a bonus!

The experiments in the next seven chapters relate to time. Through these exciting projects you will learn all about the history of the earliest time-telling devices and clocks, how the sun, the moon and the stars all determine time, and why time, at one place in the world registers differently—at the same moment—than time in another place in the world.

The seven chapters that follow help to explain some puzzling and interesting ideas about nature. You may not realize it but you are related to the dragonfly. You are also related to the pine tree and the mushroom. In fact, all living organisms are related to each other in some way. We depend on members of the plant and animal kingdoms for our food, building and clothing materials, and for our enjoyment. Plants and animals depend on each other for their survival, too. In fact, all plants and animals (including human beings like you and me) are part of a complex survival system, commonly called ecology, with every other member of the plant and animal world.

The activities in this section are designed to help you explore and understand nature, and to appreciate the connections that exist between all living things and the world around them. You will discover that you alone can do a lot to help the environment. That is the way we learn to really appreciate the plants and animals with whom we share this world, and can ensure that we will be able to enjoy them for years to come.

This is a book of discovery. All of the activities are hands-on, fun to do, and use only simple, easy-to-obtain materials. Some activities will take only a few minutes; others will last several days or weeks. Most of the activities are open-ended—meaning there are no right or wrong answers. You can do as many of the experiments as you wish, again and again, or for as long as you want. You are the scientist.

Several of the activities suggest that you keep a journal or notebook to record your observations. Scientists always do this. Buy a spiral notebook and mark it "My Nature Journal." Use your journal to keep track of the growth of a plant, the animals you see in a certain area, or how much rain fell on a certain day. Your journal will be an important record of what you did and

observed during an experiment so that you can compare it to what happens when you do the same experiment again several weeks or months later.

It's smart to be careful in whatever you do. A few of these experiments or activities call for the use of a stove, a knife, or a sharp scissors—times when you might want to ask an adult for help. Watch for the "safety bee" in some if the experiments to remind you, and do be careful.

The final chapters help you explore the science of space. Space travel came from man's imagination. The French writer Jules Verne (1828–1905) set down his dream of going to other worlds in a book entitled FROM THE EARTH TO THE MOON. It was a story about traveling in rockets.

Sir Isaac Newton's Law of Motion gave modern space scientists the principle that every rocket is based upon: for every action, there is an equal and opposite reaction. In 1926, an American, Robert Goddard, built and launched the first successful fueled rocket.

In the 1940s, while the Germans developed working long-range ground missiles, the Russians worked on building larger rockets, powerful enough to thrust them towards their dream of outer space. In 1957, the Russians launched Sputnik I, the first unmanned satellite to go into orbit around the Earth. They continued their lead in space exploration by, in 1961, placing the first human being in orbit, a cosmonaut named Yuri Gagarin.

Americans finally pulled ahead in the space race when, on July 20, 1969, Neil Armstrong became the first human to step foot on the moon. Later, through 1972, there were several other manned moon landings (*Apollo* missions). Over the years since, the U.S. has taken part in many space missions, launched many satellites and space probes, and has placed several space stations in orbit. But it is the Russians that are credited with launching and maintaining in orbit the most impressive and largest space station to date, the *Mir*.

It is the purpose of this section to give future astronauts and flight and space scientists food for thought. Here is a chance to experiment, question, think, and dream. In this section, you'll learn about Bernoulli's Principle—without it, you'd never know the basic laws of flight. You'll design an airfoil, or airplane wing, construct a simple helicopter-like toy, learn about gravity and centrifugal/centripetal force. In addition, you'll

construct flight instruments, learn about hot-air balloons, and make a variety of gliders and planes to discover how they really work. You'll also make your own kites—with flight and aerodynamics in mind. You'll even learn about the orbits and sizes of the planets, and do some great experiments to explain it all!

As space scientists, you'll learn about conditions on the moon, how conditions in outer space and lack of gravity affect space flight, and how astronauts reenter Earth's atmosphere and maintain orbit. You'll design, construct and launch a simple rocket space shuttle—and, if that's not enough, you'll learn how NASA's future astronauts are selected and trained.

Most of the materials you'll need to do the many projects in this book are inexpensive and easy to find—usually simple, everyday household items. We'll let you know, though, about the few things you may need to hunt up. So get ready to have fun and learn all about the many mysteries of science. We wish you many hours of happy experiments!

BEATING THE HEAT

Heat is a form of energy. It is what happens when molecules move around within a substance. The faster the molecules move, the hotter the substance gets.

About Heat

All things have some heat. Heat passes freely from hot to cold things. For example, you pour a hot drink into a glass with ice cubes. The heat from the drink moves into the ice, melting it, and the drink is cooled, meaning that some of the heat has been removed.

Heat affects what kinds of clothes we wear and what types of houses we live in.

We depend on heat for life, for if the sun should cool, all life on Earth would disappear. With this in mind, we should learn all that we can about heat. The study of heat in physics is called thermodynamics.

Note: The HOT symbol (shown below) will remind you to be extra careful at certain times when you will be using heat in these experiments. Always remember to use pliers, tongs, an oven mitt, or a pot holder to handle anything that may be hot. Even minor burns can be painful.

1 Make a Foil Lamp Shade

HOT!

Some of the experiments in this book use a lamp with a 100-watt bulb as a source of heat. To collect and direct the heat from the bulb toward the experiment, make a cap-shaded lamp shade out of aluminum foil. Take a small square of foil and round off the corners by folding or cutting. Place the foil on top of the cold (not lit) light bulb and shape it into a cap shape. Turn the edges of the foil up slightly, and you have a shade ready for your experiments with heat. Remember to watch for the HOT symbol (see above), and be careful.

Step on a Crack

Have you ever wondered why sidewalks are laid out in sections with spaces, or cracks, between them?

What to do: Hammer the nail into the bottom of the can. Work the nail in and out a couple of times to make sure that it slides through easily. Pull the nail out of the hole.

Turn on the lamp with the foil shade. Set the kitchen timer for two minutes. Now, using pliers or tongs, hold the nail over the lamp shade on the bulb and heat it until the timer bell rings. Be careful not to touch the hot bulb or foil shade with your hands. Try to put the nail back into the hole in the can.

What happens: The heated nail does not fit back into the hole.

Why: Heat from the light bulb excites the tiny, separate particles called molecules that make up the nail. These excited molecules move faster and spread out to take up more space. So the heated nail is now bigger than it was before and no longer fits in the hole.

Like the nail, a sidewalk's molecules also spread out on hot summer days. If there were no cracks between the sections of sidewalk, the heated molecules would have no room to expand and the concrete sidewalk would crack or break up.

Day and Night in a Can

Why do you suppose the people who design clothing use dark colors for winter coats but white or light colors for summer things?

YOU WILL NEED:

lamp (100-watt bulb) with foil shade

small can

black paint

paint brush

petroleum jelly

2 pennies

cotton swab

What to do: Prepare for this experiment by painting one side of the inside of the can black. (Be careful of sharp can edges.) Leave the other half shiny.

When the paint is completely dry, take the cotton swab and put two dime-size blobs of petroleum jelly on the outside of the can, one in the center of the dark half and one on the other side. Push a penny down firmly into each blob so that it sticks. Make sure that one penny is stuck outside the dark half, and one outside the shiny half.

With the foil shade in position on the bulb, carefully balance the can, open side down, on top of the shade. Now, turn on the lamp.

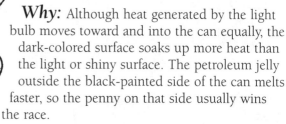

What happens: The petroleum jelly melts and the pennies drop off, of course, but the penny outside the darkened half drops first.

Why: Although heat generated by the light bulb moves toward and into the can equally, the dark-colored surface soaks up more heat than the light or shiny surface. The petroleum jelly outside the black-painted side of the can melts faster, so the penny on that side usually wins the race.

Dark colors not only retain heat better, but they also do a better job of soaking up, or absorbing, the waves of heat that come to us in the light rays from the sun. So, in winter you want a dark coat to keep you warmer. Light-colored clothing reflects, or bounces, most of the heat-making light waves back into the atmosphere, so it keeps you cooler on hot summer days.

4

Decorate a Hat

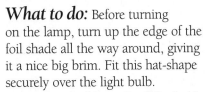

lamp (100-watt bulb)
with foil shade
box of birthday can-
dles (different colors)

How does heat change solid forms to liquids? Here's a chance not only to understand the process of melting, but to use it to make a fancy hat as well.

What to do: Before turning on the lamp, turn up the edge of the foil shade all the way around, giving it a nice big brim. Fit this hat-shape securely over the light bulb.

Turn on the lamp. Carefully, hold the tip of the birthday candle against the top of the foil hat.

What happens: After a few seconds, the candle begins to change into a liquid that quickly drips away from the wick.

Why: The heat from the light bulb excites the tiny particles, or molecules, of wax that make up the can-dle. As these molecules expand, or spread out, they begin to move about so wildly that they change into a liquid. This process is, of course, called melting, and the temperature at which a substance melts is called its melting point.

What next: Finish decorating the foil hat by letting the different-colored candles drip all over the hat and around the brim. When you are finished, turn off the lamp and let the hat cool before removing it from the bulb. Later, you can design a face on an apple or a potato and create "a someone" to wear the decorated hat.

Melt a Kiss

5

Our Earth gets its warmth from the sun's light. Fortunately, the Earth is constantly turning on its axis and is not made of chocolate.

small paper bag
water
lamp (100-watt bulb)
with foil shade
chocolate kiss

What to do: Put a little water into the bag. Swirl it around to coat the inside of the bag and pour the rest out. Put the chocolate kiss into the bag. Then, carefully, hold the bag over the shaded light bulb. Do not let the bag touch the shade.

What happens: The chocolate kiss inside the bag begins to melt, but the bag doesn't get hot.

Why: The heat energy coming from the light waves is soaked up, or absorbed, by the film of water molecules inside the bag and by the chocolate kiss.

This heat energy, which cannot be seen but can be felt, moves in circular waves away from its source, like the expanding rip-ples a stone makes when it is thrown into calm water. It is this form of heat, called radiation, which allows the sun to heat our earth, and the lamp to melt the chocolate kiss.

Color Me Warm

Warmed air rises, cools off, and sinks down. This experiment uses water to give you a clear picture of how warmed air reacts.

YOU WILL NEED:

2 clear drinking glasses
hot tap water
very cold water
food coloring
a small measuring spoon

What to do: Fill one glass with hot water, and the other with icy-cold water. Measure some food coloring into each glass.

What happens: The food coloring quickly swirls around to mix with the hot water—but not so in the cold water.

Why: Because its tiny, separate particles, or molecules, are moving faster than the cold-water molecules, the hotter water at the bottom of the glass whirls around and up to the top, taking the food coloring with it. As the water at the top cools, warmer water takes its place, and now the cooler water sinks. This process, called convection, will continue until all the water is at the same temperature.

Because there is less motion in the cold water, the food coloring sinks to the bottom of the glass and stays in place longer.

Birds on a Wire

7

If you have ever grabbed a hot metal handle of a cooking pan, you have actually felt hundreds of speeding molecules striking your hand like tiny bullets. Unfortunately, such a "hands-on" experience usually results in a painful burn or blister.

YOU WILL NEED:

paper clip or stiff wire
spring-clip clothespin
petroleum jelly
small spoon
lamp (100-watt bulb)
with foil shade
piece of waxed paper

What to do: Straighten out the paper clip to make a straight piece of wire. Clip the clothespin to one end of the wire as a handle. With the spoon, line up three separate, jelly-bean-size blobs of petroleum jelly on the wire. Try to space the blobs evenly, so that they look like birds sitting on a telephone wire.

Place the end of the waxed paper underneath the lamp's base. With the foil shade covering the bulb, turn on the lamp. Holding the clothespin, touch the far end of the wire to the bulb and hold it there. The "birds" need to be sitting on the wire over the waxed paper leading away from the bulb.

What happens: Beginning with the "bird" perched nearest the light bulb, one after the other begins to drop off the wire, until all three are gone.

Why: When one end of the wire is heated by the light bulb, the tiny,

separate particles, or molecules, in that area of the wire zoom into motion. Soon these heated molecules begin to jostle the ones next to them, then those molecules bump others nearby, until the heat is passed all the way down the wire, melting each "bird" in turn.

This passing of heat from one excited, jostling molecule to another, like a handshake sent down a line or around a circle, is called conduction.

WHY IS THERE AIR?

Air alone has no color, taste, or smell. You can't see it, and you can put your hand right through it without feeling anything. However, air is more than just nothing at all. It is actually made up of many gases, mainly nitrogen and oxygen, which consist of tiny molecules that are far apart and move about quickly. This is why gases are thin and appear invisible.

About Air

Scientists estimate that one cubic inch (16.4 cubic centimeters) of air contains about 300 billion billion molecules! Even though the molecules are so tiny, there is still plenty of space between each one. Each air molecule has enough energy to zip through space at 11,000 miles (1600 kilometers) per hour.

The Collapsing Bottle

8

The following experiment will help your recycling efforts by giving you more room in the collecting bin.

What to do: Pour hot water into the bottle until it is about half-full and swish it around for about a minute. Then pour the water out and, quickly, put the cap on and twist it tightly.

What happens: The sides of the bottle suddenly collapse inward!

Why: The hot water heats the air inside the bottle and, with the cap left off, it fills to the brim with warm air. When the hot water is poured out and the cap is replaced, the air inside of the bottle quickly starts to cool. Since cooler air takes up less space than the same amount of warmer air, there's now extra room in the bottle!

To fill that extra space, the sides of the bottle are pushed in by the force of the air pressure outside the bottle, which is constantly pressing in every direction.

The Wonderful Whistle-Stick

9

Can you turn a piece of wood into a whistle? Sure you can. It's a great experiment, and fun, too.

What to do: Use the hammer and nail to make a hole in the narrow end of the stirrer or paddle. Put one end of the string through the hole and tie a tight knot. Now, make two or three holes in the wider end of the wood. You can put the holes all in a row, or make up your own pattern.

To hear your whistle-stick, go outside or find a large open area where you can swing the stick without breaking anything. Hold tightly onto the loose end of the string and whirl the paddle around in front of you or over your head. Be careful NOT to do this experiment where people are passing by.

What happens: You hear an unusual whistling sound over and over again.

Why: As you whirl the paddle around, the air passes through the holes in it at a higher speed than the air going around the paddle. When this happens, the paddle whistles.

What next: Different numbers and sizes of holes make different whistle sounds. You might want to make several whistle-sticks—some with only a few small holes to catch the air and others with larger or a lot of holes. Then you can compare the whistle sounds that each one makes.

The Talking Coin

10

You may have heard somebody say that money talks, but until you do this experiment you have probably never actually seen it speak.

What to do: Put the quarter in the cup of water and place the empty bottle in the freezer for five minutes.

When the time is up, remove the bottle from the freezer and, immediately, cover the mouth of the bottle with the wet coin. (It is important to completely cover the bottle's mouth with the coin.)

What happens: The quarter becomes a tongue for the bottle and begins to chatter at you.

Why: When the bottle was put into the freezer, the air molecules inside of it cooled and moved closer together. Since the air in the bottle then took up less space, it left room for extra air to flow in—so it did.

When the bottle was removed from the freezer, however, the air molecules inside of it began to warm up and spread out again. It's a great example of, "There was enough room for everyone to sit comfortably in the car until we all put on coats and it was crowded." Suddenly there was no room for the extra air molecules.

It is that "extra air" that is being pushed out of the bottle as the air warms that makes the coin move up and down as if it were talking.

The Incredible Shrinking Face

11

Air has a magical quality about it, in that it can expand or shrink flexible material almost instantly.

What to do: Blow up the balloon until it is fully inflated; then hold it tightly in one hand so that no air leaks out. While holding the balloon, pick up a black or dark marker with your other hand. Draw a large face on the balloon, completely covering one side of it. Next, relax your grip on the balloon's neck and watch as you slowly let a constant stream of air escape.

What happens: Right before your eyes, the huge face that covered the whole side of the big balloon shrinks to a miniature drawing.

Why: As the air is allowed to escape, the balloon material that expanded as you blew into the balloon goes back to its original small size, taking the marker "face" with it. If your marker ink tends to smear, spray the drawing while the balloon is full of air with a clear gloss aerosol finish to keep it neat.

Launch Your Own Astronauts

12

In the same way that a hurricane can blow you off your feet, you can make a flying chamber for your own band of brave adventurers.

YOU WILL NEED:

Ping-Pong balls
blow dryer
permanent markers
(optional)

What to do: For fun, using the markers, make a face on each of the balls. You could even identify your astronauts by writing their names on the balls. Next, plug in the hair dryer, turn it to the high setting, and point it straight up.
Place one of your homemade astronauts in the dryer's airstream and let go.

What happens: The astronaut is launched toward the ceiling, but stops and bounces around in the airflow partway up.

Why: The airstream from the dryer pushes the astronaut upwards, against the force of gravity, until the upward and downward pushes are equal and the astronaut just floats.

The high pressure in the still air surrounding the airstream keeps the astronaut in the center of the visible flying chamber.

What next: Try letting two or more astronauts fly at the same time. You may be able to do this if the blow dryer's airstream is wide enough (or if you have an attachment called a diffuser that spreads out the airflow). If not, your astronauts will probably "bounce" off each other—into unknown galaxies.

The Trick Straw Race

13

This race is just for fun, but you might want to challenge someone you know is a good loser to compete.

YOU WILL NEED:

2 identical drinking glasses, evenly filled

2 striped straws

straight pin

What to do: Before the race, use the straight pin to punch 15 or 20 small holes in one end of the "trick" straw. Punch the holes where the colors change on the straw so that they will be harder to see. Place the straw, punctured end up, in your friend's drink and say, "Let's see who can drink it all first."

What happens: While your glass empties quickly, most of your friend's drink will remain in the glass.

Why: By sucking on the straw, you are lowering the air pressure inside of it, so the air pressure pressing down on your drink pushes it up the straw and into your mouth. In the "trick" straw, air rushes into the holes in the straw so that your friend can't lower the air pressure inside—at least not enough to win the race.

The Collapsing Tent

14

YOU WILL NEED:

small sheet of paper

table or countertop

Everybody knows that moving air has more power than air that is not moving. Or does it? The following experiment will help you draw your own conclusions.

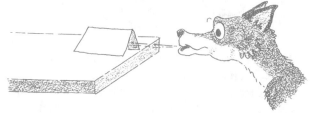

What to do: Fold the paper in half, creasing it with your finger to form a tent. Open the tent and place it near the edge of the table or a countertop, with one open side facing you. Get into position so that your mouth is level with the edge of the table, take a big breath and blow a steady stream of air through the tent.

What happens: The tent collapses, becoming a flat sheet again.

Why: When you blow through the tent, you are lowering the air pressure inside of it. This allows the higher air pressure above the tent to crush down and flatten it.

Make a Parachute

Race car-builders make their creations as streamlined as possible so that these machines cut through the air and attain the highest speeds. Parachute-makers, however, use yards and yards of billowing fabric so that their creations will grab as much air as possible on the way down.

What to do: Cut a large square piece from the front of the bag (without a seam) Trim off the corners to form an octagon, or eight-sided shape. With the nail, carefully punch a small hole near each angle of the plastic so that you have eight holes, spaced evenly, all the way around.

Tie one end of the pieces of yarn securely to each hole. Now, pull the other ends of the eight pieces of yarn together and tie them in a tight knot. Push the nail through a few of the knotted strands as a weight—this is your parachutist.

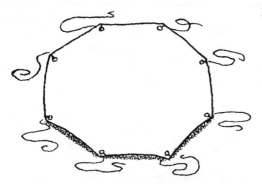

To test your parachute, stand on a sturdy chair or go outside in search of a breeze. Using both hands, hold the parachute out in front of you, high above your head, and release it.

What happens: The plastic parachute billows out and floats gently downward and away from you.

Why: It is a law of physics that the larger the surface area in contact with air, the harder it is for that object to travel through the air. So, the larger the parachute, the slower it moves—which is what you want if you are falling from a height!

But, the umbrella-like shape over a weight, like a truck parachuted out of a plane, also traps air beneath it. It is the air spilling off to one side of the parachute's top, or canopy, that makes it drift away from you.

What next: Make a very small hole in the middle of the canopy. This will make the parachute fall straighter. Now you can mark out a landing area and try to have your parachutist hit the target.

16 The Singing Balloon

Most balloons are content to just float around quietly. This mezzo-soprano is dying to let loose and sing.

What to do: Blow up the balloon, making it as full as possible. Pinch the neck of the balloon. Pull your hands apart gently to release a slow, steady stream of air from the balloon. Move your hands back and forth, stretching the balloon's neck to the music's beat.

What happens: A high-pitched squealing sound is heard. It changes tone as you pull and release the neck of the balloon.

Why: The molecules of air packed inside the balloon rub against the rubber molecules of the balloon's neck as they rush by on the way out. This causes the rubber in the balloon's neck to shake, or vibrate, and makes the squealing noise. Stretching the neck of the balloon makes it vibrate at different speeds to make different sounds.

For fun, why not form a Singing Balloon Band?

17 The Rising Notebook Trick

Even though you might think of air as a gentle, invisible "free spirit," it can be quite strong and powerful when pressured.

What to do: Place the balloon at the edge of the table or countertop with the mouth of the balloon sticking out toward you. Put the notebook on top of the balloon. Hold the balloon by the neck and blow into it.

What happens: The notebook rises.

Why: The high air pressure from your lungs causes the balloon to expand and lifts the notebook off the table. In repair garages, whole cars are lifted up in a similar way by air pressure.

Unfortunately, the air pressure in the balloon does not have a lifting effect on the grades of any homework in the notebook.

Air-Head Person

Even though you cannot actually see air, you can trap it inside something and see the shape that it makes. You can also bring that shape to life—sort of.

YOU WILL NEED:
latex balloon
square of heavy cardboard
thick nail
cellophane tape
scissors
permanent markers

What to do: Blow up the balloon and tie a tight knot in the neck.

What happens: Your once-limp balloon has taken on a round, roly-poly shape.

Why: The air you blew into the balloon with the pressure of your lungs is now trapped in there. Crammed by the balloon into the smallest possible shape, it pushes equally against all sides of the balloon, making it round.

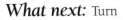

What next: Turn that roly-poly shape into an air-head person. Draw a large, rounded "W" on one side of the cardboard to make the feet. Cut around the edges of the cardboard, and then punch a hole in the center of it with the nail. Carefully poke the knotted end of the balloon through the hole in the cardboard feet. Pull the knot forward, toward the "toes," and tape the knot securely to the cardboard with some tape.

Your air-head person is now ready for a face (eyes, ears, mouth, nose, hair, glasses, mustache, or whatever you like), using the markers. And don't forget to print a name on its cardboard feet.

Decorate your room or make lots of air-heads for a birthday party, depending on how much air you have to spare.

19 Real String Soap in a Bottle

YOU WILL NEED:

plastic detergent bottle with cap

white string

scissors

a helper (optional)

By knowing a little about how air pressure works, you can make a great trick that is sure to surprise everyone.

What to do: Remove the cap from the detergent bottle. Using the scissors, bend the plastic strip inside the cap to one side, or remove it altogether. (If you have trouble doing this, ask someone to help you.) From the inside of the cap, poke one end of the string through the holes and out the top. Make sure that the string glides easily back and forth through the openings.

Then, tie a fat knot in each end of the string so that it cannot pull through the holes and will stay in place. Leaving only the fat knot outside, covering the cap opening, hide the rest of the string down inside the bottle. Now, replace the cap. To do the trick, point the bottle and give it a quick squeeze.

What happens: Watch it! A stream of white "string soap" squirts out!

Why: When the bottle is squeezed, air rushes out through the holes in the cap and the top, shooting the knot covering them into the air. Also, the air pressure inside the plastic bottle, when you squeeze it, is greater than the air pressure outside of it. This difference in pressure also helps to force the string out.

20

Underwater "Eggspert"

You probably know that eggs have yolks, but did you know that they also contain air? This "eggsperiment" will show you how to prove it.

YOU WILL NEED:

fresh egg
deep cereal bowl
hot tap water
yellow food coloring
(optional)

What to do: Carefully, place the egg in the bottom of the bowl and fill the bowl with hot tap water. Quickly add a little yellow food coloring. Watch the egg closely for several minutes.

What happens: Streams of tiny bubbles rise to the top of the water from the submerged egg.

Why: When the air inside the egg is heated by the hot water, the air molecules expand. Many of the now crowded air molecules push their way out of the egg through some of the almost 7,000 openings, or pores, in the egg's shell. These heated air molecules exit the egg, usually without cracking the shell, and rise to the water's surface as bubbles.

21

Acupuncture Balloon

Acupuncture is an ancient Chinese medical procedure often used to relieve pain. You can practice acupuncture, without a medical license, on a balloon.

YOU WILL NEED:

small latex balloon
adhesive or other strong,
sticky tape
5 or 6 sharp straight pins
string

What to do: Blow up the balloon about three-quarters of the way. Knot the end and tie the piece of string around the neck to help hold the balloon. Cut off five or six pieces of the strong, sticky tape. Press the pieces as evenly as you can around the outside of the balloon. Make sure that each piece of tape is secured tightly to the balloon.

Now, one by one, carefully stick a straight pin through the middle of each piece of the tape and into the balloon, puncturing the balloon all over.

What happens: Nothing! The balloon doesn't burst!

Why: When the pins pass through the tape, the sticky adhesive on it forms a seal around each pin that prevents the air from escaping from the balloon when you push them in. And, as you may know, a balloon only "pops" when the air is under pressure, and it is suddenly allowed to escape.

"Boil, Boil, Magical Water"

Would you believe you can boil water without using a stove? Here's the key to this old, well-kept secret.

YOU WILL NEED:

clear drinking glass
(a narrow one is easier to handle)
water
handkerchief-size square of cloth
rubber band
sink

What to do: Fill the glass about half full of water. Lay the cloth evenly over the top of the glass and push the center of it down into the water. Then, put a rubber band tightly around the top to hold the cloth edges against the sides of the glass. Turn the glass upside down over the sink. Some of the water may dribble out, but most of it will stay inside the glass.

Hold the cloth tightly around the neck of the glass, between the rubber band and the covered opening, and push down hard on the upside-down bottom of the glass.

What happens: The water starts to boil! (It may take a couple of tries to get the hang of this, but don't give up.)

Why: Of course, the water isn't really boiling, because there is no heat source. Actually, it is the air that comes in through the cloth when the water is squeezed out (by pressing on the bottom of the glass and tightly pulling on the cloth) that causes the bubbles—and makes it look as if the water in the glass is boiling.

What next: Once you can control the bubbling, use this experiment as a trick lie detector. Ask friends some questions and tell them that the water will boil if they lie, but won't if they tell the truth.

Note: You can make this trick more mysterious by tinting the water in the glass with food coloring.

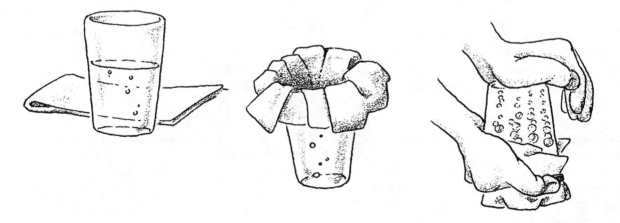

WATER, WATER, EVERYWHERE!

Water is the most common substance on Earth, covering more than 70% of its surface. Although it sometimes appears blue or green, water is a clear, colorless liquid. The thing about water that makes it different from most other liquids is that it is lighter as a solid (ice) than as a liquid.

About Water

Water is necessary to sustain life, making up most of an animal's blood, a plant's sap, and two-thirds of the human body.

Water is also a large part of our environment. It occurs as rain, sleet, snow, hail, frost, fog, dew, steam, humidity, and clouds. Not only are there lakes, rivers, oceans, and swamps that cover three-fourths of the Earth's surface, but water also accumulates in spaces between and within rock beneath the Earth's surface, supplying wells and springs and sustaining streams during periods of drought.

Water circulates constantly through our world, being used but never being used up. The glass of water that you drink today could contain the very same water molecules that a thirsty caveman enjoyed many thousands of years ago!

"I Was Here First!"

This experiment proves that two forms of matter cannot occupy the same place at the same time.

What to do: Fill the glass to about half-full of tap water. Next, put a piece of masking tape on the outside of the glass to mark the water level. Now, tilt the glass and carefully slide the marbles, one by one, down inside the glass to the bottom. Set the glass upright and check the water level.

What happens: The water level is higher than it was before.

Why: The water and the marbles are both examples of matter that cannot share space. When the

marbles are added to the glass, they are heavier than the water so they roll to the bottom of the glass and push the water there out of the way. The water level is, therefore, pushed up above the masking-tape marker.

Flowing Fountain

24

Blaise Pascal, a French physicist in the 1600s, discovered the scientific principle of how pressure affects liquids. Every time you enjoy watching water "dancing" from decorative fountains, you should thank Pascal.

What to do: Using the hammer and nail, punch eight holes evenly around the can, about two finger digits (1½ inches) up from the bottom rim.

Next, make a second row of holes, about one finger digit above the first one, except this time make

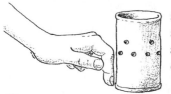

only four holes. Try to space them evenly around the can in a nice pattern.

Tear off two strips of freezer tape, each long enough to reach all the way around the can, and carefully cover each row of holes with the tape.

Fill the can with water, hold it over a sink basin, and rip off both tapes together. (You may need an extra helping hand here.)

What happens: The water flowing from the bottom holes squirts out just a little bit faster and farther than the water from the upper row of holes.

Why: The water in the lower part of the can is under more pressure, from the weight of the water above it, than the water higher up in the can.

Two Water Towers

Water towers come in all sizes, but does size make a difference to the water? Let's see.

What to do: Using the hammer and nail, make a hole about one finger digit (1/2 inch) up from the bottom rim of each can. Be sure to make the holes identical. Cover each hole completely with a small strip of freezer tape.

Fill each can to the brim with water. Set both cans on the edge of the sink, with the holes toward the basin. Rip off the tapes.

YOU WILL NEED:

2 cans
(one tall and thin; one short and bigger around)
hammer
nail (birthday-candle size)
freezer tape
water

What happens: The stream of water that flows out of the taller, thinner can is longer than the stream of water from the shorter can.

Why: It is the depth of the water that determines how fast the water flows out of the hole, and the deeper water is in the taller can. Shorter towers that are bigger around might hold as much or more water, but that water will come out slower and with less power. That is because the weight of the water pressing down, or water pressure, is less.

"I Think I'll Eat Worms"

When this experiment with bringing spaghetti to life is finished, you can amaze your friends even more by eating the "worms." They might taste a bit like pickles.

What to do: Tear the strands of cooked spaghetti into several worm-size pieces. In a bowl or jar, mix the cup of vinegar and the cup of water. Next, add three drops of red food coloring and three drops of blue food coloring to the mixture and stir to make the color purple.

Slowly add the two tablespoons of baking soda, then drop in the pieces of cooked spaghetti.

What happens: The purple "worms" seem to come to life! They swim back and forth, rising to the top of the water and then falling back to the bottom of the container.

Why: When vinegar and baking soda mix, they form tiny gas bubbles. These bubbles attach themselves to the small strands of spaghetti, raise these "worms" to the top, and then burst. The pieces then fall back to the bottom where, if more gas bubbles attach themselves, the purple "worms" will continue to swim up and down in the bowl.

The Power of Water

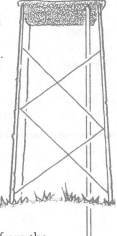

Turn on a faucet in your home until a stream of water trickles out. Then, put your hand directly under the faucet, and try to stop the water from coming out. You can't? This experiment will help you understand why you have to turn off the faucet to stop even the littlest stream of water.

YOU WILL NEED:

large-size can

hammer

nail
(birthday-candle size)

freezer tape

tap water

sink

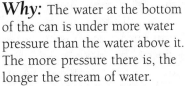

What to do: With the hammer and a nail, punch three holes into one side of the can. Put one hole near the bottom of the can, just above the rim. Make the other two holes about a finger digit (¹/₂ inch) apart, going up the side of the can, above the first hole.

Cover all three of the holes with one long strip of freezer tape, then fill the can with tap water.

Place the can on the edge of a sink, with the holes positioned over the basin, and rip off the tape.

What happens:

The water stream from the lowest hole at the bottom of the can is the longest. The water stream from the middle hole is next longest, and the stream from the highest hole is the shortest.

Why: The water at the bottom of the can is under more water pressure than the water above it. The more pressure there is, the longer the stream of water.

Your faucet is like the long stream from the lowest hole. Some cities pump water into tall tanks, or towers. The pressure of the water from these tall containers forces water through long pipes beneath the ground and into people's homes. The water from the faucet has all that pressure behind it, that's why you can't stop it with just your finger or hand.

You didn't really think that all that water was right inside your wall, did you?

28 Ice Boat Float

What strange thing about water protects hundreds of millions of fish in lakes and rivers each winter? Here's how to find out.

YOU WILL NEED:
large jar filled with very cold water
ice cube

What to do: Place the ice cube in the jar of water.

What happens: The ice cube floats like a boat.

Why: When water molecules freeze, they expand and spread out. This means that ice is not as heavy or dense as water. Because frozen water is lighter than regular water, it floats! This lucky law of nature causes water to freeze from the top down. When the layer of water on the surface turns to ice, it prevents the water below it, where the fish live and swim, from freezing, too. So, in winter, the fish's watery world is protected by a floating "sky" of ice.

29 The Floating Glass

Floating clouds, yes; but floating glasses?

YOU WILL NEED:
2 drinking glasses that fit inside each other (glass works best)

What to do: In one drinking glass, pour in just enough water to cover the bottom. Then place the second glass inside the first.

What happens: The inside glass floats. (If this does not happen, add a little more water and try again.)

Why: The amount of water in the bottom of the first, outer glass is heavier than the weight of the inside glass.

It was Archimedes, a Greek mathematician who lived over 2,000 years ago (287–212 B.C.), who discovered that a floating object displaces, or pushes out of its way, an amount of liquid equal to its own volume.

Disappearing Salt

If you have ever gone swimming in the ocean, you have probably tasted salt in the water. No matter how hard you looked, though, you couldn't see it. Why not?

What to do: Fill the glass right to the brim with warm tap water. Measure a half-cup of salt and, very slowly, pour it into the full glass of water, while stirring gently with the straw.

What happens: If you pour carefully, you can add the entire half-cup of salt to the full glass of water without any of the water overflowing.

Why: The water does not spill over when the salt is added because no extra room is needed. The molecules of water have spaces between them. These spaces are filled nicely by the molecules of salt, just like pouring sand into a jar filled with marbles. (The sand finds its way into the spaces left by the marbles.) Such a neat arrangement between two substances is called a solution.

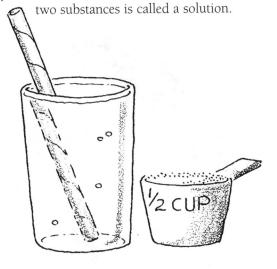

"Freeze Me and I'll Burst!"

Have you ever had the water pipes in your home burst because water froze inside them? The following experiment explains why this can happen.

What to do: Fill the jar to the brim with tap water. Cover the jar's top completely with the cardboard square. Now, carefully place the jar in the freezer and wait until the water freezes.

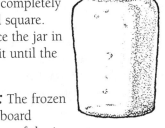

What happens: The frozen water lifts the cardboard square above the top of the jar.

Why: When the temperature of water drops below 32°F, or freezes, its molecules spread out and need more space—just like when water is heated (water is strange in this way). The freezing water molecules push up out of the jar looking for room to spread out.

If, instead of just laying a loose piece of cardboard on top, you had put a tight-fitting lid on the jar, what would have happened? The freezing water molecules would have expanded and broken the jar. This is what can happen to your water pipes in winter. To prevent their pipes from bursting, some people allow faucets to drip, drip, drip, on freezing winter nights.

1 + 1 Does Not Always = 2

You might be a good math student, but you will have to be a good physics student to figure out this experiment.

YOU WILL NEED:

large-size glass jar
masking tape
pen
cup of sugar
measuring cup
paper towel
drinking straw
warm water

What to do: Place a strip of masking tape down the outside of the jar. Pour one cup of warm water into the jar and mark the level that it reaches on the tape. Then, add a second cup of warm water and, again, mark the water level on the tape. Empty all of the water out of the jar and dry the inside of it with a paper towel. Now, pour one cup of warm water into the jar. Follow that with one cup of sugar. Stir this solution well with the straw and then check the liquid level on the masking-tape measuring strip.

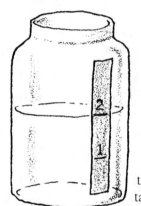

What happens: The liquid level of one cup of water plus one cup of sugar does not reach the two-cup mark of the tape.

Why: If you caught the clue word, solution, when you were instructed to stir the sugar and water together, you probably already know the answer. The substances in a solution fit neatly together, like puzzle parts. Instead of taking up their own space, the grains of sugar simply fill in the empty spaces around the water molecules to make something entirely new, a solution called sugar water... but less of it than you thought you would have when you added the sugar and water measurements.

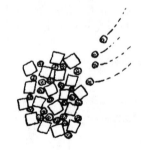

"Give Me Room!"

33

Just as you probably don't like to sit close to anyone when you are hot and sweaty, neither does a molecule of hot water.

What to do: Put some water into the bottom of the pot and place it on the stove or hot plate. Fill the jar right to the brim with water. Then, carefully, so you don't spill the water, place the jar in the middle of the pot. Turn the stove or hot plate on high heat and wait a few minutes as the water in the pot heats and begins to boil. Watch the water in the jar.

What happens: The water in the jar overflows into the pot.

Why: Like other liquids, water expands and needs more space when it is heated. As the water gets hot, the molecules in the jar start to bounce around rapidly, bumping against each other and looking for room to spread out, until they spill out over the top.

Warning: Turn off the stove or hot plate and let the water cool before removing the jar from the pot.

The Shrinking Molecule

34

When you are very cold, you sometimes huddle up, trying to make your body smaller and smaller to keep warm. What does a water molecule do when it's cold?

What to do: Fill the jar to the brim with tap water. Place the jar uncovered in the freezer. Set the timer for 30 minutes. When the time is up, take the jar from the freezer.

What happens: The water level in the jar drops below the brim, even though none of the water has splashed out.

Why: As the water's temperature gets colder, to about 39°F, its molecules contract, or huddle closer together—maybe to keep warm. As a result of this "scrunching up," the molecules of cold water in the jar take up less space than they did before.

Shy Blue

Have you ever had a shy moment, such as at a family reunion, when you wanted to run and hide? If you have ever felt this way, then you can sympathize with Shy Blue.

YOU WILL NEED:
white plate
water
blue food coloring
rubbing alcohol
eyedropper or drinking straw

What to do: Take some water and pour a small circle of it in the middle of the plate. Put three or four drops of food coloring into the water. Now, fill the eyedropper with alcohol and then squeeze it out, letting the drops fall against the circle of water. Do it again.

What happens: Shy blue trembles and shrinks back, away from the alcohol.

Why: Both the water and the rubbing alcohol have something called surface tension, a thin, invisible "skin" that holds them together. The surface tension of the water is stronger than the alcohol's, so it pulls its molecules away from the alcohol, trying to escape from its touch.

Make a "Dropper"

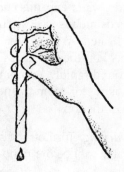

If you don't have an eyedropper (or medicine dropper) for use in some of these experiments, you can use a drinking straw. To do this, put the end of the straw into the liquid you need. Slowly and carefully, suck on the straw to pull a little of the liquid into it; then quickly put your finger over the top of the straw. Air pressure will hold the liquid inside. Next, move the straw into position and release your finger, and your "drops."

Square Bubbles from Square Holes?

Can it be done? Try the following experiment to see if you can blow a square soap bubble.

What to do: Bend the wire or pipe cleaner into a square shape with a handle. With your finger, mix some water with a few drops of dishwashing detergent in the saucer. Adding two or three drops of glycerin makes bubbles last longer. Next, dip the side of the square shape into the soapy solution. Be sure to completely cover the shape with the mixture. Lift the square form to your mouth and blow gently.

What happens: The bubble that emerges from the square form is not square, but round.

Why: The culprit is surface tension—that attraction of molecules for each other that forms a "skin" over them. In this case, the surface tension of the soapy water making up the bubble pulls it into a rounded shape, no matter what shape you use to make the bubble. The attraction of the molecules makes a sphere, or ball, because that's the shape that allows them to be closest together.

More Than Enough

Is a cup of water full when it's full? Can it be more than full? Seeing is believing.

What to do: On a table or countertop, set the cup in the saucer and fill it to the brim with tap water. Next, draw some tap water into the eyedropper. Add at least 20 drops of water, one after the other, to the full cup. Then bend over so that you are level with the cup and look at the water's surface from the side.

What happens: Without spilling, the water rises over the rim of the cup like a large bubble.

Why: When the water molecules across the surface are linked together with surface tension, they are strong enough to hold back the water so that it rises above the cup's rim without spilling. At some point, if more water drops are added, the mound of water in the cup will become so high and heavy that the surface molecules will lose their grip on each other and will tumble out of the cup and into the saucer. Ouch!

39 Water "Glue"

While water and flour mixed together make a paste that will hold paper together, water "glue" (without the flour) is really a trick your eyes play on you.

What to do: Hold the rounded part of the spoon (bottom side up) under the stream of water.

What happens: The water sticks to the spoon as if it were glued to it.

Why: The reduced air pressure under the water on the spoon's rounded bottom holds the flowing water against the spoon, rather than allowing it to splash away. But, it is the rapid movement of the running water, so fast that your eye can't following the speeding molecules, that makes it look as if the water were "glued" to the spoon.

What next: Turn the spoon over, right side up, and hold it under the stream of water from the faucet again. Does the water come unglued this time?

40 Stick Together, Stay Together

You often use water to wash off your sticky hands, but have you ever thought that water itself might be sticky? Let's find out.

What to do: Using the pencil or nail, punch two small holes in the bottom of the foam cup. Make the holes as close together as possible without allowing them to touch. Next, fill the other cup with water, hold the cup with the holes up over the sink basin, and pour the cup of water into it. Now, very quickly, using your thumb and index finger, pinch together the two streams of water flowing out of the holes.

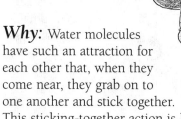

What happens: The two separate streams of water come together and form one stream. (You might have to refill the cup a couple of times until you get the pinch right.)

Why: Water molecules have such an attraction for each other that, when they come near, they grab on to one another and stick together. This sticking-together action is known as cohesion.

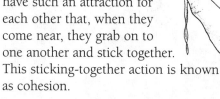

Fishing for "Clippies"

With this experiment, you can fish at your kitchen table, on your back porch, or anywhere you choose.

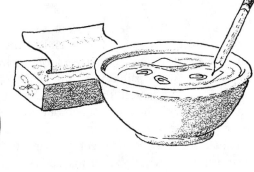

What to do: Straighten one of the paper clips, shaping one end into a hook. Open and lay the facial tissue across the bowl of water. Next, quickly but gently place the remaining paper clips, one at a time, on top of the tissue. Then, tap around the edges of the tissue with a pencil until the paper sinks to the bottom of the bowl, leaving the "clippie fish" afloat.

Now that your homemade fishing pond is stocked, use the hook that you made to see how many clippies you can catch.

What to do: If you are careful, you hook all five clippie fish. If not, the clippies escape to the bottom of the bowl.

Why: Surface tension, that invisible skin that covers the water in the bowl, holds the paper-clip fish within reach of your hook. As long as you don't break that tension, you can keep fishing and end up with the "Catch of the Day."

Unfortunately, if you break the surface tension with your hook, the weight of the clips causes them to sink.

47

42 ◆ Water-Drop Art

YOU WILL NEED:

large piece of waxed paper
wooden toothpick
5 small cups of water
red, green, yellow, and blue
food coloring
eyedropper or drinking straw
paper towels (optional)

While you have probably only used water to clean up after an art lesson, the following experiment will show you how to create a picture using water as the main ingredient.

What to do: Put three or four drops of red coloring into one of four cups of water and do the same with the green, yellow, and blue coloring to make four cups of "water paints." Leave the fifth cup of water clear. Next, spread the waxed paper out on a flat surface. With the eye-dropper, put three or four drops of each color water paint on the waxed paper.

Remember to rinse the eyedropper in the cup of clear water first when you change colors. Continue by dipping one end of a toothpick in the cup of clear water and then putting it near, but not touching, a water drop.

What happens: The water drop moves toward the toothpick, gliding easily over the waxed paper, to help create a picture or design.

Why: The water drop rolls around on the waxed paper because the wax keeps it from soaking in. The water drop is drawn to the wet toothpick because of cohesion—the tendency of molecules that are alike to stick together.

What next: Continue creating your picture or design using water drops in each of the four colors.

When you are finished, you can save the pattern by laying a paper towel over it and letting the towel absorb it. If you don't want to save your work, you can let the different-colored drops touch each other—and watch as they gobble each other up.

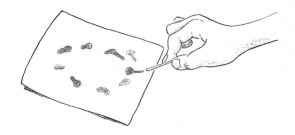

43

Oil versus Water

"Oil and water don't mix." After this experiment, next time you hear anyone say that, you'll know why.

What to do: Pull a few drops of alcohol into the eyedropper and then watch as you release them slowly just below the surface of the water in the glass.

Next, pour some cooking oil into the plastic or paper cup and refill the eye dropper with a few drops of cooking oil and add it to the water just as you did the alcohol.

What happens: The alcohol just disappears. The oil forms drops that float to the surface and stay there.

Why: Water and alcohol attract each other. On leaving the dropper, the molecules of alcohol rush to grab hold of the nearest water molecules, fitting together perfectly to form a solution.

Oil and water are the opposite. They push each other away. So the oil molecules pull together against the pressure of the surrounding water to form bubbles. Because water is heavier than oil, it presses down and the bubbles of oil are forced upward to float on the surface of the water.

44

Make a Waterwheel

Huge waterwheels are used in large rivers to generate, or produce, a certain kind of electricity called hydroelectric power. You can make a model of a waterwheel in your sink.

What to do: Using the scissors, cut six 1-inch slits spaced evenly around the outside edge of the plate to form the waterwheel's blades. Bend these blades away from the plate to make them more efficient. Next, push a pencil through the center of the plate and work it back and forth a few times so that the pencil moves easily.

Now, turn on the water faucet so that a fast stream of water flows out. Hold the pencil so that one blade of the plate catches the water.

What happens: The waterwheel will begin to spin!

Why: The water tumbles out of the faucet, pushes against one blade of the plate, then another, and another, until the waterwheel is powered into motion. This motion can be used to generate more power. That is why electricity plants are built next to dams or fast-flowing rivers.

Deep-Bottle Diver

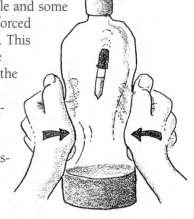

45

YOU WILL NEED:
2-liter plastic bottle with cap
tap water
eyedropper

If you have ever played submarine in the bathtub, you will like the following experiment.

What to do: Fill the bottle to the top with water. Pull a little tap water up into the eyedropper and place it inside the bottle so that the dropper floats near the top. Replace the bottle cap. Now, press the sides of the bottle in and then release them.

What happens: When you press the sides of the bottle, the eyedropper "diver" sinks to the bottom. When you release the sides, the "diver" rises again.

Why: When the sides of the plastic bottle are pressed in, it increases the water pressure equally throughout the bottle and some additional water is forced into the eyedropper. This makes it "dive." The amount of water in the eyedropper can be controlled by changing the water pressure in the bottle: pressing = more pressure; not pressing = less pressure.

The Warm and Cold of It

46

YOU WILL NEED:
2 small balloons
2 large, tall jars
cold and warm tap water

When swimming in a lake, have you ever glided down deep beneath the smooth surface and found the water there to be suddenly colder? Here's why.

What to do: Fill each of the balloons with cold water, loop the end over and tie a tight knot to keep the water inside. (If your tap water is not very cold, put some in a pitcher and add ice to cool it before filling the balloons.) Now, fill one of the jars about halfway with warm water and the other one halfway with cold water. Place a water-filled balloon into each jar.

What happens: The balloon filled with cold water sinks to the bottom of the jar of warm water but floats in the jar of cold water.

Why: Cold water is heavier than warm water because the cold-water molecules are denser, that is, stick closer together. So the weight of the cold water in the balloon drags it down to the bottom of the jar of warm water. Where the balloon floats in the jar of cold water depends on the temperature difference of the water in the balloon and the jar.

Make a Purple People-Eater

Sometimes, on a dull, rainy day, it's fun to mix up a Purple People-Eater.

YOU WILL NEED:

red food coloring
blue food coloring
2/3 cup of tap water
mixing bowl
spoon
1 cup of cornstarch
2 marbles (optional)

What to do: Put three drops of red and three drops of blue food coloring in the water to make purple. Pour the cornstarch into a mixing bowl. Slowly add the water, stirring to mix well. Now, grab a handful of the mixture and form a ball by rolling it between your hands. Stop rolling and let the mixture rest on your outstretched palm.

Why: As you have already learned, both salt and sugar dissolve in water to form solutions. Cornstarch, however, does not form a solution with water. Instead, the cornstarch particles are simply held together by the water, creating a mixture called a suspension. When you roll the mixture in your hands, it squeezes together on all sides and feels dry. But, when you stop rolling, the cornstarch particles in the mixture drift apart, creating an ooze.

What next: Press two marble "eyes" into your Purple People Eater, and you will have created a monster that any Dr. Frankenstein would be proud of.

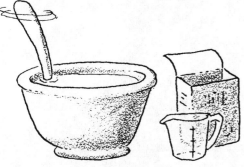

What happens: While you are rolling the mixture between your hands, it feels dry. When you stop rolling, the ball suddenly turns into an ooze!

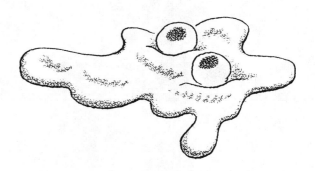

Seeing the Light

Like heat, sound, and electricity, light is a form of energy on which all life on Earth depends. Unlike sound, light can travel where there is not even any air, and it can do so at the fastest speed known—186,000 miles per second.

About Light

We see an object because light reflected from that object reaches our eyes. Over the centuries, people believed that light consisted of tiny particles. Others thought differently, although nearly everyone agreed that light traveled in straight lines. Today, scientists have learned that light sometimes acts like particles and sometimes like waves. Maybe you'll be the one to discover someday what light really is.

48 Sometimes Bigger Is Better

YOU WILL NEED:
food box or package
clear glass of water

Have you ever wondered what is in some of the food you eat? Many people do, but they don't read the ingredients listed on the side of the package because the print is so small it is hard to see. The following experiment will help you to read more about it.

What to do: Hold the food box up close to the glass and look through it at the ingredients list printed on the box.

What happens: The print on the package appears much larger and is easier to read.

Why: Because the drinking glass is curved, the light rays enter at an angle and are bent as they pass from the glass to the water. This is called refraction. The result is a homemade magnifying "glass."

49 Make Your Own Movie Screen

Have you ever wondered, at a movie theatre, how that narrow beam of light from the projection booth at the back could light up and fill a whole movie screen from so far away? Here's how.

YOU WILL NEED:
shoebox with a lid
ruler
pencil
small knife or scissors
flashlight
graph paper
(lined to make squares)
a helper

What to do: With the ruler and pencil, measure and mark out a small square in each end of the shoebox and carefully cut them out. Replace the lid of the box. Turn on the flashlight and aim the light through the square cutouts in the box while a friend or helper on the other side of the box "catches" the light on a piece of graph paper. Ask your friend first to stand close to the box, then step back one ruler length from the box, then another ruler length. Watch the light on the paper.

What happens: As your friend moves farther away from the shoebox, more and more of the squares on the graph paper are lit up, but the light's brightness begins to fade.

Why: Once the light beam passes through the holes in the shoebox, it begins to spread out. The light loses more and more of its brightness as the same amount of light from the flashlight spreads out to fill a larger area.

Also, once it reaches the paper, part of the light's energy is absorbed by the molecules in the graph paper. Other light rays bounce, or reflect, off the graph paper and scatter around the room. This is called diffusion. It is your eyes' ability to detect this reflected light which allows you to see.

The Reappearing Penny

This is a fun trick to play on your friends because your hands never touch the penny.

What to do: Put the penny in the empty dish and set it on a table or countertop. Next, while watching the penny, have your friend back away from the dish slowly until its edge just blocks the view of the penny. Tell your friend not to move, and you'll make the penny magically reappear. Then, slowly fill the dish with water.

What happens: Your friend will see the penny gradually come back into view.

Why: When you put water in the dish, it bends the light reflected from the penny around the edge of the dish to reach your friend's eye again.

---

51 Big Bold Letters

Big, bold, or fat print is easier to see than small, skinny print. Here's how to make small letters appear fatter.

What to do: Using your finger, place a dab of vegetable oil on a word on the magazine page. Gently, rub it into the paper. Now, using the eyedropper, put one drop of water on top of the oil-coated word.

What happens: When you read the word through the water drop, it looks bigger.

Why: The oil you rubbed in has coated or conditioned the paper so that the water does not soak in. As a result, the drop of water sits on top of the word and forms a lens. This lens changes the path of the light that reflects off the page and reaches your eyes and makes the word look fatter.

This same principle is used in making eyeglasses, except that it is glass, not water, that bends the light, causing it to reach our eyes at the correct angle to see better.

Amazing 3-Ring Light Show

When blue, red, and green paint are mixed together, they make black. When blue, red, and green light are mixed together... a surprising thing happens! Can you guess what?

YOU WILL NEED:

3 flashlights, same kind
sheets of cellophane
paper or transparent
plastic wrap—1 blue,
1 red, and 1 green
3 rubber bands
white wall
small table or bench
1 or 2 helpers

What to do: Using the rubber bands, fasten a different-colored sheet over the head of each flashlight.
Now, place the three flashlights on a table or bench, or get one or two helpers or friends to help you, and aim the flashlights at the wall. The two outside flashlights should be turned slightly toward the middle one, which should be aimed straight ahead.
Then, turn on all three flashlights, moving the two outer ones so that the three circles of light on the wall overlap.

What happens: A rounded triangle of white light appears in the middle of the three overlapped colored circles.

Why: Light has within it all colors, which is why it sometimes makes something called a continuous spectrum, in other words, a rainbow.

By passing the white light through the red sheet, only red light comes out. The same thing happens with the other color sheets, so you get the three primary colors: red, green and blue. When all the colors come together again, in the middle of the lights, the mixture of all the three colors forms a rounded white triangle.

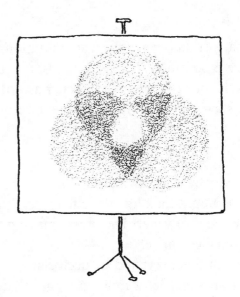

SOUNDS LIKE FUN

What you know as sound are vibrations that travel to the ear via a sound carrier. Because there is so much air, it is the most common carrier of sound, but it is also the slowest. Sound travels four times as fast in water as it does in air. Sound travels faster at high temperatures, but slower high in the atmosphere or on mountaintops where there are fewer air molecules to vibrate.

About Sound

Sound waves from vibrating objects are sent out in all directions. If you could see them, the waves might look like the circles, or ripples that spread out when a rock is thrown into a quiet pool of water. The object making the vibrations, or sound, would be in the center of the smallest circle.

Sound is measured by decibels. These measurements go from 1 (a sound that can barely be heard) to 130 or more. A sound that measures 120 decibels hurts most people's ears. Some sounds can be so high, or squeaky, in pitch that people can't hear them, but some animals can.

Deep "C", High "C"

53

YOU WILL NEED:
large jar
small jar

Sound is made up of waves that move through the air much like the rippling circles that move across the surface when a rock is thrown into a quiet pond.

What to do: First, hold the opening of the large jar to your mouth and hum into it; then hum the same way into the smaller jar.

What happens: A deeper sound is heard when you hum into the large jar, and a higher sound when you hum into the small jar.

Why: The pitch of the sound depends on the height and diameter of the jar. Because there is more room in the large jar, your humming makes longer sound waves, so you hear a deeper, lower sound in that jar.

The sound waves in the smaller jar have less room, so they are shortened, and the frequency, or pitch, of the sound you hear is higher.

What next: Try some other empty jars. How do they sound?

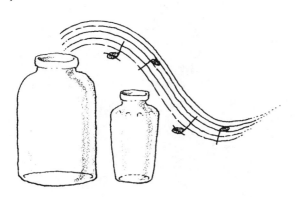

Catching Sound

54

YOU WILL NEED:
a helper
2 paper-towel tubes
a wall
clock or kitchen timer
that ticks loudly

The following experiment will show you how you can produce an echo, without leaving home in search of a canyon.

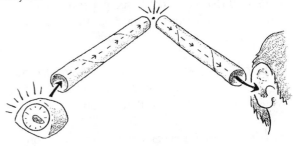

What to do: Place one end of each cardboard tube on a slant against a wall, so that they come to a point, or make at least a 45° angle.

Have your helper hold the ticking clock at the other, open end of his or her tube. Listen at the open end of your tube.

What happens: You can clearly hear the ticking sound of the clock through the cardboard tube.

Why: Normally, the sound waves sent out into the air by the ticking clock would scatter in all directions, becoming fainter the farther away from the clock they traveled.

By using the tubes, the sound waves of the clock's ticking are captured and directed down one tube. Then, if the tubes are held correctly, the sound waves bounce off the wall and shoot up through the second tube for you to hear—just like an echo.

Change places, now, so your helper is on the receiving end of the bouncing sound waves.

The Amazing Hum-o-comb

You don't need private lessons, sheet music, or even a teacher to learn how to play this musical instrument, and making it is a snap.

What to do: Wrap the tissue paper around the comb, teeth side down. Now, hold the comb up against your lips and hum loudly.

What happens: Even though you aren't blowing on the tissue paper at all, you feel it vibrating. Your humming sounds different, too.

Why: The tissue paper vibrates, just like your vocal cords, because sound waves from your humming are hitting it. The vibrations of the tissue paper molecules add a whole new sound to your humming.

What next: Don't stop with one selection. Any song that you know can be played on a comb. Get several friends together and put on an Amazing Hum-o-comb concert.

Was It Ripped or Torn?

You snag your clothing on a nail or something at school. You can tell right away, without looking, if it was ripped or torn. How? Physics tells us, listen to the sound.

What to do: Hold the edge of the cloth in your two hands and pull evenly, tearing the cloth slowly. Now, grab the cloth and yank it apart suddenly, so that it rips in your hands.

What happens: When you pulled slowly, the tearing cloth made a lower sound than when you pulled suddenly.

Why: Each time a thread in the cloth is broken, the molecules in the air around it are set into motion. When the cloth is torn, the air molecules are not bumped around as fast and the sound, or pitch, is lower.

When the cloth is ripped, however, the air molecules are bounded around at a higher rate of speed, and a higher-pitched sound is heard.

Make Your Own Sound Studio

57

Do you like to sing in the shower? Usually your singing sounds better there than it does in the family room. How come?

YOU WILL NEED:
tape recorder with
separate microphone
very large new or
clean metal bucket
a helper

What to do: Hold the microphone and turn on the tape recorder. Sing any song that you like. Turn off the tape recorder.

Still holding the microphone, pick up and put the bucket over your head. Then, turn on the tape recorder again. (You might need a friend to help you here, with that bucket over your head!)

Now, sing the same song that you sang before. Remove the bucket and turn the recorder off when you are finished singing. Rewind and play through the tape.

What happens: Your song sounds richer in tone and louder in volume when you sing with your head in the bucket.

Why: The sound waves from your voice cause the molecules in the metal bucket and air inside it to vibrate and "build up" your normal voice, much like a professional sound studio does for recording artists. The same thing happens when you sing in the shower.

The Silence of Snow

58

YOU WILL NEED:
2 paper clips
18 or 20 cotton balls
white glue
whistle

Is it quieter outside after a snowfall? It's true that the snow does provide a soft carpet for your feet, but what about all the other noises?

What to do: Glue the cotton balls to the inside of one paper cup until it is completely covered with the cotton "snow." Then, blow the whistle inside the cup with no cotton stuffing and listen to the sound. Next, put the whistle inside the snow-covered paper cup and blow again.

What happens: The whistle's sound in the first cup is loud. Inside the "snow-filled" paper cup,

however, the whistle's shrill notes sound like a flute being played in a closet.

Why: Like snowflakes, cotton balls have hundreds of tiny spaces between them. Sound waves get trapped in these tiny spaces and are muffled, like in winter when you can't hear someone trying to talk to you through a heavy scarf or muffler.

Now, you also know why there is a law requiring all cars to have mufflers.

59

Cigar-Box Guitar

Years ago, many people made their own musical instruments. They loved music, but instruments were expensive and they had little money to buy them. Today, right now, you can do the same thing.

YOU WILL NEED:
cigar box
(or similar box with rigid sides)
6 assorted rubber bands (including 1 very wide and 1

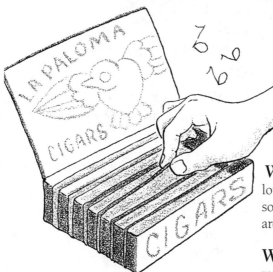

What to do: Open the lid of the cigar box and keep it open (or remove it altogether). Now, beginning with the widest rubber band, then to the next-to-the-widest, place them lengthwise around the cigar box. Try to space the rubber bands equally, about one finger-width apart.

When you have all six "guitar stings" in place, give each of them a pluck.

What happens: The wide rubber band has a low sound, the very narrow "string" has a high sound, and the sounds of the other rubber bands are somewhere in between.

Why: The wide rubber band has a low vibration rate and does not produce many sound waves.

The narrow rubber band, however, has a high vibration rate and produces a higher number of sound waves with a higher tone or pitch.

But that's not all. Pitch also depends on the degree of tightness, or tautness, of the "string." A wider but short rubber band that is pulled very tight might make a higher sound than a narrower rubber band that is put on more loosely.

What next: Listen to the sounds of each of your instrument's strings again. If needed, switch them around so that the sounds are in order, from the lowest to the highest. When you are ready, sing a tune and accompany yourself on your cigar-box guitar.

Dance, Sprinkles, Dance

60

YOU WILL NEED:

small, round oatmeal box, with top

sharp knife (ask for permission or help)

candy sprinkles

Does certain music make you want to dance like crazy? It's not wild—it's physics!

What to do: Cut an egg-size hole in the side of the oatmeal box, about 2 finger-digits (1½ inches) up from the bottom. Next, put a few sprinkles on the top of the box.

Now, put your mouth to the hole in the box and hum loudly. Begin with low notes and then move on up to the higher ones.

What happens: Somewhere, as you go up the scale of notes, the candy sprinkles will begin to dance!

Why: The molecules on the box top are set into motion when one certain note is reached. That particular note is called the box top's resonant frequency—a note that makes it all happen. When the box top vibrates, the sprinkles dance.

Other hummed notes will make the sprinkles move slightly, but only one really makes them jump!

Natural Vibrations

61

Do you know why soldiers deliberately walk out-of-step rather than march when crossing a bridge? Read on.

YOU WILL NEED:

2 small soda bottles (same kind)

a helper

What to do: Hold one of the small bottles to your ear and listen while your helper or friend blows across the mouth of the second bottle until it makes a clear sound.

What happens: The bottle that you are holding to your ear will vibrate "in sympathy," making a similar but weaker sound than your helper's bottle produced.

Why: Depending upon its size and shape, each object has its own natural rate of vibration. When two objects have the same vibration rate, like the two similar bottles, one can cause the other one to vibrate. When this happens, the two objects are said to be "in resonance."

The officers of soldiers approaching a bridge know that the bridge has a crumpling point related to its natural vibration rate. If the soldiers' even footsteps should happen to match the bridge's natural vibration rate, it could begin to swing and collapse! So soldiers are ordered to walk naturally as they cross the bridge.

62 ◆ Musical Nails

Visitors usually knock or ring the bell at your house door, but have no way to announce their arrival at a screened porch or patio door. A nail chime is the perfect welcoming sound.

What to do: Tie a string to each nail. Tie the other end of each piece of string to the straight lower bar of the coat hanger. Hang the coat hanger on a door knob and open and close the door.

YOU WILL NEED:
wire coat hanger
10 different-size nails
10 pieces of string

What happens: You hear a pleasant chiming sound as the nails jingle.

Why: When the door is opened and closed, the movement causes the nails to hit against each other and the door frame and vibrate. Each nail, depending on its size and what it is made of, makes a different note. All the nails vibrating together produce the chiming sound.

If the pieces of string were not attached to the coat hanger, and you just held them in your hand, the nails would not vibrate together or as long. Also, the sound from each nail would be much softer and quieter.

Make a Megaphone 63 ◆

Have you ever cupped your hands around your mouth when you wanted to yell a message to someone far away? You were on the right track.

What to do: Put the rubber band around the middle of the plastic jug to serve as your cutting guide. Then, carefully, force the sharp point of the scissors through the lower part of the jug, below the rubber band.

Following the edge of the rubber band, cut the jug apart. Discard the bottom half of the jug.
Now, speak in a normal voice to someone across the room. Then, talk into the mouth of the megaphone that is aimed across the room.

What happens: Your voice is louder and can be heard farther when the megaphone is used.

YOU WILL NEED:
clean plastic milk jug or well-rinsed bleach container
large rubber band
heavy scissors or kitchen shears

Why: When you just speak, the sound waves ripple out in all directions, getting weaker the farther out they go.

The megaphone, on the other hand, aims all your sound waves in one direction, like a baseball hit to centerfield. Sound waves sent through a megaphone, therefore, lose less of their energy in transit and arrive with more volume.

What next: Create an original design for your megaphone, using markers, stickers, and cutouts. Decorate it with your school colors and your name. Don't forget to take it with you next time you go to the ballpark.

Dancing Cereal Puffs

While air molecules are usually invisible, in this experiment, disguised as cereal puffs, they dance and pass along the sound.

What to do: Tie a piece of thread around each piece of cereal. Tie the other ends of the threads onto the straight lower bar of the coat hanger. Hook the coat hanger onto a shelf or the back of a chair, or ask someone to hold it for you.

Then, holding one end of the rubber band in your clenched teeth, pull the other end of the band toward, but not touching, one of the middle pieces of puffed cereal. Pluck the stretched band like a banjo. Be careful not to let it snap out of your hand.

What happens: The middle cereal puff begins to move back and forth, touching its neighboring puffs on each side.

Why: The vibrations of the plucked rubber band stir the air molecules around and inside the middle piece of cereal. Like the invisible air molecules, the puff dances from side to side and passes along the vibrations to the other nearby puffs.

The cereal pieces will continue to swing until all the vibrations, or energy, from the plucked rubber band are gone.

If the rubber band is plucked harder a second time, more of the cereal pieces will move because the sound and vibrating air molecules will travel farther. None of the cereal puffs, however, will sway very far.

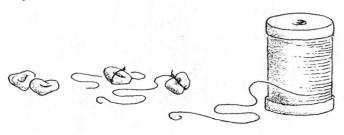

Wild Animal Calls

If you like to play jungle safari, here is a way to make your adventure sound more realistic.

YOU WILL NEED:

large throw-away plastic cup

piece of heavy cotton string, about 12 inches long

pencil or nail

toothpick

wet paper towel

What to do: Use the pencil to poke a hole in the middle of the bottom of the plastic cup. Push one end of the cotton string into and through the hole, then tie that end of the string tightly around the middle of the toothpick. Pull the string back through the cup so that the toothpick fits nicely in the bottom of the cup. (Break the ends off the toothpick, if necessary, to make it fit.)

Squeeze out any excess water from the paper towel (you don't want to get the string too wet). Then wrap the towel around the string near the cup. Now, squeezing the paper towel tightly around the string, pull down.

What happens:
A loud "screaking" sound is heard.

Why: The friction from pulling the paper towel down the string causes vibrations, which move along the string to the toothpick in the cup. From the toothpick, the vibrations travel on to the bottom and sides of the cup. Not only do these sound vibrations move farther, but they get louder because the cup also acts like a megaphone, sending the vibrations out into the surrounding air molecules.

What next: To make a variety of "animal" calls, try using different-size plastic cups. You can also experiment with different-texture strings for some really wild sounds.

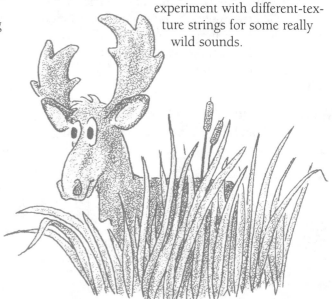

64

A MATTER OF GRAVITY

Gravity is the pull that objects have on other objects around them. All objects have gravity, which means that they are always trying to pull other objects toward them. The larger an object, the stronger its pull. Because the Earth itself is the largest object in our world, the pull of its gravity is the strongest we can feel.

About Gravity

It was in 1687 that Isaac Newton discovered and proved the existence of a force called gravity. The story goes that one day Newton was sitting under an apple tree watching the moon moving in the sky when he was almost hit on the head by a falling apple. Many people before Newton had seen apples fall to the ground, but he not only saw it happen, he also wondered why... and figured it out.

When you throw a ball in the air, gravity pulls it down. When you sit on the sofa, gravity holds you down, and when you walk, gravity keeps your feet on the ground. Without gravity we would all float off into outer space.

Feel the Force

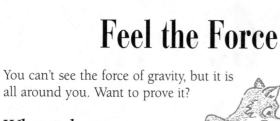

66

YOU WILL NEED:
low, sturdy chair

You can't see the force of gravity, but it is all around you. Want to prove it?

What to do: Place the low chair in front of you. Get ready, and jump onto the chair. Next, turn around, get ready, and jump down. Feel the difference?

Do it again. This time, when you jump down, close your eyes. Feel it this time?

What happens: It is a lot harder to jump up onto the chair than to jump down.

Why: Gravity is the force that pulls all objects down toward the middle of the Earth. When you jump up, you are jumping against the force of gravity, which is pulling you back. When you jump down, the force is with you. It is doing all of the work. You really only have to step off the chair seat.

Which Drops Faster?

67

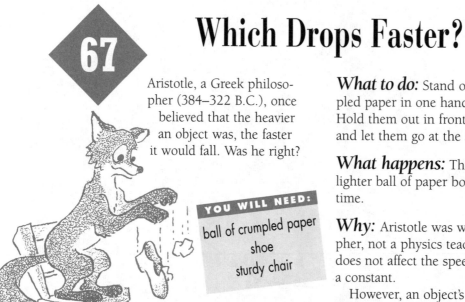

Aristotle, a Greek philosopher (384–322 B.C.), once believed that the heavier an object was, the faster it would fall. Was he right?

YOU WILL NEED:
ball of crumpled paper
shoe
sturdy chair

What to do: Stand on the chair with the crumpled paper in one hand and the shoe in the other. Hold them out in front of you as high as you can and let them go at the same time.

What happens: The heavier shoe and the lighter ball of paper both hit the floor at the same time.

Why: Aristotle was wrong. (He was a philosopher, not a physics teacher.) An object's weight does not affect the speed at which it falls, which is a constant.

However, an object's shape does affect its speed. For example, if the paper had not been crumpled into a ball, the air hitting its under-surface as it fell would have slowed its rate of fall and the shoe would have hit the floor first.

Why not get another sheet of paper and try it?

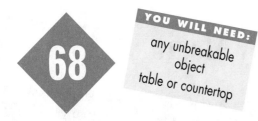

YOU WILL NEED:
any unbreakable object
table or countertop

Find the Center of Gravity

Want to find an object's center of gravity? It may sound hard, but it's really very simple.

What to do: Slowly push the unbreakable object to the table's edge. Keep pushing, pushing, pushing until—

What happens: The object suddenly falls to the floor!

Why: When the object's center of gravity passes the table's edge, the object will fall to the floor. Try to balance the object on the table's edge. When you do, its center of gravity has been found.

69 # Wacky Ball

YOU WILL NEED:
Ping-Pong ball
flat-headed straight pin
tabletop

If you have ever tried to play Ping-Pong with a ball that had a nick in it, then you have played Wacky ball.

What to do: Press the pin firmly into any spot on the ball. Now, roll the ball across the tabletop.

What happens: The ball always stops rolling with the pin head touching the tabletop.

Why: Before the pin was pressed into the ball, all of its weight was concentrated in its middle, the point known as the center of gravity.

With the pin pushed into the side of the ball, its center of gravity is shifted from the middle to the side with the pin. Now, the ball will stop rolling only when the pin is at its lowest possible point, pulled there by the force of gravity. That ball's not as wacky as it seems.

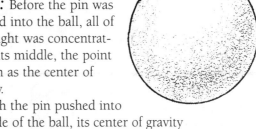

Anti-Gravity Magic

Everyone knows that water flows downwards. It has to because of gravity's pull. But here is a fun way to defy gravity and make water flow upwards…just this once.

What to do: About 30 minutes before you want to do the experiment, fill one of the bottles with cold tap water and put it in the refrigerator to make sure it's cold. When you are ready to start, turn on the hot water faucet and let the water run until it is very hot. Turn off the tap.

Put the funnel in the second small bottle, place it under the faucet, and carefully fill the bottle with hot tap water.

Set the bottle of hot water in a bowl on a table or counter top. Add three or four drops of food coloring to the hot water. Wait a few seconds until the coloring mixes with the water.

Now, remove the first bottle of cold water from the refrigerator and place the index card or cardboard over the top of it.

Next, holding the index card firmly against the bottle's mouth, with your helper's assistance quickly turn the bottle upside down and set the bottle of cold water on top of the bottle of hot colored water.

Match up the two bottle tops end-to-end, then ask your helper to hold the two bottles steady while you slide the index card out from in between.

What happens: The blue hot water flows upward into the cold-water bottle, seeming to defy gravity!

Why: Hot water is not as heavy as cold water and its molecules are more active, so it rises to the top of the cold water, taking the blue food coloring with it.

Gradually, the hot and cold waters will mix until the temperature is evenly warm throughout, and the blue food coloring will be distributed between both bottles.

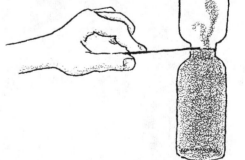

PHYSICS MIX

In earlier experiments, you have learned something about heat and air, water and light, sound and gravity.

About Physics

But there is still more, much more, to physics. There are laws of motion, natural rhythms, and strange forces that surround you and that you can learn to understand and use.

The experiments in this short section will just touch on these other areas of physics. Here you will discover the whirlpool in your home, the energy you create by brushing your hair, and the working pendulum. But when you finish these experiments, it is only a start. Physics has so much more for you to examine and study, to learn from and to marvel at. And it's all around you. All you have to do is look.

The Deep, Dark Hole

YOU WILL NEED:

mixing bowl

water

large spoon

Ever try to make a hole in water? It's easy.

What to do: Fill the mixing bowl half-full of water. Then, take the spoon and stir the water quickly until it is spinning around the bowl.

What happens: The water climbs the sides of the mixing bowl, leaving a "hole" in the middle.

Why: When you stir, the spinning water moves away from the center of the bowl because of the outward pull of centrifugal force and forms a whirlpool, or vortex.

The "hole" that forms at the bottom of the whirlpool is smaller than the one at the top because of water pressure. The weight of the water above prevents the water below it from spreading out too much.

A Gyroscope in Your Pocket

YOU WILL NEED:

large-size coin

Did you know that the reason you are able to stay up on a moving bicycle is because you are riding on two gyroscopes? Read on.

What to do: Try to balance the coin, make it stand up on end. Can you do it? Now, hold the coin straight up and "flick" it with your finger to make it spin.

What happens: Although the coin first fell over when you tried to balance it, the spinning coin balances on edge for a moment, until it slows down.

Why: As it turns, the coin becomes a simple gyroscope, or top. The spinning motion causes the coin to stand on its end. The coin's center of gravity now runs straight down through it from edge to edge, keeping the spinning coin in place and balanced.

What next: When you become an expert coin-spinner, try getting the coin to spin on smaller and narrower surfaces, like the end of a can or a glass, or on a book or a ruler.

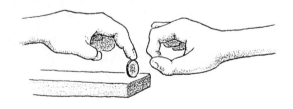

The Kissing Balloons

If kissing is frowned upon in your school, you'd better get permission for these two "kissing cousins" to visit your science class.

What to do: Blow up the balloons and tie a string to each one and hold them. Now, using the markers, carefully draw a "boy" face on one balloon and a "girl" face on the other.

When the marker ink is dry, hold the balloons and rub each face several times with the flannel or rayon cloth. Put the balloons face to face.

What happens: The balloons will begin to kiss. They will also kiss your hair and your sweater, if you let them.

Why: When the piece of flannel or rayon is rubbed across their faces, the friction, or rubbing, charges the balloons with static electricity. Made up of positive and negative electrical charges, which attract each other, it is very sticky stuff.

Unlike regular electricity that flows through

YOU WILL NEED:

2 light-colored latex balloons
2 pieces of string
piece of flannel or rayon cloth
permanent markers

wires and is very dangerous, static electricity stays in one place. Although it can give you a scary "zap" sometimes, it is really harmless.

What next: Give the balloons a few more rubs, to make more static electricity, and see what other materials or things in your home the balloons will "kiss."

Want to see static electricity? Turn out the lights and do some experimenting in the dark.

Make a Balloon Rocket

74

A balloon rocket works the same way a real rocket does, except that it is powered by air instead of rocket fuel.

YOU WILL NEED:
balloon

What to do: Blow up the balloon as full as possible and hold the end tightly closed with your fingers. Now, let go.

What happens: Although it won't head for the moon, the balloon "rockets" around the room.

Why: When you blow up the balloon, the air pressure inside presses equally in all directions and makes the balloon large and round. Everything is so perfectly balanced that the balloon simply floats as you hold it tightly.

As soon as you let go of the balloon, the air inside rushes to get out. The perfect balance of air pressure is gone.

As the air goes in one direction, the balloon goes in the other. This action-reaction motion sends the balloon zooming forward, until all of the air is gone and the balloon falls to the ground.

You have just seen Sir Isaac Newton's third law of motion, "Every action has an equal and opposite reaction," in action.

The Magic Water Bucket

75

You can pour water out, but can you sling it out?

YOU WILL NEED:
small bucket
some rope
water

What to do: Fill the bucket half-full of water. Then tie one end of the rope to the middle of the bucket's handle. Lift the bucket off the ground with the rope and quickly start to sling the bucket around, turning and pulling on the rope until the bucket is swinging around you about waist-high.

What happens: The water stays in the bucket!

Why: As you turn, centrifugal force pulls the bucket, and the water in it, upward and outward as far as the rope will allow. Because the rope holds the bucket's opening toward you, the water is pressed against the bottom of the bucket, even against the force of gravity. Everything is great... until you try to stop! As soon as you slow down, centrifugal force becomes weak or is lost and gravity takes over. That's when, if you're not careful, the water will spill.

Pendulum Sand Painting

76

YOU WILL NEED:

coffee can with plastic lid
hammer
medium-size nail
string
light sand (the clean, store-bought kind works best)
piece of poster board
broom or mop handle
2 chairs
red sand and blue sand

Sand painting is an art form. Using physics, you can create your own sand painting.

What to do: Using the hammer and nail, punch a hole in the middle of the bottom of the can. Then, punch three holes equally spaced around the top edge of the can, just inside the rim.

Cut three short pieces of string, several inches long, and tie them to the can's rim through the holes. Gather the other ends of the strings together and knot them. Cut off a longer piece of string and tie it to this knot.

Set two chairs back to back, with a space between, and slide the broom handle through the chair's slats to hold it steady.

Then, tie the string with the can attached onto the middle of the broom handle. The bottom of the can should be just an inch or two above the floor.

Snap the plastic lid over the bottom of the can and fill the can with either red- or blue-tinted (and dry) sand.

Finally, sprinkle the poster board, giving it a thin layer of white sand, and position it underneath the coffee can. Pull the sand-filled coffee can slightly off to one side, remove the plastic lid to the sand can flow out, and release the can.

To adjust the pattern or give the can a little more "swing," give the string near the can a smooth, light push.

When one color is finished or you want to change colors, put the lid back on the can, put the second color in the can, remove the lid, and start the can swinging again.

What happens: As the sand streams from the can, it makes a series of arcs on the poster board, and a unique sand painting appears right before your eyes.

Why: What you have made with the coffee can is a small version of a pendulum, like Jean Bernard Léon Foucault hung in a church in 1851 to demonstrate the Earth's rotation. Allowed to swing continuously, a pendulum makes one complete circle of arcs every day.

Here, the swinging motion of the pendulum, back and forth and side to side, forms a physics-inspired pattern of curves, or ellipses, on the white sand.

It's Crystal Clear

Crystals are everywhere. Snow, sugar, salt, parts of rocks, and precious jewels are all crystals. Crystals are made up of atoms that join together in a certain different way.

About Crystals

In this part of the book, you'll make crystals from table and rock salt, bluing, sugar, washing soda, and alum. When you're finished, you can invite your friends over for a gem show and display all the crystals you've grown.

Your Diamond Ring?
Just Another Carbon Copy!

Diamonds are carbon crystals. Carbon is a material known as an element. Volcanoes were nature's chemists. The heat and pressure of volcanoes crystallized the carbon into diamonds. When lava reaches the surface of the earth, it cools and hardens and forms a rock called kimberlite. Diamonds are found in kimberlite. Tons of kimberlite have to be washed and crushed just to find one small diamond.

The diamond is the hardest substance found in the earth. An imperfect diamond, not good enough to be mounted on a ring, makes a perfect tool for cutting hard metals. Diamonds are so hard they can cut anything. (If you find something you think might be a diamond, test it by trying to cut with it. If it doesn't cut, it is probably only a piece of glass.)

Sparkling Soda

No, we're not using soda pop in this experiment, but washing soda. That's right! Although this soda is all washed up in this activity, it still sparkles!

What to do: Pour the washing soda slowly into the water, stirring as you pour, until no more will dissolve. Set the cup aside and check the experiment often over the next few hours.

What happens: As the water cools and begins to evaporate, crystals form on the sides and bottom of the cup.

Why: When you dissolve the washing soda (solute) into the hot water (solvent) until no more can be dissolved, you put more solutes in the water than it can possibly hold when it is cool. When this saturated solution cools, the washing soda molecules hook up with each other and form crystals.

What next: Pour the washing soda crystals from the cup into a shallow disposable (frozen food) container. Place them in a warm, sunny place for 24 hours and let the water evaporate. (See "Astronomical White Asteroids.")

Astronomical White Asteroids

Asteroids are irregularly shaped, rocklike chunks in space. Like the planets, they revolve around the sun. Your washing soda, after it is chemically changed, will look very much like these rocklike chunks of space matter. The smallest and largest crystals can be compared to the largest and smallest asteroids, the smallest being less than one mile wide, the largest about 500 miles wide. Save these Sparkling Soda asteroid chunks for "The Gem Show," and use this information for your label.

79 Crazy Cave Icicles

You can make your own crystal rock formations (stalagmites and stalactites) to demonstrate how chemistry in a cave really works.

YOU WILL NEED:
hot tap water
2 one-pint jars
dishcloth
1 cup washing soda
small round dish
3 small pieces of string

What to do: Fill the two jars almost to the top with hot tap water. Stir washing soda into each jar until no more will dissolve. Twist the dishcloth and tie the ends and the middle with the strings. Place the ends of the "rope" you have made into the two jars of water, making a bridge. Make certain that the "rope ends" touch the bottoms of the jars. Place the dish under the cloth bridge to collect the drips. Allow three to five days for icicles to form.

What happens: The water and soda solution travels up both sides of the dishcloth rope and drips from the middle. The drips turn into hard soda pillars with the two columns meeting in the middle. Something similar happens in caves.

However, the buildup of cave deposits takes hundreds of years, while yours take only a few days.

Why: The water travels through the dishcloth rope by filling up all the tiny air pockets in the cloth. This is known as capillary action and it is similar to a row of dominoes falling down. The washing soda is carried along the "rope" by the water, which drips down from the middle. The water evaporates and leaves behind the hardened soda pillar. When you stir the washing soda into the jars until no more can be dissolved, you saturate it. The cooled solution's molecules then crystallize, or harden.

Chemistry in a Cave

Most caves are made of limestone. Limestone is a rock that can be easily worn away by water. Over thousands of years, this solution of water and calcium bicarbonate has gradually carved out great rooms in huge pieces of rock. This same solution drips through cracks in cave ceilings. As the water evaporates in the air, carbon dioxide is given off and the solid mineral calcite is formed. This turns into the hard lime icicle deposits, known as stalactites, found hanging from cave dwellings. Stalagmites are similarly shaped rock formations that build up from the floor, because of the dripping, instead of from the ceiling.

The Diamond Mine

80

Alum is a type of mineral or chemical salt that puts the pucker into some pickles, making your mouth feel as if it wants to close up. It looks and feels very much like table salt (sodium chloride), but while table salt in a microscope looks like ice cubes, with flat sides, alum crystals have many angular sides, or facets. Try making your own clear alum crystals and you'll think you've discovered a diamond mine.

What to do: Slowly and carefully pour the alum into the cup of water, stirring as you pour, until no more will dissolve. You'll know when the solution is saturated because you'll hear the alum grains scratching on the bottom of the cup and you'll see some floating in the water. If you put your finger in the cup and touch the bottom, you'll be able to feel the undissolved crystals. Keep the solution in the cup overnight.

The next day, pour the water into the jar and tie one end of the nylon thread around a large piece of hardened alum crystal you'll find in the bottom or on the sides of the cup. (Be patient with this. If you've ever threaded a sewing needle, you'll understand what we mean. It's hard to tie the fine nylon thread around the small alum crystals.) Wind and tie the thread around the middle of a pencil and place the pencil over the jar mouth so that the alum dangles low in the water. Keep the jar in a protected place for several days and observe the crystals from time to time.

Note: Save the other alum crystals on the bottom of the paper cup and set them to dry on a paper towel. Place them on a dark piece of construction paper and study them with your hand lens. Save these shiny, many-sided alum crystals for "The Gem Show."

What happens: If you hold the thread up to the light and view the alum crystals, you'll see what appears to be many shiny brilliant gems.

Why: Again, the crystals are formed by dissolving enough solutes or solid substances (alum) in the solvent or water to make a saturated solution. Then the cooled solution causes the alum molecules on the string to build on one another. Crystals will continue to form on the crystal string until all of the solution evaporates.

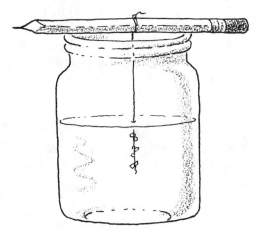

77

81

Blue Moon Rocks

YOU WILL NEED:
frozen-food tray
paper towels
disposable cup
3 tablespoons salt
3 tablespoons water
3 tablespoons laundry bluing
spoon
magnifying hand lens
newspaper

You'll think you've stepped out on the moon when you grow this crystal garden. Make certain you cover your work area with newspapers so you won't have crystals growing everywhere!

What to do: Place a folded paper towel in the bottom of the tray. Crush the second paper towel and place it on top. In the disposable cup, mix all the ingredients together and slowly spoon the mixture over the paper. With the hand lens observe what happens.

What happens: Blue bubbly crystals instantly appear in the container. (For a full garden, it will have to set for at least 24 hours.)

Why: The salt solution with the bluing becomes saturated until no more can dissolve. As the water is soaked up by the paper towels and evaporates, the salt left behind forms new crystals around the powdery bluing.

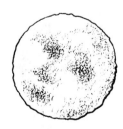

82

Rocky Mountains

Watch these beautiful rock salt crystals climb on the sides of a string and turn into sparkling mountains of diamondlike cubes. Follow the instructions as in "The Diamond Mine," but replace the alum with $1/2$ cup of rock salt. Use a strong string dangling from a pencil to catch the growing crystals. Don't rush this one! Great mountains of crystals may take as long two to four weeks to grow.

About Crystals

Crystals can be grown from a string tied to a pencil and placed across a cup or glass, or scraped with a spoon from the sides and bottom of the container. Keep the crystal solutions in a warm, sunny window. The longer the crystal solution is left to evaporate, the larger the crystals will be.

Store your crystals in a dry place and be careful handling them. If your hands are wet or damp, it is best to use tweezers or a plastic spoon.

The Gem Show

Invite your friends over for a gem show. It's easy and it's lots of fun! Display your sugar, salt, alum, and washing soda crystals in a special way. Line lids of small boxes with dark paper or cloth and place your crystals in them. Place the lids on an outside table for "crystal viewing" on a sunny day. Use information from this book to make labels for your crystal trays. Supply plenty of magnifying hand lenses for viewing. You may even give a demonstration on how to make crystals with a saturated solution.

Also, you can separate your crystals and glue some onto rings for a special display. (Plain rings can be purchased at hobby stores or made with pipe cleaners.) Try adding a drop or two of food coloring to your solutions when you make crystals. You'll be able to make simulated or fake rubies, emeralds, or sapphires. You can add these to your rings, make crystal-designed holiday ornaments, or use them in other crafts. With a little imagination, the possibilities for exciting crystal-craft projects are endless.

Hi, Sugar!

With all your experience with saturated solutions, now make a saturated sugar collection. You can use a string on a pencil to catch your crystals or leave them in the bottom of a jar or cup and collect them later. Keep them for displaying in "The Gem Show."

Unlike salt crystals, which look like cubes, sugar crystals are long and have flat, slanted sides.

THE LAB:
CO$_2$ AND YOU

In this chapter, you'll make a manometer, an exciting and great piece of chemistry equipment to put in your laboratory, a place where you, as chief chemist, will be doing your own research and studies. A manometer is easy and inexpensive to make and fun to use. With it you'll be able to test substances for carbon-dioxide (CO$_2$) gas.

But first, it's time to solve the mystery of the rising doughs and find out which contains the most CO$_2$ gas, a definitely air-raising experience!

Dynamite Dumplings

YOU WILL NEED:

small cup, for mixing

cup filled with very hot water

test substances:

1/2 tablespoon baking powder

1/2 tablespoon baking soda

1/2 tablespoon quick-rising dry yeast

flour

cool water

teaspoon

tablespoon

What substances added to flour and water produce the most carbon-dioxide (CO_2) gas? In this three-part experiment you'll make a water and flour dough three times, using a different combination of substances.

Each part of the experiment will be done separately, using the same equipment and ingredients, almost.

The only thing to change will be the substance to be tested: baking powder, baking soda, or quick-rising dry yeast. Before you start, make a hypothesis, or scientific guess, as to which substance contains the most carbon dioxide gas. Then do the tests and find out if you are right.

What to do: With a teaspoon, mix a full tablespoon of dry flour with the first test substance, the baking powder, in a cup or mug. Add a little bit of cool water, a drop at a time, and make a ball of dough. If the mixture becomes too wet, add more flour. Place the ball of dough in a tablespoon. Leave the spoon in a cool place while you fill another cup or mug with very hot water (from the tap, or warmed on the stove or in a microwave).

For about two minutes, hold the spoon with the dough over the hot water. Let the spoon touch the water, and a little of the hot water enter it. Set the ball of dough inside.

Now, repeat the experiment, but instead of the baking powder, use baking soda. Then do the experiment again with the third substance, the quick-rising yeast.

What happens: All the dough balls grow much larger.

Why: The baking powder contains bicarbonate of soda. When combined with flour, water, and heat, it produces a chemical change which produces carbon-dioxide gas. This is seen in the gas-bubble holes that appear in the dough and make it larger. The baking soda and the yeast doughs also produce chemical changes and CO_2 gas. The baking soda dough will probably grow less than the baking powder and yeast doughs, which may even double in size. Of the two, the yeast dough should grow slightly larger. Was your hypothesis corrected?

86 ◆ How to Make a Manometer

Your manometer is simply a plastic tube pushed down inside a glass bottle with the other end attached to a stick. You'll use it to test different substances for carbon-dioxide gas and have the fun of watching the colored water rise in the plastic tube, somewhat like a thermometer. You can even calibrate, or put lines on, your tube-stick with a marker pen to measure, and record, how much gas is in a substance. If the colored water shoots up the tube or even comes out of it, you'll know the test substance produces a lot of carbon dioxide gas.

What to do: Clean the bottle thoroughly. Have someone make a large hole in the bottle lid with the nail and hammer. (It will have to be large enough to hold the tube.) Push about 4 inches of the 28 inches of tubing through the hole in the lid into the bottle. (Bend the tube back and forth to straighten it). Make a small clay rope and press it around the hole in the cap to make the bottle airtight. Now take the jar lid and press clay into the bottom of it; put a little more in the middle.

At this point, you may wish to draw some measurement lines on the stick with a marking

YOU WILL NEED:

16-ounce (473 ml) glass bottle with a screw-on top

28 inches (71 cm) of home aquarium air tubing

small drinking glass half-filled with water

food coloring (any color)

wide-mouth jar lid

large nail and hammer

stick about 16 inches (40 cm) long

rubber bands or twist ties

medicine dropper

modeling clay

scissors

pen. Each line should be 1 cm from the next, starting from the middle of the stick to one end. Number the lines, starting with "1" in the middle. This makes a nice scale and lets you know how much each substance causes your manometer to register.

Now, push the stick into the clay stand so that it stands up. Bend the outside tubing to the bottom of the bottle and stand to form a lower loop and fasten the rest of the tubing to the stick with the rubber bands. The tube opening should be at the top of the stick. You are now ready to fill the lower loop with colored water.

Put a few drops of food coloring in the half-glass of water to color it. With the medicine dropper, drop one or two drops of colored water into the top of the tube on the stick. If the water separates in the tube, gently suck or blow on the straw to bring the water drops together. You now have a new piece of chemistry equipment to use in your lab experiments.

87 ◆ The Care and Use of Your Manometer

1. Work on a kitchen counter, in case your manometer blows its top (loses liquid)!

2. Keep added colored water in a small, closed bottle, to replace any water lost during experiments or storage.

3. When taking the top off the manometer bottle to add solutions, place the tube with the lid on it into another similar empty bottle so that the colored water in the tube won't escape or break up.

4. So as not to twist the tube and loosen the seal, screw the bottle into the cap instead of the cap onto the bottle.

5. Store your manometer in a small box. Make certain the cap with the tube in it is screwed tightly on the bottle.

6. Drop only one or two drops of colored water into the top of the plastic tube on the stick. If the water breaks up, gently blow and suck into the plastic tube. The colored water should come back together.

7. To do tests, pour powders first, followed by liquids, into your manometer bottle and cap it immediately. Your experiments will not work if you mix the solutions in other containers and then pour them into the manometer bottle, or if you do not close the bottle quickly enough.

88 ◆ CO$_2$ Uplift

YOU WILL NEED:

manometer
test substances:
1 tablespoon baking powder
1/2 cup vinegar
empty spare bottle
colored water
medicine dropper

How much will the colored water marker rise when certain substances are placed in the manometer? Whether you do these manometer experiments in one day or on several different days, it is very important to keep a scientific journal, or record book, and write down what happens in each and every experiment. Doing and recording these experimetns will make a real chemist out of you!

What to do: Set up your manometer on the kitchen counter or with newspaper under the container to catch any spills. Keep the bottle and stand close together so the tube makes a low loop between them. With the dropper, place one or two drops of colored water in the open tube attached to the stand. Only a few drops are needed! The water should drop down into the lower loop. If it does not do this, or if it breaks up, gently blow or suck on the tube to bring the liquid together and move it into place in the lower loop.

Now, measure one tablespoon of baking powder and ½ cup of vinegar. Take the cap off the manometer bottle and rest the tube in another bottle. Pour the baking powder into the bottom of the manometer bottle, followed by the vinegar (the liquid always goes in last). Quickly, screw the cap back on tightly and shake the bottle a little. Write down what happens and how far the solution makes the colored-water marker rises in the tube.

Wash out the manometer bottle thoroughly before going on to the next experiments, and remember to wash it again between experiments or you might invalidate, or spoil, your results.

Now test the next five combinations as you did the baking powder and vinegar experiment:

Test substances:
1 tablespoon baking soda and ½ cup vinegar
2 antacid seltzer tablets and ½ cup water
½ cup carbonated soft drink
1 tablespoon baking soda and juice of 1 lemon
1 tablespoon baking soda and ½ cup water

Note: For added experiment effects and results, try varying, or changing, the amounts of dry ingredients to liquids, and of different liquids to powders.

What happens:

The colored water in the manometer tube rises forcefully up the tube with much sputtering and bubbling, or it rises slightly but does not sputter, or it does not rise at all.

Why: There is obviously more CO_2 gas given off in some chemical reactions than in others. In the above experiments, both vinegar-and-baking-soda and vinegar-and-baking-powder produced the best results. Both mixtures drove the colored-water marker bubbling noisily up the tube.*

While there was definitely some CO_2 gas given off with the seltzer tablets, soda, and baking-soda-and-lemon solutions, the water marker did not move as much as it did with the powder and vinegar solutions. In these tests, there was little movement and no noticeable sound. But absolutely nothing happened with the baking-soda-and-water solutions, which released no CO_2 gas at all.

Note: If you did not get this reaction, do the experiments again. Be sure to put the powder in first, and to cap the bottle quickly before the CO_2 gas.

KITCHEN ALCHEMY

Most people don't think of cooking as chemistry, but when batters turn into cakes, cookies, and pancakes, and sugar crystallizes and turns into candy, it definitely is.

About Cooking and Chemical Reactions

In fact, most cooking does involve chemical change or reactions. If pizza stays in the oven too long, a black substance called carbon results. Carbon-dioxide gas, through yeast, makes bread rise, and salt causes water to leave pickles through a process called osmosis.

Don't be too surprised if these experiment-recipes become family favorites. Besides being great chemistry experiments and fun to make, they're fantastically delicious!

Spicy Infusion

89

YOU WILL NEED:

teakettle with boiling water

small kitchen strainer or a tea ball

1/2 teaspoon each of at least 6 herbs or spices: whole parts, such as a bay leaf or leaves of oregano, basil, mint, or parsley; buds or seeds, such as cloves, mustard, fennel, or anise; or cinnamon bark, etc.

teacups or mugs

spoons

paper and pencil to record solubility and tastes

Chemists often use the word infusion. Anything dissolved in hot water is called an infusion. Some people drink infusions every day in the form of coffee and tea. In this activity, you'll make your own infusions and you'll have the fun of drinking them, too!

What to do: Put one herb or spice in the strainer and place it on top of a cup. Pour some water from the teakettle over it. Let the substance steep, or soak, for two to three minutes. Remove the strainer and clean it out under cold water. Now taste your infusion "tea" and describes its taste. Repeat these steps with the other herbs and spices.

What happens: The spices and herbs steep and dissolve in the water to color and flavor it.

Why: Some herbs and spicy substances are more soluble, or dissolve more easily, in hot water, than others. The chemical composition, or the way the molecules are arranged, has a lot to do with a substance's solubility. A tea may be sweet and pleasant, or bitter and sour. It may make your mouth pucker when you taste it, or may be so weak you can hardly taste it at all. What do you like or dislike about your infusions?

Give an Infusion Party

90

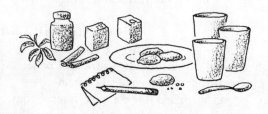

Invite some of your friends over on a wet and cold day for an infusion-test "tea" party. Provide a list of spices and herbs used but don't identify or name the samples. Have among your "teas" some made from such popular and favorite herbs and spices as nutmeg, anise seed, mint, fennel seed, allspice, cinnamon bark, and clove. Also, try thin slices of ginger root. Use sugar or honey for flavoring and supply small disposable plastic spoons and cups for sampling. Serve your infusion "teas" with some light, crispy cookies. Give each person a pencil and a small notepad and ask them to identify each infusion and its solubility, or how well-flavored it is. Have fun and enjoy!

Butter Me Up ◆ 91

You can make your own butter very easily. This experiment-recipe is made in small quantities to use immediately. (Get help with this one!) It may take about ten minutes for your cream to turn to butter but it's definitely worth it—you butter believe it!

What to do: Pour the cream into the chilled bowl. Mix on high until the cream forms yellow clumps. This will not happen right away; allow at least ten minutes. As you mix, a liquid separates from the clumps. Pour this liquid off into the measuring cup as you continue to mix.

What happens: The cream is turned into butter, and there's a good bit of liquid in the measuring cup.

Why: Cream is a combination of butterfat and water molecules. The butterfat floats throughout the water. This, again, is an example of a suspension, a solid suspended in a liquid. When you use the mixer on the cream, the molecules of butterfat collide and stick together, the clumps get larger, and you have butter, a solid substance. The water molecule part of the cream is the liquid you now have in the measuring cup. How much of the cup of cream was butterfat and how much water?

◆ 92 "Emulsional" about Mayonnaise

Don't cry over cracked eggs and when your egg whites get beaten up, send in the substitute! You're sure to get "egg-cited" about this tasty and delicious spread. Make mayonnaise in small quantities to use immediately. This serves two to four.

What to do: Place the egg substitute in the bowl. Add the mustard, lemon juice, and seasoning. Beat these with the spoon. Add the oil a little at a time, then beat. Add some more oil, and beat again. Do this until the mayonnaise gets stiff, then you can add the oil faster.

If the oil just seems to sit there (now you'll learn how emulsions act), simply add a touch more mustard and continue beating. The secret of making good mayonnaise is to keep on beating the ingredients. At the end, add a teaspoon of boiling water to keep your mayonnaise from separating.

What happens: From the separate ingredients, you have made mayonnaise, a mixture of liquids suspended or floating in one another, called an emulsion.

Why: In the case of mayonnaise, the mustard and boiling water are the emulsifying agents that keep the oil and the lemon juice from separating and keep the mixture emulsified. Without these agents, the mixture can and will separate.

Tarragon Mayonnaise Dressing
Add shredded leaves of fresh tarragon (an herb found in your supermarket's produce department) to your mayonnaise, and you have a delicious, light salad dressing. It's great on sliced tomatoes, too!

In a Pickle

93

Now make some simple delicious pickles you can eat tonight. You'll be using salt and vinegar, compounds that keep foods from spoiling.

What to do: Scrub the cucumber. Cut deep grooves down and around the length of it with the prongs of a fork. Slice the cucumber thinly, so you can almost see through the slices. Place the slices in a deep bowl and sprinkle the salt on top. Toss the slices thoroughly with a spoon to mix in the salt. Cover the slices with a small plate and place something heavy on top—a tin can will do. Let the cucumbers stand at room temperature for one hour.

Drain the slices and put them in the serving container. Mix the sugar and vinegar, and pour it over the cucumber slices. Chill thoroughly for two to three hours. Before serving, drain off the liquid and sprinkle with chopped dill, parsley, or tarragon. Enjoy!

What happens: The cucumbers turn into a simple version of crispy, crunchy pickle slices.

Why: The salt and vinegar combine to ferment the cucumber. The process, called osmosis, draws water out of the cucumbers to make pickles crisp and crunchy.

Fermentation
Salt keeps foods from spoiling. Pickles are usually made by placing vegetables, usually cucumbers, in salt water. The salty solution is called a brine. The salt draws out the juices and helps the good bacteria change, or ferment, the cucumbers into pickles while killing the bad bacteria. Chemists know that bacteria are everywhere, even in our bodies. Some cause disease, while others cause chemical changes in foods to make new foods, such as pickles.

YOU WILL NEED:

large unpeeled cucumber
1 tablespoon (15 ml) salt
1 tablespoon (15 ml) sugar
1/2 cup cider or white vinegar
small, covered serving container
1 tablespoon (15 ml) chopped dill, parsley, or tarragon (fresh or dried)
fork
knife
deep bowl
spoon
small plate and weight

Atoms Apple

94

Try rearranging the same apple atoms, and make a delicious warm dessert that serves four.

What to do: In the pot, cook the first three ingredients together for five minutes, then remove the lemon slice. Peel, core, and slice the apples, and add them to the sugar solution, a few at a time. Cook until soft, adding water as needed. To serve, move the apples to plates, pour the warm sugar syrup over the apples, and sprinkle with cinnamon.

What happens: The firm apples soften and make a delicious apple dessert.

Why: The lemon acid and sugar combine with a substance in the apples called pectin. This softens them into a jellylike mixture. The heated water helps break down the atoms of the apple or the structure of its molecules. Then it is chemically changed by "cooking," from a hard state to a soft one.

YOU WILL NEED:

large pot
1 1/2 cups water
1/2 cup sugar
lemon slice
6 small-medium apples
peeler and knife
use of stove (ask for permission or help)
cinnamon

95 Lemon Aide

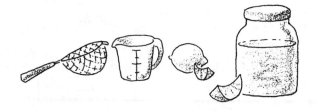

Chemistry, as you can see, is everywhere in the kitchen. Like candy, syrups are super-saturated solutions of sugar and water, and the difference between the two is the degree of heat that chemically changes in substances. In this recipe-experiment, you'll make your very own lemon syrup for instant fresh lemonade.

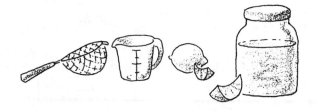

What to do: Place the sugar and water in a pot. Boil the solution for five minutes; then let it cool and add the lemon juice. Pour the syrup through a strainer and into the container. For keeping, store in the refrigerator. You'll need 2 tablespoons of syrup to one glass of ice water for a great fresh lemonade. Enjoy!

What happens: The sugar, lemon, and water solution turns into a thick, lemony syrup.

Why: The heat causes the sugar and water to mix thoroughly, then it boils away some of the water molecules through stream, or water vapor. When the thickened sugar solution cools, it chemically reacts with the lemon juice, making the syrupy mixture.

YOU WILL NEED:
a pot
2 cups sugar
1 cup water
use of stove (ask for permission or help)
strainer
1 cup lemon juice
large clean jar or covered container

Herb Dressing: To Be or Not to Be? 96

YOU WILL NEED:
mixing jar with lid
1 teaspoon herbs (chopped parsley, chives, mint, tarragon, or a combination)
1/2 cup oil
1/2 cup vinegar
salt and pepper to taste

Salad dressings don't know whether they are emulsions or not; let's make one and see why. (Makes about 1 cup).

What to do: Place all the above ingredients in the jar and shake well. Store in refrigerator, and shake before using.

What happens: When shaken, the vinegar and oil combine, but then they eventually separate.

Why: The vinegar, oil, and water are a temporary emulsion, or "colloid," of small molecular substances, which combine temporarily with other small molecular substances in a liquid. Salad dressing is not a true emulsion, as mayonnaise is, or it would not separate.

I Scream! 97

Endotherm another frozen treat by replacing the Cranberry Lemon Snow juices with 1 tablespoon instant vanilla pudding powder, 1/2 cup chilled evaporated milk, 1/2 cup low-fat milk, 1 tablespoon sugar, and 1/2 teaspoon vanilla extract. Mix the ingredients thoroughly before packing the open jar in ice. It's a delicious soft-serve vanilla ice cream!

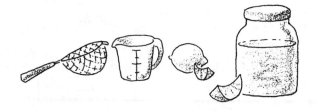

Endothermic Frozen Treat: Cranberry-Lemon Snow

Can an endothermic change, or one where heat energy is used instead of produced, make a delicious frozen treat? Let's see what happens with fruit and lemon juice. You'll have the fun of doing this great chemistry experiment and eating it, too!

What to do: Pour the fruit and lemon juice into the jar and shake. Place the open jar in the middle of the bowl. Carefully pour crushed ice around the jar up to the top. Sprinkle rock salt in and around the ice. Fold the paper towels or dishtowels lengthwise and wrap them around the bowl. Place a heavy object or two against the bowl to keep the towels in place. Be patient! It will take about two hours for your experiment to turn into an icy treat.

What happens: The juice turns into an icy slush.

Why: The salt on the ice draws the heat out of the juices in the jar and the temperature goes down below the freezing point.

YOU WILL NEED:

small, clean jar
medium-size mixing bowl or container
sheets of paper towels or 2 small dishtowels (to fold and wrap around bowl)
spoon
1/2 cup cranberry or other fruit juice
1 tablespoon lemon juice
1/2 cup rock salt (available in spice section of supermarket)
6 cups crushed ice

Maple Snow Sugar

Early colonists in America made a special maple candy called "Jack Wax." Boiled maple syrup was poured onto the snow and hardened into a sugary maple treat. You can make your own Jack Wax in just a few minutes. (Involves hot, boiling syrup! Adult help is recommended!)

What to do: Pour the syrup into the microwave-safe container. Cook on high power for five minutes. Very carefully (hot sugar can cause a bad burn), spoon the maple syrup over the crushed ice.

YOU WILL NEED:

1/2 cup maple syrup
1 microwave-safe container
medium bowl half-filled with crushed ice
spoon
fork
an adult helper

What happens: The hot syrup turns into strands of taffylike maple candy. With the fork, you can now pick out strands of taffylike maple sugar and roll it into hard bands. Enjoy them alone or as a morning treat with doughnuts, or with delicious sparkling apple cider pancakes in "Batter on the Moon."

Why: The maple syrup, boiled to the hard-sugar stage, is chemically changed so that the individual sugar crystals link up and harden together to form a solid.

Batter on the Moon

100

YOU WILL NEED:

2 cups baking and pancake mix

1 1/3 cups sparkling (apple) cider

wire whisk or mixing spoon

pouring-type measuring cup

electric fry pan, or grill and use of stove

mixing bowl

1 egg

1/2 cup oil

pancake turner

No, they don't play baseball on the moon but you can make light, delicious, sparkling apple cider pancakes that are guaranteed to be out of this world! The chemically changed mixed batter, with its bubbles and holes, will remind you of craters on the moon. You won't strike out with this experiment if you keep your eyes on the batter. (Makes 16 four-inch pancakes.)

What to do: Pour each ingredient into the bowl and mix them together with the wire whisk or spoon. Do not overmix. Pour the batter into the pouring-type measuring cup. Lightly grease the grill, pan, or electric fry pan (set at 350°F). When the grill or pan is hot, start the pancakes by pouring the batter. Pour enough to make four- or five-inch cakes onto the hot grill or pan. Let the pancakes cook on one side until bubbles appear and until the surface is somewhat dried out. Turn the pancakes over with the turner and cook until cakes lightly lift from pan.

What happens: As you mix the batter, bubbles appear in it. When you add heat, cooking the batter, it turns into light, delicious pancakes. Serve them with butter, syrup, and applesauce. Adding your "Maple Snow Sugar" candies would make this breakfast an even bigger hit.

Why: The apple juice in cider is carbonated, or creates carbonic acid. This happens when carbon dioxide is dissolved into the solution. The craters, or holes, in the pancake batter are created by the carbon-dioxide gas. This also makes the pancakes lighter and puffier. If you save leftover batter for later, the pancakes will be heavier and flatter, because the CO_2 gas bubbles will be less or gone. This is similar to when you put uncapped soda in the refrigerator and it loses its fizz.

I've Got a Crush on You

101

If your refrigerator does not have a crushed ice dispenser, ice cubes can be crushed in a special appliance, food processor, or blender, or by putting them in a towel and breaking them up with a hammer.

In an electric blender, place two cups of ice cubes into the blender container, along with one cup of water. Press the CHOP or high-speed button to blend. Turn off the blender occasionally and stir the ice with a rubber spatula or wooden spoon. This will distribute the cubes equally so that they can be crushed more evenly.

If needed, ask for help making crushed ice.

FOOD FOR THOUGHT

What makes us hungry? Why do salted potato chips make us thirsty? How does the temperature of food affect its taste? What does salt do in the pot—and in our bodies? Is it better to use honey than sugar? And more....

About Hunger and Food

Why do we cook? First of all, to make food digestible and safe. But we also cook for other reasons. We cook to make food tasty so that we will enjoy eating as we satisfy our hunger. But what makes us feel hungry?

Chemicals in the body—in our blood, our digestive hormones and our nervous system—all give us signals, sensations such as stomach movements. When these signals reach the brain, it recognizes them as a need for food.

Our sense of hunger and satisfaction is also influenced by other things. Sometimes we want and eat food when we don't need it. Maybe we eat because it's our favorite food, or because we are upset about something and think food will make us feel better. Or maybe we eat just because everybody else is eating. Sometimes, too, we refuse food even though we need it—perhaps because we are sick or worried or afraid we'll gain weight. Sometimes, we don't eat enough because we don't like the taste or smell or looks of a particular food.

Taste, Bud?

How your food tastes to you depends largely on your tongue. It has about 3,000 taste buds located on its surface. The sensation of taste arises from the activity of clusters of cells (the epitheliads) that are embedded in the small bumps (the papillae) on the tongue's upper surface.

Strangely, your nose, your sense of smell, plays a big part in tasting food. Without this important sense, as when you have a bad head cold, you cannot even recognize the flavor of foods you are eating; you just can't "taste" anything.

102 Tasting Through Your Nose

The smell of a food is as important as its taste! In fact, its smell actually influences how it tastes! If you doubt it, try this experiment.

What to do: Grate part of a peeled potato and put it on a spoon. Grate an equal amount of a peeled apple and put it on a second spoon.

Close your eyes and mix up the spoons so that you're not sure which is which. Hold your nose and taste each of the foods.

What happens: You will have trouble telling which is which!

Why: The nose shares the airway (the pharynx) with the mouth. Therefore, we smell and taste food at the same time.

Only salty, sweet, bitter and sour are pure tastes. Other "tastes" are combinations of taste and odor. Without the help of your nose, you may not be able to tell what you are eating.

103 Some Like it Hot

Believe it or not, the temperature of food affects the taste!

What to do: Taste the cold salty water. Let it stand on the table for an hour or so until it is at room temperature. Taste it again. Then heat it slightly and taste again. Bring the salty water to a boil. Let it cool slightly and taste it again.

Repeat the process with the sugary water and finally with the lemonade.

What happens: The salty water tastes saltier at room temperature than at the other temperatures. The sugary water tastes sweetest and the lemonade most sour when they are just slightly warm.

Why: The temperature at which tastes are strongest ranges from 72° to 105°F (22° to 40°C). Salty and bitter tastes are stronger at the lower range, which is room temperature. Sweet and sour tastes are stronger at the upper part of the range.

If food is really hot or cold, it is hard to taste it. The receptor molecules on the tongue can't easily capture the food molecules. Ice cream makers, for instance, have to use twice as much sugar as they would if the ice cream were served at room temperature.

However, whatever the temperature, we are all much more sensitive to bitter tastes than any others.

Certain substances can make a taste stronger—or get rid of it altogether. The cynarin in artichokes, for instance, makes everything taste sweet. It blocks the other tastes. MSG (monosodium glutamate), used in some prepared foods and in Chinese restaurants, makes salty and bitter tastes stronger.

Wilting a Cucumber

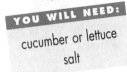

YOU WILL NEED:
cucumber or lettuce
salt

Though our bodies need the two minerals (sodium and chloride) that salt provides, too much salt—and too much of the foods preserved by salt—can cause health problems. Salt is powerful! Let's look at its effect on a vegetable.

What to do: Cut off two or three slices of cucumber or tear off several leaves of lettuce. Salt them and let them stand.

What happens: They wilt!

Why: The salt draws the water out of the cells of the vegetable. The same thing happens to our body's cells if we eat too much salt and the amount of sodium in the fluid surrounding the cells is too high. The "wilted" cells don't function properly.

Salt is an essential part of blood and other body fluids. But when we eat too much of it, too much water and potassium are drawn from the body's cells. This may cause high blood pressure or kidney damage.

Too Many Potato Chips!

Here is one way the body keeps us from getting too high a concentration of salt.

YOU WILL NEED:
salt pretzel or several
potato chips

What to do: Eat a salt pretzel or three or four salted potato chips.

What happens: You will need to take a drink of water!

Why: You want extra water to dilute the extra salt you have eaten. Thirst keeps the body functioning by making sure it doesn't have too high a concentration of salt.

When there is too great a concentration of sodium and potassium in our body fluids, the hypothalamus (a part of the brain located near its base) triggers a feeling of thirst.

An increased concentration of sodium also can be caused when we perspire. You may have heard that you should eat salt when you're sweating, but that's a mistake. Your impulse—to drink water—is right.

Too Salty!

Besides sprinkling on too much salt, what makes food taste too salty?

YOU WILL NEED:
salt
water
2 pots
use of the stove
(ask for permission
or help)

What to do: Add 2 tablespoons of salt to 2 cups of water. Stir and pour half into one pot and half into the other.

Boil the water in the first pot for 20 minutes. Boil the water in the second pot for 10 minutes. Let them cool and taste each one.

What happens: The first will taste much saltier than the second.

Why: After the boiling starts, the water turns into water vapor, an invisible gas, and escapes into the air (evaporates). Continued boiling does not raise the temperature. It just speeds up evaporation. The longer the salted water boils, the more water evaporates and the saltier the remaining water tastes.

Water, Water— Every Time

It was once believed that athletes and dancers should never drink water after working out. But today we know it's important for them to drink plenty of water before and after they perform—and even during the competition or game if it lasts long.

Not drinking enough water can cause an athlete to lose the race, miss the hoop, drop the catch. If their muscles don't have enough water, they feel weak and tired.

Although salt is lost along with sweat, the amount is less than the amount of salt in the blood. That means that we need to replace more water than salt when we sweat a lot. Doctors tell us that the safest way to replace lost sweat is with plain water.

What Pot?

Does it matter what size pot we cook in?

What to do: Pour a cup of water into each pot. Place both pots on the stove over medium heat.

What happens: The water in the short pot boils first!

Why: There is less atmosphere in the shallow pot. That means there is less air pressure keeping the molecules down and they have an easier time escaping into the air. The tall, narrow pot is under greater pressure from the air, its molecules have to work harder to escape into the air—and so its boiling point is about 1° higher.

Watch That Salt Shaker

Food tastes most salty at room temperature. When we season hot food such as potato salad that is going to be eaten cold, we can use less salt, knowing that it will taste saltier when we eat it. When we're salting cold food that is going to be reheated later, we can use a little more salt than our taste tells us—or better still, wait until after we heat it and salt it then.

Which Boils Faster— Salted or Plain Water?

What effect does salt have when you boil water?

What to do: Add two tablespoons of salt to one of the pots of cold water. Don't add anything to the other pot. Heat both pots on the stove. Which one starts to boil first?

What happens: The pot without the salt boils first!

Why: The point at which a substance changes from a liquid to a gas is called the boiling point. The more salt in water, the higher the temperature must be for the water to boil. Salt molecules turn to gas at much higher temperatures than water molecules.

So we add salt to cold water if we want our food to cook faster since it will be cooking at a higher temperature. Spaghetti and other pastas, for instance, cook well in vigorously boiling salted water. The difference in temperature between salted and unsalted water can be important when we're cooking sauces and custards that call for exact temperature or timing.

109 Poached Egg Physics

YOU WILL NEED:

tall, narrow pot
4 cups of water
slotted spoon
short, wide pot
2 raw eggs
timer (optional)
use of the stove (ask for permission or help)

In which pot—the short, wide one or the tall, narrow one—can we poach an egg faster?

What to do: Pour 2 cups of cold water into each pot. Place the short pot on the stove over medium heat. After the water boils, carefully break open one of the eggs and slip it into the water. Set the timer at two minutes or count 120 seconds. (You do this by saying, "And 1, and 2, and 3," and so on up to 120.) Then quickly remove the egg with a slotted spoon.

Repeat the process with the egg in the tall pot, again allowing it to cook exactly two minutes.

What happens: The yolk of the egg in the tall pot gets harder than that of the egg in the short pot!

Why: Because the boiling point is higher (see "What Pot?") in the tall pot, the food cooks at a higher temperature than in the short, wide pot. Therefore, it takes a shorter time to cook.

110 Salt versus the Sweet Stuff

If someone pulled the labels off identical containers of sugar and salt, could you tell which was which? There are ways to tell besides tasting them.

YOU WILL NEED:

1/2 teaspoon salt
1/2 teaspoon sugar
2 small saucepans
use of the stove (ask for permission or help)

What to do: Place the salt in one of the pans and the sugar in the other. Heat each for a few minutes over low heat.

What happens: Nothing happens to one. That one is salt. The other melts and gets brown. That one is sugar.

Why: All sugars are simple carbohydrates. They all contain carbon and hydrogen and oxygen. Heating sugar separates its molecules. At about 360°F (189°C), the sugar breaks down into water (the hydrogen and oxygen) and carbon. The carbon makes the sugar turn brown, or caramelizes it. Have you ever toasted marshmallows over an open fire? Then you've seen it happen.

97

Freezing Salt and Sugar

111

YOU WILL NEED:

1 tablespoon salt
2 cups food coloring (2 colors)
1 tablespoon sugar
water
ice cube tray with separators

Here's another way to tell whether a substance is salt or sugar!

What to do: Fill the cups halfway with water, and color each one with a few drops of a different food coloring. Dissolve the salt in one cup and the sugar in the other.

Pour the solutions into opposite ends of an ice cube tray with separators. Put the tray in the freezer for an hour or two.

What happens: The sugar cubes freeze. The salt cubes remain liquid.

Why: Plain water turns into ice at 32°F (0°C). Both sugar and salt lower the freezing point of the water. But sugar molecules are heavier than salt molecules. There are more salt molecules than sugar molecules in a tablespoon. So salt lowers the freezing point twice as much as sugar.

The Candy Trap

112

YOU WILL NEED:

1 medium-size apple
1 medium-size banana
Tootsie Rolls
pieces of chocolate

When we feel hungry, we often reach for a candy bar. But suppose we ate a piece of fruit instead?

What to do: For your afternoon snack, try a Tootsie Roll one day and an apple the next. On a third day, try chocolate. On the fourth, eat a banana.

What happens: They all taste great. But the candy leaves you hungry and wanting more. You may go on to eat three or more Tootsie Rolls and two or more ounces of chocolate. However, chances are that one apple or one banana will leave you feeling full.

Why: The sugar in candy is highly refined, and it gets digested very quickly. It doesn't stay in the stomach very long and so we stay hungry. Raisins, apples, bananas, pears, and melon contain sugar (fructose) in a form that we digest more slowly, and therefore they fuel the body more gradually.

It's possible to eat a whole pound (.45 kg) of apples before using up the amount of calories in three Tootsie Rolls! Three medium-sized bananas are equal in calories to two ounces (56 g) of chocolate.

The piece of fruit also supplies vitamins and minerals and fiber instead of just "empty" calories.

Salt and Ice Cream

When you make ice cream, you put milk or cream, sugar, flavoring and gelatin in a special container that sits in a cooling bath of ice-cold water. The water is kept liquid by adding enough salt to lower the temperature to below 27°F (-3°C). That's why salt is such an important ingredient in the making of ice cream.

The Cookie Test

Compare the taste and feel of different sugars and honey in these great cookies.

YOU WILL NEED:

1 1/2 cups (170 g) flour

1 1/2 sticks or 6 ounces (170 g) margarine or butter

2 tablespoons white sugar

2 tablespoons brown sugar

1 tablespoon honey

1 1/2 teaspoon lemon juice

bowls

wooden spoon

cookie sheets

teaspoon

use of the oven (ask for permission or help)

What to do: Preheat the oven to 350°F (175°C). Soften the margarine at room temperature before you start to mix it with the various sugars.

Using a food processor or a bowl with a wooden spoon, cream a half stick (4 tablespoons) of margarine with the white sugar. Add a half teaspoon of lemon juice. Gradually mix in a half cup of the flour. Continue mixing until the dough is smooth and beginning to form a ball.

Repeat the process with the brown sugar and then with the honey.

Drop rounded teaspoons of the dough onto cookie sheets about two inches (5 cm) apart. Press each cookie flat with the back of the spoon. Each batch makes about a dozen cookies. Bake 15 minutes or until the cookies are a light brown.

Let cool—and taste.

What happens: The cookies are equally sweet, but the tastes are different!

Why: Each sweetener comes from a different source.

White sugar—sucrose—is made either from a tall grass known as sugar cane or from the roots of sugar beets. When it is processed, impurities are removed; it is then refined, and made into the granulated, lump, or powdered form we buy in the supermarket.

Brown sugar also comes from sucrose, but it is made by coating sucrose crystals with molasses, the thick syrup left when water is boiled out of sucrose.

Honey, of course, is manufactured by bees. They make the sweet, sticky thick liquid from the nectar of flowers. Honey has 18 more calories per tablespoon than sugar, but because honey is sweeter than sugar, you need less. You used only half as much honey as sugar for your cookies.

Honey has small amounts of vitamins and minerals, but too little to offer much nutrition. Cookies made with honey, though, may stay moist longer because honey retains moisture longer while baking. It may even bring moisture from the air into the finished cookies. That's why candy made with honey tends to get sticky.

GREEN BROCCOLI
AND OTHER VEGETABLES

How do plants eat and drink? When do turnips smell like rotten eggs? How can we make beans user-friendly? The answers to these questions—and much more.

About Vegetables

Vegetables are plants grown for the parts we can eat—root, stem, leaf, flower, seed, or fruit. Sometimes, though, a fruit is a vegetable and sometimes a vegetable is a fruit!

According to botanists, the scientists who study and classify plants, fruits are the part of the plant that contains the seeds. But whether we call a food a fruit or a vegetable seems to depend on its sweetness. Both cantaloupe and squash are in the same fruit family. But squash is not all that sweet and it is served as a vegetable.

Many vegetables are eaten raw. Lettuce and other greens, tomatoes, and cucumbers are among the most usual salad ingredients. Onions and peppers are often added. Cauliflower and broccoli are often eaten raw and dipped in a spicy or creamy sauce. However, many vegetables are easier to digest when they are cooked. Others, like potatoes and yams, can't be digested at all unless they are cooked.

114 The Vegetable Game

Botanists divide the vegetables we eat into the following groups: leaf, stem, root and tuber, flower and bud, seed and seed pod, fruit-vegetable, and fungi. A carrot, for

instance, is a root, celery a stem. Potatoes are tubers, fleshy underground stems bearing a bud. Fungi are plants like mushrooms that live on other plants because they lack chlorophyll—the green coloring matter (see "How to Feed Celery"), and so cannot manufacture their own food.

How much do you know about veggies? See if you can identify the following vegetables according to the part of the plant we eat. (Answers on page 00).

a. Root	1. asparagus	17. okra
b. Tuber	2. beets	18. onion
c. Stem	3. broccoli	19. parsnip
d. Leaf	4. Brussels	20. peas
e. Flower	sprouts	21. pepper
f. Seed	5. carrots	22. potato
g. Fruit	6. cauliflower	23. pumpkin
h. Fungi	7. cabbage	24. radish
	8. celery	25. spinach
	9. corn	26. squash
	10. cucumber	27. sweet
	11. eggplant	potato
	12. kale	28. tomato
	13. leek	29. turnip
	14. lettuce	30. water
	15. morels	chestnut
	16. mushrooms	31. yam

YOU WILL NEED:
stalk of celery with its leaves
half a glass of water
1 teaspoon of red food coloring

115 How to Feed Celery

Plants feed us, but how do plants get fed?

What to do: Stand the stalk of celery in a half glass of water colored with a teaspoon of food coloring. Start it off in bright light and let it remain overnight.

What happens: The leaves turn reddish.

Why: The celery stalk is the stem of the celery plant. It absorbs water and minerals from the soil through its root hairs by means of osmosis. Osmosis is a process by which some liquids and gases pass through a membrane—a kind of skin. The water passes into nearby cells and is carried up through its center tubes to the plant's stem and leaves.

The chlorophyll in the leaves—their green coloring—turns the light of the sun into energy. This energy is used to combine some of the water from the soil with carbon dioxide from the air. The carbon and oxygen of the carbon dioxide react with the hydrogen and oxygen of the water to form carbohydrates.

This sugar and starch serve as food for the plant—and eventually for us. You can eat the celery now, or you can use it in the salad on page 00.

116 Storing Carrots

What's the best way to keep carrots, beets and other leafy root vegetables fresh and tasty?

What to do: Wrap one of the carrots with leaves in a plastic bag that has air holes punched in it. Wrap one carrot without leaves the same way. Store them both in the crisper of the refrigerator.

Wrap the other carrots in plain plastic bags without air holes and store them in the crisper, too.

Observe the carrots daily for a week. Taste each one of them.

What happens: The carrot that tastes and looks the best is the one without leaves wrapped in the plastic bag with holes in it.

Why: When the leaves are not removed from the carrots, the sap continues to flow from the root to the leaf, depriving the part we eat of some of its nutrition

and flavor. In addition, the leafy tops wilt long before the sturdy roots and start to rot the carrot.

In the bag with holes in it, the air can circulate. This prevents a bitter-tasting compound called terpenoid from forming.

Answers to the Vegetable Game

Carrots Hate Fruit!

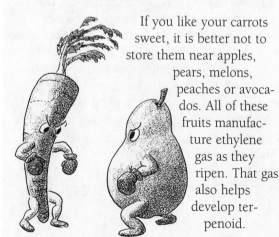

If you like your carrots sweet, it is better not to store them near apples, pears, melons, peaches or avocados. All of these fruits manufacture ethylene gas as they ripen. That gas also helps develop terpenoid.

1. c	9. f	17. g	25. d
2. a	10. g	18. c*	26. g
3. e	11. g	19. a	27. b
4. d	12. d	20. f	28. g
5. a	13. c	21. g	29. a
6. e	14. d	22. b	30. b
7. d	15. h	23. g	31. b
8. c	16. h	24. a	

*bulb—a stem enclosed in fleshy leaves.

No Way to Treat a Lettuce

YOU WILL NEED:

2 lettuce leaves
2 bowls

People have been eating lettuce since ancient times. There are many kinds—Bibb, Boston, Iceberg, Romaine, Red-leaf, among others. Most of the time, we eat these leaves raw in salads, though we can cook them in a variety of ways—even into soup. But lettuce has to be treated right!

What to do: Tear one of the leaves into bite-size pieces and place them in a bowl. Leave the other leaf whole and place it in a bowl. Let both stand for an hour or so.

What happens: The torn lettuce turns limp, while the whole leaf stays crisp.

Why: The torn leaf exposes greater areas to the air, so more of the vegetable's water evaporates and escapes into the air. Tearing also releases an enzyme that destroys vitamin C. That's another reason why it's better not to tear lettuce until just before you serve it.

Salting lettuce in advance also makes it wilt. (See page 00.)

Helping Lettuce Last

To perk up limp lettuce, soak it in cold water. The lettuce absorbs the fresh water and the leaves become crisp again.

Lettuce turns yellow as it gets older because its green chlorophyll fades, allowing its yellow pigments to show through. Lettuce will last for a week in the refrigerator. Don't separate the leaves. Wrap the head of lettuce in damp paper towels and place it in a perforated bag. That way you provide the moisture and air it needs to stay fresh.

◆ 118 Taming an Onion

YOU WILL NEED:
2 onions
running water
knife

Cultivated since prehistoric times, the onion has a number of varieties. The most familiar are the yellow and red unions that are very strong and can make people cry if they try to slice them without knowing how to handle them.

What to do: Peel both onions. Slice one under water. Slice the other without the water.

What happens: Your eyes begin to tear when you slice an onion—but not when you do it under running water.

Why: When you cut an onion, you tear its cell walls and release a gas called propanethial-sulfur oxide that turns into sulfuric acid in the air. Sulfuric acid stings if it gets into your eyes. When you slice onions under running water, you dilute the gas before it can float up into the air.

Onion Talk

Some varieties of mild onions do not irritate your eyes—the Vidalia from Georgia, the Walla Walla from Washington, and the Maui from Hawaii. All of them have a higher sugar content because of the soil and climate in which they grow.

Believe it or not, onions may be good for your heart. A number of laboratory studies find that oils in onions appear to lower blood levels of the "bad" low-density lipoproteins (LDLs), which carry cholesterol into the bloodstream, and they raise the blood levels of the "good" high-density lipoproteins (HDLs), which carry cholesterol out of the body.

Chill It!

Another way to tame the onion is to chill it in the refrigerator for an hour or so before you slice it. The cold temperature slows the movement of the atoms in the gas so that they don't float up into the air so quickly.

Taking the Starch Out of a Potato!

What is starch? It's what people sometimes add when they wash shirts, and it is an ingredient in many medicines. But it's also an important food!

Plants make starch from sugar molecules in order to store food for the winter. Plants also use starch to feed seedlings or new sprouts. The starch is stored in the seeds of corn and wheat, in the stem in sorghum (a grain similar to Indian corn), and in the roots or tuber (underground stem) of yams and potatoes.

How do we know potatoes have starch?

What to do: Grate a tablespoon or two of potato into a bowl. Squeeze the potato mush through cheesecloth or a fine strainer onto a piece of aluminum foil. Pat the mush dry with a paper towel. Then apply a drop of iodine to it.

Place the salt and the flour on the aluminum foil. Apply a drop of iodine to each.

What happens: The salt takes on the light brown tint of the iodine. The potato and the flour turn blue-black.

Why: The blue-black color tells us that starch is present. A chemical change takes place as the iodine combines with the starch. Starch is a carbohydrate, made up of carbon, hydrogen, and oxygen. In the supermarket, you may see packages labeled "potato starch." Inside is a white, powdery substance ground from potatoes by machines. Huge screens filter out the potato fiber, and the potato starch is then left to dry in large vats.

Potato starch is used to thicken sauces and gravy and to replace wheat flour in cakes, if you don't want to eat wheat.

Potato Race

120

You wouldn't want to eat starchy vegetables such as potatoes and yams unless you cooked them. You need heat to break the cell walls so the potatoes can be digested.

Water boils at 212°F (100°C). Your oven can reach temperatures up to 500°F. Which method of cooking is faster—boiling or baking?

YOU WILL NEED:

pot of boiling water
2 small potatoes of
same size
use of the stove and
oven (ask for permission or help)

What to do: Preheat the oven to 450°F (230°C).

Carefully scrub the skin of the two potatoes, but don't peel them. Place one potato on a spoon and lower it carefully into the pot of boiling water. Place the other in the center of your oven. Using a long fork, test each potato every 10 minutes until it yields to the fork.

What happens: The boiled potato cooks faster—even though your oven is set at more than twice the temperature of boiling water.

Why: In both the boiling and baking, molecules of gas or liquid circulate and transfer their heat to the food. But the molecules of bubbling water move more violently than the air currents of the oven. This is because water is much more dense than air (1000 to 1). It delivers heat more efficiently.

Tips on Saving Time and Vitamins

To cook a potato faster, always put it in a preheated oven or in boiling water. You can also make a potato bake faster by sticking two or three nails in it. They conduct the heat from the stove to the potato.

Some people wrap a potato in aluminum foil, believing it will bake faster. But foil actually slows down the transfer of heat from the oven. Also, because it keeps the moisture from evaporating, it keeps the potato's skin from getting crisp. Aluminum foil is useful, but only to keep the potato warm after it is cooked.

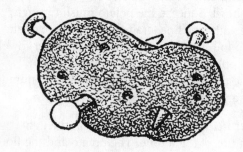

121 Milking a Potato

Plants draw water from the earth by osmosis. And food gets into our cells by osmosis. We talked a little about osmosis on page 00. What is it and what does it have to do with cooking?

3 large raw potato cubes of the same size
3 glasses of water
ruler
salt

What to do: Put each cube into a glass of water. To glass #1, add a large handful of salt. To glass #2, add a pinch or two of salt. Leave glass #3 plain. After an hour, measure the potato cubes.

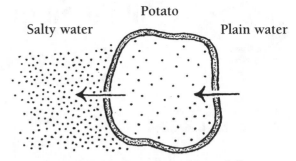

Salty water   Potato   Plain water

Arrow shows direction of liquid flow.

What happens: #1 will be smaller than it was; #2 will stay same size; #3 will be a little bigger.

Why: The more salt you add to the water, the stronger the mixture (the solution) becomes. The stronger the solution, the lower its concentration of water.

Osmosis is the flow of a liquid through a membrane (a thin wall). The liquid will always flow into a stronger solution—one where the concentration of liquid is lower.

In #1, the potato cube shrinks as the water in it moves from the weaker potato juice into the (stronger) heavily salted water. In #2, where the concentrations are equal, there is no movement. In #3, the potato juice is the stronger solution, so the water moves into its tissues and makes the cubes swell.

Making Soup

When you make soup, you want the juice to get out of vegetables and meat to flavor the liquid. That's why you add salt to the cooking pot. But when you are cooking meat or chicken as a main course, you want the juice to stay inside. Then you would start with plain water and add salt later, when the cooking is over. Cooking changes the wall of tissue so that osmosis can no longer take place. The liquid can't pass through.

Potato Soup

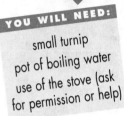

Why Do Some Vegetables Smell Bad?

It's easy to make your potato cubes into hot potato soup.

Bring the water to a boil, add a pinch of salt and pepper, and put in the potato pieces. In 20 or 25 minutes, when the potatoes are tender, put them in a bowl and mash them. Set aside 1 cup of the water in which the potatoes were boiled. Heat the milk until it just begins to bubble. Add the cup of potato water. Stir in the mashed potatoes and continue to heat the soup over low heat.

In a separate saucepan, melt the butter or margarine. Blend it with the flour and then add the milk. Cook the mixture until it is smooth and bubbly. Then gradually add it to the pot of hot soup, stirring all the while. Add the grated onion. Cover the pot and cook over low heat about 10 minutes. Add salt and pepper to taste. Sprinkle with parsley or chives.

YOU WILL NEED:

potato cubes cut into quarters
2 cups of water
salt and pepper
1 cup of milk
2 teaspoons flour
2 teaspoons butter or margarine
3 or 4 tablespoons milk
2 tablespoons grated onion
1 or 2 teaspoons parsley or chives (optional)

Some nutritious—and delicious—vegetables don't always get to our plates because of their unpleasant odor!

YOU WILL NEED:

small turnip
pot of boiling water
use of the stove (ask for permission or help)

What to do: Peel the turnip and cut it in half. Cut one half into cubes. Leave the other half whole. Place all the turnip pieces in the pot of boiling water. Test each half with a fork after 15 minutes or so, to find out if it is soft. Continue until both halves are firm but tender.

What happens: The cubed turnip cooks in less than a half hour. The other half needs more time and after a half hour it begins to smell bad.

Why: Turnips and rutabagas contain hydrogen sulfide, which smells like rotten eggs. When you cook these vegetables, you release this bad-smelling gas. The longer you cook it, the more smelly chemicals are produced and the worse the odor and the stronger the taste.

Shorter cooking time also means that you save more of the vitamins and minerals.

Other Smelly Veggies

Cabbage and cauliflower also contain smelly sulfur compounds. The longer you cook them, the worse they smell, but the better they taste! To lessen the smell, add a slice of bread to the cooking water. And keep a lid on the pot to stop the smelly molecules from floating off into the air.

Keeping of the Green

124 Green vegetables, such as broccoli, zucchini, spinach, green beans and peas, often come to the dinner table looking drab and unappetizing! Why?

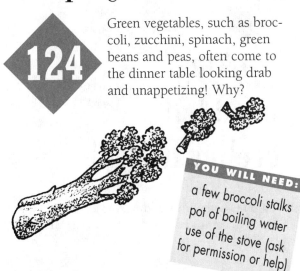

YOU WILL NEED:

a few broccoli stalks
pot of boiling water
use of the stove (ask for permission or help)

What to do: Cut off the stem and separate the broccoli flowers. Place the flowers in a pot of boiling water. After 30 seconds, scoop out half the broccoli. Let the rest continue to cook.

What happens: During the first 30 seconds, the broccoli turns a deep green. The broccoli left in the water loses color.

Why: The color intensifies because gases trapped in the spaces between cells suddenly expand and escape. Ordinarily, these air pockets dim the green color of the vegetable. But when heat collapses the air pockets, we can see the pigments much more clearly.

Longer cooking, however, results in a chemical change. The chlorophyll pigment that makes vegetables green reacts to acids. Water is naturally a little acid. When we heat broccoli or zucchini or spinach, its chlorophyll reacts with its own acids and the acids in the cooking water to form a new brown substance (pheophytin). That's what makes some cooked broccoli an ugly olive green.

125

YOU WILL NEED:
broccoli flowers or zucchini strips
pot of boiling water
1 teaspoon baking soda
use of the stove (ask for permission or help)

Looking Good but Feeling Rotten!

Restaurants sometimes add baking soda to a vegetable to make it look good or cook faster. Does it work?

What to do: Place the broccoli in the boiling water and add the baking soda.

What happens: The vegetable stays green, but after a short time it turns mushy.

Why: Baking soda is an alkali, the chemical opposite of an acid. When it is added to the water, it neutralizes some of the acids of the water and the vegetable. Because there are so few acids, the vegetable stays green—but the alkali dissolves its firm cell wall. The vegetable tissue rapidly becomes too soft.

Baking soda also destroys the vegetable's vitamins. It's a high price to pay for looking good!

126 Cold or Hot

We always start cooking green vegetables in boiling water. Why?

YOU WILL NEED:
broccoli or spinach
pot of cold water
pot of boiling water
use of the stove (ask for permission or help)

What to do: Place half of the broccoli or spinach in a pot half full of cold water. Place the other half in a pot half full of boiling water. Cook both until the vegetables are tender.

What happens: The vegetable in the cold water loses more color than that in the boiling water. Why: Plants contain enzymes, proteins that cause chemical reactions. They change the plant's color and also destroy its vitamins. The particular enzyme (chlorophyllase) involved here is more active between 150° and 170°F (66°-77°C) than at other temperatures, so less pigment is lost if the vegetables don't have to be heated through the 150°-170°F range. Water boils at 212°F (100°C). If the vegetable is put into boiling water, it avoids the lower range completely.

Keeping a Lid On

127

How can you preserve a vegetable's color better—
cooking it covered or uncovered?

YOU WILL NEED:
broccoli or zucchini
2 pots of boiling
water, one with a cover
use of the stove
(ask for permission
or help)

What to do: Cut off the stalk and separate the flowers of the broccoli or cut the zucchini into quarters.
Cook half the vegetable in a large quantity of boiling water in a covered pot for five to seven minutes.

Cook the other half in a large quantity of boiling water in a pot without a lid for five to seven minutes.

What happens: The broccoli in the uncovered pot retains its color. The broccoli in the covered pot does not.

Why: The color changes less in the uncovered pot because some of the plant's acids escape in steam during the first two minutes of boiling. When the pot is covered, the acids turn back into liquid, condense on the lid and fall down into the water.

The bad news is that, without the lid, you lose more vitamins into the air. And because it takes longer to cook without a lid, the nutrients have more time to be drawn out of the food.

128 There Must Be a Better Way!

YOU WILL NEED:
broccoli
steamer rack
(or colander)
pot with a cover
water
use of the stove (ask
for permission or help)

In the last experiment, you saw that cooking a green vegetable in a large quantity of water with the lid off prevents it from discoloring. But cooking that way, more vitamins are lost. What's the solution?

What to do: Separate the broccoli flowers and put them in the steamer rack. Place a half-cup of water in the pot and turn on the heat to medium high. When the water starts to boil, slip in the steamer rack with the broccoli, and cover the pot with a tight-fitting lid. Cook for seven to nine minutes.

What happens: The broccoli remains green.

Why: Steaming is less effective at conducting heat than water is. So the vegetable may take a few more minutes to soften than it would if boiled. But since it never comes into contact with the acids in the water, it doesn't lose its color or its vitamins.

129 Colorful Carrot

Unlike green and red vegetables, carrots do not lose their color when cooked in water!

What to do: Bring a cup of water to the boiling point. With a large spoon, lower the carrot slices into the pot of boiling water. Cook for 15 to 20 minutes.

What happens: The carrots remain orange, but you now can pierce them with a fork.

Why: Though they dissolve in fat, the coloring matter of carrots (carotenes) do not dissolve in water and are not affected by the normal heat of cooking. The carrots therefore stay orange.

Because heat dissolves some of the fiber (the hemicellulose) in the stiff carrot walls, cooked carrots are easier to digest and more nutritious than raw carrots. Cooked or raw, carrots are a good source of both vitamin A and the mineral potassium.

Strangely enough, eating huge amounts of carrots (two cups a day for several months) turns your skin yellow! Fortunately, when you stop eating so many carrots, it returns to its normal color.

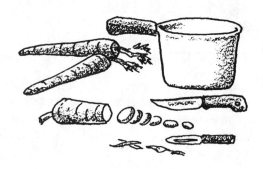

130 About Legumes

Legumes are foods such as beans, peas and lentils that come from the fruit or seeds of plants that have pods. We can eat them both fresh and dried. Kidney beans, for instance, are the dried seeds of green beans. But we call the green beans a vegetable and the kidney bean a legume!

Legumes are second in importance to grain as a source of food. They are valuable because they absorb nitrogen from the air. Nitrogen is the essential mineral of amino acids, the building blocks of the protein that helps grow and repair our body's tissues. So, in addition to fiber and essential minerals and vitamins, beans supply us with protein.

Among the thousands of beans that belong to the legume family, only 22 are grown in quantity for us to eat. These range from lima beans, split-peas and chick-peas to adzuki, used in Asian sweet dishes, and the soybeans from which soy sauce and tofu are made.

Though we call it a nut, the peanut is also a legume.

What kinds of legumes do you like to eat?

131 Culling

We cull beans to pick out small stones and other unwanted material. There is a quick, foolproof way to do it. Place the lentils or beans in a clear jar or bowl. Cover them with a half glass of water.

Most of the beans will stay at the bottom of the jar but the few defective ones will float up to the top—they are hollow and therefore lighter. You can lift them out with a slotted spoon.

132 Tough Cook, Tender Beans

Most legumes have a bland flavor. We season and flavor them to make them taste good. Mexicans add garlic and chili; Italians add garlic and oregano. The British add mustard and bay leaf. New Englanders make their famous baked beans dish with brown sugar and molasses.

Either tomatoes or lemon juice will make legumes tasty. And their vitamin C makes the iron in the beans easier to absorb. But not if our timing is off!

What to do: Cull the lentils (see above) and discard any that float to the top. Place three tablespoons in each pot and cover with water.

To pot #1, add the tomato sauce and lemon juice.

Don't add any juice or sauce to pot #2.

Simmer both pots on low heat. After 20 minutes test the lentils in both pots for softness using a fork. Retest every 10 minutes. Remove the pot from the heat when the lentils are tender but firm. Note how much time it takes them to cook.

YOU WILL NEED:
6 tablespoons lentils or presoaked beans
4 tablespoons tomato sauce or lemon juice
2 small pots
water
use of the stove (ask for permission or help)

What happens: The plain lentils take 30 to 40 minutes to soften. The lentils with the tomato sauce take much more time to soften.

Why: When you add tomatoes or tomato sauce or lemon juice before the beans are soft, the acid of the fruit or vegetable reacts with the starch of the beans to toughen their seed coat. They do soften, but it takes them much longer. That's why acidic foods need to be added only after the beans are soft.

Adding molasses before the beans have softened also interferes with the softening process because molasses contains calcium.

Salt also reacts with the seed coating to form a barrier that keeps liquid from being absorbed and makes the skins tough. It too should be added only after the beans are cooked.

Lentil Snack

YOU WILL NEED:

1/2 cup cooked lentils

1 tablespoon chopped onion (optional)

1 to 2 teaspoons (5 to 10 ml) lemon juice or

1 teaspoon (5 ml) tomato sauce

Dried lentils will swell up to two or three times their original size in the cooking. Add lemon juice to them or tomato sauce or vinegar and onions and serve your cooked lentils on crackers. They are even tastier served cold the next day.

Fabulous Soybeans

Soybeans are the only beans whose proteins are considered "complete." They contain all the amino acids that are essential for us to get through our food.

Soybeans are considered a perfect meat substitute and are ideal for vegetarian cooking. Tofu, a cheese-like curd made from soybeans, is a Japanese favorite that has become popular in the rest of the world. The secret of tofu is that it has no flavor of its own but takes on the taste and smell of the foods with which it is cooked. It can taste like eggs, cheese, chicken—even like chocolate pudding!

Sprouting Beans

133

The sprouts used in salads actually sprout from beans! You can easily sprout your own.

YOU WILL NEED:

6 tablespoons mung beans, chick-peas or lentils (use dried or fresh, not canned or frozen)

cheesecloth

string or rubber bands

labels and pencil

3 clean drinking glasses

warm water

What to do: Cull the beans.

Soak 4 tablespoons of the beans overnight in warm water. Then drain them and divide them between two clean glasses. Put a layer of cheesecloth over the top of each of the glasses and tie it on with a string or rubber band.

Store the first glass in a warm, dark place like a cupboard. Store the second in the refrigerator.

Without soaking them, place the last two tablespoons of the beans in a third glass. Label it and store it in the cupboard.

Keep the sprouts moist in all three glasses by rinsing them twice a day with lukewarm water. Drain off the excess water through the cheesecloth to prevent rotting or molding.

Note what happens after four or five days.

What happens: The batch of soaked beans stored in a warm, dark place sprouts and yields four to six ounces (112–118 g) of sprouts!

The beans stored in the refrigerator and the unsoaked beans never sprout.

Why: During the overnight soaking, the hard outer shell splits, the starch in the beans absorbs the water and the beans swell. That permits the embryo within each bean to take in water. But in addition to moisture, seeds need warmth and darkness in order to grow.

Harvest your crop and use the sprouts raw in salads or on sandwiches, or stir-fry them with scallions, soy sauce and garlic.

FRUIT OF THE VINE AND OTHER PLACES

Who calls a tomato a fruit? Why not store bananas in the refrigerator? What does pineapple do to gelatin? Where does vinegar come from? Is one end of a fruit sweeter than the other? And more.

About Fruit

Botanists call tomatoes, eggplants, cucumbers, and pumpkins fruits because they are the part of the plant that has the seeds.

But as cooks—and eaters—we call them vegetables and save the term fruit for plants that are sweeter.

All fruits grow above ground. We harvest grapes, berries, and melons from vines and shrubs. From trees, we get apples and pears, citrus fruits, bananas, figs and dates, and cherries. The largest fruit to grow on a tree is the jackfruit, native to southeast Asia. It can weigh as much as 80 pounds!

Most fruits are eaten raw once they ripen. But many fruits are also cooked—stewed, poached, baked—as well as dried, canned, frozen, squeezed into juice, baked in pies, used to flavor other foods, and made into jams and jellies. Some, like plantains, quince, rhubarb and sour cherries, must be cooked.

134 Bite or Bake?

There are hundreds of varieties of apples to choose from. Which do you bite and which do you bake?

YOU WILL NEED:

1 Red or Golden Delicious apple

1 Rome, York Imperial, Stayman, Winesap or Jonathan apple

2 to 3 tablespoons sugar or raisins

dash of nutmeg (optional)

water

baking dish

use of the oven (ask for permission or help)

What to do: Core both apples and cut away a circle of peel at the top. Place them in a baking dish. Fill the center hole of the apples with sugar or raisins. Sprinkle with nutmeg. Add water to cover the bottom of the dish. Place it in a 400°F (200°C) oven for about an hour or until the apples are tender. Taste each one.

What happens: The Delicious apple is mushy and shapeless. The Rome is firm and tasty.

Why: The Delicious apple becomes mushy for two reasons. First, it lacks enough fiber (cellulose), the part of the cell wall that keeps it firm, to hold the peel intact. Second, the Delicious apple doesn't have enough acid to counterbalance the added sugar. The apple that is less sweet remains firmer and retains more fiber. Fiber is indigestible roughage that is good for us because it helps the intestines and bowels to work better to eliminate waste products.

Of course, a raw apple contains the most fiber!

Bursting an Apple 135

Suppose you want a mushy apple!

YOU WILL NEED:

2 apples

water

parer (optional)

knife

pot with cover

1/2 cup water

1 teaspoon lemon juice or

dash of cinnamon and nutmeg

use of stove (ask for permission or help)

What to do: Wash both apples, peel them and cut them in four sections. Cut away the core and slice each quarter into cubes. Cook the pieces in a small amount of water in a covered pot until they are tender. Add the cinnamon and nutmeg—or the lemon juice—and cook a few minutes longer.

What happens: You have applesauce.

Why: With the peel removed, the pectin—the cementing material between cells that stiffens the fruit—dissolves. The water inside the apple's cells swells, bursts the cell walls, and the fruit's flesh softens. An apple turns into applesauce.

Apple in the Cookie Jar

136

YOU WILL NEED:

2 cookie jars or tins
1 slice of bread
2 slices of apple
1 slice of cake
(or a cookie)

An apple in the bread box or cookie jar will affect our bread or cake!

What to do: Place one apple slice in a cookie jar with the slice of bread. Place the other in the cookie jar with the slice of cake. Don't open the jars for a day or so.

What happens: The bread gets stale—and the cake stays moist!

Why: Sugar dissolves in water. It will absorb water from the atmosphere, if given the chance. The more sugary food draws water molecules from the other food. The apple has more sugar than the bread, so the bread loses water to the apple. But the cake has more sugar than the apple, so the apple loses water to the cake.

One End Is Sweeter!

137

Did you know that different parts of the same fruit taste different?

What to do: Peel the orange. Cut one slice across the stem end and then one across the blossom end. Taste them.

What happens: The slice at the blossom end is sweeter.

Why: The blossom end develops more sugar because it is more exposed to the sun. For the same reason, fruits grown in the temperate zone are only 10 to 15% sugar, while those from the tropics, such as bananas, figs, and dates, range from 20 to 60% sugar.

Why Are Green Apples Sour?

What makes unripe apples sour? Malic acid. All apples have it, but as an apple ripens on the tree, the amount of malic acid declines and the apple becomes sweeter. Depending on the soil and climate in which they are grown, some varieties stay more tart than others. Some people prefer apples like Granny Smiths, which stay green, just because they are sour.

How to Ripen a Fruit

YOU WILL NEED:

2 unripe peaches, nectarines or other fruit
brown paper bag
your refrigerator

All too often, the fruit we buy is not quite ripe. What do we do with it?

What to do: Place one of the unripe fruits in the crisper of the refrigerator for a day or two. Place the other in the paper bag and close it securely. Put it somewhere out of the way—on top of the refrigerator, for instance. Let it stand for a day or two. Taste both.

What happens: The fruit in the refrigerator softens—but it is not very tasty. The fruit in the paper bag softens—and sweetens!

Why: In the paper bag, you are trapping and concentrating the ethylene gas that comes from the fruit naturally. This gas speeds up the ripening process. In the refrigerator, the ethylene gas is shared with the other contents of the crisper.

Getting Juice from a Lemon

139

YOU WILL NEED:

2 lemons
knife

How do you get juice out of a lemon?

What to do: Cut the first lemon in half and squeeze out as much of the juice as you can.

Before you cut it, roll the other lemon on a hard surface like a countertop. Then squeeze out the juice.

What happens: It is much easier to squeeze out the juice after you've rolled the lemon—and you wind up with much more juice!

Why: You break up the tissues of the fruit when you roll it on a hard surface, so the juice comes out more easily.

Lemon Ices

YOU WILL NEED:

freshly grated lemon peel
1/2 cup of lemon juice (1 or 2 lemons)
1 cup of sugar (or less to taste)
4 cups of water
ice cube tray without separators, or a metal baking pan
small paper cups

Use your lemon juice to make refreshing lemon ices. Grate the peel of one lemon into a small plate or jar.

Simmer the water and the sugar uncovered over medium heat about three minutes until the sugar dissolves. Let it cool and put it in the refrigerator for about an hour until it is cold.

Combine the cold sugar syrup, the grated lemon peel and the lemon juice, and pour it into an ice cube tray. Put the tray in the freezer for about 30 minutes—until ice crystals begin to form. Then stir the mixture well and return the tray to the freezer. Keep stirring every 30 minutes until the mixture is frozen through—about 2 to 2 1/2 hours.

Spoon it into small paper cups—and lick away!

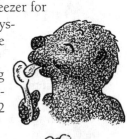

Rescuing an Apple

140

How do you prevent a cut apple from turning brown?

What to do: Cut the apple into quarters. Let one of the quarters remain on the kitchen table. Place another in the refrigerator.

Sprinkle lemon juice on the other two quarters. Place one of these on the table and the other in the refrigerator.

What happens: The untreated apple on the table turns brown first. The apple with the lemon juice in the refrigerator stays fresh longest.

Why: When you cut into apple, you tear its cells, releasing an enzyme called polyphenoloxidase. The enzyme speeds up the process by which compounds in the apple (phenols) combine with oxygen from the air. This is what produces the brownish pigment that darkens the fruit and makes it taste bad.

The enzyme works more slowly at cold temperatures than at room temperatures. It works even more slowly in an acid like lemon juice, which completely inactivates it.

If you don't have any lemon juice around, you can use orange juice, but lemon juice is better because it contains more acid.

Not in the Refrigerator

141

Bananas are picked and shipped green, but green bananas are not digestible. You can ripen them in a few days—but is it true that you should never put bananas in the refrigerator?

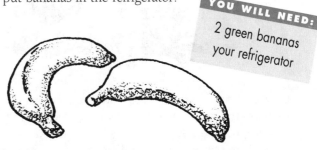

What to do: Place one banana on the counter and one in the refrigerator

What happens: Within a few days the banana on the counter turns yellow and its flesh becomes soft and creamy. The one in the refrigerator blackens and its insides remain hard.

Why: Bananas release ethylene gas naturally to ripen the fruit. On the counter, the skin's green chlorophyll disappears and reveals yellow pigments (carotenes and flavones). Also, the starch of the banana changes to sugar and the pectin, which holds the cells of the banana firm, breaks down. And so the flesh softens and is easy to digest.

In the cold of the refrigerator, the tropical bananas suffer cell damage and the release of browning and other enzymes. The fruit doesn't ripen and the skin blackens instead of turning yellow.

Once a banana is ripe it is safe to store it in the refrigerator. The skin may darken but the fruit inside will remain tasty for several days.

142 Powerful Pineapple

Gelatin is protein that comes from the connective tissue in the hoofs, bones, tendons, ligaments, and cartilage of animals. Vegetable gelatin, or agar, is made from seaweed. Gelatin dissolves in hot water and hardens with cold. We can put all kinds of fruit in it to make terrific desserts—but we're told on the package not to add raw pineapple. Why?

What to do: Stir gelatin in the cold water and let it stand one or two minutes. Then add the boiling water and stir until all the gelatin is dissolved. Pour into 2 cups or dessert dishes.

To one, add raw pineapple bits or frozen pineapple juice. To the other, add canned pineapple bits or canned juice. Put both in the refrigerator.

What happens: The gelatin with the canned pineapple becomes firm. The gelatin with the raw pineapple remains water.

Why: Pineapples, like figs and papayas, contain an enzyme that breaks proteins down into small fragments. If you put raw pineapple in gelatin for a dessert or fruit salad, this enzyme digests the gelatin molecules and prevents the gel from becoming solid. It remains liquid.

Cooking stops the enzyme from working. That's why you can add canned pineapple to the gelatin with no bad effects. Since it has been heated, it no longer contains the active enzyme.

Putting Pineapple to Work

Chefs sometimes simmer raw pineapple with a meat stew to help break down the protein of the meat and make it tender. A bonus is its sweet flavor.

143 ◆ Currying Flavor with a Lime

Sometimes "cooking" starts hours
before you light the stove.

What to do: Mix the lime juice and olive oil. Add the herbs and spices and stir. Put one of the chicken breasts in a bowl and cover it with the marinade.

Season the other chicken breast with salt and pepper and, if you wish, herbs.

Refrigerate both chicken breasts for an hour or so. Broil each one. After 10 minutes, turn them over and continue to broil for another 5 to 10 minutes. Test them for tenderness and remove them from the oven when a fork goes in easily.

What happens: The marinated chicken breast cooks faster. The lime not only flavors the chicken but also cuts down on cooking time.

Why: In marinating, the essential ingredient is an acid such as lime or lemon or vinegar that softens the tissues.

In addition to tenderizing and adding flavor, marinades sometimes preserve color. If you are marinating foods more than an hour or two, it is safer to refrigerate them. Like cooked food, marinating food needs to be refrigerated to prevent the growth of dangerous bacteria.

144 ◆ How to Make Vinegar

Vinegar is often used to flavor salads and tenderize meats. Many vinegars are made from fruit or wine (which is made from fruit). You can use apples to make your vinegar.

What to do: Cut the apples into small pieces, place them in your blender or juicer, and press out the juice. Pour half the juice into one jar, and the other half into the other. Place one jar in the refrigerator. Place the other in a warm place. Compare the color and the odor over a period of a week.

What happens: Both change, but the juice in the warm place changes much faster—weeks faster! At first you see bubbles and smell alcohol. You may see a thick film forming on top. Then the liquid begins to smell sour.

Why: Chemical changes have taken place. Yeasts from the skins of the apple and from the air act on the sugars of the apple juice, producing carbon dioxide and alcohol ("hard" cider). Within the week, bacteria in the cider turn it into vinegar.

GRAIN: THE STAFF OF LIFE

What happens when you make toast? What puts the bubbles in the pancakes? Why is baking more expensive on a rainy day? What is yeast? And more...

About Grain

Grain, whole or ground into meal or flour, is the principal food of people and domestic animals. Even Goldilocks and the Three Bears ate cereal, though they called it porridge.

Cereals, breads, rolls, muffins, buns, bagels, pancakes, waffles, spaghetti, macaroni, rice, bulgur, kasha, cookies, crackers, cake—all are grain products. They are made from wheat, buckwheat, rice, rye, oats, maize, barley, and, in Africa and India and China, millet or sorghum. Less familiar grains include amaranth, which fed the Aztecs; quinoa, a staple food of the ancient Incas; and triticale, which modern scientists developed by crossing rye and wheat.

145 What is Toast?

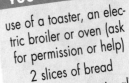

Toast is defined in the dictionary as a slice of bread browned on both sides by heat. But what causes the bread to brown?

What to do: Place the pieces of bread in the toaster, in the electric broiler, or in the oven under the broiler. Let one stay in twice as long as the other.

What happens: One turns golden brown. The one kept in too long turns black.

Why: Too much heat releases the carbon of the starch and sugar. It is this carbon that makes the bread turn black.

Toasting is a chemical process that alters the structure of the surface sugars, starches, and proteins of the bread slice. The sugars become fiber. The amino acids that are the building blocks of the protein break down and lose some of their nutritional value. Toast, therefore, has more fiber and less protein than the bread from which it is made. Some nutritionists believe that when you eat toast instead of bread you are getting color and flavor at the expense of nutrition.

146 Science for Breakfast

Hot cereal feels good, especially on a cold morning. Does it matter whether you start it in cold or boiling water?

What to do: Stir 1/3 cup of the oatmeal into a pot with 1/2 cup of the water. Bring it to a boil, lower the heat, and simmer for five minutes, stirring occasionally. Cover the pot and remove it from the heat. Let the mixture stand.

In a second pot, bring the rest of the water to a boil. Add salt and pour in the other half of the oatmeal. Lower the heat and simmer for five minutes, stirring occasionally. Again, cover, remove from the heat and let the mixture stand for a few minutes.

Taste the first pot of oatmeal. Then taste the second.

What happens: Both are cooked and taste good. The oatmeal that started in the cold water is creamier than the oatmeal that started in boiling water.

Why: As you heat the grains, the starch granules absorb water molecules, swell and soften.

Then the nutrients inside are released and are more easily absorbed by the body.

When you start cooking the oatmeal in cold water, the granules have a longer time to absorb the water. The activity starts at 140°F (60°C), well below the 212°F (100°C) boiling point. The complex carbohydrates (amylose and amylopectin) that make up the starch change. They break up some of the bonds between the atoms of the same molecule and form new bonds between atoms of different molecules. The water molecules then get trapped in the starch granules, which become bulky and eventually break, releasing the nutrients inside.

Add milk and raisins or bananas or blueberries to the oatmeal and you have a terrific dish that also furnishes vitamins, minerals, and complete protein.

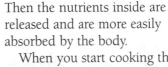 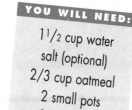

147 Why Not Eat Flour Raw?

Flour is the finely ground meal of wheat or other cereal grains. But we can't eat it raw.

What to do: Stir the sugar into one of the glasses of cold water. Stir the flour into the other glass of cold water.

What happens: The sugar disappears. The flour does not.

Why: The sugar dissolves in the water. The grains of flour are too big to dissolve. When you stir the flour and water together, you get a paste in which each grain is hanging suspended in the water.

When you chew your food—but before you swallow it—saliva works to help you digest it. Sugar molecules separate and mix with saliva immediately.

Flour, however, is suspended in the saliva, just as it is in the glass of water. The tough wall of plant cells around each grain of flour prevents the starch molecules from getting out. Nothing can get in unless the wall is broken—neither water needed to soften the starch nor the enzymes that would digest it. Heat breaks that wall. That's why flour needs to be cooked.

Popping Popcorn 148

Making popcorn gives you a good idea of how heat bursts the starch wall. Puffed cereals are made in a similar way.

What to do: Heat the pan on high heat for one or two minutes, and then pour in enough oil to cover the bottom of it. Lower the heat to medium. Add a few kernels and cover the pot. When you hear those kernels start to pop, add just enough popcorn to cover the bottom of the pot. Lower the heat. Put on the lid.

Shake the pot from time to time, but don't remove the lid while you can hear crackling sounds. When the sounds stop—within a minute or two—remove the pot from the stovetop and uncover it.

What happens: You have a mountain of popped corn!

Why: The moist and pulpy heart of the corn kernel is surrounded by a hard starch shell. When the kernel is heated, the moisture in the kernel turns to steam; the heart gets bigger—and the shell bursts. Grains of starch behave a lot like kernels of corn. When heat breaks the wall, the starch comes out and mixes with water. It is then in a form that we can digest.

All recipes that have flour as an ingredient—cake, biscuits, bread, gravies, sauces, puddings—must be cooked so that the starch in the flour can be released.

Buttered Popcorn

Many people eat popcorn exactly as it comes from the pot. But you may want to flavor it with a bit of melted butter or margarine and a pinch or two of salt.

Be sure to wait until after the kernels have popped to add the salt. Doing it beforehand makes the popcorn tough, just as adding salt before they cook toughens lentils and beans (see page 113).

149 Gluten: The Sticky Story

YOU WILL NEED:

2 tablespoons of warm water

4 tablespoons all-purpose flour

cold water

bowl

faucet with running water

In much of the world, flour is often made from wheat. There are two types of wheat—hard winter wheat and soft spring wheat. Soft wheat has more starch in it. It is made into soft, powdery cake flours and products that are meant to be tender and crumbly. Hard wheat, with more protein and less starch, is more gritty and coarse. It is better for bread baking because it forms a strong gluten. What is gluten?

What to do: Mix the flour and water. Roll it into a ball and soak the ball in cold water for 30 minutes. Gently fold and squeeze the dough under running water. Then knead the dough. The illustration shows how.

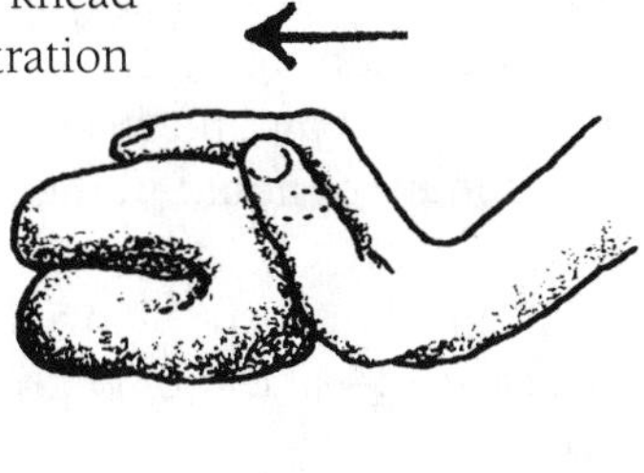

What happens: The dough becomes a sticky substance that stretches.

Why: All-purpose flour is a blend of both soft and hard flour. When you soak the dough in cold water, you wash away the starch, leaving the proteins. When you knead the dough, these proteins (gliadin and glutenin) interact to form an elastic substance—gluten. When the bread bakes, tiny bubbles of air get trapped inside the gluten. They make the dough rise a little. Without gluten, there would be no raised bread.

Only wheat produces the gluten that traps these air bubbles. That's why most bread and muffin recipes call for some wheat—even rye bread and corn muffins.

To form more bubbles within the gluten and get the dough to rise higher, bakers sometimes add other ingredients, such as yeast (see page 128) or baking soda or baking powder (see page 131).

Contents of Flour

	% Protein	% Starch
Cake flour	7.3	79.4
Semolina flour	12.3	73.5
All-purpose flour	10.5	76.1

Flour also contains 1% fat. The rest is moisture.

Whole wheat flour, graham flour, and cracked wheat all use the whole kernel—the bran (the hard, brown outer cover), the endosperm (the interior food for the germ) and the central germ (the part that sprouts). "White" flour has been refined—the brown bran and the germ have been removed.

Storing Bread

It's best to store bread in a breadbox at room temperature or in the freezer—but not in the refrigerator. Bread gets stale because the water from the interior flows to the crust where it is absorbed by the gluten (see page 125) and starch of the wheat. If bread is left uncovered, its water is lost in the air and the bread gets stale very fast. This happens fastest at temperatures like those of a refrigerator, just above freezing.

Because most of the water remains in the loaf, you can often "revive" stale bread by heating it. However, when bread becomes moldy, it is unsafe to eat.

Popovers: Gluten in Action

150

The way you mix batter or dough influences the amount of gluten that you develop and whether the baked goods will be spongy or flaky, coarse or fine, tender or tough.

YOU WILL NEED:

1 cup (112 g) flour
2 eggs
1 tablespoon (15 ml) cooking oil
1 cup (240 ml) milk
1/2 teaspoon salt (optional)
muffin tins
use of the oven (ask for permission or help)

What to do: Preheat oven to 450°F (232°C).

Beat the eggs, add the milk and gradually stir them into the flour to make a smooth batter. Beat the mixture thoroughly with an egg beater or in a mixer. The batter will be thin—like heavy cream.

Grease the muffin tins. Fill them half to two-thirds full. Bake at 450° (230°C) for 15 minutes. Then reduce the temperature to 350° (175°C) and bake for 20 minutes more. Don't open the oven door before the time is up.

What happens: The batter has baked into six to eight crisp, nearly hollow, delicious shells!

Why: When you started, you beat the dough hard to develop the gluten. In the oven, the combination of hot air and steam—formed from the large amount of liquid in the batter—causes the mixture to swell.

If you had opened the oven door, hot air would have escaped—and the popovers would have collapsed.

151 Hidden Sugar

Would it surprise you to find out that your body converts starch to sugar?

YOU WILL NEED:

pinch of cornstarch or a small cracker

What to do: Place the cornstarch or the cracker on the tip of your tongue. Mix it with saliva and let it stay for a while.

What happens: At first, it doesn't taste sweet on the tip of your tongue. But when it mixes with saliva, it becomes quite sweet.

Why: A molecule of starch is composed of a chain of sugar molecules, which can be broken into separate links by enzymes, proteins that cause chemical reactions. The enzyme (ptyalin) in your saliva splits the starch into its sugar links. The links dissolve in your digestive juices and then move easily into your intestines, through the wall into the bloodstream, and then along the bloodstream to the cells.

152 Alice's Magic Pill

In Wonderland, Alice ate a little pill and grew and grew and grew. Do you suppose it was made of yeast?

YOU WILL NEED:

1/2 cup (60 ml) of warm water
1 tablespoon of sugar
1/2 package of dry yeast
2 bowls
3 1/2 cups (392 g) of flour
measuring cup
1/2 cup (180 ml) of water
pinch of salt
wax paper or plastic wrap

What to do: Put the warm water in a cup. Test a drop of it on your wrist. It should not feel hot. Stir in the sugar and the yeast. Let it stand. Within 5 or 10 minutes, bubbles appear on the surface.
While you are waiting, mix the flour and salt and 1/2 cup (180 ml) of water in one of the bowls. Divide the mixture in two, and put half into each bowl.

Add the bubbly yeast to the first bowl. Cover both bowls with wax paper or plastic wrap and let them stand in a warm place from 45 minutes to an hour.

What happens: The mixture with the yeast doubles in size. The other remains the same size.

Why: The yeast converts the flour into sugar molecules. It eats the sugar, digests it, and uses it for energy, producing carbon dioxide bubbles, which puff up the mixture.

153 ◆ The Sugar Eater

Yeast, a tiny colorless plant, has been used for thousands of years to put air into breads and cakes.

What to do: Pour ⅔ of a cup of warm water into each of the glasses. Number the glasses. Add the sugar to #1. Add the flour to #2. Don't add anything to #3. Next, add an equal amount of the yeast to each glass. Let them stand. Observe them after 10 minutes, 20 minutes, 30 minutes. Note the differences.

What happens: Glass #1 produces bubbles in the first 10 minutes. Glass #2 produces bubbles after 15 or 20 minutes or so. Glass #3 never bubbles.

Why: Yeast is a fungus. It feeds on sugar and breathes out carbon dioxide. In the glass with sugar, it eats quickly— and soon produces carbon dioxide, which makes bubbles. In the glass with the flour, it takes longer because the enzymes in the yeast have to turn part of the flour's starch into sugar before the yeast can digest it.

In the glass of plain water, the yeast has no sugar on which to feed and so does not produce carbon dioxide. Some sugar is required for yeast to feed on.

Too much sugar, however, slows the production of carbon dioxide or even stops activity completely.

Just Right

154

Some like it hot, some like it cold, but yeast likes it just right!

What to do: Dissolve the sugar and yeast in 2/3 cup (160 ml) of water that is warm to the touch. Let the mixture stand.

Mix the flour, salt, oil, and 5 ounces (150 ml) of water. When bubbles appear on the surface of the yeast mixture, add it to the flour and mix well with a wooden spoon, or in a mixer. Knead the dough on the chopping board for 5 to 10 minutes, following the illustrations.

Sprinkle on more flour if the dough gets too sticky to handle. Keep pushing against the ball of dough, pressing into it and turning it to knead it on all sides.

When the dough feels satiny, make it into a ball and divide it in three equal parts. Place each part in an oiled bowl covered with plastic wrap.

Number the samples. Place #1 in a warm place (without a draft). Place #2 in the warmest part of the refrigerator. Place #3 in a hot place—over a radiator or in a hot oven.

What happens: Within 45 minutes to an hour, the dough in a warm place doubles in size. The dough in the refrigerator eventually rises, too, but it takes much longer. The dough in the hot place does not rise at all.

1 push it away →

2 ← **pull it back**

3 turn ball of dough

4 continue to knead and turn

YOU WILL NEED:

2/3 cup (160 ml) of warm water
2 tablespoons of sugar
1 package of dry yeast
3 mixing bowls (or cereal dishes)
plastic chopping board
felt-tipped pen, paper, scotch tape
plastic wrap
3 1/2 cups (392 g) of flour
2 tablespoons (30 ml) of cooking oil (olive or corn oil)
5 ounces (150 ml) of water
pinch of salt
1 teaspoon of cooking oil (to oil bowls)
wooden spoon
use of the oven (ask for permission or help)

Why: Yeast requires a moist, warm temperature—above 50° and below 130°F (10°–54°C). Below 50°F (10°C), it is relatively inactive, and above 130°F (54°C), it dies of too much heat.

The Pizza Test

155

Yeast consists of tiny living cells that make carbon dioxide as they breathe. Its bubbles not only puff up bread and cakes but also pizza. With the dough from the last experiment, you can see just what a difference yeast makes!

YOU WILL NEED:

Dough #1 from the previous experiment

Dough #3 from the previous experiment

2 cookie tins or pie plates

small can of tomato sauce

pinch of oregano

rolling pin or glass

2 to 4 ounces (56–112 g) of cheese (mozzarella, Parmesan or cheddar)

1 to 2 teaspoons olive oil

What to do: On a lightly floured board, punch the raised dough with your fists. Knead it for a few minutes and stretch it out or roll it with a rolling pin or the side of a glass to a circle six to eight inches (15–20 cm) in diameter and ½-inch (.62 cm) thick. Leave the edges a little thicker so they make a rim.

Put the rolled-out dough on an oiled cookie sheet or a pie plate. Let it rise for another 15 minutes. Roll out the other piece of dough, the one that didn't rise because the yeast was killed. Knead it and then roll it out onto the same kind of circle.

Preheat the oven to 450°F (230°C).

Put a layer of cubed or grated cheese on each of the dough circles. Stir a pinch of marjoram or oregano into the tomato sauce. Then pour half of the tomato sauce into the center of each pizza and spread the sauce in circles toward the rim. Top each with another layer of cheese.

Place the pie plates near the bottom of the preheated oven. Bake each pizza for about 20 to 30 minutes or until its crust is brown.

Be sure to use a pot holder when you take the pizzas out of the oven. Let them stand for about five minutes before you cut them. Taste each one.

What happens: The pizza made from the raised dough puffs up even more and has a light, moist taste. The dough of the other "pizza" is unpizza-like—flatter, heavier, and not very tasty.

Why: The yeast in the raised dough is still active and continues its action during your kneading and for part of the time that the pizza is baking. The other dough bakes as though no yeast had been added.

 156 About Baking Soda

Baking soda is sodium bicarbonate—sometimes called bicarbonate of soda. Some people use it for brushing their teeth, for absorbing refrigerator odors or as an antacid for indigestion! But we can also use baking soda to puff up bread and cake.

YOU WILL NEED:
2 teaspoons of baking soda
glass of orange juice or lemonade
glass of water

What to do: Add 1 teaspoon of baking soda to the glass of water. Add 1 teaspoon of baking soda to the orange juice.

What happens: Nothing happens in the glass of water. In the glass with the orange juice, you get bubbles. You have made orange soda!

Why: When you add an acid (orange juice) to the baking soda, you free the carbon dioxide of the baking soda—the bubbly gas.

Try adding baking soda to buttermilk, sour cream, yogurt, molasses, apple cider. They are all acidic and they will all bubble.

When baking soda is added to dough made with any of these or other acidic liquids, bubbles form and cause the dough to rise.

 157 About Baking Powder

How is baking powder different from baking soda?

YOU WILL NEED:
2 glasses of water
1/2 teaspoon baking powder
1/2 teaspoon baking soda

What to do: Add the baking powder to one glass of water. Add the baking soda to the other.

What happens: The water with the baking powder bubbles. The water with baking soda does not.

Why: Baking soda is an alkali, the chemical opposite of an acid. When it combines with an acid, it forms carbon dioxide.

Baking powder is a combination of baking soda and an acid. When you add baking powder to water or milk, the alkali and the acid react with one another and produce carbon dioxide—the bubbles. There are three types of baking powder. Each one contains baking soda. In addition, they each contain an acid—either cream of tartar (tartrate baking powder), monocalcium phosphate (phosphate baking powder) or a combination of calcium acid phosphate and sodium aluminum sulfate (double-acting baking powder).

158

Powder Versus Soda

What happens if we add baking powder to an acid?

What to do: Add baking powder to one of the half-filled glasses of sour milk and baking soda to the other glass.

What happens: The sour milk with the baking powder does not bubble as much as the one with the baking soda.

Why: When you add baking powder to an acid, you are tampering with the balance of acid and alkali. You are adding more acid than alkali. The result is that you actually reduce the amount of carbon dioxide produced. Therefore, if you want to bake with sour milk or buttermilk instead of regular milk, you could do it by eliminating the extra acid. You would just replace each teaspoon of baking powder in the recipe with 1/2 teaspoon of baking soda.

Chemical Bubbles

It wasn't until the middle of the 1800s that people started using chemicals to put air into breads and cakes. Today, instead of yeast, we often use either baking soda or baking powder—sometimes both. It takes much less time to bake with them. Batters, such as those used for pancakes and certain cakes, contain much more liquid than doughs used for breads and other cakes made with yeast. These batters are so thin that slow-acting yeast can't trap enough air to make bubbles. That's why we use the modern chemicals.

159 Model Muffins

If you want light, fluffy muffins, take care to treat the batter right! See what happens if you don't!

What to do: Grease the muffin pans. Using the smaller bowl, beat the egg with a spoon or a whisk. Then add the milk and oil.

In one of the large bowls, combine the flour, sugar, baking powder, cinnamon, and nutmeg. Make a hole in the center of the dry ingredients. Dump the liquid ingredients into the hole. Stir the mixture about 12 to 14 times, just enough to moisten the dry ingredients. The batter should be rough and lumpy.

Pour half of the batter into a second large bowl. Mix that batter until it is smooth.

Spoon a heaping tablespoon of the lumpy batter into one of the muffin cups so that it is two-thirds full. At the opposite end of the same muffin pan, do the same thing with the smooth batter. Repeat the process with the two other pans. Now you have three muffin pans, each with one muffin of smooth batter and one muffin of lumpy batter.

Turn on the oven to 400°F (205°C). Don't pre-heat it; instead, immediately put in one muffin pan. After 10 minutes, put in the second. In about 25 to 30 minutes, when the muffins are golden brown, remove them from the oven. (Use pot holders!)

Then put the third muffin pan into the hot oven and turn the heat up to 450°F (230°C). After 25 or 30 minutes, remove this pan from the oven.

Let them all cool and sample each muffin.

YOU WILL NEED:

1 cup (112 g) all-purpose, unbleached flour
small egg
3 tablespoons sugar
1 teaspoon baking powder
1/2 teaspoon ground cinnamon
1/2 teaspoon ground nutmeg
2 large bowls
wooden spoon
1/2 cup (60 ml) oil
1/2 cup (120 ml) milk
whisk (optional)
small bowl
3 muffin pans
oil or margarine for greasing
use of the oven
(ask for permission or help)

What happens: The muffins from the lumpy batter in the preheated oven—pan # 2—look and taste the best.

Why: For delicious muffins, you don't need to work hard! Overmixing develops the gluten and results in knobs or peaks on the top and long holes or tunnels inside the muffins.

It is also important to preheat the oven before you put the muffins in. If the oven is not hot enough, the muffins will be flat and heavy. That's because the baking soda isn't activated soon enough to cause the batter to rise.

However, if the oven is too hot, the carbon dioxide goes to work too soon, and the muffins will be poorly shaped and tough.

Weather and Cookies

Make the following cookies on two different days—one sunny and dry, the other rainy. The cookies will taste good on both days but…

What to do: Let the margarine stand at room temperature for 10 to 15 minutes. Then put it in a mixing bowl and add the sugar and vanilla extract. Cream the mixture well with a wooden spoon or in a food processor or electric mixer. Add the flour and continue mixing. When the dough is thoroughly mixed and smooth, remove it from the bowl and form a ball. If it is sticky, roll it in flour until it feels satiny. Wrap the dough in wax paper and refrigerate for an hour or more.

Preheat the oven to 325°F (165°C).

Cut the ball in half and roll out two logs, adding flour if the dough is sticky. Slice thin, as in the illustration, and place the circles a half-inch apart on an ungreased cookie sheet. Bake in center of the oven for 20 minutes or until the bottoms of the cookies are slightly brown.

What happens: On both the rainy day and the sunny day, you'll end up with 4 to 5 dozen great cookies. But it takes several more tablespoons of flour on the rainy day than it does on a dry, sunny day!

Why: On a rainy day, the dough soaks up water from the air, gets sticky and is harder to handle. You therefore have to use more flour than on a dry day.

What "Where" Has to Do with It

If you live in an area where the altitude is 500 feet or more above sea level (166 m), any dough with yeast or baking powder or soda will rise more quickly than it would at sea level. This is because the blanket of air (atmospheric pressure) is lighter. The carbon dioxide encounters less resistance from the surrounding air, and so it rises higher—with more force and more rapidly. This may make for tough, tasteless baked goods. The solution: Use less yeast or baking powder than you would at sea level. Some prepared commercial mixes solve the problem by directing you to add more flour at altitudes of 3,500 feet or more.

Making Food Last

How do salt and sugar preserve food? How do you change a grape into a raisin? Why freeze herbs? What is cheese? And more about making food last.

About Preservation

To make foods last longer, we try to halt the growth of the bacteria, fungi, and molds that make it spoil. Sometimes we need to destroy destructive enzymes or prevent oxidation. Either of these processes changes the color, texture, taste, or nutritional value of a food.

We use many methods: drying, salting, smoking, pickling, canning, refrigerating, and freezing, among others.

For centuries, particularly in warm countries, people used salt to preserve many types of meat and vegetables. Beef still comes to the table as corned beef, cabbage as sauerkraut, cucumbers as pickles. Salt draws moisture from food by osmosis or absorption. This discourages the growth of bacteria. In dry curing (or corning), food is buried in salt. Other techniques involve soaking food in brine, a salt-and-water solution, or injecting salt into the food.

Smoking meat, poultry, and fish is also an age-old practice. The food is hung, usually in a special smokehouse, above hickory, apple, maple, or other aromatic wood chips burning at a low temperature—sometimes for days. The longer the smoking process, the stronger the flavor and the longer the food lasts.

When we talk about pickling, we usually think of pickled cucumbers. Cucumbers turn into pickles with the help of vinegars and other acids, spices such as dill, and salt and sugar. But other vegetables and fruit as well as fish and meats can also be preserved by pickling.

Canning dates back only to the early 1800s. It involves the rapid heating of sealed sterilized containers, glass or tin. Salt is often added and so is sugar. Like salt, sugar acts as a preservative, helping to keep mold from growing on such foods as jams and jellies.

In addition to these methods, commercial food manufacturers also add chemicals to extend the time food can remain on store shelves.

161 Hocus-Pocus— Raisins

A raisin starts life as a grape and a prune as a plum. What happens to these juicy fruits? See for yourself.

What to do: Wash the grapes in cold water and remove those that are bruised. Pull out the stems and place the cleaned grapes in a strainer. Dip them into a pot of boiling water so that the skins break. Spread the grapes on one of the drying trays so that they don't touch each other. Using the empty cans, prop the second tray over the first.

There are two methods you can use.
1. For four or five days, place the trays by a sunny window, turning them every hour, so that the fruit dries evenly.
2. Or place the trays on the middle rack of a preheated oven (140°F/60°C) and let them remain overnight.

When you think they may be dry, remove one or two of the grapes. Let them cool, and test them for moisture. If they still have water in them, let the fruit dry for another hour or so. Then test. If the grape is pliable and chewy, remove the rest from the drying tray.

What happens: You have raisins! Put them in a plastic bag and they will last for months and months.

Why: Drying as a means of preservation is thousands of years old. Normally fruit rots in a week or less at room temperature. Even in the refrigerator it will rot after a few weeks.

Fungi that start as spores—tiny seedlike cells—drop from the air and feed on the fruit's sugars and starches. When you dry out the grapes, you are taking away the moisture that the fungi need in order to grow. As long as the dried fruit can't take in moisture from the air, it will stay edible for many months.

About Herbs and Spices

For hundreds of years, herbs and spices were a symbol of wealth, valued because they preserved food or disguised its smell when it was spoiled. They also served as medicines.

Spices are the dried flavorings made from the buds, flowers, fruit, bark, and roots of fragrant tropical plants. Herbs are the leaves, stems, or flowers of aromatic succulents grown in temperate climates.
• Fresh herbs will keep for a week in the refrigerator. Wrap the stems in damp paper towels inside a plastic bag.
• Cut, crush, or mince the herbs just before you use them.

Freezing Herbs

Certain herbs, such as parsley, chervil, and chives are preserved better by freezing than by drying. The secret is to package them so that you keep air out and moisture in.

YOU WILL NEED:

bunch of herbs (parsley, basil, dill, sage, thyme, or chives)
small thick sealable plastic bags
paper towels
labels and felt-tipped pen
drinking straw (optional)
pot of water (optional)
your freezer

What to do: Wash the herbs in cold water and remove any leaves that are rotting. Drain and pat them dry with paper towels.

Strip the leafy herbs from their stems. Package the leaves in small plastic bags leaving 1/2 inch (1.25 cm) of headroom. You can use a drinking straw to remove as much air as possible. Or making sure that no water enters the bag, you can dip it in a pot of water. This pushes the plastic against the food, forcing out all the air.

Seal the bag tightly, using freezer tape if the bags are not self-sealing. Label each one with the name of the herb and the date, and place the bags in the freezer, preferably at 0°F (-18°C).

What happens: At that low temperature, herbs last up to a year and maintain flavor, color and nutrients. You can add them to soups, stews, sauces, salads, and other foods while they're still frozen.

Why: Enzymes, protein molecules that speed chemical reactions, harm foods by changing their color, texture, taste, and nutritional value. Like heating, freezing slows down active enzymes and delays the spoiling process.

You remove the air because air pockets between the food and the plastic bag collect moisture from the food, which results in frost and freezer burns. As ice crystals form, the water expands and ruptures cell membranes and walls.

Because food expands during freezing, you don't fill the bag completely. The bag or other container will split if it's too full for the contents to expand freely.

If the freezer temperature is higher than 0°F (-18°C), the herbs will not keep their flavor as long. Each 10°F (-12°C) above zero cuts the storage life in half!

You can substitute frozen herbs for fresh in recipes, but remember to use them while they're still frozen. If you let them thaw, microbes and enzymes have time to wilt and darken them.

- Buy dried herbs and spices in the smallest quantity possible—they lose flavor with age and exposure to air.
- Use less dried herb than fresh—1/3 to 1/2 teaspoon of dried to a tablespoon of fresh.
- Presoak dry herbs for a few minutes in lemon juice, soup stock or oil for more flavor.
- Add herbs the last 10 or 15 minutes of cooking.
- If you've added too much of an herb, add a raw potato to the cooking pot. It will take up some of the excess flavor and save your dish from being too spicy.
- Put a bay leaf in your flour canister to help protect against insects. Bay leaves are natural insect repellents.

163  To Freeze or Not to Freeze

Is freezing a good way to preserve any food?

YOU WILL NEED:

lettuce leaves or green pepper or tomato
cloves of garlic
2 tablespoons (30 ml) of cottage cheese
3 plastic bags
labels and freezer tape
your freezer

What to do: Cull the vegetables, wash and pat them dry. Put them each in a plastic bag, whole or cut up, and remove the air as described on p. 137. Seal the bags, label them and place them in the freezer. Spoon the cottage cheese into a plastic bag. Remove the air, seal the bag, label it, and also place it in the freezer.

After two or three days, remove all the bags from the freezer and thaw the contents.

What happens: The foods are no longer appetizing. The lettuce and tomatoes have lost their crispness and become limp. The garlic has become stronger. The cottage cheese has separated and become grainy.

Why: When the water cools, it expands and turns to ice, damaging the cell walls of the foods. This loss of crispness is not so important if the food is to be cooked, but foods that we eat raw, like lettuce, tomatoes, and cottage cheese, definitely lose their appeal.

Salted foods also don't freeze as well as unsalted foods. This is because the salt lowers the freezing point and gives the enzymes more time to work.

Preserving a Pear

One great way to preserve fruit is to convert it into jam or jelly.

YOU WILL NEED:

2 pears
1 teaspoon grated peel (zest) of lemon
1/2 small can of thawed frozen apple juice concentrate or
1 cup of apple juice
1/2 cup of water (optional)
1/2 teaspoon vanilla
1 teaspoon lemon juice
a pot
clean jar with lid
use of the stove (ask for permission or help)

In the past these have been made with heavy concentrations of sugar and pectin and stored in sterile jars. In fact, for commercial manufacturers to label a product "jam" or "preserve," the U.S. federal law requires that 65% of the final product be sugar. In Europe, there is a similar requirement for products labeled "conserve." A certain amount of sugar and acidity prevents the growth of dangerous microorganisms.

But now fruit spreads, sweetened with fruit juice concentrates instead of sugar, are being sold commercially. We can easily and safely make these in our kitchen to refrigerate for up to a month or two.

What to do: Peel the pears and remove the cores. Then cut the pears into cubes. Put the cubes in a bowl with the grated lemon peel and lemon juice.

Heat the thawed apple juice, water, and vanilla for 10 minutes or so. (It's okay to use canned or bottled apple juice, but if you do, don't add water.) Add the pears and lemon juice.

Bring the mixture to a boil. Then lower the heat and, stirring frequently, cook it for 30 to 40 minutes, or until it thickens. Place it in a clean jar and refrigerate.

What happens: You have pear jam that will keep for a month or two.

Why: The acid of the lemon juice and the sugar of the apple juice prevent the growth of dangerous microorganisms.

You can make chunky preserves by slicing your pears into eighths. Add grated lemon peel and lemon juice and cook in apple juice for 20 to 30 minutes, or until soft but not mushy.

Little Miss Muffet

YOU WILL NEED:
glass of milk
pinch of salt
rubber band or length
of string
bowl
cheesecloth or a
strainer lined with a
clean cloth

Making cheese is one of our oldest ways of preserving milk. How is it done? Was Miss Muffet eating milk or cheese? And did her curds and whey come from a cow, a goat, a sheep, a mare, a camel, a llama, a reindeer or a buffalo? Milk and cheese can come from all these—and other animals!

You can make your own cottage cheese and observe the start of the process by which all cheeses are made.

What to do: Let the milk stand for two or three days at room temperature until it sours and starts to form chunks. Add a pinch of salt.

Using a rubber band or length of string, fasten a square of cheesecloth over a wide bowl. (Or line a strainer with a clean cloth—an old cotton handkerchief—and suspend the strainer on the lip of the bowl.)

Empty the sour chunks onto the cheesecloth Let them drip for two or three hours.

What happens: You have cottage cheese in the cheesecloth.

Why: Harmless bacteria act on the sugar in the milk to sour it and change the sugar into acid. The acid curdles the milk and separates it into a liquid (whey) and little solid chunks (curds). The curds contain a protein (casein), mineral salts, and the butterfat of the milk. Cottage cheese is a "fresh" cheese and lasts a relatively short time. Many other cheeses are cured—aged and ripened—by adding different molds and bacteria for varying periods of time. These give the cheeses their particular flavors and a longer life.

Why Swiss Cheese Has Holes
Carbon dioxide makes the holes in the Swiss cheese. It is released by bacteria that are added during the curing process.

Talking About Time

We use the word "time" to refer to the period when something happens or how long an event lasts.

About Time

People have measured time by the sun, by the moon, and by the stars. To measure time they have used oil and candles, water and sand, weights and pendulums, batteries and electric power stations, and the atoms of a metal called cesium.

In prehistoric times, people measured time by the seasons and night and day. Today physicists, studying particles of the atom, measure a picosecond, which is a trillionth of a second. Other scientists, including paleontologists, geologists, archeologists, and biologists, use "radioactive clocks" and "molecular clocks" to measure billions of years.

Astronomers, physicists, engineers, and statisticians, as well as blacksmiths and locksmiths, were all involved in the development of "the clock," which is the instrument for measuring time. Horologists, or clock-makers, based their inventions on the scientific theories of such scientists as Newton, Descartes, Galileo, Niels Bohr, and Einstein.

But it was natural phenomena—the spinning of the Earth on its axis and the rotation of the Earth around the sun—that provided the first means of measuring time.

Now and Then

166

We use words about time all the time. Play a game with a friend, or just challenge yourself, to see how many you can jot down in 10 minutes.

What to do: Set the timer or alarm clock for 10 minutes. Then list as many words and expressions about time as you can think of before the alarm goes off. "Then" and "before" are both examples, and so are such expressions as "in time" and "split second."

What happens: Check the list on page 143. Did you miss any? Are any of yours missing from the list?

Time to Wake Up

167

Scientists have discovered that the two sides of the human brain do different things. The left side of the brain has a strong sense of time; the right side has none. But when you tell yourself to wake up at a particular time, the right brain is the one that understands and wakes you.

See whether the two sides of your brain cooperate. Try waking at a particular time without an alarm clock—or someone else waking you.

The Time of Your Life

168

A "timeline" is a list of the dates of significant events in the order in which they occurred. You can make a timeline of your life, giving the dates of the important things that have happened to you.

What to do: Sit down and think about things that are important to you. Talk to your parents about dates that you aren't sure of. Make a list of all the things that occur to you—your birth date, when you first walked and talked, the time you entered kindergarten, when you learned to read, trips you went on, the date you first learned to ride a bike or to skate, the arrival of a sister or brother, a prize you won, a play you were in, when you met your best friend, your graduation from school.

Put them in order according to date and then make a timeline like the one on page 145. Liven it up with drawings if you wish. Later, you may want to revise your timeline because other things have become more important. And you may find it interesting to consult with your parents and your grandparents and make timelines of the events in their lives.

169

How Long Is a Minute?

Do you know exactly how much time it takes before a minute has gone by? Have fun with a friend by seeing who can come closest to "timing" a minute!

What to do: Take turns. Your helper or friend holds the watch and gives a signal. You then put your hands on your lips and keep quiet until you think one minute is up. Then you shout "Time!" Your friend will record your time. Then you take over the timing while your friend keeps quiet for what seems like a minute and you record the time. Compare your time and your friend's.

What happens: You will find that a minute can be quite a long time!

Why: Time drags when you're concentrating on time passing. But try timing a minute when you are reading or drawing or playing a game and see how short a minute can seem.

Time Words and Expressions

(Answers to "Now and Then" on page 142)

after
after a while
afternoon
all the time
already
any time
as soon as
at once
before
biennial
bimonthly
biweekly
century
chronology
circadian
concurrent
contemporary
constant
continual
continuous
daily
day
double time
diurnal
during

earlier
early
eon
epoch
equinox
evening
era
eternal
eventually
final
first
for a second, a
    minute, an hour,
    a month, a season,
    a year, a while
forever
fortnight
frequent
future
hitherto
horology
hour
immediate
in a flash
in a minute

infinite
infrequent
instantly
intermittent
interval
last month, last week,
    last year
late
later
latest
long ago
meanwhile
midnight
millennium
minute
momentary
month
morning
nanosecond
never
next month, week, year
night
nocturnal
noon
now

now and then
o'clock
on time
once in a while
once upon a time
overtime
past
picosecond
perpetual
present
previously
quicker
quickest
quickly
rapidly
seasonal
second
sequence
sequential
slower
slowest
slowly
sometimes
split second
sudden

synchronize
tempo
temporal
temporary
then
this month,
    week, year
timeless
timely
today
tomorrow
tonight
ultimate
ultrashort
vernal
week
when
while
year
yearlong
year-round
yesterday
yesteryear
yet
zero hour

TELLING TIME BY THE MOON

Some scientists, called archeoastronomists, combine the study of the stars and planets with the study of ancient civilizations. These scientists have studied 10,000 year-old bones found in Africa and Europe. They think grooves carved into them may be primitive calendars used to follow the cycles of the moon throughout the year.

Before our early ancestors became concerned with the hours of the day, they were involved with day and night, with the months and the seasons of the year. Peoples of many different cultures observed the phases of the moon and the movements of the sun and stars. They used them to keep time, so they would know when to plant and when to harvest.

The pyramids in Egypt and the Yucatan, as well as rock foundations like Stonehenge in England, all indicated those important times of the year and the religious holidays that celebrated those times and pacified their gods.

About Calendars

Calendars are orderly plans that fit days into months and months into years. As far back as 3000 B.C., Babylonians, who lived in what is now part of Iraq, and Egyptians devised lunar calendars. They were made up of 354 days with months based on the cycles of the moon. The Athenians had a similar calendar.

Later, because the floods came every 365 days, the Egyptians changed to a solar year, with a calendar of 12 months, each with 30 days. This left 5 extra days at the end of the year during which the people celebrated the birthdays of important gods.

The Romans originally had a lunar year of 355 days, but by the time of Julius Caesar, the Roman calendar was three months ahead of the sun's year. In 45 B.C., Caesar reformed the calendar, bringing it closer to the one we use today. He added almost three months to the year 46 B.C. and, like the Egyptians, devised a solar calendar of 365 days. He added an extra day every fourth year, our leap year. This calendar, called the Julian calendar, was used throughout the Middle Ages.

It wasn't until 500 years after the death of Jesus Christ that time was related to his birth. Many non-Christian societies use C.E. (Common Era) instead of A.D. (Anno Domini, the Year of Our Lord) and B.C.E. (Before the Common Era) instead of B.C. (before Christ). The Muslim Hijri calendar starts counting from A.H. (Anno Hegirae), the Year of the Emigration—the journey of Mohammed from Mecca to Medina.

Because the year was still too long by about 11 minutes, by the 16th century the Julian calendar was more than a week off. Eventually, Easter would coincide with the previous Christmas! So, in 1582, Pope Gregory XIII wiped out 10 days (October 5 became October 15), and decreed that no century year, like 1700, should be a leap year unless it was divisible by 400. That meant that three leap years would be omitted every four centuries. In addition, the calendar year was to begin on January 1 instead of March 21. September through December were to keep their original names—which meant seventh, eighth, ninth, and tenth months of the year—even though they were now the ninth to twelfth months of a year that began in January. This Gregorian calendar is the one we use today.

The Chinese calendar, devised about 2700 B.C., reckoned time with numbered months and years named for twelve different animals. It's still used for setting the dates of the festivals of the Harvest Moon and of the New Year (which is celebrated between January 20 and February 19 on the Gregorian calendar).

The Orthodox Eastern Church still uses the Julian calendar, so Greek Catholics celebrate Christmas a number of days after other Christians.

170

Calendar Timeline

4242 B.C.—Egyptian lunar calendar
3761 B.C.—Jewish lunar calendar
3300 B.C.—Possible date of first Mayan calendar
3100 B.C.—Egyptian solar calendar
3000 B.C.—Mesopotamian and Athenian lunar calendars
2680 B.C.—Egypt's Great Pyramids built
2637 B.C.—Chinese calendar invented by legendary Emperor Huangdi
1600 B.C.—Stonehenge erected in England
753 B.C.—Founding of Rome
600 B.C.—Zoroastrian calendar with year starting at vernal equinox—still used in Islamic Iran
46 B.C.—Julius Caesar revises Roman calendar
500—Dionysius Exiguus proposes using the term Anno Domini (A.D.), the Year of Our Lord

622—Hijri calendar
900s—Mayan calendar more exact than modern calendar
1077—Jalali calendar devised by Omar Khayyam of Persia
1100—Mayan pyramid built in the Yucatan
1582—Gregorian calendar
1752—Great Britain and colonies abandon Julian calendar
1844—Badi' calendar of the Baha'i faith
1873—Buddhists in Japan adopt Gregorian calendar
1917—USSR adopts Gregorian calendar
1957—India adopts Gregorian calendar

Moon Time

To know when to plant their seeds, and to fix the dates of religious holidays, many ancient peoples devised calendars based on the moon. One of the first words for moon meant "the measure of time." The word "month" comes from the moon—moonth.

YOU WILL NEED:
lamp
white tennis ball
pencil
paper

What happens: You will observe the various phases of the moon from the full moon to the half moon to a crescent sliver to the new moon when no part is lit.

You can use a lamp and an ordinary tennis ball to see what causes the various phases of the moon.

What to do: Place the lighted lamp on a table in a darkened room. Hold the ball in your hand at arm's length with your back to the light. Raise the ball high enough to allow the light to strike the ball. Note the part of the ball lighted by the lamp. This represents the full moon.

Turn around slowly from right to left, keeping the ball in front of you and above your head. Observe the change in shape of the lighted part of the ball as you make one complete turn. Stop at each one-eighth turn and draw the shape of the ball (the moon) that is lit up.

Why: Every day the moon rises and sets about 50 minutes later than the day before, taking about four weeks to go around the Earth. During that time the moon waxes from new moon to full moon and then wanes to new moon again. The same half of the moon always faces the Earth as the moon goes around it. Half of the moon is lighted by the sun and half is in darkness. Actually you see a little more than half because the Earth's gravity causes the moon to librate, to vibrate, as it rotates. At new moon the half facing the Earth is dark because the moon is between the Earth and the sun. Of course, you often see the moon in its various phases in the night sky. But you can also see the crescent moon and the half moon during the day because they rise before nightfall.

172 # Different Drummers

Some societies set up their calendars to start with the year of their rulers, with the founding of a city, or with an important event in their religion. The Greeks measured time by referring to the Olympiads, the first of which was held in 776 B.C.

Even today, the Hopi Indians express time in their language by what happens "when the corn matures" or "when a sheep grows up." Off New Guinea, the Trobriand Islanders date events by saying they occurred "during the childhood of X" or "in the year of the marriage of Y."

Do you ever measure time by thinking about events in your life?

173

String Calendar

YOU WILL NEED:
large sheet of heavy paper
paper punch or scissors
long piece of string

The string calendar, a way of recording the passing of days in a lunar month, comes from Sumatra, an Indonesian island in the Indian Ocean. You can make one for yourself by threading string through each of thirty holes in a sheet of heavy paper. It may be easier to use a printed calendar to keep track of the days of the month, but your own string calendar can amuse your friends.

What to do: Fold your paper lengthwise in half and then in half again. Punch seven evenly spaced holes in each of the first three-quarters of the page. In the last quarter, punch 10 holes, as in the illustration. On the first of the month, knot your string and thread it through the first hole. The next day, thread the string through the second hole. Do the same every day of the month. When you want to know what day of the month it is, just count the number of holes you've covered.

174

Perpetual Calendar

YOU WILL NEED:
the charts on page 148
your birth date

You can find out the day of the week on which you were born. Indeed, you can find the day of the week of any date from 1920 to 2019.

What to do: First check the Years chart for the letter next to the year of your birth. Next, on the Months chart look for your letter and find which number falls under the month in which you were born. Then, on the Days chart, use the number you just found and go down to the date on which you were born.

What happens: If you were born on July 19, 1986, for example, your letter is "B", your number is "1", and you were born on a Friday.

Amaze your friends and tell them the day of the week on which they were born. You can also find out about your parents or a historical figure, as long as you know their birth dates.

147

YEARS

1920 K	1940 H	1960 L	1980 I	2000 M
1921 F	1941 C	1961 G	1981 D	2001 A
1922 G	1942 D	1962 A	1982 E	2002 B
1923 A	1943 E	1963 B	1983 F	2003 C
1924 I	1944 M	1964 J	1984 N	2004 K
1925 D	1945 A	1965 E	1985 B	2005 F
1926 K	1946 B	1966 F	1986 C	2006 G
1927 F	1947 C	1967 G	1987 D	2007 A
1928 N	1948 K	1968 H	1988 L	2008 I
1929 B	1949 F	1969 C	1989 G	2009 D
1930 C	1950 G	1970 D	1990 A	2010 E
1931 D	1951 A	1971 E	1991 B	2011 F
1932 L	1952 I	1972 M	1992 J	2012 N
1933 G	1953 D	1973 A	1993 E	2013 B
1934 A	1954 E	1974 B	1994 F	2014 C
1935 B	1955 F	1975 C	1995 G	2015 D
1936 J	1956 N	1976 K	1996 H	2016 L
1937 E	1957 B	1977 F	1997 C	2017 G
1938 F	1958 C	1978 G	1998 D	2018 A
1939 G	1959 D	1979 A	1999 E	2019 B

MONTHS

	J	F	M	A	M	J	J	A	S	O	N	D
A	1	4	4	7	2	5	7	3	6	1	4	6
B	2	5	5	1	3	6	1	4	7	2	5	7
C	3	6	6	2	4	7	2	5	1	3	6	1
D	4	7	7	3	5	1	3	6	2	4	7	2
E	5	1	1	4	6	2	4	7	3	5	1	3
F	6	2	2	5	7	3	5	1	4	6	2	4
G	7	3	3	6	1	4	6	2	5	7	3	5
H	1	4	5	1	3	6	1	4	7	2	5	7
I	2	5	6	2	4	7	2	5	1	3	6	1
J	3	6	7	3	5	1	3	6	2	4	7	2
K	4	7	1	4	6	2	4	7	3	5	1	3
L	5	1	2	5	7	3	5	1	4	6	2	4
M	6	2	3	6	1	4	6	2	5	7	3	5
N	7	3	4	7	2	5	7	3	6	1	4	6

DAYS

	1	2	3	4	5	6	7
Monday	1						
Tuesday	2	1					
Wednesday	3	2	1				
Thursday	4	3	2	1			
Friday	5	4	3	2	1		
Saturday	6	5	4	3	2	1	
Sunday	7	6	5	4	3	2	1
Monday	8	7	6	5	4	3	2
Tuesday	9	8	7	6	5	4	3
Wednesday	10	9	8	7	6	5	4
Thursday	11	10	9	8	7	6	5
Friday	12	11	10	9	8	7	6
Saturday	13	12	11	10	9	8	7
Sunday	14	13	12	11	10	9	8
Monday	15	14	13	12	11	10	9
Tuesday	16	15	14	13	12	11	10
Wednesday	17	16	15	14	13	12	11
Thursday	18	17	16	15	14	13	12
Friday	19	18	17	16	15	14	13
Saturday	20	19	18	17	16	15	14
Sunday	21	20	19	18	17	16	15
Monday	22	21	20	19	18	17	16
Tuesday	23	22	21	20	19	18	17
Wednesday	24	23	22	21	20	19	18
Thursday	25	24	23	22	21	20	19
Friday	26	25	24	23	22	21	20
Saturday	27	26	25	24	23	22	21
Sunday	28	27	26	25	24	23	22
Monday	29	28	27	26	25	24	23
Tuesday	30	29	28	27	26	25	24
Wednesday	31	30	29	28	27	26	25
Thursday		31	30	29	28	27	26
Friday			31	30	29	28	27
Saturday				31	30	29	28
Sunday					31	30	29
Monday						31	30
Tuesday							31

175

The Wobbly Week

The week has not always consisted of seven days, except among the Jews. The Greeks had three 10-day weeks in a month; the Romans had an eight-day week. After the French Revolution, the French tried a 10-day week. That experiment lasted 10 years, until 1806. In 1929, the Soviet Union tested a shifting four-day work week with the fifth day a day of rest, but it, too, was abandoned after only two years.

• Sunday is named for the sun and Monday for the moon. The other days of the week are named for various ancient gods: Four days of the week are named for Norse gods and one for a Roman god:
• Tuesday for Tiv (the ancient German name for Mars)
• Wednesday for Woden (Mercury)
• Thursday for Thor (Jupiter)
• Friday for Frigga (Venus)
• Saturday for the Roman god Saturn, the father of Jupiter

Do you think you would like a 10-day work week? A four-day week? Why?

TELLING TIME
BY THE SUN

Our ancestors were mostly concerned with sunrise, noon, and sunset. For those, they watched the sun, or the shadows cast by trees or rocks or the distant hills.

For at least 10 and perhaps as long as 20 centuries, measuring the shadow cast by the sun was an important method of telling time. The sundial is mentioned in the Bible in an incident scholars say took place in 741 B.C.

In *Chaucer's Canterbury Tales,* written about 1400, the Parson estimates the time on the basis of his height and the length of his shadow. Characters in several of Shakespeare's plays use sundials.

Sundial Timeline

176

1500 B.C.—Fragment of earliest known sundial (now in a Berlin museum)

900s B.C.—Egyptians make T-shaped shadow timetellers with hoursmarked along their length

600s B.C.—Greek philosopher and astronomer Anaximander of Miletus introduces sundial into Greece

600-300 B.C.—An instrument is devised that doesn't have to be turned in the afternoon

200s B.C.—Chaldean astronomer Berossus describes the first hemispheric sundial

200 B.C.—Sundial commonplace in Rome

100—Sundial with gnomon (the arm on a sundial) tilted at an angle according to latitude

1528—Portable sundial with 10 faces, each at a different latitude

Where Does My Shadow Go?

YOU WILL NEED:
flashlight
darkened room

Our ancestors told the time by the shadows made by the sun. But why do we sometimes see a shadow and at other times "there's none of him at all?"

What to do: In a darkened room, place the lighted flashlight on the floor about five feet from a light-colored wall. Stand behind the flashlight. Do you cast a shadow? Now stand between the flashlight and the wall. Then move closer to the wall.

What happens: You don't cast a shadow when you stand behind the light. You cast a big shadow when you are near the light and far from the wall. As you move farther from the light, the shadow becomes smaller.

Why: You cast a shadow by blocking the rays of light. As you move away from the source of light, your shadow becomes smaller because you cut off fewer rays of light. Any object that won't permit light to shine through creates a shadow, an area of lessened light.

Why Am I Sometimes Very Tall?

This simple experiment shows how the length of a shadow changes when the source of light changes position.

YOU WILL NEED:

spool of thread
sheet of paper
2 pencils
flashlight

What to do: Put the spool of thread on the sheet of paper. Stand one of the pencils in the spool. Darken the room and hold the flashlight at different angles above the pencil. On the paper, using the other pencil, record the length of each shadow.

What happens: When the flashlight is high and directly above the pencil, the shadow is short. When the light is low and at a slant, the shadow is long.

Why: When the light is low and at a slant, the shadow is long because few rays of light pass through. This shows us why the shadows at the North Pole are longer than those at the equator. The sun hits the Earth directly at the equator and indirectly at the Poles.

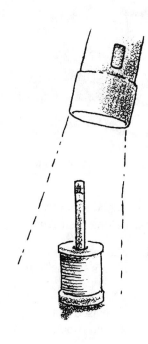

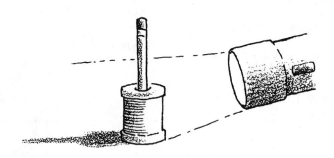

Shadow Watch

At what time of day is the shadow the shortest? You can find out by watching the shadow cast by the sun in the same way our distant ancestors did!

YOU WILL NEED:
tree
chalk or stones
pencil
paper
clock
tape measure

What to do: Find a nearby tree that is in sunlight much of the day. Using either small stones or chalk, mark off the shadow it casts right after you get up in the morning. Measure the shadow's length. Then do the same thing at noon or, if your area is on Daylight Savings Time, an hour later. Finally, mark the shadow cast late in the afternoon toward sunset and measure it.

What happens: The shadow is shortest at noon. The shadows cast in the early morning and late afternoon are both much longer.

Why: The sun is highest in the sky at noon and, therefore, casts the shortest shadow. However, your clock and the sun may have a difference of opinion about when it is noon. (See page 156 to find out why.)

◆ 180 ◆ Shadow Timepiece

YOU WILL NEED:

2 empty milk cartons
index card or piece of cardboard
tape
small compass
large piece of paper
marker

The earliest device for telling time, a crude forerunner of the more accurate sundial, was the Egyptian shadow clock. It dates from between the 10th and the 8th centuries B.C. and was made of stone. You can make your own from materials you have around the house.

What to do: Place one of the milk cartons on its side. Tape the index card, or a piece of cardboard, 1 inch from the top of the short flat end of the carton. Hold the second carton perpendicular to the first and attach it to the free end of the index card, as in the illustration.

In the morning, go outdoors and place the timeteller level on the piece of paper with the upper carton pointing east. In the afternoon, turn the timeteller around so that it points west. Check your watch clock every hour and mark where the shadow falls on the paper.

What happens: The shadow shortens as it gets to be lunchtime and lengthens again toward dinner time. And the distances from one hour to the next differ! The shadows are farther apart from one another early and late in the day and closer during the middle of the day.

Why: Only at the equator will the spaces allotted to hours be exactly equal because the sunlight hits the Earth directly. Unlike the day and the year, which are dictated by the revolution of Earth on its axis and around the sun, the hour is a division devised by people. The day runs from midnight to midnight, but it could be divided—and has been—into twenty parts or six parts or three parts instead of into 24 hours. Early Egyptians didn't talk about 2 or 3 o'clock. They agreed to meet when the shadow was, for instance, four steps long.

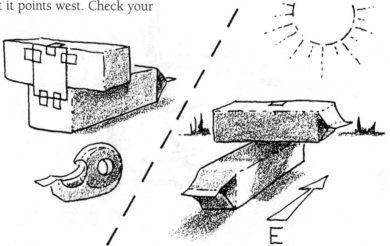

What's the Angle?

181

YOU WILL NEED:

atlas

2 pieces of heavy cardboard, approximately 6 x 8 inches (15 x 20 cm)

protractor

marker or pencil

scissors

stick, about 4 inches (10 cm) long

paste

watch

In about the first century, it was discovered that a slanting object cast a shadow that kept more accurate time than an object that stood straight up. This was especially true if the object, known as the gnomon, slanted at the same angle as the latitude of the place where it was being used. In that case, its direction was the same at any hour of the day, regardless of the season of the year. The term "gnomon" comes from the Greek word which means "know," and the gnomon was so named because it "knew" the time.

What to do: In an atlas, look up the latitude of your town—that is its distance north or south of the equator. Subtract it from 90°. (For example, 90° minus 50° equals 40°.) Using the protractor, mark that angle on one of the pieces of cardboard. Cut two wedge shapes with that angle; see illustration A.

On the second piece of cardboard, draw a line parallel to and 1 inch (2.5 cm) away from the long edge, as in illustration B.

Paste the 4-inch (10 cm) stick at right angles to the cardboard through the center of the line. With the protractor, divide the space above the line into 12 angles of 15° each. Label the middle line 12 and the bottom lines 6. Then fill in the other numbers, as in illustration C.

Paste the pieces of cardboard to the wedges so the boards touch at one edge and the hour lines of the upper board point away from the free edge. See illustration D.

Set the sundial level. Place the edge where the two boards meet so that they run east and west. A

A

B

C

D

simple way of orienting the sundial is to set it up at noon and indicate where the shadow falls. Check the sundial each hour, marking the spot where the shadow falls with a marker or pencil.

What happens: The shadow of the stick will point to the time.

Why: You have set up the sundial so that the gnomon is in the same direction as the earth's axis and the upper board is parallel to the ground at the North Pole. But it will not always agree with your watch.

Why the Difference? L.A.T., local apparent time, is time measured by the actual movement of Earth and the sun. It differs from season to season and from place to place. It is the time measured by the sundial.

L.M.T., local mean time, measures the average speed at which the sun rotates and Earth spins in its orbit. Our clocks and watches show local mean time.

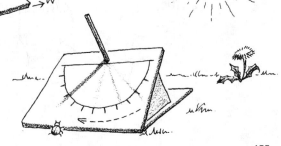

Hand Dial

YOU WILL NEED:

pencil
your two hands
sunny day

A 16th-century German woodcut shows a unique portable dial that requires no special equipment to tell time. If you know the latitude of your area, you can tell the time without a watch or sundial. Actually, you can be a human timepiece.

What to do: Look up the latitude of your area in an atlas. Using your left hand in the morning and your right hand in the afternoon, hold the pencil with your thumb. Tilt the pencil at an angle approximately equal to the angle of latitude of your area, as in the illustration below. Hold your left hand straight up toward the west. Hold your right hand straight up toward the east.

What happens: The shadow on your hands indicates the time!

Why: You have made the pencil into a gnomon and angled it parallel to the Earth's axis, as in the last experiment. But remember, your hand sundial may not agree with your clock.

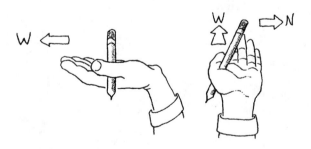

Noon Marks

Instead of noting time by the position of a shadow, you can note it from the position of a small beam of light. It is easy, but it takes patience—and two seasons.

YOU WILL NEED:

window that faces
south
hole punch
piece of black paper
masking tape
pencil

What to do: Punch a hole about 3 inches (2 cm) in diameter in the center of a piece of black paper. Tape the paper to one pane of a window that faces south. With a dot of masking tape, mark the spot on the floor where a sunbeam hits at noon on a winter's day. Then mark it again at noon on a summer's day. Connect the two spots on the floor.

What happens: Whenever the sunbeam crosses the line, it will be the local apparent noon, the time the sun (not your watch) says it is noon. Sun time and your watch will only agree on April 16, June 14, September 2, and December 25.

Why: Days measured by the sun differ in length. There are two reasons: First, the Earth moves faster when it is closer to the sun and, second, the Earth's path around the sun is an ellipse rather than a circle.

Time Zones

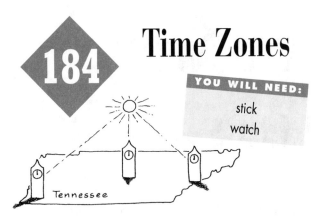

YOU WILL NEED:

stick

watch

The difference between sun time and clock time depends on where in a time zone you are located. You can see this for yourself with the shadow time-piece. See page 154 for an explanation of time zones.

What to do: Place the stick straight up in the ground. When its shadow is shortest, check your watch.

What happens: If you live in the eastern edge of your time zone, the sun at noon is earlier than the clock reading. If you live in the western edge of your time zone, the sun at noon is later than the clock reading. If you are on Daylight Savings Time, you need to take that into account; your watch will read before or after 1 o'clock.

Why: The geographical region in which the same time is used is large. It is only in the middle of the region that the sun will be highest in the sky at noon on our watches.

Noon Holes

Noon marks can still be seen in Europe's ancient cathedrals. In the Duomo in Milan, a church dating back to 1380, for example, there is a sun hole on one wall near the ceiling and signs of the Zodiac indicating the months on the marble floor. Posted on a bulletin board is a daily schedule of times the sun will shine on each month's symbol.

The Fickle Hour

We now divide the day into 24 equal parts, or hours, throughout the year, but it was not always like that. The Egyptians, for example, divided daylight into twelve parts and the darkness into twelve parts, except during the summer when days were longer, they lengthened the daylight divisions.

The Babylonians did the same thing, but they divided the day into 12 hours instead of 24. They had two systems. One of them began at midnight and divided the day into six parts, each with 60 subdivisions. The other measured the start of day from sunset and split it into twelve divisions with thirty subdivisions.

Early Hebrews divided the day into six parts, three light and three dark. While the Chinese adopted an equal hour system by the 4th century B.C., Europeans changed the length of hours according to the seasons until the 14th century. The Japanese continued to have variable hours until 1868.

CLOUDY DAY AND NIGHT TIMETELLERS

Sundials, of course, were of no use on cloudy days and at night. People used many kinds of household materials to measure time on those days and at night. They tied knots in ropes to mark the hours, and burned measured quantities of oil, incense, and specially prepared candles.

185

Cloudy Day Timeline

1400 B.C.—Egyptians and Mesopotamians produce glass

1450 B.C.—Egyptians devise water clock

700 B.C.—Assyrians acquire water clock

38 B.C.—Plato adds alarm to water clock

200s B.C.—Hourglass invented in Alexandria

250 B.C.—Alexandrian engineer Ctesibius adds gears connected to a pointer on a drum indicating time

150 B.C.—Pliny writes that the water clock replaced the sundial as the official timepiece

50—Athens acquires water solar clock

725—Buddhist monk T-Xing and Chinese engineer Liang-Zen build a water clock with an escape vent used to power various astronomical devices

875—Calibrated candles mark the passage of time

186

Candle Timekeeper

Religious candles are reminders of the candle timekeepers which date back to the 9th century. It's not difficult to make a candle timekeeper, but be sure to get an adult to help you.

5 bolts or paper clips

5 two-inch (5-cm) lengths of heavy thread

2 tall, straight not tapered, white candles

pencil

paper

ruler

2 candle holders

2 china or metal plates

matches

clock

What to do: Attach a bolt or clip to one end of each 2-inch (5-cm) length of heavy thread. Measure the candles. Write down the results. Then insert one of the candles in a holder and place it on the plate. Light the candle in the holder and let it burn for 10 minutes. Then blow out the flame.

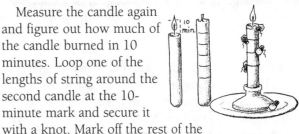

Measure the candle again and figure out how much of the candle burned in 10 minutes. Loop one of the lengths of string around the second candle at the 10-minute mark and secure it with a knot. Mark off the rest of the first candle in 10-minute segments. Measure it each time and wrap a length of string, with a bolt or clip attached, at the proper spot on the second candle. Depending on the size of your candle, you may be able to use more or less than five lengths of string.

Insert the second candle in a candle holder, place it on a plate, and light the wick. Check your watch every time you hear the clang of the bolt or clip.

What happens: Every 10 minutes, you will be alerted by an "alarm" as the thread burns off and the bolt or clip hits the plate.

By a Nose! 187

Add to eyes, ears, and touch the sense of smell in the service of time-telling! In the early 14th century the Chinese developed an incense clock. They placed aromatic powders in grooves carved into a hardwood disk and lit it. It burned for about 12 hours. Each hour was recognized by its particular scent.

What scents do you associate with various times of day?

188 Water Clock

One of the most ingenious of cloudy day timekeepers was the water clock, the clepsydra. It originated in Egypt and Babylon and came into use about a thousand years after the sundial.

The Egyptians made a small hole in a large clay bowl, which was wide at the top and narrow at the bottom and was marked with horizontal lines on the inside, one for each hour. They filled the bowl with water and as it leaked out they could tell how much time had passed by looking at the lines and the water left in the pot. You can make your own clepsydra with a plastic container.

What to do: Use your marker to make four lines equally distant from one another around the inside of the container. Then using the nail, punch a small hole in the bottom of the container. Cover the hole with a piece of tape. Fill the plastic container with water. Place the container over a large pot (or in the sink), uncover the hole, and see how long it takes the carton to empty. Write down your findings.

Fill the container again. This time note how long it takes to get to each of the lines you've drawn, as well as how long it takes for the container to empty.

What happens: It takes the same amount of time to empty during the two trials, but the time to move from one line to the next differs.

Why: The water pressure lessens as the water escapes, and so the water runs out more slowly than when the container is full.

What next: Now do the same experiment using plastic containers of different sizes and shapes. See if it makes a difference using hot water or ice-cold water from the refrigerator.

Having It Both Ways

YOU WILL NEED:

2 heavy paper cups
nail
yardstick
masking tape
large pot or bowl
water faucet
marker
watch

A more accurate water clock has water flowing in and out of containers at the same time.

What to do: Punch a small hole in the bottom of the paper cups. Hold the yard-stick up and tape the cups to it, as in the illustration below. Tape the yardstick to the side of a large pot or bowl with the cups facing inward so that they are over the pot.

Cover the hole in the top cup with a piece of tape. Fill the cup with water. Then place it under a slow-running faucet as you uncover the hole.

Every five minutes, use tape or a marker to indicate the water line in the bottom cup and the water line in the pot or bowl.

What happens: The water flows out at a regular rate and the marks are equally distant from one another.

Why: Because the amount of water that flows in comes from a cup that is always kept full, the water pressure remains the same and therefore the water flows out at the same rate.

Not Quite Perfect

Unlike the candle or rope clocks, the water clock could be used over and over. But there were problems. Although it didn't need the sun to show how much time had passed, it was not really an all-weather timeteller. When it was very cold, the water would freeze; when it was very hot the water would evaporate too quickly. And when it was dirty, whether from human or natural causes, the water ran out more slowly.

A Knotty Problem

190

For many years, it was the practice at sea to throw overboard a thin rope weighted at one end with a piece of wood and knotted at regular intervals. A seaman would hold the rope as it was dragged through the water and feel how many knots passed through his hands during the time it took for a timed sandglass to empty. In this way, he estimated the speed or "knots" at which the ship was moving. Nautical speed is still measured in knots.

Hourglass Timekeepers

191

Hourglass timers were once used for serious jobs. They timed sermons, speeches, and court presentations. Four-hour models were used aboard ship to measure watches right up to the late 18th century, when accurate ship chronometers were invented. Today the most common task of the hourglass is to time boiled eggs. But the advantages of the hourglass over the water clock is that the hourglass is portable, there is no sloshing water—and weather does not affect it.

YOU WILL NEED:

2 small clear jars
heavy paper or cardboard
scissors
nail or hole punch
sand or salt
masking tape
clock or watch

What to do: Cut a circle out of heavy paper or cardboard to fit the mouths of the jars. Punch a small hole in the center of the circle with a nail or a hole punch. Place a few ounces of sand or salt in one of the jars and cover it with the disk. Tape the second jar to the first, mouth to mouth. Make sure they are taped securely. Turn the jars upside down. and time how long it takes for the top jar to empty.

Now make the hole larger and change the amount of sand or salt. How long does it now take for the top jar to empty?

What happens: By making the hole larger or smaller, or changing the amount of sand or salt, you can change the time it takes to empty the top jar.

Why: Gravity forces the sand to drop at a steady rate. You can use your "minute glass" over and over and time longer periods—if you just keep track of how many times you turn it over. You may even find it useful.

192 Invent Your Own Clock

Timetellers have ranged from natural phenomena to manmade devices, from primitive to sophisticated, from simple to complex. The writer Albert Camus tells of an old man who thought a watch a silly gadget and an unnecessary expense. He devised his own "clock" designed to indicate the only times he was interested in. He worked out the times for meals with two saucepans, one of which was always filled with peas when he woke in the morning. He filled the other, pea by pea, at a constant, carefully regulated speed. Every 15 pots of peas it was feeding time!

Fifth graders at the Fieldston School in Riverdale, New York, invented their own timers. One made a fizzy alarm clock using vinegar dripping into baking soda; another timed how long it took heat to blow up a balloon.

Can you devise a "clock" from items around the house or activities you do often?

Telling Time by the Stars

While the ancient Egyptians built sundials to keep track of daylight hours, during the night they measured the movement of the stars across certain portions of the sky.

They associated their goddess Isis, "the lady of all the elements, the beginning of all time" with the brightest star in the night sky, Sirius. They built temples facing the point on the eastern horizon where Sirius first appeared before sunrise. Ancient Egyptian astronomers, tracking Sirius for their calendar, started a new year at the first new moon following this appearance of Sirius—and all awaited the annual floods that irrigated the land.

In the Northern Hemisphere, a February evening is a good time to look for Sirius to the side and a little below the group of stars known as Orion the Hunter. Face south at about 9 p.m. Orion is high in the winter sky but not visible in northern skies during the summer. Using the line of Orion's belt as a guide, look southeast for the Dog Star.

193 Star Timeline

3000 B.C.—Earliest Babylonian astronomical records

300 B.C.—Chinese astronomers chart position of stars

280 B.C.—Aristarchus suggests Earth orbits the sun

140—Ptolemy contends that planets orbit Earth, a theory accepted for fifteen hundred years

500—The astrolabe, developed in ancient Greece, is used for reckoning time and measuring the position of heavenly bodies. Later, mariners began to use it in navigation

1543—Nicholas Copernicus, a Polish priest, publishes theory that the sun is the center of the universe. Idea banned as challenging the Bible

1608—Hans Lippershey of the Netherlands invents first telescope

1609—Galileo Galilei confirms Copernicus's theory, but is eventually forced to recant

1620s—German mathematician Johannes Kepler proves planets move around the sun

1668—Isaac Newton invents a reflector telescope with a curved mirror replacing one lens

1739—Sextant is invented by Thomas Godfrey and John Hadley

194 Cereal Box Planetarium

YOU WILL NEED:
round box (the kind that oatmeal or raisins are packaged in)
tracing paper
pencil
glue
small nail
flashlight

You can make your own "planetarium" by creating a model of a cluster of stars you will see in the sky.

What to do: Make a circle of tracing paper to fit the bottom of the box. Then trace the illustration of the Big Dipper, the North Star, and Cassiopeia shown below onto the thin piece of paper. Glue the paper to the bottom of the box. With the nail punch holes through the box at each star.

Take your planetarium into a dark room and stand facing one of the walls. At the open end of the box tilt a flashlight so that it shines against the side. Turn the box slowly.

What happens: You get an enlarged image on the wall. When you turn the box, you will see the various positions of the stars as they seem to revolve.

Why: The Earth rotates on its axis, so the constellations appear to circle around the North Star, which remains at the same place in the sky. Therefore, you see these constellations in all positions—on their sides or even upside down. The "W" shape of Cassiopeia becomes an "M" depending on when it appears above the North Star.

Big Dipper

Pole Star (North Star)

Cassiopeia

The Sky as Compass

If you are ever lost in a forest at night, you can use the sky to find your way. Face the North Star, which is the brightest star in the northern sky, and you are facing north. Look 180° across the sky to the horizon. That is south. East is 90° to the right and west is 90° to the left.

On a clear night, ask an adult to help you practice finding the North Star.

Star Map

Draw a star map of the constellations that circle around the North Star and use it to note the changes in the sky from hour to hour.

YOU WILL NEED:
circle of cardboard
flashlight
red cellophane and tape

What to do: To make your star map, copy the illustration below onto your circle of cardboard. Then tape the cellophane over your flashlight. (The red covering will prevent it from being too bright for you to see the stars.)

At 9 o'clock on a dry moonless night, take your star map and the flashlight outdoors. Turn the chart so that the month in which you are observing is on the top. Hold the chart above your head and look for the same pattern in the sky.

On another night, go out at 7 o'clock or at 10 o'clock and match the star map with the sky.

What happens: At 7 o'clock you have to turn the chart one month clockwise to match the sky. At 10 o'clock you have to turn it a half-month counterclockwise.

Why: The North Star remains at approximately the same place in the sky—far, far away, but directly above the North Pole. This is because the Earth's axis points to it throughout the year. All the other stars and constellations, however, seem to wander around the North Star once a day, moving counterclockwise. As the Earth rotates, it looks as if the entire sky is rotating, although the stars do not change position relative to each other. Since one turn of the Earth takes only 23 hours and 56 minutes, a star seems to rise and set about four minutes earlier than the day before. This adds up to two hours (30 x 4 = 120 minutes) in a month and, of course, one hour in half a month.

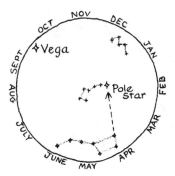

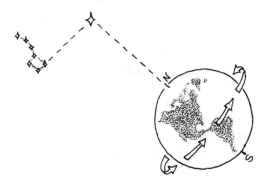

Some Timetelling Stars

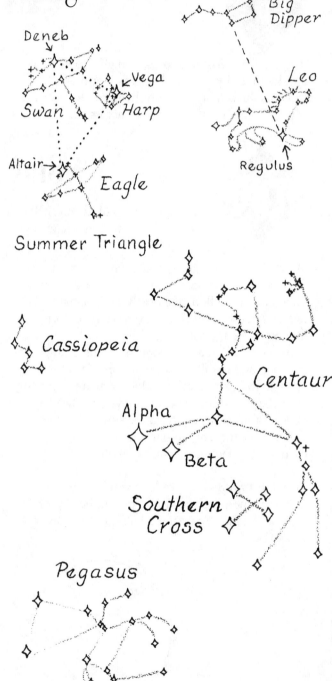

A constellation is a group of stars that long ago people named for heroes and gods and animals that they thought the patterns looked like. There are 88 constellations. We still use many of these names in Latin and in the English translation. And we still use the stars as a calendar and a direction finder.

The equator is the only place from which all 88 constellations can be seen during the course of a year. In other latitudes, you can see perhaps 60 at different times, and about 24 at any one time.

In the United States, Canada, the United Kingdom, and Europe, you can see the constellation of Leo, the Lion, with the bright star Regulus high up in the sky in the middle of April at about 9 p.m.

In August, as it gets dark, high in the southeast section of the sky you will see three bright stars—the Summer Triangle. Directly overhead are Vega, in the constellation Lyra, the Harp; Deneb of the constellation Cygnus, the Swan; and Altair of the constellation Aquila, the Eagle.

In the evening skies of October, just below the W-shaped constellation Cassiopeia, you will find four bright stars arranged in a square making up the body of an upside-down horse with wings, the constellation Pegasus, the flying horse.

In the Southern Hemisphere, the Southern Cross (the Crux) is the easiest constellation to recognize. You can see it in the evening skies of Miami and the Florida Keys in May and June, but its four stars are always visible below the equator. Looking south, observers in Australia, southern Africa, and South America can see the Crux just below the two bright stars Alpha and Beta Centauri. Some think it looks more like a kite than a cross.

Get a book from the library about stars and constellations and on a clear night, ask an adult to help you practice finding constellations in the sky.

Star Time

Stars tell us the time and direction on land, on sea, and in the air. You can have fun estimating the time by observing certain stars.

What to do: Mark out circles on two of the pieces of cardboard. Make one circle about 8 inches (20 cm) in diameter. Make the other 1 inch (2.5 cm) smaller with four 3-inch (7.5 cm) triangles sticking out as in illustration C. Cut out the two disks.

On the larger cardboard disk draw two ½-inch (1.3 cm) circles around the outer rim. Mark the outer circle with the months of the year. Mark the inner circle with the days of the month.

From the sheet of paper, cut out an oval 3½ inches (9.5 cm) deep and 4 inches (10 cm) wide. On the oval copy the sky map in illustration B.

Hold the larger disk so September is on top. Paste the sky map to the inner circle above the days of March.

On the smaller disk, 1 inch (2.5 cm) from the bottom, mark out an oval, also 3½ inches (9.5 cm) deep and 4 inches (10 cm) wide. Cut the oval section out.

Around the edge of the smaller disk draw a clock face like the one in illustration C. Notice that the numbers, like the stars, go in the opposite direction from an ordinary clock and cover twenty-four hours instead of twelve. Place the smaller disk on top of the larger disk so you can see the map through the "window" of the smaller disk.

Tape the tips of the triangles of the smaller disk

to the corners of the third cardboard. Punch a hole through the center of all three pieces if cardboard. Fit the fastener through the three center holes.

On a clear, preferably moonless, night, pick a spot where street lights, houses, and trees don't obstruct your view. Face north and look for the Big Dipper and Cassiopeia. Two pointer stars of the Big Dipper point to a fairly bright star, the North Star—also known as the Pole Star or Polaris—which is halfway between the Big Dipper and Cassiopeia. At a latitude of 40° (New York, Denver, Salt Lake City), it is almost halfway up in the sky. The farther north (London's latitude is 50°) you are, the higher up the North Star will be; the farther south (New Orleans is 30°), the lower it will be.

Rotate your Star Timeteller until it looks like the sky.

Draw an imaginary line from the North Star, one of the bright stars of Cassiopeia. For each week after September 21 subtract a half hour; for each week earlier add a half hour. If you are on Daylight Savings Time, add an hour.

What happens: The imaginary line acts as the star clock's hour hand. With a little simple arithmetic, you can find the approximate time.

Why: You add and subtract depending on when you observe the stars because the solar day is longer than the star day. The star clock runs too fast. As we have seen, it gains four minutes every day. In a week it gains about a half hour (7 x 4 = 28 minutes); in a month it gains about two hours (30 x 4 = 120 minutes). Since the earth is rotating counterclockwise, it will be earlier when you observe after September 21, so you subtract. And it will be later before September 21, so you add.

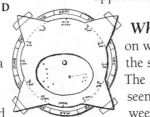

MECHANICAL CLOCKS

A kind of mechanical timeteller existed in the late 13th or early 14th century. Housed on a high bell tower, it used a heavy falling weight tied to a rope that was wound around a huge revolving drum. It had no dials and, at first, no means of striking, but it could indicate important times by means of a moving figure called a jack. It alerted the keeper of the clock, usually a monk, to sound a bell.

About Mechanical Clocks

The word clock comes from the Latin word *clocca,* which means bell. Up until this time, any instrument that measured time was known as an horologium, an hour-teller.

Huge public clocks, which struck the hours, but did not have a face with hands, appeared in Italian towns starting in the fourteenth century. Many of these—and some still exist—used a variety of jacks for entertainment.

Clocks made for royalty were even more elaborate. France's Louis XIV had a clock with models of several kings of Europe, who bowed to him before striking the hour with canes.

The cuckoo clock, with its carved wooden bird that pops out to "sing" the time, first appeared in Germany in 1730.

199 Mechanical Clock Timeline

1320—weight-driven mechanical clocks used

1350—public clocks in European towns

1510—portable spring-driven clocks invented

1583—Galileo Galilei of Rome shows that a pendulum swings at a constant rate

1656—Christian Huygens designs a pendulum clock

1660—Huygens and Robert Hooke invent the spiral hairspring (see page 171)

1668—Boston has the first town clock in Colonial America

1675—grandfather clocks available

1676—minute hands and crystal covers added to watches

1725—Nicholas Faceis of Basel, Switzerland adds jeweled bearings to reduce friction

1730—cuckoo clocks made in Germany's Black Forest

1773—Englishman John Harrison invents a seagoing chronometer

1803—Eli Terry of Connecticut begins clock mass production

1824—"time ball" standardizes timekeeping in some towns

1875—stem-wound watches replace watches with keys

1884—standardized time zones established

Yo-Yo Clock 200

If you think about how a yo-yo spins when you unwind its cord, you'll have an idea of how the earliest mechanical clocks worked. The energy of falling weights suspended from a drum were their source of power.

YOU WILL NEED:

length of heavy thread or cord

heavy button or a washer

empty thread spool

What to do: Tie one end of the cord to the washer or heavy button. Tie the other end around the spool and wind it up.

Turn the spool so that the weight hangs down, as in the illustration. Then rewind the spool. Again turn the spool so that the weight hangs down, but this time keep tapping the edge of the spool quickly with your finger.

What happens: When the weight falls, the cord unwinds and the spool turns quickly. But when you tap the spool, your finger acts as a brake. The taps stop the spool and the weight falls in small jerks with a slow and steady regular rhythm.

Why: The falling weight supplied the energy to turn the spool while the tapping finger regulated it. Early clocks worked in the same way by means of a device called an escapement. The escapement made sure the weight fell slowly and steadily and prevented the drum from rotating too fast and using up all the energy of the weight too quickly.

These early clocks, installed in bell towers, weighed hundreds of pounds and fell distances of more than 30 feet (9 m), but were highly inaccurate.

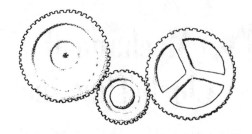

Get in Gear

201

Gears are wheels with notches or teeth. Small gears are called pinions. Wheels with 20 or more teeth are called gears. Large gears that have an even greater number of teeth are called cogs.

The first clocks had a gear at each end of a spindle, the axle of the spool. The gear on the back of the spool axle meshed with a series of gears that regulated the unwinding of the cord. The other gear on the spool—the one on the front of the spool axis—controlled a moving figure (called a jack), which beat on bells to sound the hours. Later this front gear turned a hand that showed the hour on a round dial.

It's not difficult to make your own gears, but you had better ask an adult for some help with this project.

What to do: Be sure the caps are not bent. Ask an adult to help you punch a hole through the center of each cap.

Sundials Versus Mechanical Clocks

Early mechanical clocks were inaccurate and, therefore, sundials were used to regulate them until the advent of electrical clocks in the late 19th century!

Place the caps on the block of wood close enough to one another so that they touch. Tack them down loosely with thin nails so that they turn easily.

Turn one of the caps with your finger and notice what happens to the others. Turn one of the caps in the opposite direction. Turn them slowly, then quickly.

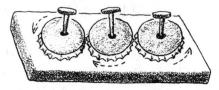

What happens: When you turn one cap, all three turn. But each gear turns in the opposite direction from the one next to it.

Why: The ridges of each cap act like the teeth of a gear and interlock, or mesh, with the ridges of the cap next to it. In addition to changing direction, gears change force or speed. Speed increases when a small gear is turned by a large one and force increases when a large gear is turned by a small one.

The set of gears of a clock changes slow turning into fast turning. It connects the axle to several wheels. As the axle turns, the wheels turn at different speeds. The regulator, called the escapement, controls the turning of the fastest of the wheels. Two of the slower wheels turn the hands on the face of the clock.

The main features of all clocks are: a device that swings at a regular rate; something that keeps the motion going by feeding energy to the swinging device; and a means of counting and indicating the swings.

Why Clocks Count to Twelve

202

Do you know how hard it is to count the chimes when a clock strikes 12? Well, imagine what it would be like to have to count 24 chimes! That's what people had to do years ago when more and more clocks were striking the hour in village squares all over Europe. That's why, in the early 15th century, a double 12-hour system took the place of the 24-hour system in many countries.

This system of dividing the day into two sets of 12 equal hours starting at midnight originated in southern Germany, scholars claim, where the sale of locally made mechanical clocks was thriving.

Most military organizations and some parts of Europe, however, still use a 24-hour system starting at midnight. For example, 12:59 a.m. is 0059; 1:00 a.m. is 0100; 12 noon is 1200; 12:59 p.m. is 1259; 1:00 p.m. is 1300; 10:59 p.m. is 2259. When you convert from a 12-hour clock to a 24-hour clock, the minutes are unchanged, but you add 12 from 1:00 p.m. on. To convert from a 24-hour clock to a 12 hour system you just subtract 12 hours between 1300 and 2359 and add p.m.

Try some conversions on your own.

Military Time

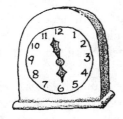

Portable Timekeepers

In 1510, Peter Henlein, a locksmith in Nuremberg, Germany, substituted small coiled springs for the huge weights in clocks and made the first table timekeepers that could be carried around. They were known as "Nuremberg Eggs" because of their oval shape. They were small enough to wear on a belt or on a chain around the neck, but they were not accurate enough to have a minute hand.

In 1660, Robert Hooke attached a small balance wheel to the mainspring, and a short, stiff hog's hair bristle to control the oscillations—the movements back and forth. Later, a fine steel wire was used instead of a bristle, but it continued to be known as the hairspring—and still is!

The watch now had a mainspring, the source of energy; an escapement and balance unit, which controlled the release of energy; and two gear trains, one transmitting the energy and another controlling the movement of the hands. It also had a mechanism for winding the clock and a frame or case to protect it.

When a mechanical watch is wound, the springs are coiled tightly around the central shaft, which is held by a gear attached to a bar with projecting levers. As the housing turns around the shaft, the spring gradually unwinds. The gear attached to the housing drives other gears that move the hands of the watch.

Jewels as Cushions

YOU WILL NEED:

2 different-sized jars
lids
tape
pencil
marbles

Sometime between the end of the 17th century and the beginning of the 18th century, Swiss watch-makers began to use chips of sapphires and rubies to ease the friction between various parts so they moved more smoothly and didn't wear out as fast. A 17-jeweled watch has seventeen of these jeweled bearings, although now the "jewels" are probably synthetic. You can see the effect of the jeweled ball bearings by using a handful of marbles.

What to do: Turn both lids so the insides are upward. Tape the smaller lid to a table. Tape the pencil to the inside of the large jar lid. Then place the large lid on top of the small one and, using the pencil as lever, spin it. Note what happens. Now fill the small lid with marbles and then spin the large lid on it. Note what happens.

What happens: In the first experiment the top lid moves with difficulty. When you put the marbles in the top lid it spins easily.

Why: When two things move in contact with one another, they resist moving. No two surfaces are completely smooth. The bumps of one surface catch on the bumps of the other. The resistance that results when the surfaces rub against each other is known as friction.

The amount of friction depends on the kinds of surfaces as well as the force pressing them together. The rougher the surfaces, the greater the friction. Too much friction produces heat and wears away parts. The smooth, round marbles reduce the amount of friction. The contact between the moving parts and the marbles is very slight, and so the friction is very low. This is the reason that the tiny, hard gems in a watch reduce wear at the principal points of friction—the delicate axles around which the various wheels revolve. The more jeweled bearings in a watch, the longer it lasts.

About the Word "Watch"

Where did the use of the word watch for a timekeeper come from? Some sources say it originated during the Middle Ages, when the man who kept the night watch proclaimed "All's well!" and also announced the time. Others say it came about because people were at last able to see the time instead of merely hearing it announced by chimes or bells. Still others claim the word came from sailors who called their duty-period—and still do—a watch.

Early watches were wound by a key inserted in a small hole under the back case. It wasn't until late in the 19th century that watches were wound by a stem. In self-winding watches, the mainspring was tightened automatically by a weight on a rotor, a revolving part that responded to the slightest arm movements of the wearer.

Pendulum Clocks

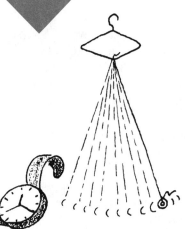

In 1656, Christian Huygens van Zulicham, a Dutch scientist, invented the first pendulum clock. Based on the principle established by Galileo's experiments in 1583, the new clock was driven by a single weight—the bob—suspended on a long rope. Because pendulum clocks were housed in tall wooden cases designed to hide the unattractive weights, they were known as tall clocks. Later these clocks became known as grandfather clocks.

What to do: Tie a weight to the longest string and suspend it from the clothes hanger so it hangs freely. Pull the string slightly to one side and let it swing. Count the number of swings it makes in 60 seconds. Then pull the string farther over to one side and let it swing again, counting the number of swings in 60 seconds. Add additional weights and try swinging the string. Again count the number of swings made in 60 seconds. Write down your results.

Do the same thing with strings of different lengths: 10 inches, 20 inches, and finally 39 inches. In each case, note how many times the weight moves back and forth in 60 seconds and jot down the results.

What happens: When the string is 39 inches long, the weight moves back and forth 60 times in one minute.

Why: A pendulum takes the same length of time to make every swing no matter how far it travels or how heavy the weight at the end of it. But the longer the pendulum, the longer the time it takes to complete its swing; the shorter the pendulum the more quickly it travels back and forth. Since it takes one second for a length of string measuring 39 inches to swing back and forth, time can be measured with accuracy.

Seconds

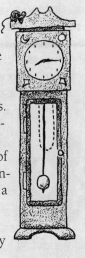

When pendulum clocks became more accurate, first minute hands and, eventually, second hands were added to clock faces. Robert Hooke, an English physicist, was the first one to use the word "second" for one-sixtieth of a minute. Since there are 60 minutes in an hour, Hooke divided a minute into 60 parts, too. He called each part a second because he was dividing by sixty a second time.

205 Railroad Timetable

Barely more than one hundred years ago every local community kept its own "official" time, calling it noon when the sun was overhead. The time was announced to the people by a town clock, by a falling time ball in the center of town, or by a factory whistle. But when railroad travel became common, this was very confusing! The country needed a uniform schedule that everyone could follow. This brought about the uniform system of time zones that we have today. It met with much opposition, however, from many people who resented being "dictated to" by the railroads.

At a meeting on October 11, 1883, four time zones were established for the United States—Eastern, Central, Mountain, and Pacific—based on the 15° of longitude that the sun travels in one hour.

The next year, by general international agreement, the entire world was divided into time zones—24 of them. Greenwich Mean Time, which had become the standard for all of the United Kingdom, was selected as the starting point from which international time zones and degrees of longitude were measured. Each zone was one hour earlier than the one immediately to the east.

The United States and its territories now have eight standard time zones including Atlantic Time for Puerto Rico and the Virgin Islands (one hour later than Eastern Standard), and Alaska, Hawaii-Aleutian, and Samoan Standard (one, two, and three hours earlier respectively than Pacific Time). Canada's five time zones range from Atlantic time to Pacific-Yukon. Newfoundland is a half-hour later than Atlantic time.

Australia and other large land masses are also divided into time zones based primarily on longitude. Australia's three time zones range from Australian Western Standard Time in the city of Perth, to Australian Central Standard Time in the North Territory and North Australia, to Australian Eastern Standard Time in Queensland, Victoria, and New South Wales, with Lord Howe Island a half hour later. China has resisted zoning—all of that vast land uses Beijing Time, which coincides with that of Western Australia, eight hours later than London. South Africa Standard Time is two hours later than London, and at noon in London it is midnight in New Zealand.

Which time zone do you live in?

206 Daylight Savings Time

Daylight Savings Time, also known as Summer Time, is a system of putting clocks ahead an hour in the late spring and summer to extend daylight hours during the time people are awake. It was first suggested—perhaps as a joke—by Benjamin Franklin in 1784, but not until the 20th century was the idea put into effect.

During World War I, Germany, the United States, Great Britain, and Australia all adopted summer daylight savings time to conserve fuel by decreasing the use of artificial light. During World War II both the United States and Great Britain used it all year—advancing clocks one hour during the winter and two during the summer.

Summer time observance was formally adopted as United States government policy in 1966, but even now it is not used in Indiana and Arizona. All of Canada observes Daylight Savings Time during the summer, but only some parts of Australia move clocks forward during their summer months starting the last Sunday in October.

Have you ever noticed that the days seem longer in the summertime? That's Daylight Savings Time!

207 International Date Line

Do you know what the International Date Line is all about? Let's take a trip around the world and find out.

YOU WILL NEED:
sheet of paper
pencil
scissors
tape
2 coins

What to do: Fold the paper in thirds lengthwise, as in illustration A. Then fold it in half three times and number the strips, as in illustration B.

Unfold the paper and fill in the times and the names of the locales, as in illustration C. Then cut the paper along the fold lines into three lengthwise strips.

Tape the strips to one another, matching the numbers so that 5 follows 4 and -5 follows -4. Tape

The one traveling eastward sets its clock ahead for each 15° of longitude to gain 12 hours. The one traveling westward sets its clock back one hour for each 15° so that it loses 12 hours.

What happens: The two clocks differ by 24 hours in one calendar day.

The problem was solved by international agreement. At the International Date Line—at 180° of longitude, located in the Pacific Ocean—travelers are required to change the date. The one traveling east moves the calendar back a day; the one traveling west moves ahead a day.

The 180° meridian runs mostly through the open Pacific. But the date line zigzags to avoid a time change in populated areas—in the north to take the eastern tip of Siberia into the Siberian time system, to include a number of islands in the Hawaii-Aleutian time zone, and, farther south, to tie British-owned islands into the New Zealand time system.

C

midnight	1 a.m.	2 a.m.	3 a.m.	4 a.m.	5 a.m.	6 a.m.	7 a.m.
Wellington, Fiji, Wake Island	Samoa	Hawaii, Aleutians	Anchorage, Yukon	Los Angeles, victoria	Denver	Chicago, Winnepeg	New York, Toronto
-12	-11	-10	-9	-8	-7	-6	-5
8 a.m.	9 a.m.	10 a.m.	11 a.m.	Noon	1 p.m.	2 p.m.	3 p.m.
Puerto Rico, Halifax	Buenos Aires	Mid-Atlantic	Cape Verde	London	Berlin	Athens	Moscow
-4	-3	-2	-1	0	+1	+2	+3
4 p.m.	5 p.m.	6 p.m.	7 p.m.	8 p.m.	9 p.m.	10 p.m.	11 p.m.
Abu Dhabi, Muscat	Karachi, Bombay	Tashkent, Calcutta	Jakarta, Bangkok	Bejing	Tokyo	Sydney	Solomon Islands
+4	+5	+6	+7	+8	+9	+10	+11

the ends (+12 and -12) to one another. Each of the numbers represents a time zone one hour later or one hour earlier than Greenwich Mean Time in England.

Let us assume it is noon on Tuesday and your two coins are going on a trip around the globe. They both start in London, but one travels east to Berlin and one goes west toward New York. Their planes meet one another on a remote Pacific island, west of Eniwetok (a coral island in the Marshalls) and east of Fiji.

International Date Line

SUPER CLOCKS

Although mechanical clocks and watches are still sold, more accurate and less expensive clocks and watches have been available for more than 50 years. These are the electric and electronic timetellers. And, of course, for true accuracy, there is now the atomic clock, but this is neither inexpensive nor available for our night tables or wrists—yet.

Super Clock Timeline

1800—Alessandro Volta makes the first chemical battery

1821—Michael Faraday uses a magnet to convert a wire carrying current to mechanical energy

1830—Joseph Henry builds the first practical electric motor

1840—Alexander Bain patents an electric clock

1881—Pierre Curie discovers piezoelectric oscillation

1894—Reliable master-clock system developed

1913—Niels Bohr and Ernest T. Rutherford develop theory of structure of the atom

1918—U.S. reliable AC current running at 60 cycles per second

1927—U.K. reliable AC current running at 50 cycles per second

1929—Warren Marrison invents quartz crystal clock

1949—Harold Lyons of the U.S. National Bureau of Standards constructs first atomic clock using ammonia molecules

1955—Dr. Essen and J.V.L. Parry in National Physical Lab in London develop atomic clock using cesium atom

1957—Electric wristwatches-battery replaces the spring

1958—First integrated circuit (microchip)

1959—Miniature tuning fork replaces the balance wheel

1965—Transistorized battery clocks

1960s—LED (Light Emitting Diode)

1969—First all-electronic watch with digital display

1967—Frequency of vibrations of cesium atom is designated definition of a second

1970s—LCD (Liquid Crystal Display)

Electric Clocks

You don't have to wind an electric clock. The spring, the pendulum, and the escapement have been replaced by a motor, which is powered by the electricity from an electrical outlet or a battery.

The first patent for an electric clock was filed as early as 1840 by Alexander Bain, a Scotsman living in London. In 1894, Frank Hope-Jones and George Boswell built a reliable electric master-clock system that had a pendulum powered by an electric battery. The system was used to power networks of clocks in railway stations and factories.

But despite these inventions, you still couldn't plug a clock into an electrical outlet until 1918 in the United States and nine years later in Great Britain. Before that, and in some places for years afterward, homes and offices were wired only for direct current (DC), which has a steady flow in one direction. This couldn't be used for clocks because clocks need current that flows in a circuit at regular intervals. That wasn't practical until a reliable alternating current (AC) was introduced. Then clockmakers were able to equip a clock with an electric motor with a rotor, a revolving part that spun at the same frequency as current from electricity-generating power stations (50 or 60 cycles a second).

Gears reduced the high speed to the slow turning needed by the hands of the clock.

Take a survey of the clocks in your house. How many are powered by electricity?

210 Make an Electric Motor

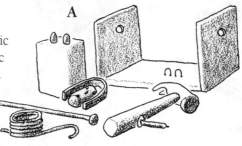

A

YOU WILL NEED:

hammer
sharp nail
2 pieces of plywood 3 inches by
4 inches (7.5 cm by 10 cm)
plastic knitting needle
glue
1 piece of plywood approx.
3 inches by 6 inches
(7.5 cm by 15 cm)
2 paper clips
cork
U-shaped magnet
covered copper wire
tape
6-volt battery
an adult helper

The electric motor in an electric clock or watch changes electric energy into mechanical energy. Inside it there may be a U-shaped magnet and a coil of wire on a rod between its poles. The electric current flows through the coil, which becomes magnetic. The forces of the coil and the magnet then push and pull on each other. This makes the coil spin around and turn a shaft. You can make a simple electric motor and see how it works, but you will need an adult to assist you.

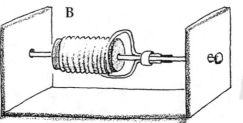

B

What to do: Use the hammer and sharp nail to punch a hole approximately 1 inch (2.5 cm) from the top of each of the smaller pieces of wood. Make sure the knitting needle moves freely in the plywood holes. Then glue one of the smaller pieces of wood to each side of the larger piece, as in illustration A. Push two paper clips into the center of the base.

Choose a cork that is small enough to fit easily between the poles of your magnet.

Cut off two 4-inch (10 cm) strips of wire to serve as lead-in wires. Scrape the ends. Leaving an inch or two free at each end, wind the rest of the wire around the cork 30 times. Then scrape the insulation from the two free ends of the coiled wire.

Insert the knitting needle through the first plywood hole, through the cork and then through the second plywood hole. Secure it with a small lump or tape. See illustration B.

Tape the coiled wire to opposite sides of the knitting needle just above the bared ends.

Connect one end of the lead-in wires to the posts of the battery. Thread the two lead-in wires through the brads and then stretch them up so they make contact with the bared ends of the wire coil. See illustration C.

Finally, hold the magnet around the coil so the coil can turn without touching the magnet. Start the motor by moving the cork with your finger.

What happens: As long as you hold the magnet around the coil, the motor will move by itself.

Why: The magnet converts electrical energy into mechanical energy. It causes the wire that carries the current to move, along with anything attached to it.

C

Charged!

You can demonstrate what goes on in a watch.

What to do: If you don't have a compass, you can make one by magnetizing a needle. Stroke the needle about 50 times in one direction with either pole of the magnet. Then float the piece of cork in the dish of water and carefully center the needle on it. Attach the wires to the two battery terminals and make contact with the needle or the compass.

What happens: The compass needle moves.

Why: When electrons flow through a wire they produce a magnetic field around it. This changes electrical energy into mechanical energy. The coil in a watch concentrates this magnetic field and so enables it to convert electric energy into mechanical energy

Coin Battery

You can make a small battery of your own. Just empty your pockets of your coins.

What to do: Pour the vinegar into the bowl. Soak the paper strips in the vinegar. Make a pile of the coins, alternating copper and the other metal. Separate each kind with one of the vinegar-soaked paper strips. Moisten one fingertip on each hand and hold the pile of coins between those fingers.

What happens: You get a slight electric shock.

Why: The vinegar, an acid, conducts the electricity created by the separated metals of the two coins. It is a wet cell, a kind of battery.

A battery is usually made up of two metals (a zinc container and a carbon rod) separated by absorbent paper soaked in a strong acid. A chemical reaction between the two metals produces a current of electrons between the two poles, and the chemical energy is converted into electrical energy. The battery is a storehouse of energy that wears out when the chemicals it contains are used up.

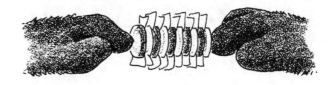

Quartz Crystal Clocks

213

The invention of Dr. Warren A. Marrison, the quartz crystal clock dates back to 1929. Electric current makes the quartz vibrate, like a violin string, at a number of frequencies depending on its thickness and the electrical power applied. This is called the piezoelectric effect.

In contrast to the balance wheel, which swings back and forth a few times a second, the crystal molecules swing back and forth at least 32,768 times a second, turning the electric current off and on each time. In an area of less than a half inch (1 cm), the modern quartz crystal watch has a crystal the size of a match head, a tiny battery the size of a fingernail, and a microchip, which is an integrated circuit containing hundreds of thousands of transistors and resistors that conduct and control the amount of current flowing through.

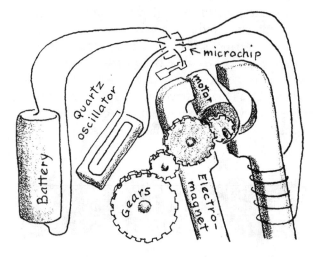

The Piezoelectric Effect

214

A simple cigarette lighter can demonstrate the effect of pressure on quartz. Ask an adult to assist you.

What to do: Apply force with your thumb to the starter.

What happens: You get a spark.

Why: Inside the lighter is a wafer of quartz. When you apply pressure to it, you create electricity. In your watch, it is just the opposite. When electric current flows through, the wafer of quartz moves. Both of these changes in a crystalline substance like quartz—creating electricity from pressure and creating movement from electricity—demonstrate the piezoelectric effect. *Piezo* comes from a Greek word meaning to press or to squeeze.

Digital Clocks

YOU WILL NEED:

pencil
paper
eraser

At first quartz clocks had dials and hands, but these were often replaced by digital "readouts" of hours and minutes and sometimes even seconds. These numbers are formed by small luminous elements controlled by electrical signals.

There are different kinds of readouts. Some are LEDs (Light Emitting Diodes). When electric current runs through these electronic devices, it gives off a bright glow, either red, yellow, or green, depending on the material used. Readouts in small timepieces are generally LCD (Liquid Crystal Display). The creamy gray liquid crystals block the passage of light and thus turn black when current is applied. The result is a black digit on a gray background. Both result in squared-off digits formed from seven-section rectangles, parts of which light up and parts of which stay dark.

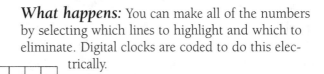

What to do: Copy the pattern above which is made up of seven straight lines forming a rectangle. Then blacken the sections of the form that make the number you want.

For instance, if you want to create a "6," blacken all the lines except F, the upper right one, and A, the top one. Then erase (or lighten) F and A. If you need to create a "5," blacken all the lines except F and C. For a "1," blacken only B and C and erase the others.

What happens: You can make all of the numbers by selecting which lines to highlight and which to eliminate. Digital clocks are coded to do this electrically.

Why: Perhaps you understand now why the shape of numbers and letters in digital readouts take some getting used to. They certainly don't resemble printed or cursive writing. The vibrations back and forth of the flake of quartz are counted by a binary logic gate, a kind of switch. Every time the count reaches the number of vibrations that a particular crystal makes in a second, the switch sends a pulse to the display unit and the watch records the passage of another second. Other switches on the same chip count 60 seconds and update the minute display; others count minutes to update the hour.

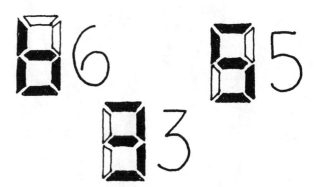

181

 216 Glowing in the Dark

Early clocks and watches were made with chimes to give the time after dark. But during World War I, when a chiming watch might have given away the wearer's position to the enemy, watchmakers developed a watch that glowed in the dark. Hands and dials were painted with radium. When radium was found to be a hazardous substance, particularly to the workers who painted with it, less dangerous materials were used.

Available today are sports watches with phosphorescent hands that glow because the phosphorus coating converts the energy of sunlight into electronic vibrations and releases it in the form of light.

Also marketed are battery-operated watches with "Indiglo night lights." The watch face is coated with zinc sulfide diluted by a small amount of copper. When you press a button, electrical energy from the battery is converted by a microchip to a higher voltage, exciting electrons in the dial material than then provide a greenish light.

Timing the Past: The Radioactive Clock 217

Scientists tell time backward by using a radioactive clock that ticks away in ancient bones, in the wood of an ancient barge, and in every material that has lived in the past 50,000 years. This radioactive clock is a slowly disintegrating form of the carbon atom called carbon 14. Plants obtain carbon dioxide from the atmosphere and animals eat the plants. After the animals and plants die, radioactive decay begins. The rate of radioactive decay is measured in terms of half-life, the time required for half of an element to decay. A once-living organism loses half of its carbon 14 in about 5,000 years, half of what's left is lost in the next 5,000 years, and half of that in the third 5,000 years. Nothing detectable remains after about 50,000 years.

To determine the age of something that once lived—from cloth to seashells—scientists figure out its carbon-14 content and compare it with the content of a modern sample.

Radioactive atoms in earth, air, and water have also provided "clocks" by which the ages of rocks and fossils older than 50,000 years can be measured. Like that of carbon 14, the rate of radioactive decay is measured in terms of half-life. In one half-life, half of the original atoms decay; in a second half-life, half of that remains, and so on. Measurements of the decay of uranium, for example, give it a half-life of about 4.5 billion years.

Atomic Clocks  218

An atomic clock is based on the action of the electrons in an atom, which vibrates naturally and whose frequency is immune to the temperature and friction problems that plague mechanical clocks.

In 1967 the General Assembly on Weights and Measurements changed the definition of a second to the frequency with which the atom of the metal cesium vibrates back and forth—9,192,631,770 times a second. The more vibrations a timekeeper makes in one second, the more accurate it is. Atomic timetellers are accurate to one billionth of a second in 24 hours.

The first molecular clock, which used ammonia gas, was built in 1949 by H. Lyons at the United States National Bureau of Standards. In 1955 L. Essen and J.V.L. Parry built the first cesium atomic clock at the National Physical Laboratory in England.

You can see this latest method of keeping time at the laboratories of the National Bureau of Standards in Boulder, Colorado. It looks like no clock you have ever seen—more like a sewer pipe—a stainless steel pipe 20 feet (6m) long with a 16-inch diameter (40 cm), which is actually a cesium-beam tube. Cesium is a soft silvery metal that looks a little like mercury.

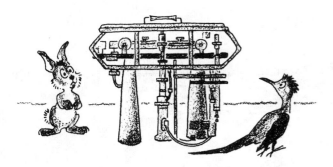

Time Machines— and More  219

A few scientists have been investigating claims that some people have actually gone back in time, that time can go backward. They are also looking into the possibility that some people see into the future. They debate whether dreams are sometimes a form of insight into what is going to happen, a form of "future time." Some philosophers through the years have suggested that time is a circle, doubling back on itself.

While it's easy to define the measuring of time, time itself is more difficult to describe. Some have questioned whether time exists at all. Everyone—from the physicist to the psychologist to the philosopher—has a different explanation. Einstein's theories—proved in laboratory atomic experiments—challenge some of our most basic beliefs about time. They indicate time slows down at speeds approaching the speed of light.

It takes light from the sun about 8 minutes and light from Pluto about 5 hours to reach Earth. But light from the nearest star—other than the sun—we now see twinkling in the sky actually has been traveling at the speed of light for more than four years. And some of the more distant stars' light has been traveling at that speed for more than 2 million years by the time astronomers see it on their telescopes.

With space exploration and the possibility of life on other planets, what more will the future teach us about the past—and the future?

UNDER GROUND

When you walk through a park, over a hill, or down a dusty road, you probably don't give much thought about the ground under your feet. But the ground is an important part of nature. The soil we use to grow our plants and the rocks we use to build our homes and highways are valuable in many ways.

About Soil and Rocks

Soil is mostly made up of rock that has been broken up into very small pieces. This sand, created over many years (hundreds of thousands), is the result of weather, erosion, and freezing and thawing. The climate and the slope of the land (hillside or river valley) also affect how fast sandy soil forms in a particular area. Soil also contains air, water, and decayed matter (known as humus). Basically, there are three types of soil: clay, sandy, and loam (a rich mixture of clay, sand, and humus that is good for growing plants).

There are also three different kinds of rocks. Igneous rock, such as granite, is formed from melted minerals, so it is often found near volcanoes. Sedimentary rock usually forms underwater, as a result of layers of material, called sediment, pressing down on other layers. Sandstone and limestone are examples of this type of rock. Metamorphic rock, such as marble, is formed by the great heat and pressure deep inside the Earth's surface.

The experiments here will help you learn about the soil and rock in your special part of the world.

220 Rock and Roll

YOU WILL NEED:

clean sand
white glue
small container
plastic spoon
oil or margarine
aluminum foil
coffee can (with lid)
water

The sand in soil is rock that has been broken up and worn down by a process called erosion. To demonstrate this, you need to make your own rocks (most outdoor rocks are much too hard).

What to do: Mix three large spoonfuls of sand together with three spoonfuls of white glue. Make small lumps of the mixture and place them on a lightly oiled piece of aluminum foil, so that they will not stick to it. Put the "rocks" in a dry, sunny location for two or three days, until hard. Then, put some of your "rocks" into the coffee can with some water. Hold the lid on securely and shake the can for four to five minutes. Remove the lid.

What happens: The rocks begin to wear down. Some rocks may be worn down into sand again.

Why: The water running over the rocks pushes them against each other, causing erosion that wears them down. In nature, this process takes many years, but the result is the same. Rocks are broken up, become smaller from rubbing against each other and, over time, wear down into sandy particles that may eventually become part of the soil near a river or stream.

YOU WILL NEED:

small clear jars
water
soil samples

221

It's a Dirty Job...

The surface of our Earth is made up of rocks, sand, humus, water, and air. All of these soil "ingredients" are necessary for plants and animals to survive. Let's find out how much air is in different soils.

What to do: Half-fill each jar with a soil sample from several places in your neighborhood. Then fill the jars with water, almost to the top.

What happens: Depending on the soil you are testing, you will see a few, some, or a lot of air bubbles rising to the top of the water in each jar. The number of bubbles tell how much air was trapped in the spaces between the soil particles.

Why: The more bubbles rising through the water, the more air was trapped which you can see escaping from the soil sample. Tightly packed soil has less space for air to be trapped than does soil that has a lot of humus or other organic matter in it to make "air pockets." Most plants tend to grow better in such aerated soil (soil with lots of air pockets) than densely packed soil (such as clay).

222 Soak It Up

Good soil, like that in a garden, always has some water in it. Here's how to find it.

What to do: Fill the can about half-full of garden soil. Tape a piece of black construction paper around the can, and place the glass or plastic plate over the top. Put the can in a sunny window or on a warm radiator for a couple of hours.

What happens: Water droplets begin to form on the underside of the lid. To prove that the water is from the soil, not the air, clean out and dry the can and repeat the experiment, but without putting in any soil. Compare the results.

Why: All soil contains some water. How much is held by the soil depends on what else is in the soil, the outside temperature, the weather at the time, and the climate in the area—wet or dry. Soil water is necessary for plant and animal growth, but most plants will need more water (from rain, rivers, or lakes) to keep growing.

223 Deeper and Deeper

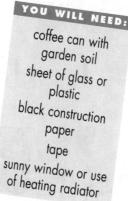

Soil is made up of different layers. Here's how you can look for them.

What to do: Find a place where you can dig a hole (be sure to ask permission first). Try to dig about 2 feet (60 cm) or so straight down.

Notice the colors of the soil layers along the sides of the hole as you dig. Measure the distance from the surface down to the different soil layers and write it down. Place a small sample of each layer's soil in a plastic bag.

At home, put some of each sample on clean white paper. Use a magnifying glass, or a microscope, to examine the samples.

What happens: Depending on where you live and dig, you may find one or more soil colors in layers as you dig down.

Why: The soil near the surface is usually a dark, rich color. This layer, called topsoil, is the thinnest and it usually contains a lot of organic matter (dead and decaying plants, insects, and animals which make up humus). Topsoil is best for growing plants and food crops. The next layer, known as subsoil, is often lighter in color and has a lot of sand and rocks in it. The last layer of soil is called the bedrock. If you dig down far enough to reach it, you will see it is the hardest layer to dig through. This is because there is no organic matter to soften it; bedrock is mostly made up of rocks, pebbles, and stones packed tightly together.

Note: Always remember to fill in any holes you make after you have finished obtaining soil samples

Nutrients Away

224

The food, or nutrients, in the soil can wash away when there is a lot of rain. Here's how it happens.

What to do: Add 1/2 teaspoon of the blue tempera paint to the 1/2 cup of soil and mix thoroughly. Set the funnel in the mouth of the jar and put a coffee filter in the funnel. Pour the soil mixture into the filter. Pour 1/2 cup of water into the funnel. Look at the color of the water running into the jar. Pour the water in the jar into a cup or container and put the funnel over the jar again; repeat this again with another 1/2 cup of water. Pour off the water, and repeat it another two or three times.

What happens: At first, the water that flows into the jar will be dark blue in color. Each time more water is poured over the same soil mixture, the color will get lighter. Eventually, the water will have no more blue in it and run clean into the jar. How many half-cups of water did it take for that to happen?

Why: The blue tempera paint you added to the soil represents the nutrients that are naturally in the ground. These nutrients are necessary for plants to grow. However, when there is a lot of rain or water runoff, these nutrients are washed away, leaving a nutrient-poor soil. Excessive rains and water runoff can remove from the soil the valuable food and minerals needed for plant growth. If you look at places in your area where a lot of soil has eroded away, you will see that there are very few plants growing there. Any plants still there are the kind that don't need much food to grow.

Making Bricks

You can make your own bricks using the same technique that the early pioneers did.

What to do: Put some ground clay (or your own "homemade" clay), straw, and enough water to make a doughy mixture in a bucket. Mix it together thoroughly. Place portions of the mixture into molds (frozen-vegetable packaging or small juice containers are good). Let them sit overnight in a warm place, then gently tear away the sides of the molds and let the bricks dry in the sun for several days. Use them to build something, like a little tower or house.

A Crystal Garden

Many of the rocks you find in the Earth's soil were formed by a process known as crystallization. This process goes on all the time and can easily be recreated in your own home. Here's how.

What to do: Wet a small piece of brick with water and place it in a small bowl. In a separate large container, mix together 1/2 cup of water, 1/2 cup of bluing, and 1/2 cup of ammonia (also from the grocery). Use a measuring cup to pour some of this mixture over the brick. Sprinkle the brick with salt and let it sit for 24 hours.

What happens: The next day you will see crystals forming on the surface of the brick.

What next: Add some more of the water + bluing + ammonia mixture to keep the blue crystals growing. Or, you can use drops of other food coloring and change some of the crystals from blue into a colorful display.

From Dust to Dust

When soil is blown from one place to another by the wind, it is known as wind erosion. This is a serious problem in many parts of the world. Is it happening where you live?

What to do: Stick some two-sided tape on one side of several different paddles. Stick the paddle handles into the ground in various places near your home. The paddles should face in different directions—North, South, East, and West (mark the direction on the paddles). At regular intervals, once or twice every week for example, look at the paddles and record the amount of dust, dirt, or soil sticking to the tape.

What happens: Depending on the amount of wind and the direction it blows where you live, you will see that certain paddles collect more dust and dirt than other paddles do.

Why: More soil sticks on the paddles where wind erosion is taking place. If there are no barriers, such as trees, plants, and grass, to slow down or stop wind erosion, great quantities of soil can be swept into the air from one location and left somewhere else. One way to prevent wind erosion is to grow trees and plants to cut the wind and cover and protect the ground. This is why wind erosion is much less of a problem in dense forest than it is in the desert, which has sandstorms!

228 Erosion Explosion

Erosion can move large quantities of soil and seriously affect the lives of plants and people. Some examples of wind or water erosion are: a sandbar in a stream or off a beach, whirling dust devils, a muddy river after a storm, sand drifted against a fence or in a gully or canyon.

Some erosion quite common in and around the home is called wear. It's caused by friction rather than wind or water. Here are some examples of wear erosion to look for:
1. Coins that are smooth from handling
2. Shoes with the heels worn down
3. An old car tire with no tread
4. A countertop with design or finish worn away

Can you list more evidence of erosion in and around your home?

229

Stem the Tide

Plants are important in many ways, but can they do anything to prevent or slow down soil erosion?

YOU WILL NEED:

2 cake pans
soil
grass seed
water
a pitcher
2 books

What to do: Fill two cake pans with soil. In one pan, plant some grass seed. Water the soil in both pans equally. Place the pan with the grass seed in a sunny location and water gently for several days. When the grass is about 3 inches (1 cm) high, place one end of each pan against a book or block of wood so that they lie at an angle. Fill the pitcher with water and pour it into the higher end of the first pan. Do the same thing with the pan that has grass growing in it.

What happens: In the pan without grass, the water flows freely across the surface. Some of the dirt is carried by the fast-running water toward the bottom of the pan. In the other pan, with the grass, less soil is washed away.

Why: The grass slows down the flow of the water over the surface and that stops much of the soil from being eroded away. You have looked at mountains or bare hillsides with very few plants and noticed that lots of soil has been washed away, except for rocks too big for the water to move. The use of plants helps keep soil in place and prevents erosion damage.

Did You Know?

230

· In the United States alone, more than seven billion tons of topsoil is eroded away into streams and rivers every year. Louisiana and Hawaii are the only states that continue to grow in physical size.

· About 75% of all the rocks on the Earth's surface are sedimentary rocks (rocks formed when small grains and particles of sediment are pressed together under tons of water for long periods of time).

· Each year, the world's deserts grow by as much as 16,000 square miles (41,600 sq km).

Water is one of the things we often take for granted. We turn on a faucet and water comes out. We turn the faucet off and the water stops. We usually don't think about what water is and just what it means to us, but we should. It is needed for our health, it is an important source of power for business and industry, and it is vital for maintaining life on Earth in all its forms.

One of the major concerns we have about water today is its purity (its cleanliness). Pollution of our water sources and resources is an increasing problem all over the world. We all need to work together to ensure that the water we want to use tomorrow is protected today.

The fun activities in this chapter will help you to learn more about water and its role in nature.

231 Compact and Loose

YOU WILL NEED:
measuring cup
potting soil
clean sandbox sand
3 same-size cans
(with ends removed)
cheesecloth
scissors
masking tape
water
3 clear jars
a helper, or a clock
with a second hand

Both water and soil are needed for plant growth. But water travels through soil at different rates, depending on how much, or the ratio of, organic matter there is to inorganic matter in the soil.

What to do: Cut three squares of cheesecloth. Shape a piece over one end of each can and tape the edges to the sides of the can. Cut out three more pieces of mesh and lay them over the tops of the glass jars. Turn the cans over, so the cheesecloth is on the bottom, and half-fill the first can with potting soil. Fill the second can halfway with sand. For the third can, combine potting soil and sand and half-fill the can with the mixture. Use your hand to pack down the soils in each can firmly, then place each can of soil on top of a cheesecloth-covered jar.

If you have a helper with you, add one-half cup of water to each can at the same time and see which one the water drips through first. If you are experimenting alone, pour the water into the cans one at a time, watch the jar and clock, and mark the time it takes for the water to leak through the soil packed into each jar.

What happens: The water you put in the can of sand runs through to the jar much more rapidly than the water in the sand and soil mixture. The water in the mixture leaks through at a faster rate than the water in the potting soil.

Why: Water flows through sand very quickly because this soil has lots of air space between the grains that lets the water pass through. Because the potting soil has organic material in it, this soil holds on to more of the water, stopping it from leaking through. This is one reason why gardeners and farmers add humus or other organic matter to the soil—to hold the water for their crops. The ability of a soil to allow water to pass through it is called permeability.

Well, Well, Well

232

YOU WILL NEED:

cardboard tube (toilet paper roll)
large (coffee) can
sand
aquarium or potting gravel
water

To get a drink of water, you probably just turn on a faucet. Many people, however, get their water from wells. How does this kind of system work? Let's build a small one and see.

What to do: Place the tube upright in the middle of the coffee can. Holding the tube, pour a layer of about 1½ inches (4 cm) of gravel on the bottom of the coffee can around the outside of the tube. Pour a second layer, this time of sand, on top of the gravel. Slowly pour some water onto the sand until the water reaches the top of the sand. Notice what happens inside the tube.

What happens: After a short time, water begins to rise inside the tube.

Why: When it rains, "groundwater" collects under the surface of the Earth. This collected water can be very shallow or deep depending on the rock formations and the kind of soil in a particular area. Some people think of this groundwater as a series of large underground lakes extending for miles and miles. Because there is a limit to the amount of water that can collect in an area, water pressure builds up in these "lakes." If a well has been dug nearby, the pressure forces water into it where it can be reached and used.

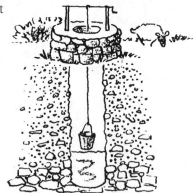

From Shore to Shore

233

Often, when we think about water pollution, we think about rivers and streams. But we need to think about our oceans, too, because much of the food we eat, the weather that affects us, the air and even the moisture in it comes from our oceans. Unfortunately, even our largest oceans are becoming contaminated—oil spills pollute the sea, litter is thrown into the water, and garbage washes up on shores all over the world.

Even though we don't drink ocean water, it is still important to human life. If you have ever gone to a beach to swim or to walk along the shore, you may have seen some of the pollution that is destroying the world's oceans. Here are three things you can do to help:

1. If you go to a beach, take along a garbage bag to pack up your own litter or any you may find there. Put it in an available trash can or take it away with you when you leave.
2. Cut apart the plastic rings that come with six-packs of canned drinks. These often find their way into the oceans and can choke and kill sea birds and other marine life.
3. Ask your parents to buy soaps and detergents that are "biodegradable" and don't poison the ocean. Regular soaps contaminate the liquid waste, which is often pumped through sewers and into the oceans, and it kills large numbers of sea animals and plants. It is important to use biodegradable products even if you don't live anywhere near the ocean.

234 More Than You Know

YOU WILL NEED:
your eyes and your nose
clean container
a helper

If a stream runs near where you live, try this experiment to find out something about the water that flows there.

What to do: With your helper or friend, visit a nearby stream. Bend down and look closely at the water as it flows by. Sniff the air. Dip your container into the water and raise some to your nose. Smell it again.

What happens: Did you notice any of the following conditions?
• Some streams have a rotten-egg smell. Often, they are heavily polluted from a lot of sewage being dumped into the water source.
• If the stream has a shiny or multicolored film floating on it, that means that oil or gasoline is seeping into the water.
• If the color of the water is very green, there is probably a lot of algae in the water. Too much algae means there isn't enough oxygen in the water for fish and other plant life.
• Foam or suds floating on the water usually means that detergent or other soapy waste is leaking into the water from nearby factories or homes.
• Cloudy or muddy water usually means that the water contains large quantities of dirt, silt, or mud. Unfortunately, this means that the animals and plants that live in the stream aren't getting enough

oxygen. It is possible that a lot of soil erosion is taking place somewhere upstream. Can you do something about it?
• Bright colors, such as red or orange, on the surface of the water is an indication that pollutants are being released into the stream by factories and industries.
• Clean, clear, or transparent water that has no smell to it is the best kind of water for aquatic plants and animals, and for us.

Why: For too long, people believed that it was OK to let streams and rivers carry away their pollutants and garbage. People put lots of things into their streams without thinking about the long-term effects. We now know that whatever we put into a stream will affect the plants, animals, and people who live downstream. Cleaning up our streams and making sure we don't put anything into a stream that does not occur naturally in that stream are important steps in maintaining these important, life-giving water resources.

235

Ocean Motion

Would you like to create an ocean that you can keep in your own home?

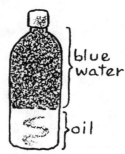

blue
water

oil

What to do: Pour cooking oil into the bottle until it is one-third full. Fill the rest of the bottle to the brim with water and add a few drops of blue food coloring. Screw the cap on very tight and lay the bottle on its side. Now, tip the bottle back and forth.

What happens: The oily water in the bottle begins to roll back and forth, moving just like the waves in the ocean do. You have created a miniature ocean in a bottle.

Why: Waves are energy moving through water. The water of the wave itself doesn't move, it's the energy passing from one water molecule to another that forms the waves. Ocean waves are caused by the gravitational pull of the moon on the Earth's surface-water, the shape (geological formation) of the ocean floor, and the spinning of the Earth on its axis. You can create similar conditions artificially in a soda bottle and observe wave action that is very much like that which occurs throughout the oceans of the world.

236 You Crack Me Up!

Here's an experiment that demonstrates how large boulders are broken down into tiny pebbles—by water!

What to do: Soak pieces of sandstone in water overnight. The next day, place several pieces of the wet sandstone into sandwich bags and seal them tightly. Place the bags in the freezer overnight. Take them out and examine them the next day.

What happens: The sandstone cracks into smaller pieces.

Why: When water freezes, it expands. The sandstone absorbs some of the water, taking it up into the air spaces between the sand particles. When the stone was placed in the freezer, the water in it froze and expanded.

In nature, water seeps into the cracks of rocks, freezes in winter, and causes the rocks to break apart. After a while, the rocks are reduced to very small pebbles and eventually to sand.

Drip, Drip, Drip

With this experiment, you'll be able to remove salt from saltwater. Let's try it.

YOU WILL NEED:

water
table salt
measuring cup
measuring spoons
large bowl
small cup
plastic food wrap
small stone

What to do: In the large bowl, mix 3 teaspoons of salt into 2 cups of water until it is thoroughly dissolved. Use a spoon to carefully taste a small sample of the saltwater. Set the small cup in the middle of the bowl. Cover the bowl with plastic food wrap and place a small stone in the center of the wrap (directly over the cup) to weigh the plastic down.

Carefully, set the wrapped bowl, with stone in place, in the sun for several hours. Look at the wrap after a while and you will notice beads of water forming on the underside of the plastic food wrap and dripping into the small cup. Later on, remove the plastic wrap carefully and taste the water that has collected in the cup.

What happens: The saltwater inside the large bowl evaporates into the air inside the

bowl. It then condenses as beads of water on the underside of the plastic wrap. With the plastic covering lower in the center, the beads of water roll down to the lowest point and drip into the small cup. The water in the cup is no longer salty!

Why: This experiment illustrates the natural process of solar distillation. Distillation involves changing a liquid into a gas (evaporation) by heating and then back into a liquid (condensation) by cooling the gas vapor. The sun's energy can evaporate water but not salt (salt molecules are heavier than water molecules), so the salt remains in the bowl. This entire process, often referred to as desalinization (removing salt) is used in many countries, such as those in the Middle East, to make fresh water from saltwater

Don't Rain on My Parade

238

YOU WILL NEED:

small (baby food) jars

pH paper and color chart (from aquarium or pet store)

rain and water samples (see below)

tweezers

Acid rain is a problem in many parts of the world, especially where there is a lot of industry. Here's how to find out if acid rain is a problem where you live.

What to do: Make sure each jar is thoroughly cleaned and dried. With an adult to help, collect several different samples of water (tap water, rainwater, well water, pool water, etc.). Collect each sample in a separate jar. Using the tweezers, dip a strip of pH paper into a sample of water and quickly compare the color that registers against the color chart. Do the same for each water sample and record the results. (You may want to collect some rainwater at the beginning of a storm and some at the end of the storm and compare the two different rainwater samples.)

What happens: You notice that the pH of the various water samples has different readings.

Why: pH indicates the amount of acid in substances. The pH scale goes from 0 to 14. Pure water, for example, has a pH value of 7 (it is neutral). Substances that have a pH value less than 7 are acids; substances that have a pH value more than 7 are bases. Acids and bases are common chemicals, many of which we have in our homes. Vinegar and lemon juice, for example, are acids; while baking soda is a base. The strength of an acid or base is determined by the pH scale (the lower the number the more acidic a substance is; the higher a number the more basic, or alkaline, it is).

Acid rain has a pH value of 5.6 or less. Rain that is considerably less than 5.6 will be more damaging to the environment than rain above 5.6 on the pH scale. Rain that falls at the beginning of a storm is usually more acidic than rain that falls at the end of a storm. Also, the rain that falls in the eastern United States is more acidic (because of the prevailing winds) than rain that falls in the western half of the country.

239

Acid Soil

There are many different types of soil. Certain plants (blueberries) like to grow in acid soils, and some plants (potatoes, peaches) prefer basic soils. You can test the pH (acidity or alkalinity) of soil with this experiment.

Collect several soil samples from various places in and around your community (about one cup of each will do). In clean jars, mix each soil sample with one cup of distilled water. (Distilled water, available in grocery stores, is neutral, having a pH of 7.) Shake each sample thoroughly. After a few minutes, dip a separate strip of pH test paper into each sample and quickly compare the strip to the colors on the pH chart. You should be able to see some difference in the pH of the soils even in your own neighborhood. Invite friends and relatives to give you soil samples from other places for testing, too.

240 Did You Know?

- It is estimated that about 14 billion pounds (6.3 billion kg) of trash and garbage are dumped into the oceans of the world every year.
- Americans alone consume about 450 billion gallons (1,710 billion liters) of water every day.
- Over 99% of all the fresh water on Earth is trapped in icebergs, icecaps, and glaciers.
- Mt. Waialeale in Hawaii averages 451 inches (1,146 cm) of rain per year, making it the wettest spot on Earth.
- There's about 9 million tons of gold dissolved in the oceans of the world.
- From the mouth of the Amazon River in Brazil pours one-fifth of all the moving fresh water on Earth.
- Canada contains one-third of all the fresh water on Earth.
- North America has more than 190,000 miles (304,000 km) of ocean coastline—more than any other continent.
- If all the world's ice melted, the sea level would rise 200 to 300 feet (600 to 900 m).
- Each year, about 2.3 trillion gallons (8.74 trillion
- liters) of liquid waste are discharged directly into United States coastal waters.
- It is estimated that acid rain costs American farmers about $4 billion a year.
- The smallest drip from a leaky faucet can waste more than 50 gallons (190 liters) of water a day.

PLENTY OF PLANTS

Plants are an important part of our environment. Without plants, animals and human beings could not survive. Plants provide us with food, oxygen, medicines, building materials, seasonings, candy, drinks, industrial products, dyes, manufactured goods, paper, and decorations.

About Plants

Plants are producers—the only living things able to make their own food. In order to grow, green plants use sunlight and store their energy in their leaves and stems. Sunlight enables plants to convert water—and also carbon dioxide, which all animals (including humans) give off as they breathe—into foods needed by the plants. This remarkable process is known as photosynthesis.

Plants are also responsible for producing oxygen—a gas necessary for animal survival. Plants add to the relative humidity of an area by releasing water vapor into the air. A plant's roots also help to reduce wind and water erosion by holding on to the soil. The fallen leaves of plants contribute to the quality of the soil, providing essential nutrients to other plants.

When the life cycle of plants is endangered by air pollution, when forests and plant life in certain areas are torn up or destroyed, or when poor farming methods are used, we are affected as well. Plants are a vital part of our daily lives and our survival

Hey, What's Inside?

Did you know that inside every seed is a very small plant waiting to grow? When the conditions are right, a new plant can begin life. What does it need?

What to do: Soak several lima bean seeds in a container of water overnight. The next day, choose some of the seeds and place them on a countertop or some paper. Ask an adult to use a knife to pry along the edge of the seed's coat (the hard covering of the seed) and open it up for you. (Knives, especially sharp ones, are dangerous and must be handled carefully.) When the two halves of the seed have separated, use your magnifying glass lens to examine the embryo in the seed (it will look like a miniature plant). You may want to look inside other seeds for their embryos, too.

What happens: You will be able to see the three basic parts of a seed— the seed coat, the food storage area, and the embryo.

Why: Many plants, such as lima beans, reproduce sexually—that is, a sperm cell from a male plant and an egg cell from a female plant combine in the flower of a plant and a seed begins to form. Inside the seed is a miniature plant called an embryo.

There is also some food material in the seed so that a newly forming plant will have a ready food source as it begins its life. Covering the embryo and food source is a seed coat that serves as protection for the seed until the new plant is ready to start. Then, when the conditions are right (moisture and warmth), the seed germinates, or begins to grow. The embryo breaks out of the seed, like a chick out of an egg, and starts its life as a new plant.

Help Me Out

Do you know what seeds need to begin growing? Here's how you can find out.

What to do: Label each small bag with a number. Cut three paper towels in half. Moisten three of the towel pieces with water. As directed below, place the towels in the bottoms of the bags. Drop six radish seeds into each bag and then finish setting up each bag as follows:

Bag 1: moist paper towel (water), no light (put in a drawer or closet), room temperature

Bag 2: moist paper towel (water), light, room temperature

Bag 3: dry paper towel (no water), light, room temperature

Bag 4: no paper towel, water (seeds floating), light, room temperature

Bag 5: moist paper towel (water), no light, keep in refrigerator or freezer

Bag 6: moist paper towel (water), no light, room temperature, seeds covered by nail polish.

Record the date and time you began this activity and check each of the bags twice daily for any changes.

What happens: The seeds in Bag 1 and Bag 2 germinate (begin to grow). You may see some small difference in the seeds in Bag 4. The seeds in the other bags do not start growing. What is wrong?

Why: Seeds need favorable temperature, enough moisture, and oxygen to germinate. Light is not needed for germination (the seeds, after all, usually germinate underground), but light is necessary later for growth. The seeds in Bag 6 can't get any air or moisture through the nail polish, so they don't germinate.

Plant Requirements

Plants have certain needs for their growth and survival, just as we do.

Air: To live, plants take two gases from the air. They use carbon dioxide, a natural product of animal life, to make food by a process called photosynthesis, and oxygen as fuel for the energy that helps them breathe.

Water: To make their food, plants need water. Minerals in the water help plants to grow and replace damaged cells. Water is taken in through a plant's roots and is carried to the leaves.

Temperature: Each plant variety requires a specific temperature range. Over many years, plants have adapted and learned to thrive where other plants could not survive. For example, a cactus or a palm tree could not live at the North Pole, where the cold temperatures would be harmful.

Sunlight: Most plants, especially green leafy ones, need sunlight to grow. The light converts a plant's food into usable energy. But certain plants, such as mushrooms, don't like light and grow only in the dark.

Soil: Land plants need some type of soil in order to grow. It is usually a combination of organic material (decayed animal or vegetable matter known as humus) and sand or clay that also help hold the plant erect. Plants also get nutrients, or minerals, from the soil.

Swell Time

In order to begin the growing process, seeds need to take in water. Here's how they do it.

YOU WILL NEED:

2 small, sealable, plastic bags

dry seeds

water

container or tray

What to do: Fill each of the two bags with dry seeds (bean seeds work best). Finish filling one of the bags with as much water as it can hold, then seal both bags and place them outside or on a tray or in a container in a sunny location.

What happens: After several hours, the seeds in the bag with the water begin to swell up. Eventually, the expanding seeds pop the bag open and seeds spill out all over the place.

Why: To begin the growing process, or sprout, seeds need to take in water. Water is absorbed through the skin of the seed (seed coat), and the seeds begin to expand. Because the bag had been filled with the dry seeds and now all the seeds in the bag were absorbing water and expanding, there wasn't enough room in the bag. So, the expanding seeds forced the bag open and spilled out. In nature, seeds take in water and expand in the same way.

Top to Bottom

Plants need both roots and shoots in order to develop properly. To watch the growth of both plant parts at the same time, do this.

YOU WILL NEED:

several large seeds

2 small sheets of glass or clear plastic

blotting paper

string

baking pan

water

bricks

marker or masking tape

What to do: Trim the blotter to fit the glass or plastic sheets. Wet the blotter well and lay it on top of one. Arrange some seeds on the blotter, placing them at least 2 inches (5 cm) in from the edge. Put the other clear sheet on top. Tie the "seed sandwich" together securely with string and place it on edge in the pan. Support it upright, at an angle of about 45°, with one or more bricks. Put ½ inch (1 cm) or so of water into the pan. Add more when needed, to keep the blotter wet.

What happens: In a few days, the seeds will sprout, the shoots going up and the roots going down. Use a marker to make lines on the glass or a thin strip of masking tape to mark the daily or weekly growth of the seeds.

Why: The seeds sprout because you have provided them with water, light, and air. The roots always grow downwards and the actual plant upwards. Depending on the seeds used, you may see tiny leaves form. All seeds in nature demonstrate this same type of growth.

245 ◆ A Growing Enterprise

Some seeds are easy to grow, while others are more difficult. Fruit-bearing plants are very hard to grow from seed. That is why many fruit farmers use other ways to start growing new fruit trees, such as grafts (attaching a part of one plant to a part of another plant) or root stocks (sections of root) instead.

To try growing some fruit plants at home (keep in mind, however, that the success rate is very low), you need some seeds. The easiest way to get them is to buy a couple of your favorite fruits (not the seedless variety). Take the seeds from the fruit, wash the seeds in water (don't use soap), and let them dry well in a warm place.

Some fruits you can try growing from seeds: apple, pear, pumpkin, orange, grape, cherry, peach, banana, fig, apricot, plum, quince, nectarine, lemon, lime, tomato, melon, persimmon, grapefruit.

When you are ready to plant, get several small plastic cups and fill each one with some potting soil. Moisten the soil and plant four or five seeds from one of the fruits in each cup. Plant as many different varieties of fruit seeds as possible and note which ones were the easiest to grow and which ones were the most difficult.

After you have sprouted one or more fruits and then have reached a height of 5 or 6 inches (13–15 cm), you may want to transplant them outdoors.

Hawaiian Harvest ◆ 246

Almost everybody loves the taste of pineapple. Now you can grow this delicious fruit in your own home.

Buy a whole pineapple. Have an adult cut off the crown of the pineapple (top part, with the green leaves) leaving about 1 to 2 inches (3–5 cm) of the fruit attached. (Even with a sharp knife, cutting the pineapple may not be easy.) Let the crown dry for 36 hours, then put it in a large container of potting soil to root. Place the container in a warm location—about 72°F (2°C) is ideal. Keep the soil evenly moist (but not too wet).

Pineapple develops on the top of a long stem that may need to be supported by sticks or secured upright with string when the fruit grows large. If no fruit develops, put the whole plant (with its

container) inside a large plastic bag. Place a rotting apple or lemon inside the bag, close it up, and leave it for several days (the ethylene gas produced by the rotting fruit will help stimulate fruiting).

Later, you may want to transplant the fruit to a larger container or, if you live where it is very warm, outside in loose, sandy soil.

247

YOU WILL NEED:
fresh stalk of celery
2 glasses of water
red food coloring
dinner knife

Green Highways

Plants must be able to carry water and nutrients to all their parts in order to grow, but can you prove that they actually do it? Sure, you can! Here's how.

What to do: Put the two glasses of water side by side. Place four drops of red food coloring into one of the glasses. Cut off the dried bottom end of the celery stalk and then cut the stalk up the middle from the bottom of the stalk to the leaves. Stand half of the celery stalk in the glass with clear water and the other in the glass with the red water. For the next several hours, go back every hour and check on your celery stalk experiment.

What happens: The celery in the glass of plain water shows no change, but telltale streaks of red move up the stalk of the celery standing in the colored water.

Why: All plants have special tubes in their stems that act something like drinking straws. These tubes move water, and the nutrients in it, from a plant's roots up into the leaves. Slight pressure differences in the long, tube sections actually "pull" the water up the stalk, using a process called osmosis. This allows the plant to get the water and food needed for it to grow and develop, By putting red food coloring into the water, you are able to track the water's path up the stalk, and prove your theory.

248

The Name Game

How would you like to spell your name with plants? Here's how.

Fill a large flat cake pan with soil. Smooth it over so that the soil is level and moisten it with water. Using a toothpick or the end of a knife, trace your name into the surface of the soil. Open a packet of radish seeds and carefully plant the seeds in the grooves you made for the letters of your name. Be sure to follow the directions for proper planting depth and distance between seeds given on the seed packet.) Cover the seeds with soil and place the pan in a sunny location and water occasionally. After a few days, the radishes will sprout into the shape of your name.

Later, you may want to write your name in plants again, using different varieties of seeds (grass seed and mung bean seeds work especially well).

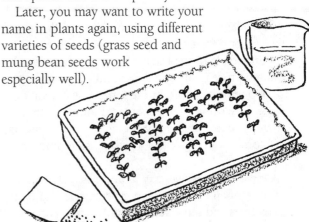

Water In, Water Out

YOU WILL NEED:

small potted plant
clear plastic bag
water
tape or string

Plants take in water in order to grow, but they also give off water.

What to do: Water the plant thoroughly. Place the plastic bag over the green, leafy part of the plant and close it up gently around the stem with tape or string. Place the plant in a sunny location for several hours.

What happens: Water droplets form on the inside of the bag.

Why: Plant leaves have tiny openings called stomata in them. In most plants, stomata are located on the underside of the leaves. During a plant's food-making process, air is taken in and released through these opening. Water, in the form of water vapor, is also released through the stomata into the atmosphere. You can see that water vapor, as it condenses and forms water droplets, on the inside of the plastic bag.

One of the reasons why a jungle is so humid is because of all the water vapor being released by the many trees and the vegetation in the area. The amount of water a plant loses varies with the weather conditions as well as the size and shape of its leaves.

Don't Crowd Me

Do plants like togetherness, or wide-open spaces?

What to do: Fill the shoe box with potting soil. At one end of the box, plant six bean seeds very close together. At the other end of the box plant six more seeds, but space them about 1½ inches (4 cm) apart. Water the soil thoroughly, being careful not to wash it away from the seeds. Set the box aside and watch what happens to the seeds. Record the number of seeds that sprout, and continue to grow, at each end of the box.

What happens: The side with the seeds planted closer together has fewer sprouts, and they grow more slowly than the seeds planted farther apart at the other end.

Why: Plants need space in order to grow properly. When plants are crowded together, they have to compete for the limited resources available. As a result, the sprouts may not get all the soil nutrients, sunlight, and water they need to grow strong. To achieve full growth, there must be enough space left between plants. In nature, seeds are scattered over a large area, so that many are able to sprout and grow in an uncrowded environment. This is why gardeners and farmers are very careful not to plant their crops too close together.

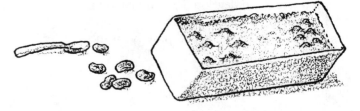

Breathe Deeply

Follow that Light

YOU WILL NEED:

elodea plants (from aquarium or pet store)
aquarium or deep container
clear funnel
test tube

Do plants breathe? If so, how?

Do plants always grow toward the light? Here's a great experiment to prove that they do.

YOU WILL NEED:

2 shoe boxes
a healthy plant

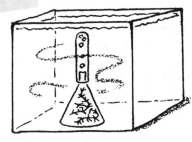

What to do: Cut two corners of the cardboard from one of the shoe boxes. Tape the pieces inside the other shoe box as shown. Cut a hole in the top side. Place a healthy plant (a growing bean plant is fine) in the bottom and place the lid on the box. Put the closed shoe box in a sunny location. Every other day or so, remove the lid for a moment and quickly water the plant.

What to do: Fill the aquarium or container almost to the top with water. Place several elodea plants inside, close together in the middle, and cover them with the clear funnel (wide mouth, over the plants and narrow neck pointing upwards). Dip the test tube in the water, making sure that it fills with water.

Then, still underwater, turn the test tube over into the stem of the funnel, making sure no water escapes. Place the aquarium in a sunny location for a few days and watch what happens in the top of the test tube.

What happens: You will see oxygen building up in the top of the test tube (pushing out the water).

Why: The elodea plants (like other aquatic plants) produce oxygen. This oxygen is released into the water, where it becomes available to organisms that need it, such as fish. In this experiment, the oxygen collects in the top of the test tube, replacing the water.

What happens: The plant grows toward the light source, even bending around the cardboard pieces to do it.

Why: All green plant life needs light in order to grow. Through a process known as phototropism, plants grow in whichever direction is toward the light. In your experiment, the plant grew toward the sunlight, even though the cardboard pieces were in the way. One of the reasons we turn our potted houseplants occasionally is so they will be able to get equal amounts of light on all sides and grow straight. If we did not, the plants would "lean" in the direction of the light.

253 ◆ Hanging On

The previous experiment showed how plants always grow toward a light source. This experiment will now demonstrate how powerful that process is.

YOU WILL NEED:
small potted plant with a strong root system
2 large sponges
string

What to do: Carefully remove the plant from its pot (try to leave as much soil around the roots as possible). Wet the two sponges, wrap them around the root system, and tie them together with string. Turn the plant upside down (roots upwards) and hang it from the ceiling near a sunny window. Check the plant occasionally, and keep the sponges moistened.

What happens: After a few days, the stem and top of the plant will turn and begin to grow upwards toward the light.

Why: The leaves and stems of a plant will grow in the direction of a light source, following the process of phototropism, even if the plant is made to "stand on its head!" Also, a plant's roots will always grow downwards, trying to reach the necessary nutrients in the soil.

254 ◆ See Me Grow

Have you ever wondered how plants grow under the ground? Here's a neat way to find out.

YOU WILL NEED:
shoe box
sheet of clear acetate or plastic
scissors
masking tape
variety of seeds
pebbles
potting soil
water

What to do: Cut a section from the side of a strong shoe box, leaving about a 1 inch (2.5 cm) border all around. Tape the acetate inside, tight against the opening. Punch some small holes in the bottom of the box. Put in a layer of pebbles and fill the box with potting soil. Plant several seeds in the soil, placing them up against the acetate so you can see them behind the sheet. Water the seeds, place the box outside or in a tray in the window. Watch the seeds for several days.

What happens: The seeds germinate and plants begin to grow. You can watch the growth of the plant upwards, and the roots reaching down underground as well.

Why: Plants need roots in order to take in water and other nutrients from the soil. They do this through tiny roots called root hairs. Roots generally grow in a downward direction to obtain the water and nutrients necessary for the plant's growth.

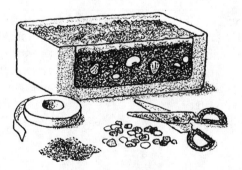

Flower Power

255

How can a little plant grow right up through a sidewalk? Let's see.

YOU WILL NEED:

any healthy potted plant
2 small boxes
sheet of clear acetate or plastic
paper clips

What to do: Put the potted plant on a sunny windowsill. Place the two boxes on either side of the pot (the boxes should be just a bit higher than the plant). Be careful not to shade the plant. Lay the clear acetate or plastic across the boxes. Make two identical "chains" of paper clips and lay them over the clear sheet so that the ends hang down the sides of the boxes. Arrange the chain ends evenly, and mark their positions on the sides of the boxes. Water and care for the plant as you would normally. Check the positions of the chains now and then.

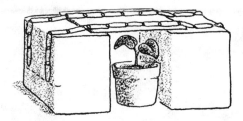

What happens: As the plant grows, it pushes upwards against the clear sheet. The rate of growth is seen and measured by the markings made by the ends of the clip chains when they move up the sides of the boxes.

Why: Plants are incredibly strong. They are able to push up through the toughest soil as well as through rocks and cement to reach the light. This is why weeds can push up through the tiniest sidewalk cracks looking for sunlight—a necessary "ingredient" for their growth.

A Powerful Force

256

Plants often push their way up through even the tiniest crack in rocks or sidewalks, sometimes breaking up those hard objects. This is one way plants have of breaking apart large rocks into much smaller pebbles and stones.

You can see this for yourself. First, get some plaster of paris from a craft or hobby shop. Soak a few bean seeds in water overnight. The next day, plant two or three of them in a plastic cup filled with potting soil. Moisten the soil thoroughly.

Mix the plaster of paris according to the package directions, until it is like a thick milkshake. Pour a layer of the mixture, about 1/2 inch (0.5 cm) thick, on top of the soil in the cup. Put the cup in a sunny location and watch what happens (if you use a clear plastic cup and plant the seeds near the sides, you will be able to look through and watch the growth process). You will probably see the developing bean plants push up and through the plaster of paris—just like weeds are able to push up and through small cracks in a sidewalk.

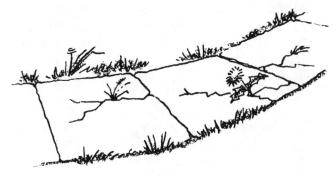

257 ◆ Hold That Mold

YOU WILL NEED:
3 slices of white bread
3 small sealable plastic bags
water
magnifying glass

Would you believe that there are millions of plants growing right in your kitchen?

What to do: Take two slices of bread and wet them lightly (don't soak them). Carefully, rub one slice across a kitchen table or countertop (do it gently so you don't tear the bread). Place the slice of bread in a plastic bag and seal it. Then take the second moistened slice and gently rub it over the surface of the kitchen floor. Put it in a second bag and seal it. Now place the third (dry) slice of bread in the third bag and seal it. Place all three bags in a closet or other dark place for a couple of days.

What happens: You find mold growing on the surfaces of the two slices of bread that were moistened, rubbed over the kitchen surfaces, and placed in the bags. There may be some mold on the "dry" slice, too (some bakeries use preservatives to keep their breads fresh longer). Examine the moldy plants with the magnifying lens, or under a microscope. Try this experiment with other types of bread (wheat, rye) or rub slices over other surfaces (fence, wall, sidewalk, tree trunk).

Why: Molds and other microscopic plants are everywhere. In order to grow they need special conditions, such as moisture, warmth, and darkness instead of light.

258 ◆ My Bud-Bud-Buddy

YOU WILL NEED:
2 packets of dry yeast
2 small, sealable plastic bags
1 teaspoon of sugar
1 cup of lukewarm water

Yeast is a plant used by cooks and bakers. The way it grows makes it a very special plant.

What to do: Put ½ cup of lukewarm water in each of the bags and add the contents of one yeast packet to each bag. Put the spoonful of sugar into the second bag. Close both bags, squeezing out as much air as possible before sealing them. Shake the bags well for a minute, then place them in a warm or sunny location.

What happens: The bag with just the water and yeast shows little change. But the bag with the water, yeast, and sugar has changed a lot. Bubbles have formed inside, and the bag is swelling up!

Why: Yeast is a plant that needs food in order to grow well. Sugar is a good food source for yeast. Yeast grows by producing one or more bumps, or buds, that break off and become new yeast plants. As it grows, the yeast also produces carbon-dioxide gas. Yeast is often added to bakery products, such as cake or bread, to make the dough rise. Without yeast, breads would be very flat.

All plants need food in order to grow. This is true for simple plants, such as yeast, and more complex plants, such as redwood trees; they all need nutrients. Without them, plants could not grow or survive.

259 Adopt a Tree

YOU WILL NEED:
string
measuring tape
plastic bags
drawing paper
pencil and crayons
your journal

Trees are some of the most beautiful plants in the world. Some are also so common that people don't even notice them. Here's an activity to help you learn more about one special tree.

What to do: Select a tree near where you live. If possible, locate a deciduous tree (one that sheds its leaves each year). The tree should be in a place that is easy to reach, because you will be visiting your tree for the next 12 months. To start, draw a picture of your tree (or photograph it) and write down in your journal any unusual markings, characteristics, or patterns you notice. Measure 3 feet (90 cm) up the tree trunk from the ground and tie a piece of string around the tree at that point. Measure the section of string to determine the circumference of the tree (how big around it is).

Collect some of the tree's leaves and save them in small plastic bags. Place a piece of paper against the bark of the tree and rub a crayon over the paper until the pattern of the bark appears. What other kinds of learning activities can you do with your "adopted" tree?

What happens: Trees change during the year. They grow, shed their leaves, grow new leaves, serve as a home for all types of animal life, and contribute to the balance of nature in your local community.

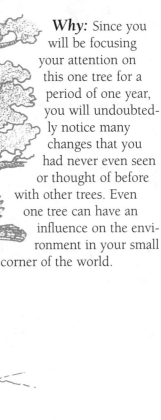

Why: Since you will be focusing your attention on this one tree for a period of one year, you will undoubtedly notice many changes that you had never even seen or thought of before with other trees. Even one tree can have an influence on the environment in your small corner of the world.

Plants Breathe, Too

YOU WILL NEED:

3 bean plants (may be grown from seed)
petroleum jelly
measuring tape or ruler
drawing paper
coloring pencils

What do you think happens to plants if there are lots of pollutants in the air? Let's find out.

What to do: Place the plants on a windowsill so they will all get the same amount of sunlight. Label the plants "A," "B," and "C." Draw a picture of each plant and measure and record its height. Rub some petroleum jelly on the top side of all the leaves on plant A and under all the leaves on plant B. Leave plant C as it is. Water the plants every so often as you normally would. Every other day, record the height of each plant and draw pictures of any changes that have taken place.

What happens: Plant C shows the most growth. Plant A shows less growth. Plant B shows little growth and begins to die.

Why: Clean air is necessary for the chemical reaction called photosynthesis (when a plant produces its own food) to occur. The air enters the plant through the stomata on the underside of the leaves. When the air is polluted or when the leaves are covered by something (such as petroleum jelly) that acts as a pollutant, photosynthesis cannot take place and the plant dies.

- The leaves of a Venus flytrap can close over an insect in less than half a second.
- The giant sequoia tree does not begin to flower until it is at least 175 to 200 years old.
- The roots of a redwood tree are capable of holding more than 130,000 gallons (494,000 liters) of water.
- There are more than 250,000 species of flowering plants in the world.
- Pacific giant kelp can grow more than 17 inches (43 cm) a day, and may reach lengths of up to 200 feet (9,000 cm).
- Bamboo may grow as much as 3 feet (90 cm) each day.
- An average apple tree will lose up to 20 quarts (19 liters) of water a day through its leaves.
- The plant life of the oceans makes up about 85% of all the greenery on the planet.
- Tree rings are a good record of earthquakes.
- In tropical rain forests, certain plants known as epiphytes grow on the highest branches of trees. They have no roots and get their water and nutrients directly from the humid air.
- A mature saguaro cactus may weigh up to 10 tons—and 80% of that weight is water.
- The largest seed in the world is the coconut.
- Lemons have more sugar in them than melons or peaches do.

I'm Impressed!

Preserve the flowers and leaves you collect by using a simple plant press. Get help to make this one.

HOT!

YOU WILL NEED:

an adult helper
use of hand or machine drill
2 sheets of plywood or fiberboard, 10 by 13 inches (25 by 33 cm)
standard size pieces of cardboard (cut from box)
white construction paper
4 bolts and 4 wingnuts

What to do: Ask an adult to drill holes (to fit your bolts) in each corner of the two sections of wood. The holes should be about 1 inch in from the top and side of each corner (drill the two boards together and the holes will be sure to match).

To use the press, put the connecting bolts through one board and lay it down so that the bolts stick upwards. Lay a piece of cardboard on top of this board. Next, place a sheet of paper on top of the cardboard, and whatever you want to press (a flower or leaves) on top of the paper. Put another sheet of paper on top of the specimen, and then other pieces of cardboard.

Repeat this process, making plant material "sandwiches," until you have a stack of several cardboard pieces. Put the second piece of plywood on top of the last cardboard piece on the stack, threading the bolts through the holes. Put a wing nut on each bolt and tighten them until you feel pressure. Then carefully tighten each bolt in turn as much as you can, putting even pressure on the stack.

The specimens will be pressed flat and will dry within a few weeks (check them occasionally if you wish). Later you may want to glue your pressed plants onto sheets of colorful construction paper and place them in paper frames from a hobby or arts and crafts store for display around your home.

What happens: The wooden press you made puts pressure on the plant specimens placed in it and keeps them flat. The pressure is gentle, but constant. Any "juices" squeezed from the plant material are absorbed by the white paper so that the plant dries out rapidly.

Why: People have been collecting and pressing plants, flowers, and leaves for many years. These pressings have been used in decorative displays and are a way of preserving some of nature's beauty long after a plant would normally die.

WONDERFUL WILDLIFE

Do you have a pet at home? Have you been to a zoo or an aquarium? Have you seen birds flying overhead, bees buzzing in the summertime, or snakes slithering through the grass? No doubt you have seen many kinds of animals wherever you live, for animals are a part of all our lives, and an important part of the world of nature, too.

About Wildlife—and You

Humans have always been fascinated by animals. We keep animals as pets and we observe animals in special places such as zoos and wildlife parks. But it is important to remember that animals are affected by the actions of humans. If we throw garbage into a stream, the fish and insects are affected; if we destroy nests and burrows during construction projects, those animals can no longer live there, and if we pollute the air, birds and, in fact, all breathing animals are affected. In other words, humans affect the survival of every living thing.

Learning about the animals in your area of the world will help you appreciate the rich variety of wildlife that surrounds you, and that look to you to help keep them safe.

263 Feathered Friends

Birds are important members of every environment and they are fun to watch. Here's how to attract more birds to your house.

YOU WILL NEED:
clean plastic milk container
scissors (with pointed tips)
an adult helper
wild birdseed
some strong string

What to do: Have an adult cut a panel from the side of the milk container, leaving a border around the opening. Tie the string tightly around the top, fill the container with some birdseed, and hang the new feeder in a nearby tree so you can see it from your window. Watch the birds that visit the feeder. What types of birds come to eat? How many, and at what time of day? Record your observations in the journal.

What happens: The feeder, if kept filled with food they like, attracts all kinds of birds. A book will help to identify the species, or types, of birds that live near you. You may learn to recognize certain individual birds that return often.

Why: Birds are affected by climate and by the availability of food. They adapt, or get used to, an environment and will stay as long as they have the food, water, and shelter they need in order to live and raise their young. Offering them clean water (bird bath), a bird house, and pieces of string and hair during nesting season are ways to encourage birds to stay nearby.

Well Fed 264

HOT!

In cold weather, birds need to eat fat to maintain their body temperature. Here's how to help.

What to do: Have an adult melt the fat or suet in a heavy pot. Then add birdseed (twice as much seed as fat) to the liquid fat and stir carefully. Let it cool and thicken overnight.

YOU WILL NEED:
fat, lard, or suet (from butcher or supermarket)
use of stove and pot
an adult helper
birdseed
tin can
nail and hammer
3 feet (90 cm) of string
can-size circle of cardboard

Carefully, using a hammer and nail, punch a small hole in the middle of the can bottom (an adult can help here, too) and the cardboard circle. Thread the string through the hole in the can and out the top. Pour the soft seed mixture into the can (if it is too liquid, you may have to seal the hole with clay or gum). When the fat has hardened, gently remove the can and push the string through the cardboard. Knot the string, then tie your seed feeder to a nearby tree, and watch the birds that visit it. (Experiment with other containers for different-shape feeders.)

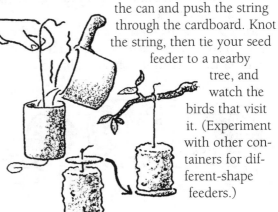

Feed Me, I'm Yours!

With a little imagination, you can create bird feeders from almost anything in your home. Here are five ideas to get you started. Place them outside, and watch what happens. How many other bird feeders can you create?

1. Cut a half circle from the plastic lid of a coffee can. Nail or tape a small board to the side of the can and put some seed inside. Put the lid back on, so that it covers the bottom half, and lay the feeder outside.

2. Cut an orange in half. Scoop out the insides and make four small holes around the edge. Tie pieces of string to the holes around the orange half, fill it with seed, and hang it in a tree or bush.

3. Tie a string to a pinecone. Fill the crevices in the cone with peanut butter and roll the cone in some birdseed. Hang the cone from a tree branch.

4. Tie some unsalted peanuts onto various lengths of string. Hang these in a tree.

5. Tie a string to the stem of an apple. Roll the apple in some fat or bacon grease and then roll it in some birdseed. Hang it from a tree branch.

Woodside Restaurant

Here's a great feeder for you to make for your feathered friends. Fill it with your own homemade nourishing treat or our super recipe for World's Greatest Birdfood (see page 215) and they will enjoy it all year long.

Find a 12- to 15-inch (30–40 cm) length of wood, about 2 inches (5 cm) square. Ask an adult to drill a number of holes in the wood with a 1 inch (2.5 cm) drill bit, staggering the holes down each side. The holes should be about 1/2 inch (2 cm) deep. Fasten an eye screw to one end of the stick and pass a long piece of strong string through it. Stuff the holes of the feeder with some sticky type of birdfood mixture, then hang the feeder in a nearby tree. Place it about 4 feet (125 cm), at least, off the ground so that the birds who come to eat will be safe from cats. Watch to see who comes to visit.

Remember to put fresh food in the holes every so often to keep your Woodside Restaurant open for business, and its feathered customers happy and coming back for more.

World's Greatest Birdfood

Home Sweet Home

This nourishing recipe will keep birds coming back to your feeder all year—but especially in the winter.

What to do: With the help of an adult, cut the suet into small pieces and melt it slowly in a large frying pan. (Be very careful of spatters; hot fat can cause bad burns.) Let the melted fat cool until it becomes solid, then reheat it again and allow the liquid fat to cool off once more.

Thoroughly mix all of the other ingredients into the soft suet. Spoon the mixture into small plastic containers and put them in the refrigerator. When the mixture is firm, spoon some of it into the feeder holes of the Woodside Restaurant or some other bird feeder. Keep the remainder of the mixture refrigerated until needed.

Note: Because of the cost or availability, you may want to experiment with different quantities or ingredients—for example, mixing together just peanut butter and sunflower seeds during the summer months, and adding the suet (for the fat that birds need) only during the wintertime.

YOU WILL NEED:
suet, from butcher or supermarket (1 cup melted)
1 cup each, chunky peanut butter, chopped nuts, sunflower seeds, and cornmeal
1 tablespoon crushed eggshells
frying pan
an adult helper
use of the stove

YOU WILL NEED:
binoculars
tweezers
magnifying glass

Some of the best "builders" in the animal kingdom are birds. Let's find out how they do it.

What to do: In late fall or early winter, take your binoculars outside to look for one or more empty bird nests. If, when you find one, it is high up, ask an adult to get it down for you. Be careful. Try to keep the nest as intact as possible and be sure that there are no eggs in the nest—that it is not still in use! At home, use tweezers to carefully separate the pieces making up the nest. Examine them closely with the magnifying glass. Make a list of what was used to build the nest.

What happens: You see the nests are constructed of many different types of materials, including twigs, grasses, straw, string, leaves, hair, feathers, etc. You will also notice that the sizes and shapes of nests vary depending on the species of bird that built it.

Why: Birds build their nests in different ways and use different materials. The construction of a nest depends largely on what material is available and how the eggs and young birds need to be protected while they are in the nest. As you continue to examine the nests of different species of birds you will notice many different variations in nest construction.

Look Ma, No Hands!

Can you imagine how difficult it is to build a nest from
things like twigs, grass and feathers that you may find lying
on the ground?

What to do: Take a walk around your neighborhood or park and locate several different bird's
nests. Look carefully at how the nests are constructed (be careful not to disturb any occupants). Using
the materials listed above (and any others you think
might help you—but no glue!), try to build a bird's
nest. Work with just your two hands and make a
round nest that has room for two or three eggs.

What happens: You discover that nest building
is not as easy as it may look. Hmmm, those birds
must be smart!

Why: Birds are able to construct their nests with
just their feet and beaks (no hands). And most
birds seem to have learned the construction process
by only seeing—and from sitting inside it—what
their parents once built!

It's amazing to think that bird's nests are some of
the most complicated homes in the animal kingdom—homes that are able to withstand bad weather and protect young birds as they grow and develop. So, the next time anyone calls you a "bird
brain," be sure to thank them for the compliment.

270 Worm World

Would you be surprised to learn that earthworms are some of the most useful animals to human life? Be prepared to be surprised.

YOU WILL NEED:

large wide-mouthed (pickle) jar

tin can

gravel or small pebbles

soil

5 or 6 earthworms (from a garden, bait shop, pet store, or garden supply store) dark construction paper

What to do: Stand the tin can in the middle of the jar. Place a layer of gravel or small pebbles about ¹/₂ inch (1.2 cm) deep on the bottom of the jar, between the can and the jar sides. Fill the jar with garden soil up to the height of the tin can. Place the worms on top of the soil. Wrap the dark construction paper around the outside of the jar to keep out the light.

Note: Check the condition of the soil every so often and moisten it as needed.

What happens: The worms will begin burrowing into the soil. After several days, they will have dug a series of tunnels. You will be able to see these tunnels by carefully removing the construction paper from the sides of the jar. (Replace the con-

struction paper after observing their work so the worms will continue to tunnel in the darkness.) You should be able to watch the worms' behavior, without harming them, for three or four weeks, but then you should put them back outside.

Why: Worms feed by taking soil through their bodies, creating tunnels as they go. These tunnels aerate the soil—providing plants with the oxygen they need to grow. If it weren't for earthworms, many varieties of plants would not be able to survive. Farmers consider earthworms some of the best "friends" they have.

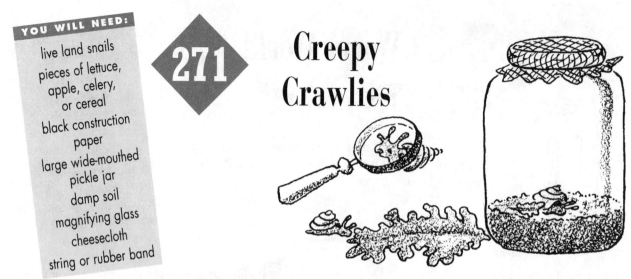

YOU WILL NEED:

live land snails
pieces of lettuce,
apple, celery,
or cereal
black construction
paper
large wide-mouthed
pickle jar
damp soil
magnifying glass
cheesecloth
string or rubber band

271 Creepy Crawlies

What do snails do? What do snails eat? How do snails travel? Here's how to discover the answers to those questions.

What to do: Find some land snails from around your home (look in the moist soil of gardens in the early morning hours). Put a 2-inch (5 cm) layer of damp soil in a large clear jar and place the snails in it. Place some cheesecloth over the jar opening and fasten it down securely with string or a rubber band to keep the occupants inside (snails can crawl up glass).

Sprinkle the soil every so often to keep it wet. Keep the jar in a cool shady place. Put in some pieces of lettuce every so often. You will be able to keep and observe the behavior of the snails for several days.

Move one or more of the snails to a sheet of black construction paper to see it better. Place a snail in the middle of the sheet and surround it with bits of feed—a slice of apple, a lettuce leaf, a piece of celery, some cereal—and watch what happens.

What happens: The snails leave trails behind them on the paper as they slowly move toward the kind of food they prefer. Did you turn one over to see how it moves over the paper?

Why: As snails travel, using only one foot that pushes them along, they produce and leave a trail of mucus behind them. This mucus protects them from sharp rocks and other harmful objects they travel over in their environment. (A snail can even travel over a razor blade without hurting itself.) Most snails enjoy eating food that has a lot of moisture, such as fresh leaves and other vegetation. That is why they are considered a pest by home gardeners.

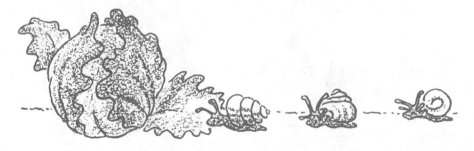

The Ants Go Marching...

272

You may not want to invite ants to your next picnic, but here's a way to invite them to your house for a short visit.

What to do: Look outside for a rotting piece of wood, which ants love, or an area with lots of ants. Scoop up into the glass jar some of the soil nearby, along with a healthy collection of ants. Put the lid on until you get the ants home. Then, cover the jar with black construction paper so that it is completely dark inside. Put some water in the cake pan, put the saucer upside down in the middle of it, and place the jar on the upturned saucer before removing the lid (the water prevents the ants from escaping from the jar). Sprinkle some sugar water over the soil and place two or three small bits of fruit inside.

What happens: The ants begin to dig tunnels in the soil. If it is dark enough, they dig their tunnels next to the sides of the glass. If you remove the black construction paper every week or so, you can see the progress they have made in their tunnel building.

Why: Many kinds of ants live in large colonies underground. Each of the ants has a job to do in order to keep the colony running smoothly. Many ants, known as "workers," are responsible for building the tunnels and the small caves that are home to the ant colony. It is in these tunnels that all the ants in a colony live, work, sleep, and eat.

Did you know that there are more than 12,000 different varieties of ants in the world?

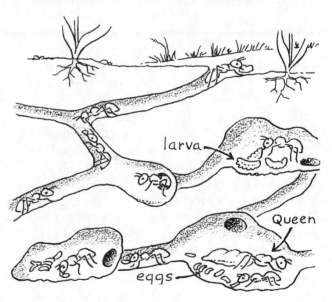

Cricket Critters

You might never have thought of keeping crickets as house pets, but in some countries, such as Japan, they are valued members of the household.

HOT!

YOU WILL NEED:

large round (oatmeal) box

an adult helper with a sharp knife

sheer nylon stocking (light color)

coloring markers or poster paints

dry soil

twigs

bottle cap

small bowl

toilet paper rolls

shredded paper

crickets (from pet store)

bran or oatmeal cereal

apple or potato slices

What to do: Draw large "windows" on the sides of the empty round box. Leave frames around the windows as shown. Have an adult cut out the windows using a sharp knife (this can be very hard to do and you might get hurt, so don't do it yourself). Remove the remaining label from the box and decorate the outside with poster paint or markers.

Place the small bowl in the "cage." Fill the bottom of the box, and the bowl, with dry soil until you can just see the rim of the bowl. Push the bottle cap down on top of the soil. Carefully, pull a nylon stocking up over the box. Put shredded paper and a toilet paper roll or two in the cage. Water the soil in the bowl, and keep it moist. Fill the bottle cap with fresh water for drinking. Put in six or seven crickets and close up the top of the stocking to keep the critters in. The crickets can be easily cared for by feeding them some bran or oatmeal cereal, keeping the bottle cap filled with fresh water, and occasionally placing a slice of apple or potato in the cage.

What happens: The crickets thrive in this miniature environment. The females lay their eggs in the moist soil of the bowl (be sure the soil is always damp). If you're lucky you'll see the cricket eggs hatch into small crickets (called nymphs) and grow into adults in about eight weeks.

Why: Crickets enjoy simple surroundings. As long as they have a constant food supply and some moisture they will thrive in almost any environment.

Note: When you get your crickets from the pet store, be sure you have both males and females. Crickets look the same, except that females have a long slender rod, called an ovipositor, protruding from their back end. They use this ovipositor to lay their eggs.

274 Web Warriors

Spiderwebs come in all shapes and sizes. Here's how you can preserve a few.

YOU WILL NEED:

clear plastic adhesive sheeting from hardware or variety store

masking tape

black construction paper

hair spray

What to do: Taking hair spray, masking tape, and black construction paper, go outside and find a spiderweb nearby (make sure the spider isn't at home). Make five rings of masking tape, sticky side outward, around the fingers of one hand. (Now you can hold the construction paper flat and vertical, and it won't fall.) Carefully, place the hand with the construction paper just behind the spiderweb. With your other hand, gently hair-spray the web from the front, so that it pushes against the construction paper.

Slowly and gently (the web is fragile), move the web stuck on the construction paper away from where it is attached. When you get home, place some sticky clear plastic sheeting over the web and construction paper around the back. Collect several different kinds of spiderwebs this way and compare them.

Note: This takes practice, so don't get discouraged if everything doesn't work out quite right the first time around.

What happens: When you use the hair spray, the spiderweb is pushed against the construction paper and sticks to it. The sticky plastic sheeting seals the web against the paper. If the sheeting covers the back of the construction paper as well, the specimen is airtight, so it is preserved and doesn't get damaged.

Why: Spiderwebs are as varied as the number of spiders in the world. Spiders use their webs for homes and to help them collect the food they need to survive. When insects and other tiny animals become trapped in the threads of a spiderweb, they are food for the web's owner. Spiders also "wrap" trapped insects to eat later.

Did you know that a spiderweb, in the early morning with dew glistening on its threads, is considered one of the most beautiful sights in nature?

275 Net Gain

Here's a handy insect net to help you capture some of the bugs that fly or jump by.

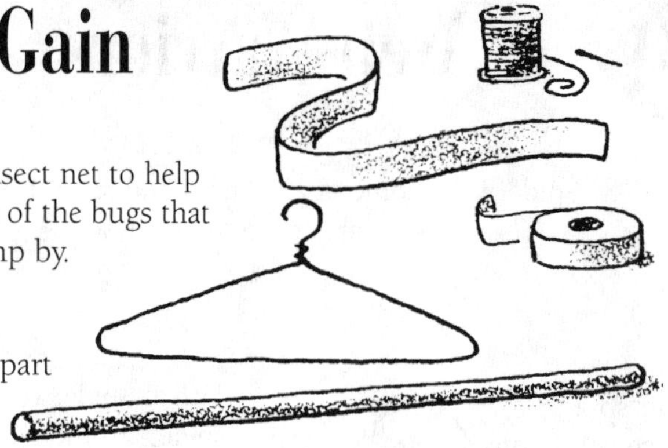

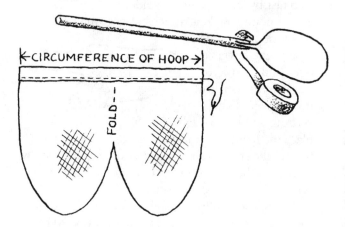

What to do: Shape the triangle part of the hanger into a circle, and straighten the hook. Tape the straightened hook to the end of the pole with the duct tape.

Using the measuring tape, measure the circumference (distance around) the wire circle. Cut the nylon netting into the shape shown here, making the straight edge the same length as the measurement around the wire loop. Sew the cotton strip to the straight edge of the net, and then sew the side seams. Attach the net to the hoop by folding the cotton strip over the wire frame and sewing it to itself.

Use your insect net to collect various types of bugs, but stay away from bees or wasps or you could be stung! When you catch something, twist the handle quickly to "close" the net and trap the insect inside. (You may have to practice with the net awhile to "close" it.)

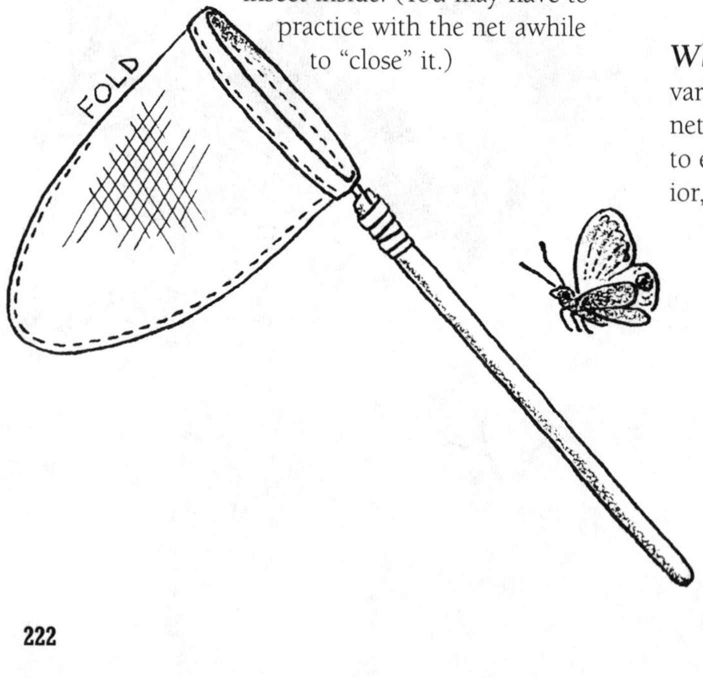

←CIRCUMFERENCE OF HOOP→

FOLD

FOLD

What happens: You'll be able to capture a wide variety of flying insects with your nature collector's net. You may want to keep some insects a few days to examine them—noting their body shapes, behavior, and what they eat—before releasing them again.

Mealworm Magic

276

Here's an animal you don't think about much, but you can keep in your home for a good while and maybe see some strange things.

YOU WILL NEED:

mealworms, from any pet store (they usually come in large or small sizes)

plastic shoe box (from variety or department store)

bran

flour

bread

apples

What to do: Fill the plastic shoe box about two-thirds full with a mixture of bran, flour, and small pieces of bread. Place 20 to 25 mealworms in the box and put on the cover. Lift the cover every few days, or have an adult drill several small holes in the lid to let some air in. Keep the box in a warm location—between 75° and 80°F (24° and 26°C). Put in a slice of apple and replace it with a fresh piece every few days.

What happens: That depends on how long you keep and watch your mealworms and just how old they are.

Why: The mealworm is the larval stage (part of the life cycle) of the darkling beetle. The larvae, which are young mealworms, grow for about six months. They then turn into the pupae, a stage which lasts for about three weeks. Afterwards, the adult beetles emerge from the cocoon. The cycle is then repeated (male and female beetles mate, eggs are laid, the eggs hatch into mealworms, the mealworms turn into pupae, the pupae turn into adult beetles). You can watch each stage of insect growth (egg, larvae, pupae, adult) by looking through the sides of the plastic box or carefully sifting through the bran mixture with your fingers. The bran provides the nourishment

these animals need, and the apple slices provide the necessary moisture.

Mealworms are raised primarily to serve as a food source for other animals (lizards and salamanders love them). They are a big part of many environments, living deep within the soil. By adding to the bran mixture and replacing dried-out apple slices, you can keep your "colony" of mealworms for some time. Later, you may want to release them to a new home, a warm and moist area near a rotting log, for example.

Bee Home, Be Careful

Bee stings can be dangerous, but bees are important to the environment. Here's how to help them survive.

YOU WILL NEED:

25 large drinking straws
masking tape
modeling clay
string
an adult helper
(optional)

What to do: Gather about 25 drinking straws. Plug up one end of each straw with modeling clay. Mix up the straws so that some plugged ends face one way and some the other. Tape the bundle together tightly. With string or tape, fasten it sideways (horizontally) underneath a windowsill, rain gutter, or the roof overhang of your house (if high up, have an adult help you place the straw bundle). The bundle must be in a sunny location. You may want to place bundles in several places outdoors.

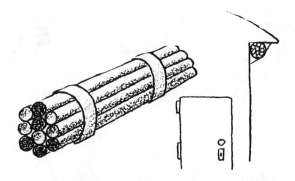

What happens: Bees may move into their new "home" and set up housekeeping. You'll see them coming and going.

   Note: Be careful not to interfere with them, or you might get stung.

Why: A bee's nest is full of small cells and tunnels. They use these to care for their young and to store the honey they make. Your "straw hive" offers the bees a place that is very similar to their regular hives. However, depending on where you live, the time of the year (early spring is best), and the type of bees that live in your area, you may or may not be able to attract bees to your nests. Several varieties of bees are very particular about where they live.

Sea Shrimp at the Seashore

YOU WILL NEED:

brine shrimp eggs
(from a pet store)

kosher or non-iodized salt

2-quart pot or container

water

teaspoon

medicine dropper

magnifying glass or microscope

aged tap water
(see below)

Brine shrimp, though tiny, are some of the most amazing animals! Let's grow some.

What to do: Fill the pot with 2 quarts of water and allow it to sit for 3 days, stirring it occasionally. (Most city water has chlorine in it, which would kill the shrimp. By letting it "age" for a while, the chlorine gas can escape from the water.) Dissolve 5 teaspoons of non-iodized salt into the water. Add ½ teaspoon of brine shrimp eggs to the saltwater and place the pot in a warm spot. Use the medicine dropper to remove a few eggs from the water, and observe them with your magnifying glass or microscope. Examine a drop of water every day. You can draw a series of illustrations in your journal to record the growth of your brine shrimp.

What happens: The brine shrimp eggs begin to hatch in about two days. They will continue to grow in the water until they reach their adult stage. You can watch this growth process over a period of many days.

Why: The brine shrimp eggs purchased at a pet store are the fertilized eggs of very tiny animals known as brine shrimp. The eggs you buy are dried so that they can be stored for very long peri-ods of time (especially when kept in a dry place). When these eggs are placed in saltwater, however, they "wake up" and begin to grow. Although they are very small you can watch them grow for many days.

Note: Brine shrimp eggs are sold as food for aquarium fish.

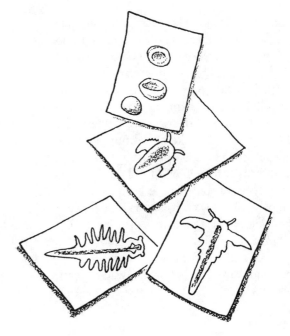

279 Can't See Me!

In order to survive, smaller animals sometimes need to hide from larger ones. One way that certain animals avoid being seen, and protect themselves from being eaten, is to use a protective coloring as camouflage. These animals match their body color to the colors in their environment so that they "blend in" and almost disappear.

What to do: Ask your helper or friend to mix up all 200 toothpicks and to spread them out over a certain area of grass (your front lawn or a section of a park, for example). The area should be about 25 yards, or meters, square. As you pick up the toothpicks, have your partner time you for 1 minute, 2 minutes, and 3 minutes. Put the found toothpicks aside in bunches each time.

What happens: After several minutes, you probably notice that you are finding and picking up more red toothpicks than green toothpicks. Later, you can count the red and the green toothpicks you found, and record in your journal the exact number of each color you found during each time period.

Why: Because the green toothpicks were closer to the color of the test environment (the green grass) than the red ones, the green ones were harder to see and find. Animals that are able to blend into their environment have a better chance for survival than those who have colors that make them easy to see. The ability of animals to match the colors of their surroundings, or use camouflage, helps them to protect themselves. Green lizards are able to hide better in an area with lots of green shrubs and plants than would red or yellow lizards. Their predators (animals that hunt and would eat them) have a more difficult time locating them.

YOU WILL NEED:
100 green and 100 red toothpicks (from party store or large grocery)
a helper
watch or stopwatch

Find Me If You Can

Camouflage is the ability of an organism (plant or animal) to blend with its surroundings. In doing so, the organism is able to escape detection and "hide" in certain parts of its environment.

The katydid, for example, is an insect that looks like a leaf, making it hard to see in a plant or tree. Because of their dull color, certain types of caterpillars look like bird droppings when they roll up, so they do it when danger is near and avoid being eaten by birds and other enemies. Some types of spiders have features that look like the parts of a flower. By sitting on a flower, they can avoid being a predator's next meal. Some desert plants, called lithops, resemble small rocks in shape and color and so avoid being chewed for their moisture. It is only when water is easily available that they bloom to spread their pollen.

Mimicry, the ability of one species to imitate the coloring or behavior of another, is also a form of protection. Some small animals or insects are unpleasant or dangerous, so larger animals avoid them. To survive, the other animals and insects "copy" the colors and body movements of the dangerous ones. By pretending to be what they're not, these "copycats" are left alone and live longer lives. One type of fly, for example, looks like a dangerous and poisonous wasp; one very tasty butterfly looks just like a bad-tasting moth; and one caterpillar has body markings that make it look like the eyes of a giant bird.

How many of nature's copycats can you name?

280 ◆ I'm All Yours!

"Adopt" an endangered animal. Write to:
The American Association of
Zoological Parks and Aquariums
4550 Montgomery Ave., Suite 940N
Bethesda, MD 20814
and ask about their animal adoption program. (Ask a parent first.) For a few dollars, you will be assigned an endangered animal and receive a photograph and a fact sheet about your "adoptee." The money you send will be used to feed and care for the animal.

Share this project with your teacher and classmates. By collecting money or contributing small amounts each, your entire class can adopt an endangered animal and learn about it.

281 ◆ Track Record

Animals leave tracks wherever they go. Here's how you can record those tracks.

YOU WILL NEED:

large-size milk carton, cut
into 1- inch (2.5 cm)
square strips (remove top
and bottom)
old bowl or pot
plaster of paris (from craft
or hobby stores)
water

What to do: Find an animal track or print in some soft dirt or mud (it can be a cat or dog track, or maybe a deer or some other wild animal in your area). Put a milk carton square around the track and push it partway down into the soil. (Be careful not to disturb the track.)

Mix the plaster of paris and water together in an old bowl or pot according to the directions on the package until it is like a thick milkshake). Pour it into the mold up to the top of the cardboard strip. Wait for about an hour until the plaster cast hardens. Remove the cast from the ground print and take off the cardboard strip.

What happens: You now have a model or cast of the animal's foot that made the print. (The cast is a raised model of the print.) You may want to make casts of several different animal tracks for display.

Why: When animals walk on damp ground, they leave impressions of their feet, or footprints, just as we do. By studying these tracks, we can tell a lot about the animal, and how and even why it was moving the way it was. If the track is very deep, the animal may have been very heavy. If the track is deeper at the front of the print than at the back, the animal was walking rapidly (or even running). If the depths of the four tracks (of a four-footed animal) are uneven, the animal may be limping from an old injury or may be hurt.

Sound Off

282

You may be surprised to discover the wide variety of animal sounds you can find in your neighborhood.

What to do: Tape the microphone handle to the end of the pole or broom (be sure not to put tape over the microphone itself). Go outside on a clear and calm day and place the microphone near one or more wildlife homes (a bird's nest, beehive or wasp's nest, for example). It helps if you know the animals are at home, but be careful.

You can either hold the microphone on the pole near the animal's home, or stick the pole into the ground. Take care doing this so that you do not disturb any birds or animals nearby. (It may be a good idea to have an adult along in case a "star" or friend nearby gets upset.) Turn on the microphone and record the sounds and noises the animals make.

Don't forget to take some "field notes" for your nature journal about the types or numbers of animals you see and have been able to "catch" on tape.

What happens: Your nature recordings will help you discover the many different sounds that the animals in your neighborhood make.

Note: It's important to make your recordings on non-windy days, since microphones often pick up wind sounds that "mask" the sounds animals may make.

Collect the neighborhood animal sounds and combine them with photographs, illustrations, and "field notes" on the behavior and habits of the animal. This data can be collected into an attractive notebook or display box for sharing with friends and family.

Why: Animals such as birds and insects make all different kinds of sounds as they go about their daily chores. Some of the sounds they make are used to "talk" to others of their species, some are for protection, some to help locate mates, and some sounds they make can call others to a food source or tell them where food nearby can be found.

Did You Know?

283

The roundworm lives for only twelve days; the lake sturgeon (a fish) can live more than 150 years.

- Crickets have hearing organs in their knees.
- An ant can lift 50 times its own weight—with its mouth.
- The common snail has close to 10,000 teeth—all on its tongue.
- A frog must close its eyes in order to swallow.
- Texas horned toads can squirt blood from the corners of their eyes.
- The tumbler pigeon can do backward somersaults while flying.

- The praying mantis is the only insect that can turn its head without moving any part of its body.
- If it were possible to weigh all of the land animals on the surface of the Earth, ants would be 10 to 15% of the total weight.
- Scientists have determined that the common housefly hums in the musical key of F.
- To make one pound (2.2 kg) of honey, bees must collect nectar from approximately 2 million flowers.
- Most mammals live for about 1_ billion heartbeats.
- A mosquito has 47 teeth.

ECOSYSTEMS NEAR AND FAR

An ecological system, ecosystem for short, is made up of organisms that live together. These ecosystems include plants, animals, and a combination.

About Ecosystems

All living things that come together in one place make up a community. Plant or animal, community members depend on one another for survival. Some animals eat plants, some plants live off other plants, and some animals eat other animals. All living things are part of one or more food chains—energy and materials are passed down the line from one living thing to another in the form of food.

While living things depend on one another, human life needs a variety of plants and animals in order to survive. Understanding how all living things rely on each other is an important part of nature study. The experiments in this chapter will allow you to journey into the ecosystems that exist where you are.

◆284 Life in a Square

You may be surprised to discover a wide variety of life—right in your own backyard!

What to do: Go into your yard or a nearby park. Push the pencils into the soil in a 1-foot (30 cm) square pattern. Tie string around them, making a miniature "boxing ring" on the ground. Get down and look closely inside the square. Make a note of all the different types of plants you see there, as well as the varieties of animal life and their behavior as they travel (jump, crawl, slither) through it. Go back regularly over several weeks to observe and record what you see.

What happens: You have a long list of natural life that lives in or has passed through your marked-off square. In fact, you are probably amazed at the many different forms of life that you found in just that very small space!

Why: Life is everywhere! Take the time to stop, see what is going on around you, and wonder at all the life forms that share the environment you call home. You may discover animals and plants, living in your own backyard, that you never knew existed!

◆285

Houses and Homes

Where do animals live? What kind of dwelling places or "houses" do they call home? Let's take a look around.

What to do: With an older friend or adult, take a walking "field trip" around your town or neighborhood. Look for places where animals live. These may be nests, burrows, tree trunks, ant hills, under rocks, in and near logs, holes in the ground, even cracks in the sidewalk. If you have a camera, take a photograph of each habitat, or place where an animal lives, or draw a picture of it. Later, name the animals and match their pictures with the pictures of their "houses." An older brother or sister, parent, or high school student might enjoy helping you learn the scientific names of the animals to add to your journal or field trip report.

What happens: You will be amazed to discover the wide variety of animals living in homes in and near your own house. You will probably discover that you've found many more than you thought you would.

Why: Animals are everywhere: from high in a tree to far under the ground. The homes that animals live in are designed to protect their young, shelter the animals from the weather, help them defend against their enemies, and are located where they can find the food they need. In fact, aren't those the same reasons why humans live where they do?

Happy Habitat

How would you like to be the creator of your own miniature ecosystem?

YOU WILL NEED:

2- or 3-liter plastic soda bottle

an adult helper with a knife

pebbles

aquarium charcoal

soil

water

small plants (see below)

small animals (see below)

string or rubber band

piece of lightweight cloth

What to do: Have an adult cut off the top of the plastic soda bottle. Cover the bottom of the bottle with a layer of small pebbles mixed with bits of aquarium charcoal. Put in a layer of soil about twice as deep as the first layer. Sprinkle the soil with just enough water to keep it moist (you may have to add water occasionally.

Place several plants, such as mosses, ferns, lichens, or liverworts (available from garden or aquarium shops), into the soil. You could sprinkle a few grass seeds on the soil, too. Place several rocks or pieces of wood into the bottom of the bottle.

Some small land animals (such as snails, earthworms, a tiny turtle or frog) can also be added. Cover the top (to allow the humidity to build up), then open and ventilate (allowing some fresh air in) by placing some lightweight cloth over the top and holding it on with a rubber band or tying it there with a string. Keep the bottle out of direct sunlight and be sure to feed the occupants of your habitat regularly.

What happens: Your miniature ecosystem will grow and flourish as long as you add some moisture occasionally. If you put animals in the bottle, check with your local pet store for an appropriate food supply.

Why: This ecosystem is similar to a wetlands or woodlands ecosystem in nature. Plants and animals are able to survive because they are dependent on each other and because all of their "needs" (air, water, food) are provided in their immediate environment.

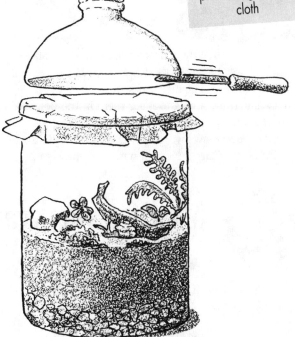

A Simple Community

287

Here's how you can construct a simple and inexpensive aquarium in your own home.

What to do: Wash and rinse out the large jar thoroughly. Wash and rinse the gravel and sand, too. Washed (clean) sand can be obtained at an aquarium store. Place a ½ inch (1 cm) layer of gravel and a 1 inch (3 cm) layer of sand on the bottom of the jar. Fill the jar almost to the top with tap water and allow the jar to sit undisturbed for three to four days so that the chlorine that is in the water can evaporate.

Get two or three aquatic plants (such as elodea) from an aquarium store and place them in the bottom of the jar (make sure they are firmly rooted in the sand). Place a few, two or three, goldfish and also snails in the jar. Place a piece of wire screening over the top of the jar—to keep in the snails!

What happens: This miniature environment will be able to sustain itself for some time (so long as you put in some fish food occasionally). The plants and animals will thrive for a good while, but you may need to obtain an inexpensive air pump later to keep your aquarium going.

Why: Plants and animals need each other in order to survive. In an aquatic environment, such as your aquarium, the plants provide necessary oxygen for the fish and snails. The fish provide nourishment (with their wastes) for the plants (and the eventual growth of small plants such as algae). The algae serve as a food source for the snails.

When properly maintained, this miniature ecosystem will be "in balance."

YOU WILL NEED:

large (commercial-size) mayonnaise jar (from your school cafeteria or a local restaurant)

gravel

washed sand (from an aquarium store)

aquatic plants (see below)

guppies or goldfish

water snails

wire screen

288 My Own Backyard

Did you know that your backyard can qualify as a nature preserve—a place where plants and animals are protected?

The National Wildlife Federation has what is known as a Wildlife Habitat Program. If you ask, they will provide you with information and details about establishing your backyard as a wildlife preserve. Then, for a small fee, you can send them a plan of action and they will certify your backyard as an official Backyard Wildlife Habitat.

For more information write:
National Wildlife Federation
Backyard Wildlife Habitat Program
1412 16th Street, NW
Washington, DC 20036

Bags of Bananas

Decomposition, the natural decay of dead organisms, is a continuing process in nature. You can learn about it by doing this experiment in your own home.

What to do: Label each one of the four bags: "A," "B," "C," and "D." In Bag "A" put several slices of banana; in Bag "B" put several slices of banana and a packet of yeast; in Bag "C" put several slices of banana and some water; and in Bag "D" put several slices of banana, some water, and a packet of yeast. Seal all the bags and place them on a sunny windowsill for a few days.

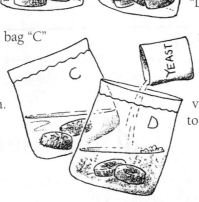

What happens: The banana slices in bag "A" darken slightly. The yeast in bag "B" grows very slowly, but there is some change in the banana slices. The slices in bag "C" show some decay and some mold. The banana slices in bad "D" show the most decay. In that bag, the banana is breaking down. The liquid is bubbling, and carbon-dioxide gas is forming and expanding the bag. The bag may pop open and release a powerful odor into the room.

Why: When plant and animal life die, they serve as a valuable food source for micro-organisms. These micro-organisms feed on the dead materials and break them down. Yeast is made up of millions of such micro-organisms that grow under the right conditions: when moisture, food, and warmth are present. As they grow, the micro-organisms in bag "D" break down the banana slices.

The same process takes place in nature. As a result, micro-organisms can reduce large animals and plants into valuable nutrients for the soil. In other words, when an organism dies it provides what other organisms need in order to live.

290

It's Absolutely Degrading!

YOU WILL NEED:

slice of fruit (apple, orange, peach)

slice of bread

piece of lettuce

plastic or foam cup

piece of aluminum foil

shovel

water

ice cream sticks

pencil or felt-tip marker

Do you know what the word "biodegradable" means? Here's how you can find out about this continuing process and how it works.

What to do: Find a place in your or a friend's yard where you can dig some small holes for this experiment. Dig five holes, each about 8 to 12 inches (20-30 cm) deep. Place the fruit slice in one hole, the bread in another hole, the lettuce in another, the cup in the fourth hole, and the foil in the last hole. Cover each hole with soil and water each one thoroughly. Place a marker stick labeled with the words "slice," "bread," "lettuce," "cup," or "foil" (or anything else you are testing for biodegradability) at the location of each hole. After 4 to 5 weeks, return to the filled holes and dig up what you buried.

What happens: The fruit, bread and lettuce have probably "broken down" or disintegrated (in fact, you may find it difficult to even locate these

items). The rate at which these items have biodegraded depends on the amount of moisture in the soil and the soil's temperature. The cup and the piece of foil, however, will be whole and easy to locate.

Why: When organic matter (fruit, bread lettuce, even dead plants and animals) is left on or in the soil, it starts to "break down." This natural (and constant) biodegrading process caused by micro-organisms releases nutrients into the soil so that other organisms can grow. The cup and the foil are not biodegradable, the micro-organisms can't affect them, so they will never decompose. Landfills are filled with lots of non-biodegradable materials that take up valuable space without returning anything to the environment.

291

Did You Know?

- Americans consume about 55 million tons of food from the oceans each year, and dump 90% of their garbage into landfills.
- Homeowners in the United States use ten times more toxic chemicals per acre (on their gardens and lawns) than do farmers.
- Each year, more than 27 million acres (10.8 million hectares) of tropical rain forest are destroyed—an area about the size of the state of Ohio, or of Iceland.
- Although rain forests cover only about 6% of the Earth's surface, they contain more than half of all the plant and animal species.
- The rain forests of the Amazon region produce about 40% of the world's oxygen.

NATURE PROBLEMS TO SOLVE

How we care for the Earth and its inhabitants today will have a big impact on the world we live in twenty or fifty years from now. It will determine the kinds of food, recreation, and quality of life available to us in the years to come. Becoming a conservator (a caretaker) of the Earth is important for every man, woman, and child.

About Nature's Problems

We are faced today with many problems that affect the way we live and the ways in which our plants and our animal friends live, too. Air and water pollution, toxins and trash, and the destruction of the ozone layer (which filters out the harmful rays of the sun) may someday threaten all our lives.

These problems are not simple ones, and they require more than simple solutions. But if we care about our environment, and understand how we and the animals and plants must all exist side by side in order to survive, then we need to start now to work together to preserve nature.

Preserving nature won't be easy. It will take lots of planning and people working together to ensure a natural and healthy life for ourselves and for our biological neighbors. The experiments in this chapter will alert you to some of the problems we face, and suggest what you and your friends can do to help preserve our fragile environment.

A Plethora of Pollution

Pollution can take many forms. Some of it can be seen, but many types that we don't see are just as dangerous

What to do: Label the four jars "A," "B," "C," or "D." Prepare each jar as follows: fill the jar halfway with aged tap water (see page 00), put in a ½ inch (1 cm) layer of pond soil, add 1 teaspoon of plant fertilizer, then fill the jar the rest of the way with pond water and algae. Allow the jars to sit in a sunny location or windowsill for 2 weeks.

Next, treat each separate jar as follows: in jar "A" add 2 tablespoons of detergent; in jar "B" add enough motor oil to cover the surface; in jar "C" add ½ cup of vinegar; and leave jar "D" just as it is. Allow the jars to sit for 4 weeks more.

What happens: With the addition of the detergent, motor oil, and vinegar to the first three jars, the healthy growth that took place in the jars during the first two weeks of the experi-ment has severely changed. In fact, those jars now probably show little or no growth taking place, while the organisms in jar "D" continue to grow.

Why: Detergent, motor oil, and vinegar are pollu-tants that prevent organisms from obtaining the nutrients and oxygen they need to continue grow-ing. The detergent shows what happens when large qualities of soap are released into an area's water; the motor oil shows what happens to organisms after an oil spill; and the vinegar shows what can happen when high levels of acids are added to an ecosystem such as a pond or stream. When indus-try, factories, homeowners, and other consumers put these and other kinds of pollutants into streams, rivers, and other sources or water, it can seriously affect and even destroy the plants and animals that live there.

Eggs Over Easy

Pollution is a problem all over the world. Let's take a look at one specific pollution problem: oil

What to do: Label the four bags "A," "B," "C," or "D." Fill each bag with ½ cup of water and ½ cup of motor oil. Place a hard-boiled egg in each bag. Remove the egg from bag "A" after 15 minutes; remove the egg from bag "B" after 30 minutes; remove the egg from bag "C" after 60 minutes; and remove the egg from bag "D" after 120 minutes. Each time you remove an egg from a bag, carefully open and peel off the egg shell.

What happens: The eggs in the oil-polluted water the longest showed the most pollution. The egg in bag "D," for example, had more oil inside its shell than the bag "A" egg.

Why: When an oil tanker accident spills oil into the water, the oil slick that forms affects all manner of living things. The oil sticks to the bodies and surfaces of birds, plants, fish , and other aquatic creatures and prevents them from doing what they do naturally. (Birds cannot use their wings or fly, fish cannot breathe, and plants cannot carry out the process of photosynthesis.) The longer the oil remains on the organism, the more damaging it is. Many living things die as a result of oil spills.

Oil Change

Repeat the "Eggs Over Easy" experiment opposite, but this time also put ½ cup of liquid detergent into each bag. Shake each bag gently and allow it to stand for the designated time. Notice what effect the liquid soap has on the pollution of each hard-boiled egg.

For another variation, put the ½ cup of detergent into each bag just before you remove the eggs. While the soap might remove some of the oil pollution from the outside of the eggs, does it have any effect on the eggs themselves?

Not in My Air!

YOU WILL NEED:
petroleum jelly
3 index cards
masking tape

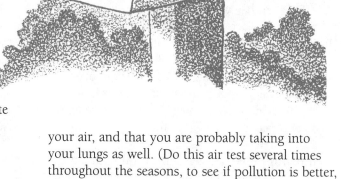

Do you know if there is air pollution in your area, and how much? Here's a way to find out

What to do: Smear a thin layer of petroleum jelly on one surface of each of the three index cards. Tape two of the cards in different locations outside. For example, one card can be taped to the side of your house and the other hung from the tree branch in your backyard. Or, one card can be taped to a mailbox and the other to a garage door. The third card should be taped someplace inside your home. Check the cards every week or so to see how much particulate matter (dust, odd bits and pieces of material, pollen, and other small particles that float in the air) have collected on them.

What happens: After some time (depending on where you live) you will find that the two cards placed outside have collected a good amount of particulate matter (the one placed inside the house may have considerably fewer particles on it). The amount of matter collected on the two outside cards indicates the amount of pollution that is in

your air, and that you are probably taking into your lungs as well. (Do this air test several times throughout the seasons, to see if pollution is better, or worse, at some times than at other times.)

Why: Air pollution is a serious concern in many industrial areas. Factories, trucks and cars, and incinerators are just a few of the causes of air pollution. The polluting particles, often very small, can affect the environment nearby and far away (blown great distances by the wind). The pollutants settle on the ground and on buildings, and sometimes we inhale them into our lungs. Your cards will show you how serious the air pollution is where you live.

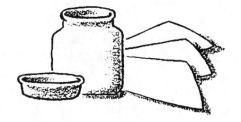

A Band of Bands

Here's another experiment to demonstrate how much air pollution is in your area.

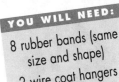

What to do: Bend each coat hanger into a rectangular shape. (Some hangers are harder to shape than others; you may need help with this.) Slide two rubber bands onto one end of a coat hanger and two over the other end. The rubber bands should be fairly tight to be sure to stay on. Do this for both hangers. Hang one of the coat hangers outside (in a tree, for example), making sure it is out of the sun. Place the second hanger in a plastic bag and seal it. Keep it in your room.

What happens: Depending on the amount of air pollution in your local area, the rubber bands on the hanger hung outside start to deteriorate. They begin to decompose, split, or break apart.

Why: Pollution in the air can affect all kinds of things, even those made of rubber, so the condition of the rubber bands on the hanger placed outside is a good indication of the severity of this problem in your area. If the rubber bands break down in only a few weeks, then it probably means that there is a great deal of air pollution in your area. If, however, the rubber bands take longer to break down, there may not be as much pollution. You'll also notice that the rubber bands on the coat hanger that you kept inside the plastic bag showed no breakdown at all. This shows what can happen when air pollution is reduced or eliminated.

Acid from the Skies

297

YOU WILL NEED:

3 jars with lids
masking tape
marking pen
lemon juice
water
3 growing bean plants
tablespoon

Acid rain is a danger to plant life in many parts of the world. Here's why.

What to do: Label the three jars and put ½ cup of lemon juice in each, then add water as follows: jar "A," add ½ cup of water; jar "B," add ½ cup of water; jar "C," add ½ cup of water. Label the three bean plants A, B and C, and place them on a sunny windowsill. Every day, water each plant with four tablespoons of the lemon juice solution assigned to it (plant "A" gets solution "A").

What happens: Plant "A" shows the effects of the "acid rain" first. The leaves start to curl and shrivel. Its growth slows down or stops, and it starts looking sickly. The other two bean plants eventually show these problems, too.

Why: Acid rain is caused by air pollutants pumped into the atmosphere through the smokestacks of factories and industry. The pollutants gather in dense clouds and fall back to earth when it rains. The pollutants, which are acidic like the lemon juice, build up in the soil and affect the growth of plant life (like the lemon juice solutions did to your plants). The more acidic the rain (like solution "A"), the sooner the plant is affected. Over time, the plants will die; and new plants won't be able to grow because of the highly

That Cookie Is "Mine"

298

When resources such as coal are taken from the ground, does it affect the local environment?

YOU WILL NEED:

2 chocolate chip cookies
use of freezer
sunny window
toothpicks
a clock or stopwatch

What to do: Put one cookie in the freezer for an hour, and the other in a sunny window. Then, pretending you are a coal miner, take a toothpick and "mine" as much hard "coal" (chocolate chips) from the cold cookie as you can for four minutes. Then stop, and try for four minutes more to dig the soft chips out of the cookie left in the window. How many chips can you remove from each in four minutes?

What happens: You find it hard to "mine" the chips and, in both cases, probably had to destroy or alter the "landscape" of the cookie in order to get chips out. You also notice that it is easier to "mine" hard chips than to remove soft ones.

Why: The hard and soft chips in the cookies represent two basic types of coal: anthracite (hard) coal and bituminous (soft) coal. When coal is mined, it can damage the surrounding area. Over several years, a good deal of harm can be done to the environment. It is often difficult or impossible to reverse the damage done by mining, just as it would be difficult to repair your cookies after removing the chocolate chips.

Gumming Up the Works

Oil spills are dangerous to the environment, so we are always looking for ways to prevent them, and to contain them when they do happen. How? Try using bubble gum to contain your own home-grown oil spill!

What to do: Put a piece of chunk-style bubble gum in the freezer and leave it overnight. Fill the pie plate halfway with water. Carefully release about 10 drops of oil into the middle of the water (use a toothpick to pull the oil-spill drops together). Take the bubble gum from the freezer and ask an adult to grate it into small strips onto a sheet of paper. Carefully, lift the sheet and sprinkle the grated gum onto the oil spill. Let a little of it fall into the water as well. Wait for about thirty minutes.

What happens: The gum begins to absorb the oil in the water. Depending on the amount of gum you sprinkled into the oil, all or most of the spill will be absorbed. The gum strips that fell on the water don't absorb anything.

Why: Gum consists of a type of particle known as a non-polar molecule. A non-polar molecule will absorb another type of non-polar molecule. Water, however, is made of polar molecules. Thus, the gum (which is non-polar) will not absorb the water (which is polar), but will absorb the oil (which is also non-polar). So, in order to contain or absorb oil spills in the ocean, it is necessary to put a non-polar absorbing material on the spill. In this way the oil is absorbed by the material, but the sea water is not. The material and the oil spill can then be skimmed or pumped from the surface of the water.

Did You Know?

- The average American family produces about 100 pounds (45 kg) of trash and garbage every week.
- According to some scientists, more than 99% of all the plant and animal species that have ever lived are now extinct.
- In California alone, more than 200 million tons of pesticides are used every year.
- In the Imperial Valley in California, there is a power plant that burns about 900 tons of cow manure daily.
- Every year, landfills in the United States are crammed with 24 million tons of leaves and grass clippings that could have been composted and recycled for use in gardens.
- By recycling a ton of paper, we can save close to 10 cubic feet (.28 cubic m) of landfill space—and 17 trees!
- Every year, humans add six billion tons of carbon dioxide to the atmosphere. Most of this comes from burning fossil fuels, such as coal and oil.

Making a Difference

Kids can and do make a difference! When you and your friends, classmates, or other neighborhood kids take an interest in preserving nature, we can all work together to care for the plants, animals, and environments that are part of our world. Sometimes it may mean putting up a bird feeder in your backyard, picking up litter along the side of a road, or writing to groups and organizations for information and brochures on what you can do to help. All our efforts are important, because if we don't take care of nature, who will?

A group called Renew America collects stories about people and groups who are working to preserve the environment. You may be interested in learning about some of the nature activities that kids all across the country are participating in— true stories about kids who are making a difference. If so, write to them and ask for information:
Renew America
Suite 710
1400 16th St., NW
Washington, DC 20036

YOU'RE ON THE AIR

Yes! You're definitely on the air in this chapter. You'll learn about the principles of flight, or Bernoulli's Law. Once you understand this, you'll know what keeps aircraft in the air.

About Air and Air Travel

Besides constructing many types of airfoils, or models of an airplane wing, you'll learn about air currents and how they circulate around and act on a plane's surface. This circulation of air, both fast and slow, lifts the airplane up into the upper atmosphere.

In addition, you'll construct toy helicopters, rotary motors, flying propellers and real cardboard plane models that fly.

The simple everyday materials needed are explained clearly, but if you have any trouble measuring and cutting out parts, get help.

With a few simple materials, and a little effort, you'll be on the air in no time.

Ruler's Uprising

302

This is one ruler that will be uplifted, even do a back flip! And it's all due to Bernoulli's Principle.

What to do: Place the cardboard strip on the ruler so that it is touching one end and extends toward the middle. Push the strip upward a bit to form a slight arch, or curve, about an inch (1.5 cm) in height. Tape both ends of the strip to the ruler.

Place the ruler on a table and balance it on the pencil. The ruler should extend about 3 inches (8 cm) off the edge of the table.

Now, blow a steady stream of air over the top of the cardboard strip and down the length of the ruler. If nothing happens, or if the ruler just moves down the table on the pencil, adjust the balance point of the ruler on the pencil and try again.

What happens: The ruler rises, springs up and does a back flip.

Why: Bernoulli's Principle is used when a plane lifts into the air. The same principle applies to our cardboard wing, or airfoil, taped to the ruler.

The air traveling over an airplane or cardboard wing has to travel farther and faster, so the pressure over the wing is less. Because the flow of air is slower on the wing's flat underside, it produces greater pressure and forces, or pushes, the aircraft upward.

Blowhard

303

Blow hard and recreate Bernoulli's Principle of Liquid Pressure. Simulate, or copy, an airplane's wing in this simple but uplifting experiment.

What to do: Place one end of the paper just below your lower lip and blow hard over the top of it.

What happens: The paper rises and flaps in the air.

Why: Again, a fast-moving flow of air passes over the top of the paper, producing lower pressure, while the slower air flow beneath the paper causes greater pressure. The difference causes lift and pushes the strip of paper upward.

Let's Wing It!

304

Do you love experiments? This one's a breeze!
Design an airplane wing, or airfoil, and see how it reacts
to a rapid air stream.

What to do: Prepare two pieces of notebook paper, about 4 by 5 inches (11 by 14 cm). (You can also cut a sheet of typing paper into quarters, use two now, and keep the other two quarters for the next experiment.) Keep one piece of paper flat and form a slight arch, loop, or hill on top with the other, as shown.

Tape the curved piece of paper to the outer edges of the flat piece, and you have made a copy of an airplane wing, or airfoil.

Now, carefully straighten a large paper clip (adult help may be needed) and poke it through the middle of both pieces of paper. Bend the clip slightly underneath, if needed, to hold the paper.

Gently but rapidly, blow some air over the short, front side of the airfoil, followed by blowing again just underneath it. Be careful to blow only for short periods, and to rest in between blowing. (Your body needs air, too!)

What happens: When you blew a short burst of air over the curved side of the airfoil, it lifted; while no movement was noticed when blowing a stream of air under the wing.

Why: Again, Bernoulli's Principle, or Rule, explains it. The lower air pressure on the top of the wing and the greater pressure on the bottom caused lift. (See "Ruler's Uprising.")

Foiled Again!

This time you're going to start rolling, and then square off, and find out what happens.

YOU WILL NEED:

notebook paper
straightened paper clip
from "Let's Wing It"
tape

What to do: From a notebook, take a small sheet of paper and roll it into a cylinder or tube, and tape it. Take another piece of paper, fold it in half, then open and fold each end to the center crease. Shape the creased sheet to form a box. Tape that, too.

Again, have someone poke the straightened paper clip into the middle of each shape and test each separately. Make certain the hole is large enough so the airfoil slides up and down the paper clip.

As you did in "Let's Wing It," blow over the top of each shape and then under it. Again, remember to rest between blowing. Did you notice any difference in the movements between the airplane foil, the cylinder or the box? Do you think how an airplane wing is designed is important?

What happens: The cylinder airfoil rises very little, while the box wing does not move at all.

Why: The push of air against a wing of a plane is called drag. Instead of helping the plane move smoothly through the air, it breaks up or blocks the airflow, so holds the plane back.

This is why the design of an airplane wing is so very important. Out first airfoil created a smooth flow of air around the wing, while the curves and angles of the cylinder and box caused much drag, or breaking up and blockage of air.

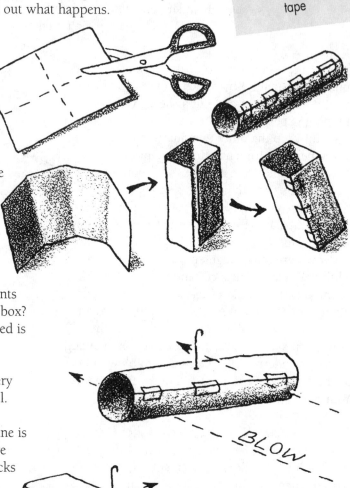

Oddballs

Air affects aircraft in many ways, both lifting and pushing. See how two balloons react to each other in this oddball experiment.

What to do: Blow each balloon up to large-orange size and knot them closed. Tie a balloon to each end of the string. Hold the string up in front of your face, or arrange the string over a high fixture or lamp, so that the two balloons hang evenly, next to each other, about 2 inches (5 cm) apart.

Now, blow a rapid stream of air between the two balloons and try to separate them more. Be sure to rest, stop blowing, a few minutes between tries. You do want to do your best…and not run out of breath!

What happens: The fast-moving air stream does not separate the balloons, as you might think, but instead brings the balloons closer together.

Why: When you blew between the balloons, the fast moving air between them caused a reduction in air pressure there, and the greater pressure on the outside of each balloon pushed them together.

Try "High Rollers" and other Bernoulli experiments for more air pressure information.

High Rollers: A Big Wind!

307

Sound like a Las Vegas game? No, you won't have to gamble on this simple and successful experiment. It's just Bernoulli's Principle of Air Pressure again, demonstrating lift.

YOU WILL NEED:

2 cardboard toilet
paper rolls
drinking straw
a flat, steady table

What to do: Place the two cardboard tubes about an inch (2.5 cm) away from one another. With the straw, blow a steady stream of air between them. (Place the tubes on a thick, heavy book to raise the experiment higher off the table, and easier to do.)

What happens: The stream of air blown through the straw causes the two cardboard rolls to come together. (Now you know why this experiment is called "High Rollers.")

Why: As the fast-moving air from the straw passes between the two tubes, the air pressure there is less than on the outer sides of the tubes. The difference in air pressure is enough to bring the two tubes together.

Whirlybird

In the next two experiments, you'll become an expert on helicopter flight. With a simple pencil and piece of light cardboard, you'll duplicate the effect of the spinning blades, or rotor, of a helicopter.

What to do: Place the middle of the cardboard strip on the top of the pencil eraser and press the tack through the strip to attach it. Make certain the tack is in tightly, as you bend the two ends of the strip upward from the middle. Your rotor blade, or cardboard strip, should have a slight V-shape at the eraser.

You are now ready to launch your model. This experiment can be done indoors or out. For best results, it can be launched from a height, such as a deck or staircase. Because high places can be dangerous, ask an adult to help you—you'll want someone to witness your launch anyway!

To launch properly, rapidly roll the pencil between your hands and release it. Be certain you roll and drop it the same way each time you conduct the experiment. (It should spin and turn as it drops downward.)

Do this many times, conducting many trials, before you decide how your model helicopter performs or flies.

What happens: With practice, your model helicopter with the cardboard-strip rotor should turn and spin and whirl through the air as it gently floats downward.

Why: Like an airplane, the rotors, or wings, of a helicopter are an airfoil and are designed to catch the slower-moving air under them rather than the fast-moving air over them.

These crowded or dense air molecules cause the rotors and craft to be pushed upward. The small side rotor on the tail end of the helicopter stops what is known as torque, balancing it and keeping the whole craft from turning, while the main rotor helps the craft to lift and turn, according to its position.

Although, our cardboard/pencil model with its rapid hand-spin thrust does not lift the model very much, it still reduces the fall rate as it descends.

Twirly-Whirlies

Twirly-what? Whirlies! In "Whirlybird," you made a simple pencil-and-paper helicopter-like toy. Now, let's replace that straight and simple blade with a circular pinwheel-and-cross rotor. Will the design of the different rotors make your model stay up in the air longer? Turn and fly better?

Do longer or wider rotors make a difference? Let's try different shapes, sizes, and widths of rotors to find out what works best.

What to do: Cut a circle between 4_ and 8 inches (11 to 20 cm) in diameter from the light cardboard. Cut four slits opposite each other in toward the center, but leave the center uncut. Fold one side of each slit to form a pinwheel.

Next, cut a strip 2 by 8 inches (5 by 20 cm) long and fold the strip in the center to form a V. Lastly, cut a 6-inch (15 cm) square of cardboard and cut out 2-inch (5 cm) squares from each corner to form a cross. Turn the cross ends up.

Now, tack the middle of each cardboard rotor to the top of a pencil eraser. Make certain the thumbtack is securely in place on all three models.

To launch, rapidly roll a pencil between your hands and release it. Again, see "Whirlybirds" for help and hints!

What happens: With our test models, the 2-by-8-inch (5 by 20 cm) strip worked fairly well but was somewhat clumsy. The pinwheel airfoil was very clumsy, did not turn or rotate, and fell to the ground without catching the air currents. However, the 6-inch (15 cm) cross rotor flew very well, with smooth and gentle spinning or rotation as it softly fell to the ground.

Why: The cross rotor was probably more like a real helicopter's airfoil than the other models. The wide blades with the four upturned ends, when rotated by hand, caught the denser, closer air underneath it and reduced the rate of drag from air holding it back as it fell to the ground. See "Whirlybird."

What now: Do this same experiment but see if you can make a perfect airfoil, or helicopter rotor, by adjusting the variables, other things that can affect spinning and flight.

For example, will longer or wider rotors make a difference? Or heavier or lighter paper or cardboard? Will making a drive shaft or spinning launcher help? In the next experiment, you'll find out!

Rotor Motor

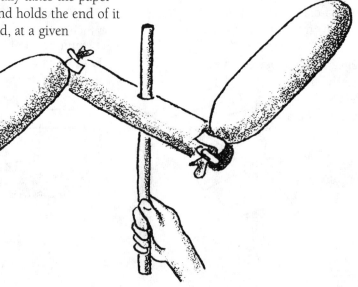

YOU WILL NEED:

cardboard paper towel roll

scissors

2 large oblong balloons

paper clip

wooden dowel, 1/2-inch by 18 inches (45 cm)

tape

a helper

You can make a jet-propelled, helicopter-like rotor, or blade, whirl, using nothing but 100% balloon power.

What to do: Ask an adult to help by using a sharp scissors tip to punch two holes completely through the cardboard tube, through both sides, at a point midway along its length. The holes need to be exactly opposite each other so an inserted dowel will fit right across. Place the dowel through the holes in the tube and turn, or rotate, the tube on the dowel many times until it spins freely.

Next, blow up one of the oblong balloons, twist and clip it, and carefully tape it to one end of the tube. (Be sure to fasten it well.)

Blow up the second balloon, twist and clip it, and fasten it to the other end of the tube, making certain the balloon opening is facing opposite the first balloon.

Now, get ready for the action! To do two things at once, you'll need the help of your assistant. While your helper carefully takes the paper clip off one of the balloons and holds the end of it closed, you do the same—and, at a given signal, both of you release your balloons.

What happens: As soon as you release the balloons, the tube whirls and spins.

Why: The rush of air from the balloons mounted on opposite ends of the tube pushes them forward, turning the tube around the dowel. The air being expelled by the balloons causes this push. Sir Isaac Newton's Third Law of Motion explains it best: for every action there is an equal and opposite reaction. The reaction of the balloons is to move forward. What would happen if the two balloons were placed on the dowel with their neck openings in the same direction?

thread, about 26 inches (70 cm)

scissors

pencil with eraser

light cardboard, 2 by 3 inches (5 by 7 cm)

thumbtack

tape

construction paper, 6 inches (15 cm) square

an adult helper

An American Yank

If you are careful to follow these clear and simple directions, this spinning airfoil won't let you down. It's time to pull some strings, give your helicopter a good old American yank, and watch it take off. You'll be flying high in no time!

What to do: Wrap the cardboard rectangle around the pencil to form a cylinder and tape it. Make certain the tube is loose enough for the pencil to turn inside it (drive shaft).

Next, cut 2-inch (5 cm) squares from each corner of the construction paper, forming a cross (see "Twirly Whirlies"). Place this cross-shaped rotor on top of the pencil eraser and fasten it with the tack. Make certain the tack is in tight enough so the rotor won't fall off. Bend the blades upward for better flight.

Lastly, place just the pencil point, or about an inch (2.5 cm) of pencil, into the drive-shaft cylinder. Wrap the thread around the pencil above it, as you would wind kite string around a stick—keeping it smooth, straight and tight.

Although it is not necessary, it's best to test-fly this experimental craft from a higher point to a lower area to observe the results. Ask for help if needed.

Pull the thread rapidly but smoothly and watch your helicopter turn with a whir and lift into the air.

If your helicopter doesn't work as it should, look for these variables, or other things that could be affecting its upward flight:

1. Is the thread wound too high on the pencil?
2. Is the pencil too deep in the drive shaft?
3. Is the tack holding the rotor loose or crooked, or still tight and in place?
4. Is the drive shaft too tight around the pencil?
5. Did you use string instead of thread? (String fibers are rough and cause drag by catching on the drive shaft and pencil.)

What happens: As you pull the thread away from around the pencil, the pencil is made to rotate, or turn, making a gradual but noticeable whirring sound and the craft lifts into the air.

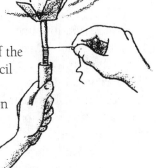

Why: The rapid action of the rotating, or spinning, pencil causes the moving rotor blades to lift up in reaction to the air being forced or pushed down.

I'm Banking On You!

312

Would you like to make the kind of instrument that helps pilots determine an airplane's position in flight? The artificial horizon will tell you whether you are flying level, or banking, or tilting, right or left. You're bound to crash in on the fun.

What to do: Flatten and cut the ends off the shoe box lid and cut the flat, rectangular piece of cardboard in half. Cut one of the halves an inch (2.5 cm) shorter.

Cut a 3-inch (8 cm) square from the plastic bag. With one of the marker pens, draw a straight line across the center of the piece.

Now, cut a 2½-inch (7 cm) circle from the center of the longer piece of cardboard and tape the clear plastic piece with the line on it to one side. Again, make certain the line is centered in the middle.

On the second, shorter piece of cardboard, draw a different colored line. It should be in the center, so as to divide it. Now draw a 90° straight line vertically or straight up from the center of the other line. You should have what looks like an upside down T.

Lastly, place the two cardboard pieces together—the window-lined piece on top of the inside shorter T-piece. Make certain both lines are matched up with each other.

Have someone punch a hole in the top center pieces of the cardboard, as you would a hanger on a picture, and position the bolt and nut, or fastener, in it.

The back, shorter, piece should move freely back and forth, much like a pendulum on a clock. Your flight instrument is now ready to be tested.

The line you drew on the plastic window represents the wing, while the cardboard with lines attached to the window shows the horizon, the line between the earth and sky.

Hold the attached longer piece level with the floor and slowly but gradually tip the instrument to the right and then to the left.

What happens: When tilting, if the horizon line is below the wing, the airplane is headed upward. If the line is above the wing line, the plane is angled downwards.

Why: A real artificial horizon helps a pilot navigate accurately even if he or she cannot see ahead. It tells the pilot whether the plane is going up, down or flying level.

The instrument shows two lines, one of which represents the horizon, the other, the wing. The horizon line is balanced by a gyroscope or a spinning wheel that keeps the horizon line level with the real horizon. This instrument is so accurate, that it keeps the two horizon lines steady, even if the airplane is not.

Note: Your artificial horizon must be matched up, line for line, carefully in order to register correctly, to give you an accurate reading.

313 Meter-Made

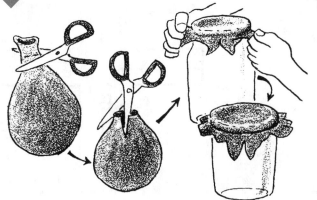

YOU WILL NEED:

16-ounce wide-mouth jar

scissors

straw

ruler

tape

clay

large balloon

Make an aneroid barometer, which is similar to an airplane's altimeter (altitude meter). Although your liquidless barometer won't measure altitude above sea level, it will teach you the highs and lows of air-pressure changes.

What to do: Cut the neck off the balloon and make a 1-inch (3 cm) cut on its side. Open it up and stretch it over the mouth of the jar, as you would spread skin over a drum. It should be put on tight, but not too tight. Done correctly, it will not slip off the mouth of the jar but will form an airtight seal.

Next, place the straw in the middle of the balloon skin and carefully and gently tape it.

Lastly, form a ball with the clay and stick the end of the ruler with the lower numbers into it. The clay will form a stand for your ruler-scale. Place the ruler close to the straw and record any numbered up and down movements.

What happens: The straw will move up or down to record any air pressure changes in the jar.

Why: When the straw moves up the numbered ruler, the pressure is higher; when it falls, the pressure is lower.

The aneroid barometer you made is similar to an airplane's altimeter, but it has no liquid in it. Too, unlike the airplane's device, it only shows altitude changes above sea level.

As a plane ascends, or climbs, the air pressure becomes less and is recorded as a drop on the altimeter. Air pressure at sea level exerts a greater force and affects all things on Earth.

Note: In order to show accurate barometric pressure changes, keep your barometer safe and undisturbed in a sheltered area for an extended, or long, period of time.

Tailspin

HOT!

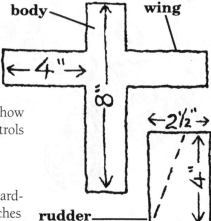

body — wing

← 4" →

8"

← 2½" →

4"

rudder —

You'll get into a real tailspin when you learn how the rudder, or tail section, of an airplane controls its left and right turns.

What to do: In the middle of the piece of cardboard, draw a line with the ruler, about 8 inches (20 cm) long. Place the ruler next to the line and draw the remaining lines around it to form the outline of the ruler. You should have drawn a long rectangle.

When done, you want an airplane pattern, with a wingspan, on each side, that measures 2 by 4 inches (5 by 10 cm). So, about 2 inches (5 cm) down from the top of the rectangle, draw a line, from one side 4 inches (10 cm) across. Do the other side the same way as to form a cross. This is the wing. Since it is wider than the body of the plane, draw a line opposite each end of each 4 inch (10 cm) line that measures 2 inches (5 cm). Fill in the remaining opposite 10-cm lines on each side to form the complete wing section.

With the remaining cardboard, cut out a rectangle, that measures 2½ by 4 (6 by 10 cm). This piece will represent the rudder.

Now, cut out both plane and rudder patterns. Cut out a slanted piece on one side of the rudder.

Align the plane pattern and attach it with thumbtacks to the narrow side of the toothpaste carton.

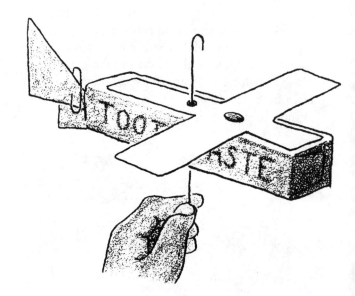

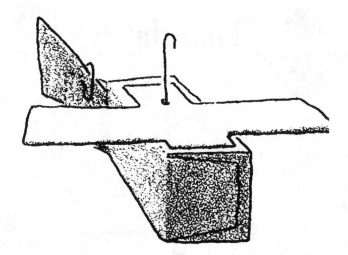

Pull out the main end flap of the toothpaste carton (near the tail-end of the airplane pattern) and attach the rudder to the flap with a paper clip (with the straight side of rudder facing away from the airplane pattern).

Puncture wounds can be dangerous, so get an adult to open and carefully straighten part of a paper clip. The straight end of the paper clip needs to be pushed through the middle underside of the box (underneath your attached plane pattern and behind the wing) and up through the top side. For safety, and to keep the plane on the clip, the straight, exposed part of the paper clip should be bent downward. (A small nail may be helpful in starting the holes.)

Your model plane is finished and is now ready to be tested.

To do this, look behind the model and push the rudder toward the right wing. Now position the plane, the front toward you, while carefully holding the underside paper clip, and gently blow a stream of air toward the rudder.

Now, repeat this action while reversing the rudder as far as it will go to the left. (Since the rudder is attached to the right side of the flap, it will be necessary for you to push and press it to the left as much and as hard as you can.)

What happens: Blowing on the rudder at different angles will move the model plane right to left.

Why: When you blew a stream of air against the rudder, while it was turned to the right, the air hit its right side, turning the plane's nose to the right. When you blew a stream of air against the rudder, while it was moved to the left, the air force again pressed against it, this time moving the plane's nose to the left.

What next: Keep your model airplane for more flight experiments (see "Flap-Happy").

315 Flap-Happy

YOU WILL NEED:

toothpaste-carton air-
plane from "Tailspin"

pencil

scissors

ruler

In "Tailspin," you made a model airplane with a rudder that controlled left and right turns, called "banking." Here, you'll go one step further, and cut flaps in the wings of your model airplane. These flaps will further control turns. In addition, you'll learn a lot about giving right-left directions—right? No, left!

What to do: Using your "Tailspin" model, mark off a 2-inch (4 cm) space on each side of the wings, making certain the marked space is in the same area on both wings.

Now, draw vertical or straight lines about an inch long (2 cm) from the end marks of each two-inch area on each wing. These will represent the wing flaps, or ailerons. Now make a cut on each vertical line—you should make two cuts on one wing; two cuts on the other. By folding, you will now have movable flaps on each side of the wings.

Look in the back of your model's wings to determine right wing, left wing. Turn the right aileron up and the left aileron down and the rudder to the right. Now blow a steady stream of air against the upturned flap. Which way does the airplane turn? Remember, to consider right-wing/left-wing, consider the turn from the back side of your model and not the front, and also remember to line up the model with your right and left hand.

Now, turn the flaps in the opposite direction, with the left aileron up and the right aileron down and the rudder pushed to the left. Again, blow a stream of air toward the front of the model. Which way does the airplane turn?

What happens: When you turned the right aileron up and the left aileron down and the rudder to the right, the model turned to the right. The plane turned to the left when the left aileron was up and the right aileron was down and the rudder was pushed to the left.

Why: Again, as in "Tailspin," the model turned to the right when the right aileron was up and the rudder was pushed to the right. The plane turned to the left when the left aileron was up and the rudder was pushed to the left.

Again, in both cases, the air stream hit the flat surfaces that were turned toward it and moved the model accordingly.

316 Flight Pattern

When you take your plane outside and throw it, you must remember that this is a scientific experiment. Like all scientific experiments, launching your model plane must be conducted scientifically. If your plane does not fly well or does not fly at all, there's probably a scientific explanation.

Again, go back to "What's All the Flap About?" Did you correctly trim and adjust the weights on your plane? Did you streamline the wings, body (fuselage), rudder and stabilizer by cutting rounder corners? If not, your plane may be too clumsy and awkward to fly.

Adjust paper clips on the nose of your plane and do not be afraid to add more, take away some, reposition clips, or add larger and heavier clips.

Remember, this is an experiment and you want to know which features will make your model fly best. Be adventurous and don't be afraid to try different things to make your plane fly longer, higher and straighter.

Also, you might want to try making different sized models with different designs by slightly changing the directions in "What's All the Flap About?" Larger planes usually glide longer distances and turn less. The possibilities for having your plane do what you want it to do are endless.

To make the best throws, find the center of gravity of your plane. If it has clips on its nose, place a finger and your thumb under the wing. When your model does not fall off your fingers and is perfectly balanced, you'll have found the center of gravity. This is where you should hold your plane; for ours, it was just behind the wing.

When you hold your plane at its balancing point, you'll get straighter, smoother and longer flights every time.

So have fun! Your plane experiments will never be boring but will leave you flying high with excitement.

What's All the Flap About?

WING

STABILIZER

YOU WILL NEED:
light cardboard, 12 inches (30 cm) square
scissors
paper clips
pencil
tape
ruler

You know something about aileron and rudder flaps; testing a practically stationary or non-movable model. Now, you'll go further. You'll throw and fly a real model with movable flaps. You'll even add a stabilizer, the horizontal, flat piece of the tail, to your experimental aircraft. Both will make your model even more interesting.

What to do: Draw the parts of your model plane. First, draw a 10-inch (25 cm) long rectangular box (ruler width) across the middle of the cardboard. When folded as shown, this will form the fuselage, or the body of the plane, with slits for the wing and stabilizer pieces.

Add a tailpiece to the fuselage, by drawing a 3-inch (8 cm) line up from the top left end of the rectangle; and then a 2-inch (5 cm) line across to the right, toward the front of your model. Finally, draw a line diagonally downward, to meet the top of the rectangle. This up-and-down part of the tailpiece, attached to the fuselage, is the rudder of your plane.

For the wing, draw another ruler-width 10-inch (25 cm) rectangular box.

Next, draw another, shorter rectangle. Make it about 2 by 5 inches (5 by 12.5 cm). This will represent the plane's elevator, or stabilizer; the flat and even part of your model's tailpiece.

To assemble your model plane, cut out the fuselage (body) with its attached rudder, the wing, and the stabilizer (flat part of tail assembly).

Make a crease, or fold, down the center of the fuselage. Fasten it with a paper clip. The clip can be removed later, as the plane is further assembled.

Now, 2 inches (4 cm) from the front of the plane, in the middle of the folded-over fuselage, draw a 2-inch (4 cm) line. Here, have an adult cut through the doubled-over fuselage to form a slit. This is where the wing will go. Make a similar line and slit toward the back of the plane, at the base of the rudder. Insert the stabilizer and the wing into their slits and adjust them. Reinforce the positions of your stabilizer and wing by taping them to the fuselage.

If your model's parts are large and it flies awkwardly, streamline it. Cut the areas at the ends of the wings, rudder and stabilizer to round them off. Cut the nose at an angle, trimming it, and place 4 or 5 paper clips on the nose assembly to balance and weight the model while removing any unnecessary clips on the fuselage.

Last-minute trimming and the adjusting of weights is necessary to make your model stable, steady, and most important, able to fly well.

Before cutting flaps in your plane's wing, rudder and stabilizer, take it outside and test it for flight. How you launch, or throw, your plane and the scientific methods you use are important variables. See "Flight Pattern" for help.

Once your plane flies well, cut flaps an equal distance apart on the wings, stabilizer and rudder. Adjust flaps up on the stabilizer to make your plane climb, or down to make it dip. Adjust ailerons (wing flaps) and rudder (flap at back) to the left or right to make turns. Let it fly!

What happens: Your model plane flies differently depending on how the flaps are positioned.

Why: When you turned the left wing's aileron up and rudder flap to the left, the air stream pushed toward the flaps and turned the model in that direction. The opposite applies when the right aileron and rudder is in the opposite direction.

Also, the movable flap in the stabilizer, the flat tailpiece, moves the plane according to how the air stream is hitting it. When lowered, the plane dives, when raised, it ascends, or climbs.

Forward, March!

In the last experiment, you learned about Newton's Law of Motion. Simply put, it states that for every action there must be an equal and opposite reaction.

When rushing fueled-air in a jet plane's engine is activated or ignited, the heated air that is released from the rear of the plane, pushes the plane forward. This is a perfect example of thrust. You can further see this law in rockets and planes by doing a few important but simple experiments:

What to do: First, blow up a few balloons and release them. When you blow the balloons up and let them go, the air comes out of the neck and propels them forward. A similar reaction occurs in planes and rockets.

You can make a simple rocket (you'll construct and develop more interesting rockets later on) by rolling a piece of paper into a cylinder and taping it.

Next, cut a piece of masking tape about 6 inches (15 cm) long and stick it on the neck of the balloon. Forming a bridge with the balloon and tape, stick the sides of the tape to the cylinder. You should be able to put your finger in the space between the tape and the cylinder. Also, the neck of the balloon should be facing the inside of the cylinder but with the opening out far enough to allow you to blow into it.

Now, blow a stream of air into the balloon and hold the end until it is ready to be released. If the tape starts to loosen or the balloon is stuck hard to the tape, readjust the tape or the balloon or start over. When ready, release the balloon and watch what happens.

The simple cylinder rocket is propelled forward as the air released from the neck of the balloon rushes through it.

319 ◆ A "Prop-er" Engine: A Wheel Deal!

YOU WILL NEED:

medium cup with plastic lid from a fast-food restaurant

cardboard

scissors

ruler

lump of clay (size of a large marble)

drinking straw

tape

rubber band

Modern jet planes use a mixture of fueled, hot, compressed rushing air to turn a series of wheeled fans on rods, or axles, called turbines.

This compressed, or flattened and pressed, air is then forced out of the plane's tail and pushes, or thrusts, the craft forward. Early turboprop planes used propellers and turbines to do the same job, but not as well as modern jet crafts. Find out how early jet-prop planes worked in this simple, easy, and fun experiment—it's a "wheel" deal!

What to do: Cut a rectangular section in the middle side of the cup that extends half way down its sides. Poke a hole in the middle of the bottom of the cup and cut the flap off the straw hole in the plastic lid.

Draw two circles 3 inches (8 cm) in diameter on the cardboard and divide each into eight parts, like circles used for teaching fractions.

Next, make _-inch cuts on the lines in the circles and bend the sections back and forth to represent the blades of a fan. Use tape to reinforce cuts and repair any tears.

Poke holes in the middle of the circular fans and push the straw through them. Each fan should be in the middle of the straw and about 2 inches (5 cm) from the other.

Fit the fan-and-straw assembly through the bottom hole of the cup while securing the plastic lid and straw into the top. Test the assembly to see if it turns easily. If not, cut larger holes to accommodate the straw, so that it will turn freely.

To make the propeller, cut a 1- by 5-inch (2.5 by 13 cm) propeller-shaped piece out of the cardboard.

Cut small slits into the center of each side and gently bend each part in opposite directions. This will give the propeller its third-dimensional shape.

Assemble the propeller by wrapping the rubber band around the straw securely where it pokes up through the lid. This will act as a buffer between the propeller and the lid, so that the propeller will stay forward and turn more freely. Next, place the propeller on the end of the straw (it will be necessary to poke a hole in the middle of the propeller), in front of the wrapped rubber band.

Finally, secure the propeller in place by shaping a nose for your plane out of clay and pushing it into place on the straw in front of the propeller.

Now you are ready to test your model jet prop. Blow a steady stream of air to the sides of the propeller and watch what happens.

What happens: By blowing a stream of air to the sides of the propeller, the compressor-turbine fanned parts are turned around.

Why: Although our experimental turboprop model is fun to make and test, it does not necessarily show how a real turboprop works. This model essentially was made to show how the movement of turbine parts is needed in the jet propulsion process. In a real turboprop engine, the turbines turn the propellers; while in our model, it is the propeller that turns the turbine parts.

Again, in a modern jet engine, incoming air at the front of the plane is compressed or squeezed together by engine parts. The jet's fuel is ignited or burned in a chamber and the hot gases are blown out of the rear of the plane. The thrust, or the forward push of the plane, is explained by one of Newton's three laws of motion, put forth in the year 1687, that every action has an equal and opposite reaction.

Traveling Bags: They're High and Mighty

Mankind could never keep eyes, and feet, on the ground. Watching birds soaring high, people dreamed of joining them—they never stopped trying.

About Hot Air Balloons

As early as the 1600s, long before the invention of the airplane, people talked of attaching baskets to flying spheres or balls. For years, they experimented with such balloons and large bags filled with lighter-than-air gases. Finally, in 1783, a French papermaker, Etienne Montgolfier, was credited with the first successful man-balloon launch—using hot air.

Air expands when heated, becoming lighter than the air surrounding it. One problem with early hot-air balloons was that the air inside would cool off. Then came the propane burner, which could be made to hang beneath a balloon, and the problem was solved.

Today, hot-air ballooning enthusiasts still enjoy just floating quietly on air currents. But balloons have been used to explore the atmosphere, gather data and weather information, even communicate. So, get ready for some "air-raising" experiences with air pressure and heated and expanded air, and learn about communication using helium balloons.

Airbag Balancing Act

HOT!

You'll have lots of fun learning how hot air behaves in this enjoyable, magical experiment. It's easy to put together and involves everyday materials you'll find around the house. However, you will need an assistant and a steady hand.

Note: An adult assistant is recommended. This experiment involves work with a lighted lamp bulb. Also, keep your materials for next experiment.

What to do: Open fully the two lunch bags. Place a paper clip on each flat, closed end of the bags.

Cut the string in half and tie each piece securely to each paper clip on each bag. Finally tie each stringed paper bag to each end of the ruler. You have now made a simple balance.

Ask your adult helper to remove the shade from a table lamp. The lamp should be low enough so you or your assistant can hold one end of the bag-balance over it.

Now, you or your assistant should balance the ruler on the end of the pencil. When equally balanced, notice how both sides are the same.

For a few minutes, hold one of the bags slightly over the heated bulb. Again, you'll need a steady hand, and you and your partner will need to watch what happens. Can you or your helper tilt one end of the balance, with the heated bulb, so that it will fall?

What happens: After a few minutes, one end of your bag-balance should slightly tip or lean to one side and finally fall.

Why: The molecules of warmed air rising from the light bulb are moving very fast and are expanded or farther apart. It is this warmer, expanded air that is responsible for pushing against the bag and slightly lifting it.

Toy Balloons and Old Bags: Still Rising to the Occasion

YOU WILL NEED:

balloon
string
tape measure
lamp or other heat source
an adult helper
pencil
paper

You can simply and easily prove that air expands when heated—very hot news for toy balloons and old bags (hot-air balloon bags, that is). So go ahead and blow up a few balloons and measure some hot air. You're sure to be bursting with excitement! It's definitely nothing to take lightly!

What to do: Blow up a balloon and tie it off with a string. Measure the circumference of the balloon, distance around the widest part. Write down the measurement. Now, with the help of a parent or adult friend, dangle the balloon above a lit lamp bulb. (It's not necessary to remove the shade.)

To thoroughly warm the balloon, you'll need to rotate, or turn, the balloon above the bulb for two to three minutes. Then, without removing the balloon from the heat source (you really need an extra hand here), measure the balloon's circumference, widest part, again. Record your information.

What happens: The balloon measurement is bigger than before!

Why: When the balloon was heated, the air inside became warmer, causing the air molecules to move faster, bump into each other and spread out. This action, in turn, increased the size of the balloon.

322

Spinning Wheel: It's Wheel Science At Work!

YOU WILL NEED:

aluminum foil circle, 4 to 5 inches (10-13 cm) in diameter

sewing needle or pin

scissors

bendable straw

an adult helper

boiling water on stove

Because air molecules expand when heated, the hot air in a hot-air balloon is much lighter than the surrounding air. It's this difference that causes a hot-air balloon to lift off from the ground.

Now you can discover how another gas rises to the occasion to turn a toy's head (a pinwheel, that is).

HOT!

What to do: Cut six 1-inch (2.5 cm), equally-spaced slits around the aluminum disk or circle. Fold the shiny side down and bend the cut sides downward and back to form vanes or flaps. You should have something that looks like an upside-down pinwheel. Poke a very tiny hole directly in the center of the disk.

Cut a 1-inch (2.5 cm) piece from the bendable straw to use as the balancing piece. Have an adult poke the needle or pin through the center of the straw to form a T. The eye or pin head should be sticking out above the crossed section.

Now, shiny side down, place the upside-down pinwheel over the eye of the needle. Also, adjust the flaps or vanes of the circle so that they lay smoothly, with a slightly downward bend.

Bend the flexible straw to form a pipe and place the pointed end of the needle into the bent end of the straw.

The next step must be done carefully and with help. Have an adult put about a cup of water on the stove to boil. When the water begins to simmer and steam, have them hold the straw and extend the pinwheel over the hot water. Watch carefully.

What happens: The aluminum pinwheel disc gradually and slowly begins to turn.

Why: Although hot air and steam are not quite the same, they are both gases. Both can "lift" and do work, such as steam engines, hot-air balloons.

The steam here is hot water vapor, a gas. Like hot air, the molecules move faster and take up more space. In turn, they have much energy to move or push an object. Here, the foil pinwheel is turned by the loose, escaping, uprising heated gas molecules.

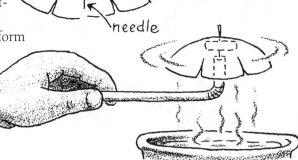

piece of straw

needle

A MATTER OF GRAVITY

Astronomers, mathematicians, and scientists once believed the planets followed circular paths or orbits around the sun; holding constant speeds as they orbited. Actually, the planets move around the sun in an ellipse, or oval, and according to their distance, or nearness to it and its gravitational pull, they speed up or slow down just enough to keep from being pulled in!

But getting down to Earth! As a resident, your body is being pulled down toward the center of the planet. Your weight on its surface reflects this pull.

About Gravity

In other words, your weight is the result of the pull of Earth's gravity on your body On Mars, your weight would be one-third of your Earth weight, because Mars is smaller. On the moon, with only one-sixth of Earth's gravity, you would weigh even a smaller fraction of your weight on Earth.

Another way of looking at it: the bigger the planet or moon, the more mass and gravity it possesses. So, on larger planets you would weigh more; and on smaller planets you would weigh less.

In this chapter, you'll not only do experiments about the speeds, orbits, and gravity of other planets, but learn how this important force affects our world as well. We know you'll find this chapter very attractive; we're pulling for you!

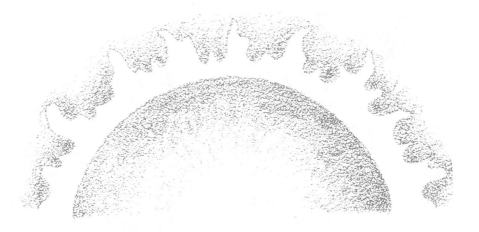

Curve-Ball Trajectory

YOU WILL NEED:

soft, light ball
(for safety)

a helper (optional), to
throw and return ball

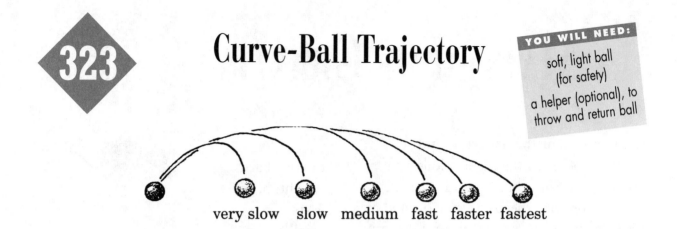

very slow   slow   medium   fast   faster   fastest

Throw a slow or fast ball and watch what kind of curved path, or trajectory, it takes.

What to do: Throw a ball upward into the air and follow the path, or trajectory, it takes each time you throw it. Repeat the throws, varying or changing the speed of your throw each time; for example, from slow, to slower, to even slower.

Then, throw some fast balls and notice if the speed has anything to do with changing the curved path or trajectory the ball takes.

What happens: All the thrown balls take a curved path once they are released, some following a steeper curve than others.

Why: The balls you threw into the air curved and were pulled back to Earth by its gravitational, or pulling, force. This curved path, called the trajectory, in all cases imitates the curvature of the Earth.

When you threw the ball slowly, you could see the curve it took more easily than when the ball was thrown fast. A slower throw, then, will definitely take a steeper, more noticeable path.

Spooling Around

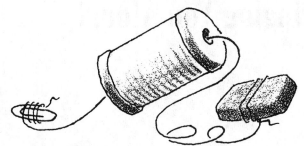

YOU WILL NEED:
rubber eraser
paper clip
string, 20 inches
(50 cm) long
empty thread spool

Make a simple twirler, an eraser suspended from a string through a spool, and learn about centripetal force—while spooling around!

What to do: Tie the string tightly around the eraser and then thread it through the spool. Wrap the other end of the string around the paper clip and tie it securely. The clip will act as the anchor, to stop the string and eraser from flying off.

Now you're ready for a test. Hold the twirler straight out, away from your body and above your head. Make sure no one is nearby or in your path.

Gently but rapidly rotate, or spin, the spool. and then allow it to slow down and then to stop.

Continue to repeat this action and carefully watch what happens. Please note! It's not necessary to do this with any great force or movement.

What happens: As you rapidly spin the spool, the eraser will spin away from the spool and will rise upwards. When you slow or stop the spinning, the eraser will be pulled downwards and eventually stop.

Why: The eraser on the string is like gravity on the Earth. The string (gravity) pulls the eraser toward it (the spool). What actually is happening is called centripetal force. This is the force that

directs movement to the center of the object. When you spun the spool, string and eraser around you, you pulled the eraser toward you and the force caused the string and eraser to move up and away from its center.

Weight Lifter: Stringing You Along!

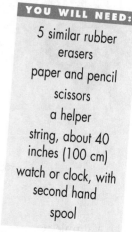

In these whirling experiments you'll use several eraser weights, and learn what this tells you about the planets, their gravitational pull, and how they revolve around, or circle, the sun. So, enjoy twirling and whirling away with no strings attached—well, maybe one!

What to do: As in "Spooling Around," tie one end of the string around an eraser and thread the string through the spool. Tie an eraser to the opposite end of the string. For each trial, you will add one eraser to the bottom of the string. Your assistant's job will be to use the watch or clock to time each 15-second trial and then to record the number of weights and the results.

When you're ready to start each trial, have your helper stand at a distance, ready to start timing. First, get your twirler spinning well, before the official start time. Be sure to pull, hold, and keep the bottom-weighted string in the same position for every experiment.

At your start signal, have your helper silently count off 15 seconds as you quietly count the number of turns the eraser makes around the spool before your assistant calls "Time." Call out the number of turns to record, then add another eraser—to two, three, then four—and repeat the trial. After each trial, your helper writes down the number of weights used and the revolutions, or number of turns.

What happens: The more weights or erasers you add to the bottom of your twirler, the more revolutions, or turns, the top one will make in the 15-second allotted time.

Why: The planets, like Mercury and Venus, that are closest to the sun have to travel faster than those that are at a distance. If these planets did not orbit fast enough, they would be pulled into the sun by its powerful gravitational force.

The twirler with many weights represents the greater gravitational force of the sun on its nearby planets (such as Mercury) and therefore such bodies need to make more revolutions. However, the sun's gravitational pull on the more distant planets—Uranus, Neptune and Pluto—is much less than on the planets closer to it—Mercury and Venus.

The twirler with one weight (again, the weight represents the gravitational pull of the sun) is like Pluto, with fewer revolutions, or turns, around the sun and, therefore, a smaller number of spins around the spool.

326

The Big Three: Mercury, Jupiter, Neptune

YOU WILL NEED:

light cardboard or poster board, at least 22 by 28 inches (56 by 71 cm)

scissors

marbles

tape

watch with second hand

pencil and paper

What to do: Cut three circles from the cardboard, one 10 inches (25.5 cm) across, the other 12 inches (30.5 cm), the third 14 inches (35.5 cm). Next, cut a slit from the outside edge of the circles to the center or middle. Form the circles into cones and tape the outside slits together. Make certain you shape each cone so the angle or height of the walls are the same. (The trick to doing this accurately and easily is placing the second and third cones inside the first!) When finished, get ready for the fun!

Orbiter I: Operation Mercury

Take the first 10-inch, orbiter cone and drop the marble into its center. The center will represent the sun; the marble, Mercury; and the cone, Mercury's orbital path around the sun.

While holding the cone in the palm of your hand, gently rotate or whirl it, keeping the marble orbiting as close to the center as possible without it actually dropping into the center.

Once the marble starts moving in a continuous orbit, with smooth, even rotations or circles, use the watch with the second hand, to time its orbits.

To do this, time and record, the number of times the marble makes one full revolution or circle in 15 seconds.

Since Mercury is closest to the sun, our hypothesis, or guess, will state that it will have to move faster around the sun in order to avoid being pulled into it. After you complete the other two experiments, you can chart and compare your results.

327

Orbiter II: Operation Jupiter

Next, place the marble (Jupiter) into the center hole (the sun) of the 12-inch orbital cone.

Again, repeat the steps as in "Orbiter I," but this time, whirl or rotate the marble so it makes a wider path or orbit, almost touching the cone's edge. The wider cone represents Jupiter's wider orbit or path around the sun.

328 The Big Three: Countdown!

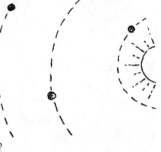

Using what you already know about the orbits of these three planets, write down or chart your experimental orbital speeds and compare them with our real planetary average estimated speeds.

Mercury speeds around the sun at 108,000 mph. It takes Mercury only 88 Earth days to revolve around the sun.

Jupiter has an average speed around the sun of 29,400 mph. It takes Jupiter practically 12 Earth years to move around the sun.

Neptune's average orbital speed around the sun is 12,200 mph. It takes Neptune over 160 Earth years to travel around the sun.

Is there a connection between your experimental orbital speeds, the distances of orbits from the sun, and the actual estimated speeds of the planets?

To be certain there are no other variables, or things that can change the results, make certain the cones are all evenly smooth circles, and securely taped. For best test results, do at least three or four such trials and compare them to the actual estimates.

329 Orbiter III: Operation Neptune

Now that you've done the first two experiments, try the third. Yes, you've guessed it! Neptune has a much wider orbit around the sun than the other planets. Use the larger, wider, 14-inch cone for this one. Repeat the steps, but now whirling the marble in a much wider orbit.

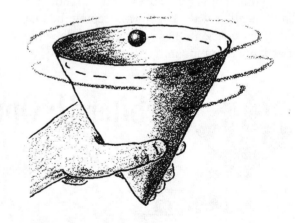

I Get Around

330

A marble's in a bottle The bottle is turned upside down. The marble stays inside! How? A full-of-surprises trick that will have your friends standing on their heads.

YOU WILL NEED:
2-liter plastic bottle
small marble

What to do: Drop the marble in the bottle and ask your friends if they can turn the bottle upside down without having the marble drop out. And no, they can't simply hold the marble inside!

Impossible, they say. Now it's your turn. Holding the bottle upright, with your hand underneath, move the bottle to start the marble whirling in a circular orbit within it. While continuing to swirl the bottle and the marble within, gradually move the bottle to a horizontal and then to an upside-down position.

What happens: The revolving whirling marble doesn't fall out of the bottle, even when the bottle is turned upside down.

Why: When your friends simply turned the bottle, not whirling it, the Earth's gravity pulled the marble down and out. However, by whirling the bottle, the marble was pulled up away from the neck to the side of the bottle by centrifugal force.

Slam Dunk

Gravity is a lot like a slam dunk, pushing a basketball forcefully down through a hoop. But gravity's force pushes everything down. In order to fly, an airplane's lift, must be greater than the downward pull of gravity. This experiment shows that gravity is a persistent force; the results are the same, even if you try to change them.

YOU WILL NEED:
large hardcover book
2 rulers
table
2 coins

What to do: Place the book on the table so one end hangs off the end. Place a ruler about an inch (2 cm) away from the book, with an end hanging over it. Place one coin on the end of the extended part of the ruler; the other at the top of the end of the book in the space next to the ruler. Now, use the other ruler to forcefully strike the end of the extended, overhanging ruler so that both coins are pushed to the ground.

Will forcefully pushing the ruler to the side to hit one of the coins greatly affect its fall? Which coin will hit the floor first?

What happens: Both coins hit the floor at the same time.

Why: The force of gravity is always the same. In our experiment, a forceful side hit to the coin by the ruler was greater than the force that caused the coin to drop off its extended end. However, even this effect was not enough to alter or change the rate of fall.

Gumdrop

YOU WILL NEED:

eraser
sheet of paper
sheet of aluminum foil
paper clip

Will a large eraser hit the floor before a small paper clip? What about a flat sheet of paper or aluminum foil? Does size, shape, and weight affect the rate of fall, or how fast an object falls to Earth? Try these experiments and erase all doubt!

What to do: With an aluminum foil sheet laying on one hand, and a paper sheet on the other, extend your arms. Drop both sheets at the same time and observe what happens.

Now repeat the experiment, but replace one sheet with an eraser. Follow this by dropping the paper clip and a sheet. Lastly, drop the eraser and paper clip at the same time.

What happens: The paper and the foil, in general, float down to the floor at the same rate, while the eraser and the paper clip hit the floor before either the foil or the paper sheet. Finally, both the eraser and paper clip hit the floor at the same time.

Why: The size and the weight of the clip and eraser do not affect the rate of fall. This is because most of their mass is inside. The amount of metal and eraser forming their surface areas are small, so drag from air resistance is reduced. Gravity pulls on both objects with the same equal force, ounce for ounce.

However, the flat sheets of paper and foil, with their masses spread out over a wider surface area, met much more air resistance. It was this greater drag that affected their rate of fall.

Balance Beam & Airheads

YOU WILL NEED:

dowel, 1/2 inch (0.5 cm) in diameter
string
4 balloons
safety pin
overhead fixture, from which to hang dowel

333

Here you'll stretch one experiment into two. First you'll find the center of gravity in "Balance Beam" and then the "Airheads" will show you their stuff.

Balance Beam

What to do: Loosely tie one end of a long piece of string to something high up and let the string hang down. Tie the dowel to the other end of it.

Yes! That's right! All you have to do for this experiment is simply adjust the dowel on the string so it is perfectly balanced. In other words, find the dowel's center of gravity, the point on the dowel where its weight, or mass, is centered. At this point, the dowel will be balanced on the string, and hang there horizontally. You'll find the dowel's center of gravity somewhere in the middle of it.

Airheads

What to do: Cut four more 15-inch (40 cm) strings. Tie and space two on one side of the dowel, and two on the other.

Inflate the four balloons equally. Knot the necks or tie the openings tightly with string, then tie each balloon onto one of the four separate strings on the dowel. The balloons should be equally spaced and the dowel's center of gravity balanced.

With the safety pin, pop one of the balloons. Adjust the dowel's center of gravity. Pop a second balloon. Now, with only two balloons remaining, readjust the balance and pop one of the last remaining balloons.

What happened: When you popped one of the two remaining balloons, the dowel, and the one remaining balloon, dropped and fell to one side.

This proves you should never take air lightly. It has weight and it is heavy—it's definitely a weighty subject!

Flypaper

A long time ago, someone took a sheet of paper, folded it, aimed it, and threw it. It became the first flying paper, or glider.

Here's your chance to build an assortment of gliders and, in the interest of science, your teacher or parents can't really complain. You'll find out which materials are best to use, what designs fly best and which attachments or parts make a difference to flight.

Now, get ready to build gliders with different designs, parts, and with ailerons or flaps—and prepare to soar.

334 Flight: Up in the Air?

YOU WILL NEED:
sheet of paper
measuring tape or stick

Still confused about the ups and downs of flight? No problem. You'll start out working with a basic glider and add or take away "extras," the variables, that make your plane fly great, good, well. Well, maybe not so well!—but you'll be air-minded in no time.

What to do: Fold the paper in half lengthwise and crease. Open the fold, and fold the two corners at one end in toward the center line. Crease at the fold.

Now, bring each of the two folded edges of the triangle to the center line. Align the folds against the center line, and crease the new folds.

Finally, turning the glider, align one fold against the center line and crease. Then do the same on the opposite side. Hold the glider up and position the wings outward. If done correctly, the nose tip of the glider should point slightly downward.

You're now ready to test your craft. It should be thrown each time by the same person and in the same way. After each throw, the distance traveled should be carefully measured and noted.

What happens: With each throw, your glider should soar, circle, swoop or descend swiftly, traveling a good distance.

Why: Your glider is an excellent example of an airfoil. If you examine the wings, you'll notice they curve slightly on the top and are flat on the bottom. The air passing over the top of the wing is forced to travel faster, due to the raised shape, and the faster air becomes thinner than the air passing under the wing.

Because the air underneath is denser, or thicker, because it is traveling more slowly, the denser air pushes the plane upward, into the thinner air. It is this process, or law of nature on air movement, that keeps your glider soaring aloft, or in flight.

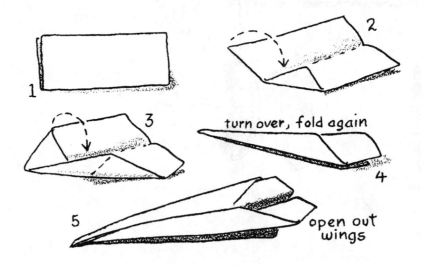

1

2

3

turn over, fold again

4

5

open out wings

335 Clipped Wings

Flaps or clips, which do you prefer? Maybe both? Try flight experiments with paper clips placed in different places on the planes to stabilize them, make them fly steadier and straighter.

Fly each separate design against your basic, no-frills model. In each case, test distance traveled and smoothness of flight. For example, test the basic plane against one that has a clip on the end of each wing, then test another design, and so on. This example of experimentation, comparing a basic model against one that has been altered or changed in one way, is called controlled.

You can also try taping the wings of one model together, cutting adjustable flaps in each wing-ending of another, or attaching a rudder or tail to a third.

There are countless combinations or possibilities—try them all or just a few. After you have thoroughly experimented with your altered or changed models and compared them with the basic glider, form a hypothesis, or guess, on why some models fly better than others. Can you now test out your hypothesis? With each test, keep accurate and careful records: distances traveled, smoothness of flight, less than successful landings. Remember, you can learn more from mistakes and failures than from smooth sailing. Every obstacle provides an opportunity to learn. By making and flying gliders, you can learn a lot about flight.

Kite Tales

A legend tells that once upon a time in the land of Woo, a Chinese province, a man named Sun-Wing was very lonely. Waion, the god of the wind, was very lonely too.

To please Waion, Sun-Wing tied and placed two thin birch sticks across very thin paper and attached it to cord. Sun-Wing let Waion catch his paper windbird and lift it on high. Suddenly, both Sun-Wing and Waion realized they were no longer lonely. On Waion's command, the paper wind bird danced, glided, swooped and dived.

You, too, can make your own paper wind-bird and, under Waion's command, maybe it, too, will dance, glide, swoop and dive.

336 ◆ Our Fantastic Mini-Box Kite

HOT!

YOU WILL NEED:

sheet of paper

scissors

hole punch or nail

ruler

tape

string

This mini-box kite is fun to make and fly, and you only need a few simple materials. You'll need, too, some measuring skills, but not to worry—it's all here in black and white. This experiment won't leave you up in the air—but the kite will.

What to do: On the paper, measure and draw a 6½-by-8-inch (17-by-20 cm) rectangle. Cut the rectangle out, then fold it in half, and crease. Next, open it and fold in each end of the sheet to the center line and crease again. Open and you have the makings of an open-ended box shape with sides measuring 2 inches (5 cm).

Now, you need to make four fairly equal rectangular "windows" in each of the four box sides. To do this, flatten the sheet, lay a ruler against the inner side of each crease and draw lines across, to help guide you. Now, ⅜ inch (1 cm) in from each guide line and ½ inch (2 cm) in from each edge of the paper, draw the 1½-by-5 inch (3-by-13 cm) windows in each side. Lay the ruler across the windows to check that they align and are centered, then cut them out.

A real, old-time box kite looks more like the one shown in the illustration. Using straws and long strips of light paper, why not try making a small model and see if it flies. Then, you can try toothpicks and smaller strips of tissue paper for an even smaller version! Where will it all end?

Build a Simple Kite!
It's a Breeze!

HOT!

Get the family together for some high-flying fun! Kitemaking is an "exact" science and an art involving designing work, stringing, framing, and bridle, so it's nice to have adult help.

You can learn a lot about the principles of aerodynamics when you build and fly one of the earliest and oldest flying toys and machines, the ever-fantastic kite!

What to do: Ask an adult to cut small grooves or notches on the ends of each wooden dowel or stick. String will be run through these slits to make the frame, so the notches need to be deep enough to hold it.

Find the middle of your 28-inch (70 cm) cross stick—14 inches (35 cm) in from the ends. Mark it.

Next, mark a place on the upright main, or mast, stick, 8 inches (20 cm) from one end. Placed toward the top, this is the point where the two sticks will meet to form a cross. Using a figure-8 wrap, tie the two sticks together carefully with string until they are fastened.

Work a long piece of string into the end notches of each dowel as you form the frame of the kite. Pull the string slightly to tighten it around the frame, then tie it off.

You will probably need two sheets of tissue paper to form the skin, or sail, of the kite. If so, lay one tissue paper sheet over the other, leaving a 1-inch (2.5 cm) margin overlap. Carefully tape the sheets along the seam, both front and back.

Lay the kite frame on the tissue paper. Leave an edging of at least 2 inches (5 cm) of paper to fold and glue down. Cut around the frame as shown.

When finished, glue the overlap or end flaps (a glue stick works well) down over the string frame. Keep your scissors handy. It's important to trim away extra paper so that the end sticks are free and clear. Also, pull the tissue slightly so that it is taut on the frame, but be careful not to rip the paper.

What happens: If all the variables are right (kite construction, bridle, tail, wind direction and speed), your kite should be lifted up high into the air and stay there, dancing against the sky.

Why: The action of air lifting a kite is similar that on an airfoil or an airplane wing. The air flowing over it has a longer way to go and has less force than the air against its near surface. As a result, the air pressure exerts a greater force on the front of the kite than on its back and the kite is pulled up, up, and away!

The string you pull toward you, on the other hand, holds and steadies the kite, balancing it in the air

338 Hightail It to the Bridle Party

Let this be a family project—a bridle party and a kite launching. Your tail and bridle, the string harness attached to the main or flying string on your kite, needs to be made and attached carefully—and with your aerodynamic mind, you should be highly successful.

To make a bridle, or kite harness, attach a long string to the ends of the upright stick. The string should be slack, or loose, enough so it pulls out.

Next, attach a shorter string to the ends of the dowel that make up the cross stick and make them meet a little below it. Adjust the bridle

strings so they are equal and tight, and tie the flying string to where the bridle strings meet.

At this point, it's important to test your kite to see if it "catches the wind" properly—if not, it will not fly at all or will fly incorrectly. With the bridle and flying string attached, stand in the wind and pull the kite toward you. If the top of the kite pulls upwards and the kite tilts and seems to be gathering in the wind, your bridle is correctly attached. If this is not the case, adjust the cross string to a higher or lower position and try again.

To add a tail (to help balance the kite), cut rectangular pieces of colored tissue (multi-colored or a variety of colored pieces show up best). Space and tie them, using smaller pieces of string, every 7 to 8 inches (18–20 cm) along a 6 to 8 foot (2–3 m) tail string.

Tie the tail to the bottom end of the upright stick and get ready to soar—and have a high-falutin,' high-flyin' time!

EXPLORATION IN OUTER SPACE?
OUT OF THIS WORLD!

From Skylab, the American space station put into orbit in 1973, to the space shuttle *Endeavor* launched in 1993, to recent cooperative efforts in the long-lasting Russian *Mir,* and Pathfinder's invasion of Mars, space exploration has never been more exciting.

In this chapter, you'll do experiments that teach you about the conditions in outer space, watch the reentry of a space capsule, make your own space food, and even design a space station and man it.

And, you'll create conditions and craters on the moon and design logo space patches for imaginative and creative fun. So, get ready to blast-off for an out-of-this-world adventure!

339 Signs from Space: An Emblematic Concern

Astronauts often wear specially designed emblems, known as patches, on their clothing to indicate their unit and tell, in pictures and words, something about the unit's mission in space. The Gemini and Apollo crew members wore such patches on their sleeves, and future astronauts will certainly wear their own similar emblems proudly.

You can design your own emblem, or badge, simply and easily. First, pick up some heavy posterboard—sold at stationary and variety stores, art supply or drugstores. Use your imagination and brightly colored markers, crayons, or pencils, creative lettering and a variety of space scenes to turn out exciting, creative crew badges.

Create a space scene, circling suns or draw some alien terrain, or ground surface. Will your badge-emblem show a planet with several moons, or a landscape with huge craters, deep surface cracks, or volcanoes? Will you have a rocket on your badge or a futuristic space shuttle or space station? The possibilities are endless and with ideas all around you, you'll have no problem getting started.

Give your pretend outer-space mission a name—remember the Discovery and Columbia missions?—and include your mission name on your badge. Use imaginative lettering for an extra-special effect. Select an interesting shape—square, triangle, circle, oval, or maybe a shield—for each badge. When you finish your emblem, cut out the shape and attach a small safety pin to the backside of each badge, using small pre-cut strips of masking tape. Now, your crew is ready to explore flight and space and to let their imaginations soar.

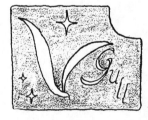

Reentry Splashdown

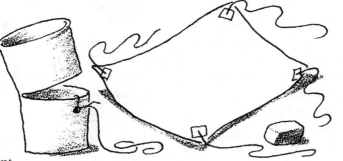

340

Ever wonder how early astronauts used to get back to Earth, before shuttles, after rocketing into space? This simple experiment will show you, with a few simple, easy-to-find materials, how it was done.

What to do: Cut away the top of a disposable cup, leaving only a 2-inch deep bottom portion. With the hole punch, make a hole about _ inch (1 cm) from the top of the cup and tie the long string to the cup.

Next, assemble the parachute and space capsule portion of the experiment. To do this, tape the four 12-inch (30 cm) strings to each corner of the paper towel. Gather the other ends of the strings together and tie them around the eraser. Test your parachute-capsule. Try balling it up in your hand and tossing it into the air a few times. The parachute should open easily and be balanced to float the eraser to the ground.

Now, to demonstrate how an orbiting space-capsule re-enters Earth's atmosphere, take all your experimental props (chute-capsule and beverage cup) outside. You'll need room to whirl your space capsule over your head without worrying about it hitting things or someone nearby.

Place the eraser in the bottom of the cup. Gently pack the paper chute on top of the eraser. Don't stuff it all the way down into the cup. It is easier to do the forced re-entry simulation if it is loosely packed.

Find a clear spot outside and begin whirling your space capsule overhead. Start slowly, and gradually increase the speed. The parachute will stay in place in the cup as long as you continue to whirl it smoothly. Now, slow the whirling motion and purposely jerk the string sharply. You may have to do this several times and in different ways before you get the hang of ejecting the parachute-capsule.

Always remember that scientists often try many different ways of doing something before they find not only an acceptable way, but the best way. If, after several tries, your capsule does not eject or the parachute does not open properly, check the weight of your eraser, how it fits the cup—maybe too tightly?—and readjust and repack the parachute.

What happens: After you slow the whirling motion and jerk on the string, the parachute and capsule eject, or pop out of the cup. The chute opens and floats the capsule easily and gently to the ground.

Why: You have demonstrated how space capsules used to be recovered or brought back from Earth's orbit and make a soft landing. The slowing of the whirling motion and the jerking of the string represented the firing of retrorockets that slowed the capsule's forward motion so that gravity would pull it toward Earth.

The string represents the balance of gravity and centrifugal force that kept space capsules in orbit so they would not fly out into space. The space capsule's orbit was similar to your turning and whirling the string-cup parachute.

To prepare for and deploy your parachute capsule for re-entry, you slowed the whirling motion and jerked the string. This was like firing retrorockets and, once a space capsule reached Earth's atmosphere, the parachute automatically opened to float the capsule to Earth.

The real space capsule landings were made at sea—called "splashdowns!" Today, astronauts travel into space in modern spacecrafts, called shuttles. They are pushed into orbit by orbiter and booster rockets that return to Earth, are recovered and reused. Astronauts now fly their shuttlecraft back to Earth like planes, to be used again and again, unlike space capsules. Some early capsules that were saved and studied after splashdown are on display in space museums.

341 Moonscape I: Mark-It Research

YOU WILL NEED:

cup plaster of paris
1/2 cup boiling water
shallow, flat disposable frozen food or aluminum pan
plastic spoon or other throw-away utensil
an adult helper
use of stove
magnifying glass

HOT!

To really see close up, and even touch the moon, make your very own model moonscape. It's easy and you'll find out how some lunar features or surface marks were formed. As a bonus, you can name the craters, mountains, and seas on your moonscape after anyone you want!

What to do: While a parent or adult brings the half-cup of water to a rolling boil on the stove, pour the half cup of plaster of paris over the bottom of the shallow, flat pan.

Then, again with help, pour about half of the hot, boiling water carefully into the pan and stir it briefly to moisten all the plaster. If needed, add more water to dry sections. Don't worry about a few lumps. They're meant for great things!

When the mixture cools slightly, and is partially solid, pour off any excess water. Place the pan where it can be left undisturbed for about an hour to dry.

After the plaster mix has completely dried, take your model moonscape and observe its features, the surface areas, with a magnifying glass. Map out and pencil in names and areas on your model; name the seas, or maria; the rougher, patchy areas; the mountains; lumpy areas; and the craters, those different-sized holes you find. Look at the moonscape in the early morning or late afternoon sunshine, or use a flashlight to see how the different features cast shadows on the moonscape.

What happens: As the plaster of paris hardens, the lumpier areas grow in size to form mountains, holes of various sizes appear in the surface to form craters; and rough, flat surfaces become the seas or plains.

Why: Billions of impact holes or craters cover all of the moon's surface, the mountainous areas as well as the flat sea, or plains, areas known as maria. These "seas" (not bodies of water at all but wide areas of volcanic rock) were formed billions of years ago as the flowing hot lunar surface cooled.

Evidence from the Apollo explorations and moon landings have proven that many lunar features or surface marks were caused by underground forces, as the moon's molten, or hot liquid, center cooled deep beneath the hardened crust.

When our hot plaster mixture cools, like the surface of the moon did long ago, it also forms craters, rough areas, and large lumpy, mountainous, areas. These features are due, again, to the heating and cooling of the surface, the contraction or shortening and the expansion or lengthening of its crust.

Moonscape II: A Heavy Hitter!

YOU WILL NEED:

small, flat container (disposable pan or food tray)

1 cup flour, baking soda, or fine sand

a "meteor"—small ball, large marble or lump of clay

ruler or yardstick

pencil

paper

newspaper

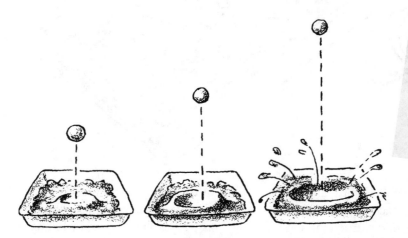

Go one step further and find out how the size of asteroids and meteorites, speed and distance affect the size and distance of moon craters. Careful, this is messy! Do it outside, wear old clothes, and put newspapers under your experiment pan to make it easy to clean up your mess when you're done.

What to do: Pour the cup of flour, baking soda or sand into the container. Mound it first into a hill in one corner of the tray then level it down, smoothing it off with your hand from that corner to the others. This will represent the surface of the moon.

Next, take the "meteor" and drop it from a height of 4 to 5 inches (10-13 cm) above the filled tray surface. Measure the hole or crater it made in

the powdery surface, across from one rim, or outer circle, of the impact, or hit, to the other. Record the distance of the "meteor" fall to the surface in the tray and the diameter of the crater the drop made. If it helps, draw a picture and put in both measurements as labels.

Level or smooth off the surface powder and try again. Double the distance of your last drop. Again, use the yardstick to measure the height of the drop and the ruler to find the diameter of the crater made by the impact. Repeat several times, and gradually increase the height of your drops, smoothing the surface powder before each. Keep good records and illustrations.

According to your notes and measurements, what did you observe between greater-distance drops and closer-distance ones?

Moonscape III: Making a Good Impression

Simulate or copy the conditions on the moon and Earth and then compare each. Unlike the Earth, the moon has little or no erosion or surface breakdown. A crater, footprint or any other impression or mark on the surface could last for millions of years!

What to do: Fill each container with _ cup of soil and 1 cup of sand. Mix each well with a trowel or spoon. Press the imprinting object firmly into each surface. If the print does not come out well, smooth over the surface and try again.

Place one of the trays in an undisturbed location and label it "Earthscape". Also write day one and date. For clearest test results, place the exposed "Earth" sample in an unprotected, open area where wind, rain and other elements can do their work.

Place the other dish labeled "Moonscape" in an additional undisturbed location. Also, place the box lid over the dish and weight it with a heavy object. Better yet, if an outdoor cabinet or shed is available, use it to enclose your "moon sample," with or without the lid.

Again, label the experiment as you did in the "Earthscape" sample. Observe each sample over a 7-to-14-day period and write down what you see.

What happens: The Earthscape experiment tray that was left outside unprotected, soon is broken down, wears away until little or any of the original print or impression is left.

The Moonscape experiment dish covered with the box lid and/or in the closet remains as it was originally. There is little erosion and the impression or print remains clear.

Why: Since the moon has no atmosphere, there is no wind, water, rain and snow or other atmospheric elements that would cause surface break-down or erosion. This, too, is somewhat like our protected experiment.

When comets, asteroids and meteors hit the lunar surface, there is no weathering force to affect the impact or craters they form.

The Earth's atmospheric conditions, however, produce wind, water, rain and snow. These same conditions, similar to our exposed experiment, cause weathering and erosion or a natural wearing away of rocks and soil.

344 Moving Picture

Since the moon revolves or moves around the Earth, how does a space craft going to the moon hit its moving target? Find a couple of friends and try this fun demonstration. It definitely will move you to think.

What to do: Mark off a large circular running area or arrange to use a school track.

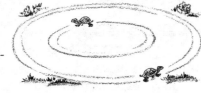

Have someone time how long it takes a runner to go around the large outside track once at a constant rate of speed. Record the time. Have a second runner run a smaller circular track within the larger track. Again have someone time this runner and record the results.

Now, start both runners running their tracks at their same rates of speed. When ready, or at your signal, the runner moving on the inner track should gradually and steadily increase the diameter of the running circle in order to join up with the runner on the outer track.

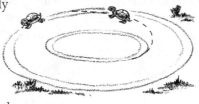

Again, the person with the stop watch should record the time it takes for the inner runner to join the outside runner.

What happens: The inside runner has a hard time trying to join up with the runner on the outer track, and likely has to speed up or slow down to do it.

Why: In order for a spacecraft to intersect the moon, timing is very important. Calculations are made before launch so that fuel is not wasted in slowing down, speeding up, or changing course in flight. The speeds of both the craft and the moon have to be taken into account, and also the speed necessary for the craft to overcome the force of Earth's gravity. Actually, to "catch" the moon, the spacecraft must be directed ahead of it, where the moon will be. Now have your runners try joining up again and see if they can better their time.

345 Plan-It Plus

Now that you've mastered the compass and distances of inner planets and sizes, why not do a large diagram of all the planets. You'll need a large white poster board and some information on the outer planets.

With the information provided below, you can mathematically calculate or figure out the scaled distances of orbits and the sizes of the outer planets.

Jupiter	over 483 million	about 90,000
Saturn	over 886 million	about 71,000
Uranus	1.783 billion	30,000
Neptune	2.790 billion	over 27,000
Pluto	3.670 billion	over 3,000

346 ◆ Plan-It!

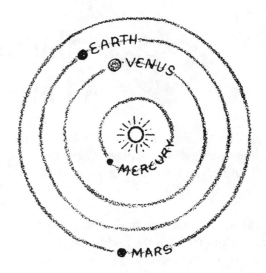

Plan a diagram or chart of the inner planets, showing their orbits and sizes. It's simple and easy and these instructions show you how.

Find a cleared desk or table for a workspace. First, you'll need an inexpensive pencil compass for making circles. For additional accuracy, an inexpensive circle stencil or template, showing the diameter of circles, can be bought at the same store. However, if you insist on drawing freehand, that's okay too!

Finally, you'll need a standard sheet of paper. For a bonus effect, you can use colored markers, pencils, crayons or colored construction paper.

Our sun is about 865 million miles in diameter (almost 1.4 million km across). One hundred Earths could fit inside the sun.

Draw a circle in the middle of your paper about the size of a quarter. If using a stencil, a 5/16-inch circle will do. If you wish, you can decorate your sun with flame-like spokes to represent the sun's outer area or corona.

Next, set your compass to the ½ inch (2 cm) mark and place its point in the middle of the sun. Carefully move the paper or the pencil around so the compass pencil-point marks the paper.

Helpful hint: Holding the center pointer down as you move the pencil around will help prevent skipping or moving. This circle represents Mercury's orbit around the sun.

Place a small pea-size circle on this path or 3/16 inch on the stencil to represent Mercury. Actually, next to our sun, Mercury is merely a grain of sand. Mercury is only about 3,030 miles wide and is 36 million miles or (58 million km) away from the sun.

Position your compass on 1_ inch (4 cm) for Venus's orbit and follow the same marking procedure as you did with Mercury's orbit. Venus's path around the sun is over 67 million miles (about 108 million km) from the sun. Nearly Earth size, it is about 7,500 miles across (about 12,000 km). Draw a circle on the orbit about the size of a large pea or ½ inch (0.8 cm) circle on the stencil.

Our planet Earth comes next. Set your compass to the 2-inch (5 cm) mark and follow the marking procedure for the other orbits. Since Venus and Earth are close to the same size, use the same circle for Earth as you did for Venus. Our Earth is just under 8,000 miles in diameter (7,927 actually, or about 12,757 km). It is about 93 million miles from the sun, or about 150 million km.

The last inner planet is Mars. According to its orbits, it's at least 50 million miles away from Earth; 142 million miles away from the sun and over 4,000 miles wide (over 6,700 km). Use a 6.5 cm setting on your compass for an orbit and a slightly smaller size than Earth or Venus for diameter or width of this planet. For continuation with the outer planets, see "Plan-It Plus."

Shuttle Wrap-Up: A Closed Case!

347

YOU WILL NEED:

2 empty soda cans

scissors

clay (enough to close can openings)

2 to 4 rubber bands

paper

pencil

2 small clear jars (remove labels)

hot tap water

a helper

2 thermometers

sheets of paper towels

paper bag

aluminum foil (enough to wrap layers twice around one can)

How do space shuttles withstand the extreme cold and heat of outer space? Do this heated experiment and find out. It's cool!

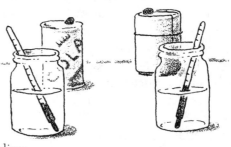

What to do: Layer the three types of paper, with the foil in the middle, the paper bag on the inside and the paper toweling on the outside.

Fill both cans with hot tap water. With your assistant's help, form two clay balls (about the size of a quarter) and press one against the hole in each can. The clay ball should be pressed against the hole and not into it.

Work quickly as you wrap the paper layers around one of the cans and secure it with rubber bands. The other can should remain as it is, without a wrapper

Four hands are faster than two and this experiment must be done quickly before water cools and thermometer temperatures change.

Patiently wait 30 to 40 minutes for the water to cool. Record the time. Again, you must work quickly to get accurate results. First, make certain both thermometers register the same temperature. If not, run them under warm or cool water to get similar readings.

While leaving the wrapper on the can, quickly pour its contents, the water, into one of the jars. Do the same with the other can into the other jar. Place the cans behind each jar so as not to confuse the sample test waters. Place a thermometer in each jar and let it stand for 2 to 3 minutes. Do not remove the thermometers from the jars when recording temperatures. Rather, press each to the side of the clear surface as you write down each number.

What happens: The can with the wrapper showed a 3 to 5° recorded temperature difference. In other words, the water in the wrapped can was 3 to 5° warmer than the can that was unwrapped.

Why: There are extreme areas of heat and cold in outer space, so space craft must be protected by wrapped blankets of insulating materials. These materials can be used to prevent or stop the loss of heat or even to cool.

Scientifically speaking, molecules vibrate more quickly in warm parts of a material and transfer heat energy to their slower moving cousins in colder parts. This process is called conduction. Knowing about this process, space scientists use materials to absorb heat or to reflect it. In general, metals conduct or carry heat best, while wood, paper, plastic, water and air are poor conductors.

348 Thermal Underwear: A Heated Problem

In places where it's very cold, people often wear thermal underwear. These long coveralls, worn under regular clothes, are designed with air pockets to keep body heat in.

In "Shuttle Wrap-Up: A Closed Case!" we put a type of thermal wrap on a can, best described as thermal outer wear. Try doing the same experiment, but substitute different layers of wrapping and rearrange them in different ways. Does what is inside or outside the other layer make much difference in final results or do the results remain the same?

Also, create some new experiments with thermal outer wear. Try using different containers with different coverings and thicknesses to scientifically "wrap-up" your final results.

349 Travel Agent

HOT!

YOU WILL NEED:
fork, nail or metal object
cup of very hot water
pencil, stick or wooden object
plastic spoon, drinking straw
an adult helper

How well does heat travel through metal, plastic or wood? The right answer, important to space exploration, will keep you out of hot water.

What to do: Heat water on a stove or microwave a cup of water on high for one minute. (Get adult help, as very hot water can cause a bad burn.) Put all three objects in the cup with ends separated and upright, like wheel spokes.

After five minutes, touch the middle of each object, where they meet the lip of the cup. Also, remove each object and feel the ends that were covered with the hot water. Of the three, which feels the warmer?

What happens:
Parts of the metal object feel warmer than that of the wooden or plastic object.

Why: Metals are better conductors of heat than plastic or wood. Electrons are looser in metals and can carry heat better. This explains why the metal object in our experiment felt warmer than the plastic or wood.

Now, you can see how this information would be helpful and very important to space scientists for insulating or protecting spacecraft and astronauts for the extreme temperatures of outer space.

350 Space Food: Can't Keep It Down!

Want to pretend you're an astronaut, and eat space-style? Enjoy this easy and fun experiment.

What to do: Pour the drink mix into the freezer bag. Fill it one-third full with milk. Seal the bag securely and shake thoroughly. Open one small corner of the bag and insert the straw. Sip your astromeal!

What happens: The food-in-a-bag demonstrates how food is eaten in space—sucked through a straw.

Why: Astronauts need to keep their foods contained in outer space. Without closed pouches, liquids and other loose foods would simply separate, and float away—all around the cabin! Messy, huh?

Space foods are dehydrated (dried), like our powdered breakfast drink, and rehydrated (water added) in outer space.

What next: Look for other dried foods found here on Earth and rehydrate them by adding water or milk. Also, experiment with ice cream, and other juices and foods that you can serve and eat spacestyle using plastic bag containers. It's a neat and fun way to eat—without all the mess.

351 Man Your Station

Make a simple space station and then man it, or place a crew member or members on its deck, whirl it, and learn what centrifugal force can really do.

What to do: Cut a rectangular opening in the narrow side of the box, leaving an inch of cardboard at either end. Have someone poke a hole on each side of the box, thread the string through both ends, and tie each side off. You now should have a string handle and a rectangular opening in the box.

With tape, attach a pair of cardboard rolls to each side. You should have what looks like an opened box with a pair of doubled-tube wings.

Lastly, place one object, followed by two to four, inside the box, or module, of your space station. While holding the string, rock the model slowly, then make several full circle swings. Start the string whirling slowly, gradually increase the speed, and then, very slowly, come to a stop.

What happens: With a slow, rocking swing, the objects move and rattle around in the box. With a faster, full, over-the-head whirl, the objects stay in place and do not move, while a slower, coming-to-a-stop type swing starts the objects moving and eventually they fly from the box.

Why: The overall force that kept the objects in your make-believe space station module from flying out, was called centrifugal force. When you rapidly whirled the station above your head, you pulled the objects inside the box toward you (centripetal force, see "Spooling Around") and the objects, in turn, pulled outward or away from you.

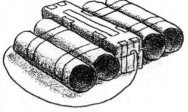

352 So You want to be an Astronaut

The future is waiting for you. If your goal is to be a part of it, out there, now is a good time to start thinking of how to turn your dream of going into space into reality. Here, from the agencies involved in space work and exploration, is information on how you can take your place as an astronaut.

353 Designer Craft

To design a more authentic, realistic space station, bring out marker pens, scissors, cardboard, toilet paper and towel rolls, tape, string and lots of imagination. The illustration on this page will help you.

For starters, use a paper towel roll for the different parts, or modules, of your craft. Since the roll is similar to the cylinder shape of a real station, this will add realism.

Also, cut out two or three rectangular pieces from the ends or middle of the tube. You might need an adult to help with this task. This will make the modules look authentic, or real. You may wish it to hold objects and put it into orbit as you did in "Man Your Station."

Draw circular and side lines to show the different modular parts. Add rectangular cardboard pieces to your model to show the many solar panels that are attached to such crafts.

Lastly, if you wish, attach string and astronauts, and put your craft into orbit as you did in "Man Your Station." Have fun!

Astronaut Selection and Training

In the future, the United States, with its international partners Japan, Canada, and the European Space Agency, will operate a manned Space Station. From that orbiting depot, explorers will continue on their journeys to the moon and Mars. As these plans come closer to reality, the need for qualified space-flight professionals will increase.

To fill the upcoming need, NASA accepts applications for the Astronaut Candidate Program on a continuous basis. Candidates are selected as needed, normally every two years, for pilot and mission-specialist categories. Both civilian and military personnel are considered for the program. Civilians may apply at any time. Military personnel must apply through their parent service and be nominated by their branch of service to transfer to NASA.

The astronaut candidate selection process was developed to select highly qualified individuals for human space programs. For mission specialists and pilot-astronaut candidates, there are several education and experience requirements: at least a bachelor's degree from an accredited institution in engineering, biological science, physical science, or mathematics. Three years of related, progressively responsible professional experience must follow the degree. An advanced degree is desirable and may be substituted for all or part of the experience requirement (i.e., master's degree = 1 year of work experience, doctoral degree = three years of experience)....

Applicants who meet the basic qualifications are evaluated by discipline panels during a week-long process of personal interviews, thorough medical evaluations, and orientation.

Selected applicants are designated astronaut candidates and are assigned to the astronaut office at Johnson Space Center for a one-year training-and-evaluation period. During this time, candidates take part in the astronaut training program designed to develop the knowledge and skills required for formal mission training upon selection for a flight and are assigned technical or scientific responsibilities. However, selection as a candidate does not ensure selection as an astronaut.

Final selection is based on satisfactory completion of the one-year program. Civilian candidates who successfully complete the training and evaluation and are selected as astronauts are expected to remain with NASA for at least five years.

Portions reprinted courtesy of the National Aeronautics and Space Administration and the Lyndon B. Johnson Space Center, Houston, Texas

ROCKETRY: THE THREE R'S (READY! REACTION! REPLAY!)

The many mini-experiments in this chapter are based on a balloon-straw-string rocket. You may have seen balloon-string rockets in experiment books before, but not the way they're presented here. This experiment absolutely shot the works, with balloons, weights, balances, and counterbalances to explain the concepts or ideas of thrust, acceleration, deceleration, and booster and retro rockets.

You'll be doing experiments with rockets, space shuttles, and retrorockets in mind. This even adds a jet-propelled toy car for fast thinkers, and you won't need expensive or dangerous propellants or fuels—it's all 100% balloon power.

So, power up! You'll need lots of balloons, both large round and oblong ones, and perhaps a helper, but you'll soon be bursting with fun and ideas. And all the experiments are fuel-proof!

Rocket Scientists Don't Fuel Around

Space scientists are very serious when it comes to getting a spacecraft off the ground. Fuel is a very important part of any space launch and this fuel-proof experiment will have you sputtering, hissing and roaring with excitement. An assistant is recommended

What to do: Place 3 teaspoons of baking soda on the coffee filter and spread out evenly into a long column. Fold over evenly to form a long tube package and secure with rubber bands. This will represent your fuel package. Pack the aluminum foil into a 5-inch (13 cm) rocket, making certain the bottom end fits snugly but not too tightly into the bottle. It should be still loose enough to move up and down. Take your bottle of vinegar, fuel package and rocket outside to a location that can be easily washed down.

The next steps must be done carefully and quickly. Make certain the long fuel tube is not broken or leaking and can be easily inserted into the bottle.

Next, drop the fuel package into the bottle, quickly followed by the rocket. When the chemical reaction occurs, poke the rocket down into the bottle and watch what happens.

Continue to poke the rocket down into the bottle until the reaction stops.

What happens: The vinegar and baking soda chemically combine to produce CO_2 gas. The gas in turn, overflows from the bottle, hisses, steams and slightly moves the rocket.

Why: Your model rocket on its launch pad (bottle) simulates or copies a real rocket or spacecraft launched into outer space. In a real craft, two liquid fuels are combined and explode, causing pressure and giving the craft its lift or thrust. The chemical reaction, hissing, steam and overflow and slight lift when the model rocket is pushed back into the bottle copies the built-up pressure, exhaust and lift of the real thing.

Designing a Rocket

How about being creative and designing special features on your 5-inch (13 cm) aluminum rocket? And, since the rocket is waterproof, you can use it over and over. Better yet, why not try modeling extra rockets of different designs and sizes for future launches?

With a little imagination, waterproof permanent markers, extra aluminum foil, straws and other waterproof household materials, you can do much to change the design and shape of your rockets.

Try forming strips of foil in separate bands around the width of your missile to show the different parts or stages of the rocket. Also, reshape the nose of your model or construct tail fins. You might even add booster or end rockets (straws work best) to make your craft look more realistic.

Lastly, use permanent markers to draw U.S.A. or other logos or signs on your project. Have fun!

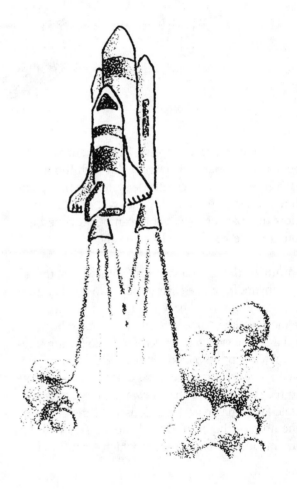

Shuttled About

YOU WILL NEED:

outdoor location
thread
a helper
tape
drinking straw
paper clip
large, long balloon
scissors
large foam cup
stopwatch or watch
with second hand
paper
pencil
clip, clothespin, or
pushpin

Watch the space capsule fall off your model rocket as it reaches its target. Although modern spacecraft use a space shuttle system with a plane-like orbiter, your simple rocket will demonstrate how one part of a spacecraft can be launched into outer space with the help of another.

What to do: Tie 4 to 5 yards (or meters) of thread lengthwise from one chair or object to another as a free, or removable, line. On the end of the free or removable line, thread the straw (see "Line Item"). An assistant is recommended for the following steps:

Blow up the balloon, twist the end and clip it. With a very long piece of tape, fasten the balloon to the underside of the straw, making certain the hole faces the chair. Next, loosely fit the cup over the nose or the front of the balloon. This will represent earlier space capsules which were fitted onto the end of rockets.

You now are ready to launch your rocket. Remove the paper clip from the balloon while holding the end of it closed. When ready, release the balloon and time how long it takes your rocket to leave its launch pad and reach its target.

What happens: When released, the balloon races along the string and reaches its target while the cup or capsule falls off.

Why: Your balloon rocket demonstrates the law of Sir Isaac Newton: for every action there is an equal and opposite reaction. Your rocket shows how the principles of jet propulsion work. The backward push of the air escaping from the balloon, propels or pushes the balloon forward.

Line Item

357

The clip, clothespin, or push-pin is used to attach or pin one end of the rocket-balloon thread line from one object to another, such as a chair. One end of the line can be permanently tied to an object but the other should be free. This is done so balloon rockets (slipped on a thread line through a straw attached to a balloon) can be changed or altered when needed. Since there are many mini-experiments with these balloon rockets, this free line should be helpful.

To easily get the thread through the straw, tie one end of it around the head of a straight pin and drop it through the straw. Leave the pin on the thread to act as a plumb or weighted line. The pin can be draped over a push pin or attached by a clip to another object.

Booster Shot

358

Now that you've got the bang of it, why not try a booster shot! You'll keep the same set-up and do the same experiment as in "Shuttled About," but now you'll add an extra balloon or booster rocket. Will it make any difference in the rate of speed and time your rocket reaches its target? Be a big shot and find out!

What to do: As you did in "Shuttled About," again blow up the original balloon taped to the underside of the straw. (If the balloon is now too stretched out or doesn't work well, replace it with a new one.) Twist the end and clip it.

Now add a new long balloon to the side of the original balloon. Again, tape, twist and clip the end of the balloon.

With your assistant's help, and the clock ready, unclip and release both balloons at the same time. Time how long it takes for your booster rocket to reach its target. Is there a big difference between the booster's time and the one in "Shuttled About?"

What happens: Your balloon rocket with its booster rocket, races along the string with more force than your original rocket.

Why: With two rockets, the jet propulsion rate is doubled and thus the rate of travel is faster.

359 Completely Exhausted

You'll love this effect for your balloon rocket. It simulates, or copies, the real thrust and propulsion of the jet rocket engine. It also gives you an idea how the stages of a rocket work. Now as a surprise bonus, there's a bit of fake smoke for realism! The materials are easy to find and it's absolutely guaranteed not to leave you exhausted.

What to do: Do this experiment as you did the others. However, before you blow up the balloon and attach it to the straw, place the funnel inside the opening of the uninflated balloon and fill it with about 1 teaspoon of flour. Use the spoon to stir the flour around in the funnel and into the balloon. Inflate the balloon, shake it so the flour reaches the opening, attach it to the straw, tie it off with the clip and get ready to shoot the works.

What happens: If done correctly, the balloon rocket races along the string, leaving a trail of smoke behind it.

360 Four Going Retro

Now, using the same thread line and materials used in "Shuttled About," try doing these next four mini-experiments on retrorockets, those small secondary or additional rockets that produce a thrust opposite to that of the main rocket. Retrorockets are often used to slow down a spacecraft's reentry or to "soft land." You can also try extending your thread line, buy larger balloons, or increase the number of balloons for added thrust.

Get your whole family, or at least a friend, involved in these experiments. You'll need the help of an assistant anyway! Now get moving and have a blast!

Retrorocket I: Watch the Tube!

With cardboard tubes, this rocket looks and acts like a real one, with retrorockets.

What to do: With tape, attach the two cardboard tubes from the top sides of an inflated balloon and attach it to the straw.

Hint: It's easier to tape from the inside of the tube out. Release the balloon from one end of the line and observe what happens.

What happens: The balloon pushes or shoots down the line, but with less force, and does not reach the end of it.

Why: The rolls, like retrorockets, act as a counter-force, a force or action acting against the main thrust of the rocket balloon. This, in turn, slows down the main thrust of the rocket balloon and makes it unable to reach its target.

Retrorocket II: A Perfect Roll Model

Now try the same experiment, but with a difference!

What to do: Inflate the balloon and, with tape, securely fasten the cardboard tube to the bottom of it and then to the straw.

Next, roll and tape the newspapers into a tight cylinder and place them into the attached balloon roll. Release the balloon from one end of the line and observe what happens.

What happens: The rocket moves only to the middle of the thread line, and then stops.

Why: The retrorocket-like tube-cylinder, due to its weight, acted as a greater counter or opposite force, and it slowed down more than its tubed cousin.

363

Retrorocket III: Bully for You!

The balloon rocket in this experiment is a regular bully, but it shows you, forcefully, the opposite thrust of a retrorocket.

What to do: Thread two straws at the beginning of the removable end of the free thread line.

Next, inflate three oblong balloons; two fully inflated, the other, half inflated. With tape, attach the two fully inflated balloons together on one of the straws—twist and clip the end of each balloon. Do the same with the half inflated balloon on the other straw.

Important: The balloons should be facing each other, with back openings facing the ends of each line.

Hold your balloons about a quarter of the distance away from the end line while your assistant does the same with the half inflated balloon.

At an announced signal, release the balloons and watch the action carefully.

What happens: The two-balloon rocket pushes the half-inflated balloon to the other side of the line.

Why: The two-balloon rocket represents a forceful retrorocket, slowing and forcefully pushing the small rocket (representing the main rocket) back to its end line.

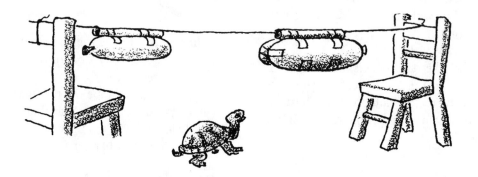

Retrorocket IV: You're Canceled!

YOU WILL NEED:

line hookup with
2 straws
2 oblong balloons
2 paper clips
tape

What will happen if two fully inflated balloons, moving in the same direction, meet?

What to do: Repeat the steps in "Retrorocket III: Bully for You" but replace these balloons with two fully inflated balloons facing each other with openings behind and facing the end lines.

What happens: The two balloons shoot to the middle of the line and stop.

Why: The thrust or push from each balloon was the same and, when they met, pushed against each other, stopping or canceling one another out.

Forgoing Retro

A toy car moving in one direction can be redirected into an opposite direction. How? Not rocketry, but a reverse trick using counter forces.

What to do: Fold the strip of cardboard in thirds lengthwise to make a walled track. Push it up against a wall. Then blow up the balloon and knot or twist it closed. Clip or tape the balloon to the lower wall and floor, or to the track so it becomes a barrier at the end of the it.

Hold the long tube at a downward angle, adjusting it as needed at the track opening oppo-site the balloon, and drop the car into it.

What happens: The car slides down the tube and onto the track. When it hits the balloon, the car is pushed backwards on the track. It's not a retrorocket, but another way a forward-moving object can be sent in another or opposite direction.

YOU WILL NEED:

toy minicar
long cardboard tube
strip of cardboard, 6-inches (15-cm) wide
paper clip
round balloon
the floor near a wall
tape

GLOSSARY

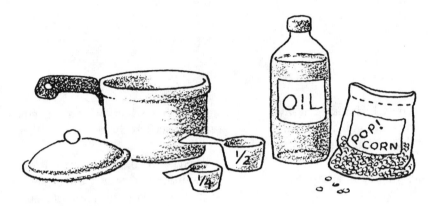

The following terms appear in the section containing experiments with food:

acids—a large class of compounds that are capable of neutralizing alkalis and which range from benign sour-tasting citric acids, like lemons, limes and oranges, to hazardous, poisonous sulfuric and hydrochloric acid.

alkalis—also known as bases—any of numerous bitter-tasting, soapy-feeling substances that dissolve in water and neutralize acids to form salts. These include carbonates, like sodium bicarbonate (baking soda) and sodium carbonate (washing soda), and caustic hydroxides like lye, limewater and ammonia, useful commercially and in the home.

amino acids—the building blocks of proteins. The body manufactures all but nine amino acids. These must be obtained from the food we eat. Meat, fish, poultry, dairy products and eggs contain all nine essential amino acids.

baking—dry heat method of cooking, especially in an oven.

boiling point—point at which a liquid turns into a gas.

broiling—cooking by direct exposure to high heat, over a grill or under an electric element.

calorie—a measure of energy. A calorie is a quantity of food capable of producing the heat and energy needed to raise the temperature of one kilogram of water one degree centigrade. An ounce of carbohydrates or protein is equal to 115 calories; an ounce of fat is equal to 255 calories. A person's daily calorie need depends on age, weight, and level of activity.

carbohydrates—the sugars and starches that supply energy help the body use fat efficiently, or provide fiber. They are compounds made of carbon, hydrogen and oxygen, most of which are formed by green plants. Simple carbohydrates are honey, sugar and fruits. Complex carbohydrates are grains and cereals, dried beans, root vegetables and potatoes.

enzyme—protein molecules that break down or build up materials inside the body but are not changed themselves (catalysts). Human digestive enzymes break up proteins into individual amino acids and starch into individual glucose units.

digestion—the changing of food to a form the body can use.

fiber—the parts of cereal grains, fruits and vegetables, seeds, legumes and nuts that cannot be digested. Fiber aids digestion and elimination by carrying waste products with it as it leaves the digestive tract and by absorbing fluids that make wastes soft enough for easy passage.

fungus—a plant like mushrooms or yeast that cannot manufacture its own food but lives off decaying organisms around it. This kind of plant is called saprophytic.

minerals—small amounts of minerals such as magnesium, phosphorus, flourine, potassium, chlorine, copper, iron, iodine, sulfur, and zinc are needed for teeth, bones and health. Larger amounts of calcium and sodium are needed.

molecule—one or more atoms that are the smallest particle of an element of compound that retains the properties of the substance.

organic compound—a group of compounds containing the carbon necessary for life.

proteins—a group of organic compounds containing nitrogen, which our body needs to build and repair tissue, red blood cells and enzymes.

osmosis—the flow of a liquid through a thin membrane from an area of greater concentration to an area of lesser concentration of water.

vitamins—special nutrients needed in small quantities but essential to life. A, D, E and K dissolve in fat and can be stored for a long time in the body. Eight B vitamins and vitamin C dissolve in water. Because they are not stored in the body very long, foods providing them must be eaten daily—whole grains, meat or beans for the B's, citrus fruits, melons, berries or leafy green vegetables for the C.

yeast—a group of about 160 species of single-celled microscopic fungi, some of which spoil fruits and vegetables or cause disease. Others are used in making bread and alcoholic drinks.

The following terms appear in the section containing experiments with time:

Balance spring-the hairspring, a long, fine, spiral spring that determines the time of the swing of the balance.

Constellation—a cluster of stars that make up a pattern. Ancient peoples saw these as pictures, giving them names like Big Bear, Leo the Lion, Orion the Hunter, etc.

Diode—an electronic device that has two terminals and converts alternating current to direct current.

Earth's Axis—an imaginary line from the North to South Pole. It takes a day for the Earth to make a complete turn on its axis.

Equinox—the days when the Sun is directly above the equator and day and night are of equal length. March 21 is called the vernal equinox, September 21 is the autumnal equinox.

Escapement—a device that regulates the speed of the train of gear wheels of a clock or watch. It usually consists of a wheel with teeth and an anchor that releases one tooth on the heel at a given interval.

Frequency—the number of complete cycles or swings per second.

Gears—toothed wheels that intermesh so that one wheel turns to drive the other. A screw (a worm) or a toothed shaft (a rack) may replace one of the wheels.

Hertz (HZ)—a unit of frequency equal to one cycle per second, named for physicist Heinrich Hertz.

Horologists—clock-makers.

L.A.T.—local apparent time, which is time measured by the actual movement of Earth and the Sun and differs from season to season and from place to place. It is the time measured by the sundial.

Latitude—the distance in degrees of a point on Earth from the equator.

LCD (liquid crystal display)—an alphanumeric display on digital watches and calculators made up of a liquid sandwiched between layers of glass or plastic. It becomes opaque when an electric current is passed through it. The contrast between the opaque and transparent areas forms visible characters.

LED (light emitting diode)—a semi-conductor electron tube that converts electric power (applied voltage) to light and is used in digital displays, as a digital watch or a calculator.

L.M.T.—local mean time, which measures the average speed at which the Moon moves in its ellipse and Earth spins in its orbit. Our clocks and watches show local mean time.

Longitude—the distance east or west on Earth's surface, measured in degrees up to 180í, or the difference in time between the meridian passing through a particular place and the prime meridian at Greenwich, England.

Megahertz (MHZ)—one million cycles per second.

Meridians—imaginary lines running along Earth's surface from the North to the South Pole.

Oscillator—an instrument that produces a steady rhythm of swings or vibrations.

Piezoelectric effect—electricity created by pressure or pressure created by electricity, especially in a crystal like quartz.

Planetarium—an optical device for projecting astronomical images; a model or representation of the solar system.

Summer solstice—longest day because the tilt of Earth lets the Sun shine longest (June 21 in the Northern Hemisphere, December 21 in the Southern Hemisphere).

INDEX

B

N

Nails, 170
NASA, 292
National Bureau of Standards, 183
National Wildlife Federation, 232
Nautical speed, 161
New Guinea, 146
New South Wales, Australia, 174
New Year, 145
New York, 175
New Zealand, 174, 175
Newfoundland, 174
Newspaper, 78
Newton, Isaac Sir, 65, 72, 141, 250, 259, 260, 296
Niels, 141
Nitrogen, 24, 112
Non-biodegradable, 234
Non-polar molecule, 241
Noon mark, 157
North Pole, 152, 200
North Star, 164, 165
North Territory, Australia, 174
Nuremberg, Germany, 171
Nutrients, 187, 200, 206, 233, 236
Nutritional value, 137
Nuts, 215

O

Oatmeal, 123
Oats, 122
Ocean, 192, 193, 241
Olympiad, 146
Onion, 104, 108
Orange, 117
Orange juice, 131, 132
Orbit, 265, 269, 270, 287
Oregano, 86, 130
Organic clay, 188
Organic matter, 185, 186, 191, 234
Organism, 182, 205, 233, 236, 237
Orion the Hunter, 163
Osmosis, 101, 107, 135
Ovipositor, 220
Oxygen, 24, 97, 101, 105, 119, 200, 205, 234, 236

P

Pacific Ocean, 175
Pacific time zone, 174
Paleontogists, 141
Pancake mix, 91
Papillae, 92
Parachute, 281
Parer, 116
Parsley, 86, 88, 108
Particles, 141
Pathfinder, 279
Pea, 162
Peaches, 197
Peanut butter, 214, 215
Peanuts, 112
Pear, 139
Pectin, 116, 119
Pendulum, 69, 73, 177
Pendulum Clock, 173
Permeability, 191
Perth, Australia, 174
Petroleum jelly, 20, 23, 210, 238
pH chart, 197
pH paper, 196
pH scale, 196
Phenols, 119
Pheophytin, 109
Philosopher, 183

Q

R

T

Y

Z